Communication Link

a Dictionary of Signs

Written and Compiled by

Cath Smith

illustrated by

David Hodgson

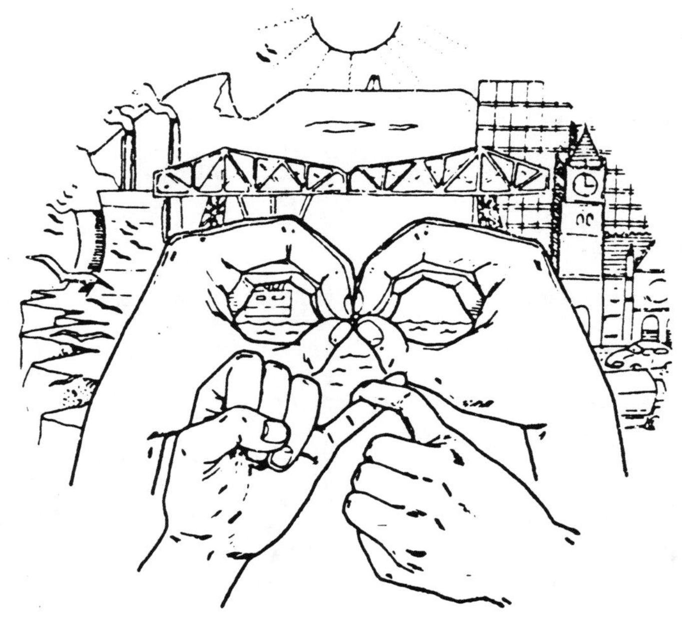

Beverley School for the Deaf
Middlesbrough

FIRST EDITION ACKNOWLEDGEMENTS

PROJECT DIRECTOR
Terry Morris, PhD, MSc

PRODUCTION TEAM

Cath Smith — Consultant and Compiler

Dave Hodgson — Supervisor Illustrator
Bill Dawson — Supervisor
Joyce McLennon — Graphic Designer
Sally Robinson — Assistant Artist
Joanna Brelstaff — Assistant Artist
Fiona Hack — Secretary
Tony Beckett — Video Production
Mark Kegney — Video Technician
Ian Wilson — Computer Programmer
Gary Catchpole — Computer Programmer

Cover Idea — David Smith

ACKNOWLEDGEMENTS
Much credit is due to the staff of Beverley School, and in particular, those members who were involved in the Education Signs Committee:

Brian Brayford, Dorothy Barlow, Carmel Hayward, Elaine McBean, Margaret Shaw, Francis Wade, Margaret Wallen.

Gratitude is expressed to the following for contributions at various stages and in various ways, to the production of this dictionary.

At Cleveland College of Art & Design:

Bill Hill, Rob Jobson, John Cooke, Fred Littlejohn, John Tempest, Ron Walding, Frank Cullingford, Bob Carr, Martin Cook, John Samson, Kevin Whitehouse and other members of the teaching, technical, administrative and ancillary staff.

Martin Colville — BSL Research Project, Moray House, Edinburgh.

Mary Plackett — RNID Librarian.

Scottish Educational Signs Committee, Edinburgh.

Geoff. Bell — Imperial Chemical Industries PLC.

Finaly thanks are due to the Deaf Community of Cleveland for their valuable suggestions and contributions to the preparation of this book.

SPONSORSHIP AND FUNDING
Sponsored by Cleveland County Council Education Department.

Publication cost through the Department of Research and Intelligence, Cleveland County.

Additional financial assistance from P.C. Werth Ltd., Audiology House, 45 Nightingale Lane, London.

PUBLISHED BY AND ENQUIRIES TO:

Beverley School for the Deaf,
Beverley Road,
Saltersgill,
Middlesbrough,
Cleveland TS4 3LQ.

Tel. (0642) 850366 or 815500

First Published 1985

Printed in the U.K. by:

County Purchasing and Supplies unit,
Central Print,
Civic Centre,
Middlesbrough.

Typesetting by:

Owens Ltd., Middlesbrough
and
The Printing Department at
Cleveland College of Art & Design.

SECOND EDITION ACKNOWLEDGEMENTS

Our sincerest thanks to the Working Party formed by the Cleveland Deaf Community who gave so generously of their time and expertise to assist in the revision of this dictionary.

Elizabeth Cannon, Cathy Duxbury, Ken Duxbury, Pauline Hodgson, Frank Johnson, Sandella Johnson, Pat Manton, Don Read, Doris Tait, Dave Walker, Keith Williams, Eddie Williams.

ISBN 1 871832 00 4

FOREWORD

On behalf of Cleveland County Council I would like to wish users of Communication Link improved success in their ventures to educate or nurture young people who have problems in acquiring spoken language.

At one time the audience for such a publication would have been perceived to have been exclusively that of teachers and social workers involved with the deaf. Nowadays there is a growing awareness amongst both parents and professionals concerning the vital importance of establishing communication in the early years of the life of deaf children. The growth of partnership between parents and professionals to facilitate the early establishment of total communication is welcome, and this dictionary should go a long way towards facilitating this development. Similarly, teachers and speech therapists working with pupils with severe learning difficulties, and or with specific speech and language impairments, are gradually appreciating that, for those pupils who will always depend upon a signed supplement for their communication development, the use of a system based upon British deaf signs and which can reflect the grammar of English, provides the pupils with a method of communication which can be utilized in the world of the deaf.

The County of Cleveland is proud to be associated with the production of Communication Link, and acknowledgements are due to the Research and Intelligence Department for their funding, and to Community Programme Agency and Manpower Services Commission for the establishment and maintenance of the essential resources team, and lastly and most importantly, to Dr. T. Morris, Cath Smith and the staff of Beverley School for the Deaf, Middlesbrough, for the many, many hours spent refining the contents of this innovative publication.

Roger Lanyon,
Adviser, Special Educational Needs.

I am delighted to have been asked to write this brief introduction for Communication Link. An enormous amount of hard work and considerable expertise has been put into the publication, both by Beverley School staff and the Community Programme Agency/Manpower Services Commission Project Team. I feel sure that it will serve as a major resource for those concerned and committed to the education of hearing impaired children through the medium of total communication. In addition, Communication Link provides marvellous reference material for parents, families and friends of hearing impaired children, and promises to be a publication which I feel will be much used.

Congratulations to all concerned.

John Logan

Chairman of Beverley School Governors &
Chairman of National Deaf Children's Society (Cleveland Region)

CONTENTS

INTRODUCTION
(SECOND EDITION)

In the introduction to the first edition of **Communication Link,** it was pointed out that this dictionary of signs was by no means complete and would require updating and revising at regular intervals.

This we have attempted to do in conjunction with the Working Party of the Cleveland Deaf Community named in the acknowledgements.

Every sign contained in the first edition has been analysed, and the resultant changes are in three main areas;

a) A large number of signs have been redrawn to improve the clarity of presentation.

b) Some changes have been made in the selection and detail of signs.

c) Identifying invented 'School' signs with the symbol (S).

The first edition was compiled in a very short space of time due to financial constraints, but our over-riding concern was, and still is, the urgent need for such a resource. In spite of it's limitations, the response to **Communication Link** has been overwhelming, a fact which seems to confirm such need. The distribution of thousands of copies nationally has made us aware of our responsibilities to a much wider group of people than originally anticipated.

During the course of developing a Total Communication approach at Beverley School, consultation was made with various sources, mainly educational, and a Sign Committee was formed to establish a consistent sign vocabulary base, taken from British Sign Language (B.S.L.) and to develop a system which could reflect the grammar of English. This involved making decisions as to which B.S.L. signs to use where there was a variety to choose from, and inventing or adapting signs for a number of commonly occurring English words, to help in the teaching of English. Unfortunately, in the absence of a B.S.L. dictionary, some signs were invented unnecessarily.

The first edition contained a mixture of all such signs, whether B.S.L. or invented, and this has lead to confusion in some cases, particularly for people learning B.S.L.

Whilst it is outside the scope of this book to deal with the grammar of B.S.L., or to give details of regional sign variations, we felt it was important to identify invented signs and to improve the selection of B.S.L. vocabulary.

Perhaps the most important change in this second edition is that an attempt has been made to remove invented and adapted signs. Those remaining in the main text of the book are marked by the (S) symbol, to clarify the fact that the sign is either totally invented or has been changed from it's original B.S.L. format in some way for school use, and is not in general use within the deaf community.

The improvements to the B.S.L. vocabulary include close attention to details, such as handshape, and some changes in the choice of signs, particularly where it has been possible to replace an invented sign with a B.S.L. sign. A number of new words have also been added.

Thus it is hoped that this dictionary will be of use to all persons involved in the acquisition and development of signing skills whether this be in the mode of British Sign Language (B.S.L.) Signs Supporting Engish (S.S.E.) or Signed English (S.E.). However, we would wish to reiterate what was pointed out in the introduction to the first edition of **Communication Link,** that this is not a ''teach yourself'' manual, but simply a record of signs. We would also wish to stress again that signs vary considerably according to INDIVIDUAL choice, REGIONAL variation, and, most importantly, according to CONTEXT. We therefore continue to recommend that the best way of developing the skills needed for communicating effectively with deaf people is through attendance at classes designed for this purpose, and contact with the deaf community.

CS TM
November 1988

INTRODUCTION

We sincerely hope that **Communication Link** will enable and encourage normally hearing persons to communicate more effectively with deaf children and adults.

Communication is a very broad term and we would like to start by defining what we mean by **Communication Link** .

COMMUNICATION	LINK
"Giving a share of: revealing: to have something in common with another: succeeding in conveying one's meaning to others".	"A ring in a chain: that which connects: a unit in a communication system".

We feel that the signs in this book should form a link between deaf and hearing people, provide common ground, and be used as part of a whole range of ways to convey meaning.

This publication is an attempt to record the signs used by the teachers, staff, and parents of hearing impaired children, involved in total communication programmes in the County of Cleveland.

It was never intended or envisaged that this dictionary of signs be viewed or used as a 'teach yourself to sign' manual. It is recommended that the best way of developing the necessary skills needed for communicating effectively with deaf persons is through regular attendance at a class specifically designed for this purpose and through contact with the deaf community. Consequently this dictionary of signs is a basic but useful reference book which will enable the reader to look up and remember a forgotten sign, as well as refresh their knowledge of other signs.

Communication Link provides a record of some 1700 signs which are used in the education of deaf children at Beverley School. The majority of these signs are those commonly used by the deaf community.

It should be appreciated that some of the signs used by deaf people may vary according to individual, regional and contextual usage. Therefore we have attempted to record signs that are widely used and understood by deaf adults. As the signs are recorded alphabetically, it has been necessary in most cases, to give a single word to each sign, regardless of context. However when communicating with deaf children, we support the use of signs according to meaning, rather than a 'sign for a word' approach which is used in some educational establishments. For instance, in a phrase such as 'the party's over', the meaning of *over* in this context implies **finished,** and should be signed accordingly.

Included in this book are some additional signs and modifications to root signs which have been taken from various sources to facilitate the teaching of English. A section dealing with these modifications (markers) can be found at the back of this publication and some of the more commonly occurring ones are included in the main dictionary.

Often the same sign is used for a variety of words with similar meaning, e.g. *angry, cross, furious, mad.* These are distinguished by emphasis, facial expression and lip pattern.

In other instances, several signs exist for the same word, e.g. *about, by, before.* This is because the same word can have different meanings depending on the context it is used in. We have therefore attempted to record as many signs as possible to cover different meanings, but not to provide the same sign repeatedly for words that have similar meaning unless the link is not immediately obvious, for example, *allow* and *let, true* and *real, cold* and *winter.*

If a sign can't be found for a word, another sign with a similar meaning may be used, e.g. *job/work, everybody/everyone, benefit/advantage.*

Many signs are based on mimed actions and some have been drawn to give examples of the basic idea, but not all. For example, sports such as golf, badminton, table tennis, netball can be conveyed by miming the appropriate action. It will be noted that *bat* has been drawn so as to illustrate a table tennis bat. However a cricket bat or rounders bat would be signed by the appropriate mimed action. So too would *brush* e.g. toothbrush, sweeping brush, clothes brush, etc. Also *wash;* to wash hair, face, hands, etc. would involve the appropriate mimed action.

Other signs have been drawn in a fixed position, but would be changed in context. For example, *operation;* knee operation, appendix operation, ear operation, and so on, would involve the sign for *operation* being made on the appropriate part of the body.

When communicating with deaf people it is necessary to use imagination and common sense. If one was signing *hearing aid* and the type referred to was a body worn model, then this would be indicated on the body. Parts of the body are normally indicated by pointing to them.

Less obviously, some signs change direction depending on context. For example, *give* moves away from the signer in 'I give you', but in 'you give me' the sign moves towards the signer. Similarly the sign for *help* moves forward in 'I'll help you', and towards the signer in 'you help me'. The same principle applies to such words as *owe, remind, visit.*

Fingerspelling is an integral part of manual communication. Signs do not exist for all words, for example, places and names, and therefore fingerspelling is necessary to convey meaning. It may be noticed in the book that some signs are actually fingerspelt words (e.g. *Mr.* and *Mrs.*) or derived from fingerspelling (e.g. *about*). These examples show the importance of a knowledge of fingerspelling and how it can be used in communication.

It is envisaged that the role of fingerspelling in communication will progressively increase as deaf children develop their literacy skills. Individuals differ greatly in many respects,and application of signed communication may vary in different situations to meet individual needs, at different stages of development. There is a need for flexibility and adaptability.

Just as speech represents one element in the way thoughts and feelings are communicated between hearing people, so signs and fingerspelling constitute only a part of the total approach necessary for effective communication with deaf people.

It is perhaps true that because of the lack of comprehensive sign reference books, many hearing persons wishing to acquire total communication skills spend not only a great deal of time re-learning forgotten signs but expend much mental energy trying to recall poorly internalised signs. This is at the expense of the development of the other important aspects of sign communication. We hope that this book will help to redress this imbalance and be conducive to a quicker acquisition of fluent communication skills.

Although this dictionary of signs is by no means complete and will require up-dating and revising at regular intervals, we do hope that it will provide immediate and practical help to parents, brothers and sisters of deaf children and to any individual involved with deaf persons either professionally or socially.

TM CS
March 1985

GUIDE TO CAPTIONS

In this book, signs and finger-spelling are described and drawn as if the person making them is right handed. Naturally, left handed people will sign and finger-spell using the left hand as the dominant hand.

The captions are intended to add extra information to explain the movement of the hands which cannot always be shown in a drawing. Where possible, a full description of the sign is given, but in some cases the hand shapes may not be given if they are clear from the drawing.

To avoid misunderstandings, and lengthy descriptions, we have used set terms to describe:

1 Parts of the hand
2 Common hand shapes
3 Directions

PARTS OF THE HAND

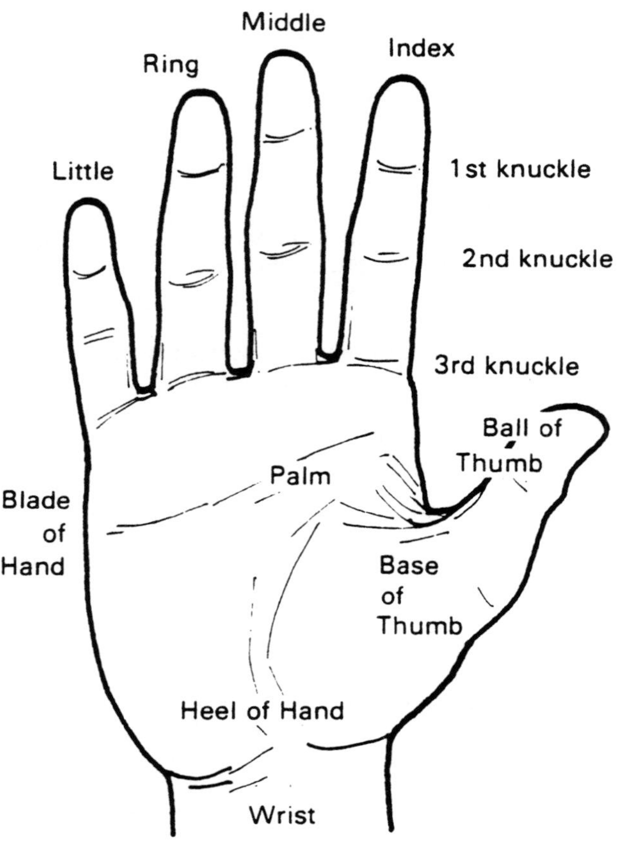

The right hand is always written as Rt.
The left hand is always written as L.

BASIC HAND SHAPES

Flat Hand

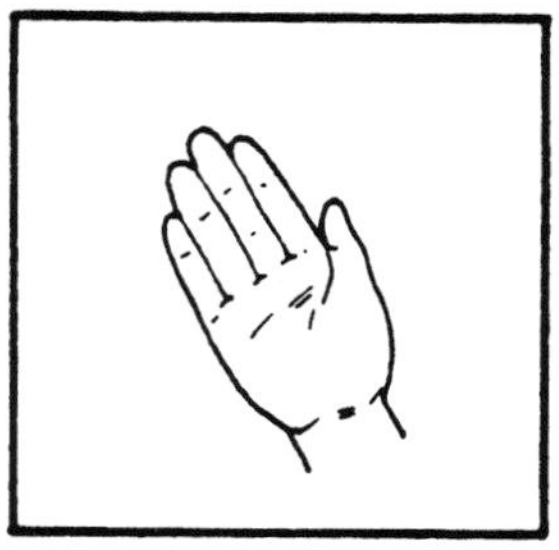

Open Hand

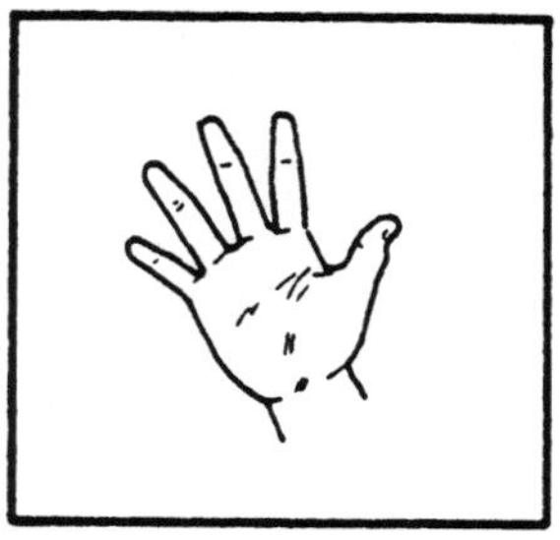

Clawed Hand

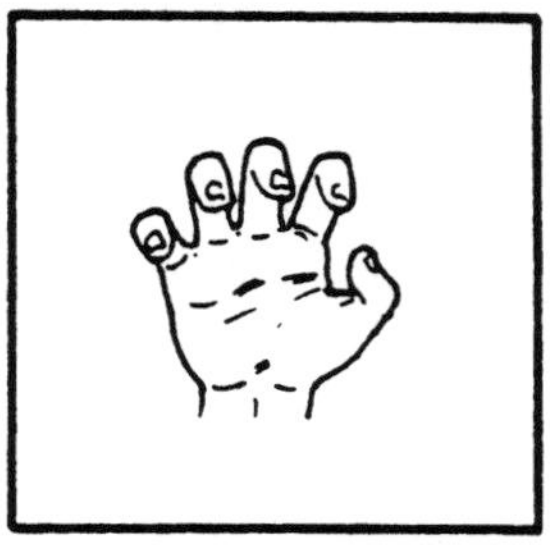

Fist

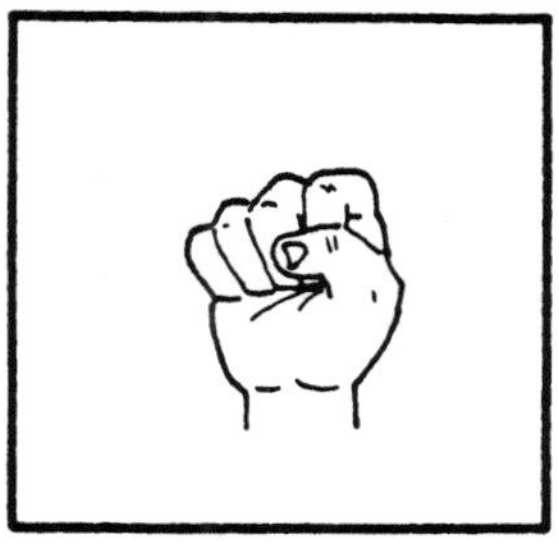

Closed Hand

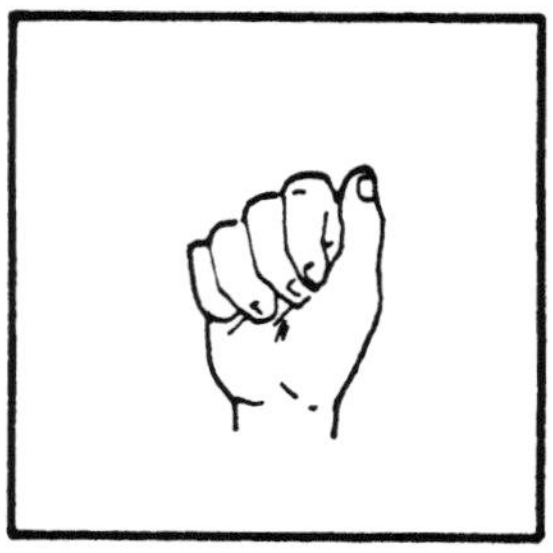

Bent Hand

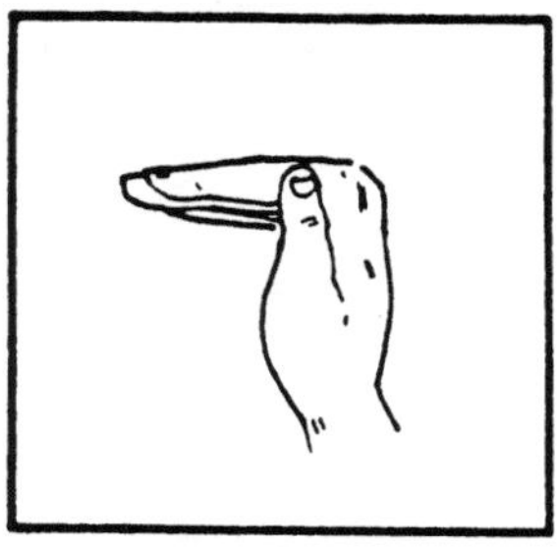

Bunched Hand

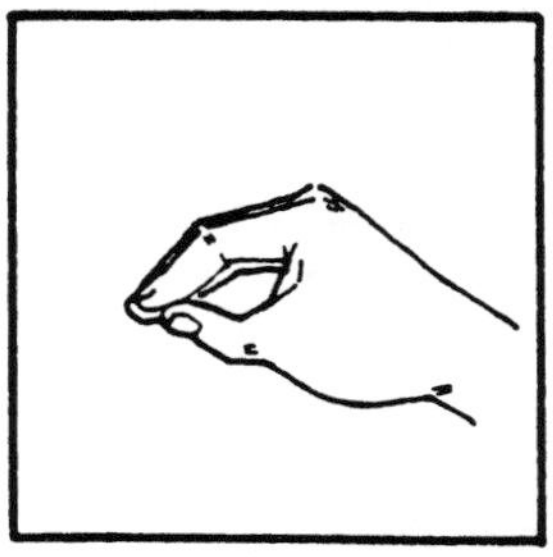

"O" hand

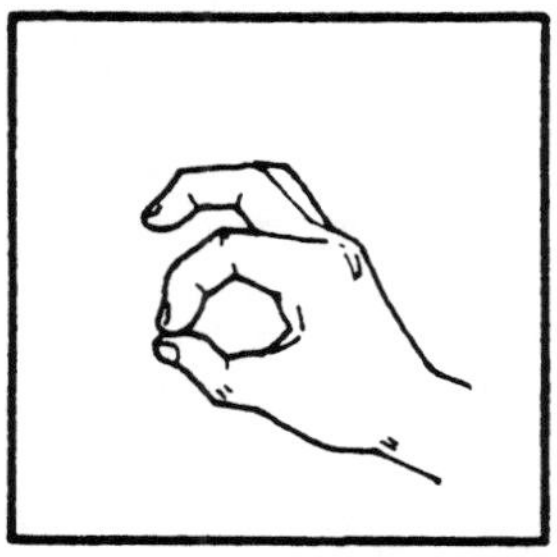

Cupped Hand

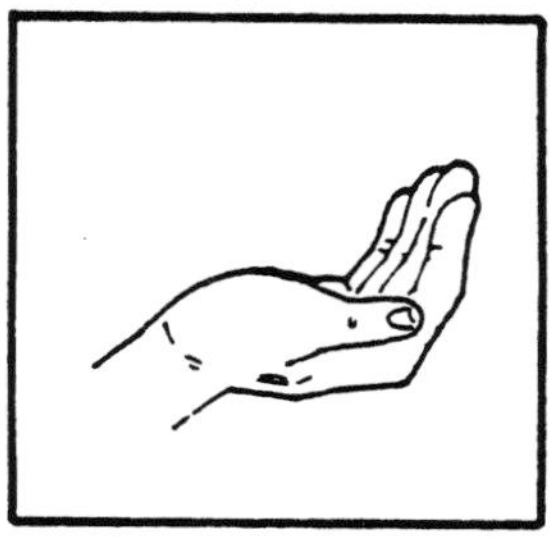

Full "O" Hand

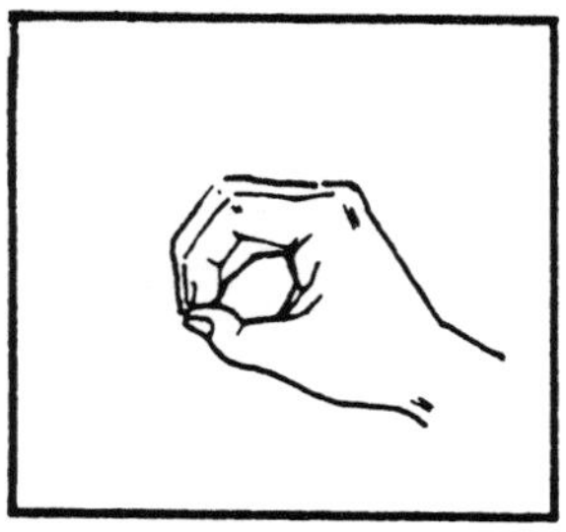

Hand shapes based on the **Right hand** shape of British two-handed finger-spelling.

"C" Hand

Full "C" Hand

"M" Hand

"N" Hand

"R" Hand

"V" Hand

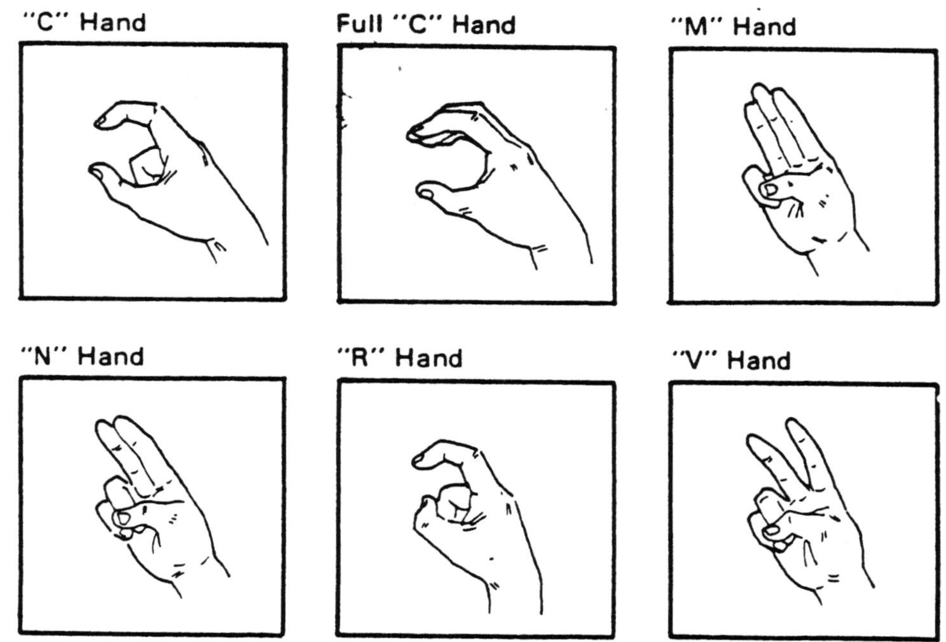

These are the most common hand shapes, but do not cover every shape used in signing. They may be further clarified, e.g. Rt. hand loosely cupped, L. hand slightly bent, two "V" hands, fingers bent, etc.

If the caption says, e.g. index, middle finger and thumb extended, then it is understood that the other fingers are closed.

DIRECTIONS

The terms used to describe the directions in which the hands are facing, pointing and moving, are as follows:

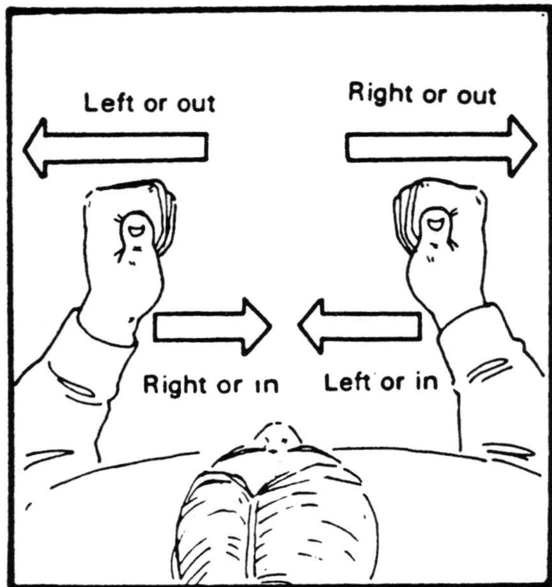

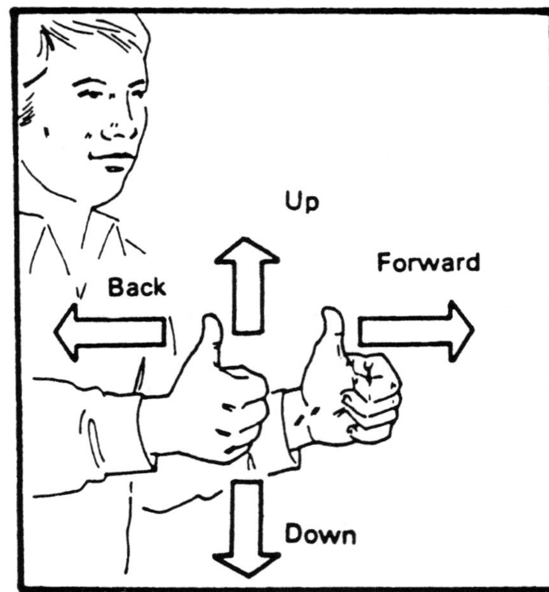

FACING

The direction the palm of the hand faces is given as "palm up", "palm back", etc. even if the hand is closed.

In the above illustrations, the Rt. hand is palm left, the L. hand is palm right. They may also be described as palms facing.

POINTING

The hand may be described as "pointing" up, forward, etc. even if the fingers are bent in a different direction, or closed.

In the above illustrations, both hands are pointing forward, thumbs up.

MOVEMENT

Where a movement or position is diagonal, it is described as "forward/left", "back/right", etc.

Many movements are described as "hands move **alternately**". This means that they move at the same time in opposite directions as in "up and down", or continuously in the same circular direction, alternately.

Some signs need a full description of hand shapes and positions before any movement is made, this is then called a **formation**, this means they keep their position together as they move.

GUIDE TO DRAWINGS

The following types of arrows mean:

A broken movement.

Movement in one direction then the other.

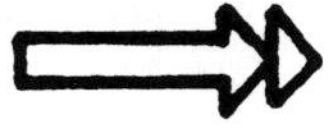

Repeated movement.

Hands move apart.

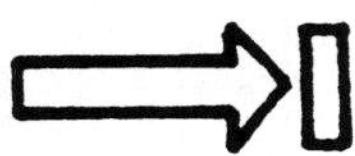

The sign ends with stress.

Hand or fingers open then close.

Open hand closes.

Closed hand opens.

Impact on point drawn.

Very small repeated movements.

Indicates sign invented or adapted for School use.

Hands drawn in dotted lines show the **start** of the sign. Hands drawn in solid lines show the **finish**.

Signs that are mimed actions of holding objects may have the object drawn in dotted lines to help people understand and remember them.

NUMBER SYSTEM

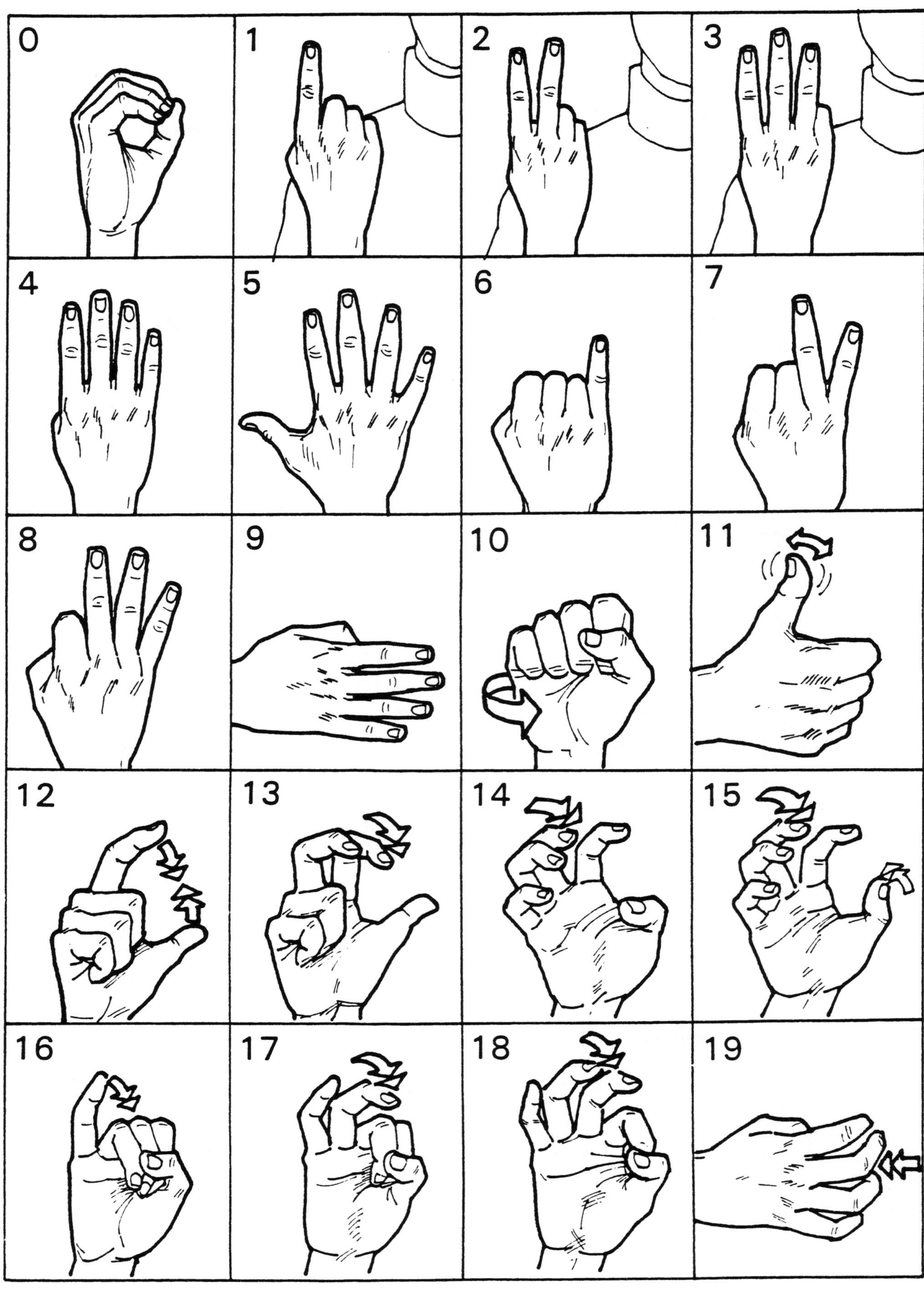

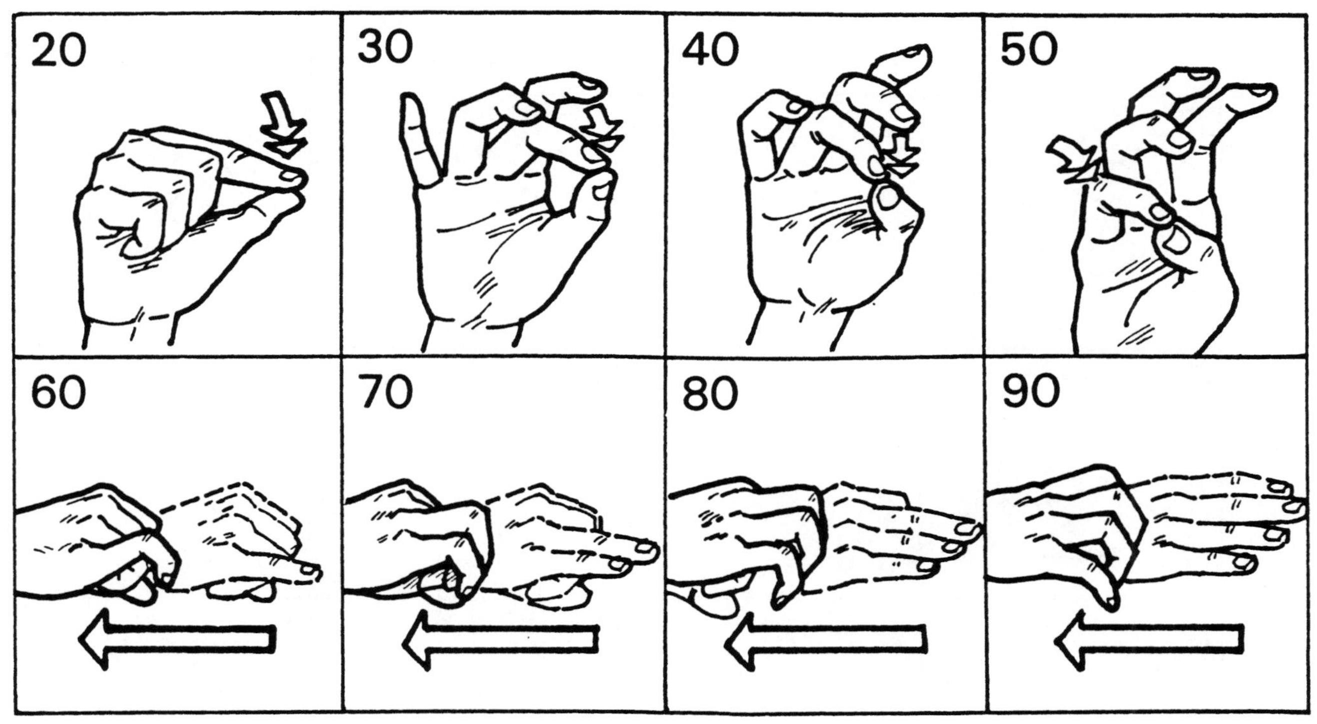

HUNDRED

THOUSAND

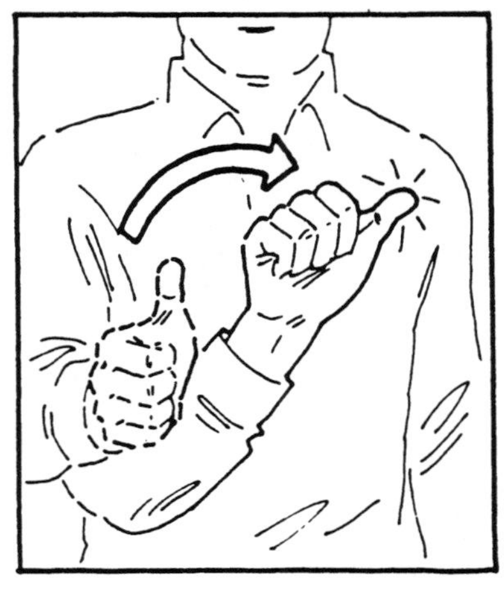

MILLION

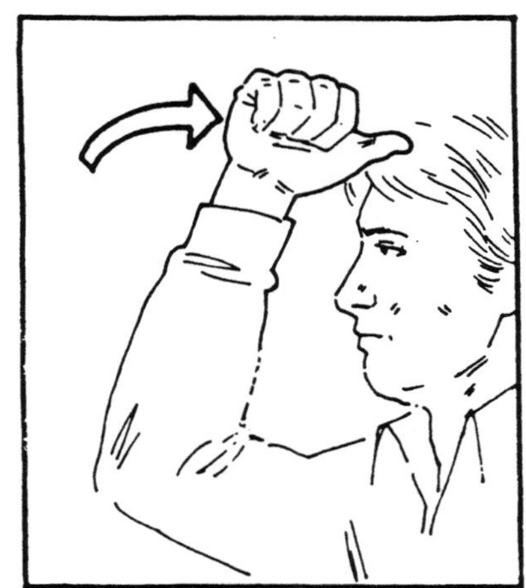

BRITISH TWO-HANDED FINGER SPELLING ALPHABET

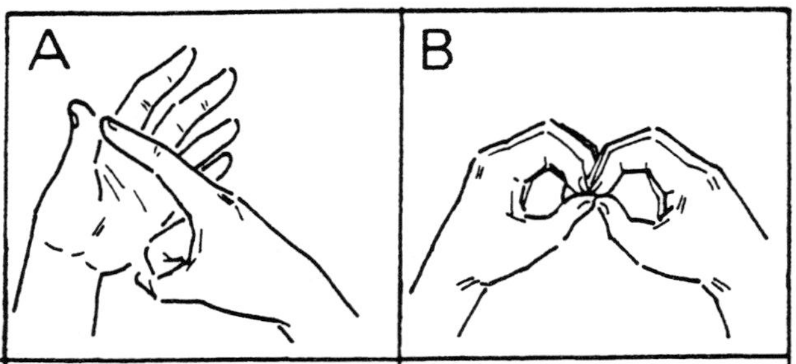

A

B

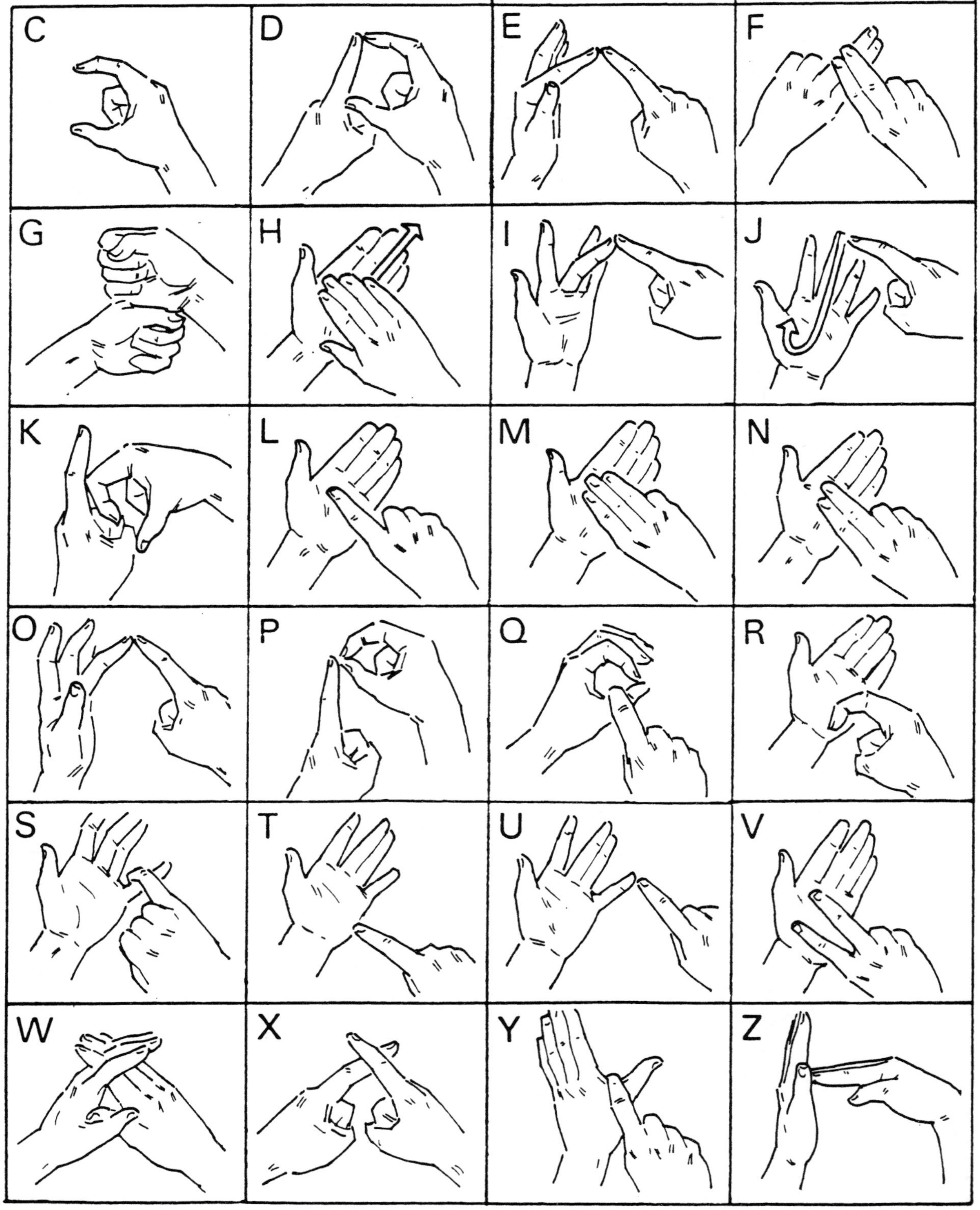

C

D

E

F

G

H

I

J

K

L

M

N

O

P

Q

R

S

T

U

V

W

X

Y

Z

DEAF-BLIND ALPHABET

The Rt. hand is represented as that of the sender forming the letters onto the passive L. hand of the deaf-blind recipient.

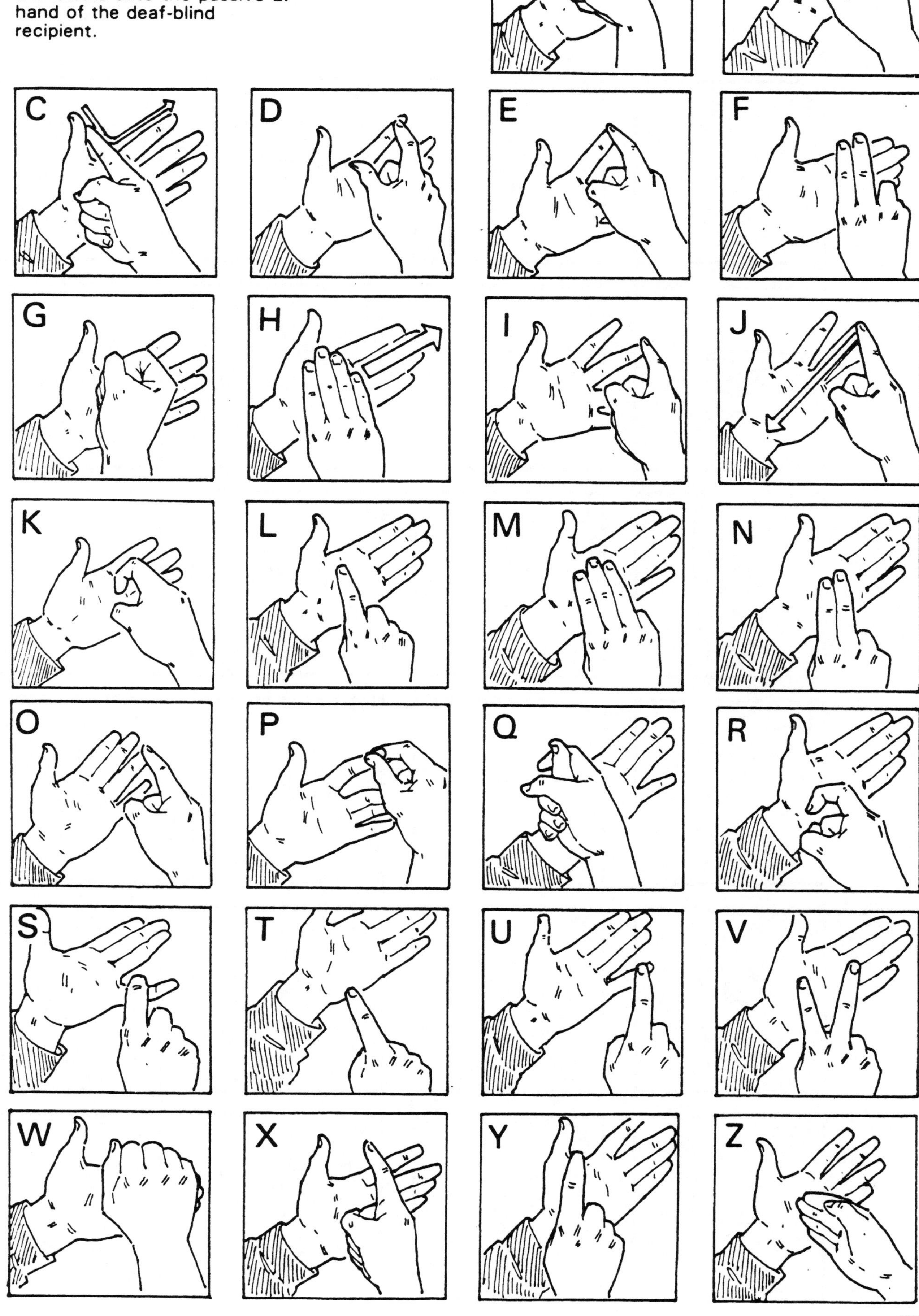

AMERICAN ONE-HANDED FINGER SPELLING ALPHABET

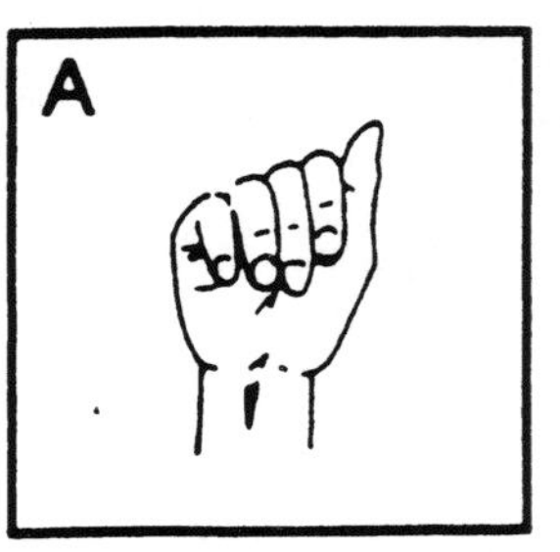

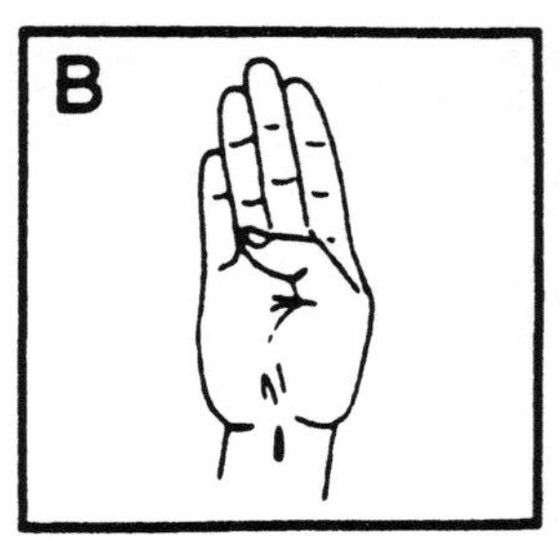

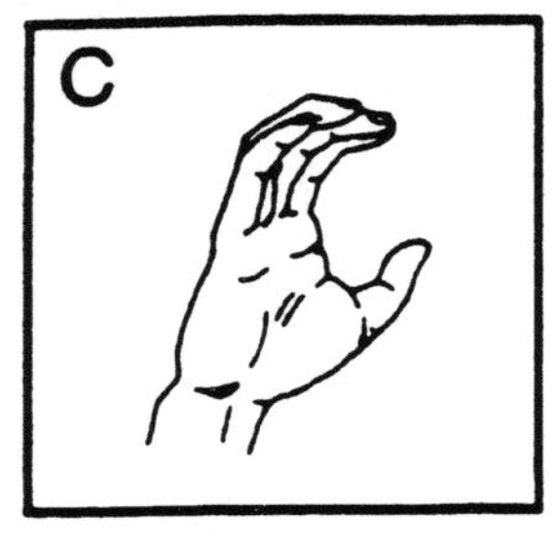

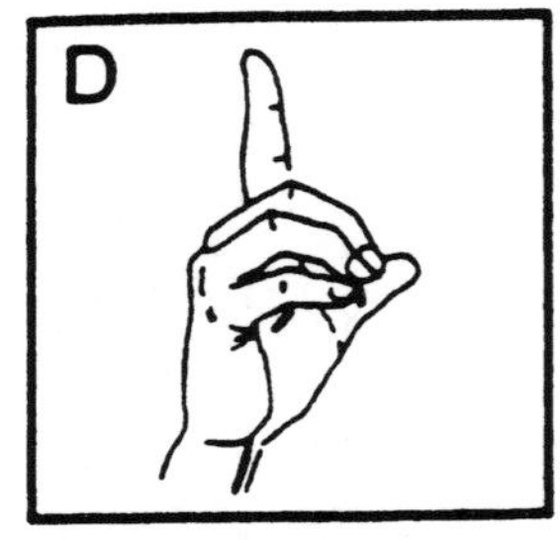

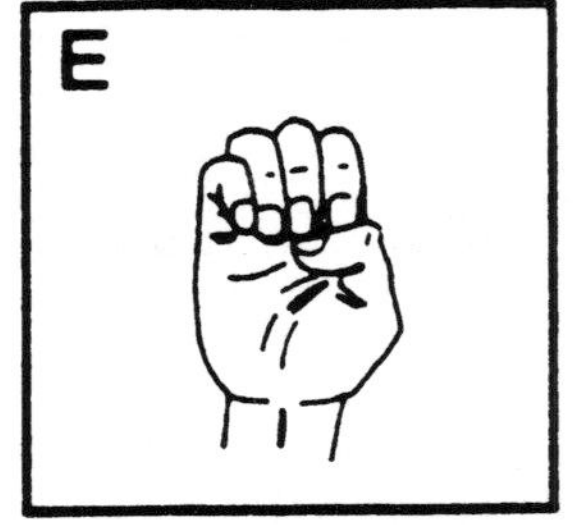

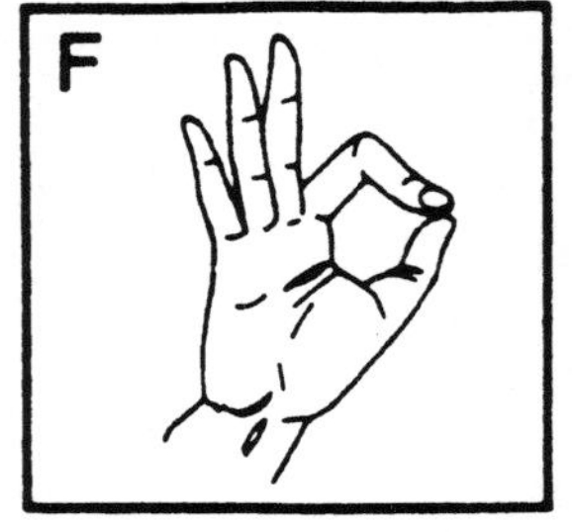

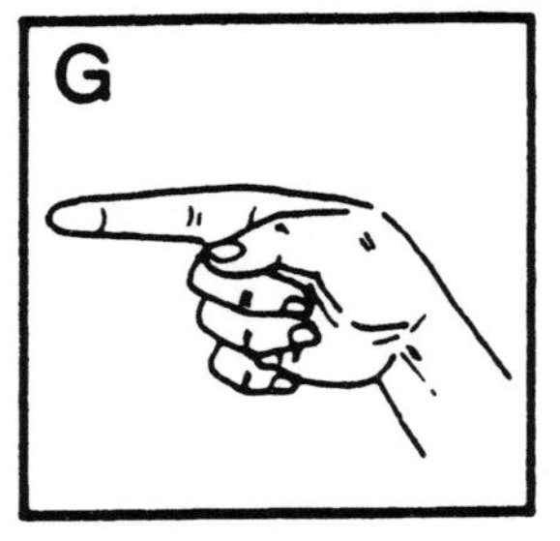

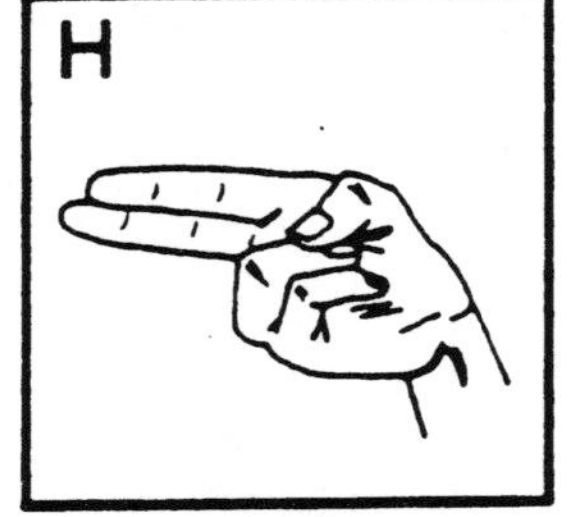

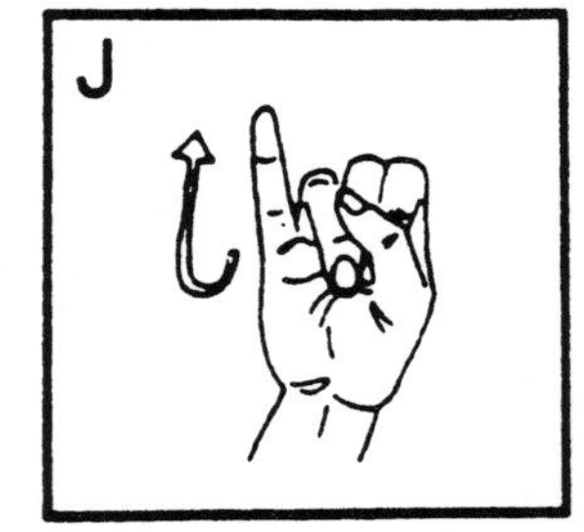

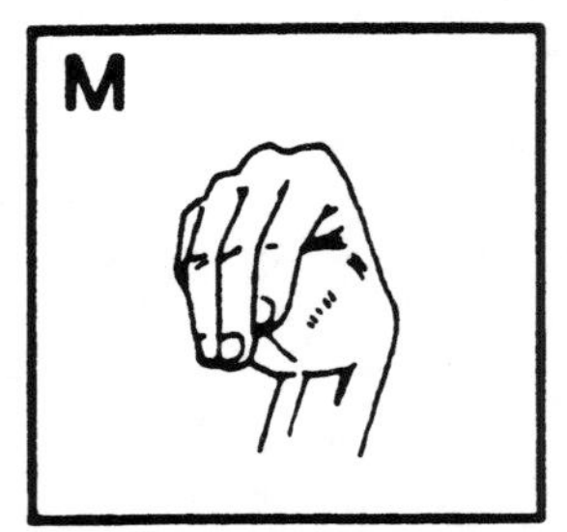

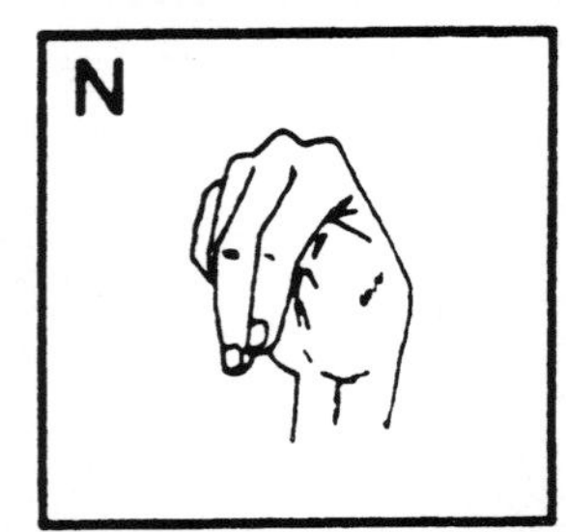

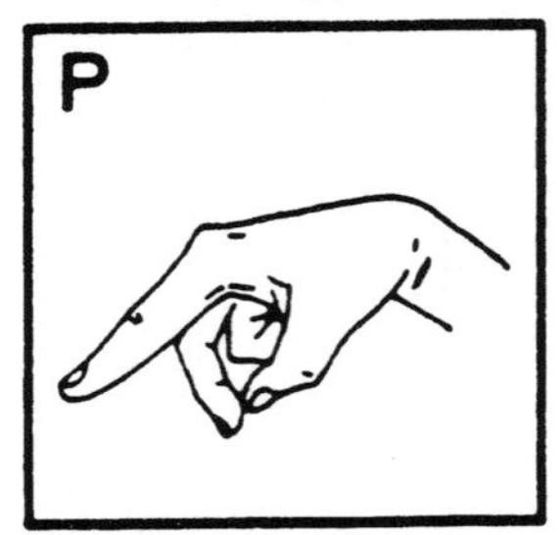

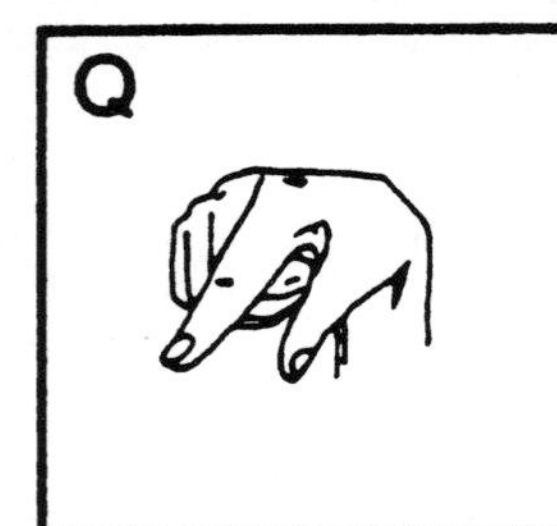

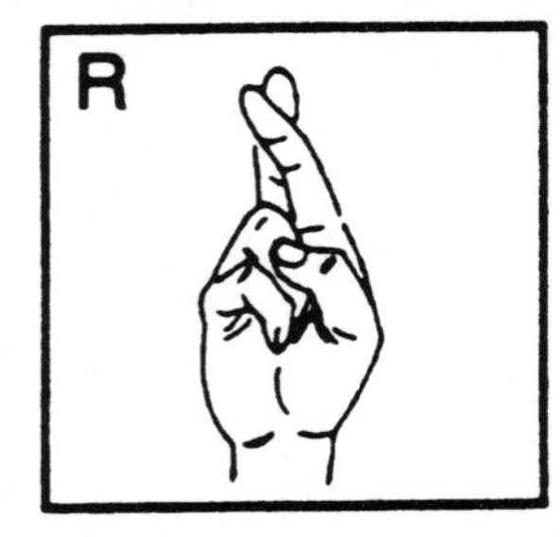

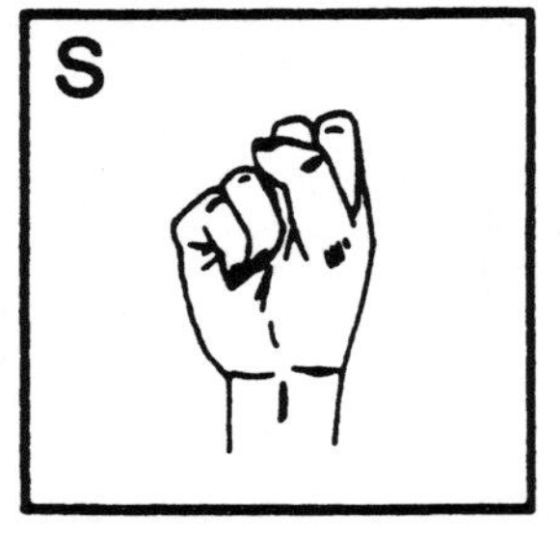

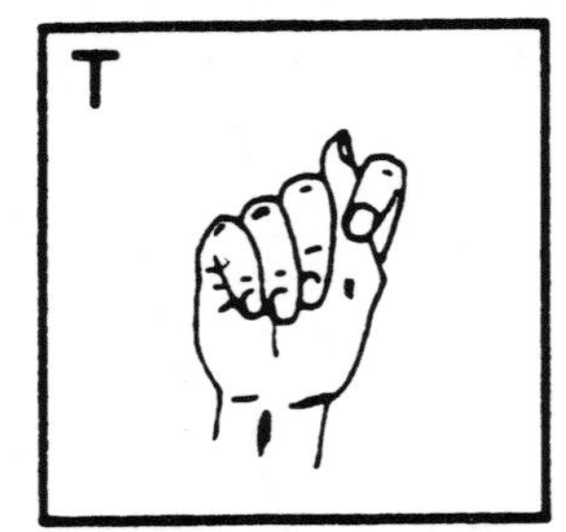

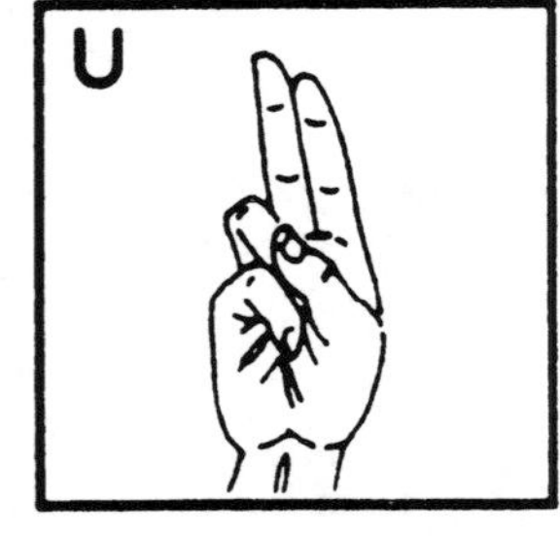

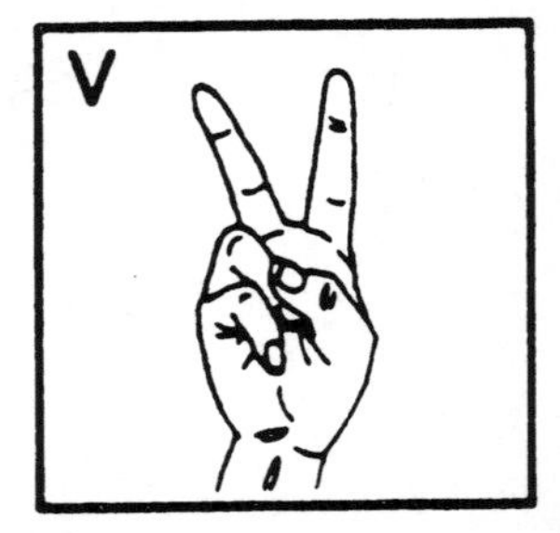

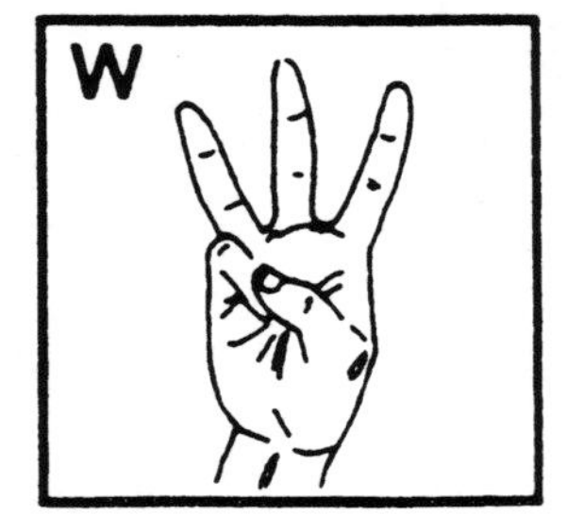

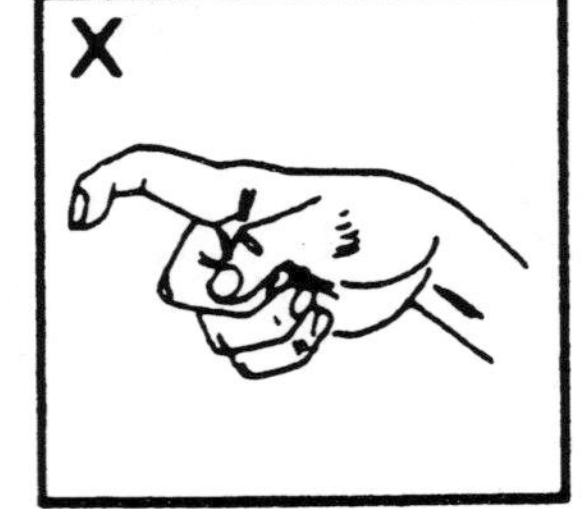

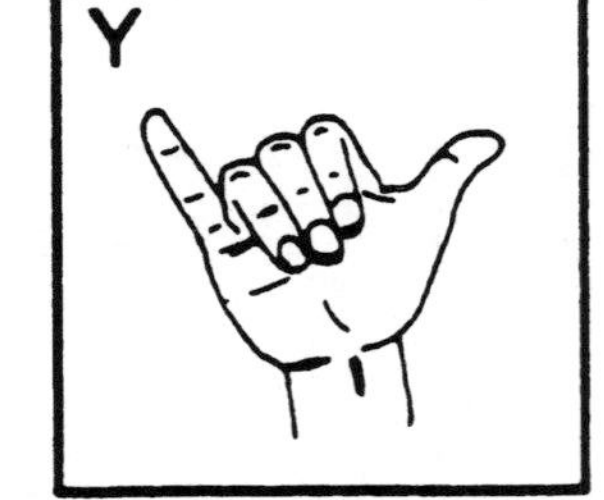

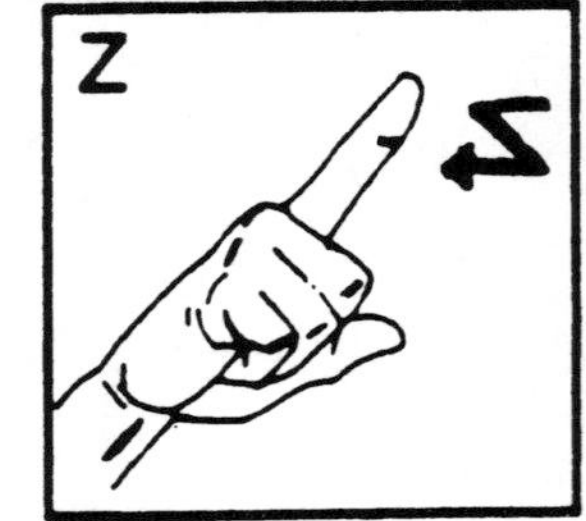

SIGN VOCABULARY

We wish to stress that signs vary considerably according to INDIVIDUAL choice, REGIONAL variation and most importantly, according to CONTEXT.

We recommend that the best way of developing skills is through attendance at classes and contact with the deaf community.

A

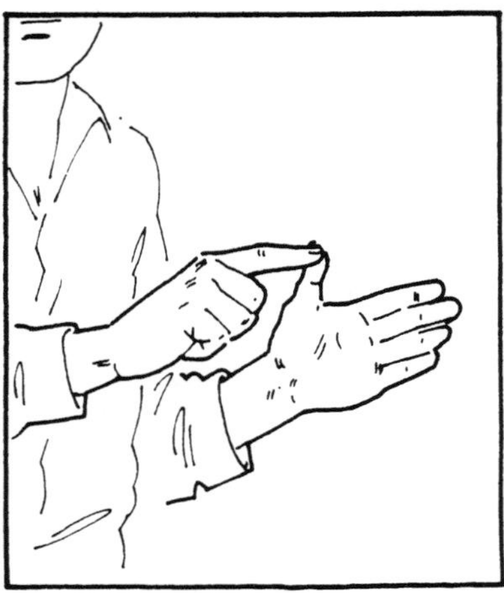

Fingerspell "A"

ABOUT (approx.)

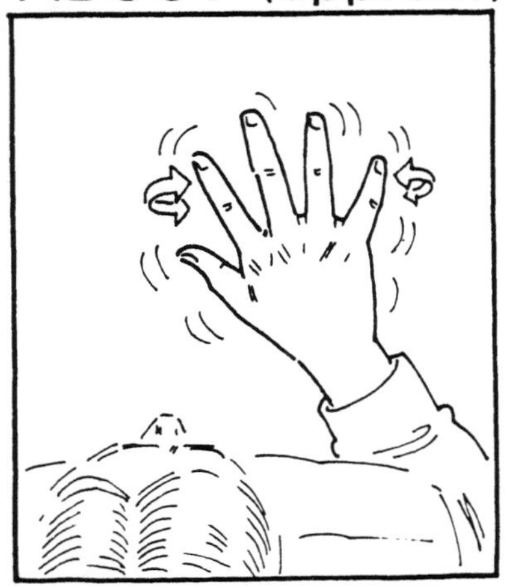

Rt. open hand palm down pointing forward. Hand waggles.

ABOUT (concerning)

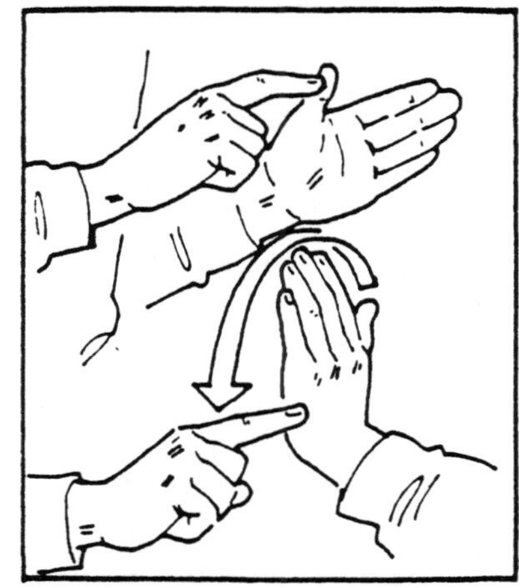

Fingerspell "A", then sweep Rt. index finger over L. fingertips to spell "T".

ABOUT (the area)

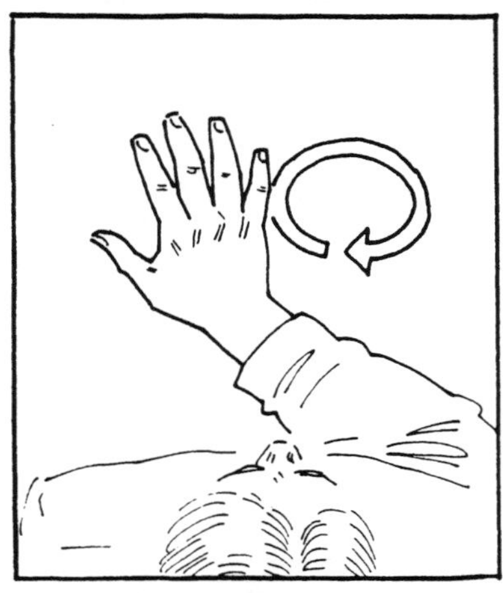

Rt. open hand palm down makes small horizontal circle.

ABOVE

Two bent hands facing each other, Rt. hand moves up in small arc to finish above L.

ABROAD

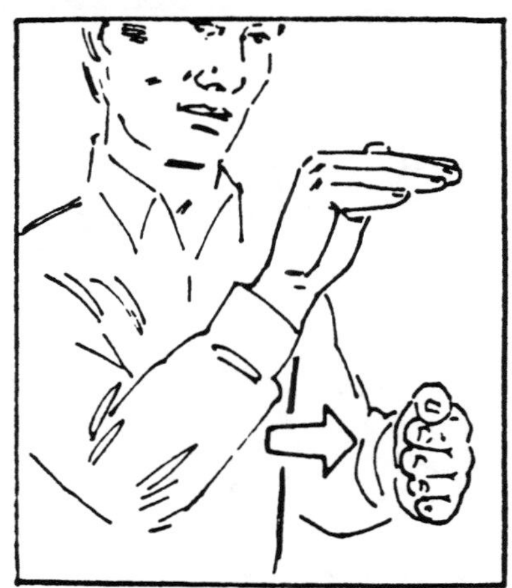

Left arm held in front of body. Rt. bent hand moves forward making contact with right forearm on L. hand.

ACCIDENT

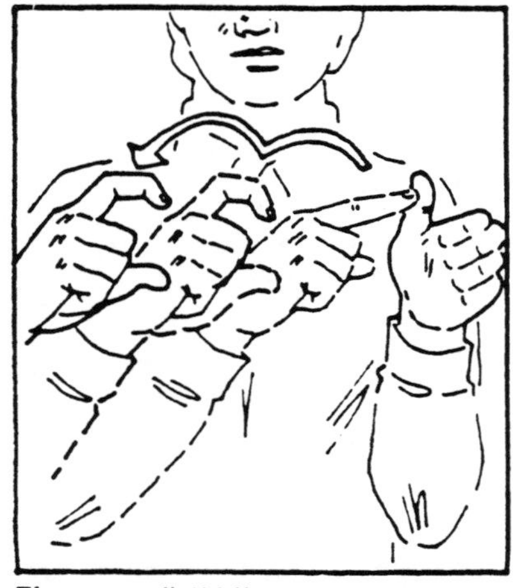

Fingerspell "A", then form letter "C" and move Rt. hand away to the right in two hops.

ACROSS

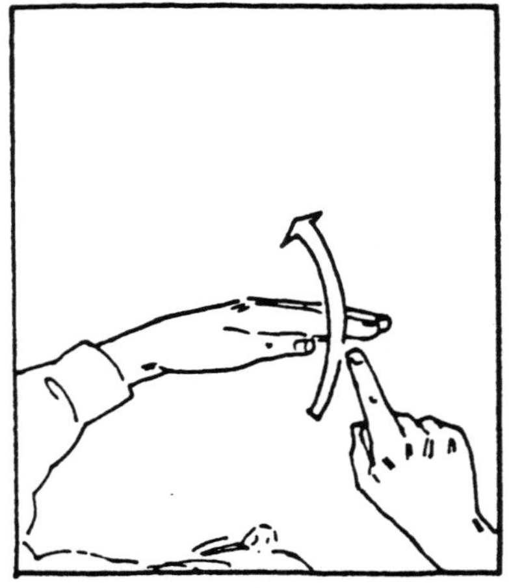

Rt. index pointing forward starts behind palm back L. hand and moves in forward arc over L. hand.

ACT (drama)

Two closed hands held on chest move up and down alternately.

ACTUAL

Two "O" hands, palms forward, held at sides of head, make small movement forward, twice.

ADD

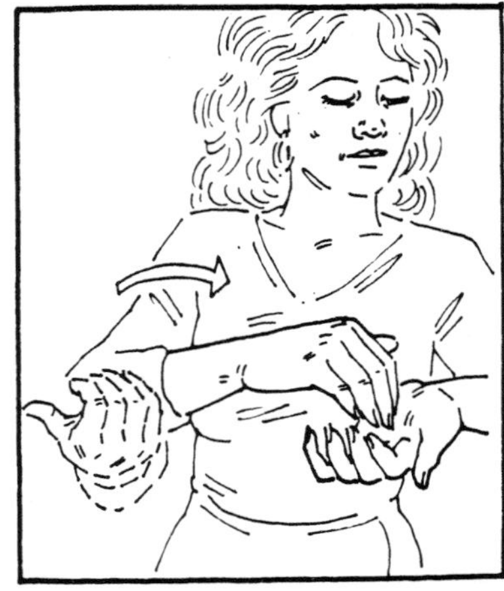

Two slightly bent hands palms up, mime tipping contents of Rt. hand into palm of L.

ADDRESS

Two flat hands, palms facing about 6" apart jerk forwards twice.

ADOPT

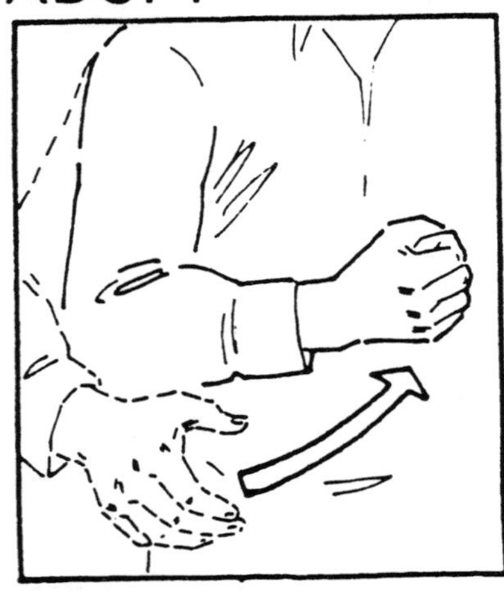

Rt. clawed hand move back towards body as hand closes.

ADULT

Rt. hand, palm down held above head to indicate height.

ADVANCE

Flat hands, palms back held in front of body. Move both hands forward in small arc.

ADVANTAGE

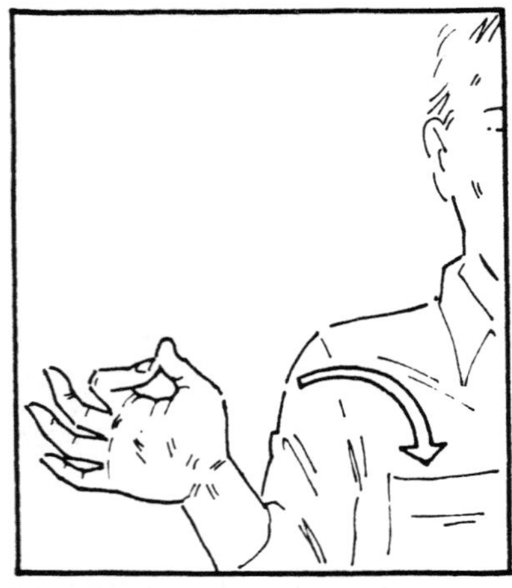

Rt. "O" hand starts palm up then moves up and over as if putting imaginary coin in pocket.

ADVERTISE

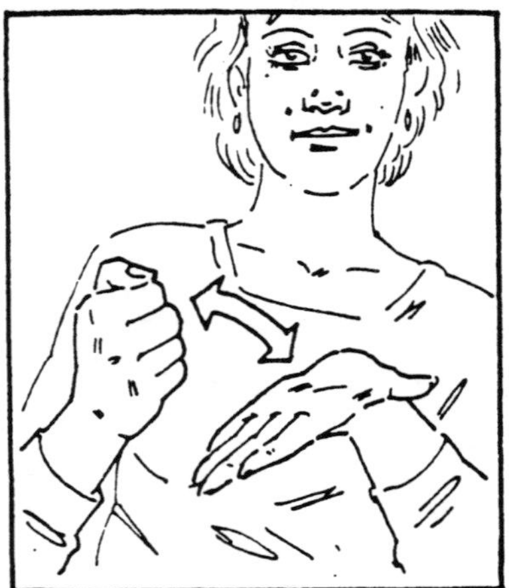

Knuckles of Rt. closed hand contact L. palm, then move off, twisting to palm up.

AEROPLANE

Rt. closed hand, thumb and little finger extended held near head, moves forward and up.

AFRICA

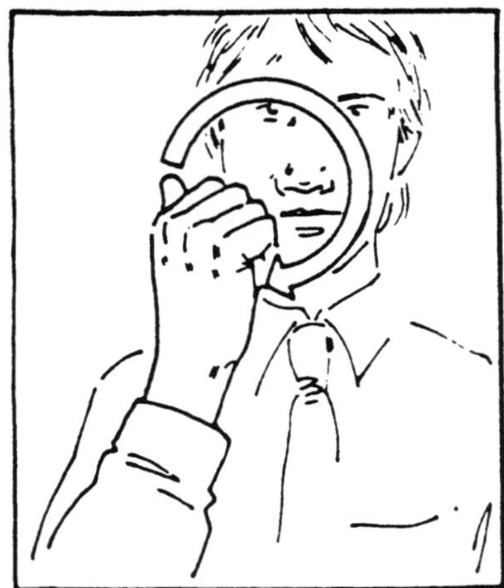

Rt. closed hand palm back makes a circle in front of face.

AFTER

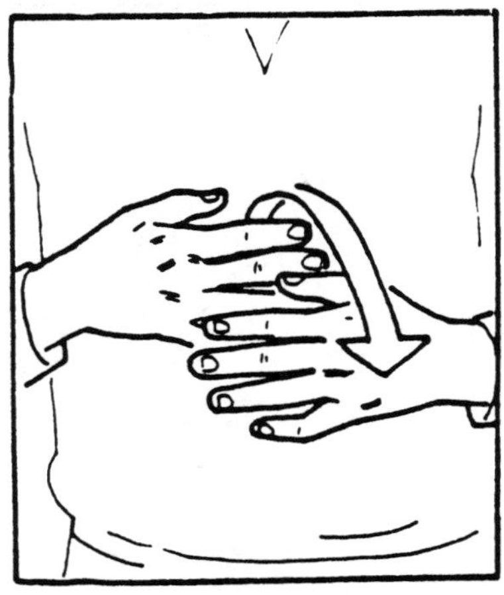

Two flat hands, palms back, Rt. behind L; Rt. jumps over to finish in front of L.

AFTERNOON

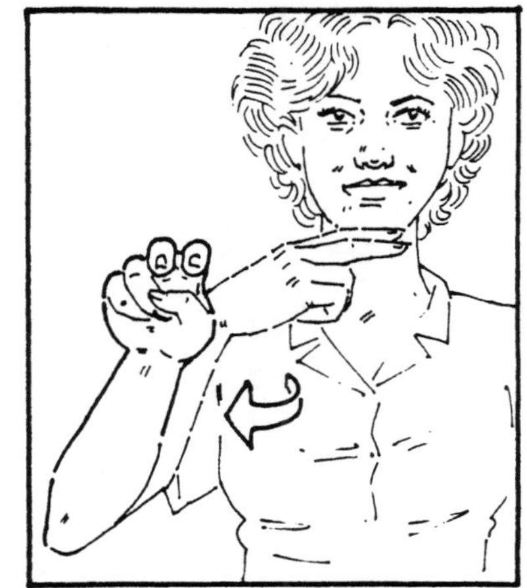

Rt. index and middle fingers touch chin then twist to point forward.

AGAIN

Rt. "V" hand palm left, shakes downwards twice.

AGAINST (vs.)

Two closed hands indexes extended 6" apart, move towards each other in sharp movement.

AGE

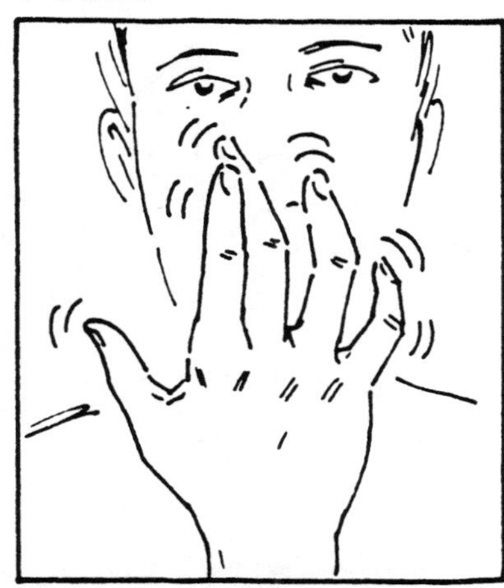

Fingers of open hand flutter in front of nose.

AGREE

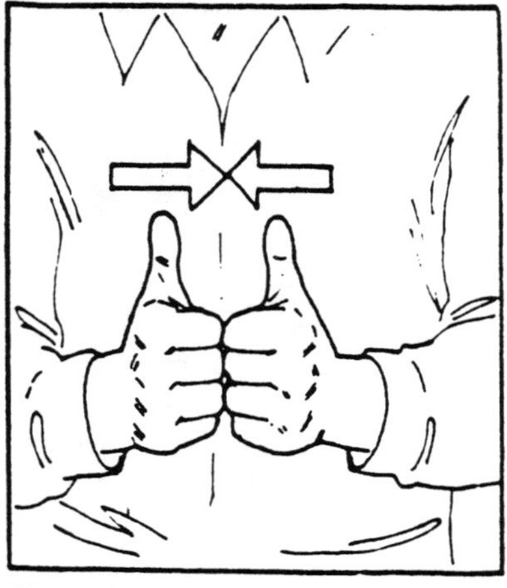

Two closed hands thumbs up held about 6" apart move together and touch.

AHEAD

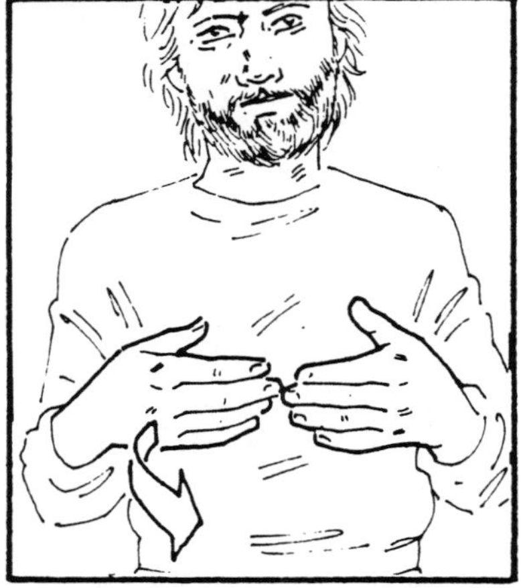

Two flat hands, palms back held in front of body; Rt. hand moves to the right and forward in small arc.

AIM

Rt. flat hand moves towards extended L. index finger.

AIR

Rt. hand. wafts towards side of face several times.

AIRPORT

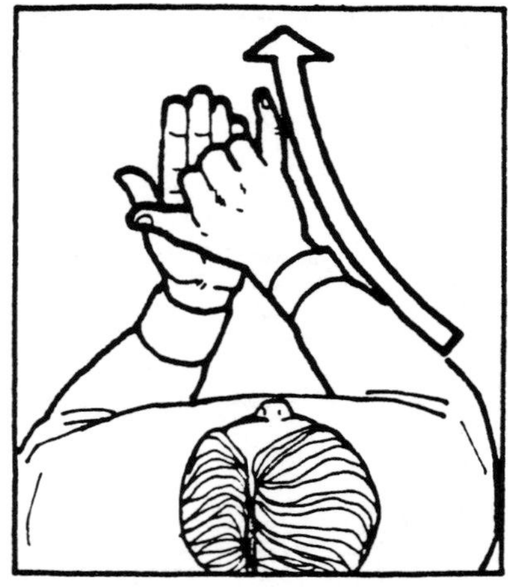

Sign for "aeroplane" moves to land on L. palm.

ALARM

Rt. index pointing up supported by L. hand waggles from side to side like an alarm bell.

ALL

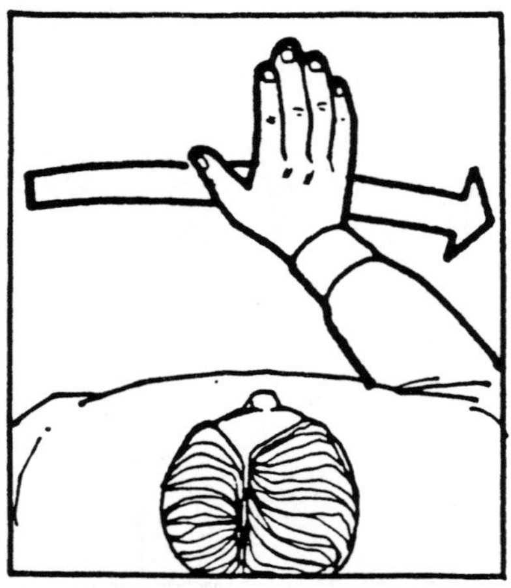

Flat hand moves in front of body in horizontal sweep.

ALLOW

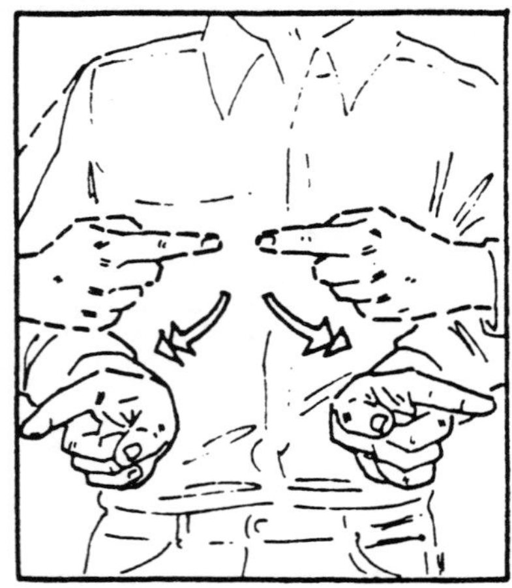

Tips of index fingers touch, then swing open and apart.

ALONE

L. hand·palm back, Rt. index extended placed above/behind L; Rt. moves down then to the right.

ALPHABET

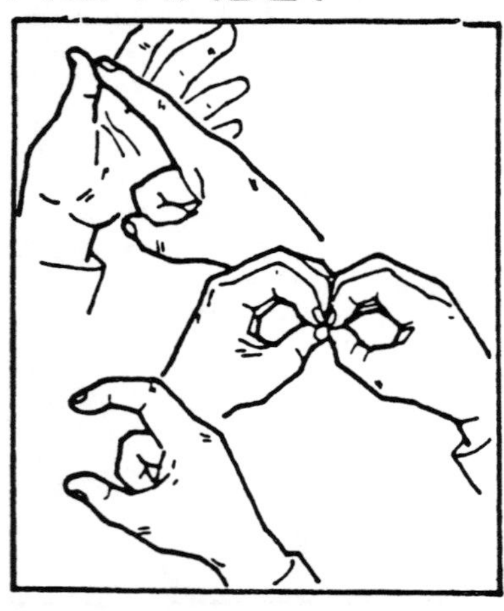

Fingerspell "A" "B" "C".

ALREADY

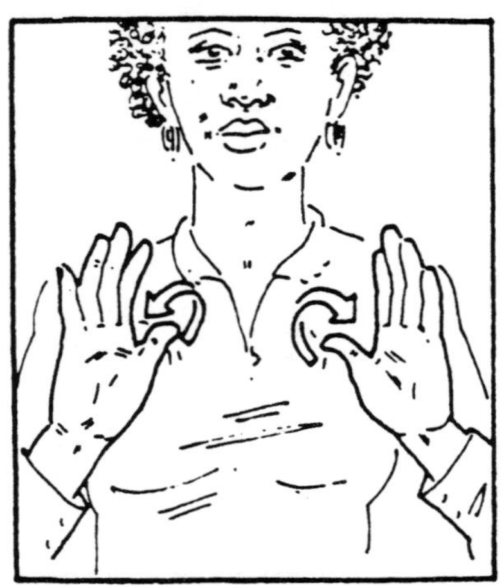

Thumb tips of open hands contact chest twice.

ALRIGHT

Rt. closed hand, thumb extended makes clockwise circle above L. palm then comes down onto L. palm.

ALSO

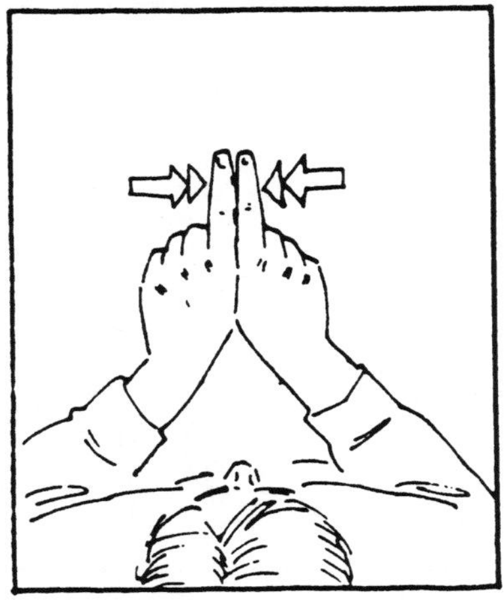

Index fingers tap together twice.

ALTERNATE

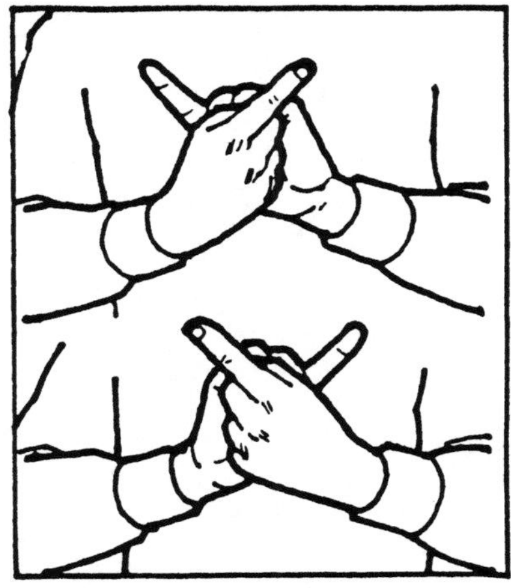

Index fingers extended, palms together - swivel Rt. in front of L. then L. in front of Rt.

ALTOGETHER

Two open hands, palms forward twist round and down and finish as two bunched hands, palms back.

ALWAYS

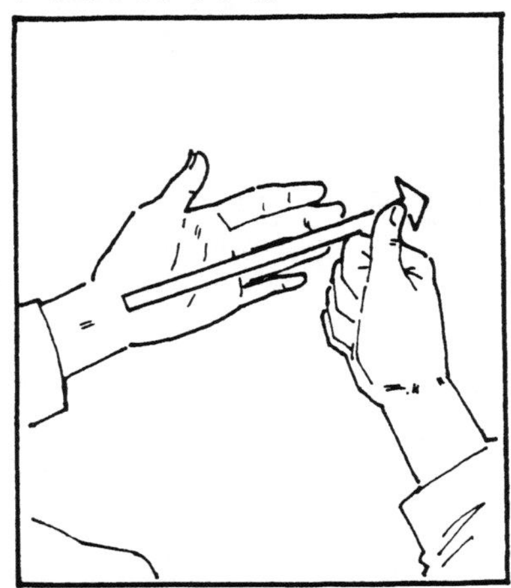

Rt. closed hand, thumb extended contacts heel of L. hand and sweeps along to L. fingertips.

ALL THE TIME

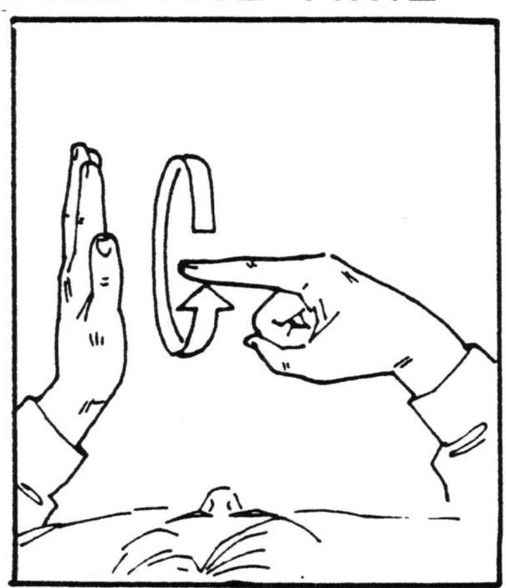

Rt. index makes repeated forward circular movements, pointing towards the L. palm.

AMAZE

Two "N" hands palms facing held in front of face move apart sharply.

AMBULANCE

Mime steering, then draw cross on left upper arm with Rt. thumb.

AMERICA

Two open hands fingers meshed make horizontal circle in front of body.

AND

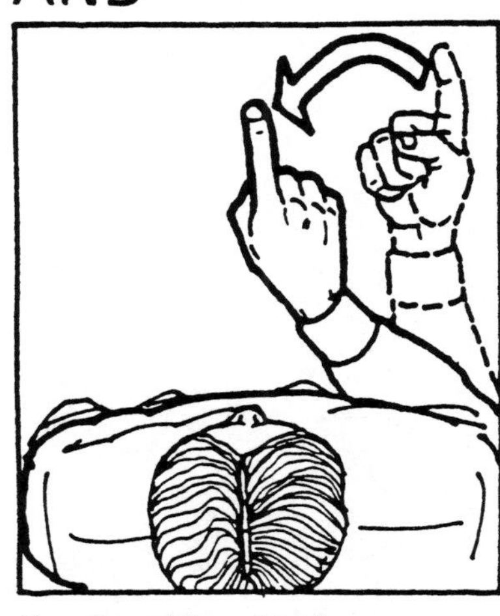

Rt. closed hand index extended, palm up, flips over to palm down.

ANGEL

Two flat hands crossed at wrists, held against chest.

ANGLE

Heel of Rt. flat hand contacts fingertips of L. flat hand and pivots slightly upwards to form angle.

ANGRY

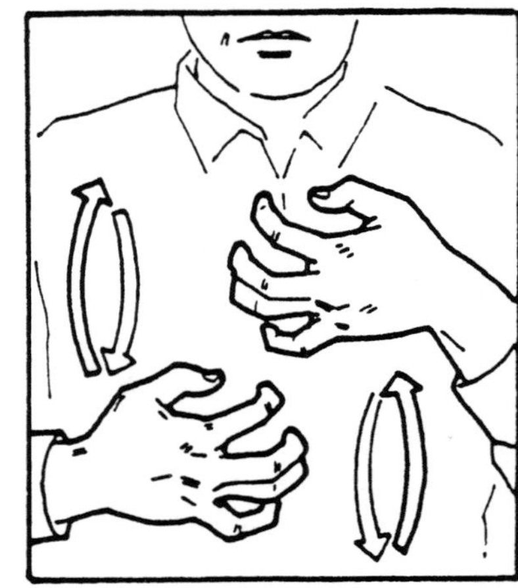

Clawed hands alternately claw up body several times.

ANIMAL

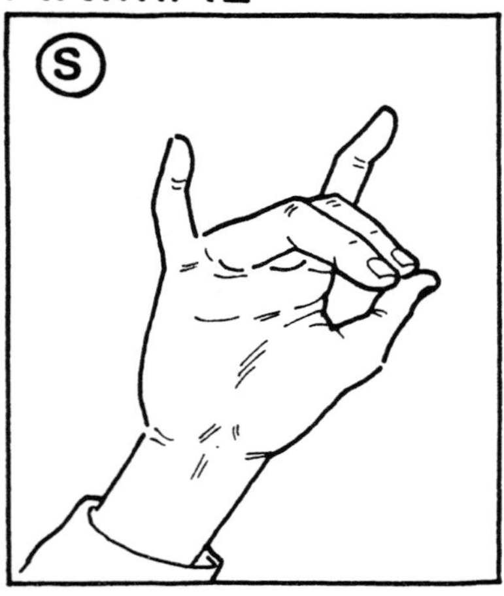

Rt. hand palm forward index and little fingers up, middle, ring and thumbtips touching.

ANNOUNCE

Index fingers touch sides of mouth then sweep forward and apart.

ANORAK

Mime pulling on hood then zip up.

ANOTHER

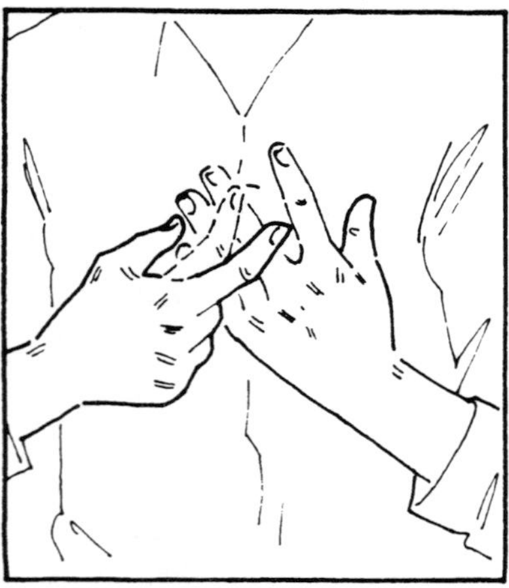

L. open hand fingers up; flick back of middle fingertip with Rt. index twice.

ANSWER

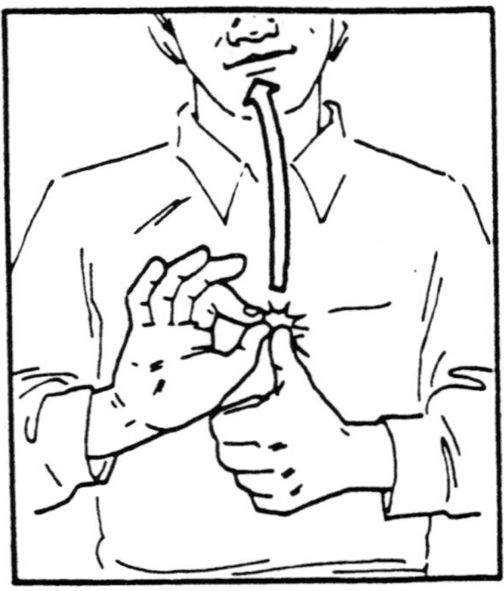

L. hand thumb up; Rt. "O" hand contacts tip of L. thumb and moves to mouth.

ANY

Rt. closed hand, thumb and little finger extended, sweeps from left to right in front of body whilst waggling.

ANYWHERE

Two closed hands with thumbs and little fingers extended, start crossed then pull apart waggling.

APOLOGISE

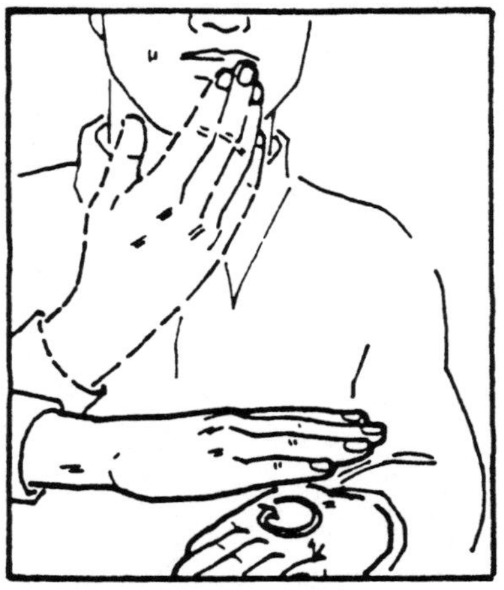

Touch mouth with fingertips of Rt. flat hand, then make small circles on palm of L. hand.

APPLE

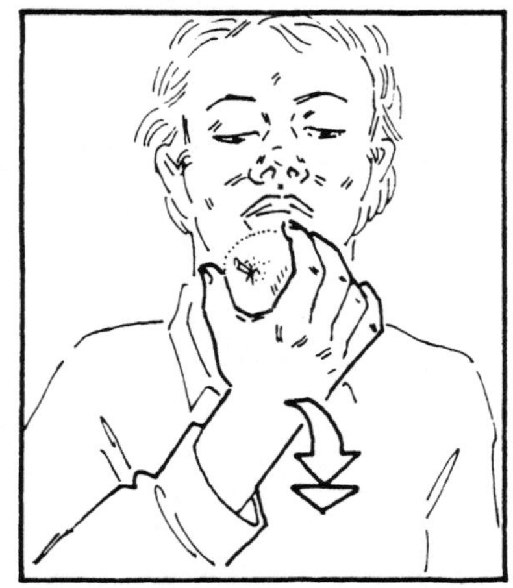

Mime holding apple in front of mouth twist from wrist as if taking a bite.

APPOINT

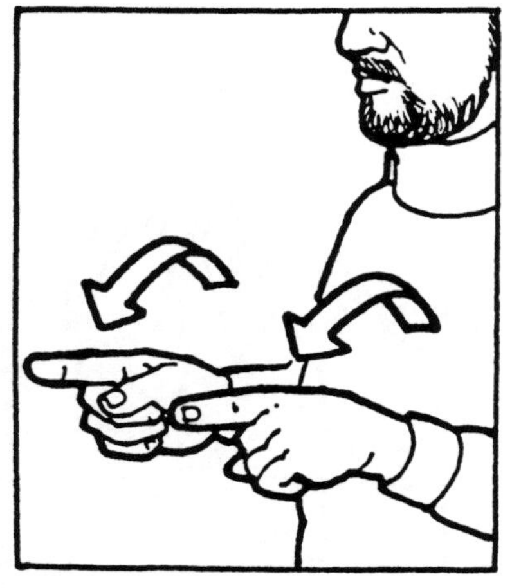

Two indexes extended, pointing forward/up move forward in small arc and point forward.

APPOINTMENT

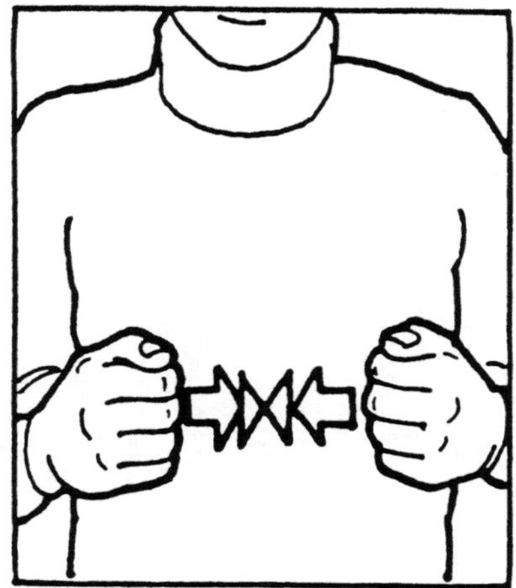

Two closed hands knock together twice.

APPRENTICE

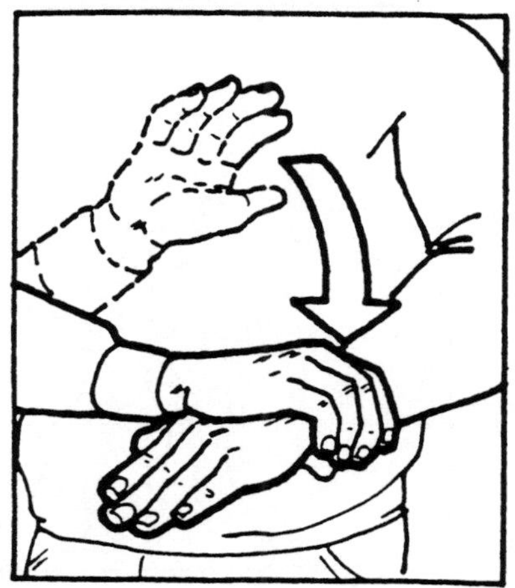

Bring Rt. hand down to grasp L. wrist.

APPROACH

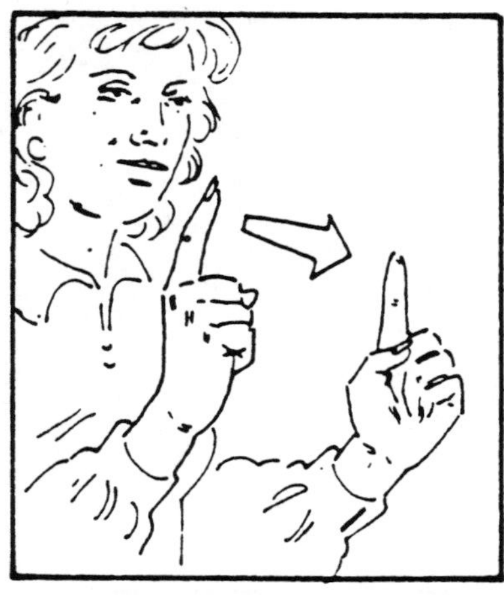

L. index held away from body; Rt. index moves from near body towards L.

APPROVE

Palm down closed hands, thumbs extended, make downward movement.

ARGUE

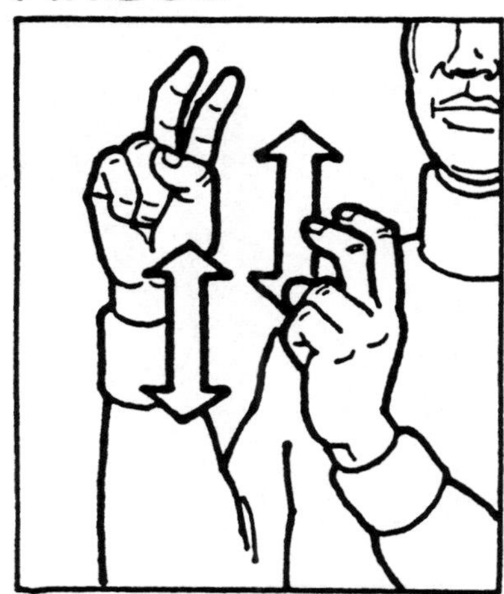

Index and middle fingers open and bent, face each other and move alternately up and down.

ARITHMETIC

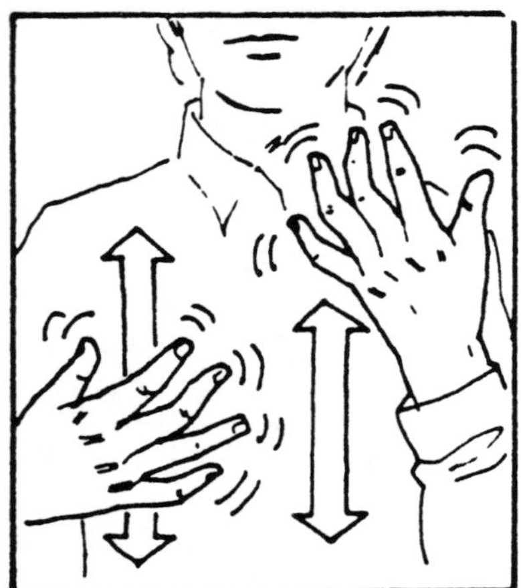

Two open hands move alternately up and down in front of body, fingers fluttering.

ARMCHAIR

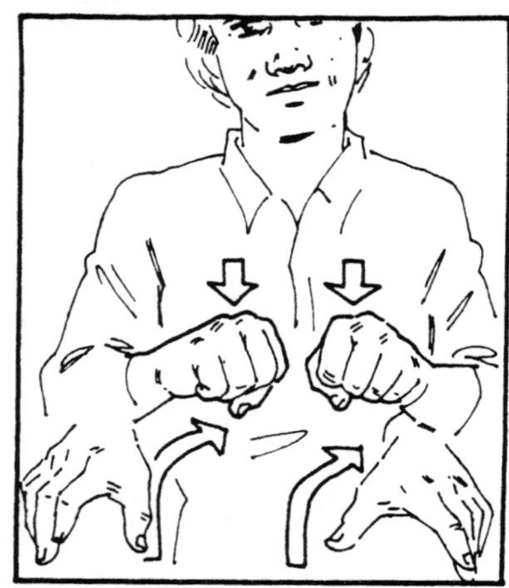

Cupped hands, palms down pull back to indicate chair arms, then sign "chair".

ARMY

Rt. flat hand, palm left, pointing up touches right then left upper chest.

ARRANGE

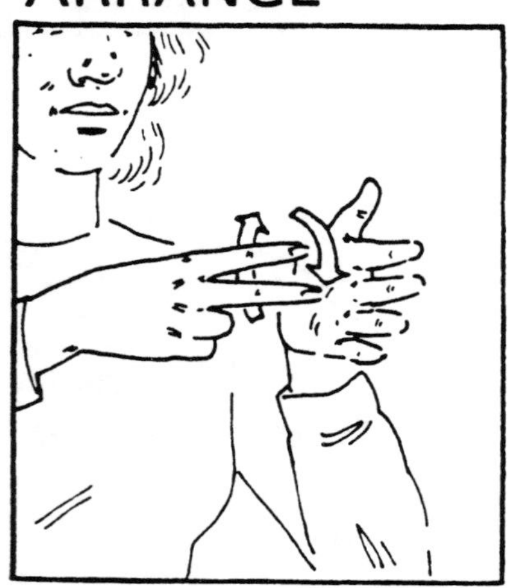

Tips of Rt. "V" hand contact L. palm alternately in twisting movement.

ARREST

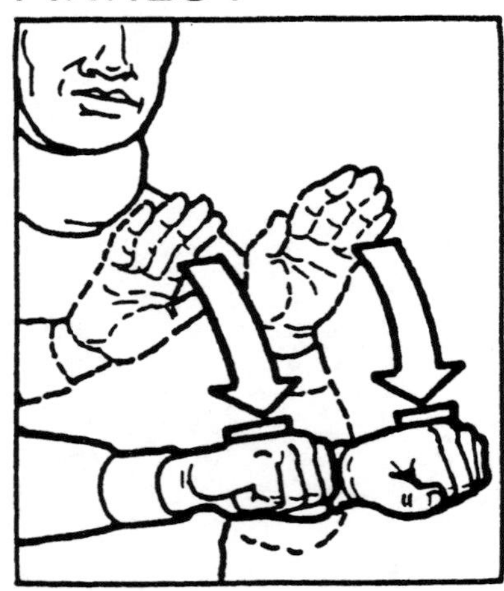

Two flat hands, slightly bent, palms down, move down sharply and close.

ARRIVE

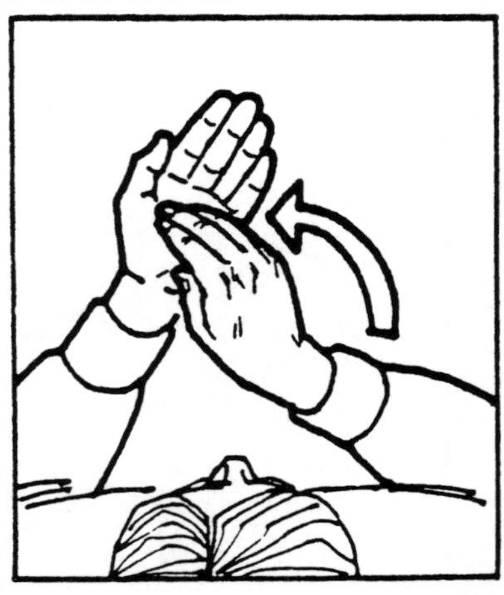

L. hand held away from body, Rt. bent hand moves forward/left in slight upward arc to touch L. palm with tips.

ART

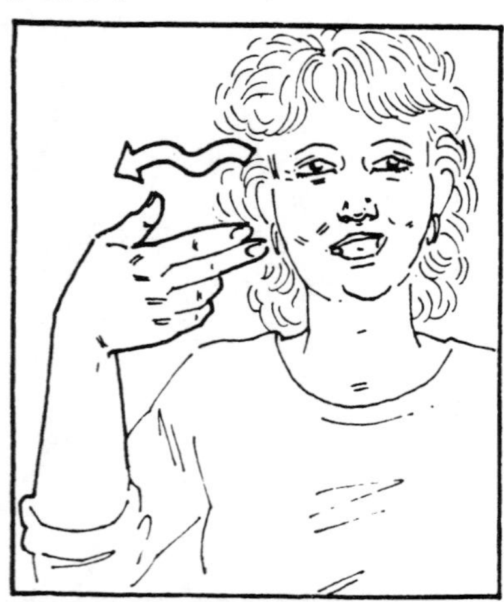

Rt. hand palm back, waggles from left to right.

ASHAMED

Open hand, palm back fingers pointing up, moves up in front of face in sharp movement.

ASIAN

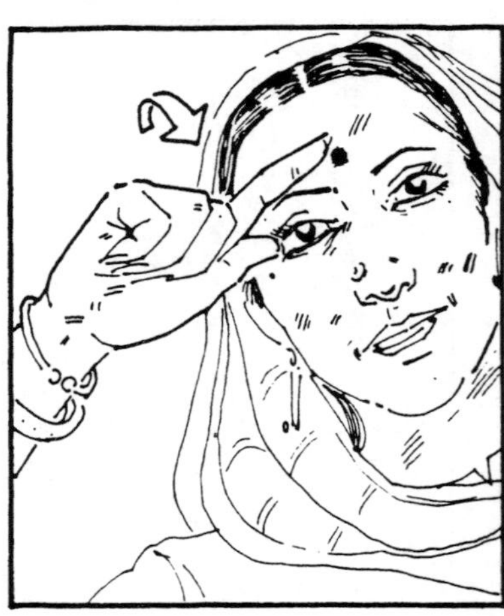

Rt. index points to middle of head and twists.

ASK

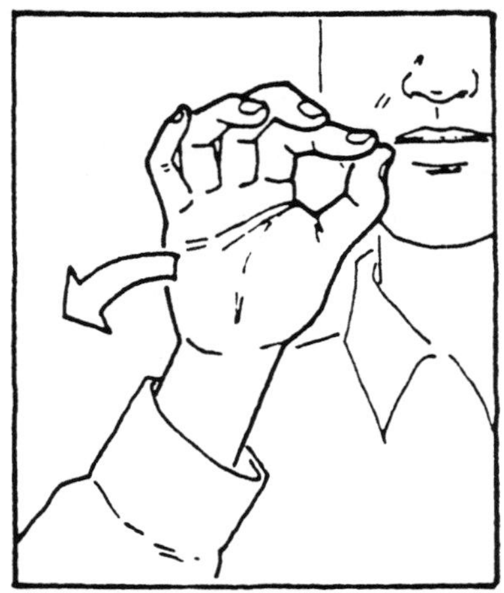

Rt. "O" palm forward moves forward from side of mouth in small arc.

ASLEEP

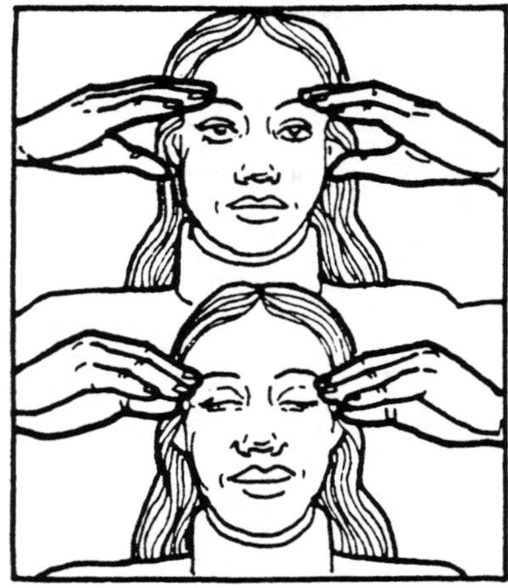

Hands held at temples snap shut to indicate eyes closing.

ATTITUDE

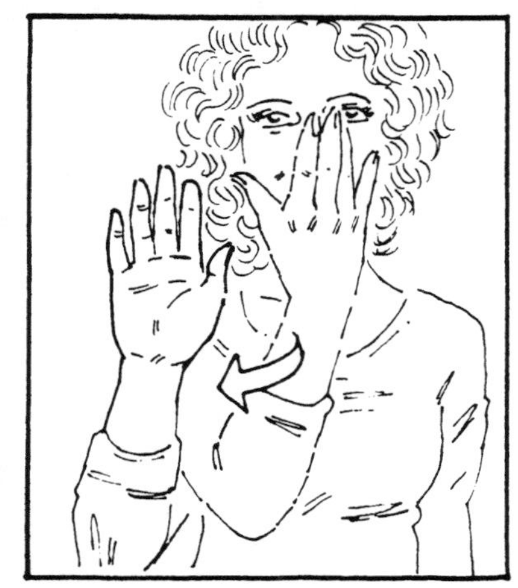

Rt. flat hand palm back in front of face moves forward and twists to palm forward.

ATTRACT

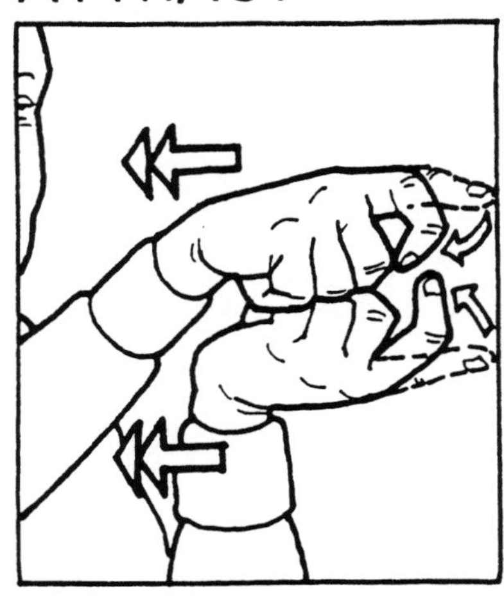

Two closed hands indexes extended, Rt. on top of L. Draw formation back twice and flex indexes.

AUNTIE

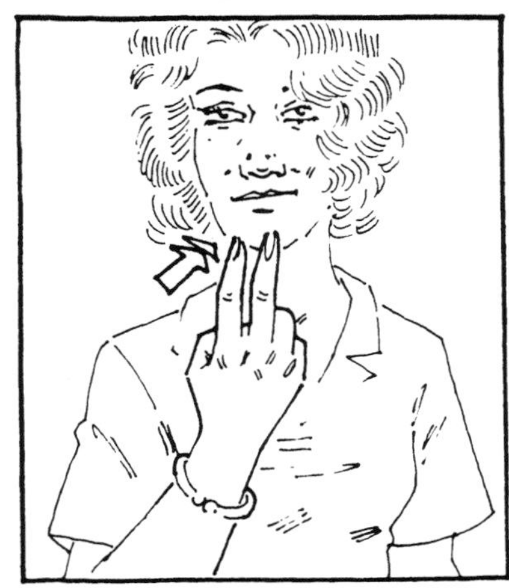

Rt. "V" hand taps chin twice.

AUSTRALIA

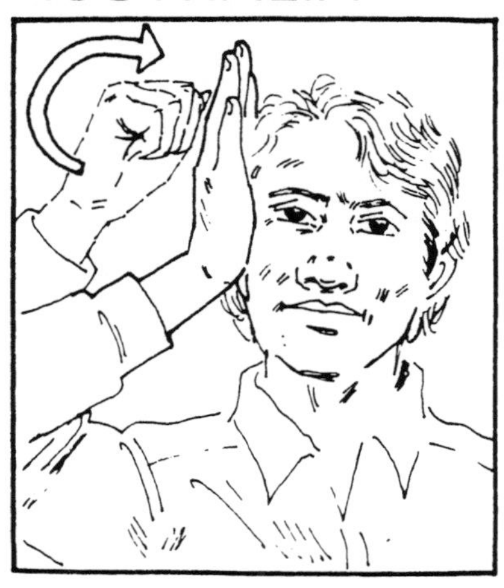

Tap right side of head with Rt. closed hand then with flat hand.

AUSTRIA

Both hands in bent "V" shape, held in front of body, crossed at the wrists.

AUTUMN

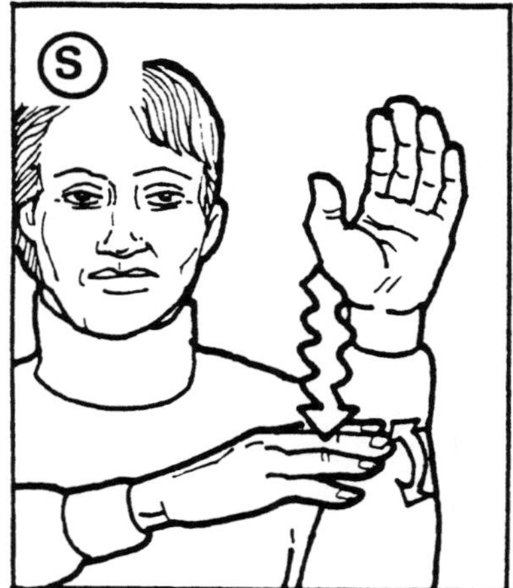

Rt. hand moves down from L. fingers fluttering, palm down, to indicate leaves falling.

AWAKE

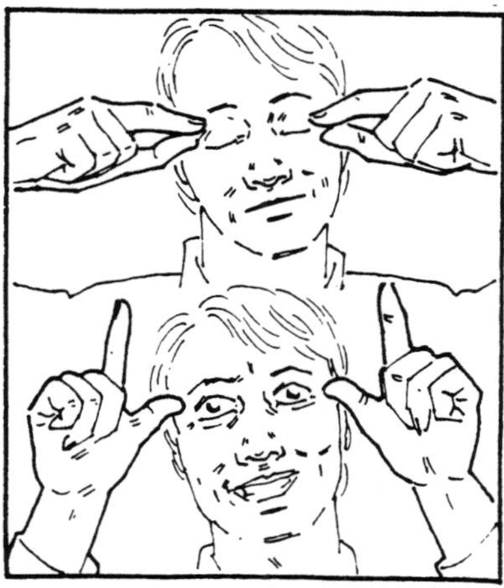

Indexes and thumbs flick open at sides of eyes.

AWAY

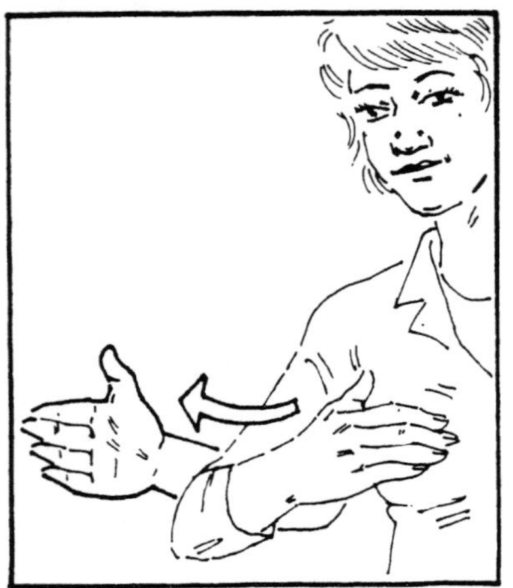

Rt. flat hand sweeps forward/out.

AWFUL

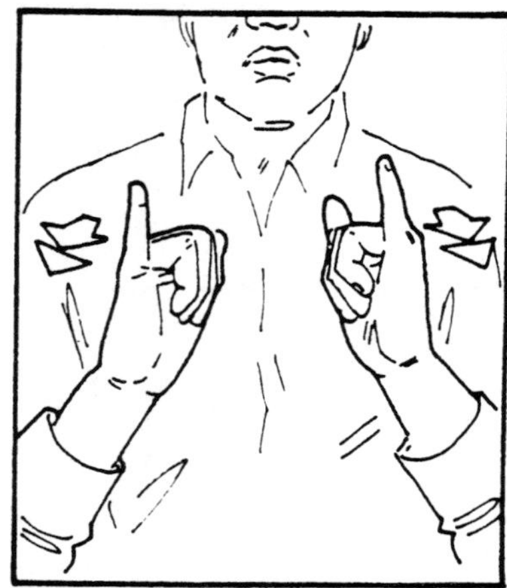

Both little fingers extended make two small movements forward, with appropriate facial expression.

AUDIOLOGY

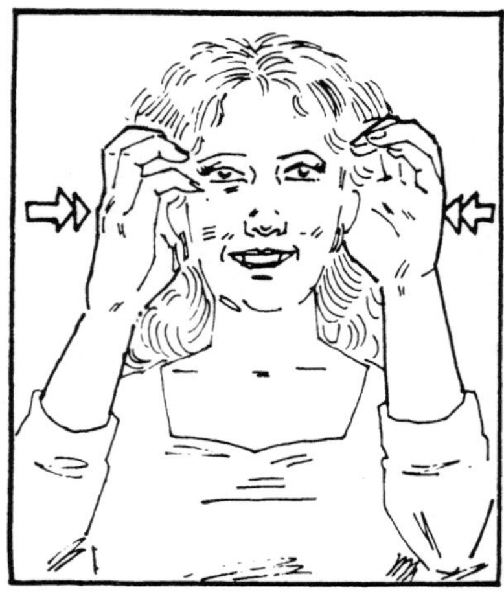

Clawed hands held over ears, tap head twice.

BABY

Mime cradling a baby in the arms and rock.

BABYSIT

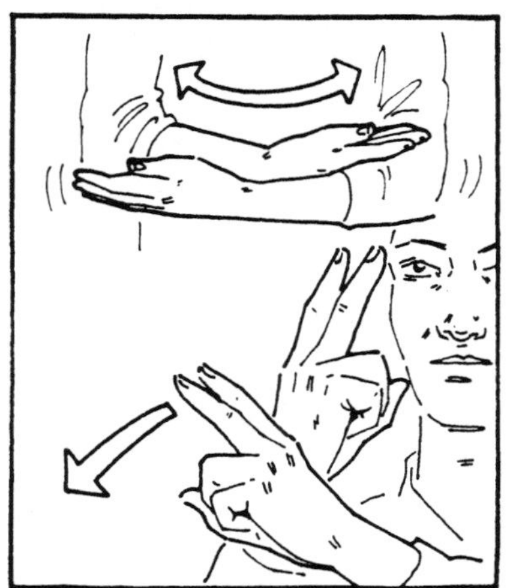

Sign "baby", then two "V" hands, Rt. on top of L. move forward/down from eye.

BACK

Rt. closed hand thumb extended jerks back over right shoulder.

BACKWARDS

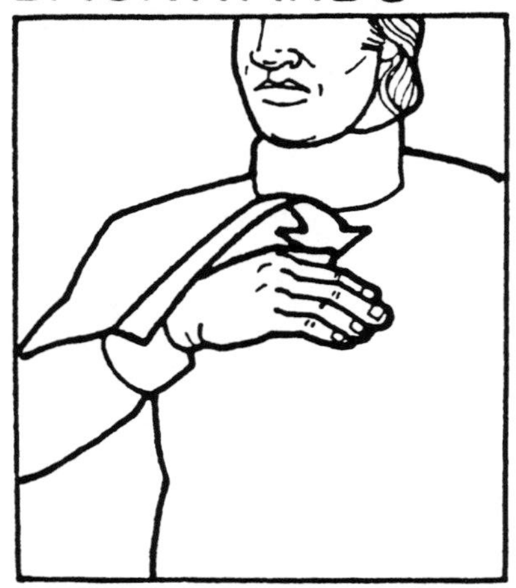

Rt. hand palm back held away from body, moves backwards in small arc.

BAD

Little finger held up.

BAG

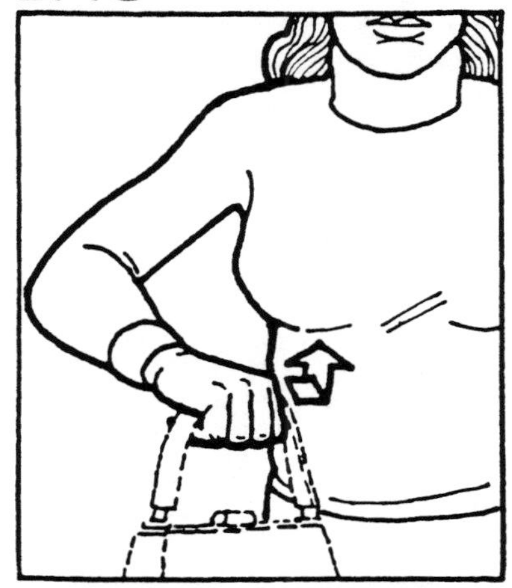

Mime holding a bag and move up and down slightly.

BAKE

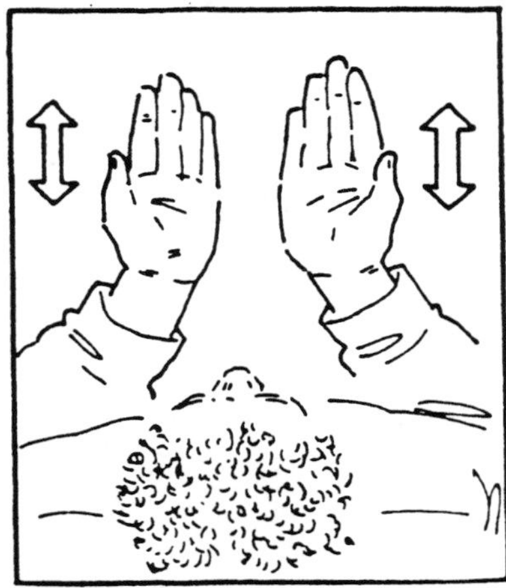

Palm up flat hands make small movements forward and back.

BAKED BEANS

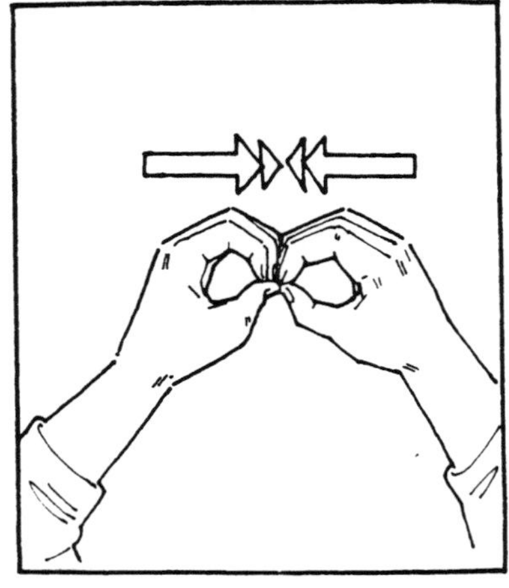

Form the letter "B" and tap together twice.

BAKING

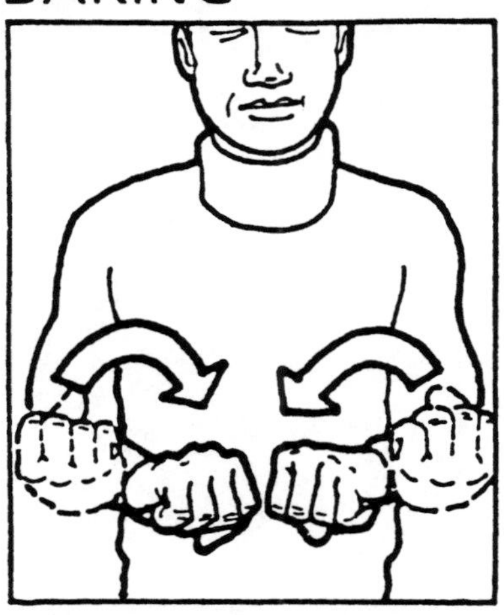

Closed hands start palms up and turn to palms down in a kneading action.

BALANCE

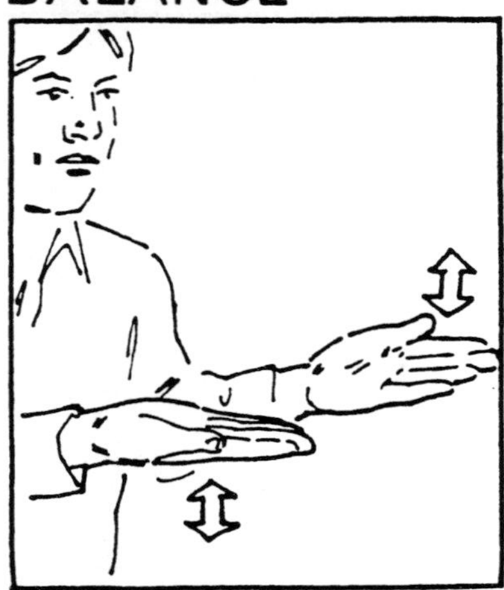

Palm up flat hands move alternately up and down.

BALL

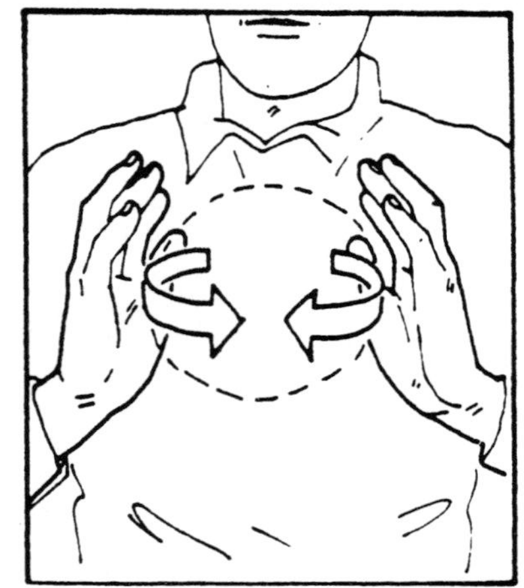

Fingers of both hands open and curved; hands swivel to touch thumbs then little fingers, to indicate shape of ball.

BALLOON

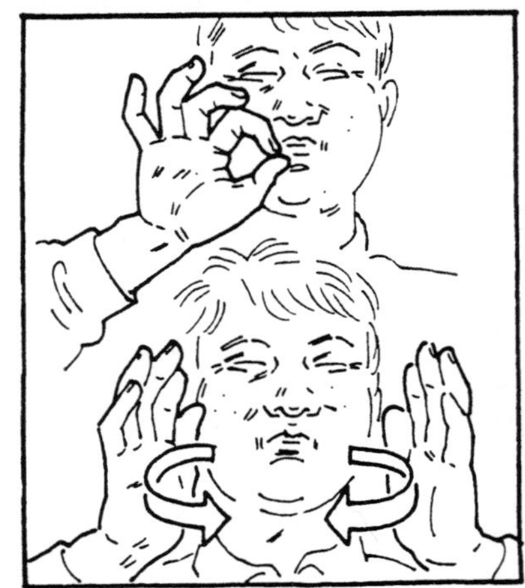

Hold imaginary balloon to the lips, then outline shape of balloon with both hands.

BANANA

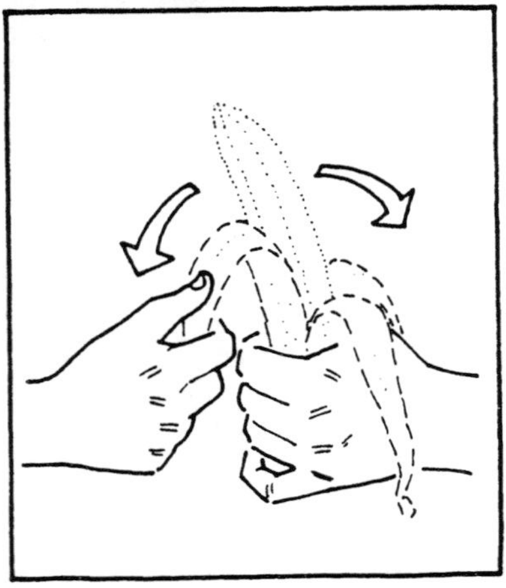

Mime holding and peeling a banana.

BANDAGE

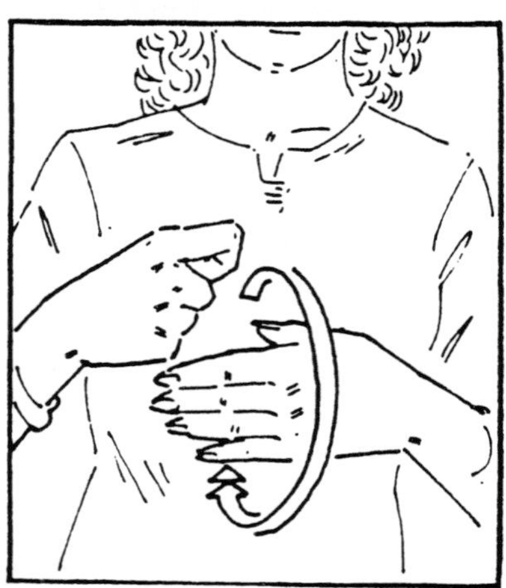

Rt. hand moves in circular motion around L. in action of holding and winding a bandage.

BANK

Stamp blade of Rt. closed hand on L. palm.

BARE

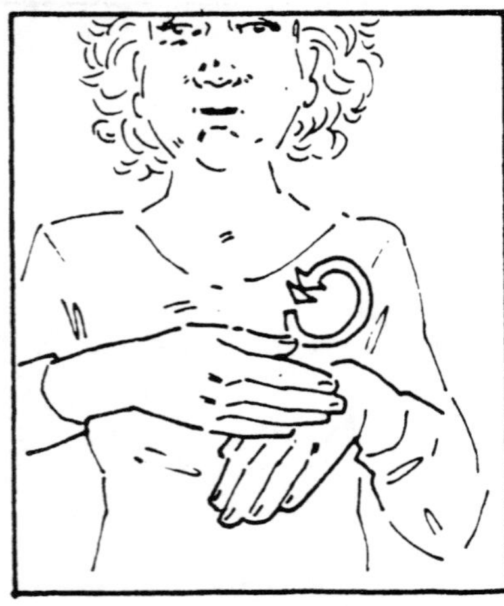

Rt. flat hand moves in circle on back of L. hand.

BASIC

Blade of Rt. fist rests on back of L. hand; formation moves down with stress.

BAT

Mime holding and striking with a bat.

BATH (A)

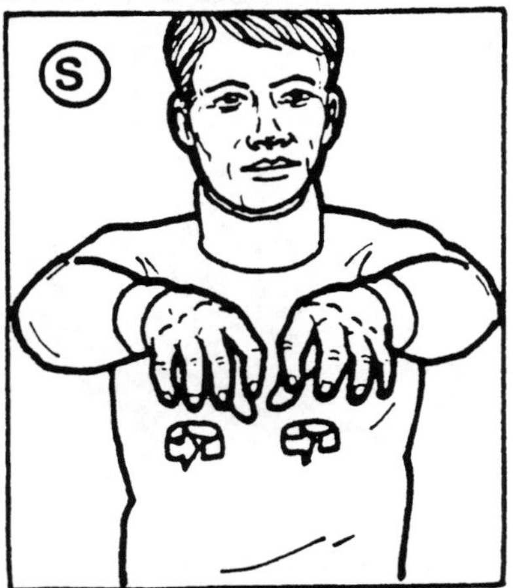

Mime turning taps with arms fully extended.

BATH (TO)

Mime drying with towel across shoulders.

BEACH

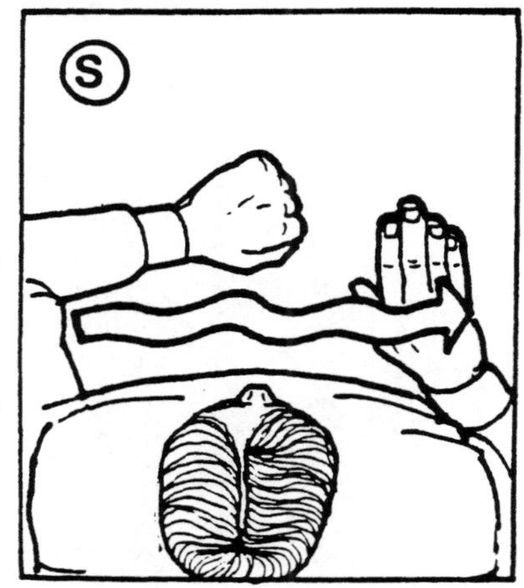

L. closed hand, palm down. Rt. flat hand, tips towards L. move along left arm in wavy motion.

BEAN

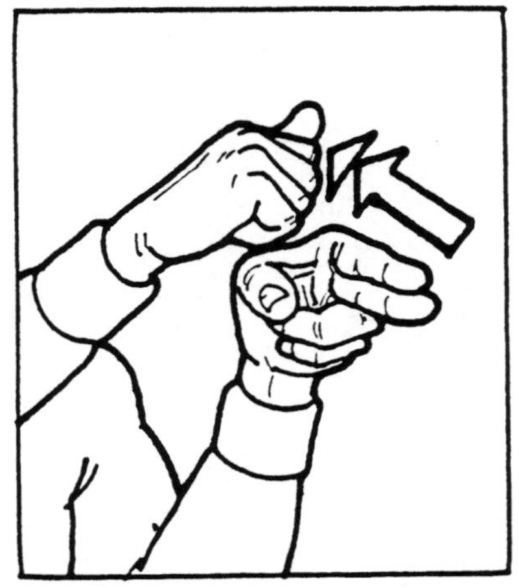

L. "N" hand palm right, scrape back along index with Rt. thumb twice.

BEAR

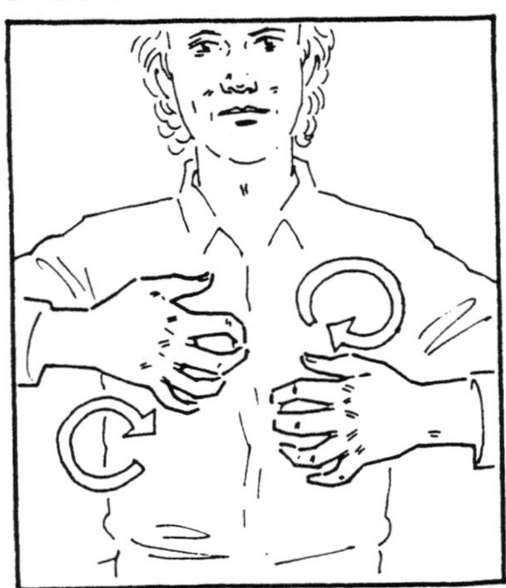

Palm back clawed hands move in alternate circles in front of body.

BEAT (game)

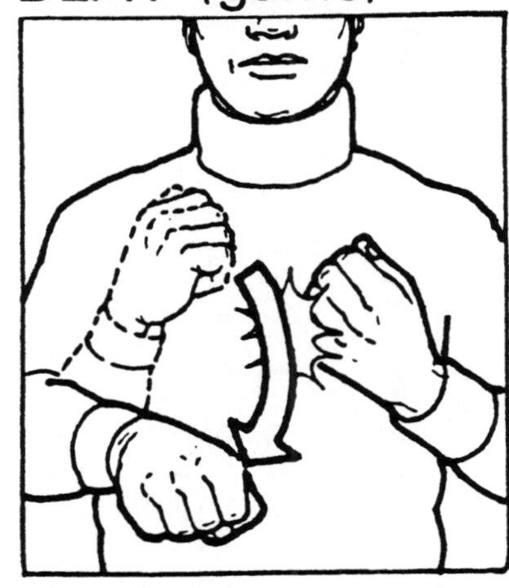

Two closed hands, palms back. Strike L. hand at second knuckles with Rt. in downward movement.

BEAUTIFUL

Full "O" hand held in front of mouth springs forward to open hand.

BECAUSE

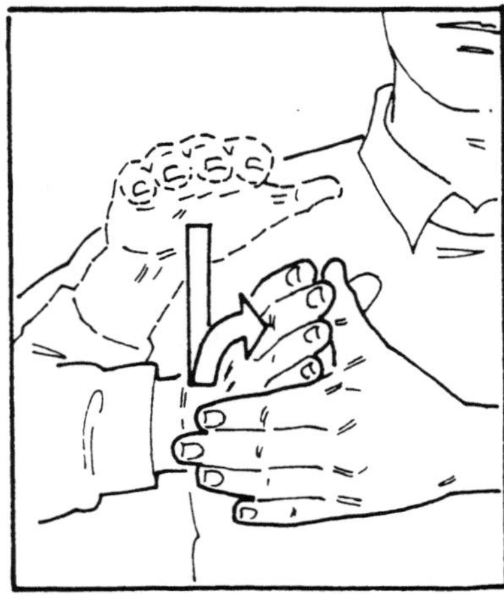

L. flat hand, thumb up. Bring Rt. flat hand down onto edge of L. index, then tap against L. thumb.

BECOME

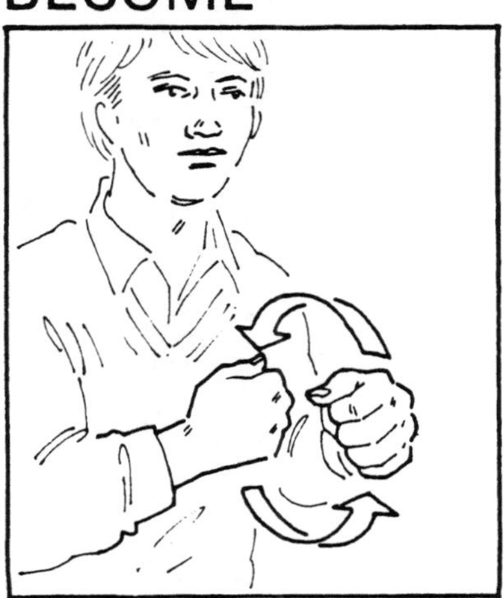

Two closed hands palms back, one in front of the other circle round each other alternately back towards body.

BED

Rest head against palm-together hands.

BEEF

Prod side of neck with thumbtip of Rt. hand.

BEEFBURGER

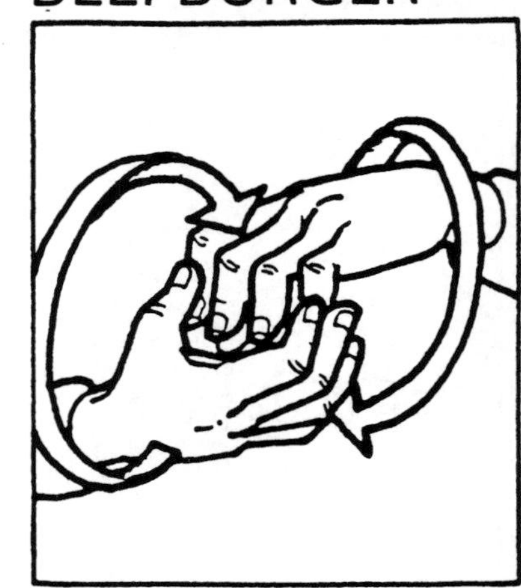

Two clawed hands Rt. on top of L., reverse to L. on top of Rt.

BEEN

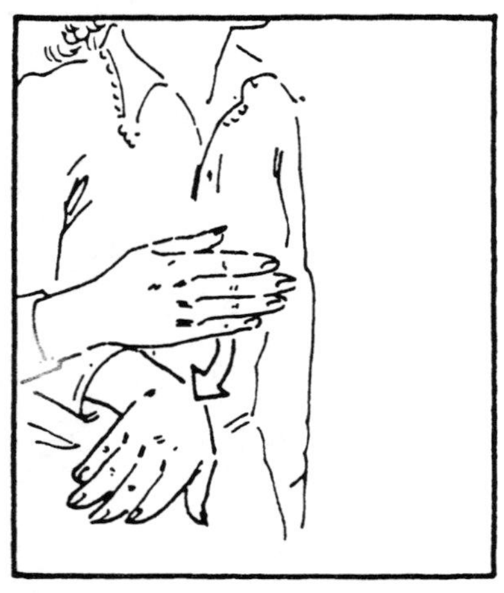

Flat hand flips over to palm down in quick movement.

BEER

Mime holding a beer glass, and make circular movement near mouth.

BEETROOT

Rt. index touches lips then makes circular movement on L. palm.

BEFORE

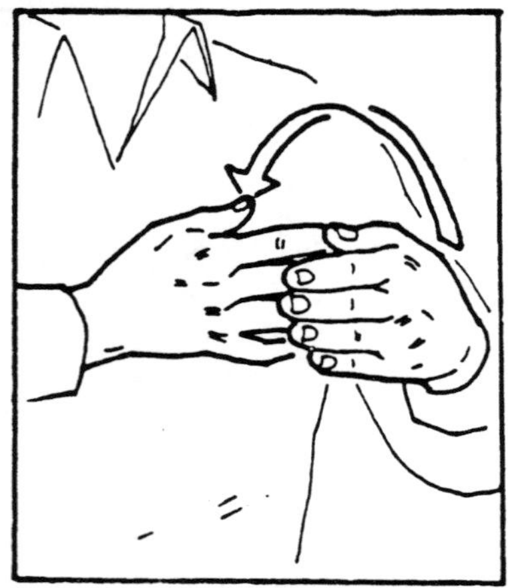

Two flat hands Rt. in front of L. Rt. jumps over to finish behind L.

BEFORE (past)

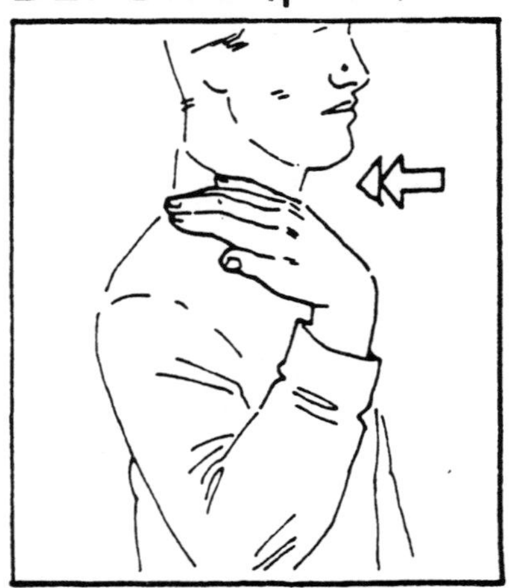

Rt. hand palm back makes backward movement over right shoulder.

BEHAVE

Raise Rt. index and move forward slightly; change to flat hand and brush down body.

BEHIND

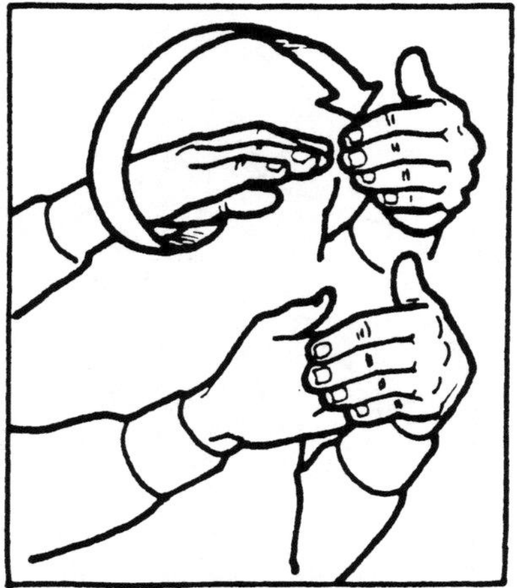

L. flat hand palm back; Rt. hand palm down swivels down and round to finish behind L.

BEGIN

Palm down open hands move up slightly and twist to palm forward, closing to fists.

BELIEVE

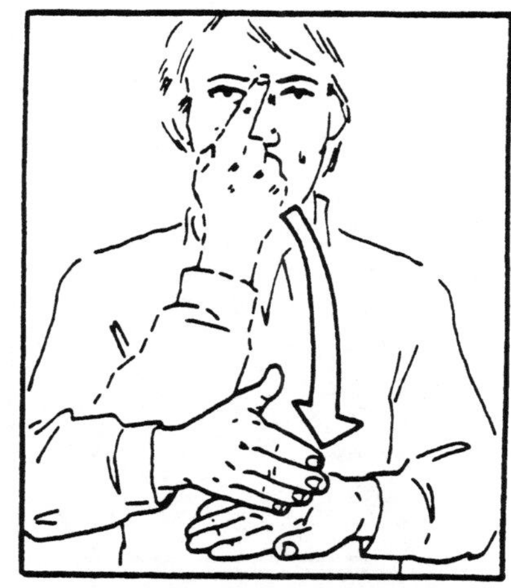

Rt. index points to forehead then moves down to finish with blade of flat hand on L. palm.

DON'T BELIEVE

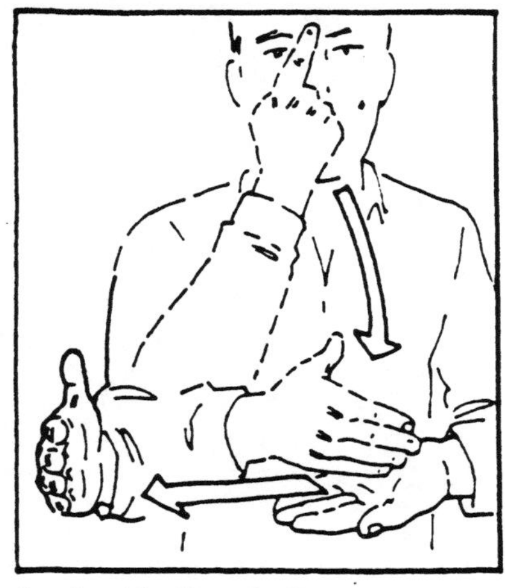

As for "believe", finishing with Rt. hand brushing sharply off L. hand.

BELL

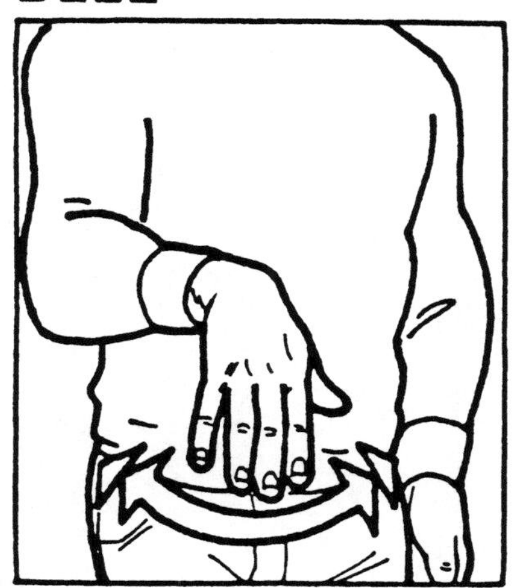

Rt. open hand palm back shakes from side to side.

BELONG

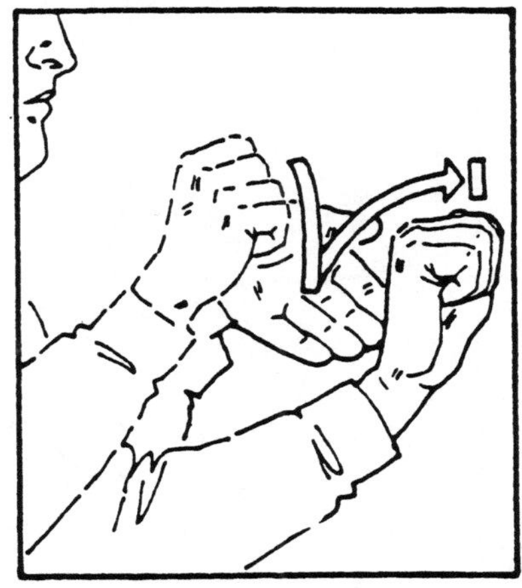

Rt. closed hand brought down onto L. flat hand bounces off and twists forward.

BELOW

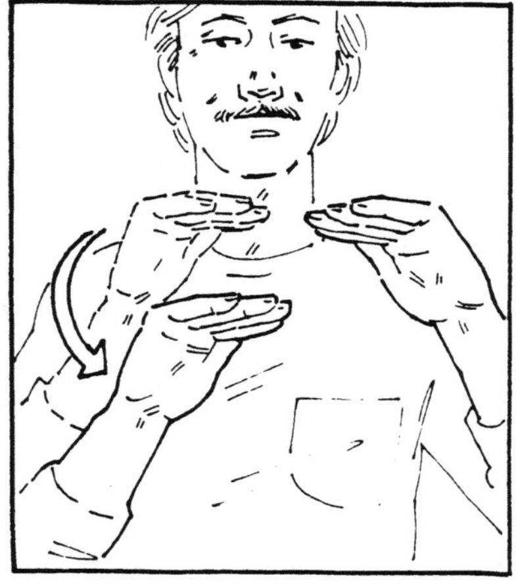

Two bent hands facing each other; Rt. hand moves down in small arc to finish below L.

BELT

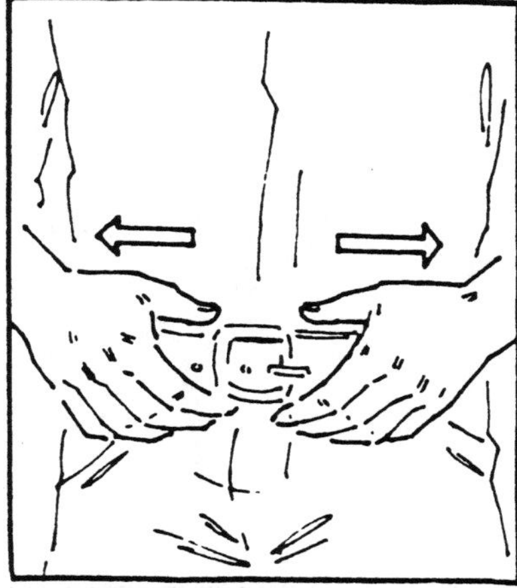

Indicate outline of belt at waist.

BERRY

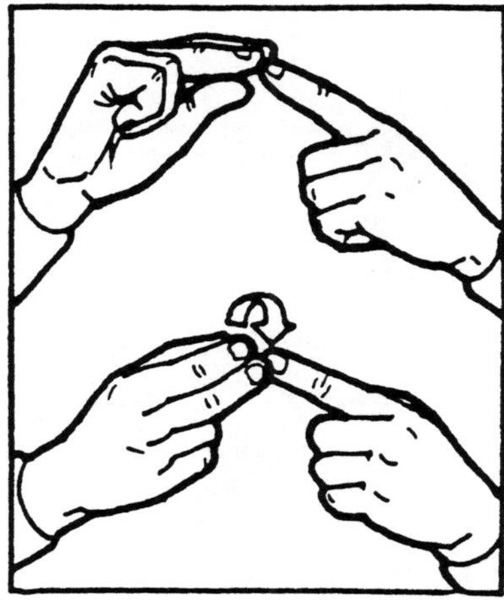

Tips of extended index, middle and thumb of Rt. hand twist off end of L. index.

BESIDE

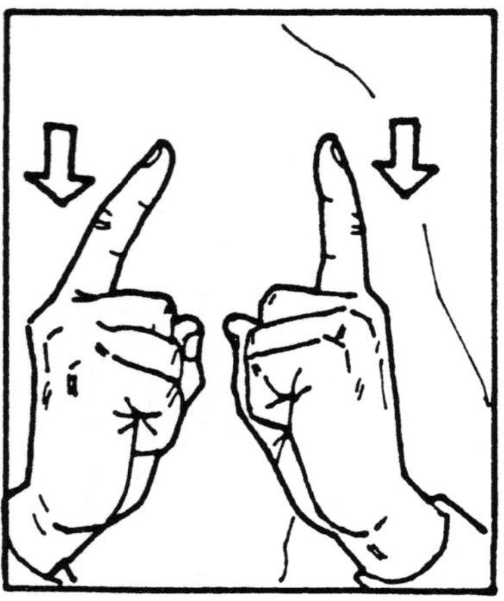

Two closed hands indexes extended held at side of body make slight downward movement.

BEST

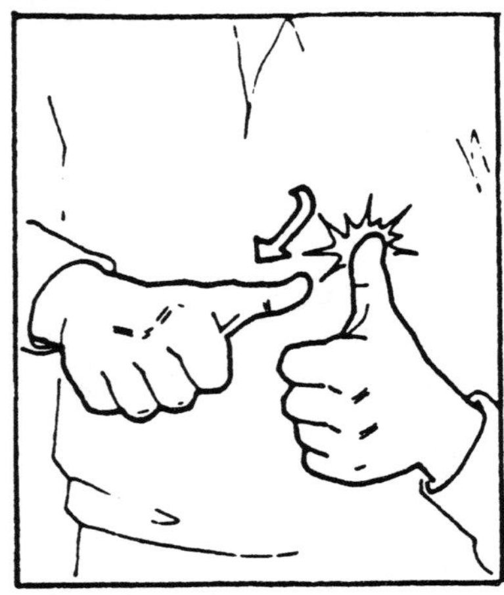

Rt. thumb strikes tip of L. thumb once in forward movement.

BET

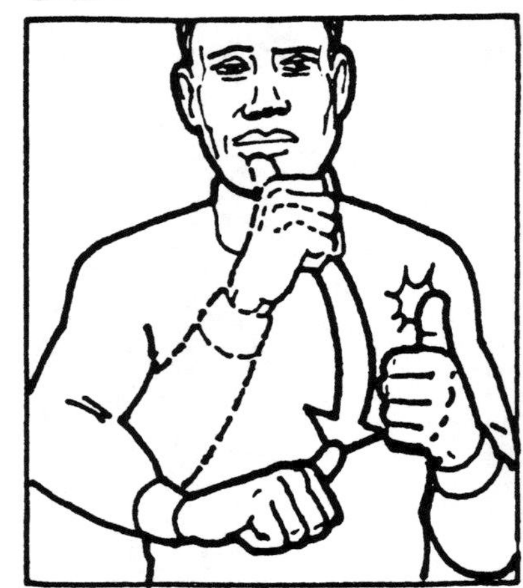

Rt. thumb moves from mouth to strike L. thumb in downward movement.

BETTER

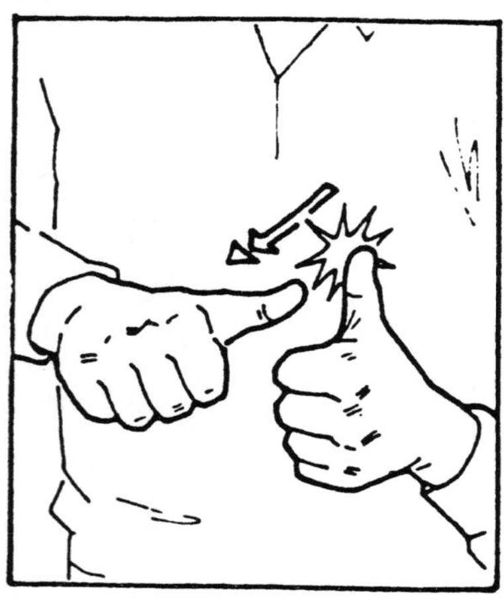

Rt. thumb strikes tip of L. thumb twice in a forward movement.

BETWEEN

Blade of flat Rt. hand waggles between middle and index finger of L. hand.

BICYCLE

Two fists held a few inches apart make pedalling action.

BIG

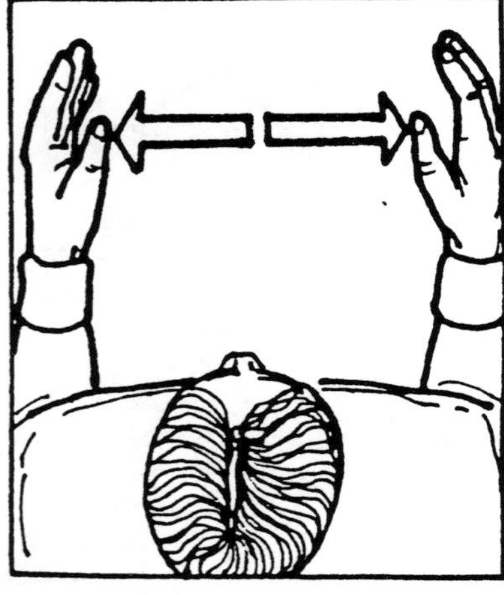

Hands move apart with emphasis.

BIRD

Index finger and thumb open and close in front of mouth like a beak.

BIRTHDAY

Blades of flat hands on either sides of waist move forward/in then up and sweep apart.

BISCUIT

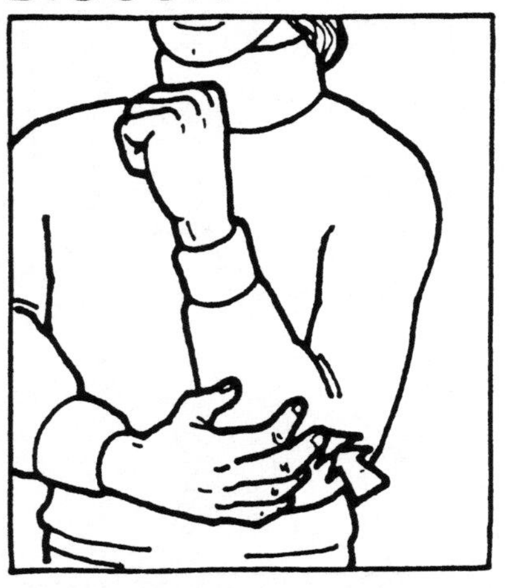

Fingertips of Rt. clawed hand tap near left elbow twice.

BISHOP

Indicate shape of bishops hat.

BIT

Little finger flicks out from under thumb.

BITE

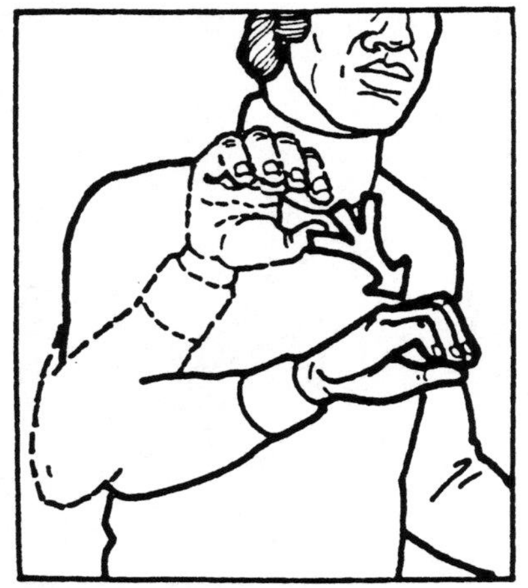

Full "C" hand moves forward and fingertips close sharply onto thumb.

BITTER

Make small circle on chin with tip of little finger.

BLACK

Closed hand moves forward from side of cheek.

BLAME

Indexes flick out as hands move forward slightly with stress.

BLANK

Rt. hand makes short sharp movement along L. palm.

BLANKET

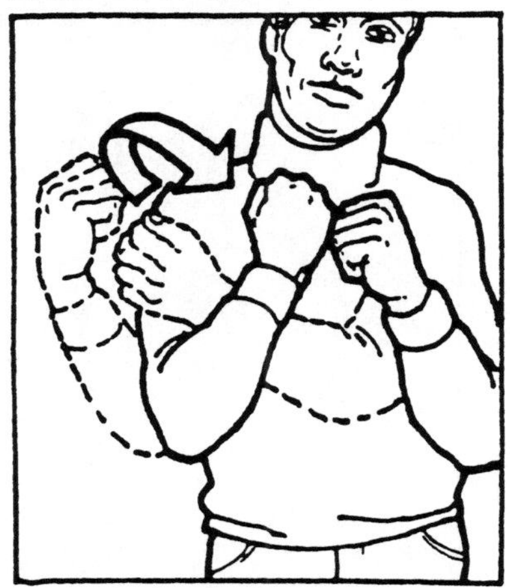

Two fists held at shoulder move forward and down together and shoulder also moves forward.

BLESS

Two closed hands thumbs extended palms up. Move up slightly and twist over to finish palms down.

BLIND

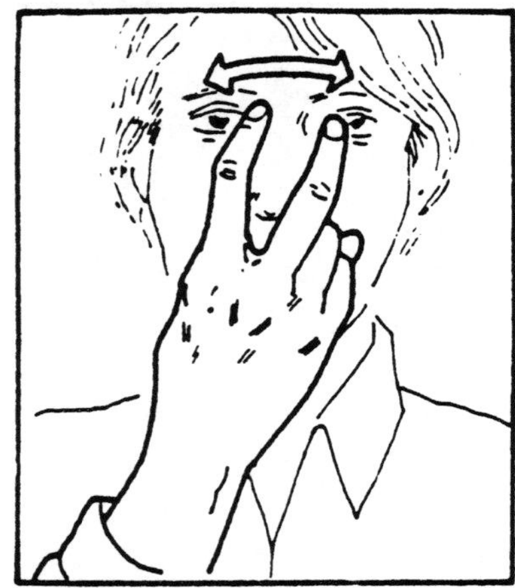

Rt. "V" hand fingers slightly bent held in front of eyes, move from side to side twice.

BLONDE

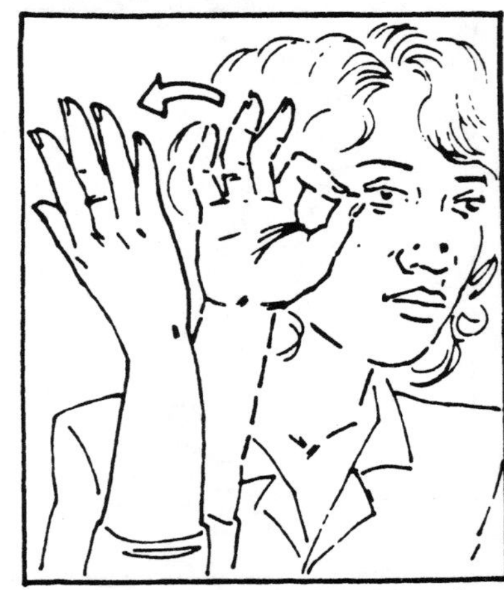

Rt. "O" hand held at side of head. Move hand back and change to open hand.

BLOOD

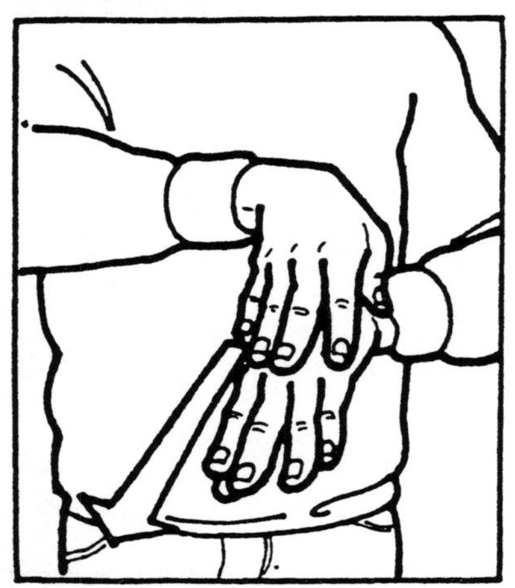

Two open hands pointing forward. Rt. on top of L. Rt. hand moves forward/down off L.

BLOUSE

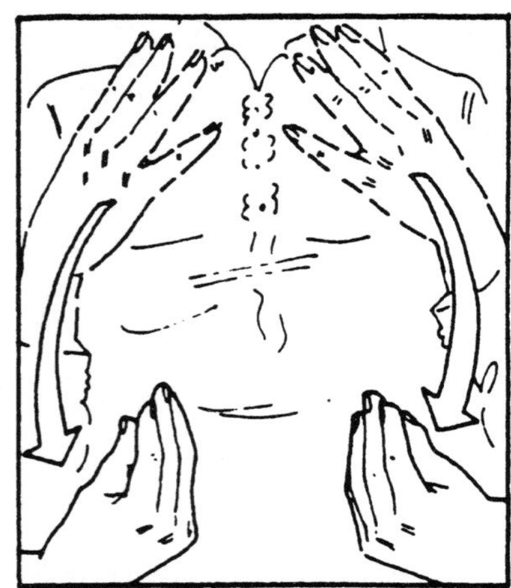

Hands move down body, closing to bunched hands to indicate the shape of a blouse.

BLUE

Rub back of L. hand with Rt. index.

BLUSH

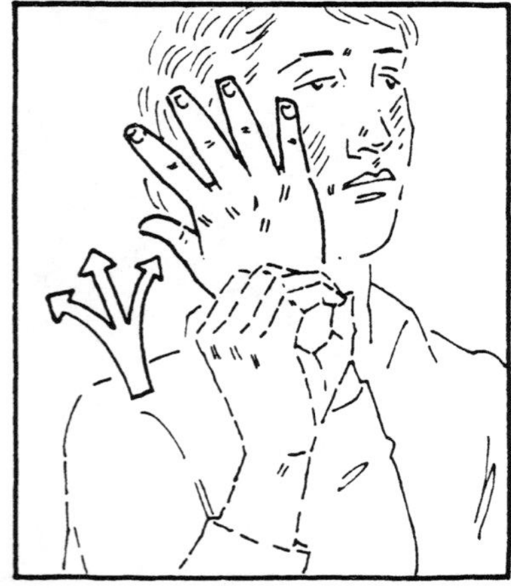

Full "O" hand held at side of chin, moves up side of face, as it changes to open hand.

BOAST

Thumbs extended, move in backward circles and stroke down chest alternately as shoulders waggle.

BOAT

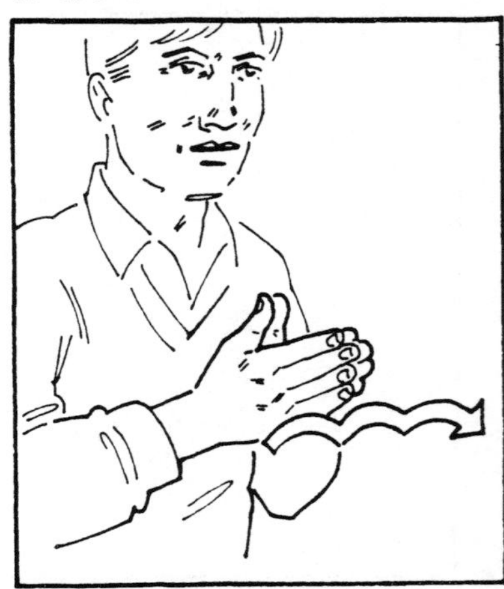

Tips of fingers touching, hands at an angle, move forward bobbing up and down.

BODY

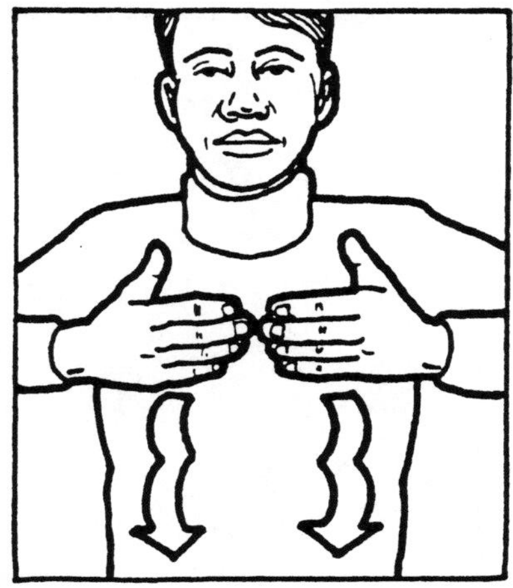

Two flat hands, contact upper, middle and lower parts of trunk simultaneously.

BOIL

Indexes point up and move in alternate small upward circles, like bubbles rising.

BONE (dog's)

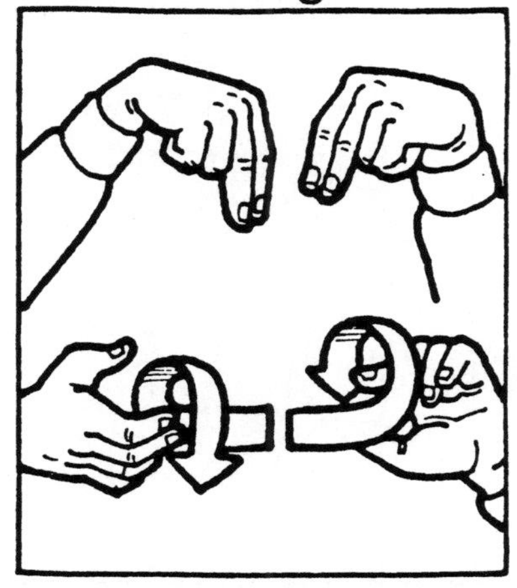

Sign "dog" then make bone shape with twist at each end.

BONE (human)

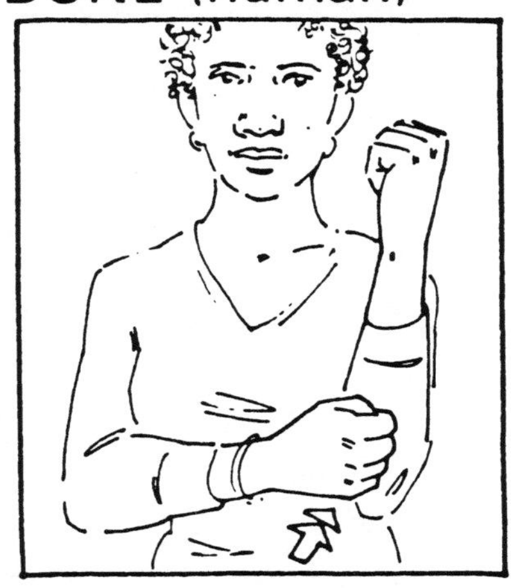

Knuckles of Rt. closed hand tap left forearm twice near elbow.

BOOK (a)

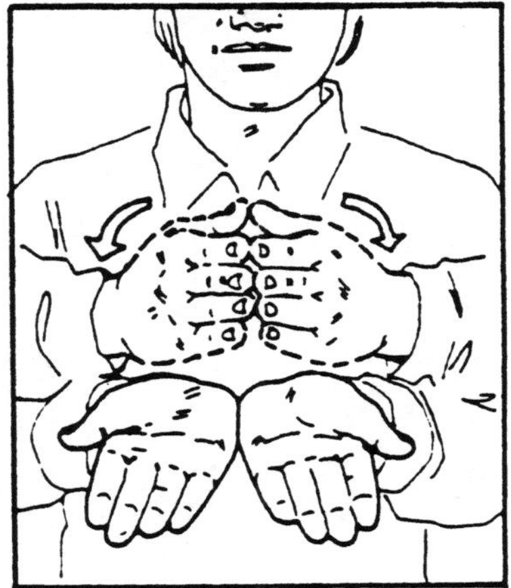

Two flat hands pointing forward, palm to palm, open to palms up.

BOOT

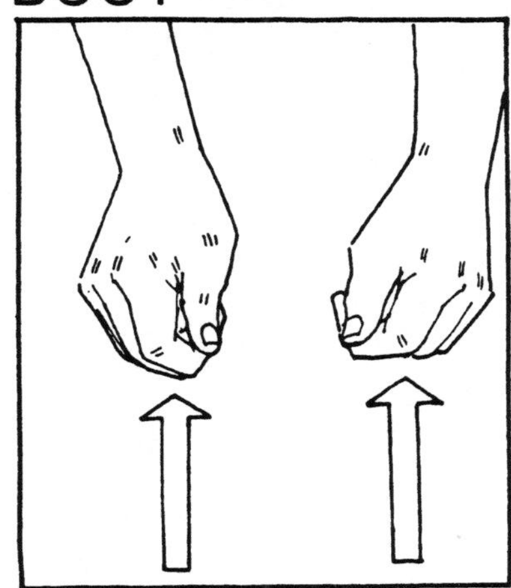

Indicate pulling on boot near leg.

BORED

Rt. hand taps mouth several times as it stifling a yawn.

BORN

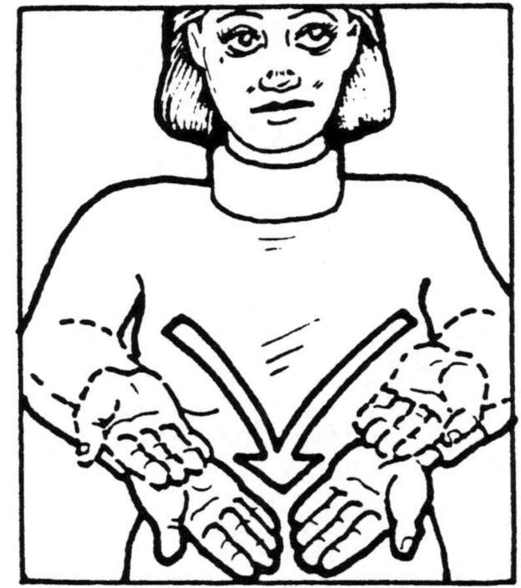

Blades of flat hands held either sides of waist, move forward and in.

BORROW

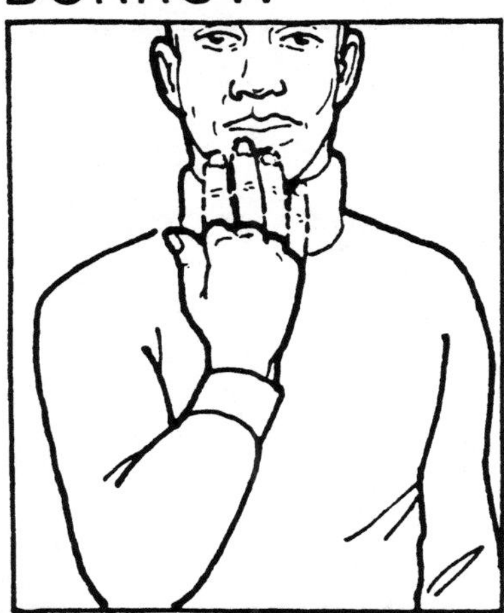

Fingertips of bent hand touch chin then flip down to touch heel of hand.

BOSS

Index held up at side of head with slight movement. Both hands may be used.

BOTH

Rt. "V" hand palm back shakes left to right.

BOTTLE

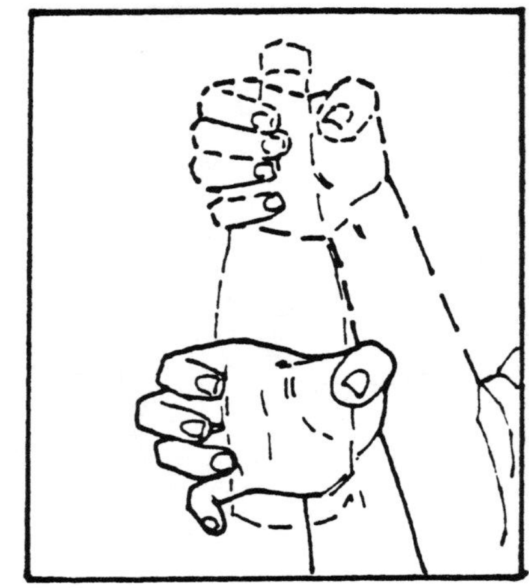

Rt. hand, fingers curved, moves downwards as thumb opens to indicate shape of bottle.

BOTTOM

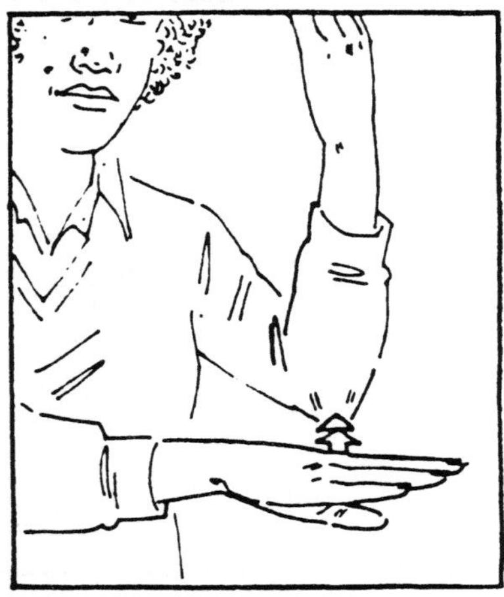

Rt. hand taps left elbow twice.

BOWL

Indicate shape of bowl using cupped hands, blades together curving apart.

BOX

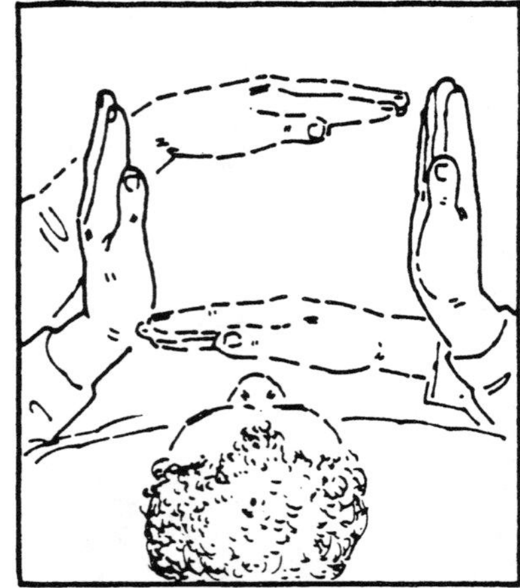

Flat hands palms back, L. in front of Rt. move to palms facing indicating sides of box.

BOY

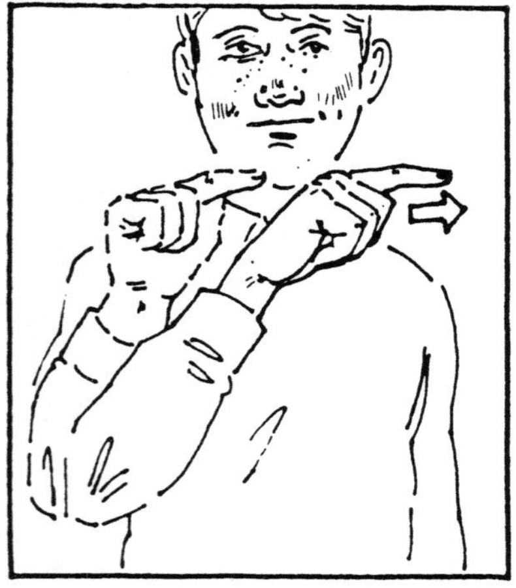

Brush Rt. index pointing left across chin.

BRA

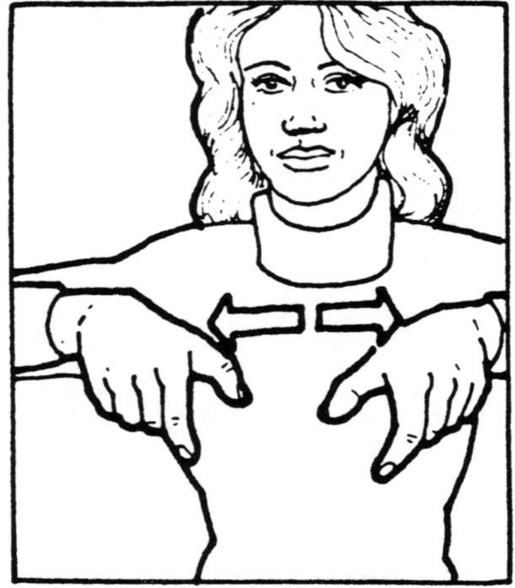

"C" hands, palms back move apart on chest.

BRACELET

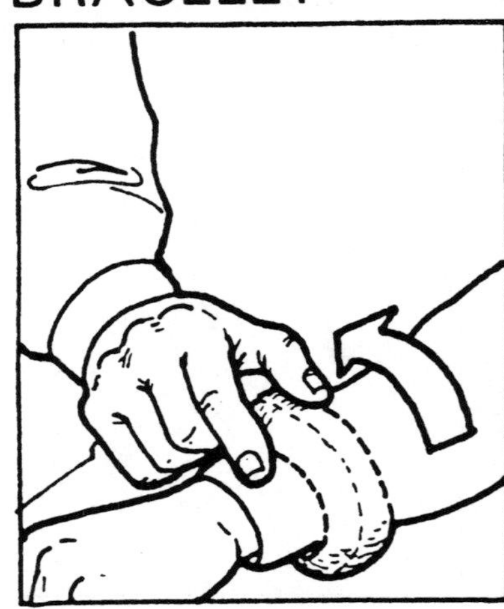

Indicate outline of bracelet on L. wrist using Rt. thumb and index.

BRANCH

Left arm vertical, fingers bent; Rt, full "C" hand, palm forward moves out from L. wrist.

BRAVE

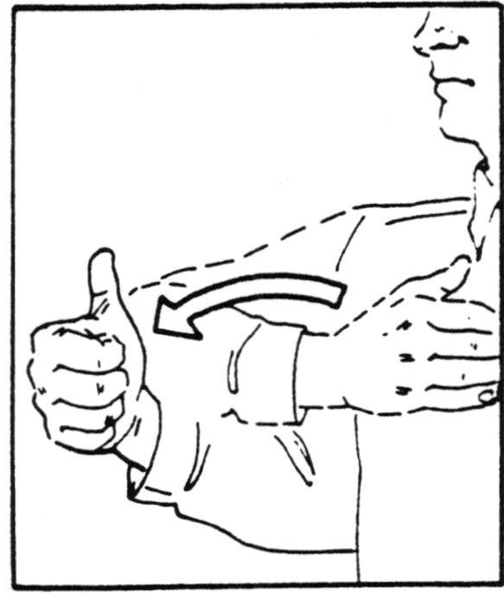

Rt. flat hand on chest, move forward to closed hand thumb extended in sharp movement.

BREAD

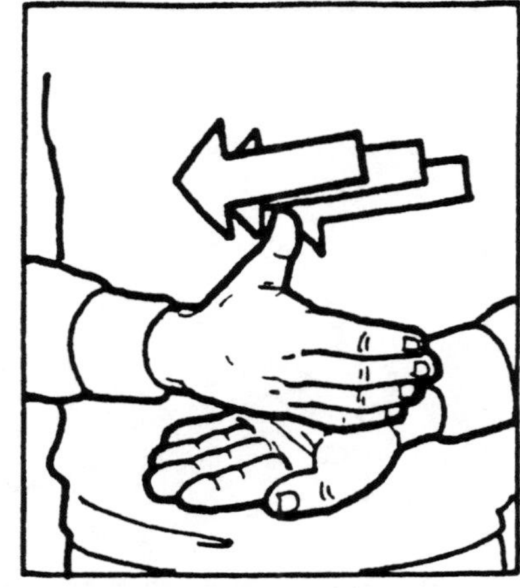

Mime slicing bread on L. palm using blade of Rt. flat hand.

BREAK

Two fists palms down, held together twist apart as if snapping something.

BREAKFAST

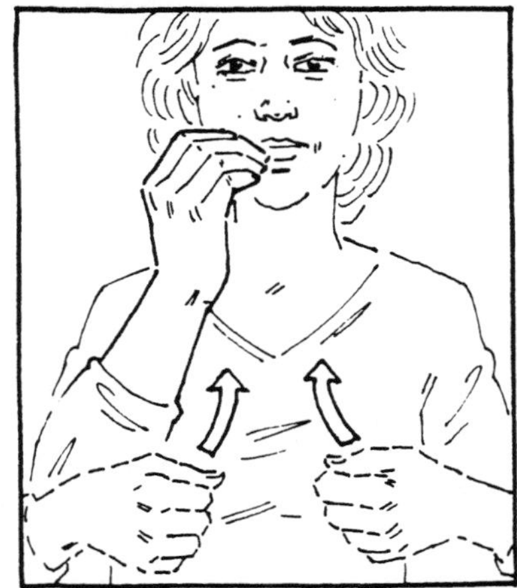

Closed hands move up body several inches from waist, then bunched hand moves to mouth.

BRIBE

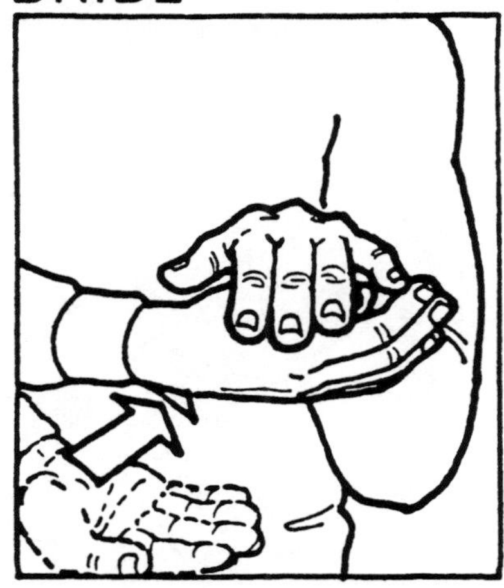

Rt. bent hand, palm up, moves up/left under L. palm down bent hand, twice, at left side of body.

BRICK

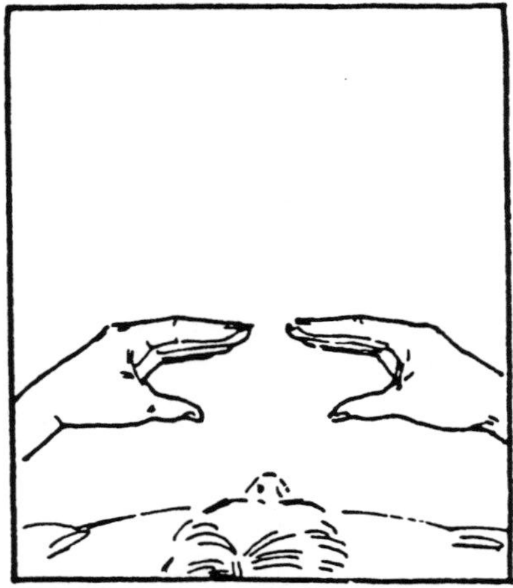

Cupped hands with thumbs extended indicate the shape of a brick.

BRIDE

Mime holding a posy and move slightly forward.

BRIGHT

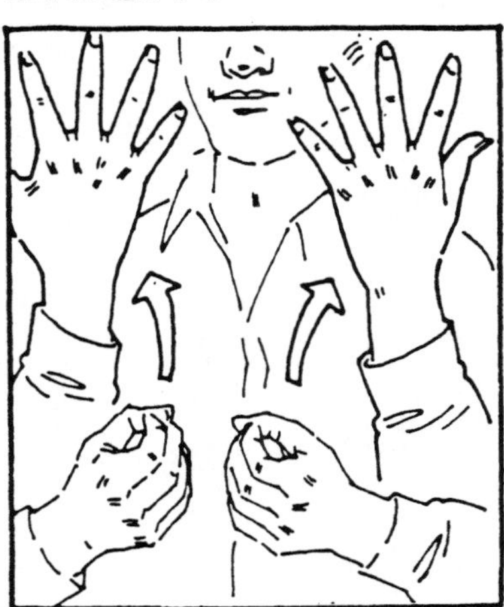

Hands move sharply upwards and apart, springing open from full "O" hands.

BRING

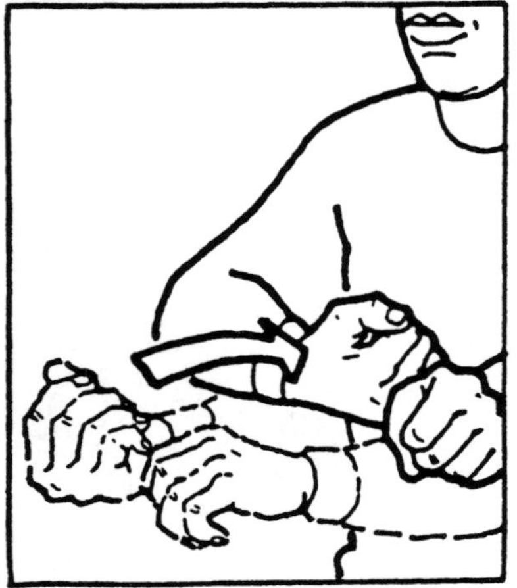

Rt. hand in front of L., pull hands back/left in small arc to body closing to fists.

BRITAIN

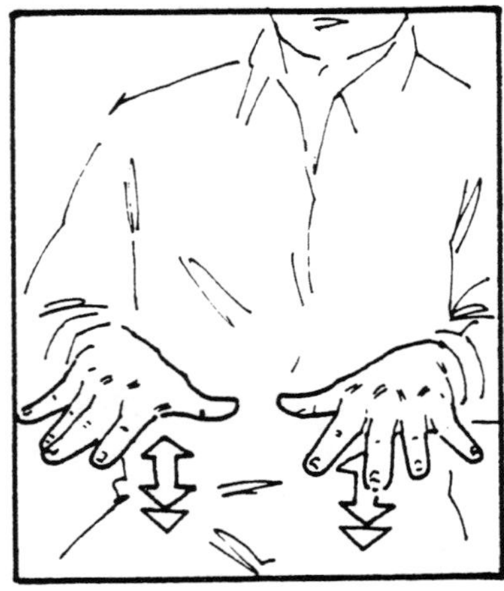

Palm down open hands make two small downward movements.

BROTHER

Two closed hands, thumbs up, rub together at 2nd knuckles.

BROWN

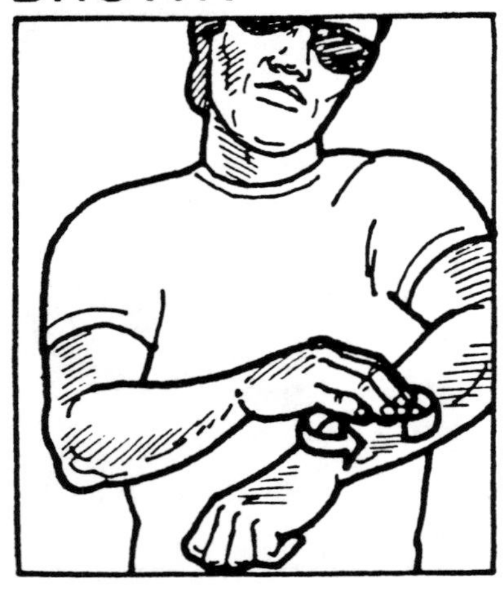

Flat hand palm down makes small circular movement on left forearm.

BROWNIE

Make the Brownie salute.

BRUSH (A)

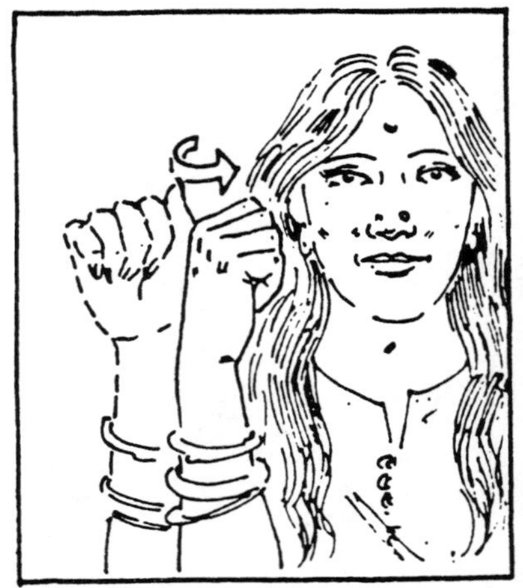

Mime holding brush and make small twist from the wrist.

BRUSH (TO)

Mime holding brush and make the action of brushing.

BUCKET

Flat hands indicate the shape of a bucket, then the closed Rt. hand indicates the handle.

BUCKLE

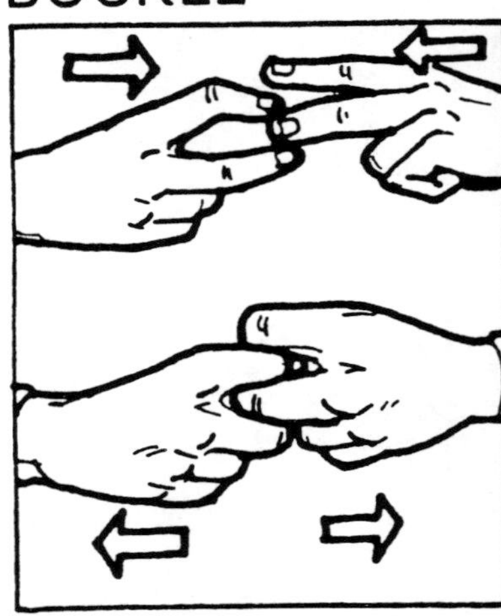

Bent index and middle fingers of each hand lock together at waist, and make slight pull against each other.

BUDGIE

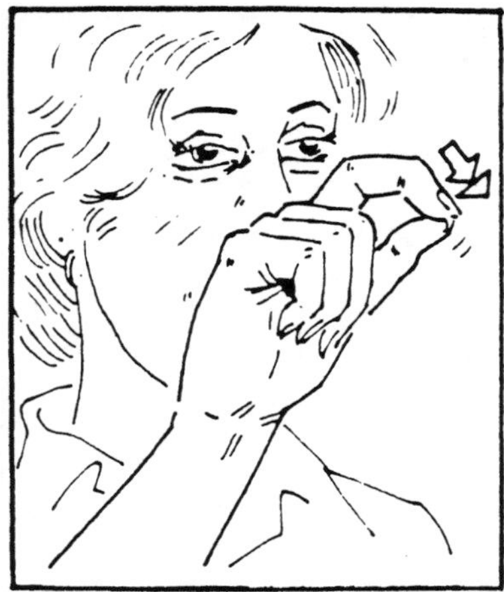

Bent index and thumb held in shape of beak in front of nose makes small pecking movement.

BUILD

Two flat hands palms down Rt. above L. then L. above Rt. Repeat upwards.

BUILDING (a)

Two bent hands, L. above Rt. Move formation up with slight stress.

BULB

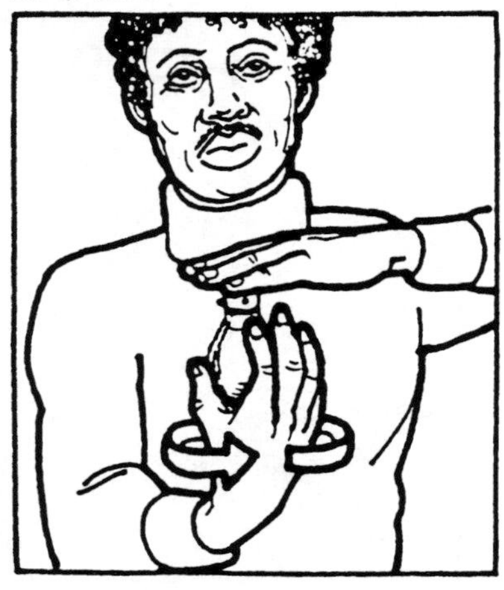

L. flat hand palm down. Mime screwing in bulb with Rt. hand into L. palm.

BULL

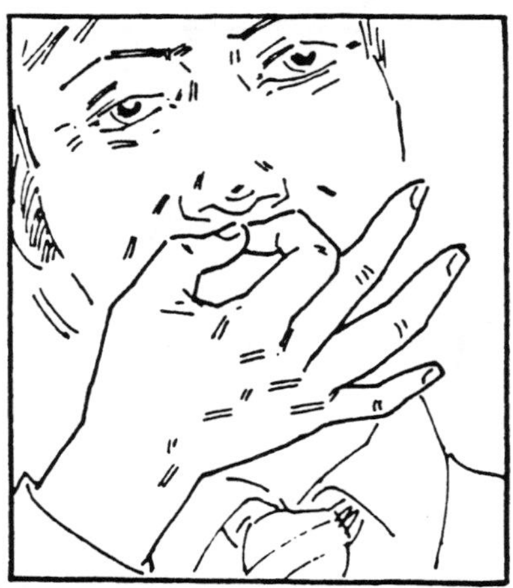

"O" hand held near nose to indicate ring in bull's nose.

BULLY

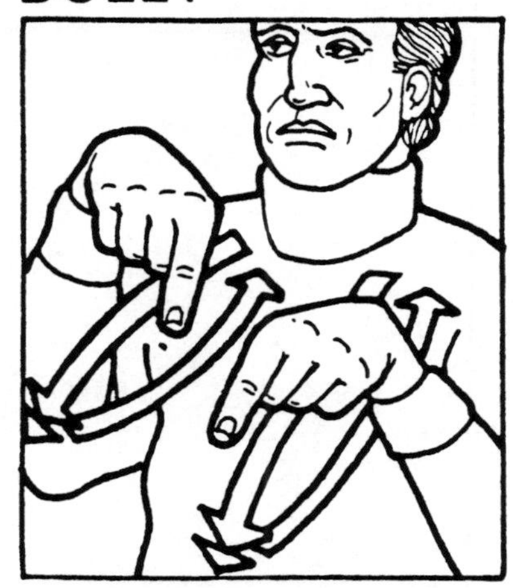

Both indexes pointing forward, palms down simultaneously jerk forward in slight circular movement.

BUN

Fingertips of Rt. full "O" hand contact back of L. closed hand.

BUNK BEDS

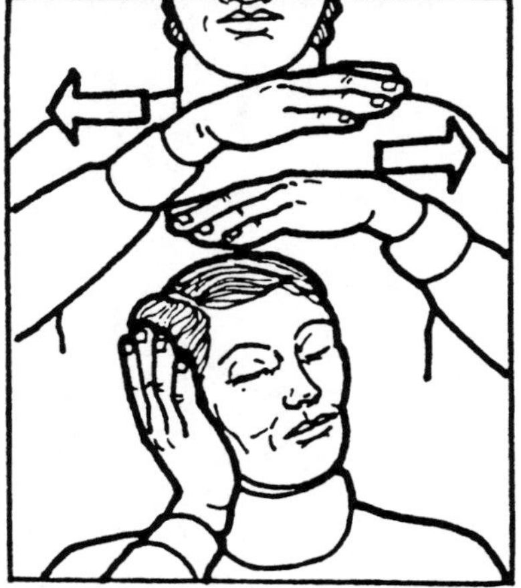

Flat hands, Rt. above L. pull apart to indicate bunks, then rest head on Rt. hand.

BURN

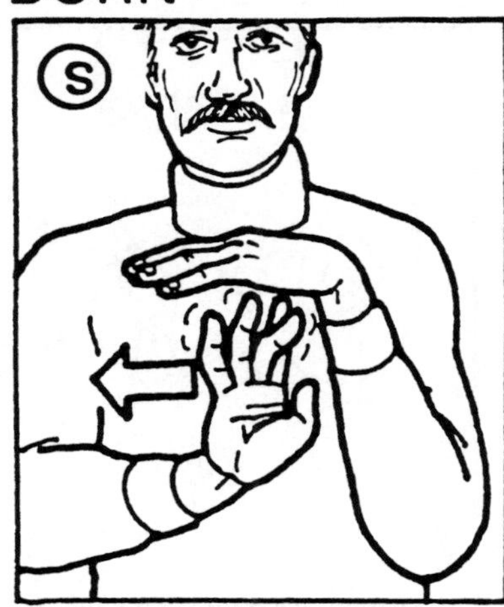

L. flat hand palm down. Rt. fingers pointing up flicker along underside of L. palm.

BURY

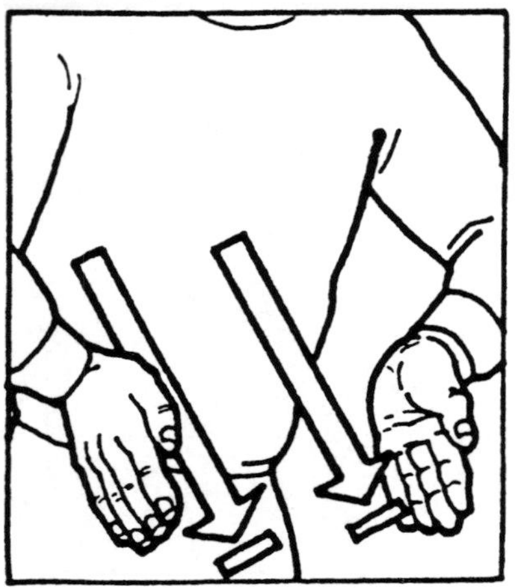

Two flat hands pointing forward/down move down with stress.

BUS

Mime steering then bring up Rt. thumb to press imaginary bell.

BUSH

Heel of palm forward clawed hand rests on left forearm.

BUSINESS

Blade of Rt. cupped hand taps twice into right side.

BUSY

Blade of Rt. flat hand swivels forward/down over edge of L. twice.

BUT

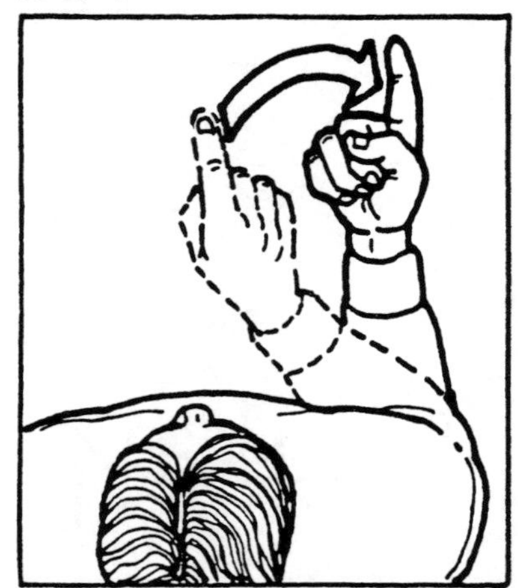

Rt. index extended and pointing forward palm down. Twist over to palm up.

BUTCHER

Rt. thumb and little finger extended, jab side of neck with thumb, twice.

BUTTER

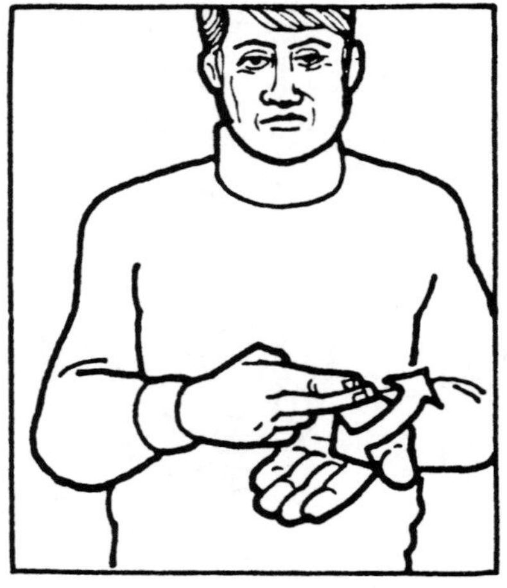

Mime spreading butter with extended Rt. index and middle fingers onto L. palm.

BUTTERFLY

Flat hands palms back, wrists crossed thumbs locked. Bend and straighten fingers a few times like wings.

BUTTONS

Index, middle finger and thumb make small twisting movement to indicate buttons.

BURST

Closed hands start crossed and pull sharply apart.

BUY

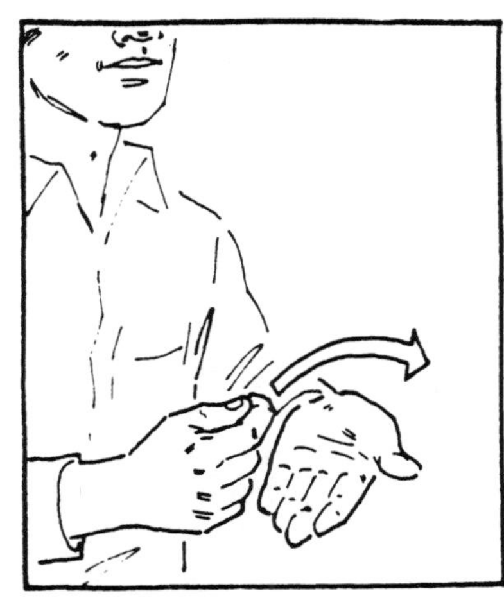

Thumb tucked into bent Rt. index, move in forward arc from L. palm.

BY (beside)

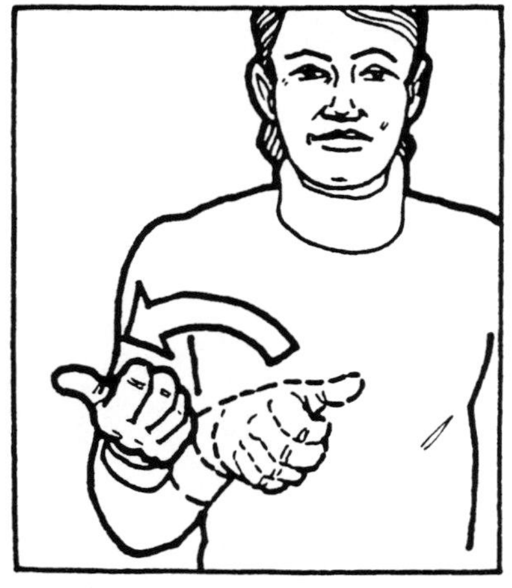

Rt. thumb extended twist over to palm up.

BY (past)

Rt. flat hand pointing up sweeps forward/down.

CABBAGE

L. fist palm back; make chopping action with Rt. flat hand on knuckle edge of L. fist.

CAKE

L. closed hand, palm down; Rt. clawed hand, palm down on top of L.

CALENDAR

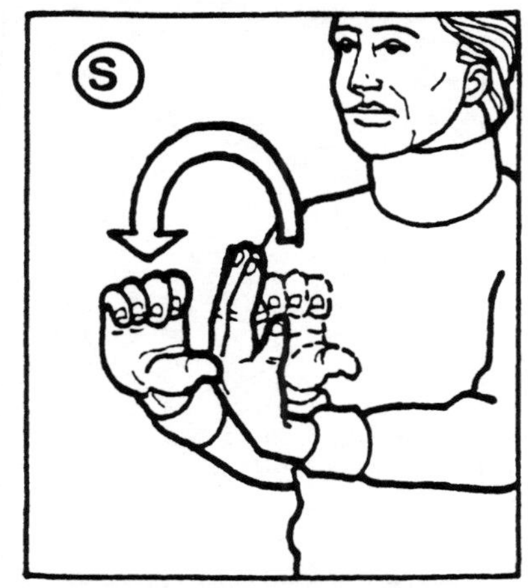

L. flat hand palm back; blade of Rt. full "C" hand on L. moves up and over L. hand.

CALL

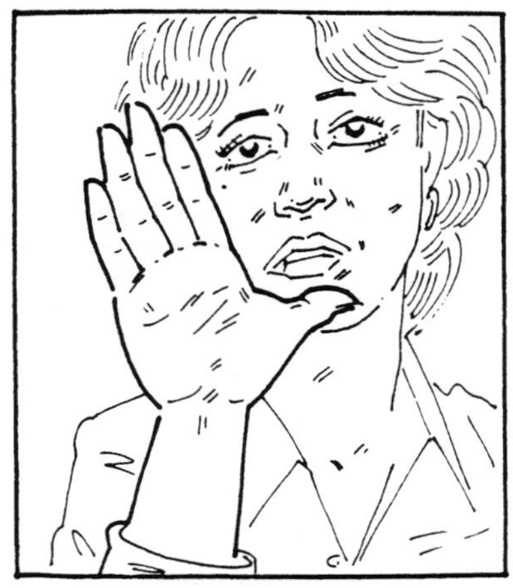

Flat hand, thumb out, palm left held at side of mouth.

CALM DOWN

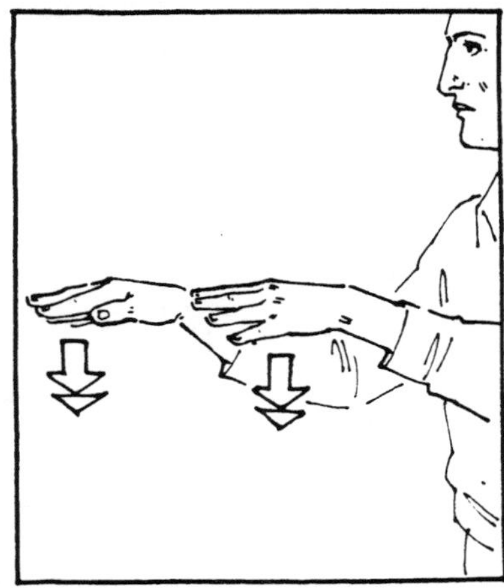

Palm down open hands, held forward, make repeated downward movement.

CAMEL

Make sign for "Animal" with Rt. hand; outline humps down right forearm with L. index and middle finger.

CAMERA

Index extended at side of head, click down and up again as if using a camera.

CAMP

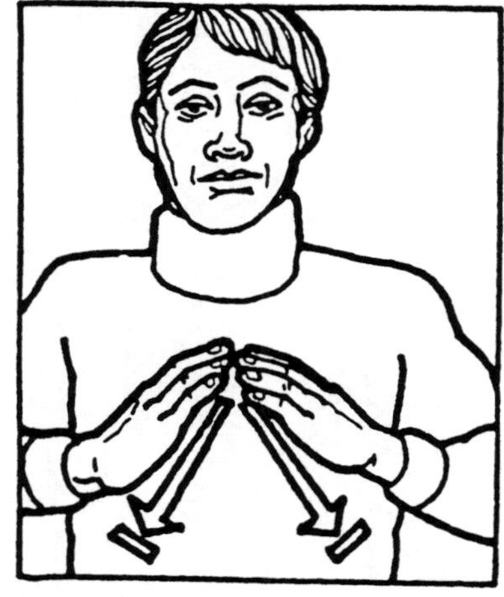

Tips of two flat hands touching, heels apart, move sharply down and apart.

CAMPAIGN

Closed hands hold imaginary banner and make repeated small movement backward and forward.

CAN

Rt. "C" hand palm back in front of face - pull away from face and flex fingers slightly.

CAN'T

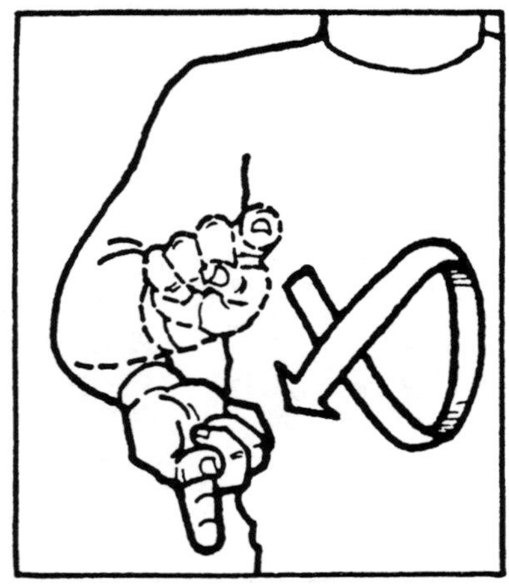

Index points slightly up and forward, moves down and loops over to palm up (like an X in the air).

CANCEL

Rt. index makes a cross on the L. palm.

CANDLE

Rest heel of Rt. hand on tip of L. index and flutter fingers.

CAR

Mime holding and moving a steering wheel.

CARAVAN

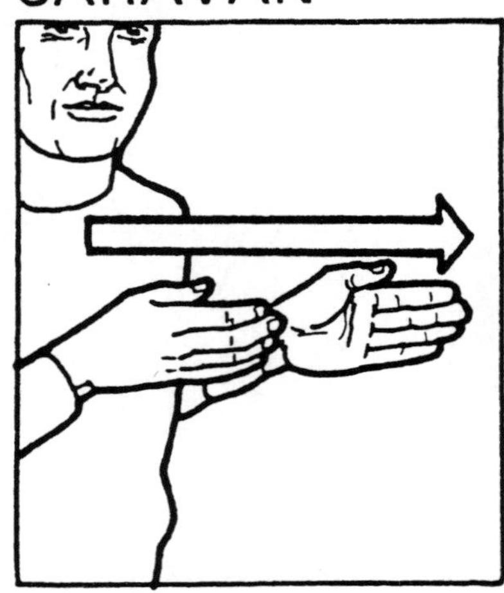

Two flat hands, L. in front of Rt. Move both forward.

CARDBOARD

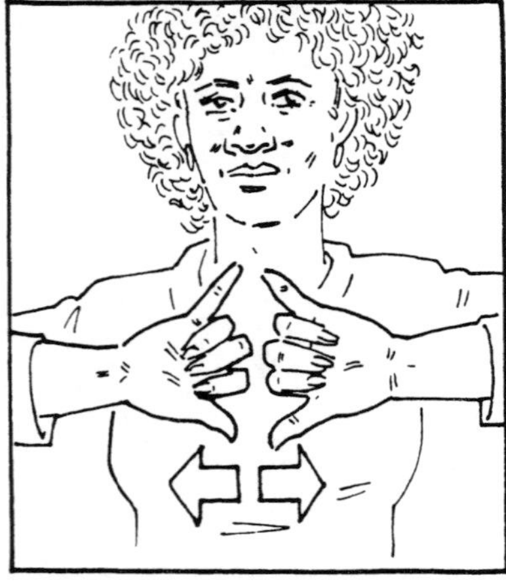

Thumbs and little fingers extended, palms forward, pull apart.

CARE

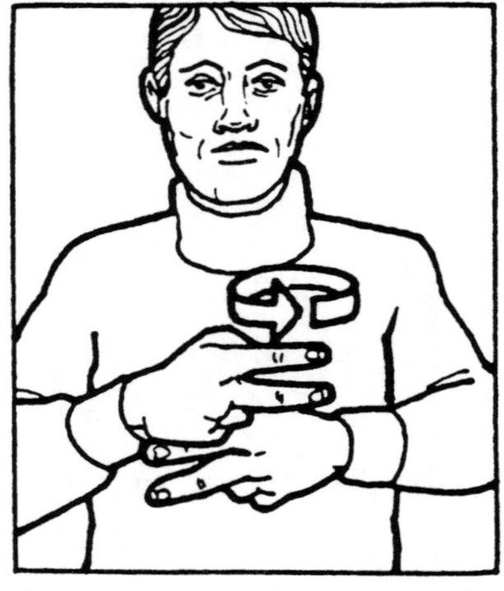

Two "V" hands Rt. on top of L., move formation in horizontal circle.

DON'T CARE

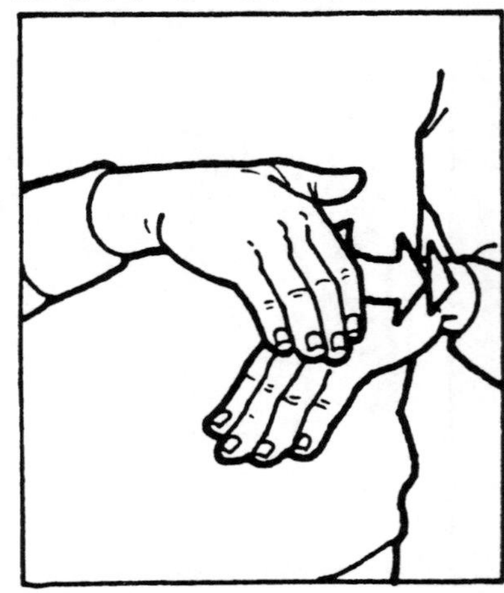

Brush tips of Rt. hand forward twice off back of L.

CAREFUL

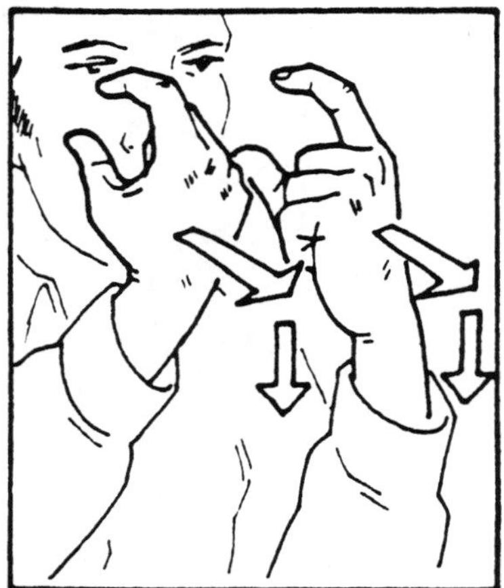

Two "C" hands, palms back held under eyes, move forward then down.

CARELESS

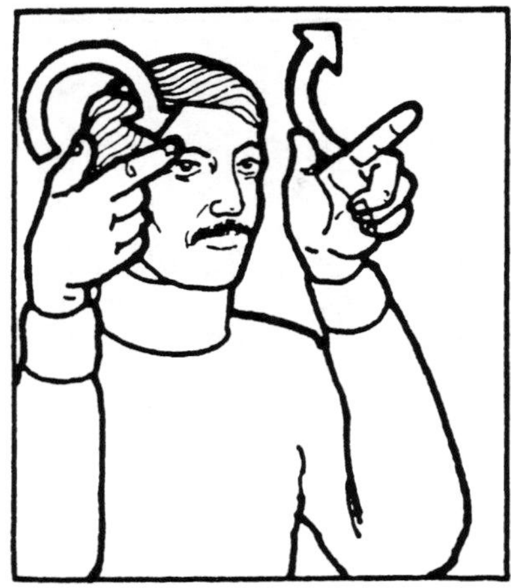

Closed hands indexes and thumbs extended held at temples make small forward circles alternately.

CARPENTRY

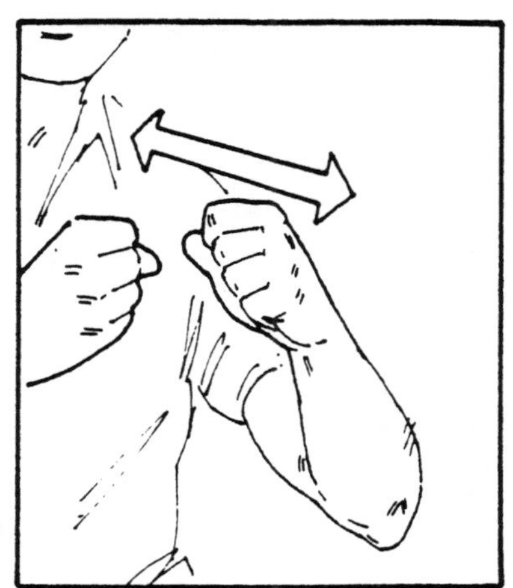

Hands move simultaneously backwards and forwards in the action of using a plane.

CARPET

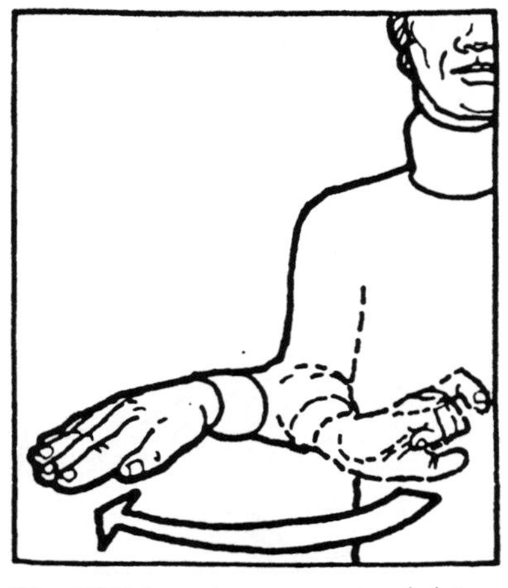

Rt. "C" hand sweeps to right changing to flat hand palm down.

CARROT

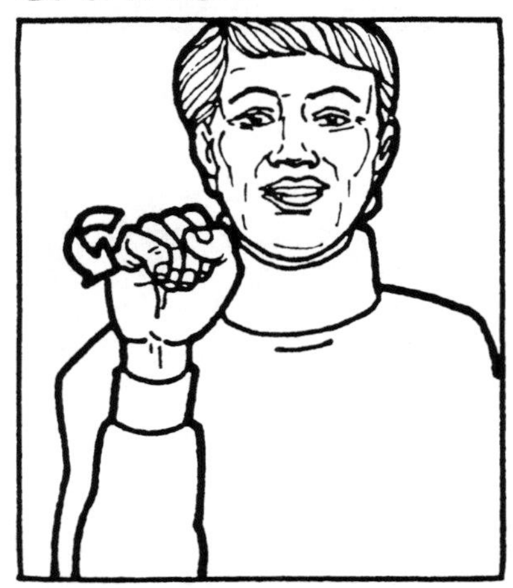

Rt. fist, palm forward twists at side of mouth as if taking a bite.

CARRY

Two cupped hands move together from left to right.

CASTLE

Two "N" hands move apart and down flexing several times, to indicate battlements.

CAT

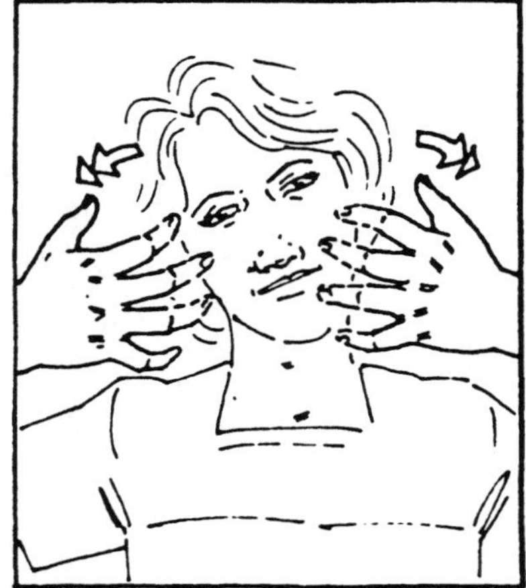

Open hands at sides of mouth move out slightly twice whilst flexing to indicate whiskers.

CATCH

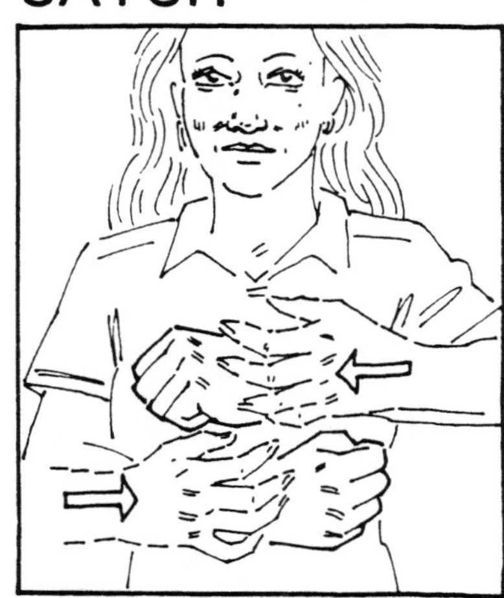

Mime catching something

CATERPILLAR

Rt. extended index moves up left forearm whilst flexing.

CATHOLIC

Make a cross on forehead with thumb.

CAULIFLOWER

Place L. fist into loosely cupped Rt. hand.

CEILING

Bent hand held above head moves forwards twice to indicate ceiling.

CELEBRATE

Thumbs and little fingers extended, hands make vertical circles whilst rotating at wrists.

CEMENT MIXER

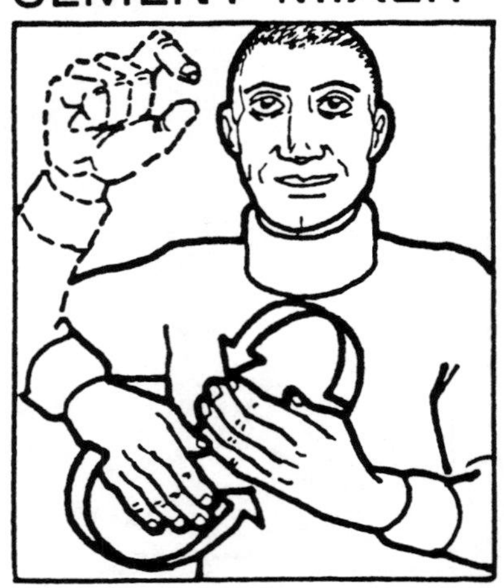

Form letter "C" then revolve hands round each other, to indicate mixing.

CENTRE

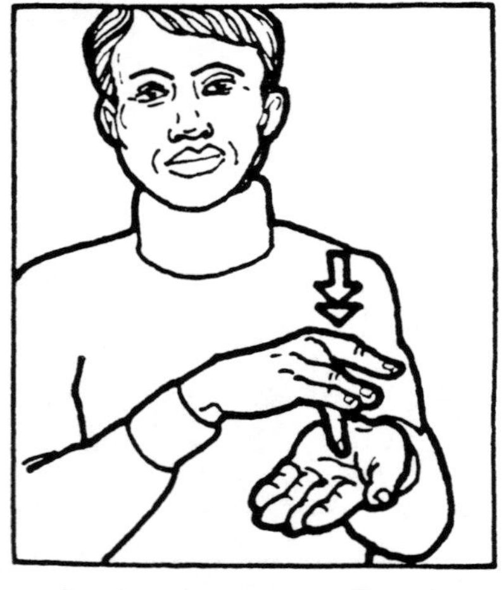

L. flat hand palm up. Tap tip of bent Rt. middle finger in centre of L. palm twice.

CHAIN

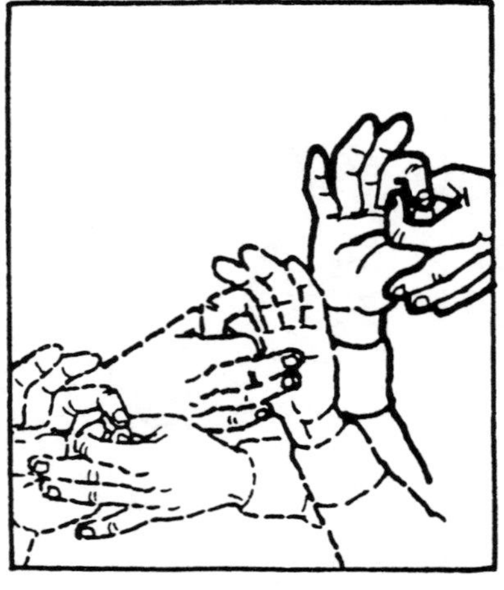

Alternately interlink "O" hands to indicate chain.

CHAIR

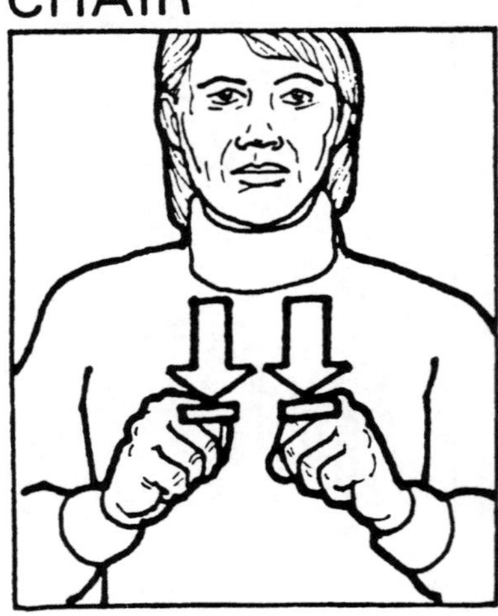

Two closed hands, move down slightly with stress.

CHALLENGE

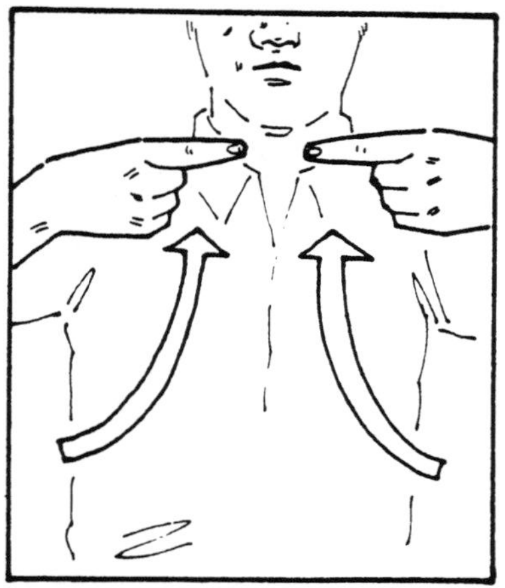

Indexes move up sharply to point towards each other.

CHANGE (alter)

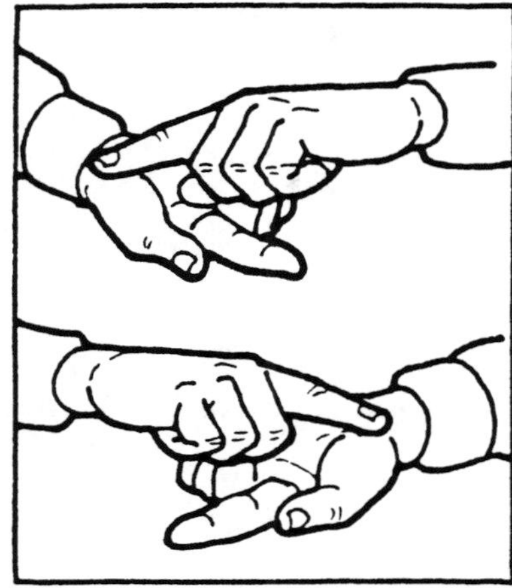

Indexes extended, L. hand on top of Rt.; rotate round to finish Rt. on top of L.

CHANGE (cash)

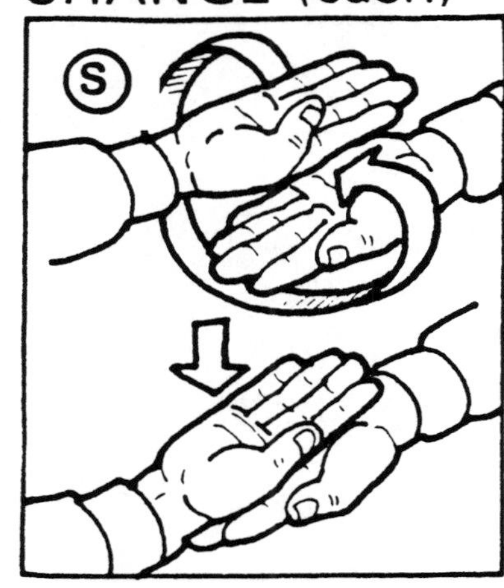

Two flat hands, Rt. on top of L.; Rt. makes full circle round L. then comes back down onto L.

CHARGE (law)

Index points up/forward, then sweeps sharply back/left.

CHARGE (price)

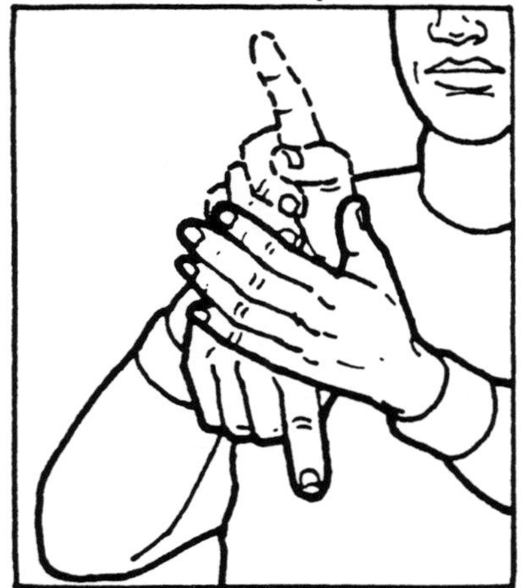

Index pointing up behind L. hand moves sharply to point down.

CHASE

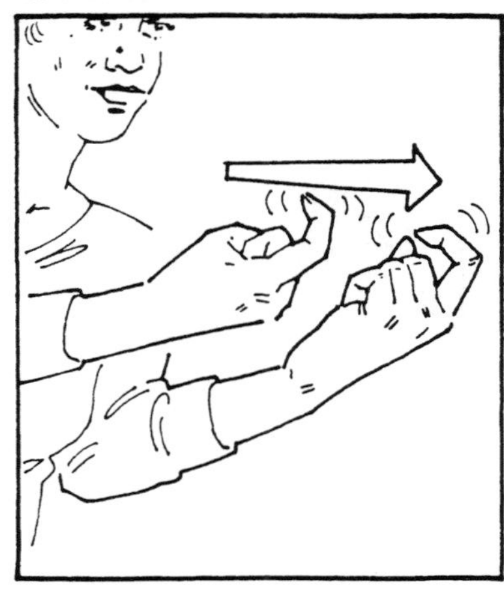

Index fingers flex repeatedly, as both hands move forward, one "chasing" the other.

CHEAP

Two "N" hands, Rt. above L., Rt. hand moves down sharply.

CHEAT

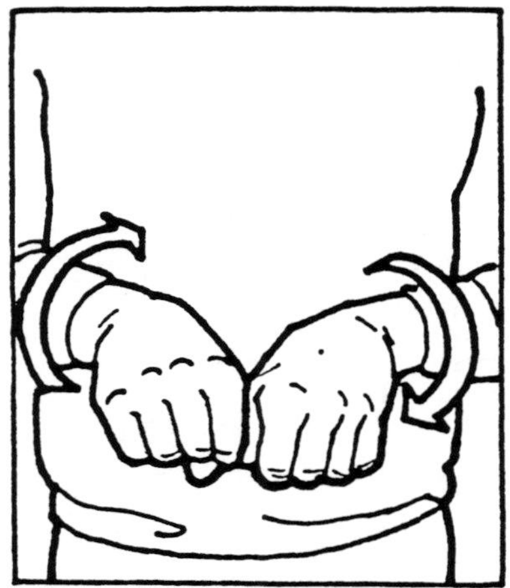

Two fists held together, twist against each other.

CHECK

Two closed hands thumbs and little fingers extended. Move down waggling.

CHEEKY

Grasp and waggle the cheek.

CHEESE

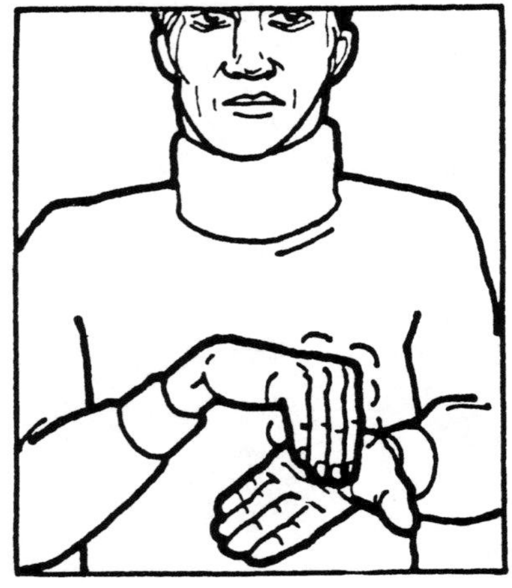

Fingertips of Rt. bent hand touch L. palm. Hand rocks slightly indicating wedge.

CHEQUE

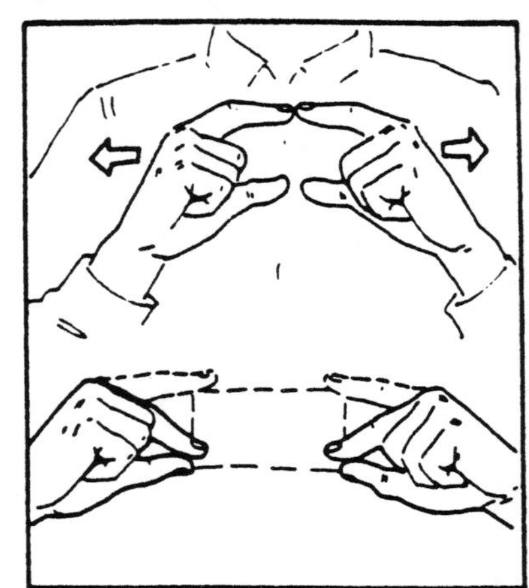

Indicate outline of cheque with indexes and thumbs of both hands.

CHERRY

Rt. "V" hand pointing down, palm back shakes at side of right ear.

CHEW

Two closed hands Rt. on top of L. rub against each other.

CHICKEN

Make sign for "bird" whilst moving elbow in and out.

CHILD

Rt. hand slightly bent indicates head of child.

CHILDREN

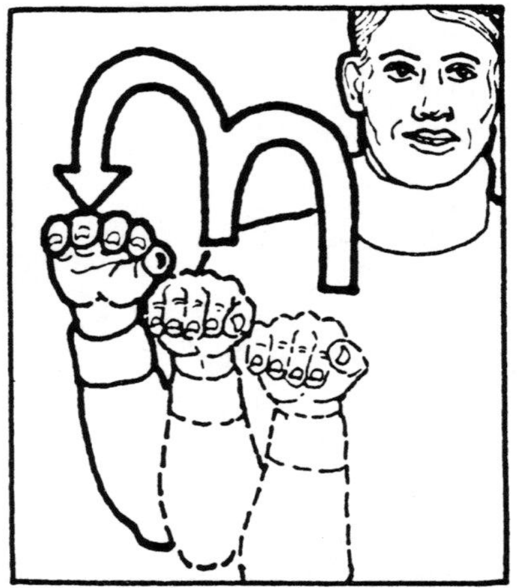

Rt. hand slightly bent indicates heads of children.

CHIMNEY

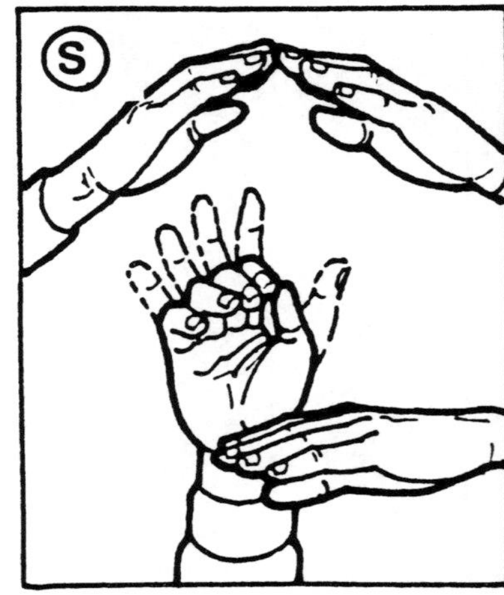

Indicate roof with both hands, then open and close Rt. bunched hand several times.

CHINA

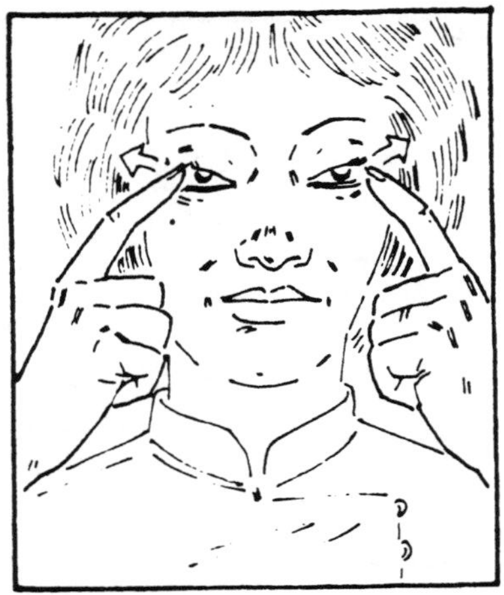

Indexes make small movement at sides of eyes.

CHIPS

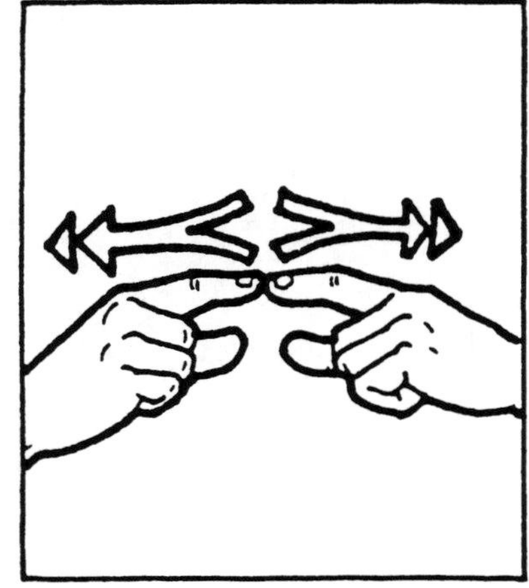

Indicate shape of chips, with indexes and thumbs, several times.

CHOCOLATE

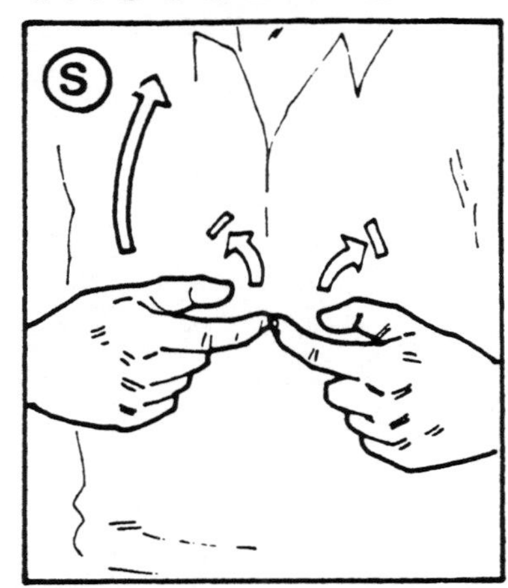

Tips of two "C" hands touch, then twist from wrists to point up. Rt. "C" then nods towards mouth.

CHOOSE

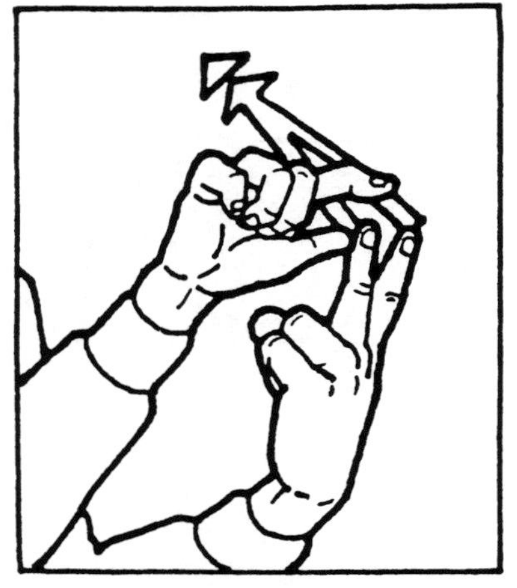

L. index and middle fingers extended, pick at one then the other with Rt. thumb and index.

CHOP

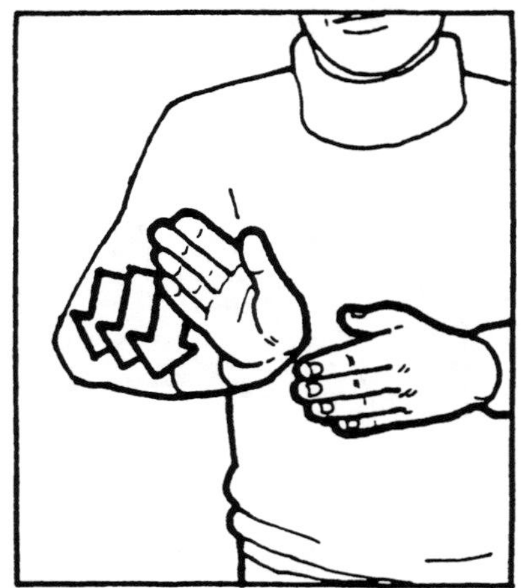

Two flat hands palms facing. Rt. hand moves away from L. in a chopping action.

CHRISTMAS

Indicate long beard by stroking hand down off chin.

CHURCH

Two fists, Rt. on top of L., move together up and down.

CINEMA

Heel of Rt. open hand palm forward rests on L. index and shakes from side to side.

CITY

Rt. clawed hand moves from behind L. around fingertips in small hops, to finish in front of L.

CLASS

Two "C" hands touch at fingertips swivel from wrists to finish with blades touching.

CLAIM

Palm up Rt. flat hand, held slightly forward, makes small sharp downward movement.

CLEAN

L. flat hand, palm up. Sweep palm down Rt. flat hand along L. palm.

CLEAN (TO)

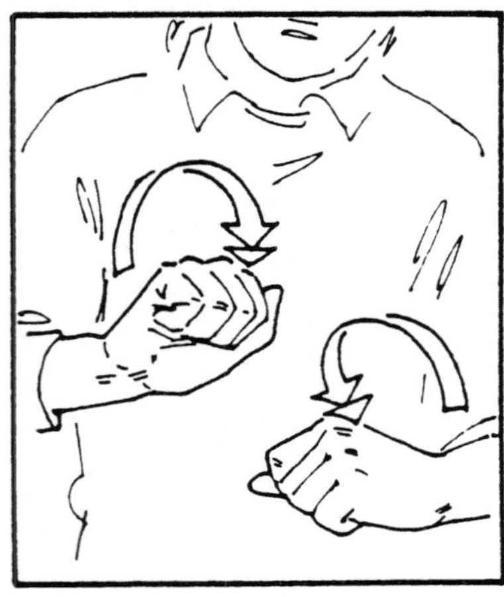

Palm forward closed hands move in alternate circular movements, in action of cleaning.

CLEAR

L. flat hand, palm up. Sweep blade of Rt. flat hand along L. palm twice.

CLEVER

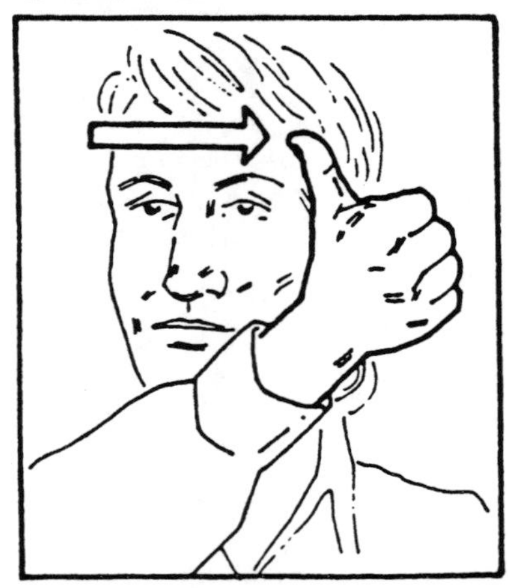

Rt. thumb moves across forehead in sharp movement.

CLIMB

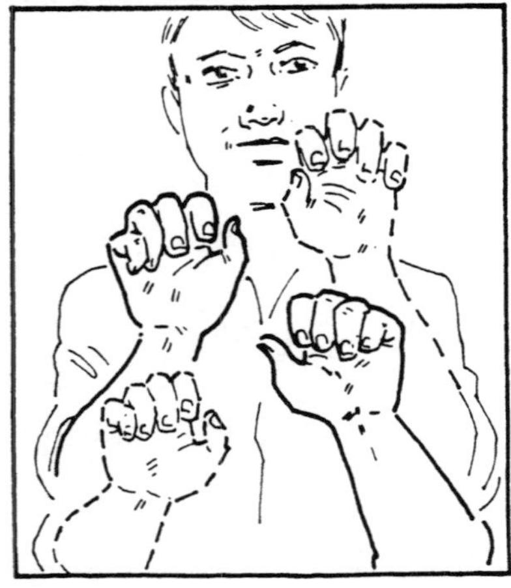

Clawed hands palms forward mime climbing action alternately.

CLOCK

Rt. thumb and index extended, thumb maintains contact with L. palm; index "ticks" round.

CLOSE (door)

L. flat hand palm back. Rt. flat hand palm left moves to "close" on back of L.

CLOTHES

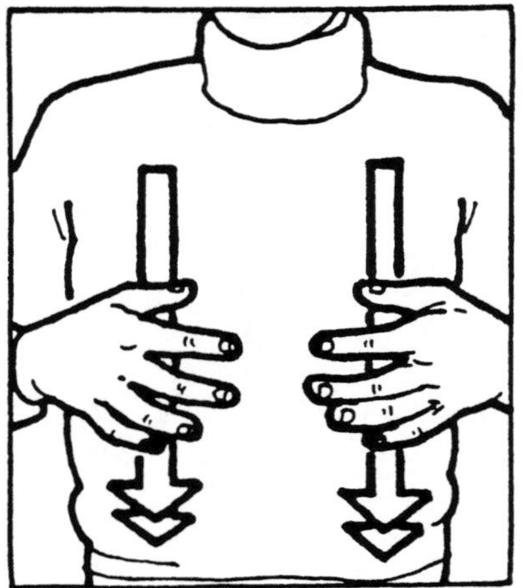

Hands brush down body twice to indicate clothing.

CLOUDS

Two clawed hands, palms forward make small vertical circles in the air at head height, alternately.

CLOWN

Twist tips of tight clawed hand in front of nose.

CLUMSY

Rt. fist palm back strikes forehead twice then index of Rt. moves forward.

COACH

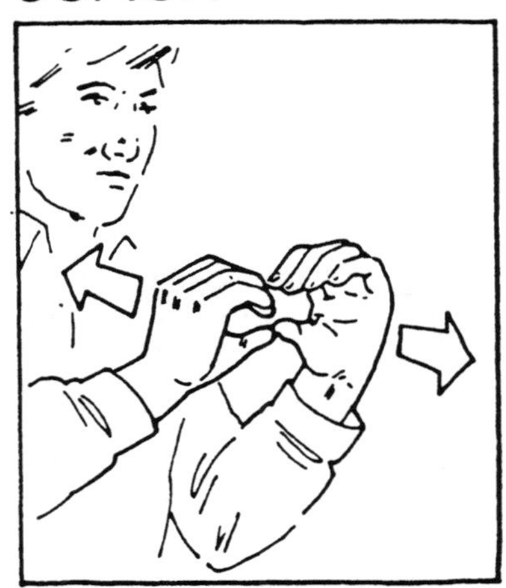

Two full "C" hands, palms facing pull apart, L. forward/ left, Rt. backwards/right.

COAST

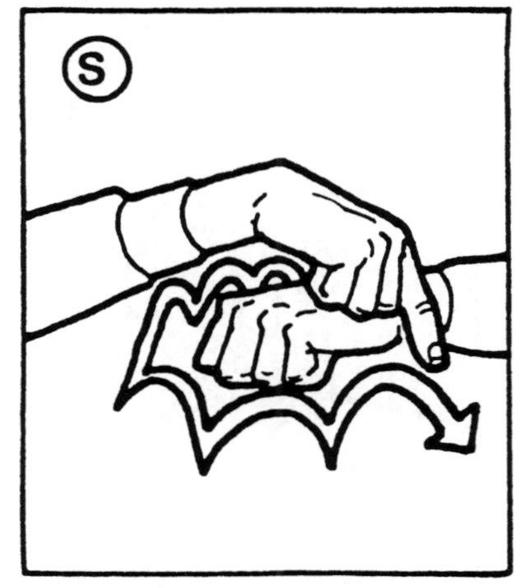

L. closed hand palm down; Rt. index points down and makes jabbing movement around L.

COAT

Mime pulling a coat over shoulders.

COCONUT

Mime holding and shaking a coconut near the ear.

COFFEE

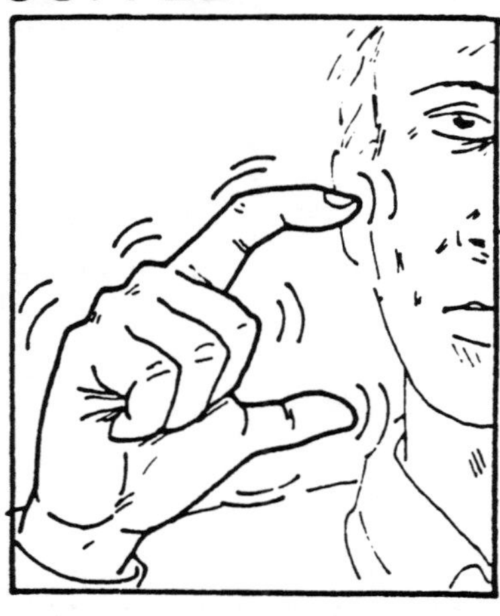

Rt. "C" hand palm left waggles from wrist at side of mouth.

COIN

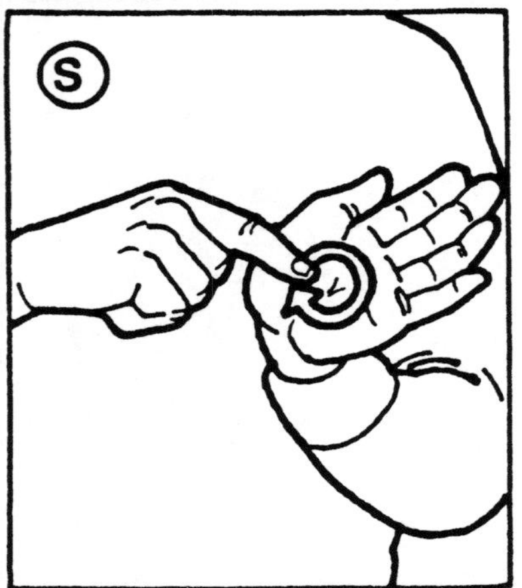

Indicate outline of coin with Rt. index on L. palm.

COLA

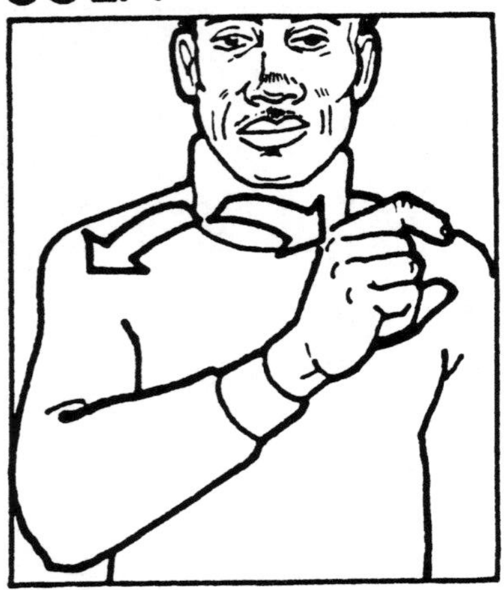

Rt. "C" hand moves left, then right.

COLD

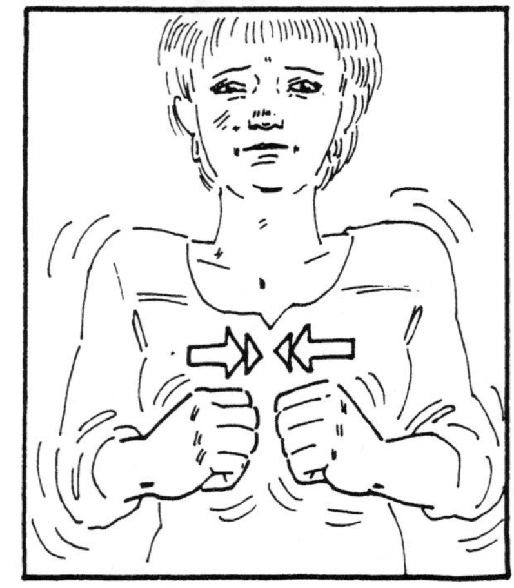

Closed hands held close together in front of chest; elbows pull into body in shivering action.

COLD (A)

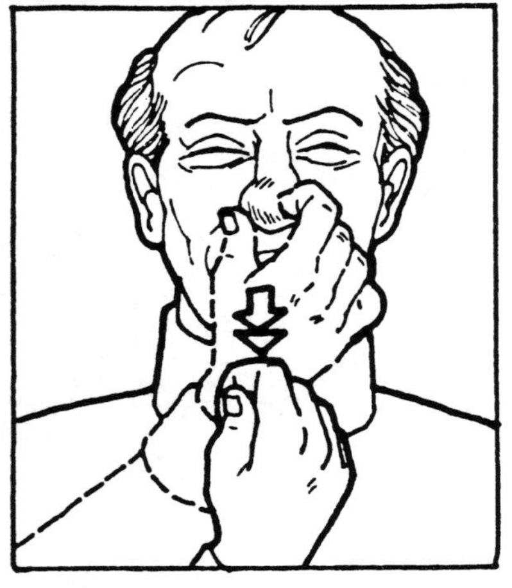

Mime wiping nose with repeated action.

COLLECT

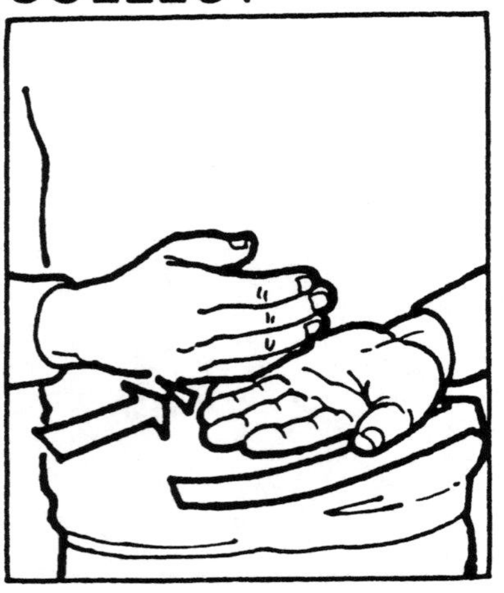

Rt. cupped hand strokes palm of L. towards body several times, as formation moves right to left.

COLLECTION

Rt. cupped hand sweeps onto palm up L.; formation then moves up and down.

COLLEGE

"C" hand waggles at temple.

COLOUR

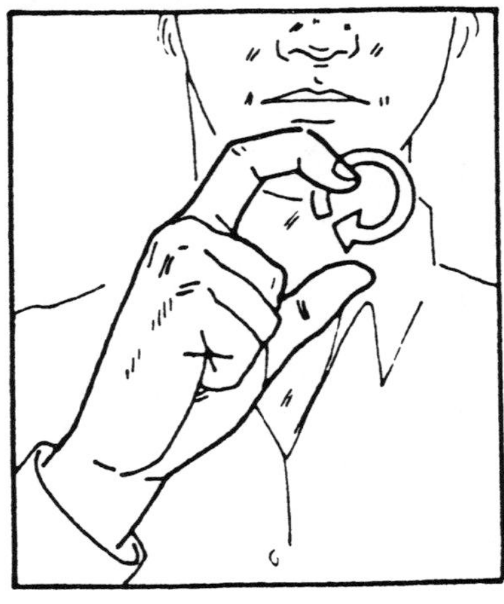

Rt. "C" hand palm left makes small vertical circles in front of chin.

COLUMN

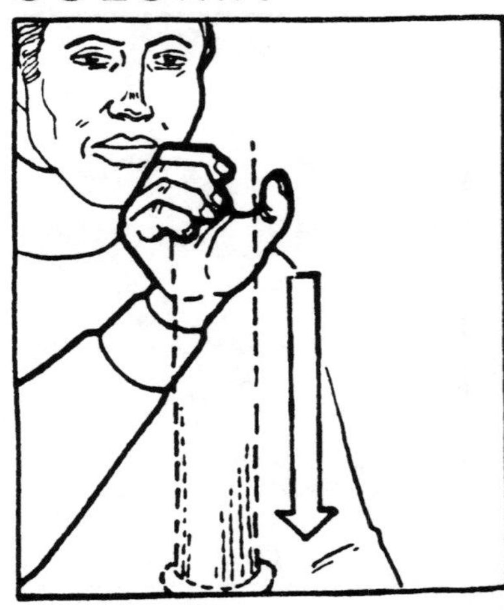

Indicate shape of column with Rt. full handed "C".

COMB

Hand moves in action of using a comb.

COME

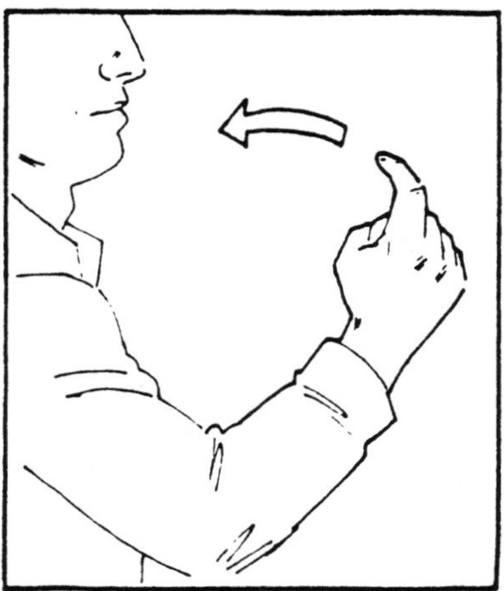

Rt. closed hand index extended held away from body, moves back towards body.

COMFORT

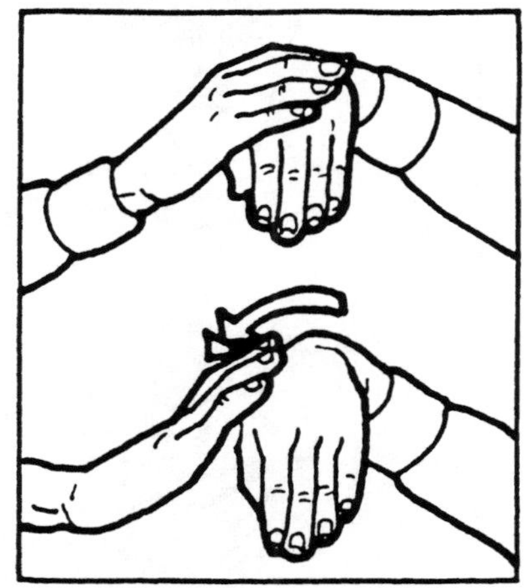

Two flat hands, palms down, Rt. strokes back of L. twice.

COMFORTABLE

Shoulders wriggle alternately as Rt. hand strokes back of L.; then L. of Rt.

COMMUNICATE

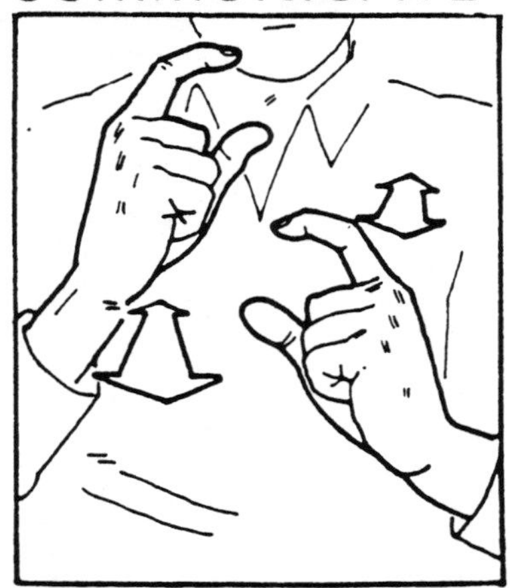

Two "C" hands, palms facing move alternately backwards and forwards.

COMPETITION

Indexes jerk towards each other several times whilst moving down.

COMPLAIN

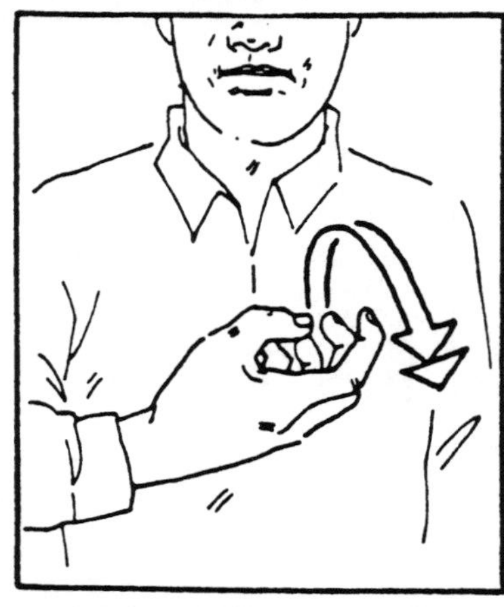

Rt. clawed hand, palm up, brushes up chest several times.

COMPUTER

Two "C" hands make vertical circles simultaneously.

CONCENTRATE

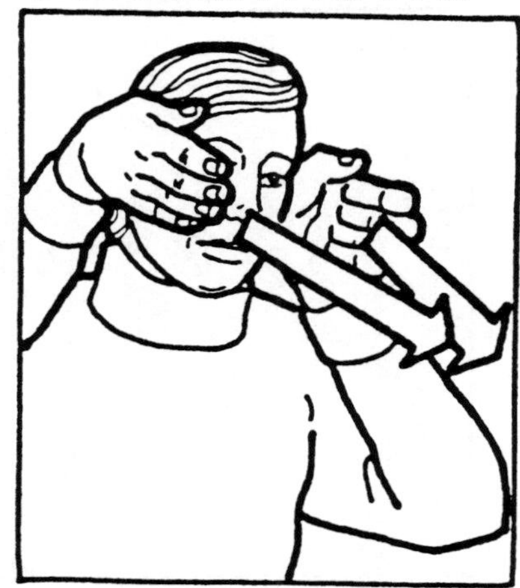

Two flat hands, held at each side of temples move forward and slightly in.

CONFERENCE

Indexes extended L. palm up Rt. palm down make alternate horizontal circles.

CONFESS

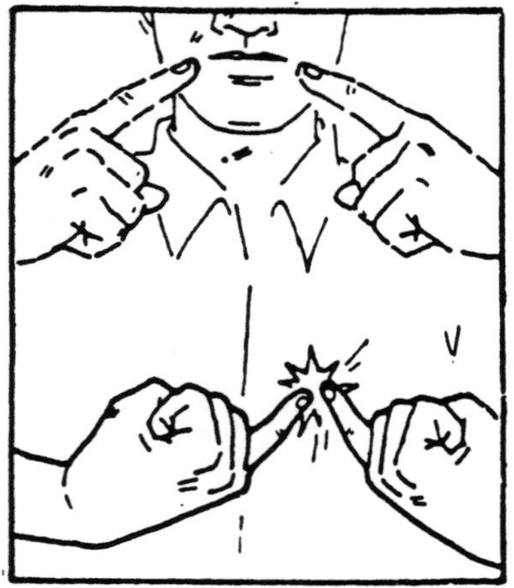

Indexes point to mouth, then move down to closed hands little fingers extended contacting left side of chest.

CONFIDENT

Rt. "C" hand taps twice against chest over the heart.

CONFLICT

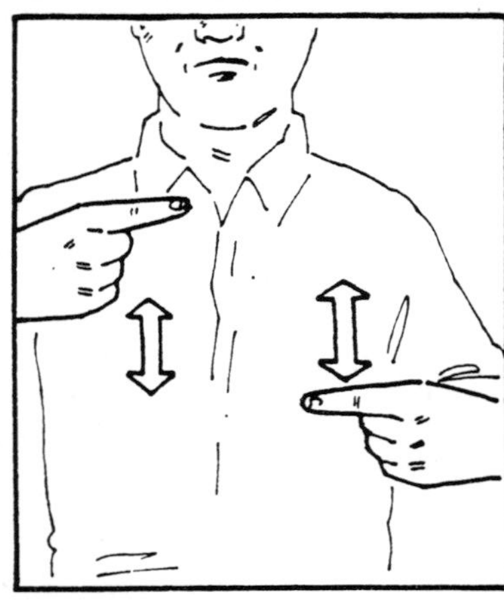

Indexes point towards each other, and move up and down alternately.

CONFUSE

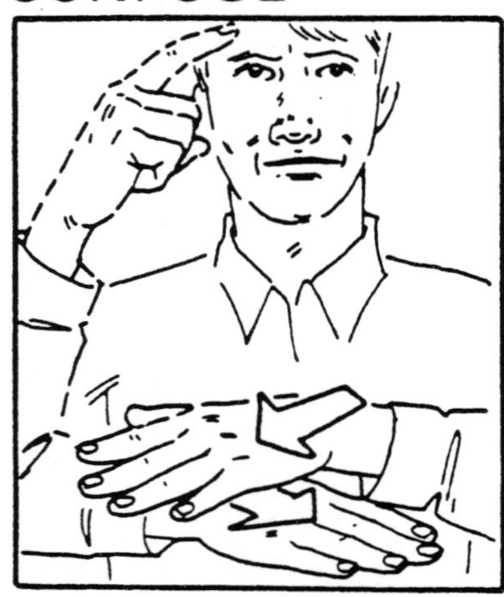

Point to temple with Rt. index, then two open hands cross sharply.

CONGRATULATE

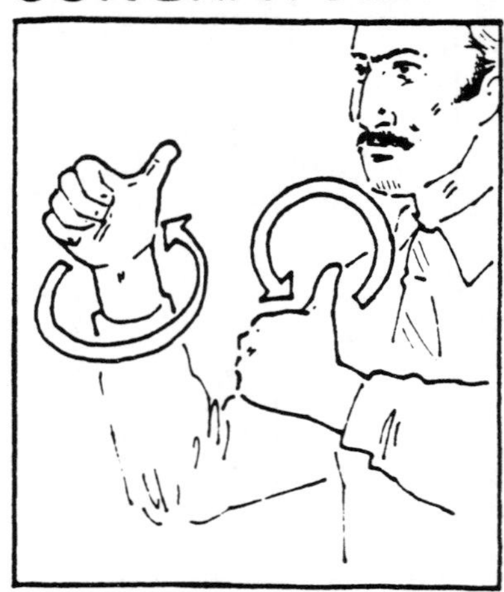

Two closed hands, thumbs extended make forward circles alternately.

CONTACT

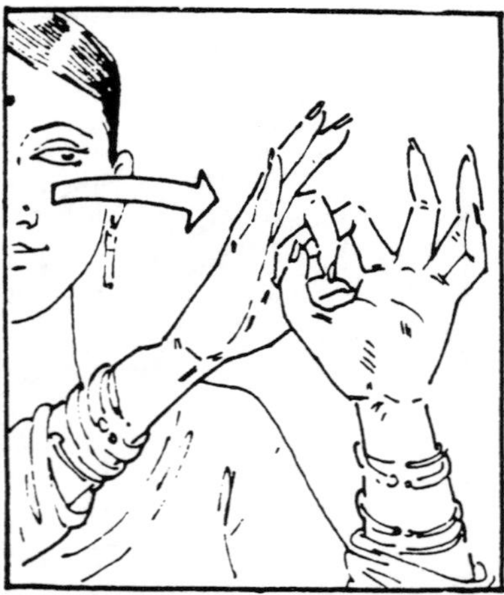

Rt. hand moves towards L. and fingers of "O" hands interlock.

CONTINUE

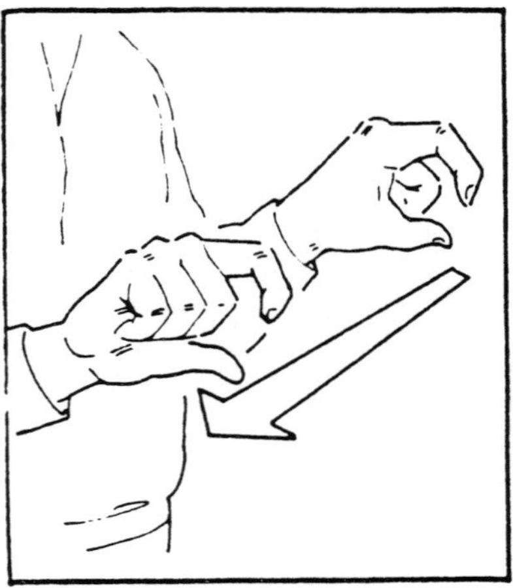

Two "C" hands move from left to right.

CONVERSATION

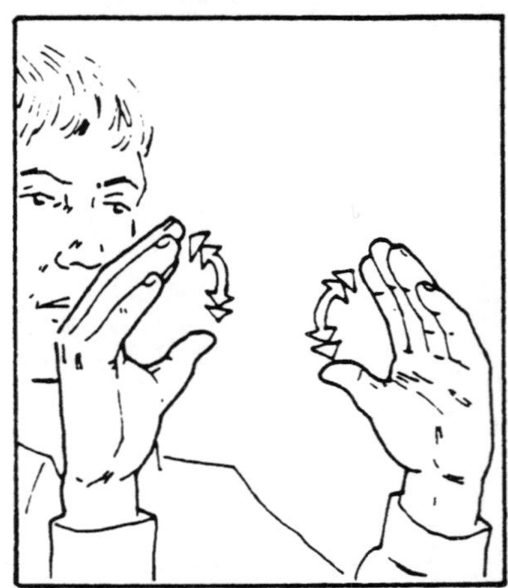

Hands face each other, one in front of mouth, one held forward. Fingers open and close onto thumbs to indicate people talking.

COOK

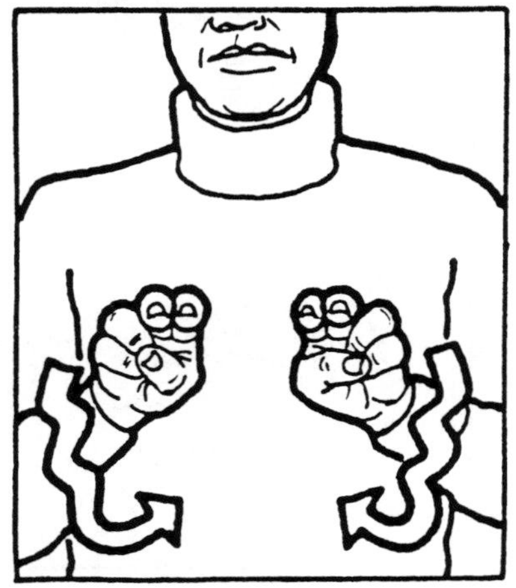

Two "N" hands point forward and move down with twisting movement.

COOKER

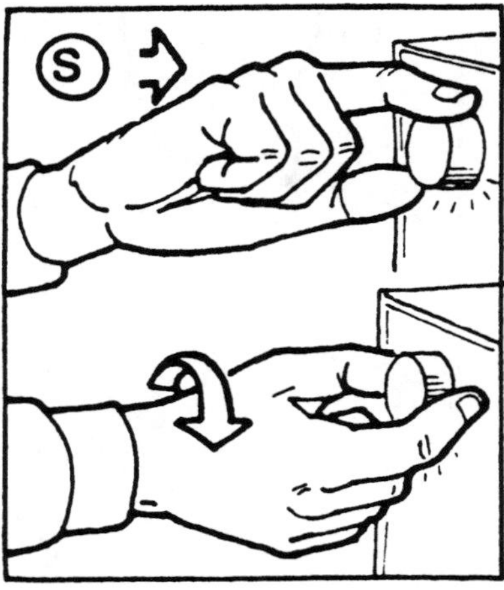

Mime pressing in knob and turning.

COOKERY

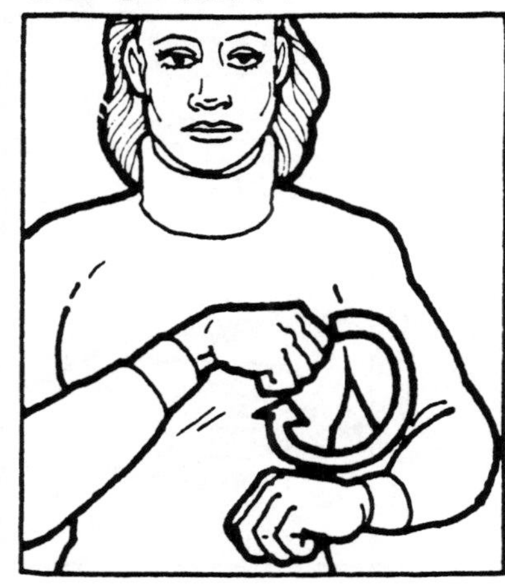

Mime mixing in bowl.

COOL

Two flat hands fingers pointing up/back, waft alternately up and down in front of face.

COPY

Rt. full "C" hand, fingers and thumb straight. Move up sharply off L. palm, closing fingers onto thumb.

CORNER

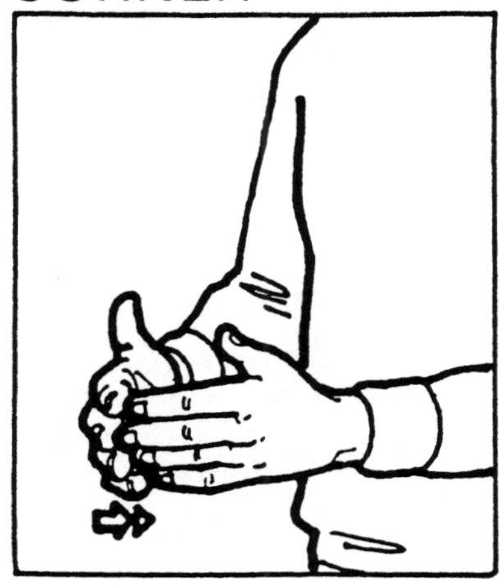

Fingers of two flat hands form an angle and tap together twice.

CORNFLAKES

Mime holding and shaking a cornflake packet.

CORRESPOND

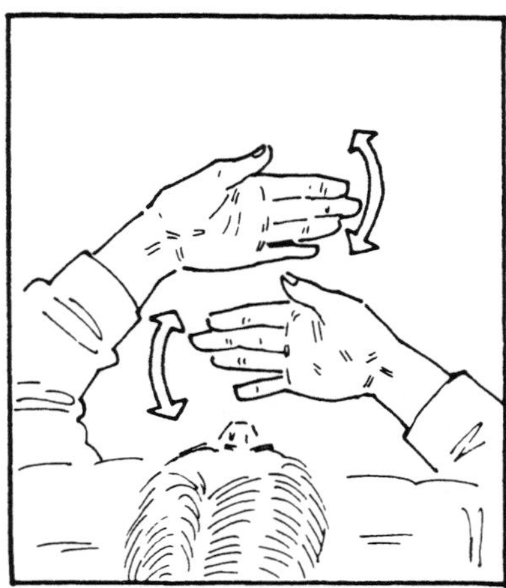

Palm up flat hands move alternately backward and forward across each other.

COUGH

Fist thumps against chest several times.

COUNT

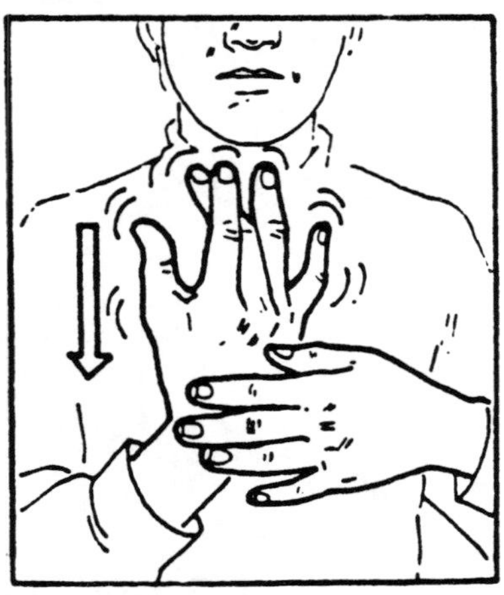

Rt. open hand behind and above L. moves down with fingers waggling.

COUNTER

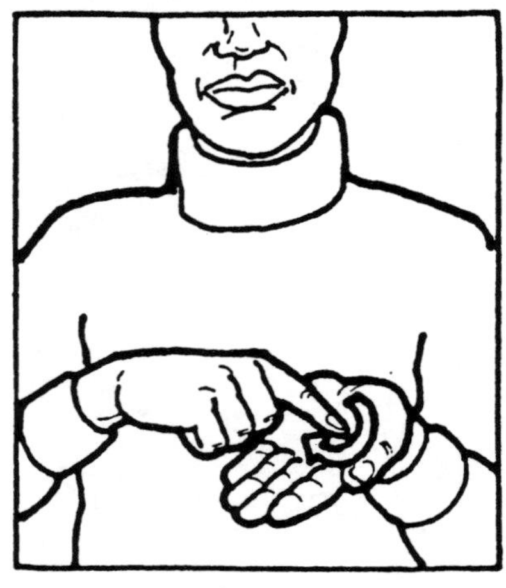

Make small circle on L. palm with Rt. index.

COUNTRY

Rt. hand starts at L. fingertips and sweeps forward and left up left arm.

COUPLE

Index and middle of Rt. hand open and close. Heel of Rt. hand supported by L. hand.

COURAGE

Contact trunk with fingertips then move hands forward closing sharply to closed hands, thumbs extended.

COURSE

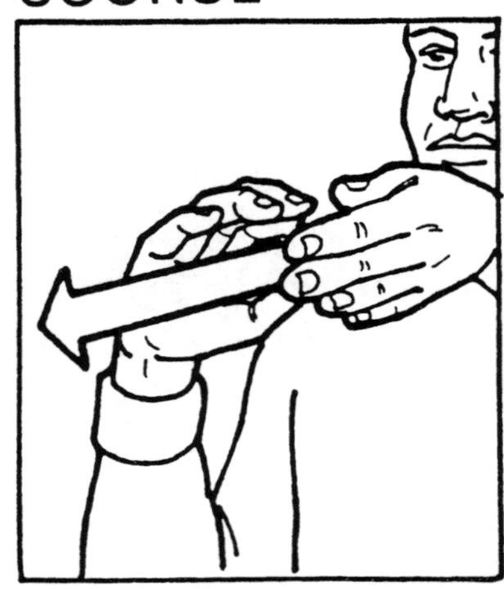

Full "C" hand moves forward from heel of L. hand.

COURT (law)

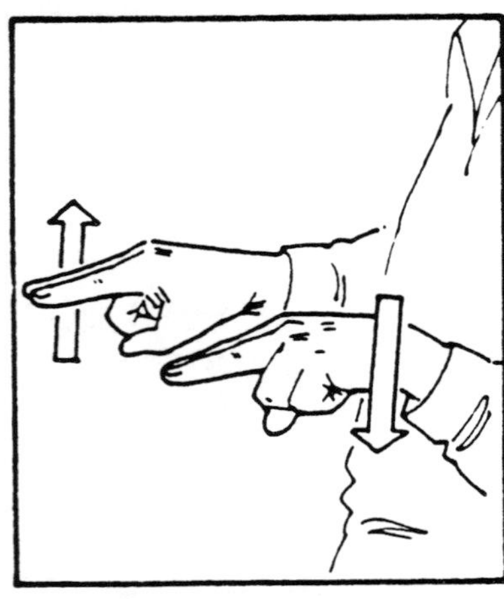

Two "N" hands pointing forward move up and down alternately.

COUSIN

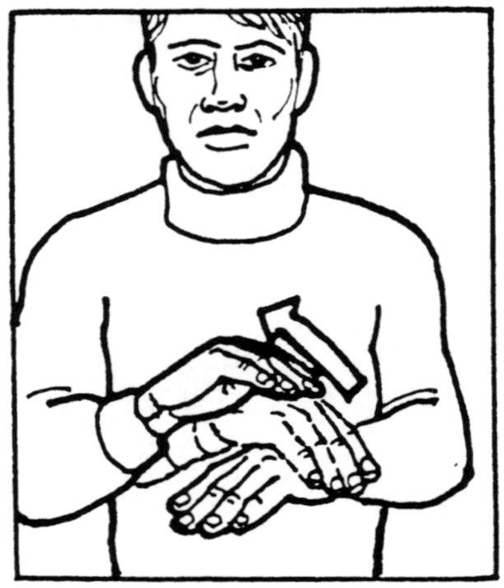

Tips of Rt. hand hold L. wrist then pull away closing thumb on fingers.

COW

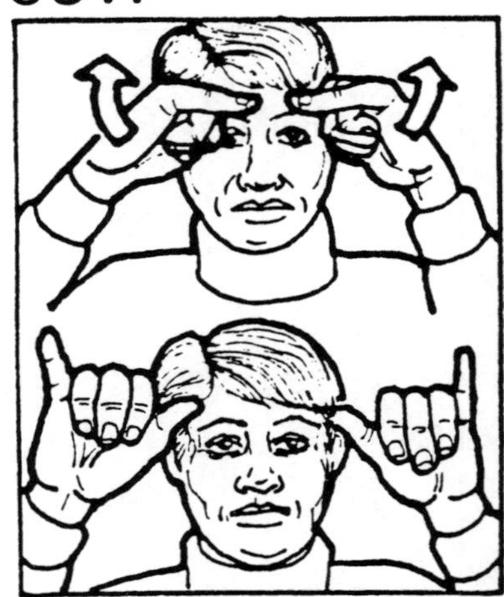

Thumbs and little fingers extended; thumbs on temples, twist from palm down to palm forward.

CRAB

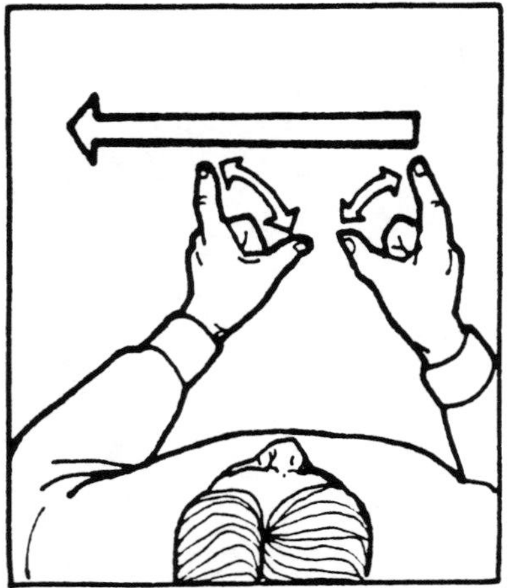

Thumbs and indexes open and close to indicate pincers whilst moving to the left.

CRANE

Clawed L. hand moves up whilst Rt. hand makes small winding action.

CRASH

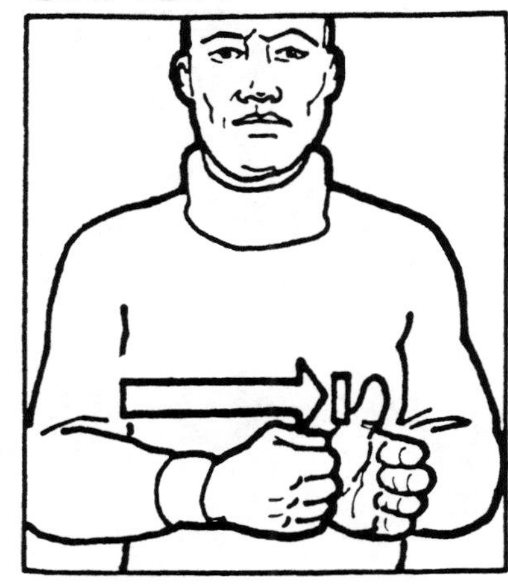

Rt. fist hits L. palm.

CREAM

Rt. hand rubs back of L. in small circular movements.

CREAM (milk)

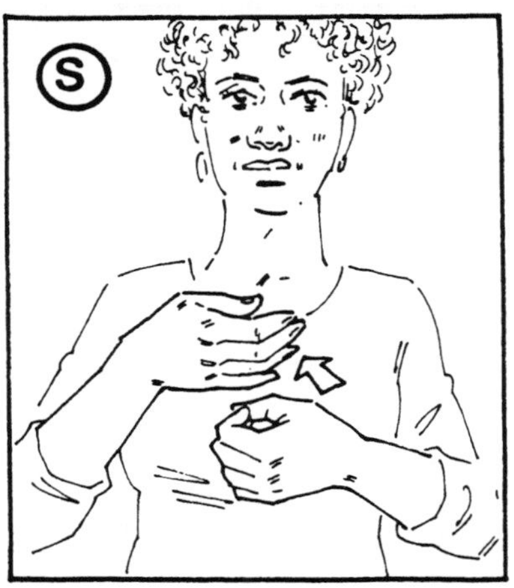

Rt. hand fingers curved scoops across top of L. full handed "O".

CRICKET

Mime batting with cricket bat.

CRISPS

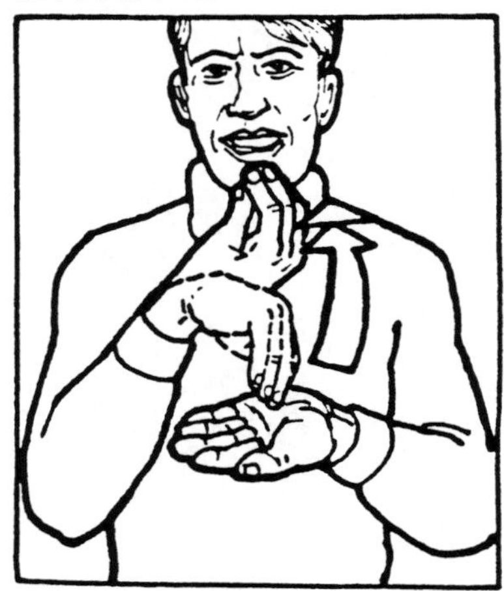

L. flat hand palm up. Rt. bunched hand starts with tips on L. palm and moves up to mouth.

CRITICISE

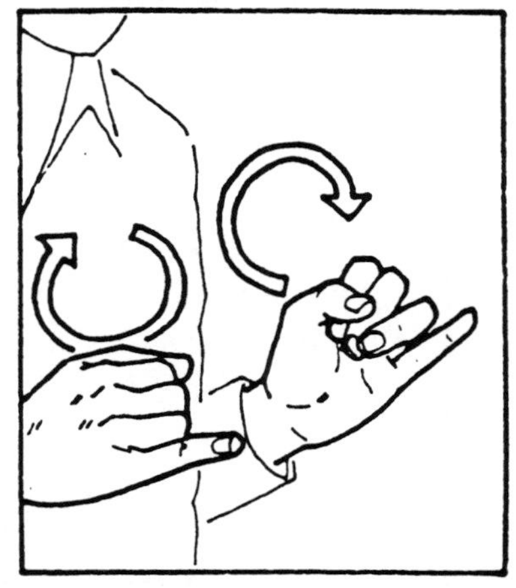

Hands closed, little fingers extended palms facing make alternate forward circles with hands.

CROCODILE

Two flat hands pointing forward palms together, open then shut.

CROSS

Draw cross in air with "C" hand.

CROWD

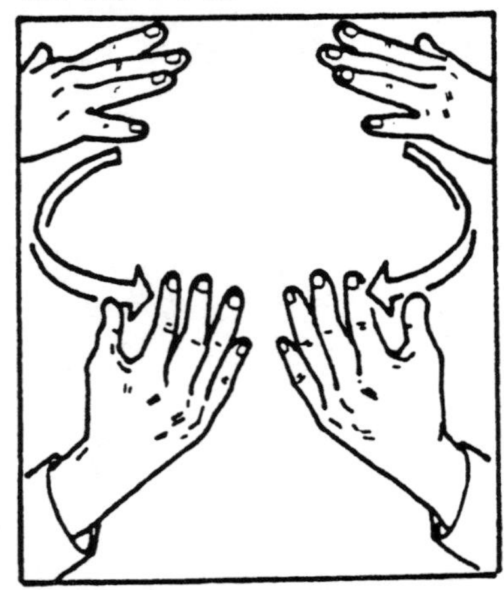

Open hands, palm down pointing in at sides of head swing out and twist to point back.

CROWDED

Closed hands pulled into body, body rotates slightly, shoulders hunched.

CROWN

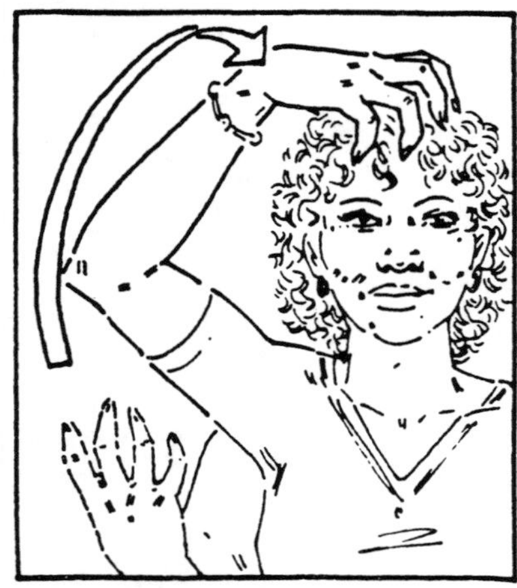

Clawed hand, palm up moves to palm down on top of head.

CRUCIFY

Hit L. palm with Rt. fist then Rt. palm with L. fist. Raise two flat hands to head height.

CRUEL

Closed hand, palm forward, index extended and pointing into side of neck, twist to palm back.

CRUSH

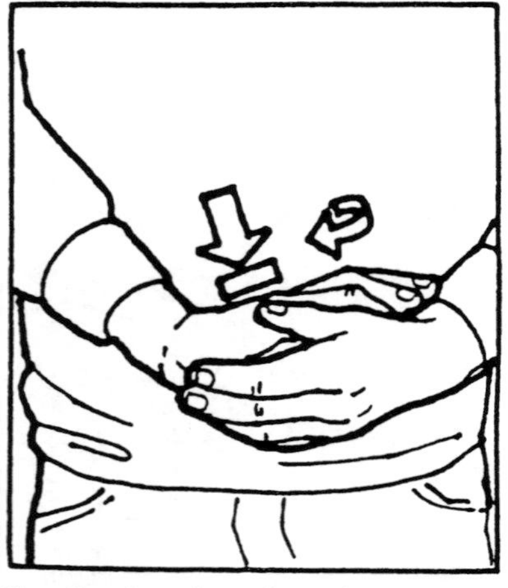

Rt. flat hand pushes down against L. palm and twists.

CRY

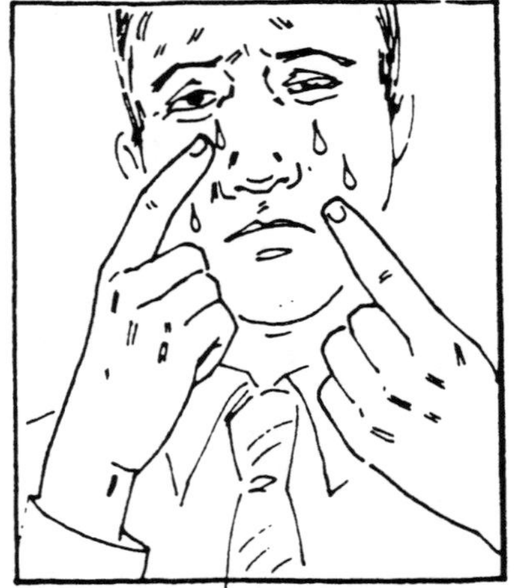

Index fingers move down face from eyes to indicate tears.

CUCUMBER

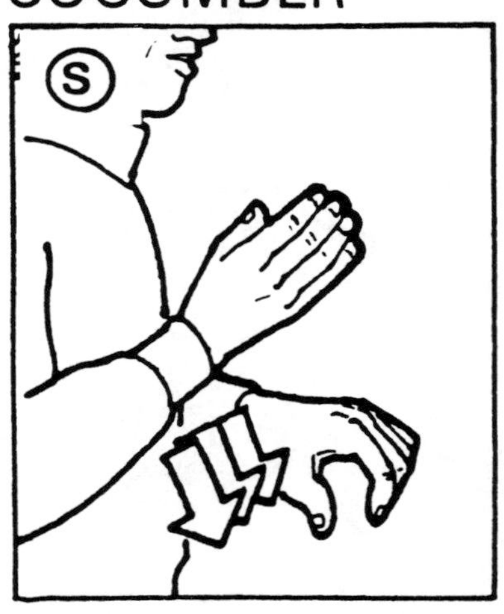

Whole L. "C" hand palm down; Rt. flat hand makes slicing movement against L.

CUP

L. flat hand, palm up. Rest blade of Rt. wholehanded "C" on L. palm.

CUPBOARD

Outline shape in the air with indexes, then mime opening doors.

CURRICULUM

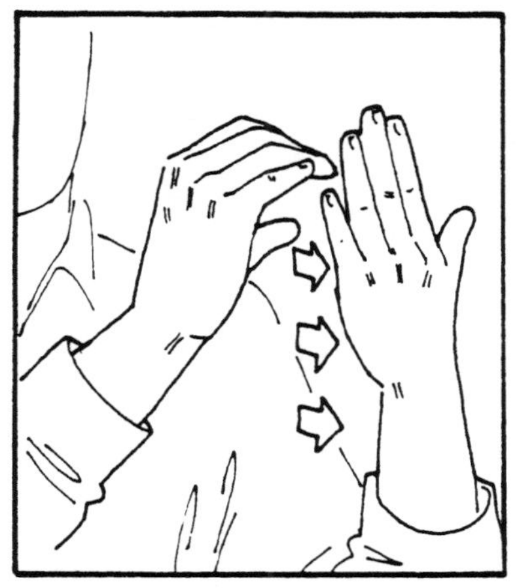

Edge of Rt. full handed "C" moves down L. arm in series of small hops.

CURTAIN(S)

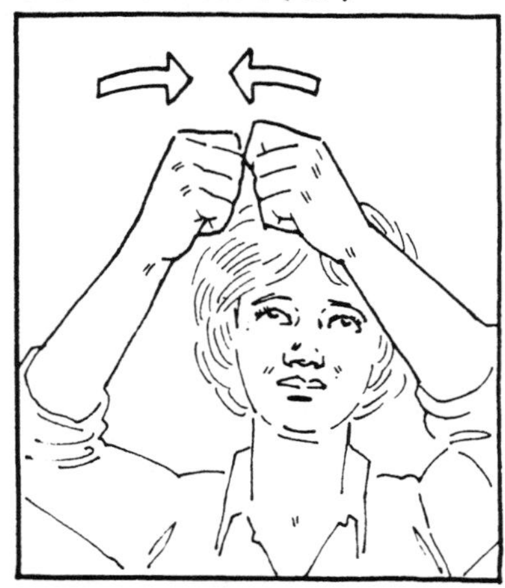

Two closed hands held above head mime action of drawing curtains together.

CURVE

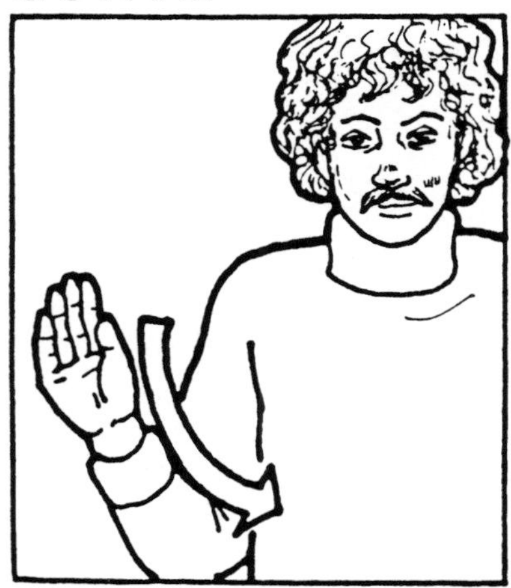

Flat hand fingers slightly bent swings in small downward curve to finish palm up.

CUSTARD

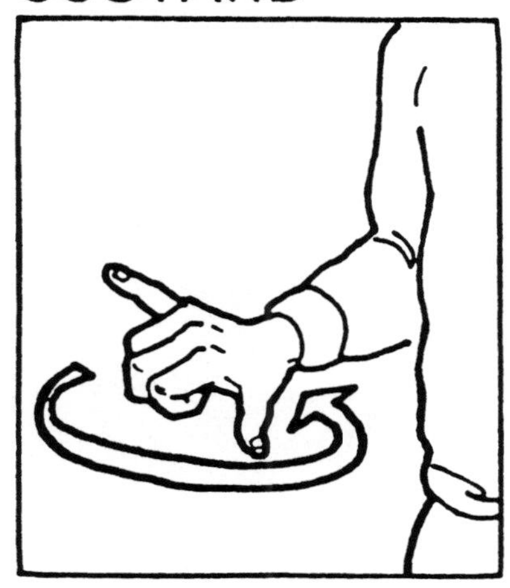

Thumb and little finger extended, tilted to thumb down make circular movement.

CUT (scissors)

Fingers of "V" hand open and shut, whilst hand moves forward/left.

CUT (knife)

Two "N" hands, fingers of Rt. resting on top of L. at right angles make small sawing action.

DAMAGE

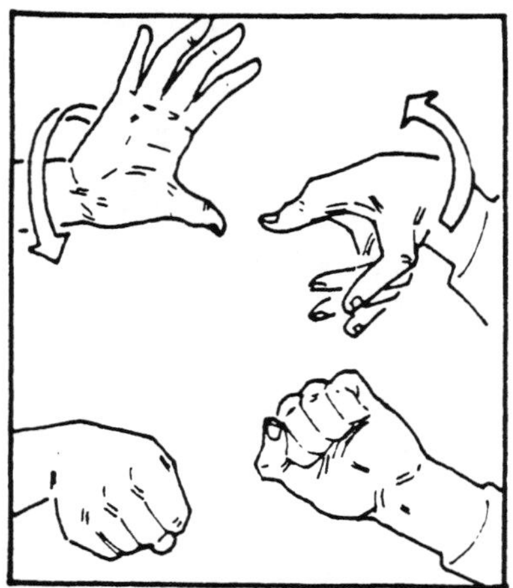

Clawed hands close sharply and twist in tearing movement.

DAMP

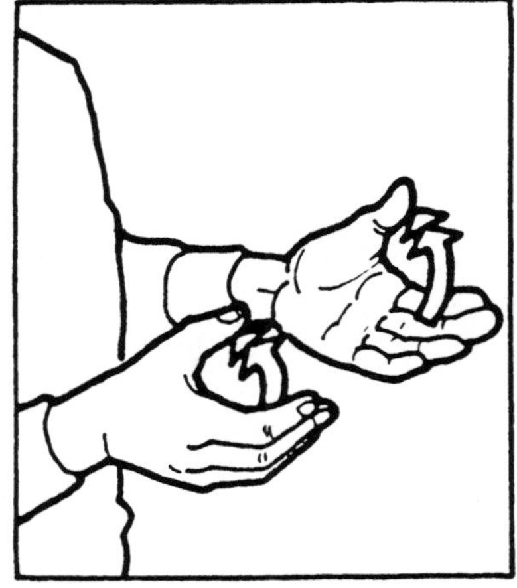

Both hands palms up, fingers close onto ball of thumb, twice.

DANCE

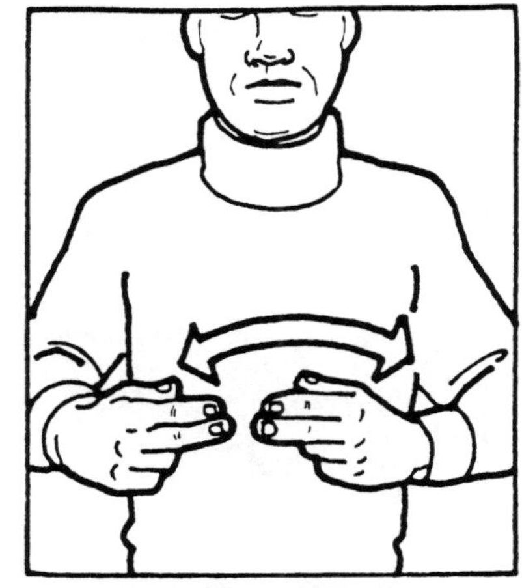

Two "N" hands palms back, move from side to side and simultaneously flick in downward movement from wrist.

DANGER

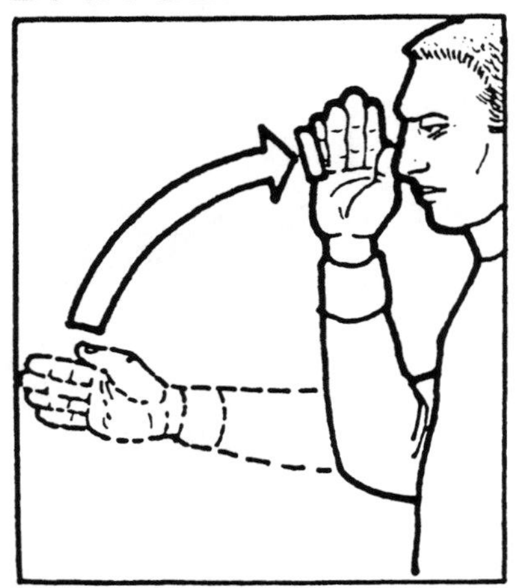

Rt. flat hand pointing forward, palm left moves up sharply in front of nose.

DARK

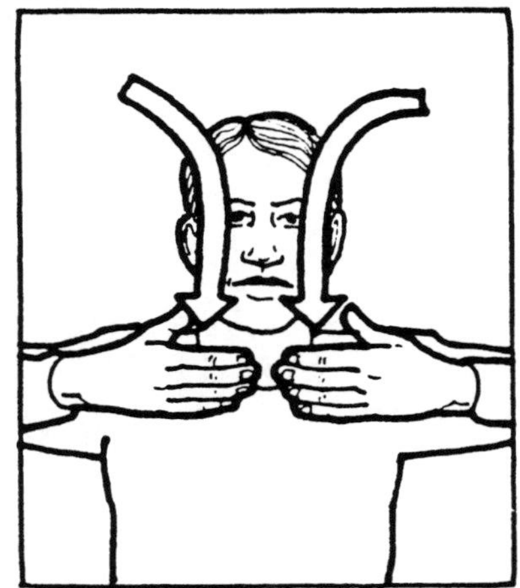

Two flat hands held at either side of head swing down to finish fingers towards each other.

DATE

Closed hand palm left knocks against side of chin twice.

DAUGHTER

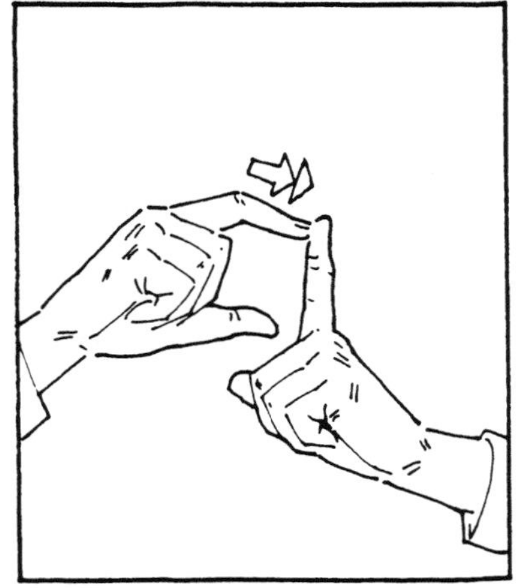

Form fingerspelt "D", and tap twice.

DAY

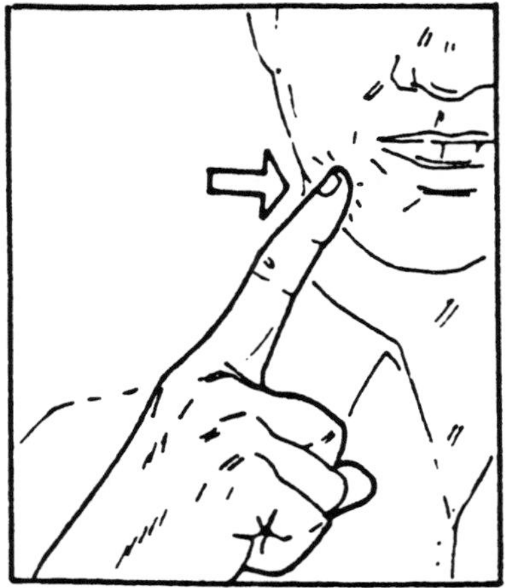

Rt. closed hand index finger extended, touches side of face.

EVERY DAY

Backs of fingers stroke forwards on side of face.

DEAD

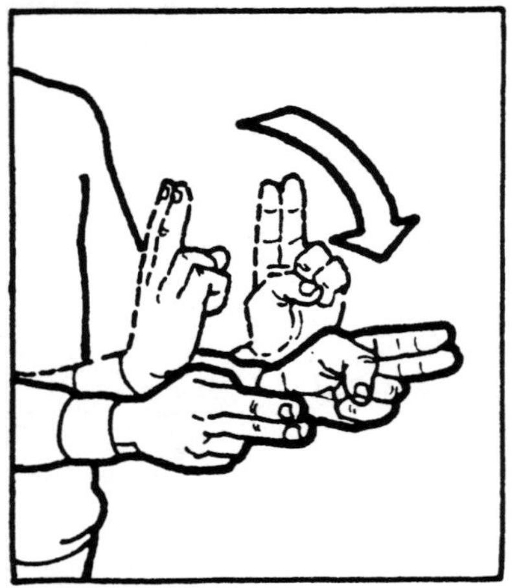

Two "N" hands palms facing drop from wrists to point forward/down.

DEAF

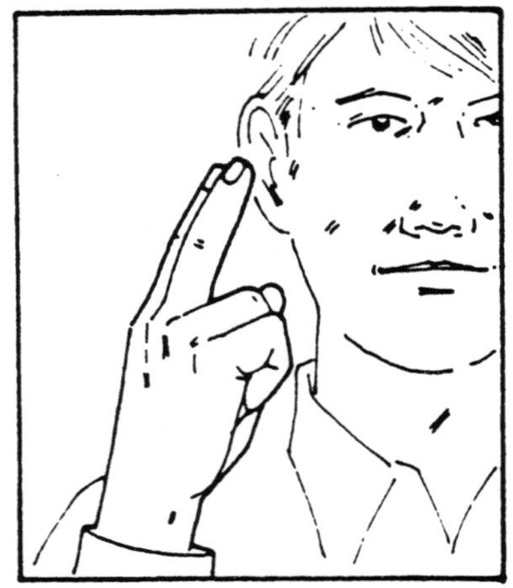

"N" hand pointing up, palm left touches ear.

DEAF CLUB

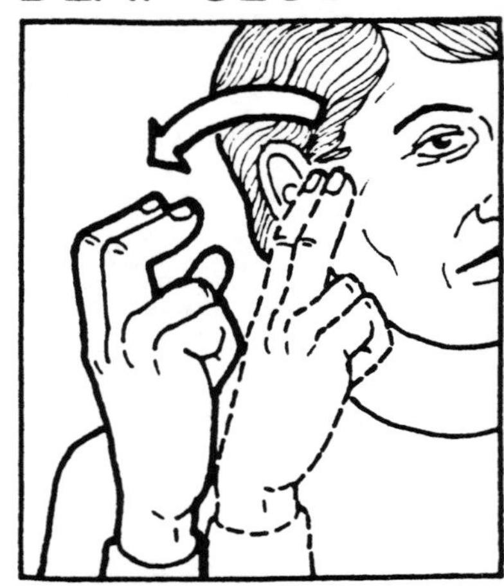

"N" hand touches ear, then moves out to form "C" with index and middle fingers.

DEAR (costly)

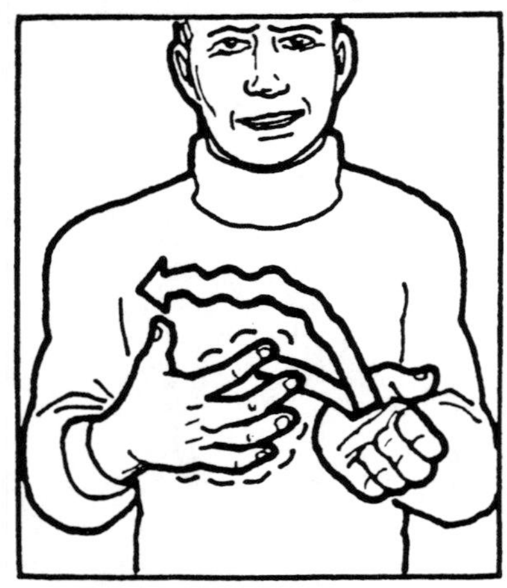

Fingertips of open Rt. hand touch palm of L. flat hand, then move to right, shaking at wrist.

DECIDE/DECISION

Rt. index touches forehead, then moves down sharply onto L. palm, with one tap for decide, two taps for decision.

DECREASE

Two "N" hands, palms facing, Rt. above L.; Rt. moves in two small movements down to L.

DEEP

L. flat hand palm right. Rt. index extended moves up and arcs over and down side of L.

DEER

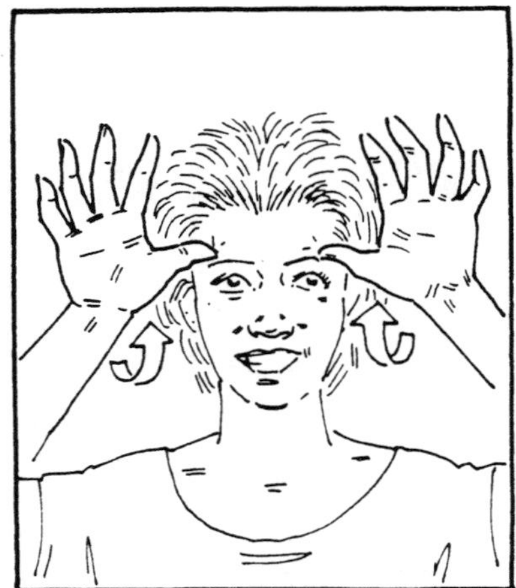

Open hands pointing forward palms down, thumbs touching temples, twist up to palms forward.

DEFEND

Palm forward closed hands, crossed at the wrists, make small movement forward with stress.

DEJECTED

Index edge of palm down flat hand brushes emphatically down chest in one movement.

DELAY

Two "O" hands, palms down move simultaneously to left in small arc.

DELIBERATE

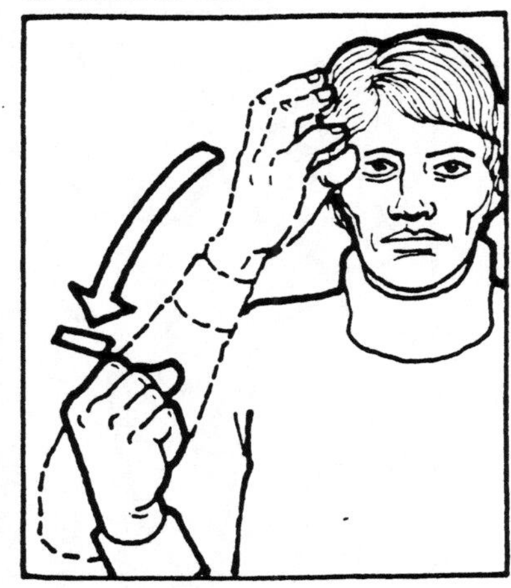

Clawed hand at side of head moves down sharply to closed fist.

DEMAND

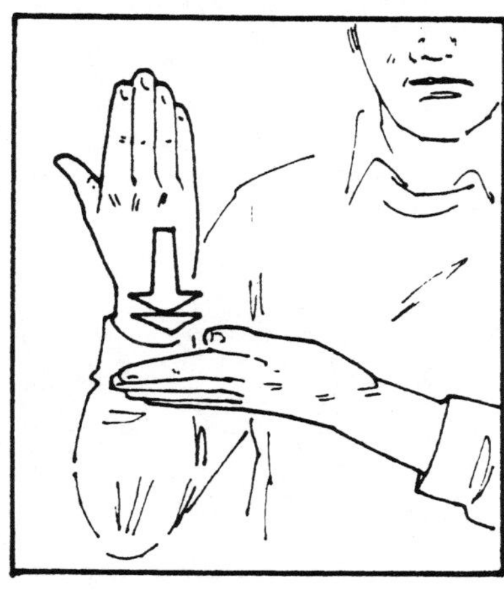

Back of palm up Rt. flat hand contacts L. palm twice, with emphasis.

DENMARK

Index, middle and thumb extended palm back, move up and down across chest.

DEPEND

L. hand palm forward, Rt. index hooked over L. thumb. Move formation down, with slight stress.

DEPOSIT

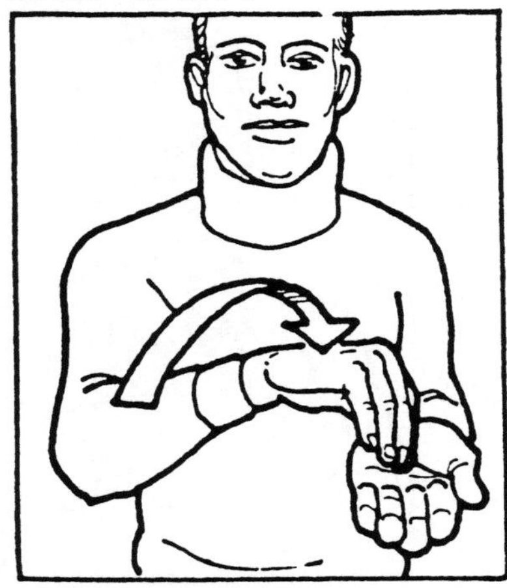

Rt. bunched hand twists from palm up to palm down, tips contacting L. palm.

DEPRESSED

L. flat hand, on top of Rt. index; hold in against body, move formation down with stress.

DESCRIBE

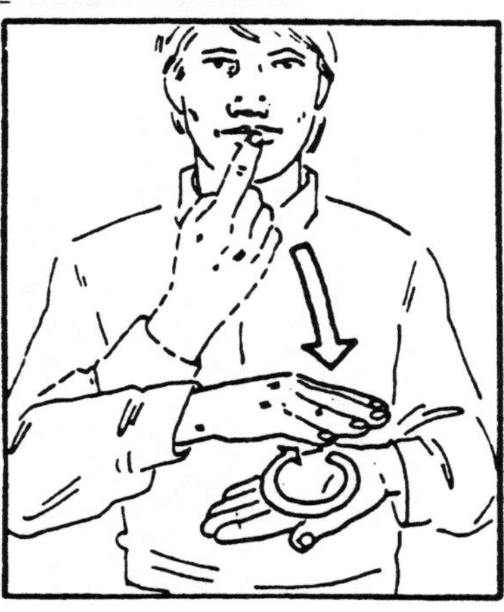

Rt. index points to lips, moves down to flat hand above L. Hands move in alternate horizontal circles.

DESTROY

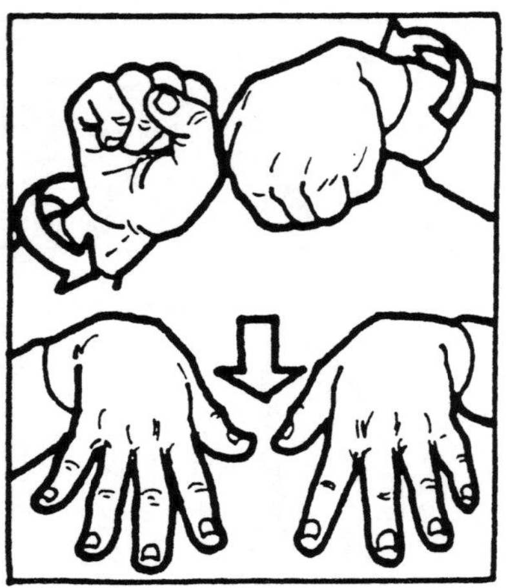

Fists twist against each other, then spring open, palms down.

DETECTIVE

Mime turning lapel over, with twisting movement from wrist.

DETERMINED

Rt. "R" hand, palm left held at side of face, twists so tip touches chin.

DEVELOP

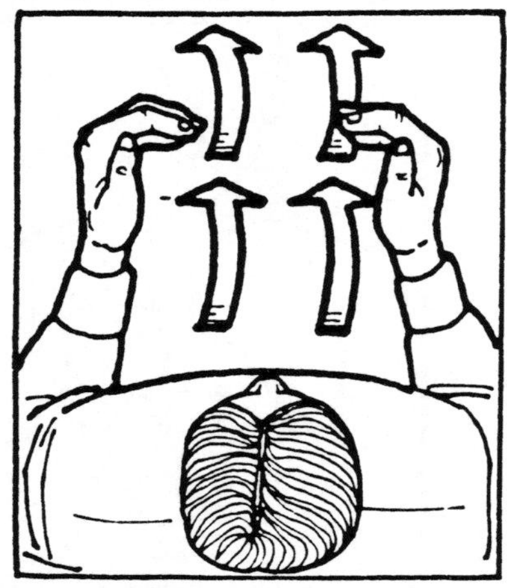

Two bent hands palms facing move forward simultaneously in two small hops.

DEVIL

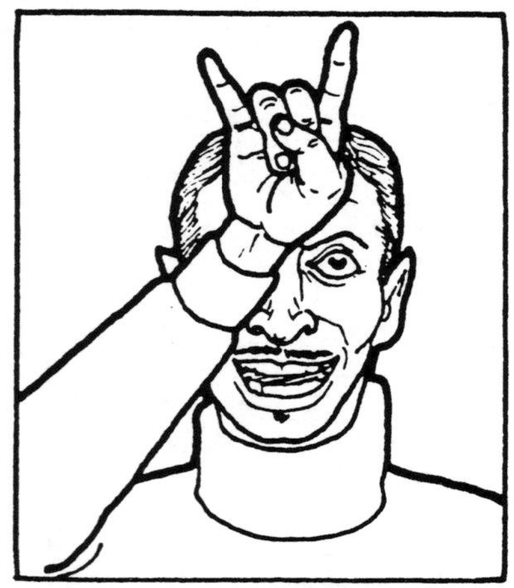

Rt. closed hand index and little finger extended moves up to forehead.

DICTIONARY

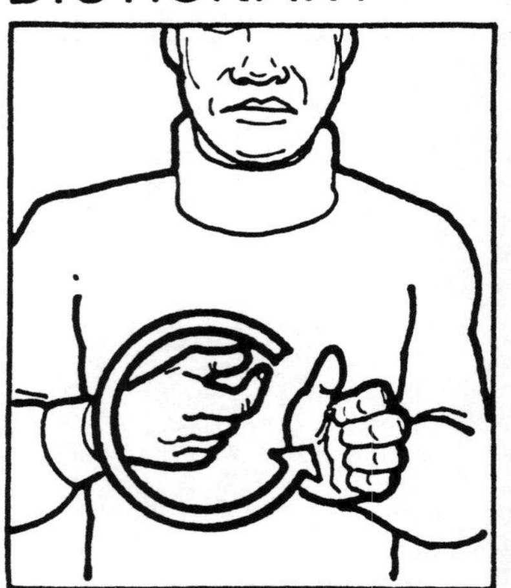

L. flat hand, palm right; Rt. "C" hand makes circular movement up L. palm.

DIFFERENT

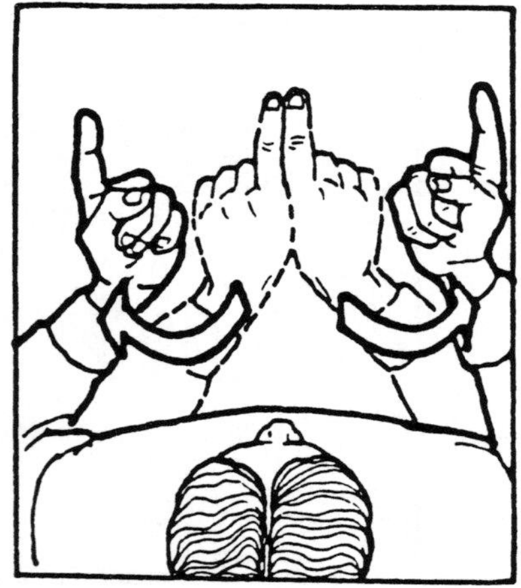

Indexes together, pointing forward palms down, move apart, twisting to palms up.

DIFFICULT

Rt. thumbtip prods L. palm twice.

DINNER

Two "N" hands palms back move alternately up to mouth.

DIRTY

Rub wrists of two closed hands together at right angles.

DISABLED

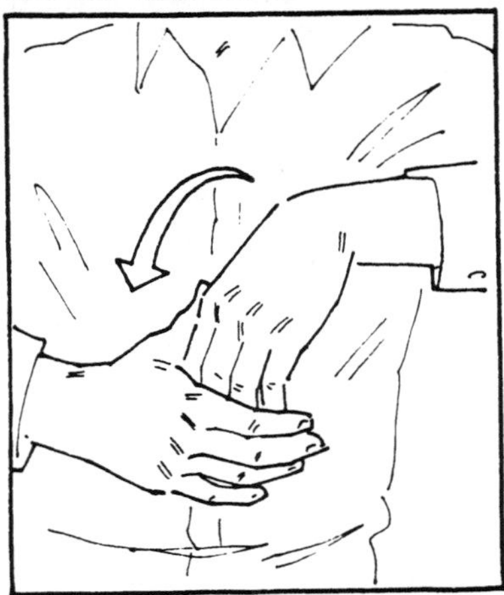

Fingers of Rt. hand push fingers of L. flat hand down/back.

DISAGREE

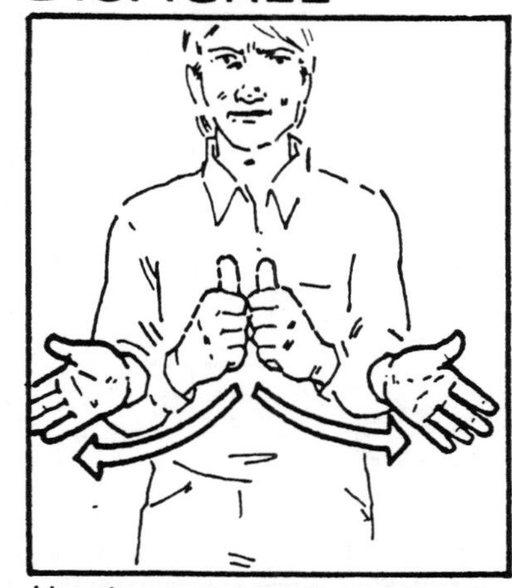

Hands start together, thumbs extended, then swing apart as fingers open in sharp movement.

DISAPPEAR

Two "V" hands thumbs out move towards each other, cross and pull sharply apart, closing fingers onto thumbs.

DISAPPOINT

Tips of "V" hand pointing up/back, jab into throat.

DISH

Two cupped hands, palms facing, move together, twisting to palms up.

DISTANCE

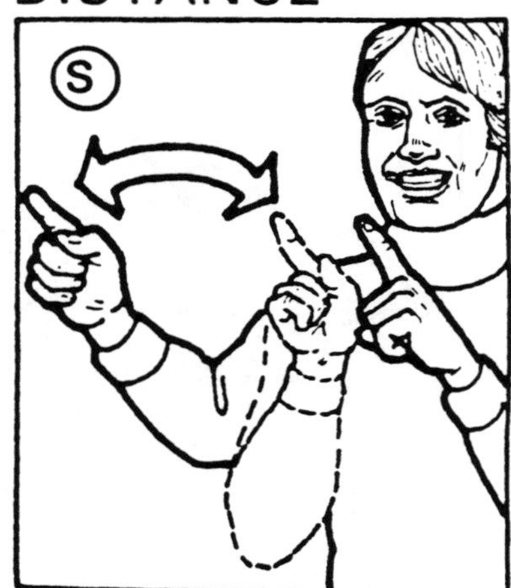

Two closed hands indexes extended start together then Rt. moves forward and back to L.

DISTRIBUTE

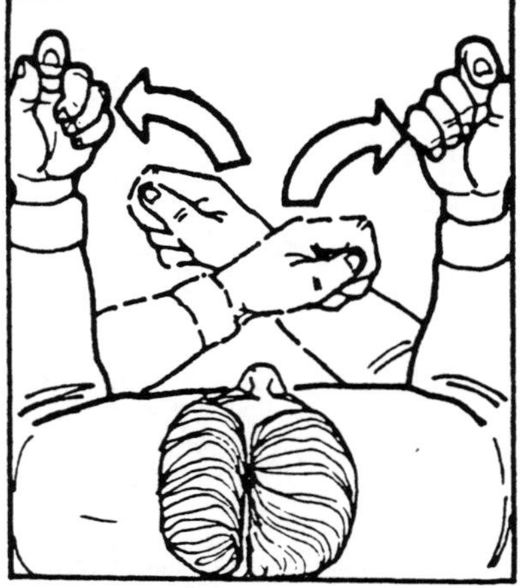

Thumbs tucked into bent indexes; hands start crossed, then swing apart.

DIVIDE

With Rt. index make a straight horizontal line with a dot above and below.

DIVORCE

Two closed hands indexes extended, start crossed then swing out.

DIZZY

Index contacts forehead then makes horizontal circles at side of head.

DO

Rt. fist strikes top of L. fist.

DOCTOR

Tap L. wrist with tips of Rt. index and thumb twice.

DOG

Two "N" hands pointing down, move up and down slightly, like dog begging.

DOLE

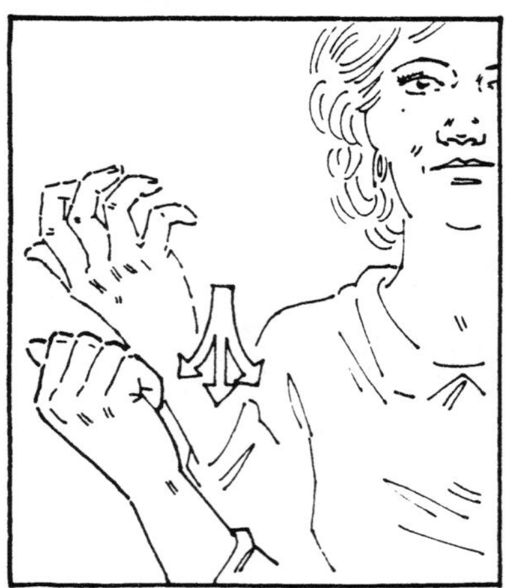

Clawed hand moves down slightly, closing in quick repeated grasping movement.

DOLPHIN

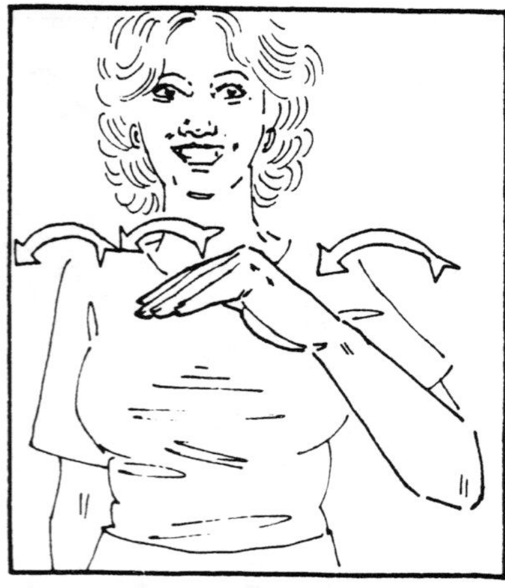

Bent hand moves in up and down diving movement.

DOMINOES

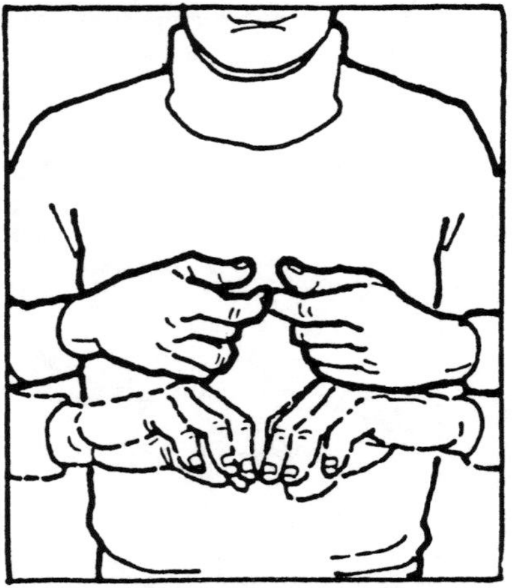

Mime picking up dominoes and turning them over to look at them.

DON'T

Rt. fist strikes top of L. fist, then open hands swing apart.

DONKEY

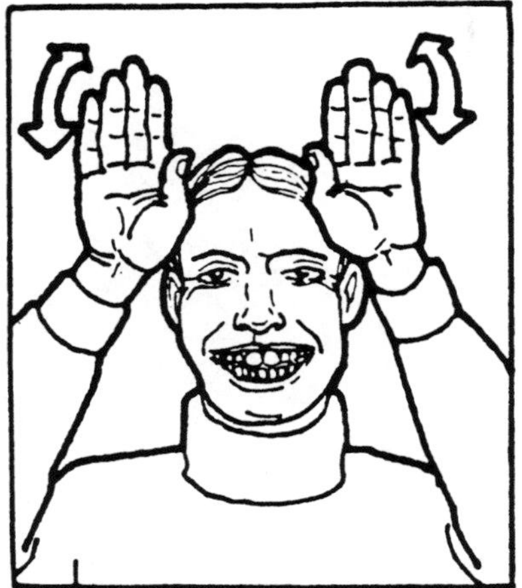

Bent hands palms forward held at temples, straighten and bend.

DOOR

Two flat hands together, Rt. in front of L., Rt. pivots from wrist to point forward, and back again.

DOUBLE

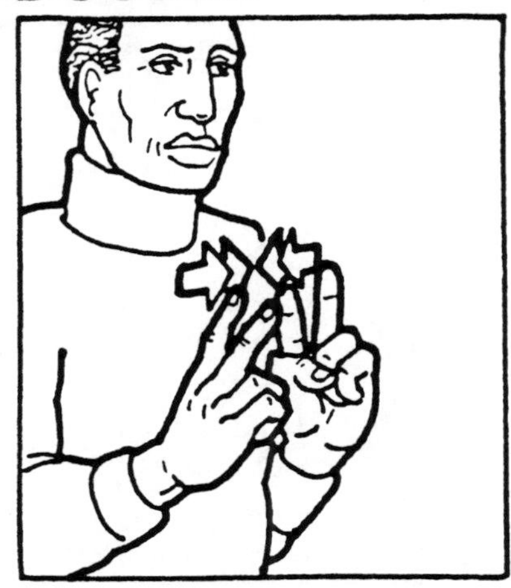

Tips of two "V" hands at an angle, tap together twice.

DOUBT

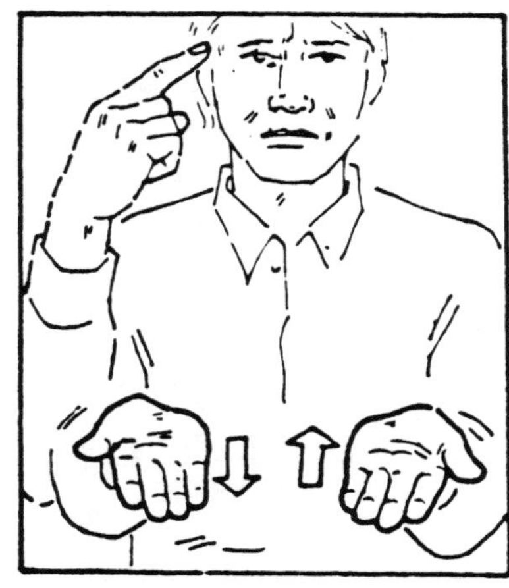

Rt. index points to temple, then both hands, palms up move up and down alternately.

DOWN

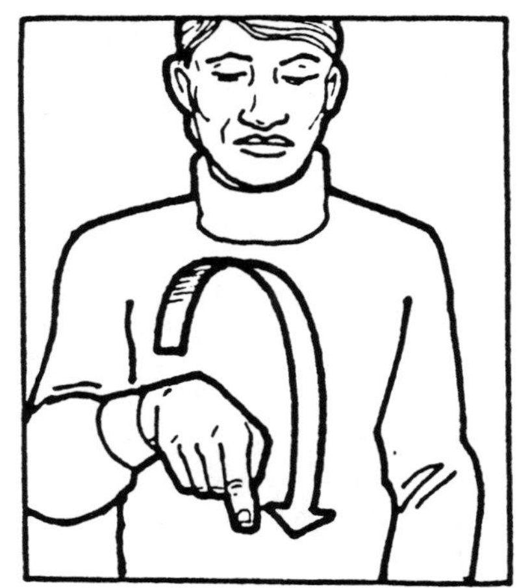

Rt. index points down.

DRAW

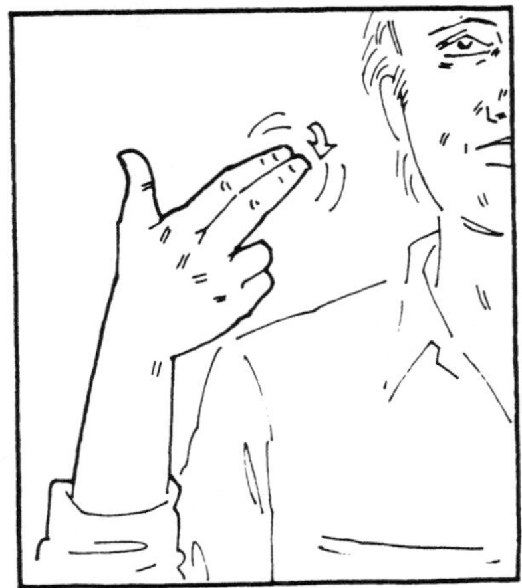

Palm back "N" hand makes small repeated movements.

DRAWERS

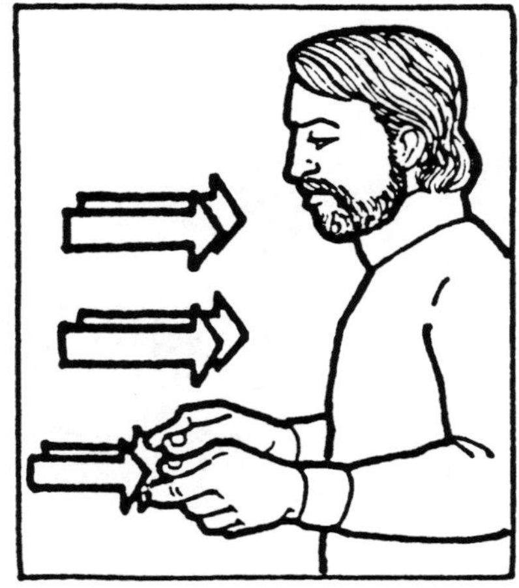

Mime pulling out drawers.

DREAM

Tips of Rt. "M" hand contact forehead, then hand moves out in small arcs, eyes closed for emphasis.

DRESS

Two open hands, palms back. Brush down body.

DRESSING GOWN

Mime pulling on dressing gown then tie cord.

DRESSING TABLE

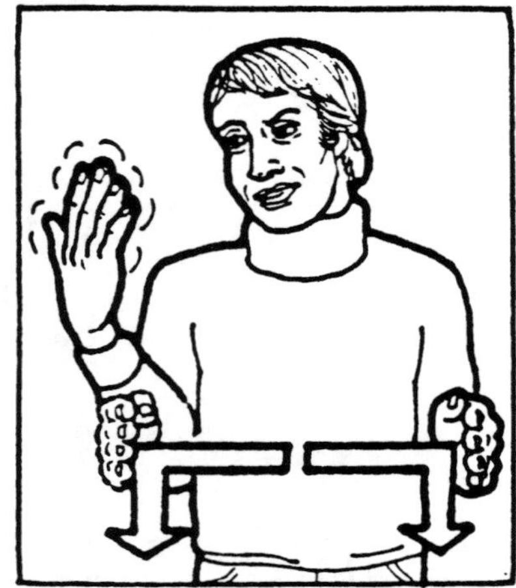

Sign "table" then "mirror".

DRINK

Mime having a drink.

DRIVE

Mime holding steering wheel and move formation forward.

DROP

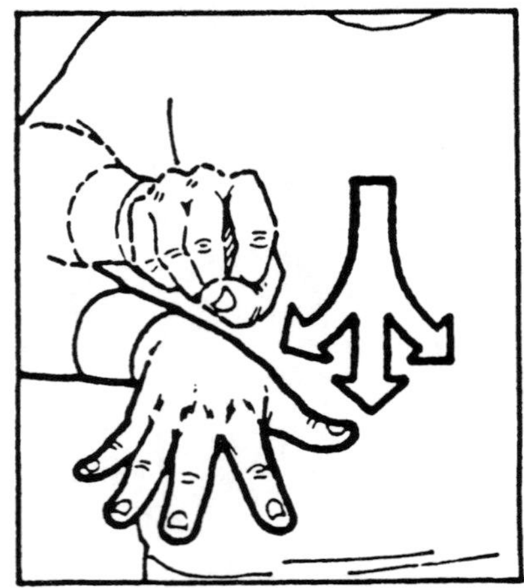

Rt. loose fist, palm down moves down and springs open.

DROWN

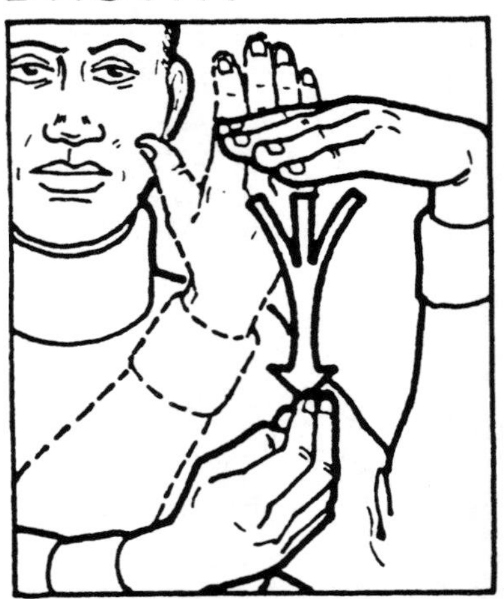

Rt.hand palm back behind L. hand, pulls down closing to bunched hand.

DRUM

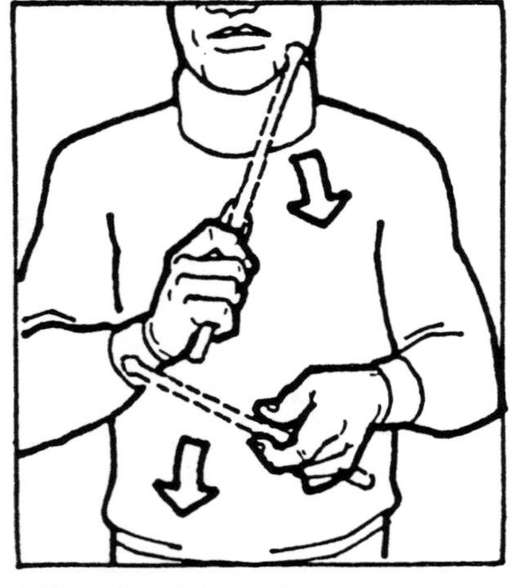

Mime beating a drum.

DRUNK

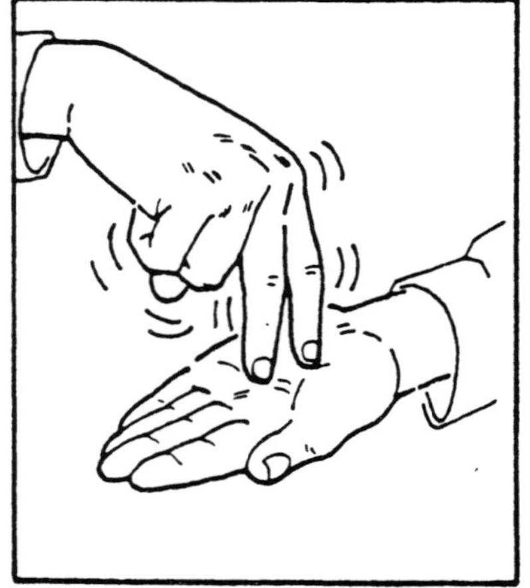

Tips of R. "V" hand contact L. palm, Rt. hand rotates slightly.

DRY

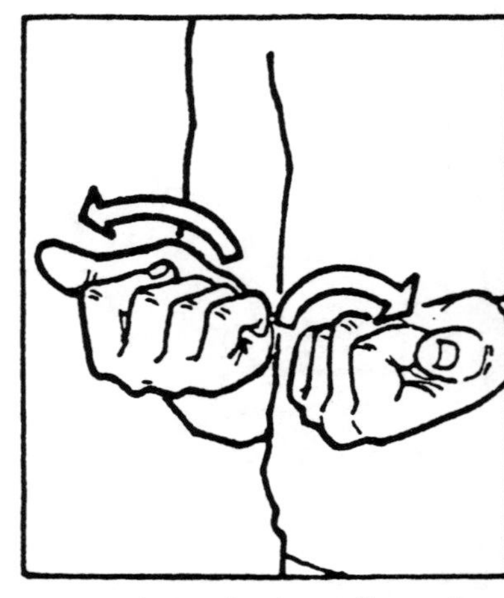

Thumbtips rub along fingertips starting at little fingers.

DUCK (bird)

Index, middle finger and thumb open and close, to indicate ducks bill.

DUCK (to)

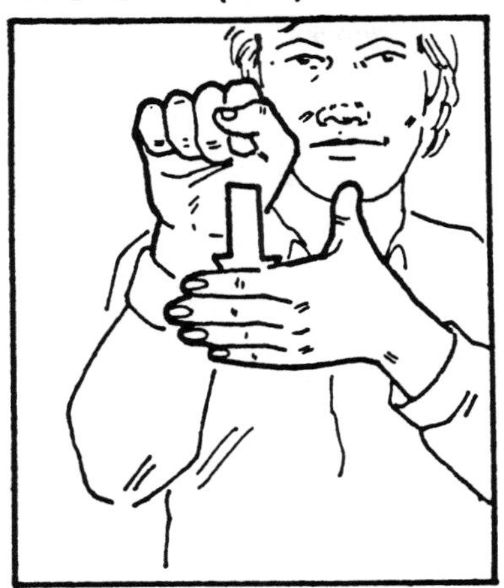

Rt. fist "ducks" down behind L. flat hand, to emphasise the simultaneous head movement.

DURING

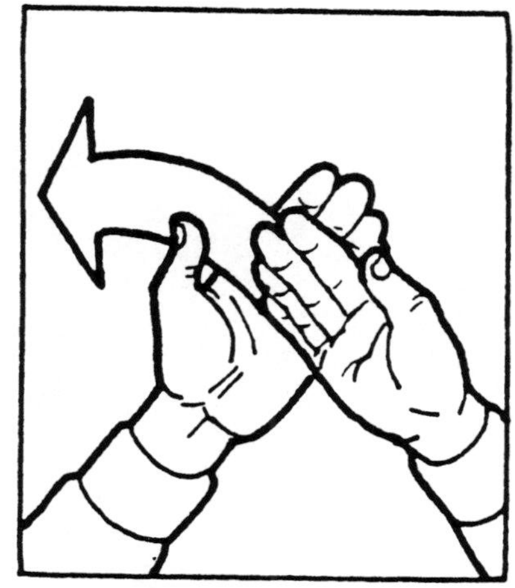

Blade of Rt. flat hand strokes across palm of L.

DUTY

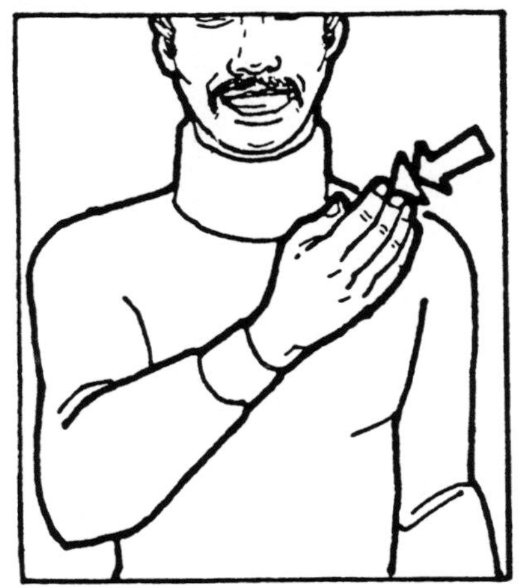

Tap left shoulder with fingers of Rt. hand, twice.

DYE

Two "O" hands, palms down dip down and up.

EACH

Rt. closed hand index extended move from left to right in three hops.

EARRINGS

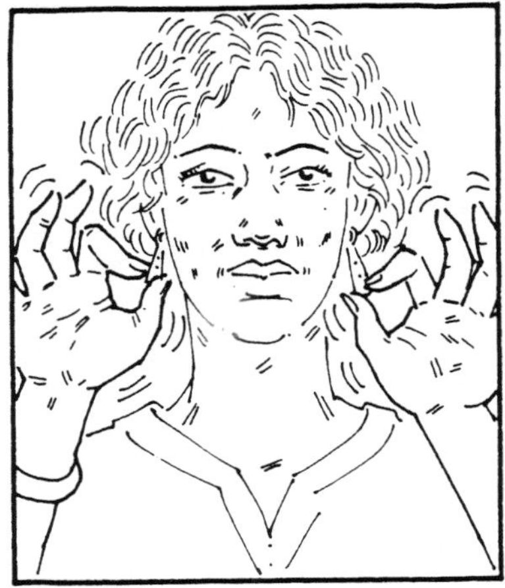

Two "O" hands held at ears waggle slightly.

EARLY

Rt. index and thumb extended, thumb maintains contact with L. palm, index jerks back in two movements.

EARMOULD

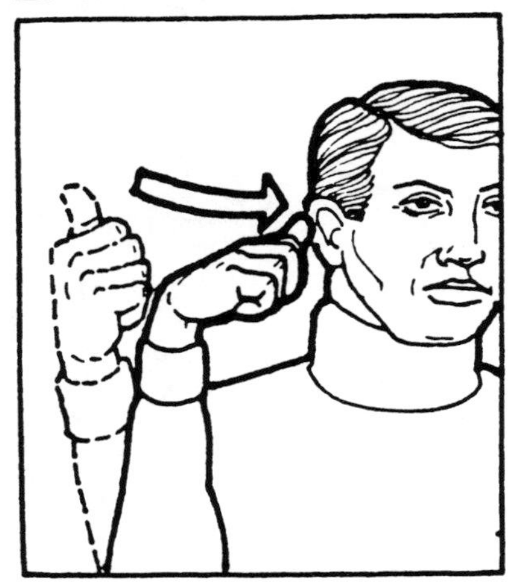

Rt. thumb pushes into ear.

EARN

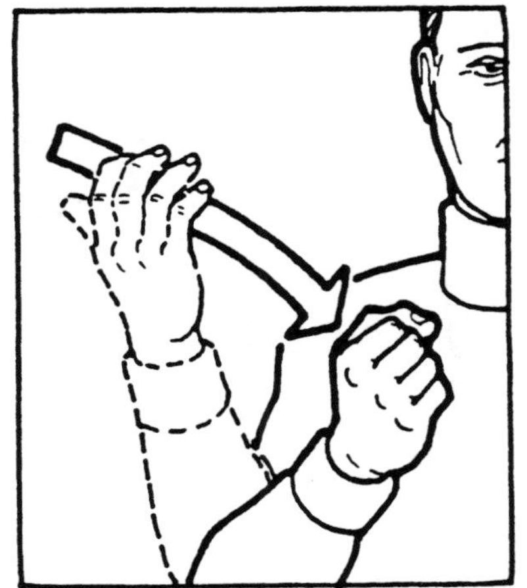

Rt. open hand, fingers slightly bent held up to right moves in to body and closes to fist.

EAST

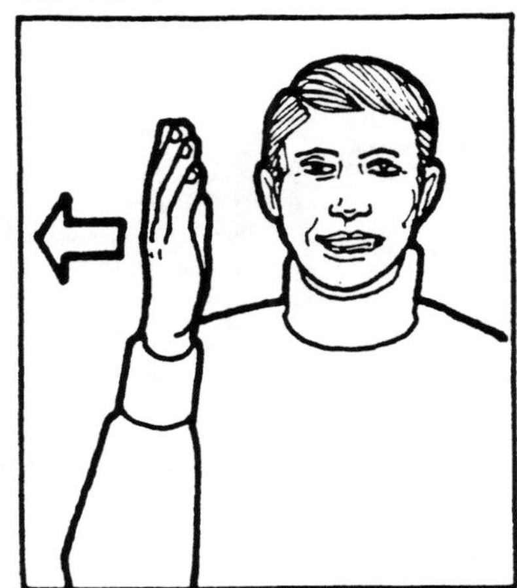

Rt. flat hand palm left moves to right.

EASTER

Hands held to indicate shape of Easter Egg, tap together twice.

EASY

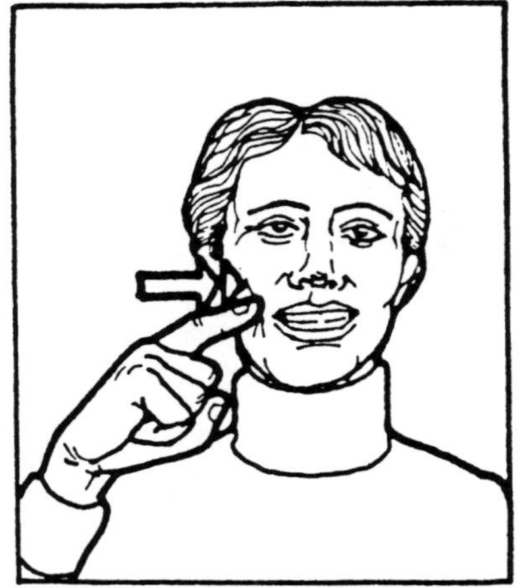

Rt. index prods cheek twice.

EAT

Bunched hand nods toward mouth twice.

EDGE

Run Rt. index along blade of L. hand palm down.

EDUCATION

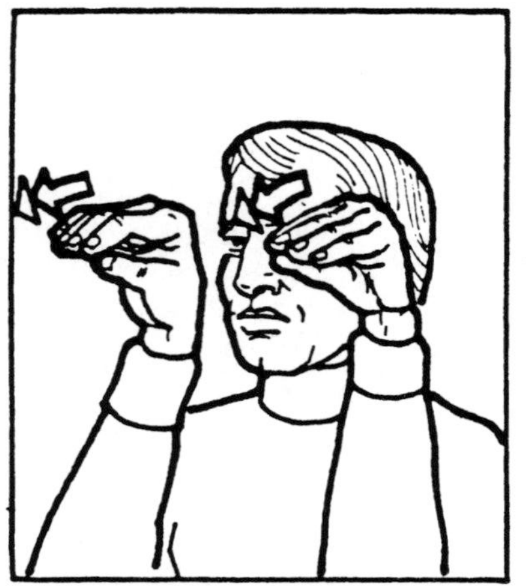

Bunched hands, pointing forward, held at temples jerk forwards twice.

EGG

Mime slicing top off an egg with Rt. "N" hand, palm up, across top of L. fist.

EGYPT

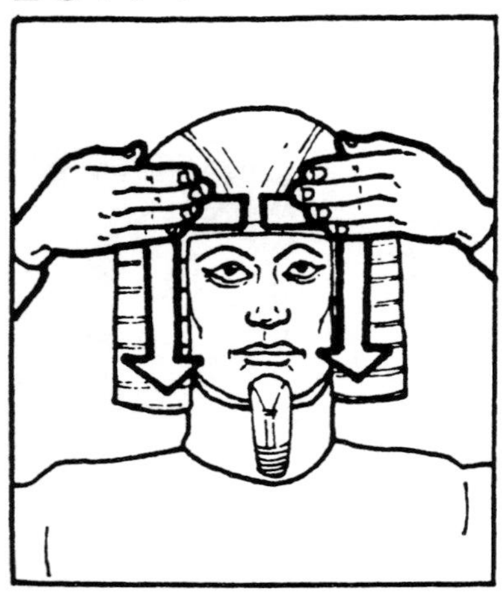

Two flat hands move out across forehead, then down to touch shoulders.

EITHER

L. index and thumb extended; Rt. little finger and thumb extended swings from side to side behind L.

ELASTIC

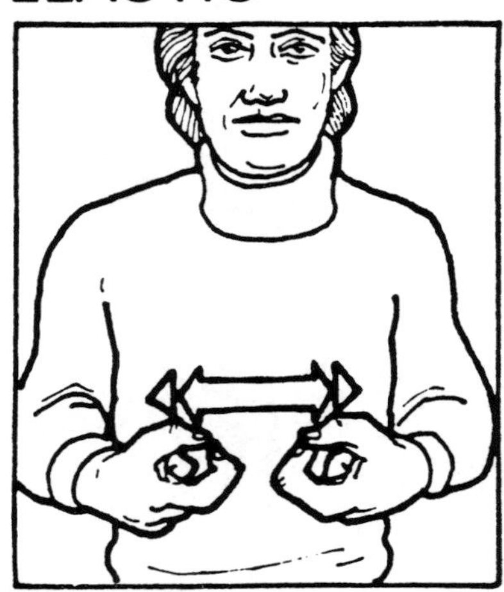

Tips of indexes and thumbs touching, palms up; pull hands apart as if stretching elastic.

ELECTRIC

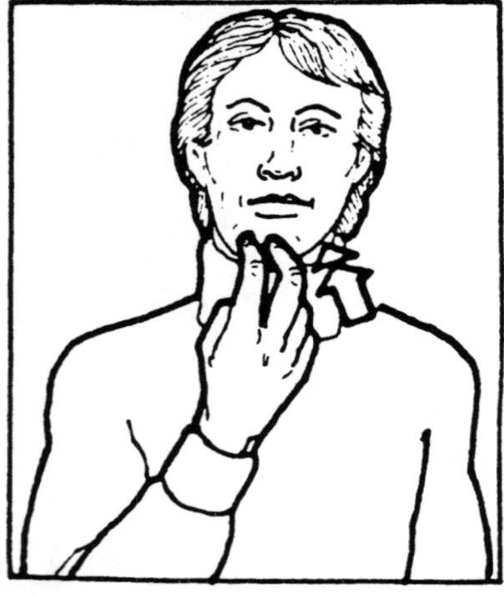

Tips of Rt. "V" hand, fingers bent, tap chin twice.

ELEPHANT

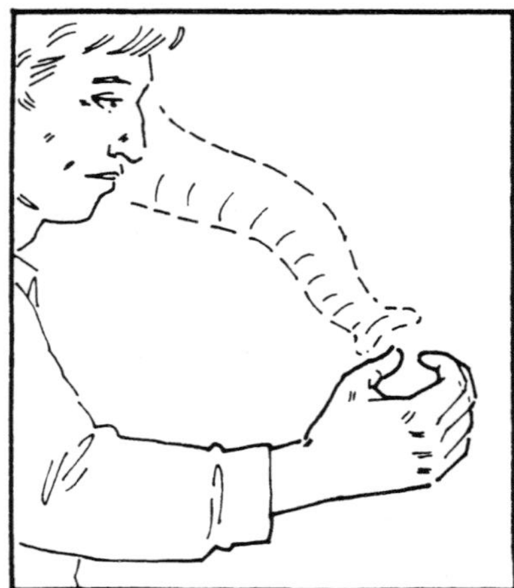

Full handed "C" moves from face to indicate trunk.

ELSE

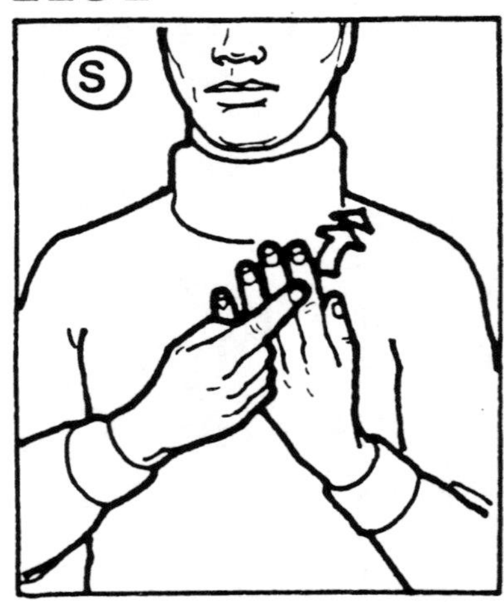

Tip of Rt. index flicks back of L. index twice.

EMBARRASS

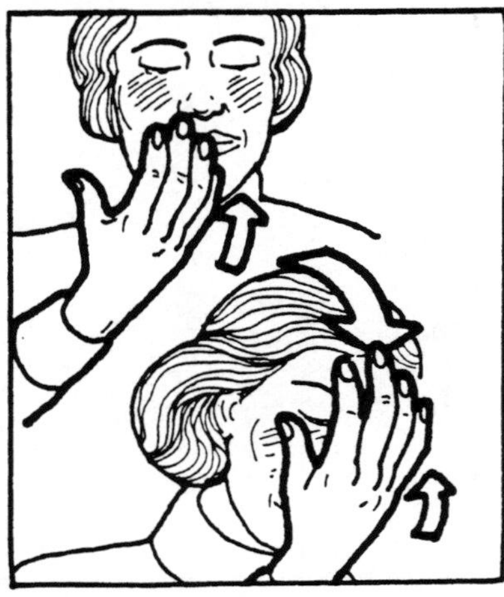

Open hand moves up face, as head tips slightly down and to the side.

EMPLOYER

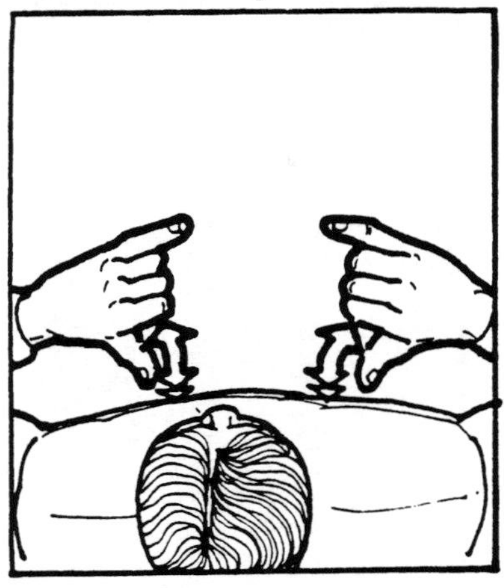

Closed hands, thumbs and little fingers extended; thumbs prod upper chest twice.

EMPTY

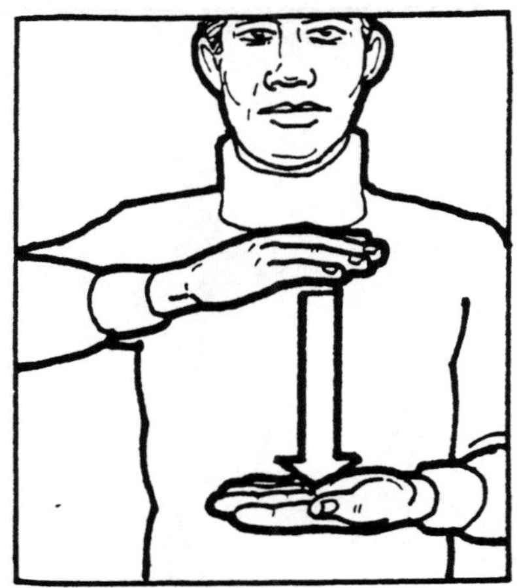

Two flat hands, Rt. above L. Rt. hand moves down onto L.

ENCOURAGE

Both hands thumbs up, push forwards twice simultaneously.

END

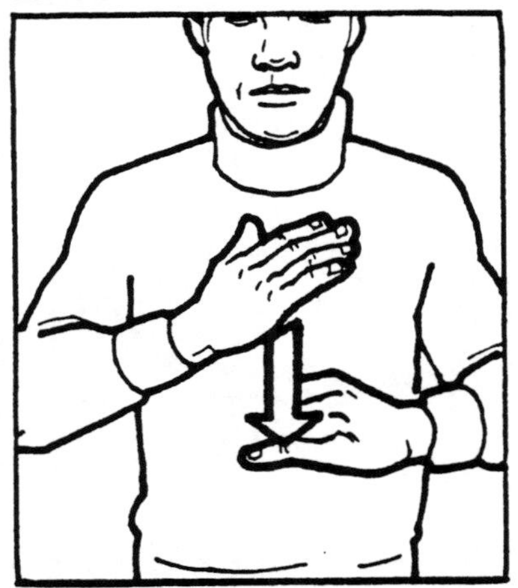

Blade of Rt. flat hand comes down onto L. extended little finger.

ENGAGED

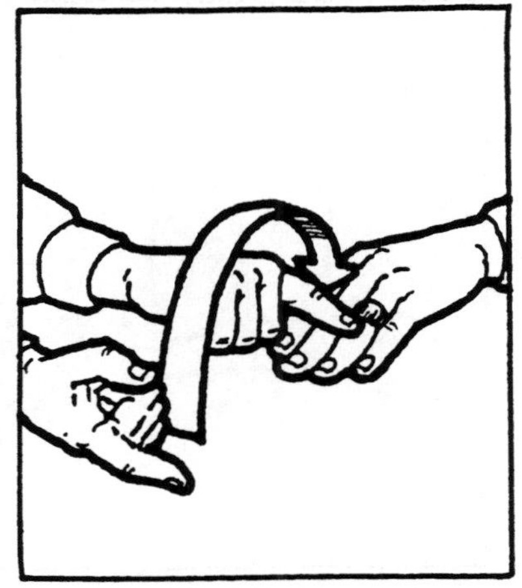

Extended Rt. index flips over from palm up to palm down on L.ring finger.

ENGINEERING

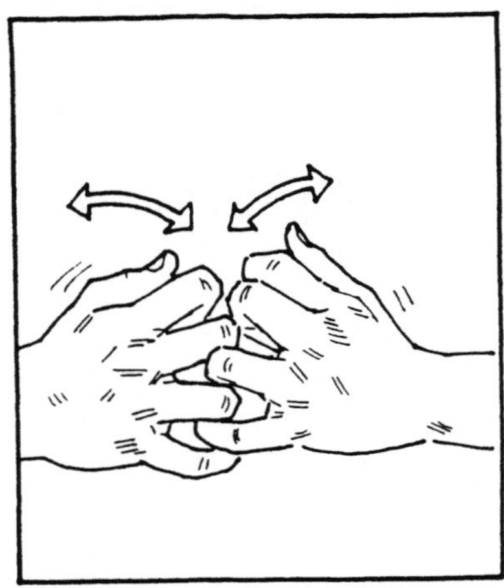

Clawed hands palms back, swivel to interlock at knuckles, then apart.

ENGLISH

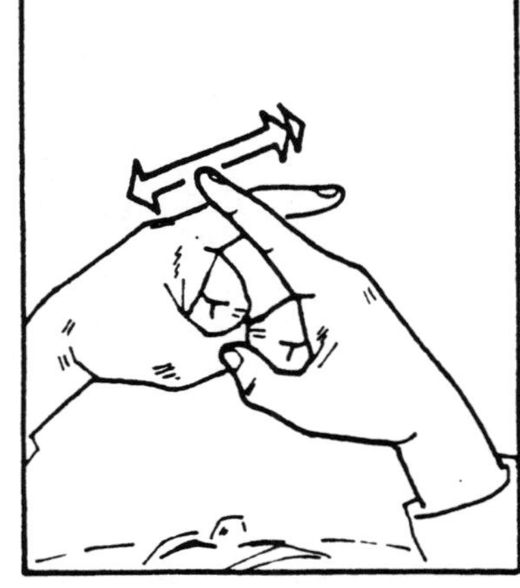

Rt. index extended rubs along L. extended index several times.

ENJOY

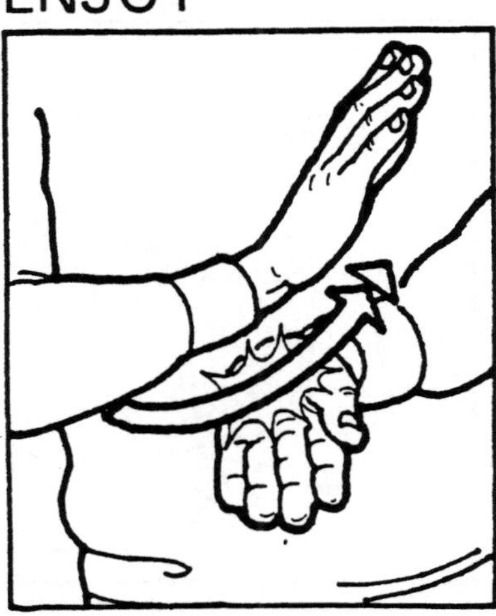

Clap Rt. palm onto palm of L. twice, in sweeping motion.

ENOUGH

Bent Rt. hand strokes up under chin twice.

ENTER

Rt. index moves under L. hand changing to flat hand.

ENVELOPE

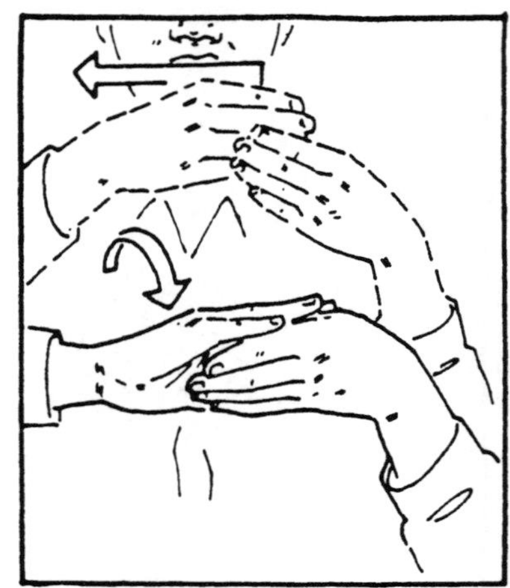

Mime action of sealing envelope.

EQUAL

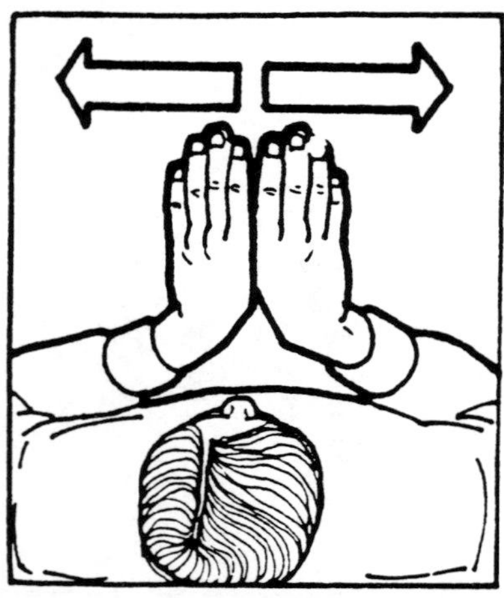

Flat hands held together palms down, move apart.

ESCAPE

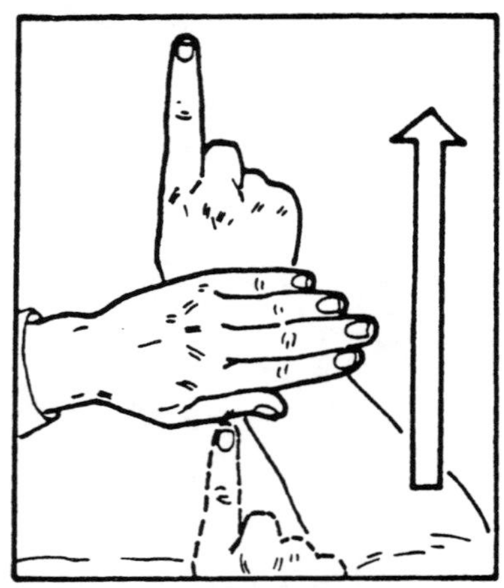

Rt. index extended passes under L. hand in sharp movement.

ESTABLISH

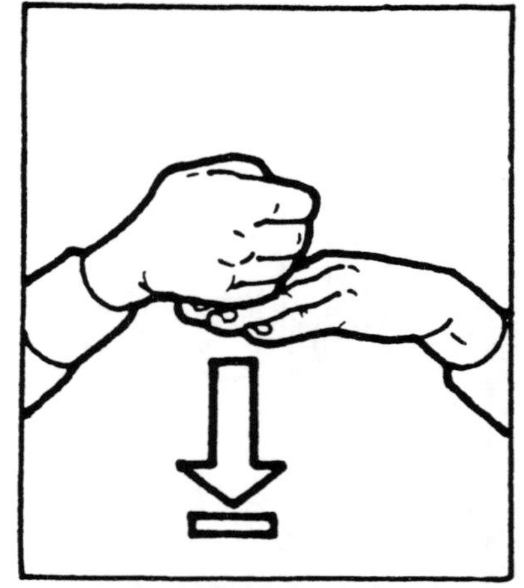

Blade of Rt. fist rests on back of L. hand; formation moves down slightly with stress.

ESTIMATE

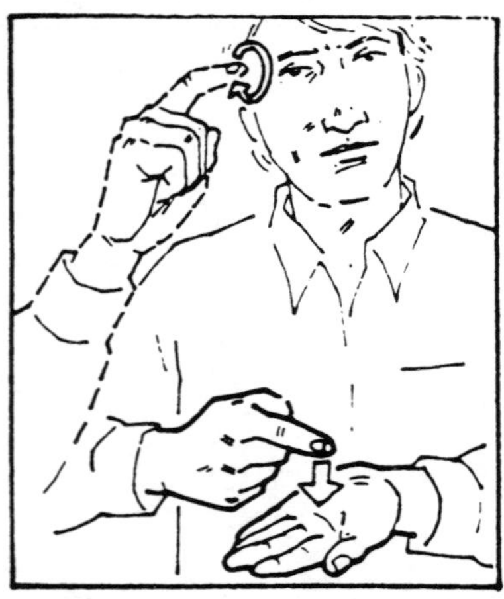

Rt. index makes circular movement on temple, then moves down sharply onto L. palm.

EUROPE

Fingers bent at 2nd knuckles tucked behind thumb; hand makes horizontal circle.

EVEN

Bent hands fingertips touching move apart.

EVENING

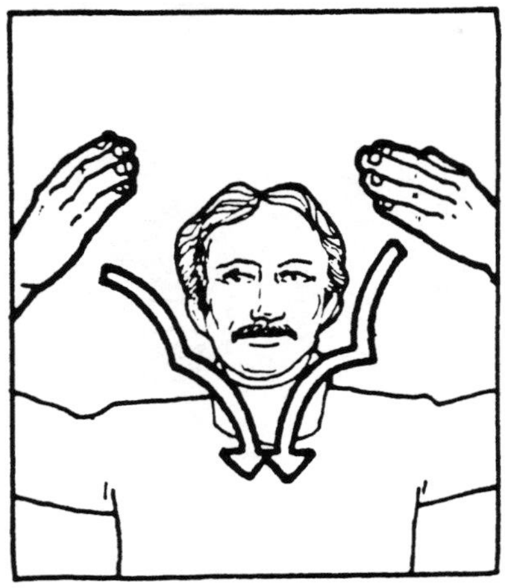

Flat hands, palms back at head height, make two short movements in and down.

EVENTUALLY

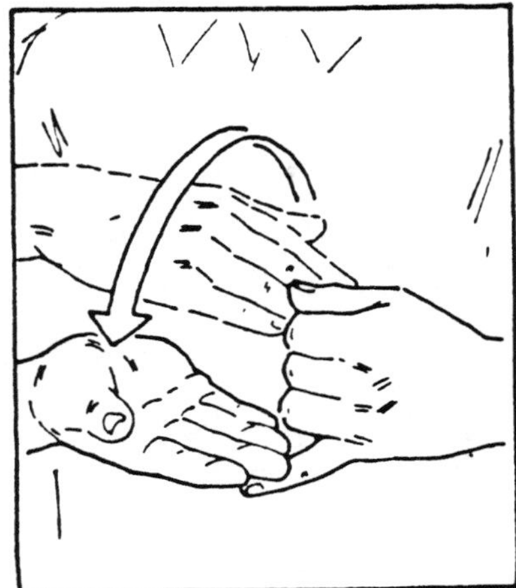

L. little finger extended, Rt. hand palm down sweeps over and forward to land palm up on L. little finger.

EVER

Tips of indexes touch, Rt. moves away to right with spiralling movement.

EVERY

Back of Rt. hand fingers against side of chin; hand swivels forward and fingers brush across cheek.

EVERYONE

As for "every", then Rt. index moves from left to right in small hops.

EVERYTHING

As for "every", then tap blades of hands together twice, indexes extended.

EXACT

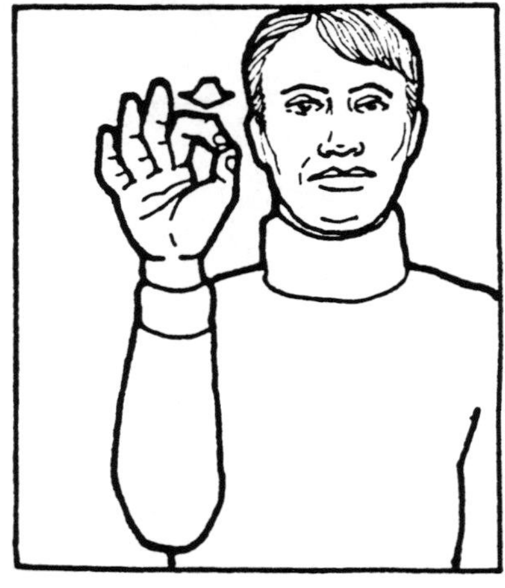

Rt. "O" hand makes small sharp movement from temple.

EXAM

Index edge of Rt. "N" hand rubs backwards and forwards on L. palm.

EXAMPLE

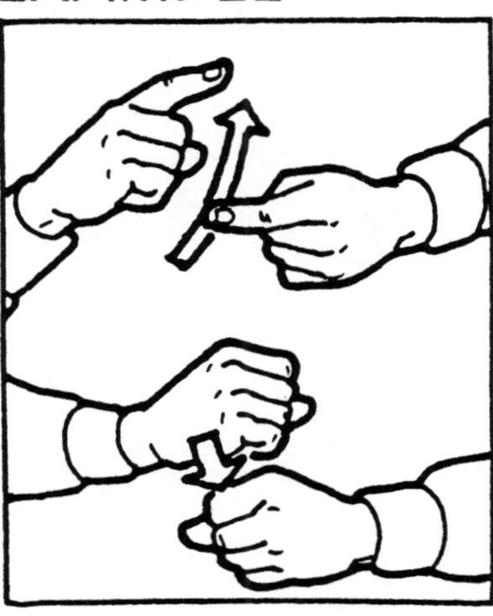

Tip of Rt. index brushes up against tip of L. index, then hands form "G".

EXCEPT

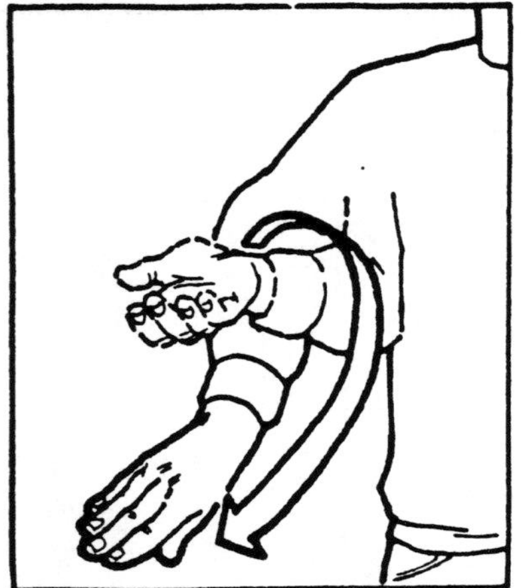

Cupped hand palm up moves down and twists away from body.

EXCHANGE

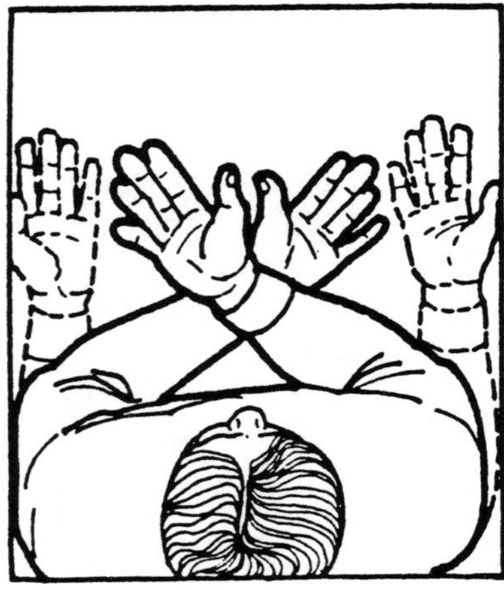

Flat hands, pointing forward, move in to cross at wrists.

EXCITING

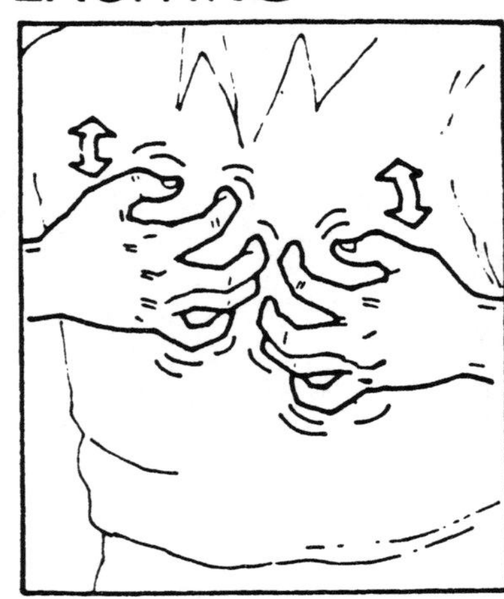

Rub clawed hands up and down on chest alternately in quick movements.

EXCUSE

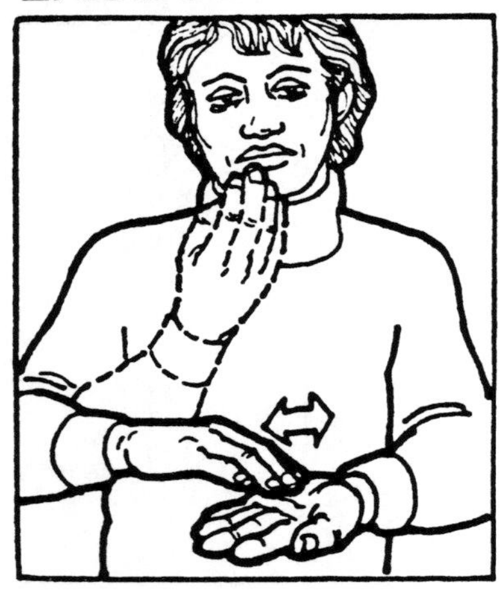

Tips of flat hand touch lips then make small rubbing movement on L. palm.

EXPECT

Two "R" hands, palms back move slightly forward from near eyes.

EXPENSIVE

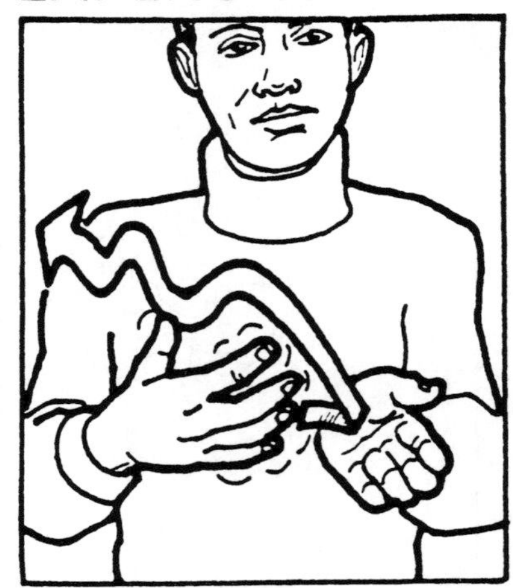

Tips of Rt. open hand bounce against L. palm, then Rt. hand moves to the right, shaking with emphasis.

EXPERIENCE

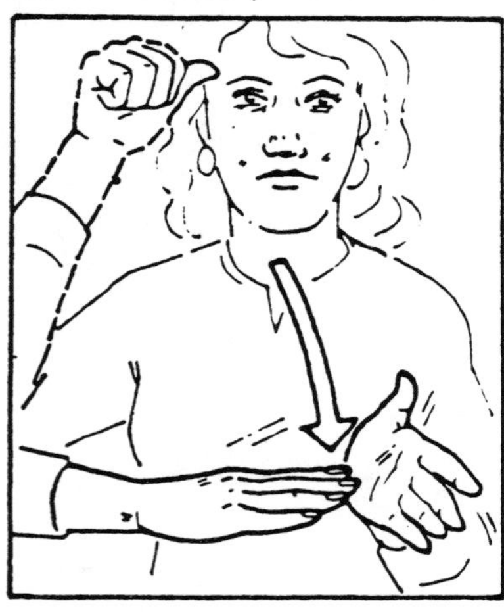

Rt. thumb touches temple, moves down changing to flat hand and brushes down across L. palm.

EXPLAIN

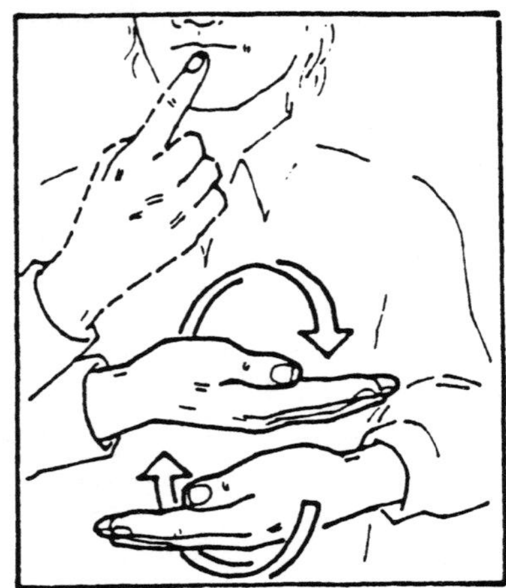

Rt. index touches mouth, then two flat hands rotate round each other in forward circles.

EXTRA

Mime tipping contents of Rt. slightly bent hand into L. palm in two movements.

FACTORY

Closed hands, thumbs extended held in front of upper chest, pull apart sharply, L. forward/left Rt. back/right.

FAIL

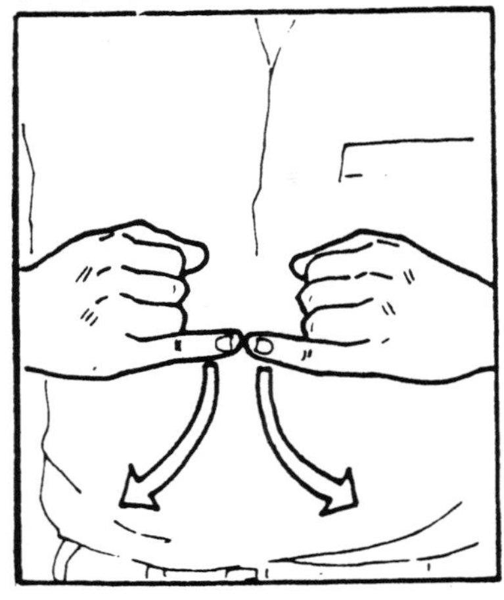

Tips of little fingers touch then hands twist from wrists so that fingers point down.

FAINT

Two "V" hands, fingers touching, pull apart, head held on one side, as if in faint.

FAIR (GROUND)

Indexes extended Rt. hand above L. makes circular movements around L. as formation moves to the right.

FAIR (just)

Flat hands palms down, move up and down alternately, come together, then move apart sharply.

FAIRY

Hands flap near shoulders, to indicate wings.

FALL

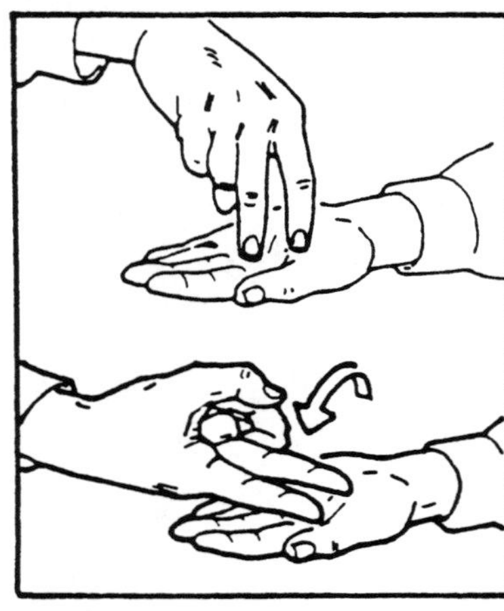

Rt. "V" hand "stands" on L. palm, then falls over to finish palm up on L. palm.

FALSE

Middle finger extended touches nose, then moves forward whilst twisting to point forward.

FAMILY

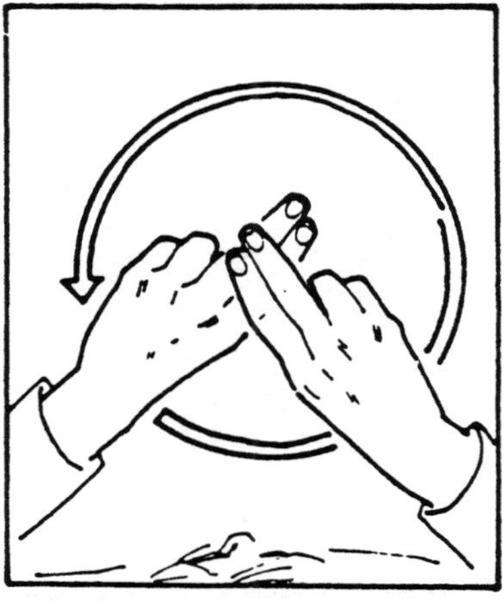

Make fingerspelt "F" then move formation in horizontal circle.

FAMOUS

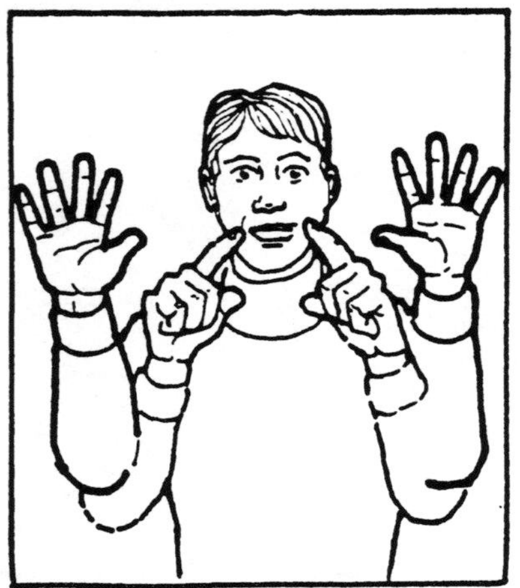

Indexes point to sides of mouth, then hands spring open and move forwards.

FAR

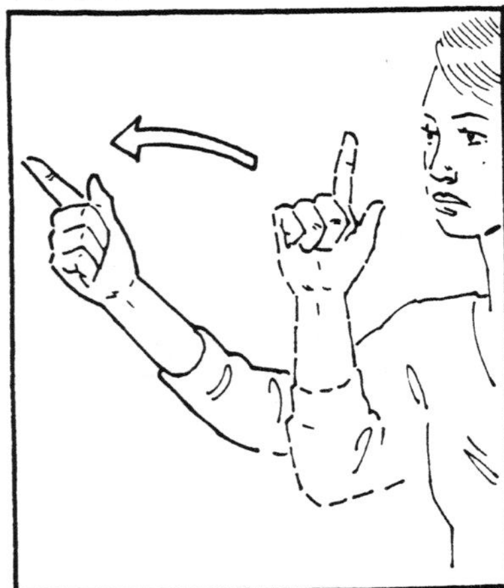

Rt. thumb and index extended, pointing up; move in large forward arc with emphasis.

FARM

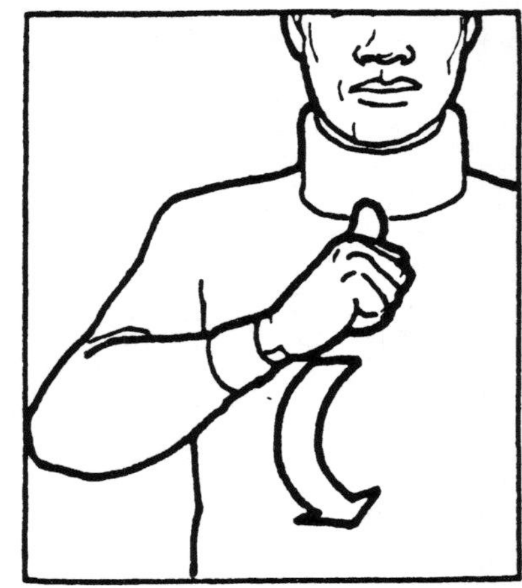

Rt. thumb extended held against upper trunk, move in arc forward and down to finish blade of hand against lower trunk.

FARMER

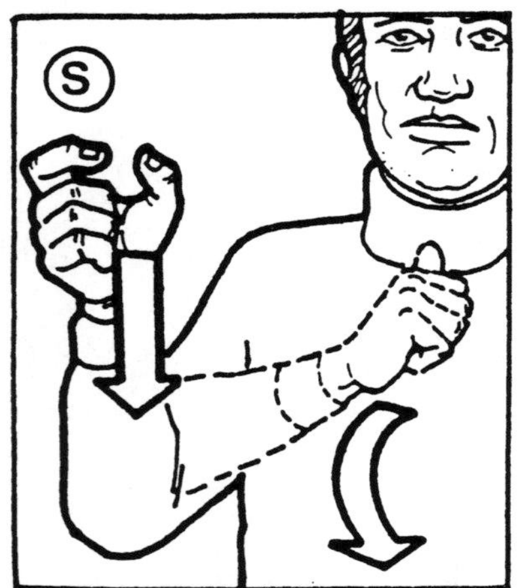

Sign farm, then "C" hand moves down to indicate person.

FASCINATE

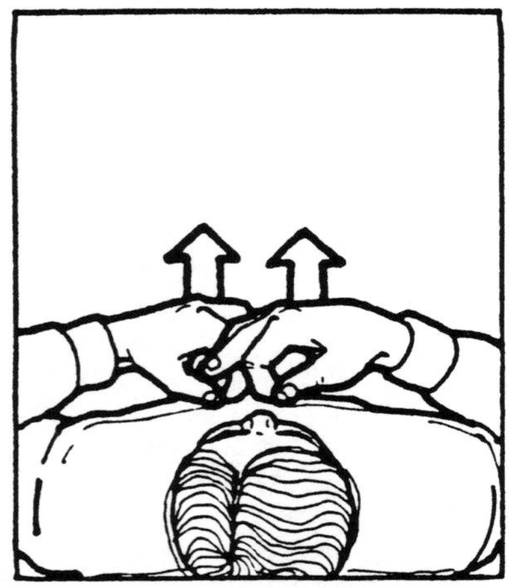

"O" hands, Rt. above L. pluck clothing of upper trunk and draw forward.

FAST

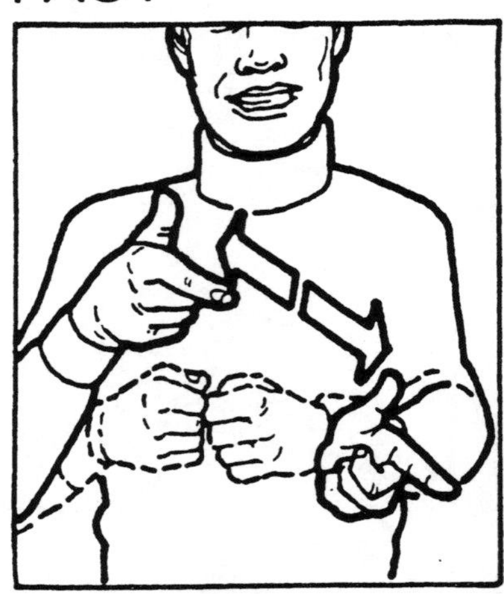

Closed hands indexes flexed on ball of thumbs. Flick indexes out pulling hands apart sharply, L. forward Rt. back.

FAT

Flat hands on lower trunk move forward and slightly apart.

FATHER

Tap fingers of fingerspelt "F" twice.

FAULT

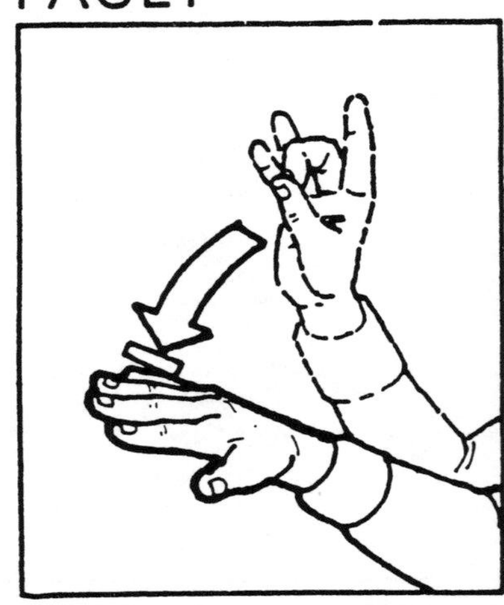

Middle finger flexed on ball of thumb, palm forward, flick finger out and throw hand forward/down.

FAVOUR

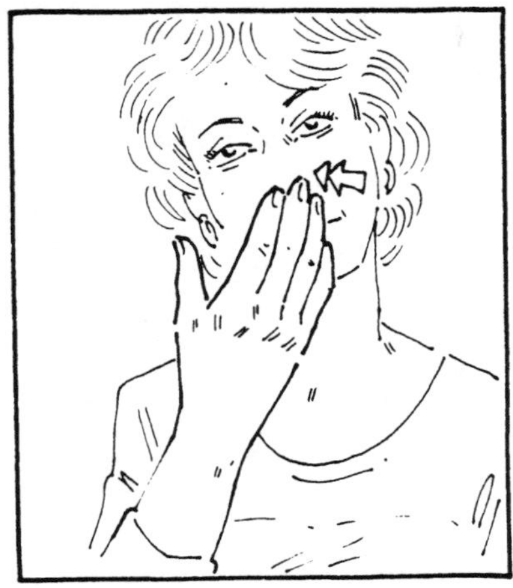

Tips of Rt. flat hand tap nose twice.

FAVOURITE

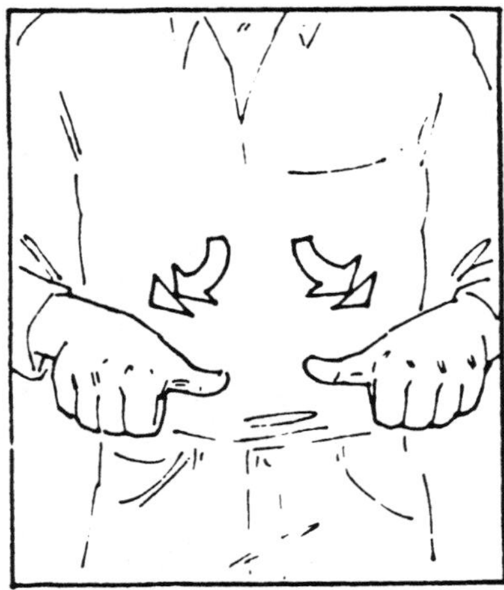

Two closed hands, thumbs extended make two jerky movements forward/down.

FEATHER

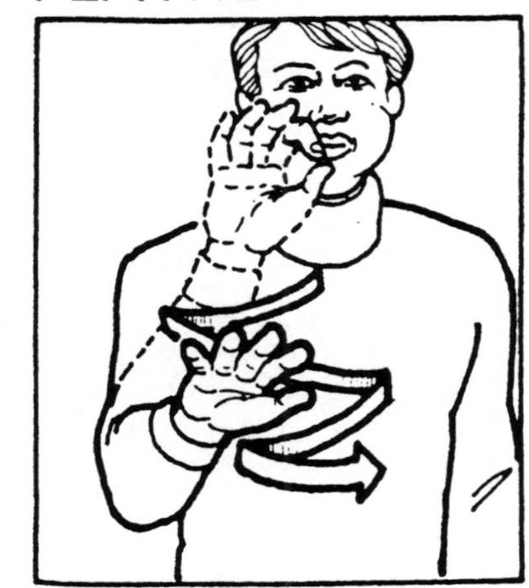

Mime blowing feather, then mime motion of falling feather, with flat hand.

FED-UP

Rt. hand, slightly bent is brought up sharply under chin.

FEED

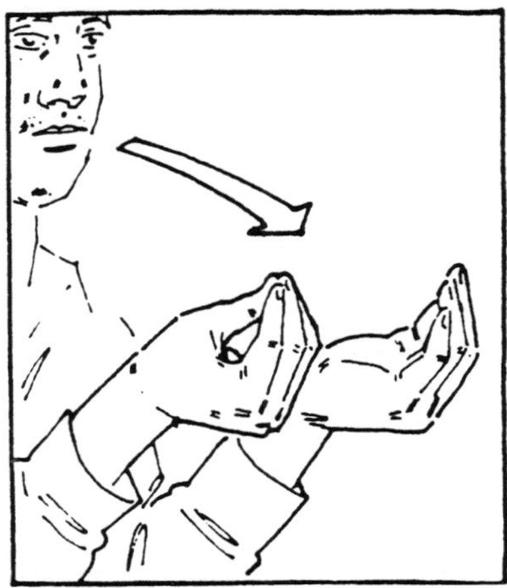

Bunched hands move forward from near mouth.

FEEL

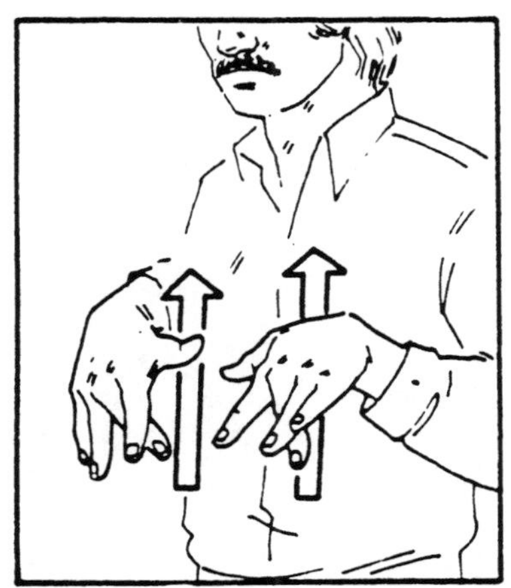

Tips of middle fingers brush up body from waist to upper trunk.

FENCE

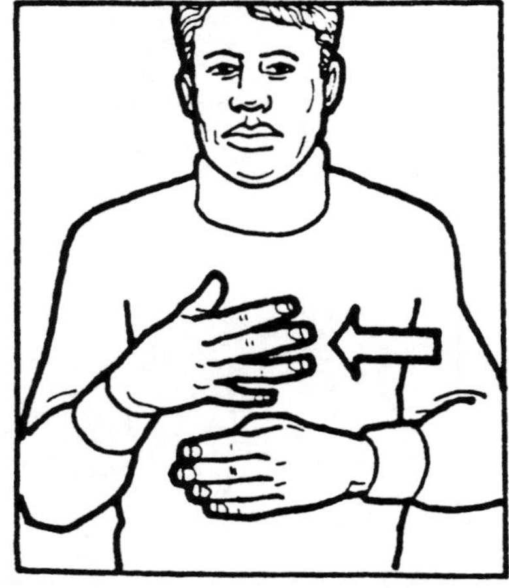

Little finger edge of Rt. open hand brushes down left arm, from elbow to fingers.

FEW

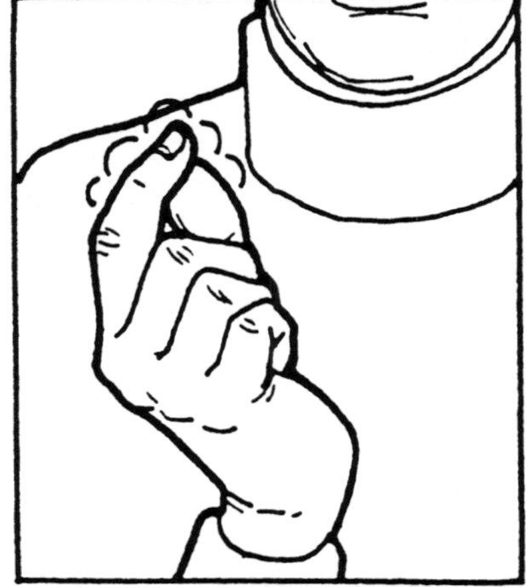

Tips of bent index and thumb rub together several times.

FIELD

Rt. palm sweeps along left forearm up to shoulder.

FIGHT

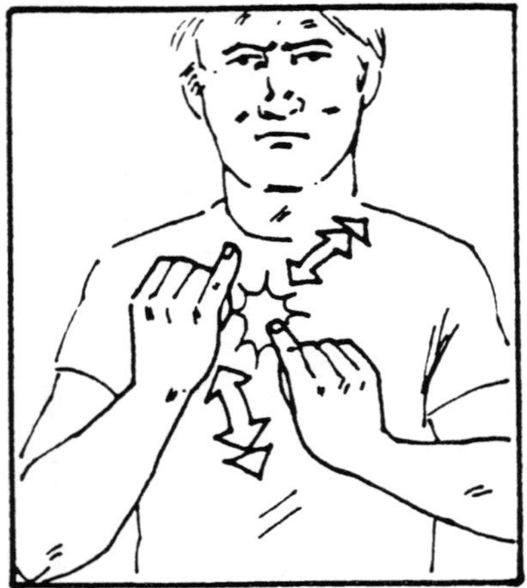

Little fingers extended, move up and down banging together several times.

FILE (system)

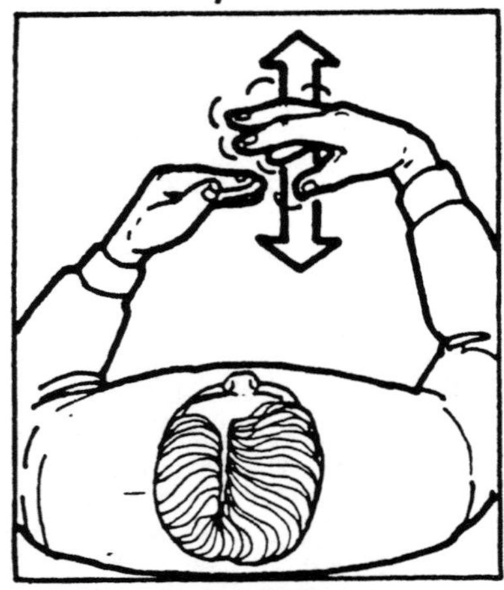

Rt. hand moves forward and back, fingers fluttering, in front of L. bent hand.

FILL

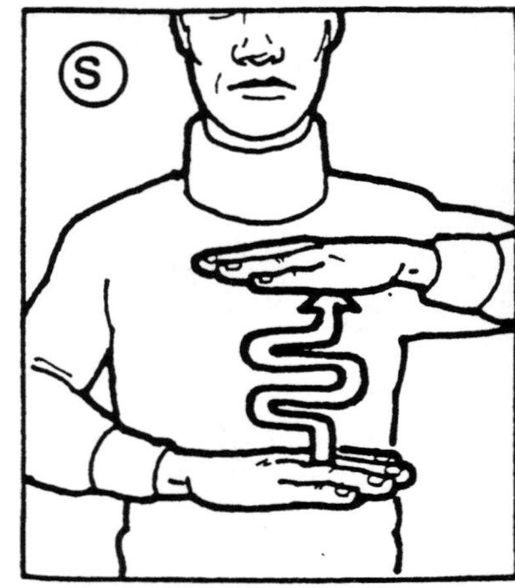

Flat hands, L. above Rt; Rt. hand moves up in wavy movement to touch L.

FILM

L. flat hand palm right, held to side of face; Rt. closed hand makes winding motion in front of face.

FIND

Index points to eye, then moves away, and grasps upwards to fist sharply as if finding something.

FINE (pay)

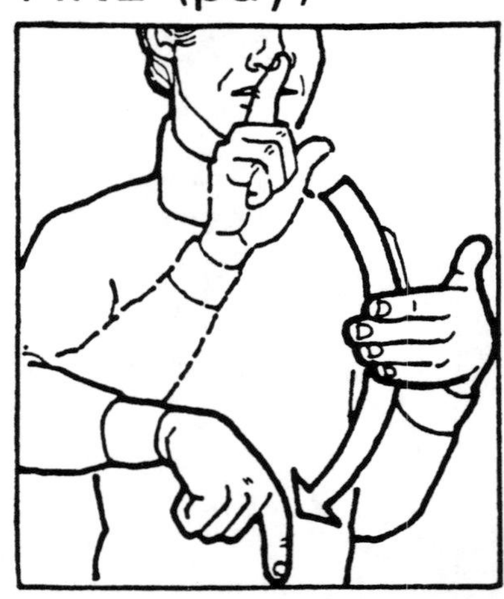

Rt. index strikes sharply down L. palm.

FINGER SPELL

Fingers and thumbs point towards each other, formation moves from left to right, fingers fluttering.

FINISH

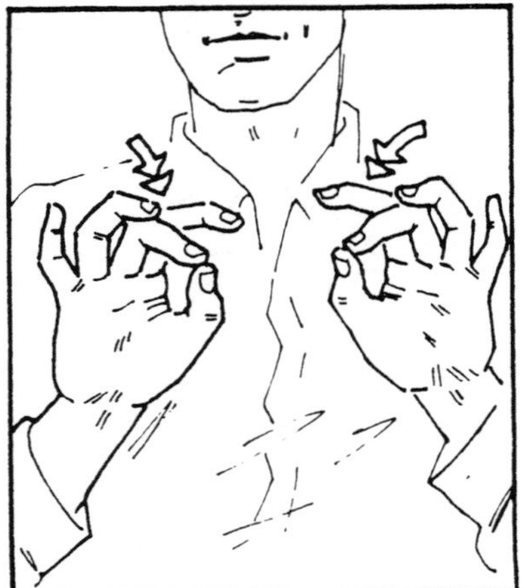

Middle fingers close onto ball of thumbs several times, quickly.

FIRE

Open hands, fingers pointing up, move upwards, fingers flicking.

FIRE ENGINE

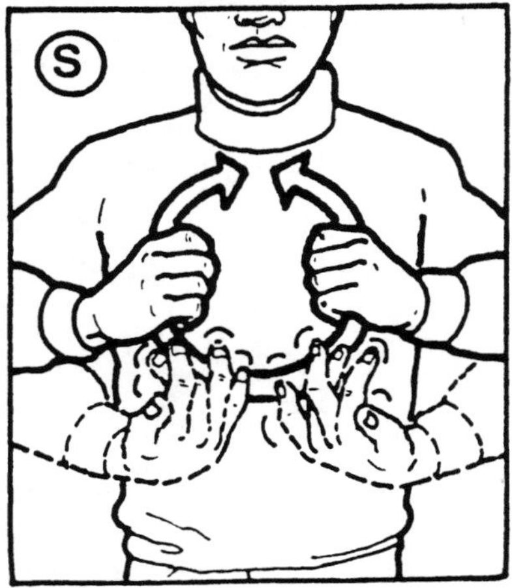

Sign for "fire" then sign for "car".

FIREMAN

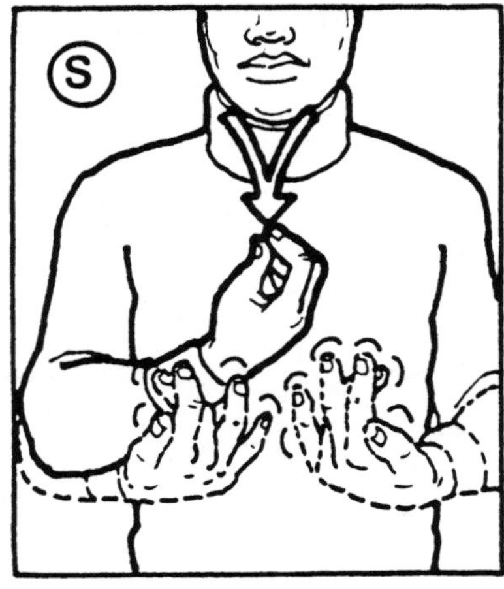

Sign for "fire" then sign for "man".

FIREPLACE

Hands palms facing move up and down alternately in circular movement, fingers flicking.

FIRST

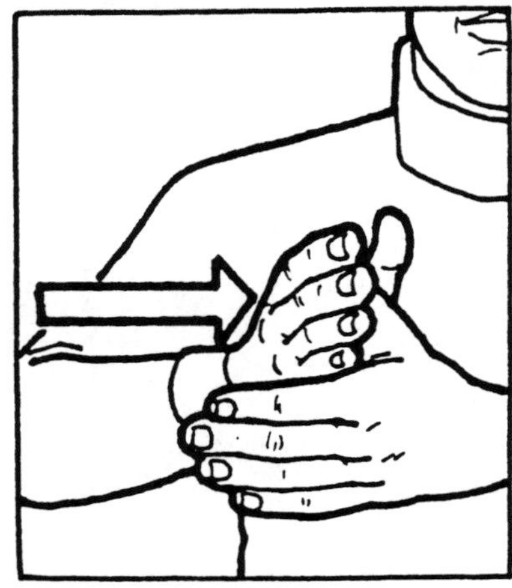

Fingers of Rt. flat hand strike inside of L. thumb.

FISH (A)

Rt. flat hand waggles forward like a fish swimming.

FISH (TO)

Mime casting out with rod.

FISH FINGERS

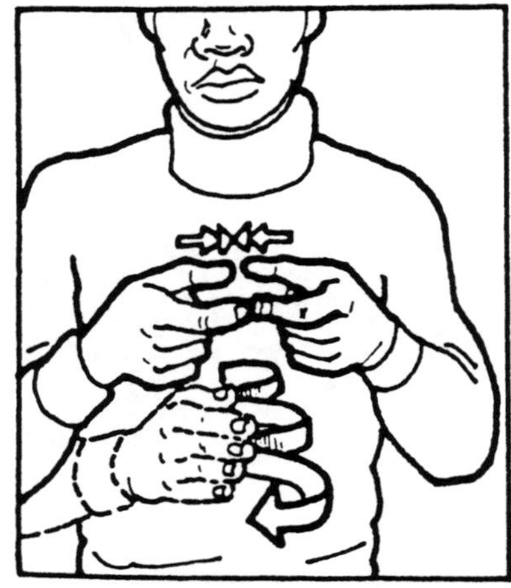

Sign "fish" then tap tips of indexes and thumbs of both hands together, twice.

FIT (healthy)

Thumbs brush down upper trunk, then move away from body and twist out slightly.

FIT (together)

Two "O" hands touching L. in front of Rt., change to Rt. in front of L. and back again.

FIX (fasten)

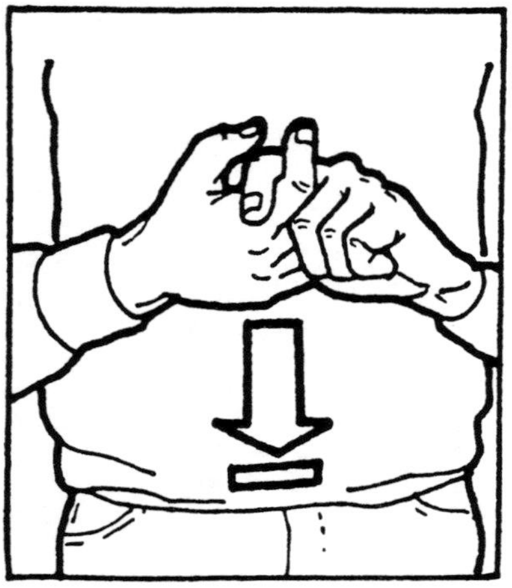

Indexes hooked together; move formation down slightly with stress.

FIX (mend)

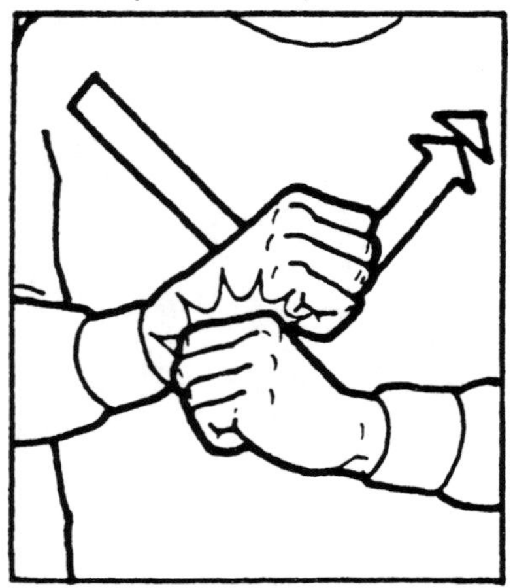

Blade of Rt. fist strikes L. fist and bounces up, twice.

FLAG

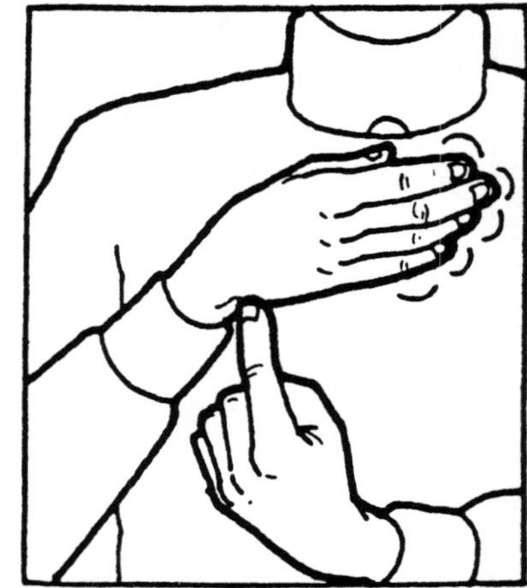

Rt. flat hand pivots on tip of L. index in waving motion.

FLAME

Rt. index and thumb open and close whilst moving down, in shape of a flame.

FLAT

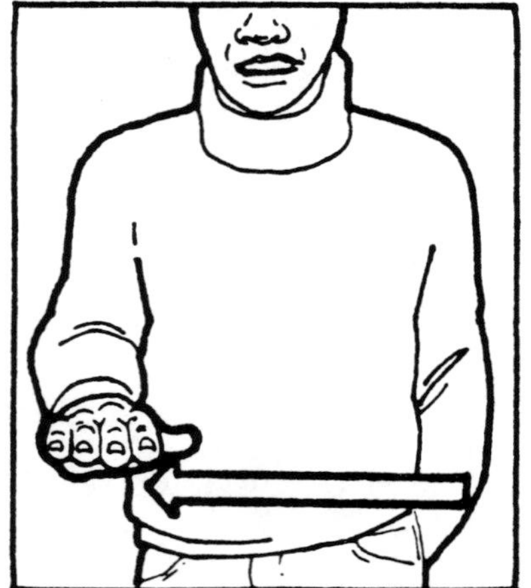

Rt. hand flat, palm down moves across in front of body in straight line.

FLOAT

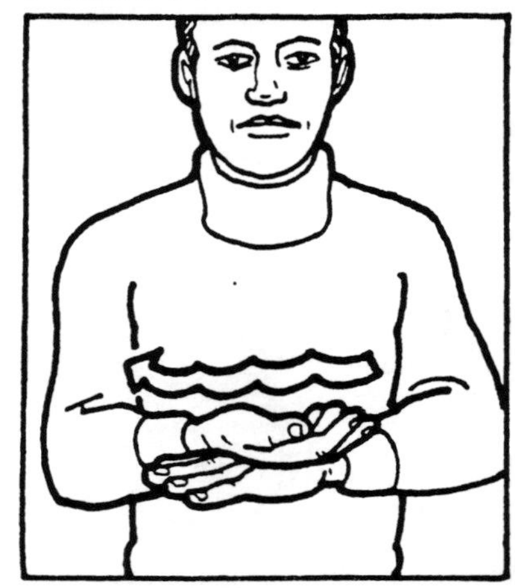

Rt. hand palm up rests on L. hand palm down, formation moves from left to right in wavy motion.

FLOUR

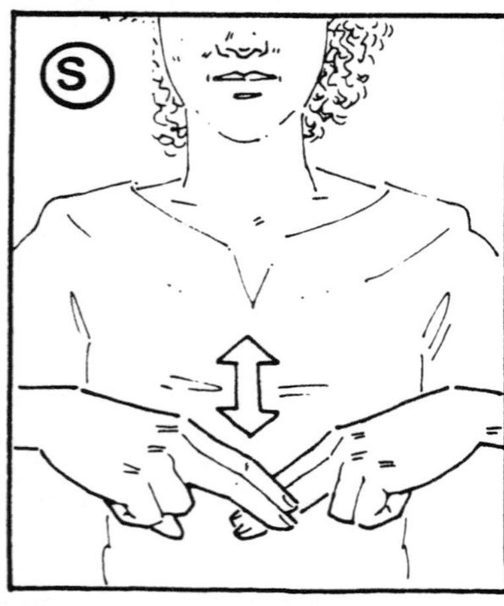

Form "F" and move formation up and down, as if sifting flour.

FLOWER

Bunched hand held under nose twists from side to side as if smelling flower.

FLY

Flat hands, thumbs hooked together, move forward/up and flap like wings.

FOG

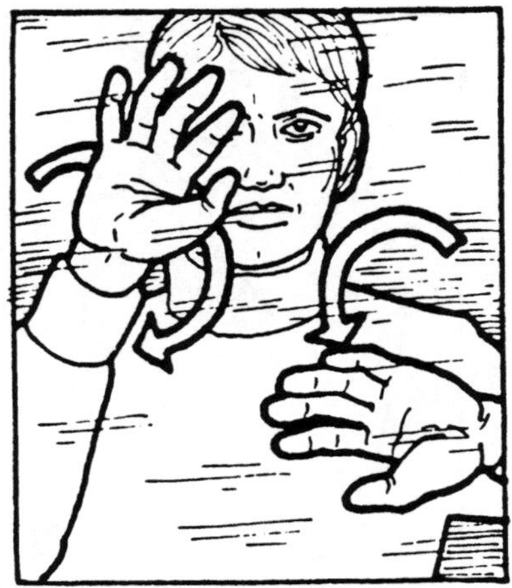

Two open hands palms forward, move in front of face in alternate, slow circular movements.

FOLD

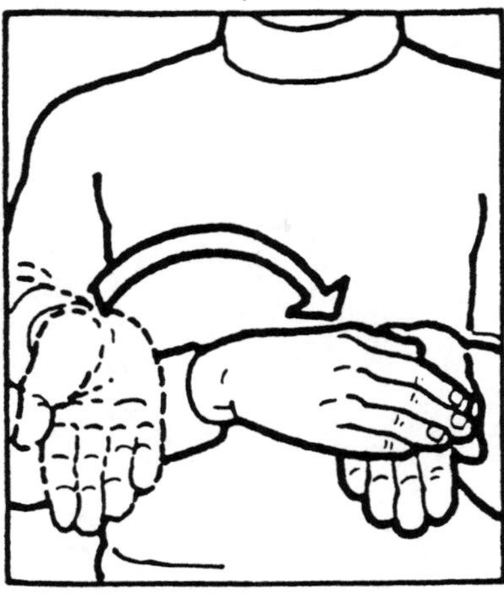

Rt. flat hand, palm up, "folds" over onto L.

FOLLOW (car)

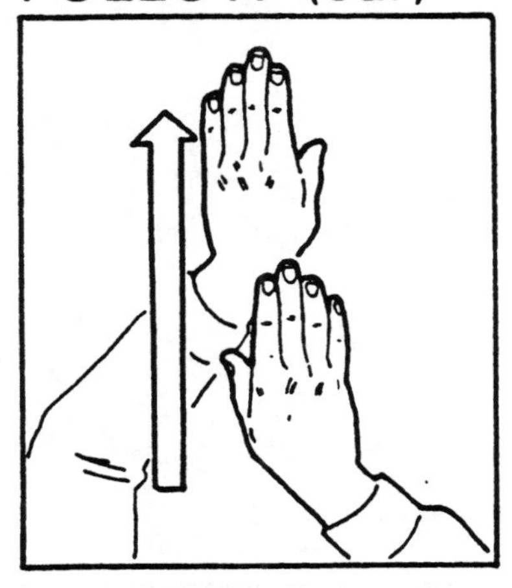

Two flat hands move forward, one in front of the other, representing vehicles.

FOLLOW

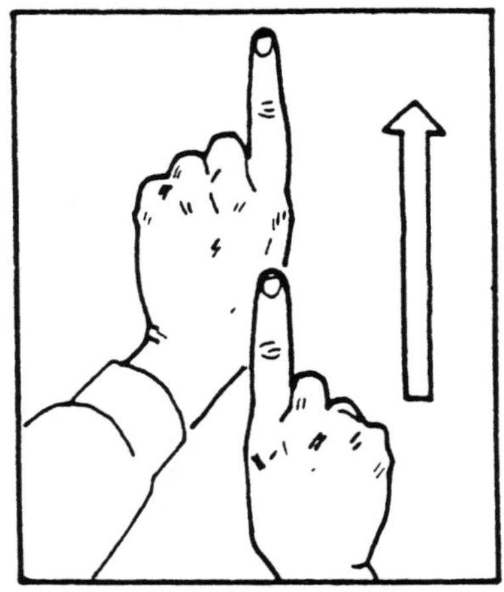

Indexes pointing forward, Rt. behind L. move formation forward.

FOOD

Rt. bunched hand held near mouth.

FOOL

Thumb of Rt. "C" hand taps head twice.

FOOTBALL

Two "N" hands pointing down, L. hand flicks up to indicate kicking.

FOOTBALL (A)

Indicate kicking a football with "N" hands, then outline shape of ball.

FOR

Rt. index points to middle of forehead then twists and moves forward.

FORCE

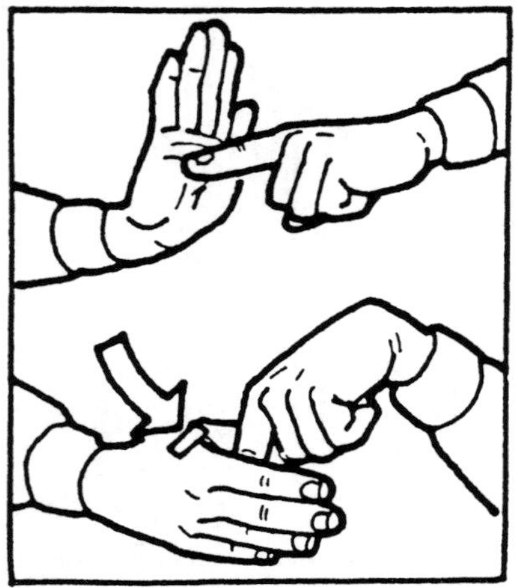

Rt. hand "forces" L. index down and back with stress.

FOREMAN

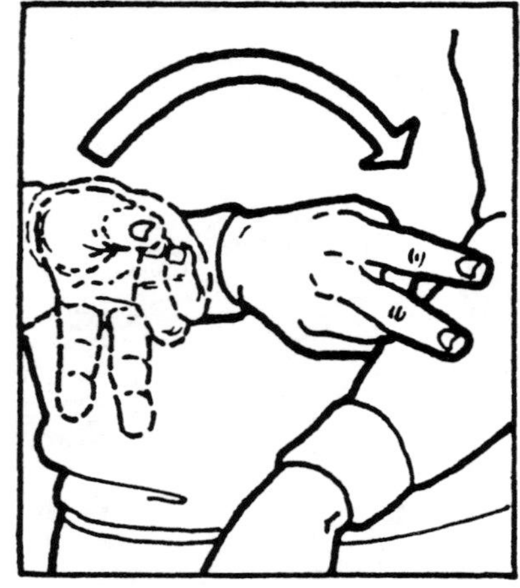

Rt. "V" hand, palm up flips over onto left forearm.

FOREST

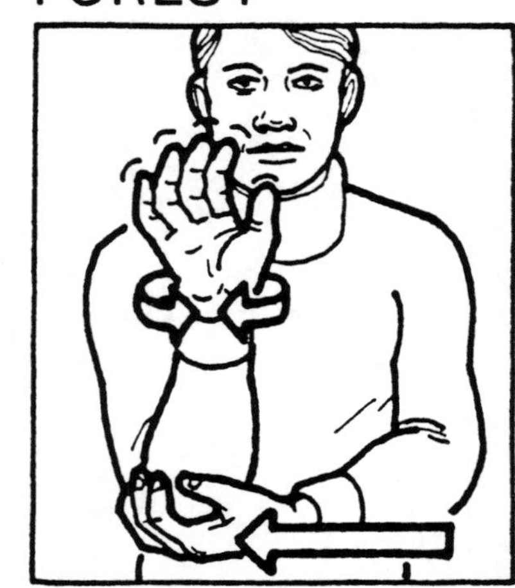

Right elbow cradled in L. hand; Rt. clawed hand swivels at wrist as formation moves left to right.

FOREVER

Tips of indexes touch, Rt. moves away to right with spiralling movement.

FORGET

Rt. full "O" hand touches temple, then springs open and forward.

FORGIVE

Fingertips of Rt. hand touch lips then rub on L. palm in circular movement.

FORK

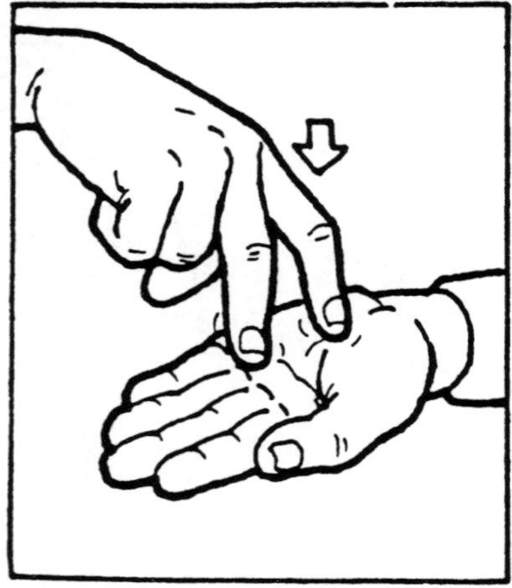

Tips of Rt. "V" hand prod L. palm.

FORTNIGHT

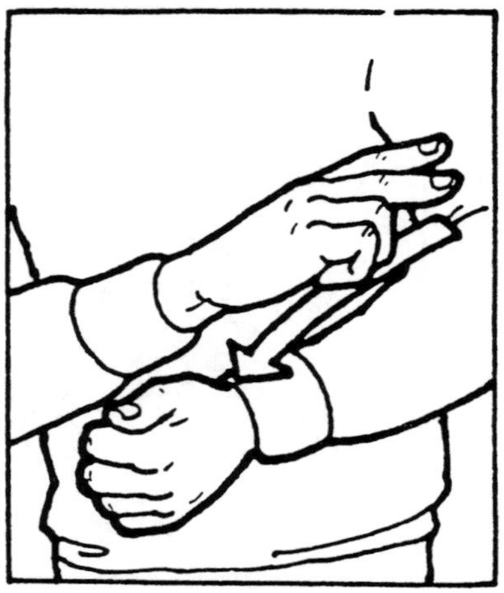

Left forearm held out, Rt. "V" hand moves down left arm from elbow to wrist.

FORWARD

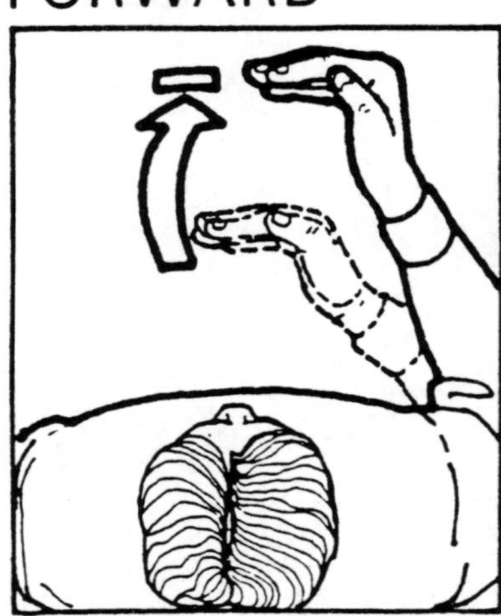

Rt. bent hand moves forward in small upward arc.

FOURTH

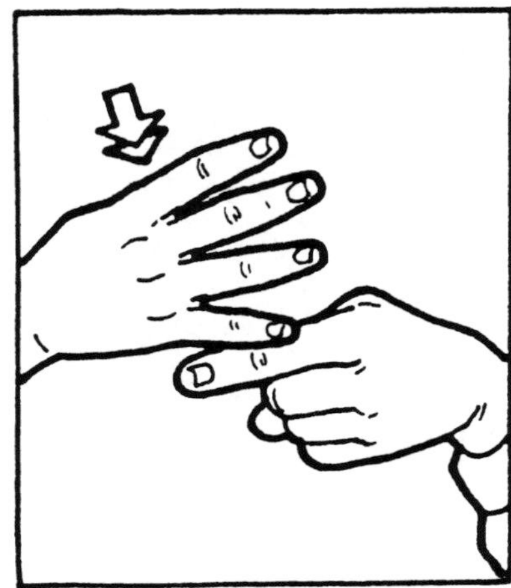

Rt. open hand, thumb tucked in; tap little finger edge on L. extended index twice.

FOX

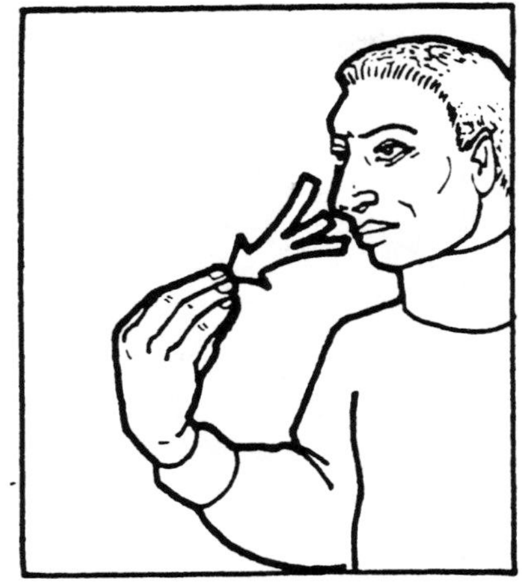

Rt. open fingers and thumb point back to face, then pull forward and close sharply to bunched hand.

FRACTION

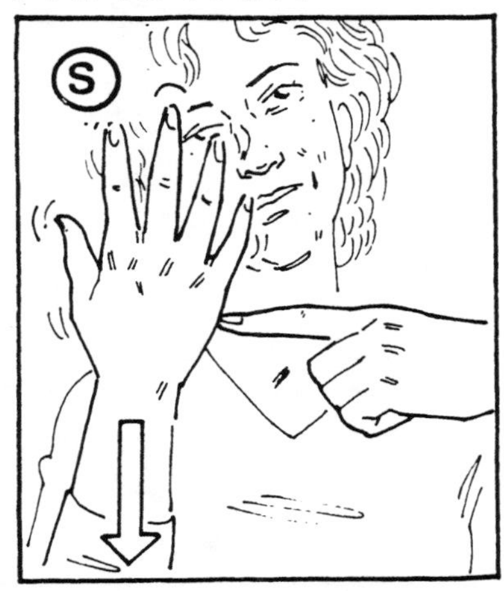

Open Rt. hand above and to the side of L. index; flutter fingers, move down about 6" and flutter again.

FRANCE

Indexes and thumbs move out slightly from upper lip twirling imaginary moustache.

FREE (to)

Two fists, crossed at wrists, spring apart.

FREE (gratis)

Form "F", brush Rt. formation forward off L. twice.

FREE

Thumb tips of open hands contact chest, then hands move and twist forward.

FREEZE

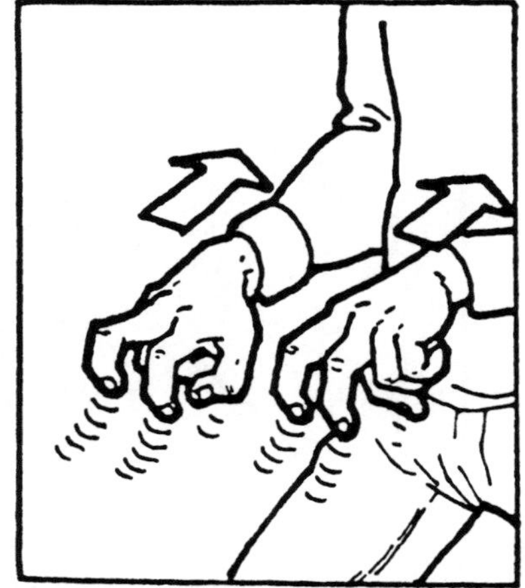

Indexes, middle fingers and thumbs bent palms down pull back towards body.

FRESH

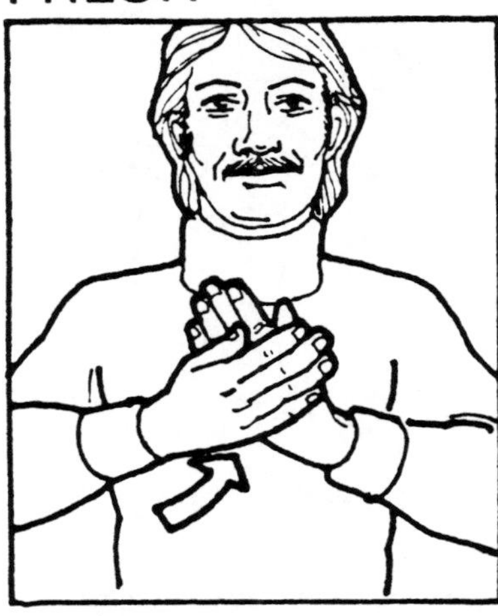

Rt. flat hand strokes sideways/ up back of L. palm.

FRIDGE

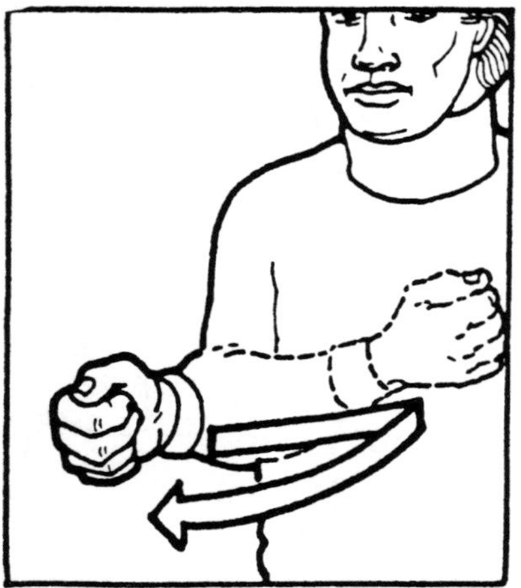

Closed hand, pointing forwards, swings back towards body, and out again.

FRIEND

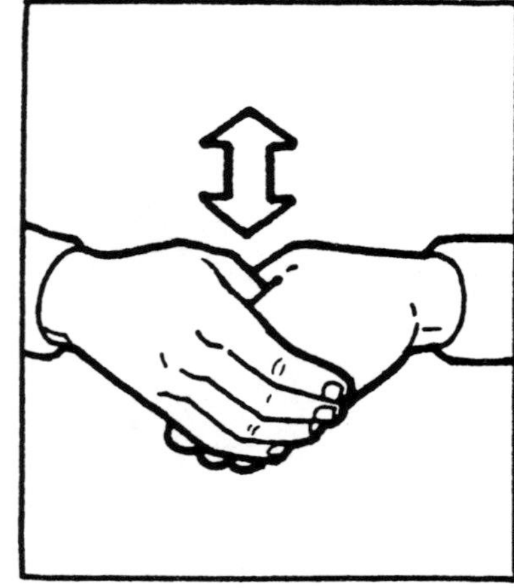

Clasp hands and shake.

FRIGHTENED

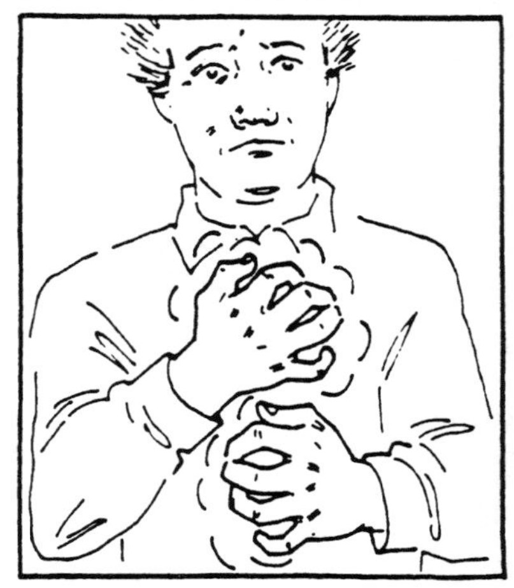

Two clawed hands Rt. above L. quiver into body.

FROG

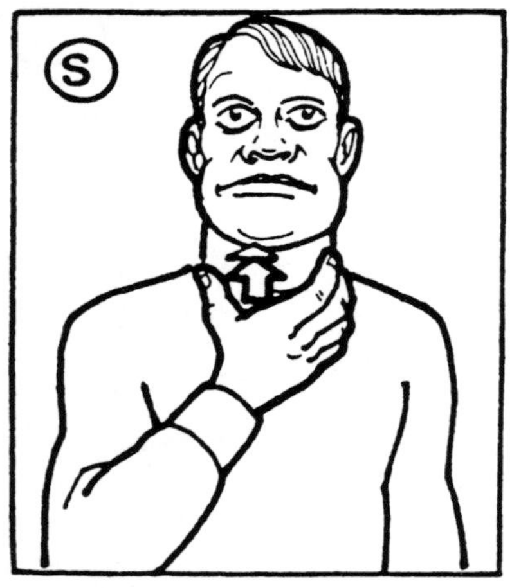

Full "C" hand moves into throat twice.

FROM

"M" hand makes small movement down in twisting movement from wrist.

FRONT

Flat hand contacts chest.

FROZEN

Rt. "V" hand, fingers bent held palm left at side of chin, twists to palm back in front of mouth.

FRUIT

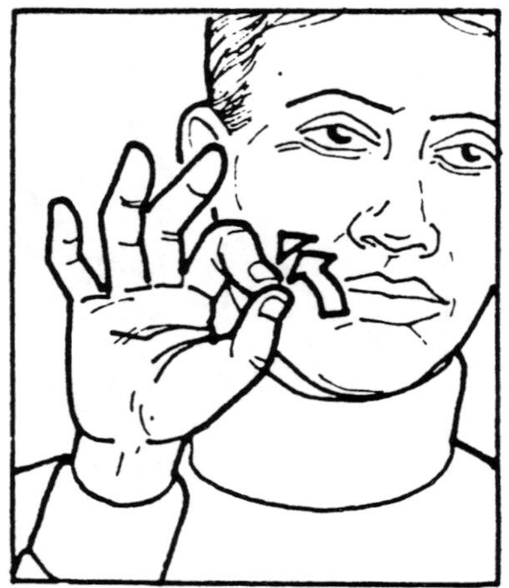

Rt. "O" hand, palm left at side of mouth, strokes backwards on cheek twice, in small movements.

FRY

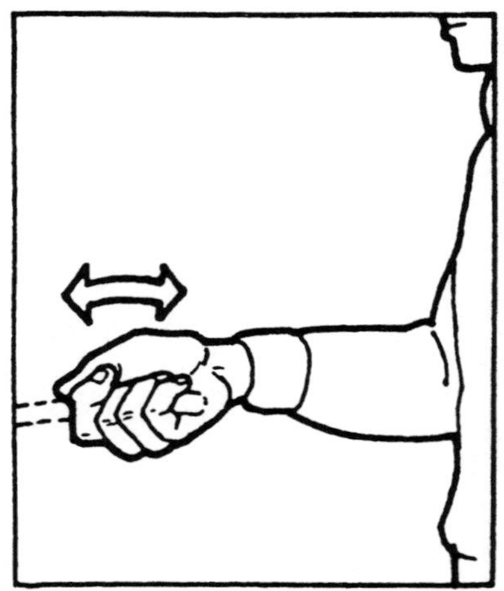

Mime holding pan and shake backwards and forwards.

FULL

Two flat hands, Rt. above L. Move L. hand up to touch Rt.

FUN

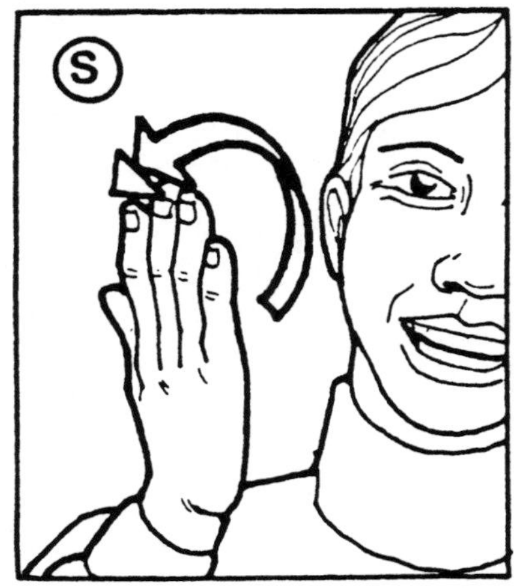

Rt. hand makes small outward circular movements at side of face.

FUNNY (ha ha)

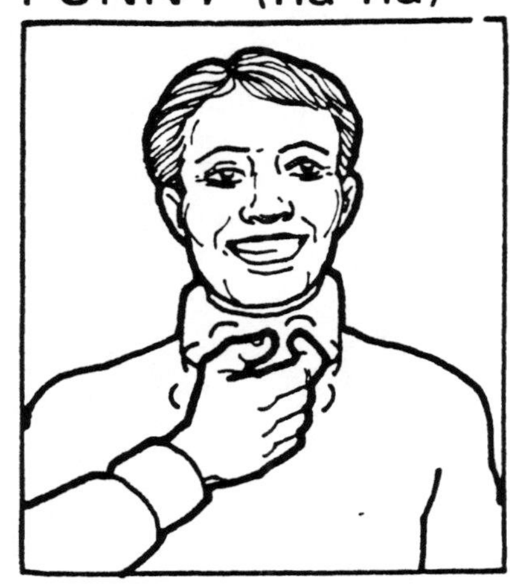

Rt. index and thumb extended and bent, shake slightly side to side under chin.

FUNNY (odd)

Rt. index flexed on ball of thumb at side of chin flicks out across chin.

FURNITURE

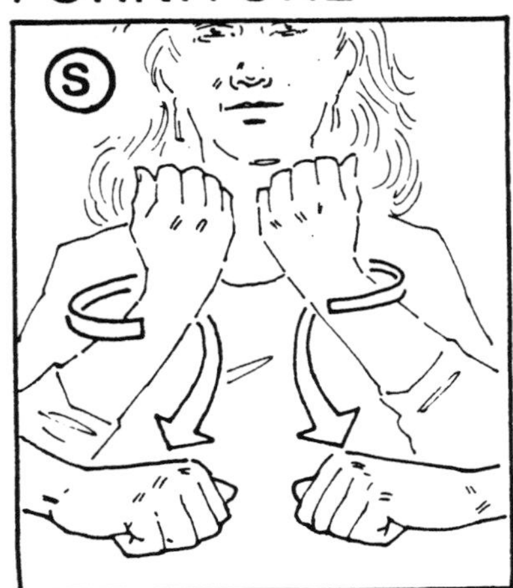

Two closed hands, blades touching move apart in horizontal circle, then turn palm down and move down.

FUTURE

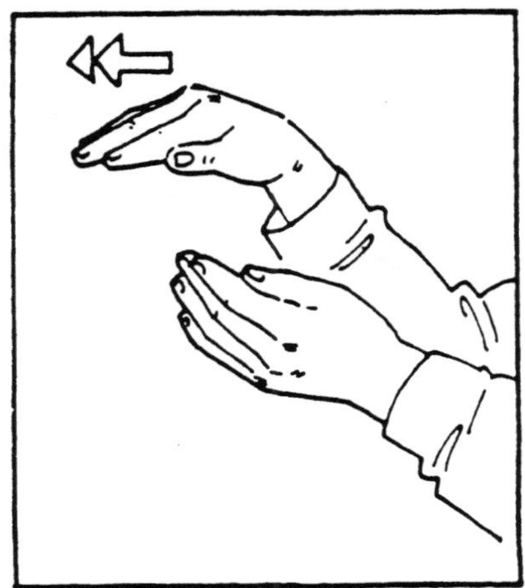

Rt. bent hand moves forward in two movements, forearm contacts L. hand.

GAME

Hands held palms facing, fingers clawed, twist backwards and forwards alternately.

GARAGE

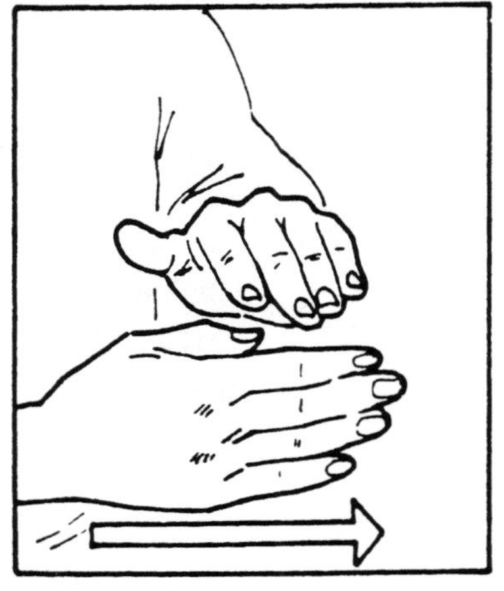

Rt. flat hand moves to stop under L. bent hand.

GARDEN

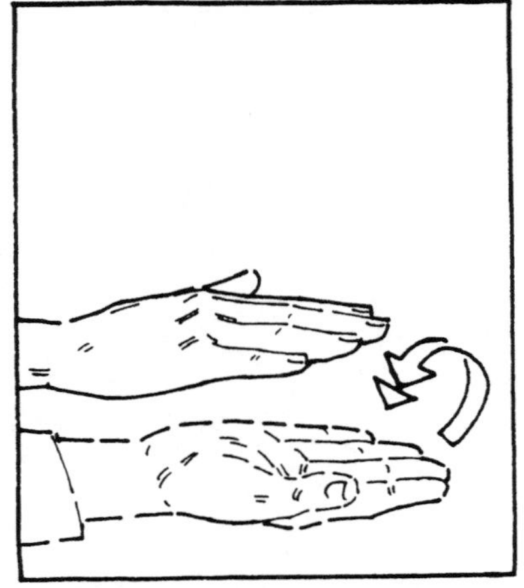

Flat hand flips over from palm up to palm down, twice.

GAS

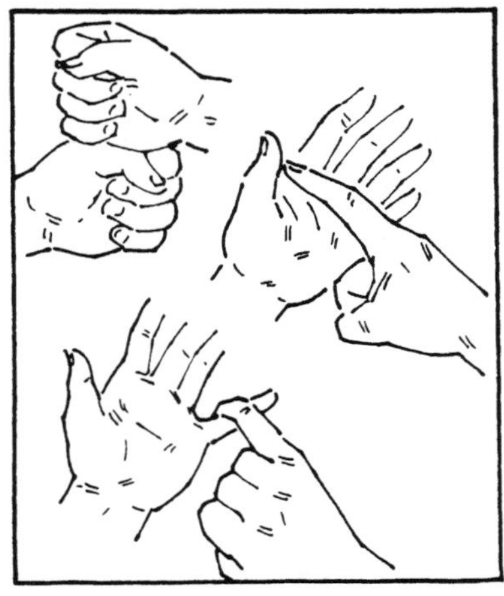

Fingerspell "G" "A" "S".

GATE

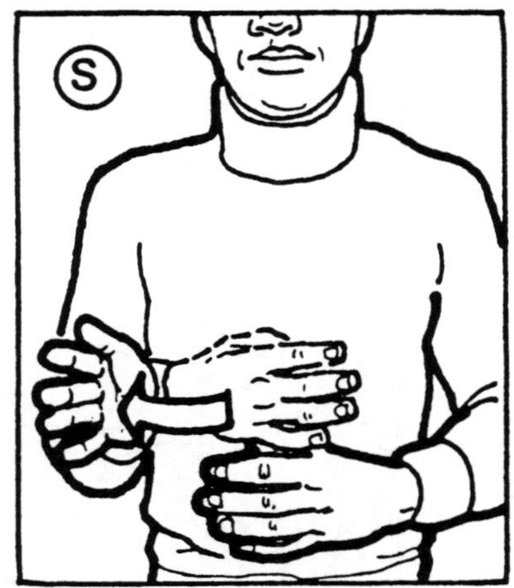

Rt. open hand palm back rests on L. then swings open like a gate.

GENERAL

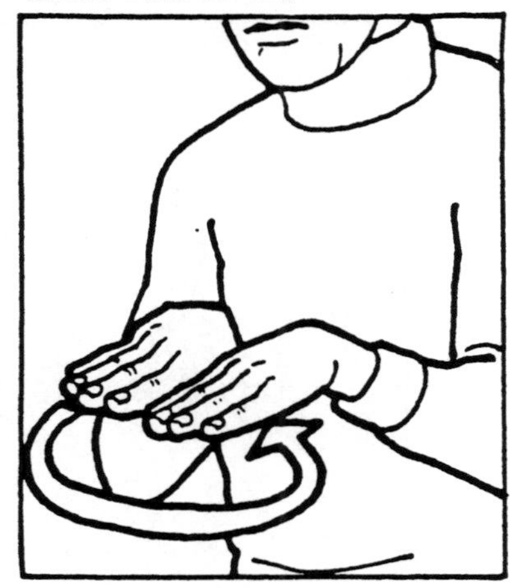

Flat hands together move round in horizontal circle.

GENERATION

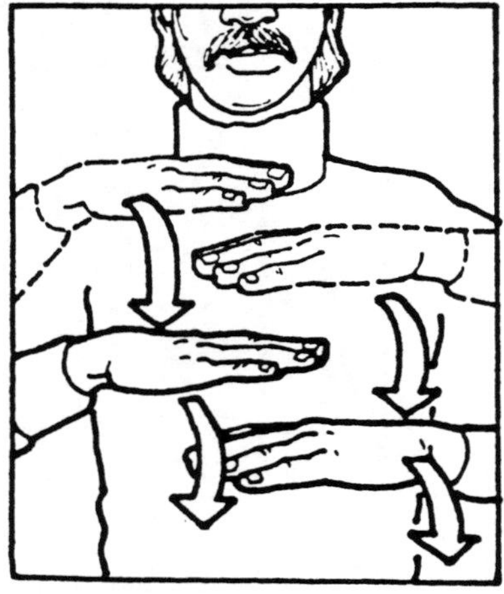

Flat hands palms down make alternate "steps" forward and down from Rt. shoulder.

GENEROUS

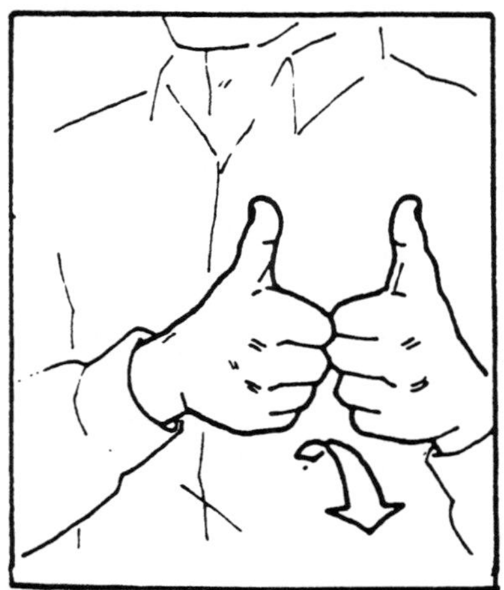

Closed hands, thumbs extended held together over heart, move forward in small arc.

GERMANY

Rt. closed hand index extended held on forehead, palm forward.

GET

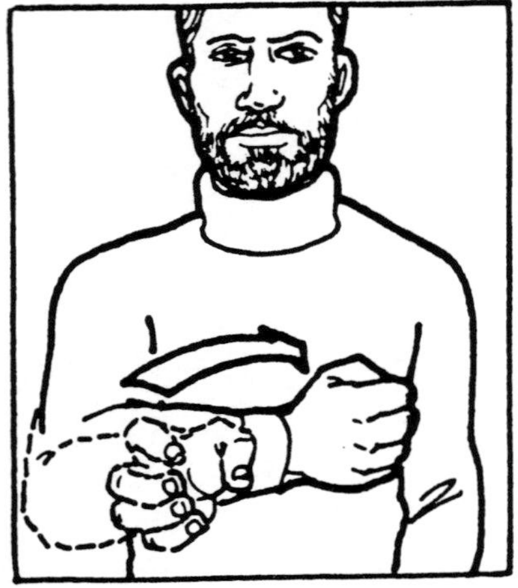

Rt. clawed hand, palm left moves left and closes sharply.

GHOST

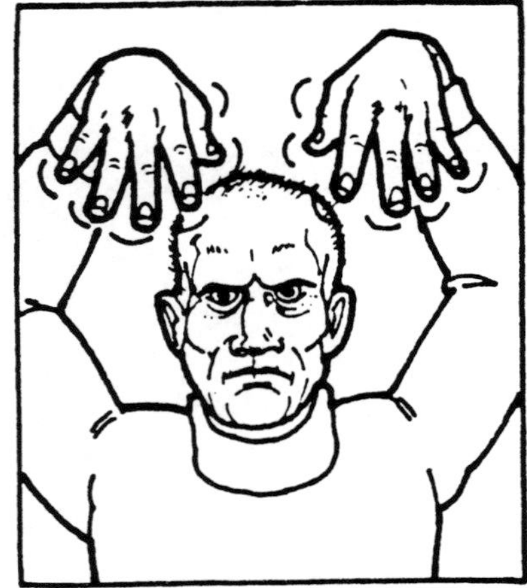

Open hands pointing down, held above head, shake from wrists.

GIRAFFE

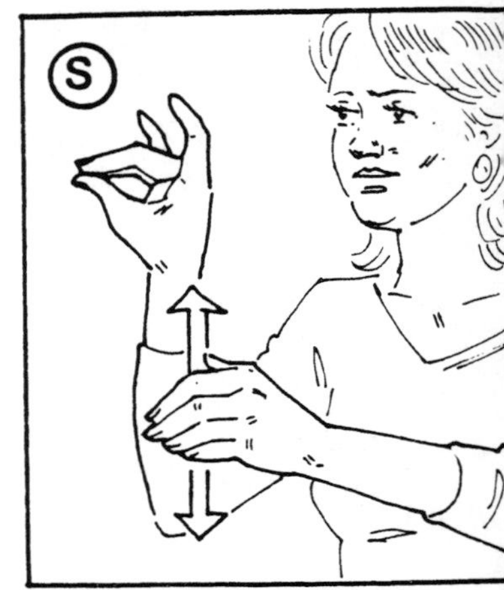

Rt. hand makes sign for "animal". Cupped L. hand moves up and down right forearm to indicate long neck.

GIRL

Stroke Rt. side of mouth with side of extended Rt. index, palm forward.

GIVE

Two flat hands, palms up, move forward in small arc, or towards person concerned. For "give me", hands move back to self.

GLASS (drink)

Mime holding glass in hand.

GLASS

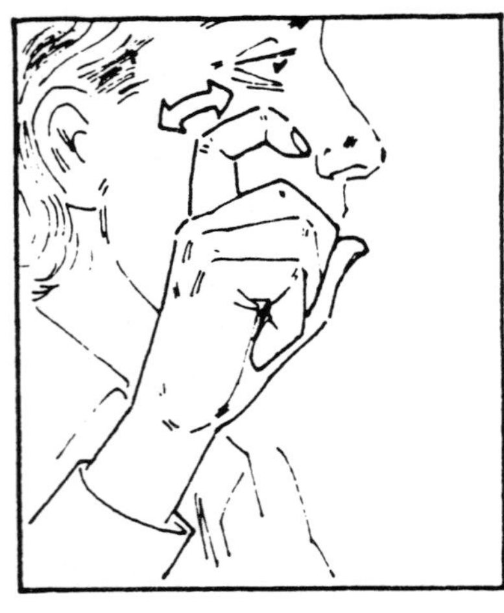

Index edge of "R" hand rubs upper cheek.

GLASSES

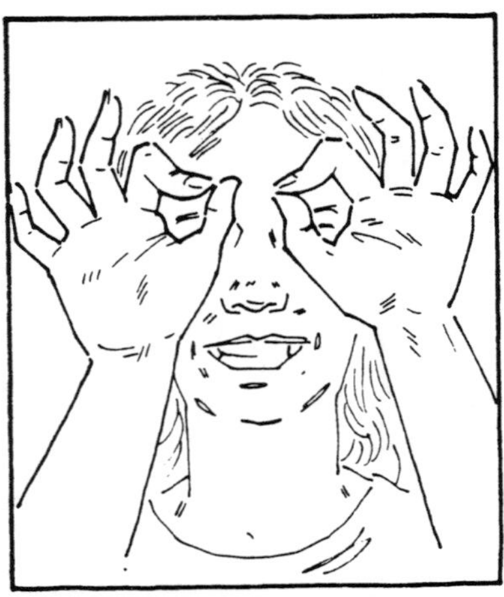

Two "O" hands held in front of eyes to indicate spectacles.

GLOVE(S)

Rt. hand mimes pulling glove over L. open hand. Reverse to L. over Rt. for "gloves".

GLUE

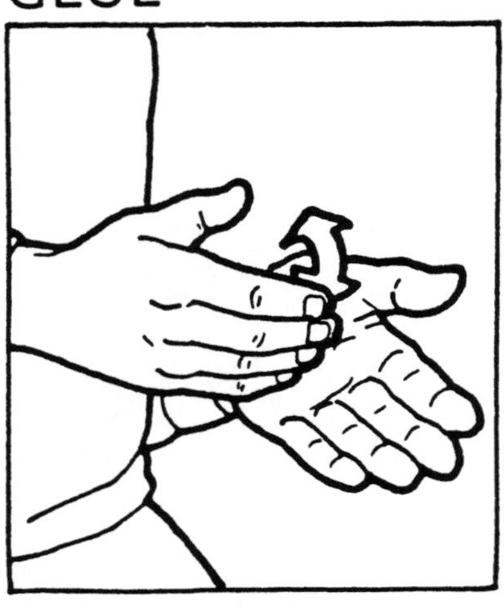

Fingers of Rt. hand press onto L. palm, lift slightly, tips maintain contact as if stuck.

GO

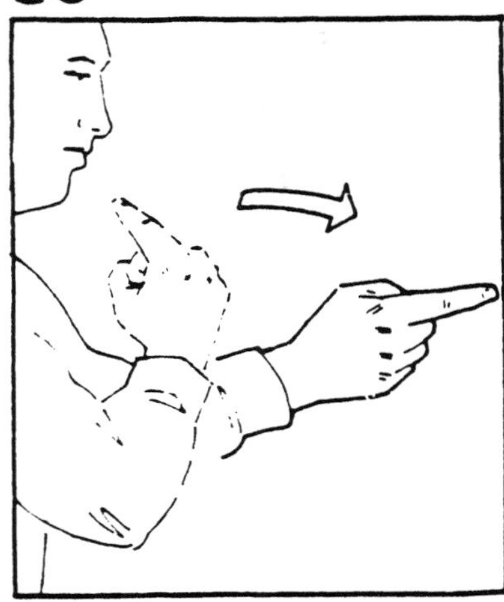

Rt. hand index extended swings forward and points away from body.

GOAL

Index of Rt. hand shoots through index and little finger of L. hand.

GOAT

Fingers and thumb tips on chin, slightly clawed, pull down and close tips together.

GOD

Rt. index points up and moves forward slightly with stress.

GOING TO

Thumb extended, held on upper trunk, prods into body in two small quick movements.

GOLD

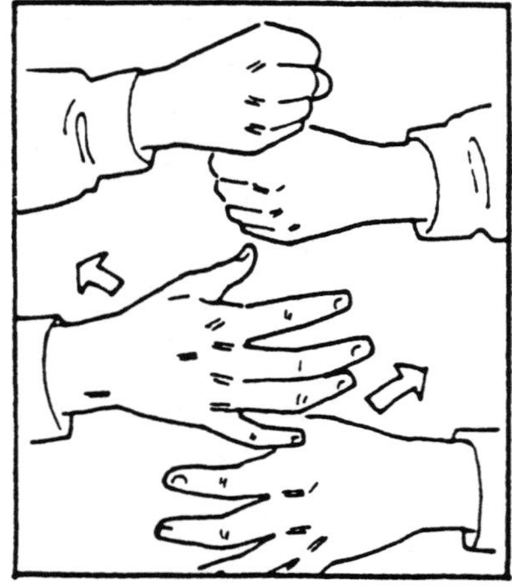

Form "G" then both hands spring open and slightly apart.

GOLDFISH

As for "Gold", then Rt. hand waggles forward like a fish.

GOOD

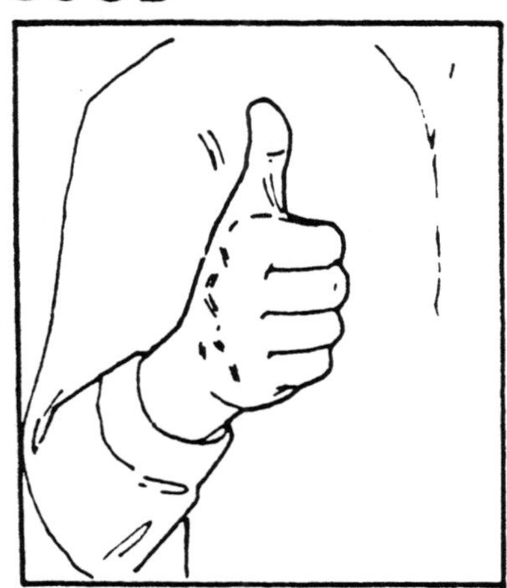

Thumb held up.

GOOD MORNING

Closed hands thumbs extended move up from waist, twisting from palm down to palm back.

GOODBYE

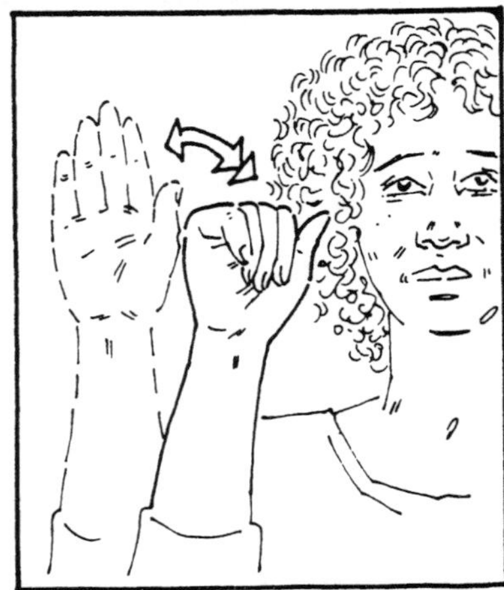

Wave goodbye.

GOOSE

Index and middle fingers open and close onto thumb as hand moves forward from mouth indicating beak and long neck.

GORILLA

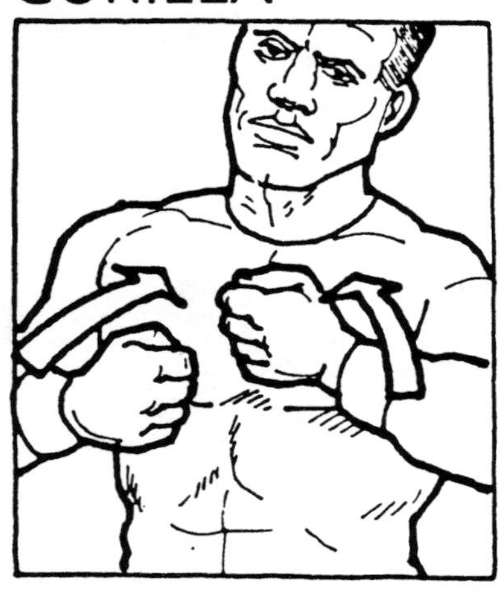

Bang chest alternately, with closed hands.

GOSSIP

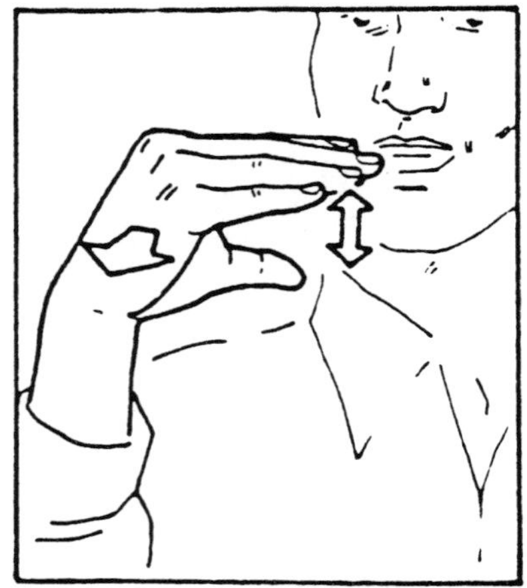

Fingers open and close onto thumb whilst moving forward from mouth.

GOVERNMENT

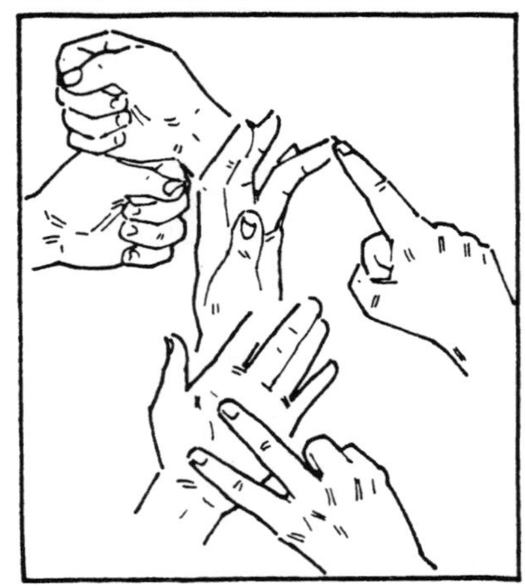

Fingerspell "G" "O" "V".

GRAMMAR

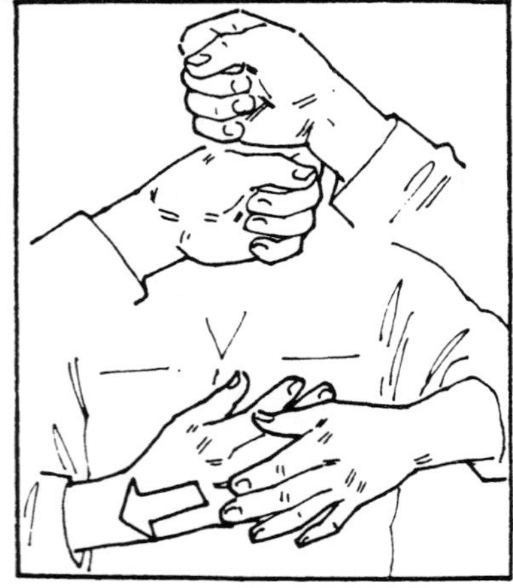

Fingerspell "G", then draw backs of fingers of Rt. open hand along L. palm.

GRANDFATHER

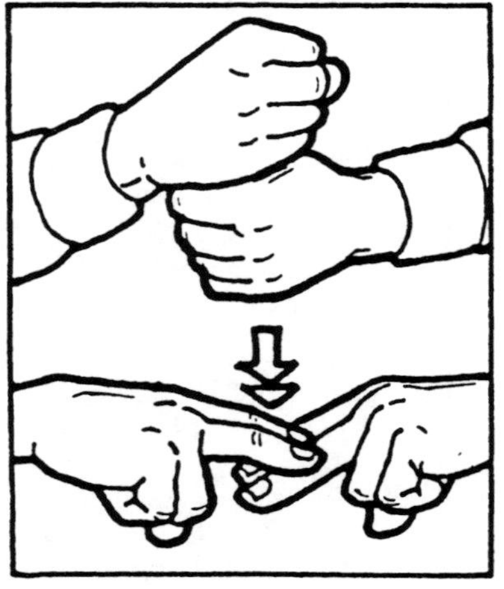

Fingerspell "G" then tap fingers of "F" twice.

GRANDMOTHER

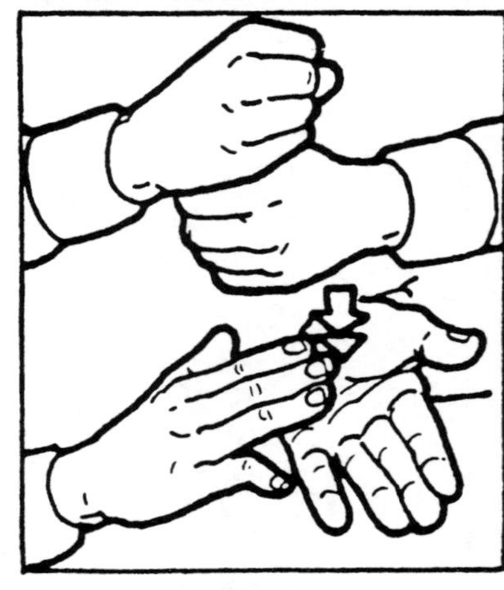

Fingerspell "G" then tap fingers of "M" twice.

GRAPE

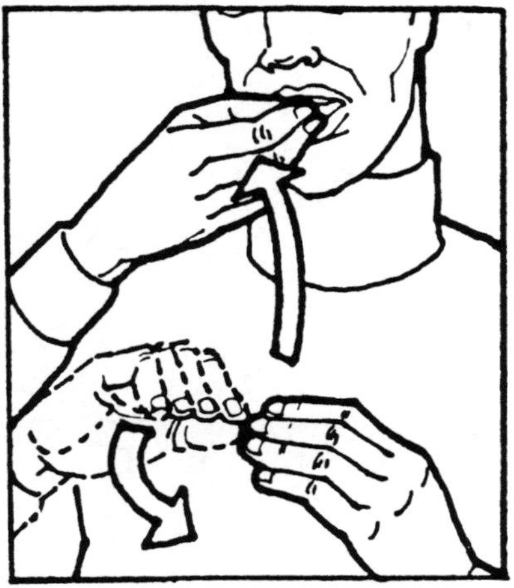

Tips of bunched hands touch, Rt. hand twists as if pulling off grape and moves to mouth.

GRAPEFRUIT

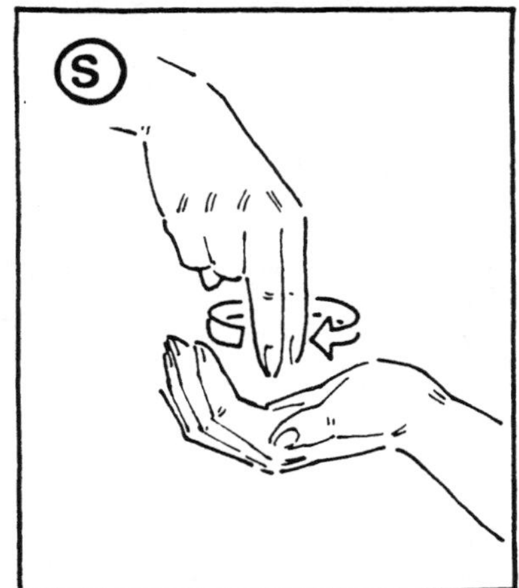

Rt. index and middle fingers make circular movement in L. cupped hand.

GRAPH

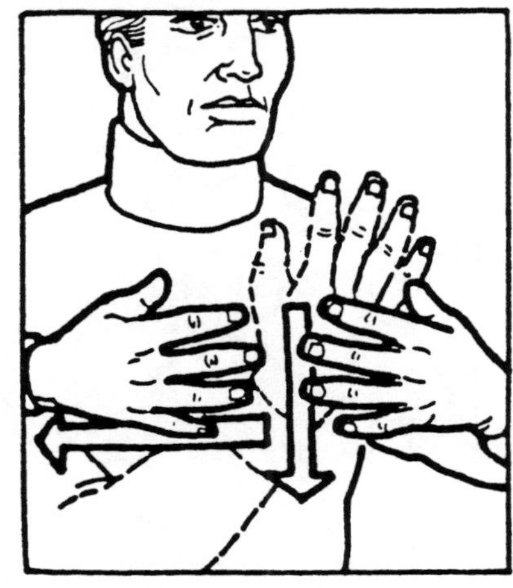

Rt. open hand moves down behind L. open hand, then left to right along L. palm.

GRASS

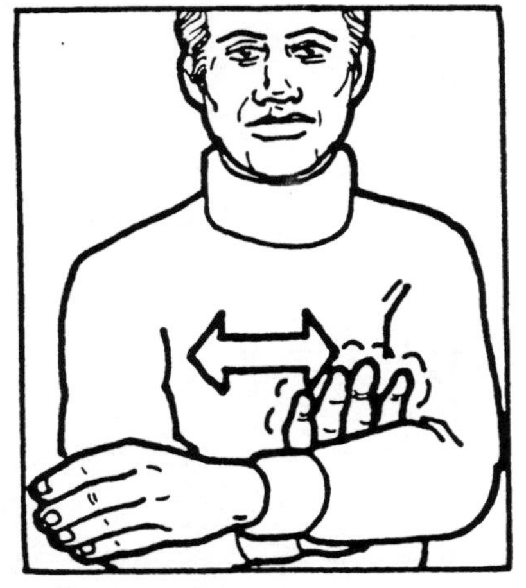

Left forearm held in front of body, Rt. hand moves side to side behind arm, fingers fluttering.

GRAVY

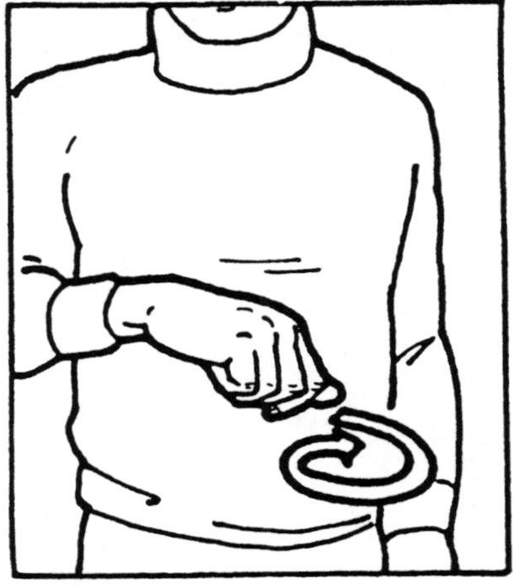

Mime pouring gravy on plate.

GREASE

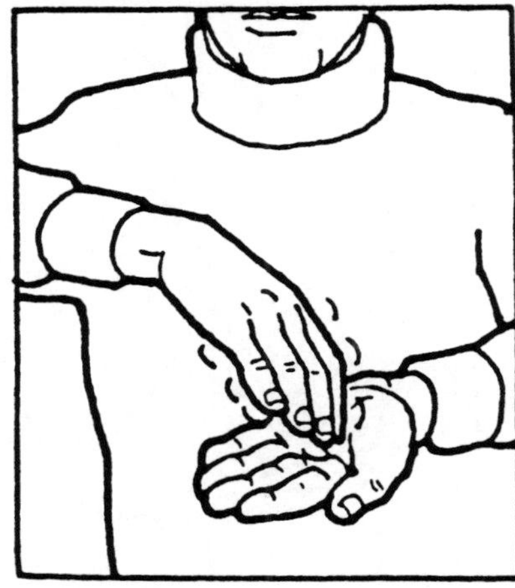

Fingertips of Rt. hand rub on palm of L. as if greasing a tin.

GREECE

Bunched hands palms back at shoulder height shake slightly forward and back.

GREEDY

Extended Rt. thumb jabs into lower trunk twice.

GREEN

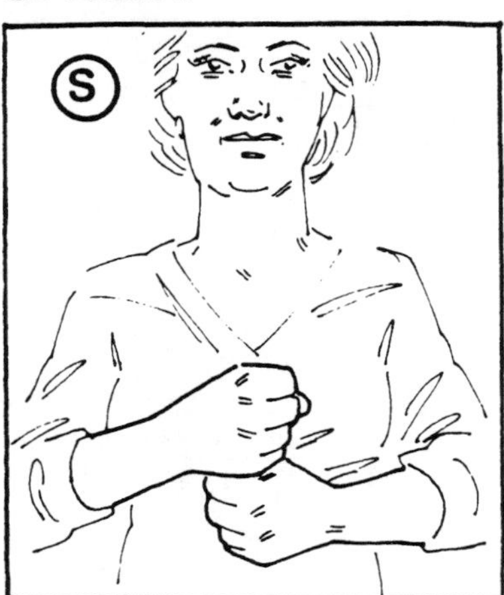

Form "G".

GREY

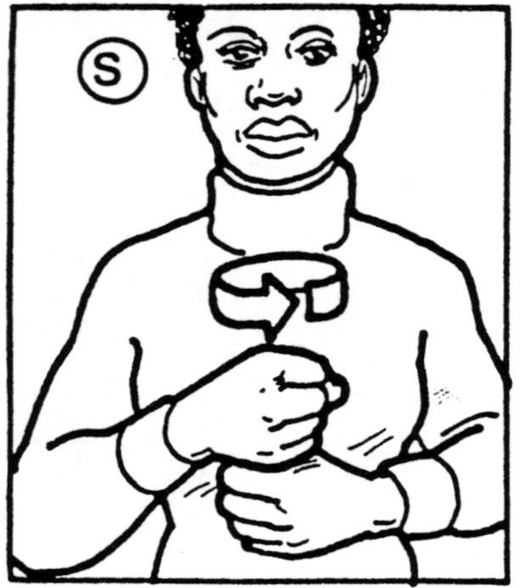

Rt. fist moves in circle on top of L. fist.

GRILL (cook)

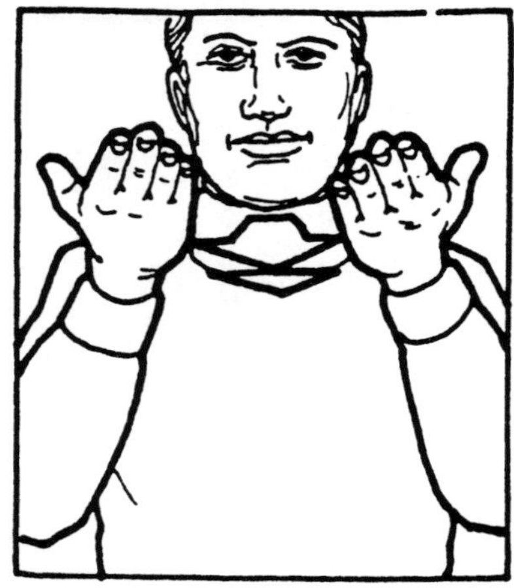

Open hands palms up, jerk forward twice at shoulder height.

GROUP

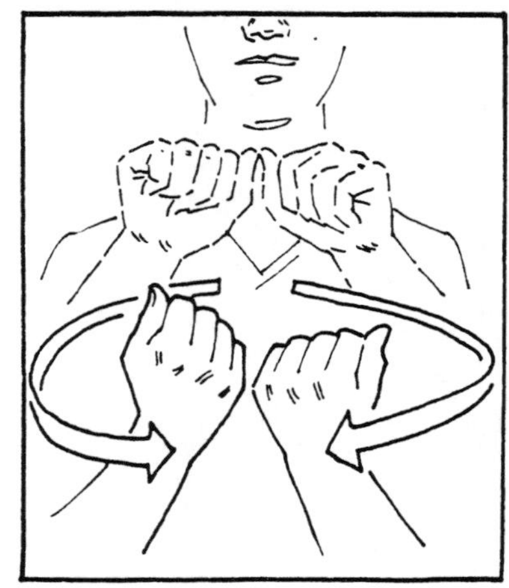

Closed hands thumbs touching held in to body, move apart in forward circle, finish blades touching.

GROW

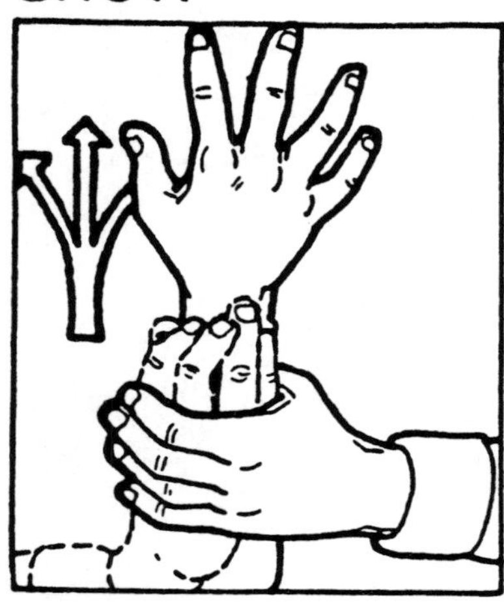

Rt. bunched hand moves up to open hand through L. full "C" hand.

GUESS

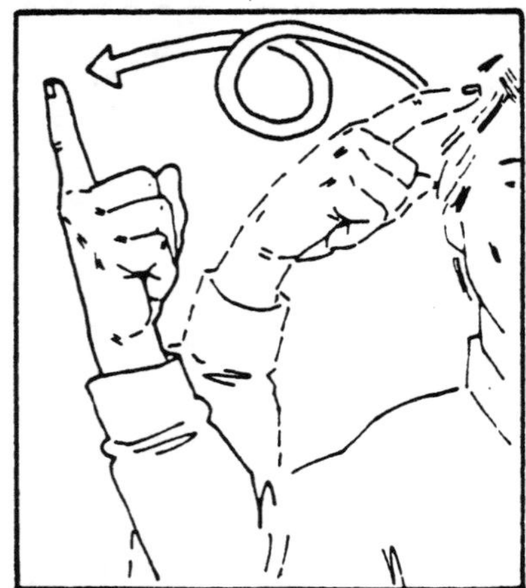

Rt. index moves away from head in looping movement.

GUIDE (lead)

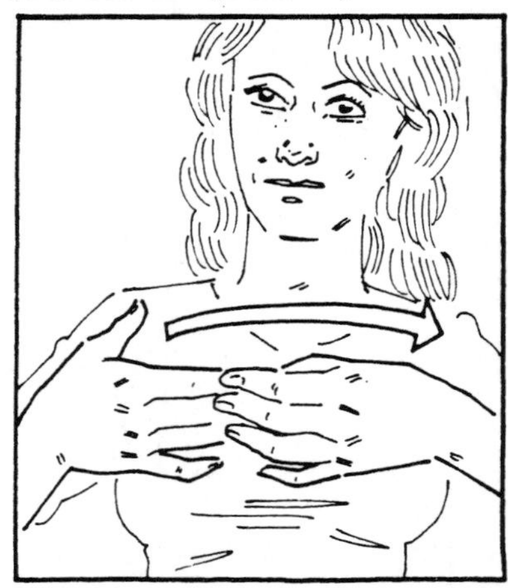

L. hand holds fingers of Rt. and pulls them to the left.

GUINEA-PIG

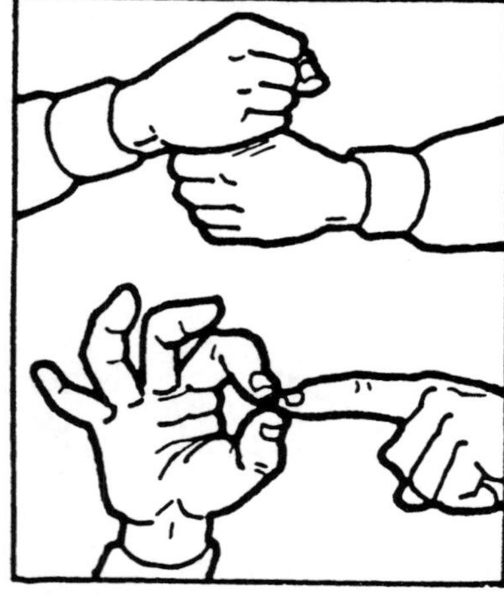

Fingerspell "G" then "P".

GUITAR

Mime playing a guitar.

GUN

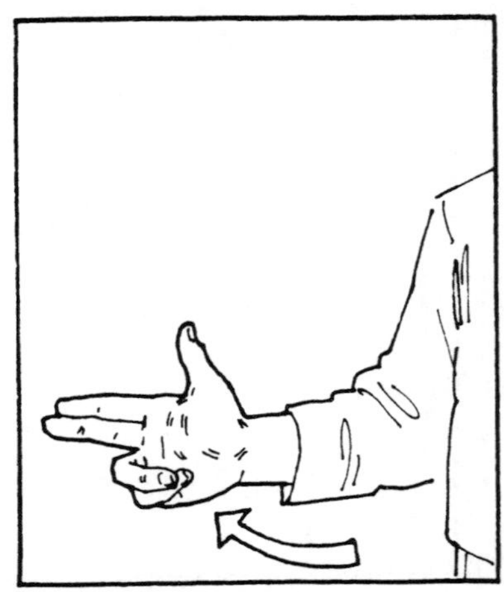

Mime pulling a gun from holster.

GYM

Hands on shoulders, move up, back to shoulders, then out.

GYPSY

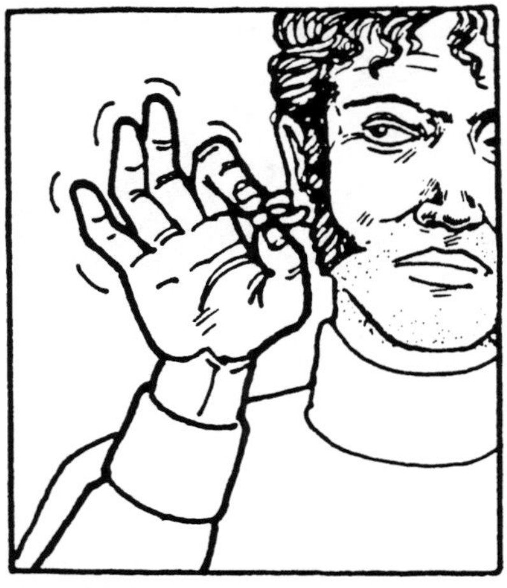

Hold ear-lobe with index and thumb and shake slightly.

HAIR

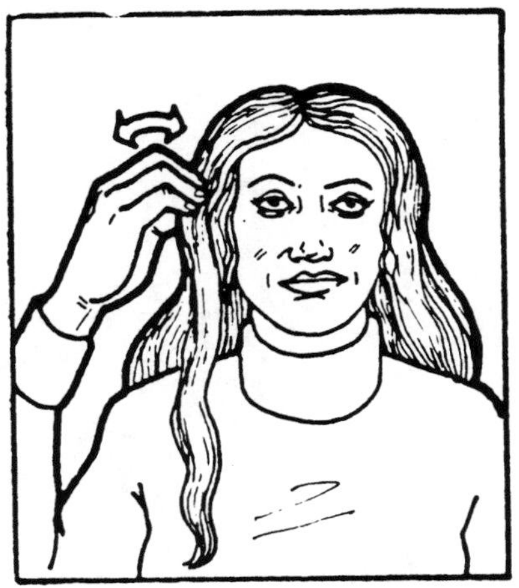

Hold strand of hair and pull slightly.

HALF

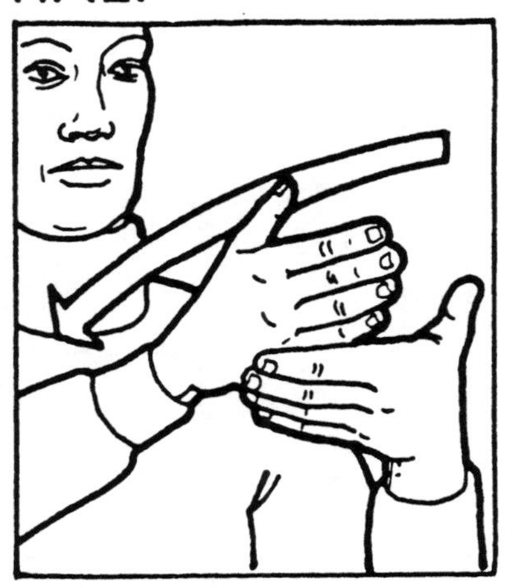

Rt. blade slices down middle of L. palm.

HALL

Two slightly bent hands touching at tips move forward.

HALT

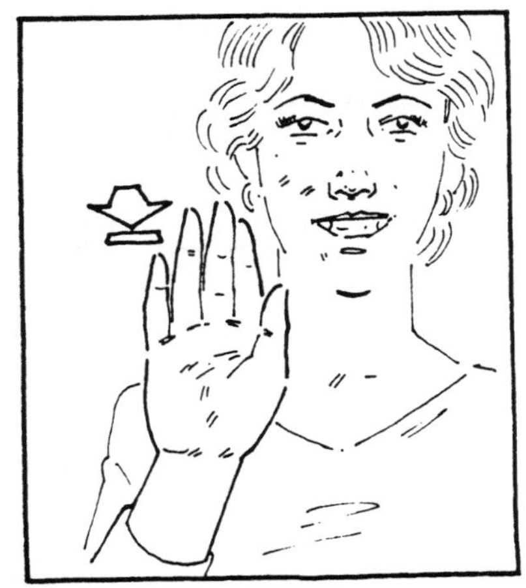

Palm forward flat hand moves forward slightly with stress.

HAMMER

Mime holding hammer and hammering.

HAMSTER

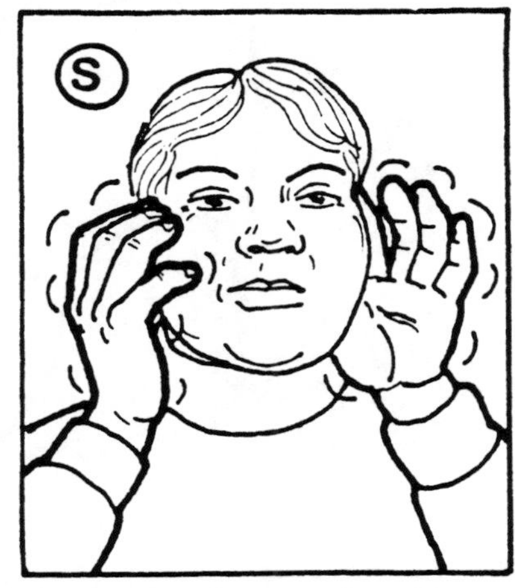

Clawed hands move in and out slightly at sides of face.

HANDICAP

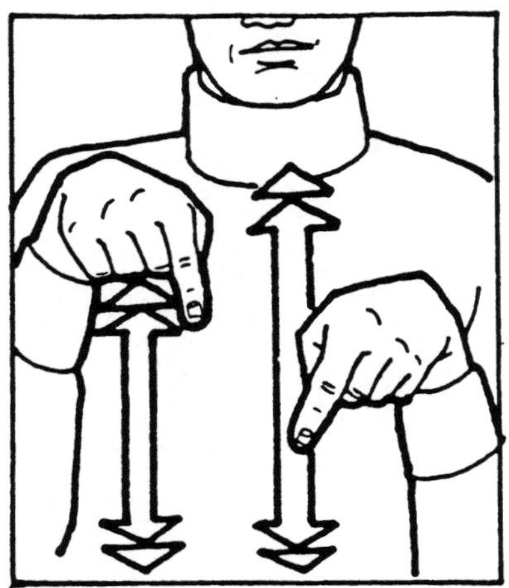

Two closed hands indexes extended and pointing down, move up and down alternately.

HANDLE

Mime holding handle and turning.

HANDSOME

Index circles round face then moves out to closed hand, thumb up.

HANG

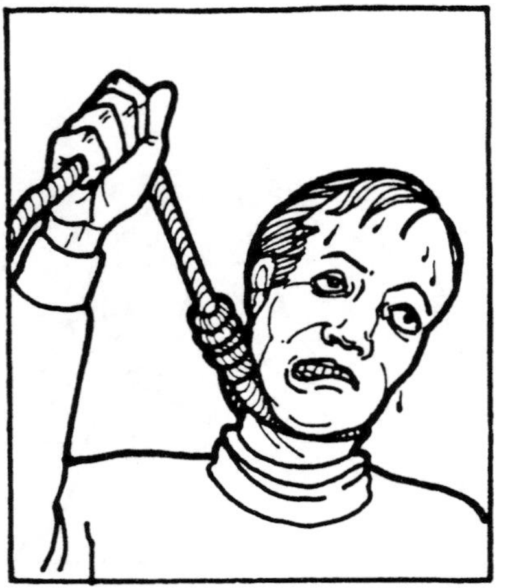

Mime holding rope and pulling, head bent over to the left.

HAPPEN

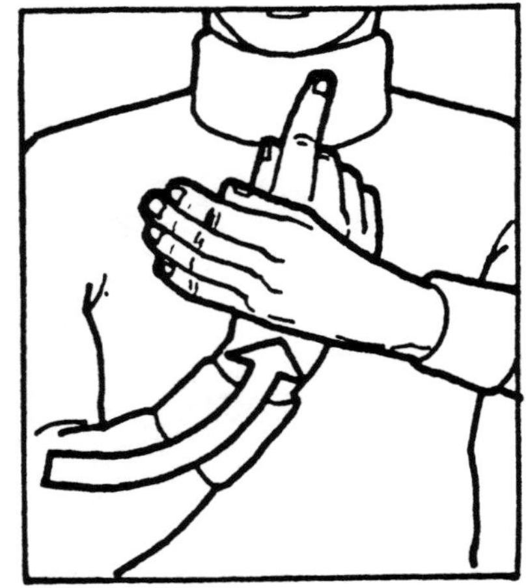

Rt. index extended moves up sharply behind palm back L. hand.

HAPPY

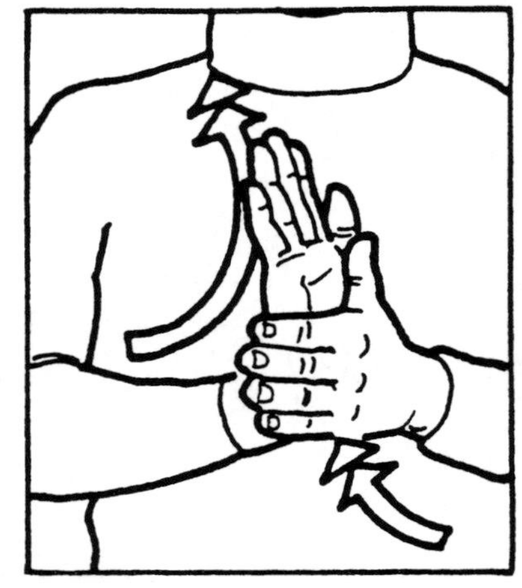

Hands clap together in circular movements.

HARD

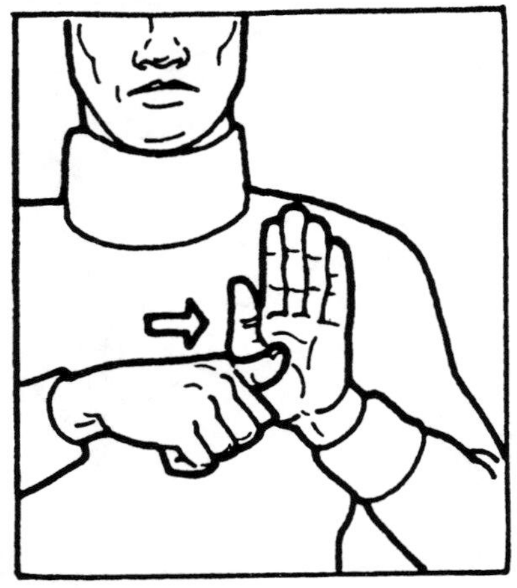

Rt. thumb presses into L. palm.

HARE

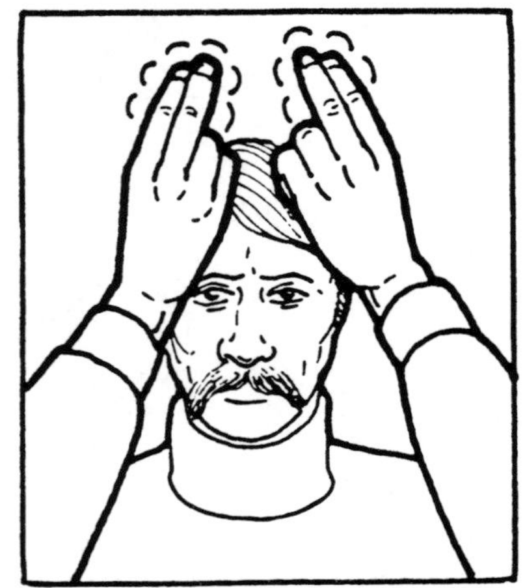

"N" hands palms back held at sides of head; fingers waggle up and down like hares ears.

HAT

Mime placing hat on head using bunched hands.

HATE

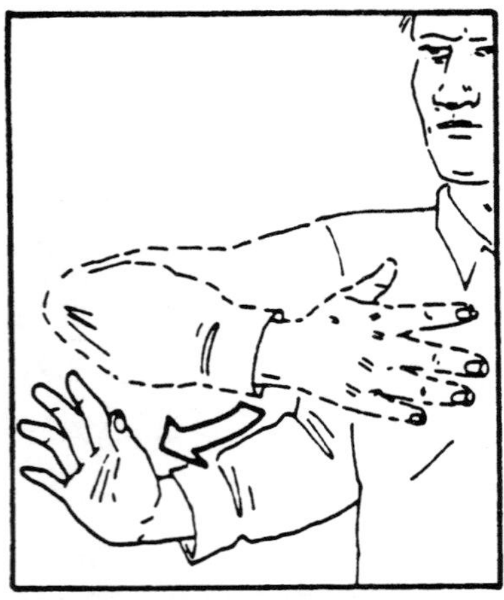

Open hand on upper chest twists to palm forward and pushes away from body with distaste.

HAVE

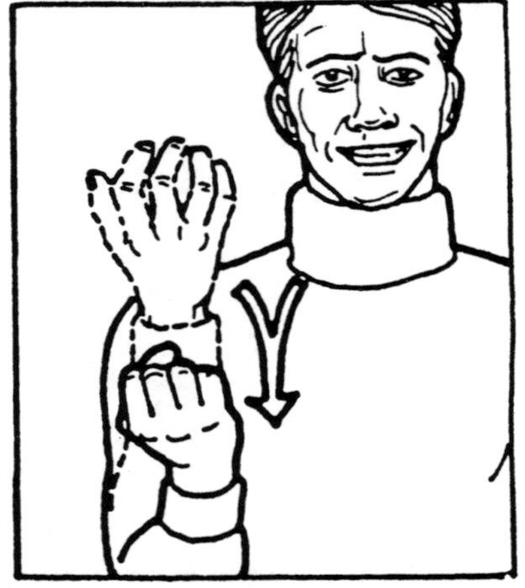

Clawed hand held at shoulder level palm up moves down and closes sharply to fist.

HE

Index and thumb stroke down chin, then index points forward, or to person concerned.

HEADLIGHTS

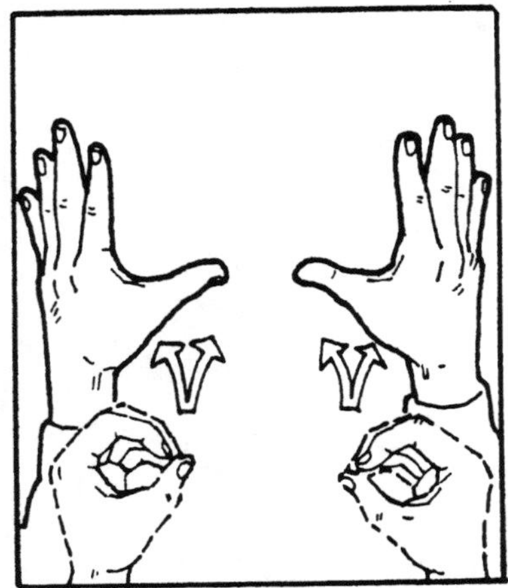

Fingers of both hands spring open from full "O" hands with slight forward movement to indicate car headlights.

HEADMASTER

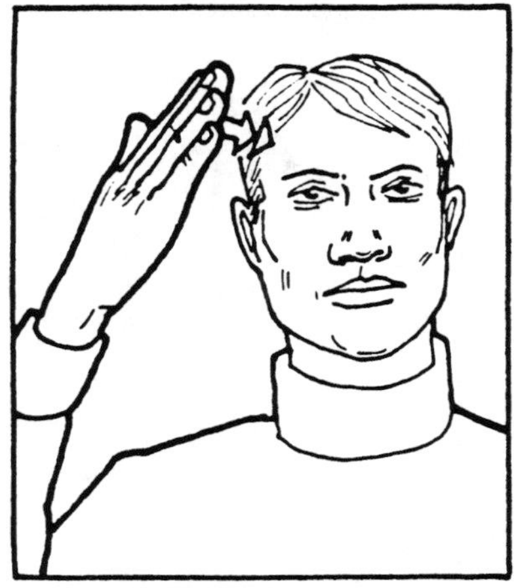

Tap right side of head with flat hand several times.

HEALTH

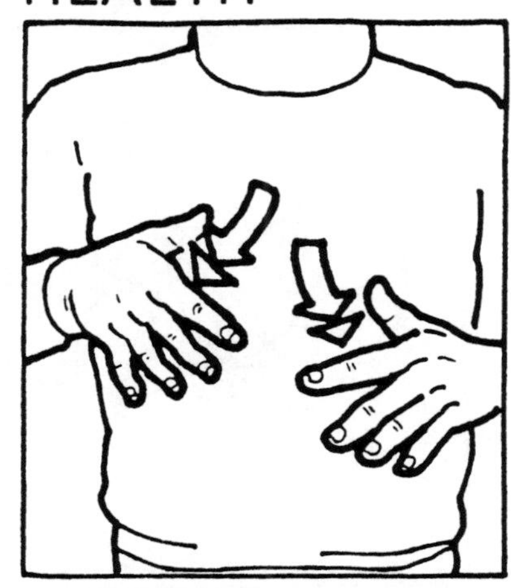

Thumbs of open hands brush alternately down chest, several times.

HEAR

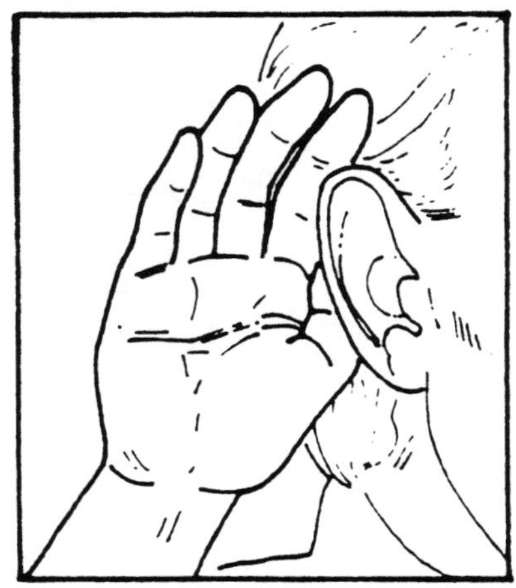

Slightly cupped hand behind ear.

HEARING

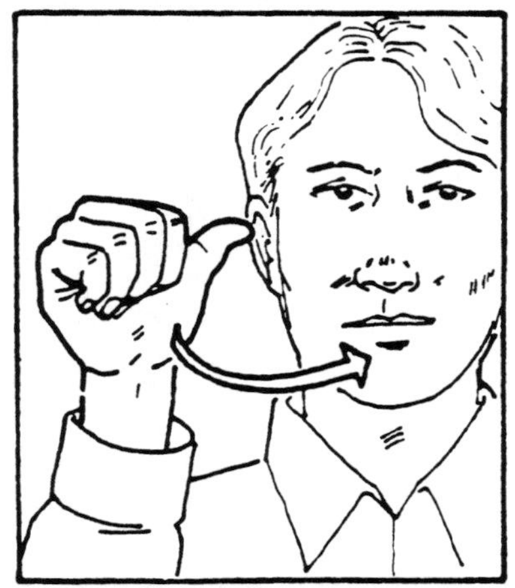

Closed hand thumb extended moves from ear to mouth.

HEARING AID

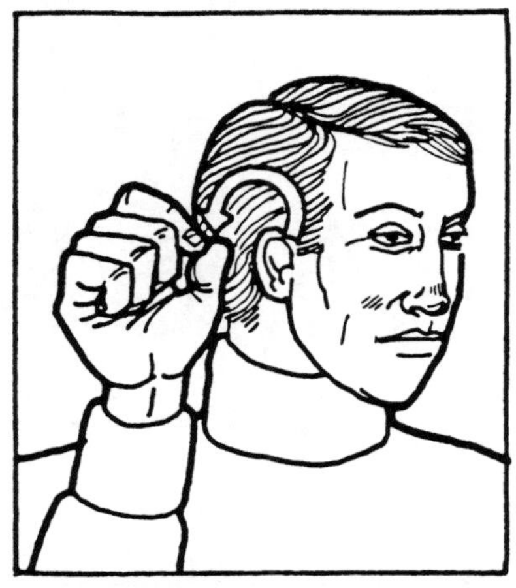

Index and thumb almost touching outline shape of aid above ear.

HEART

Tap chest over heart twice.

HEAVEN

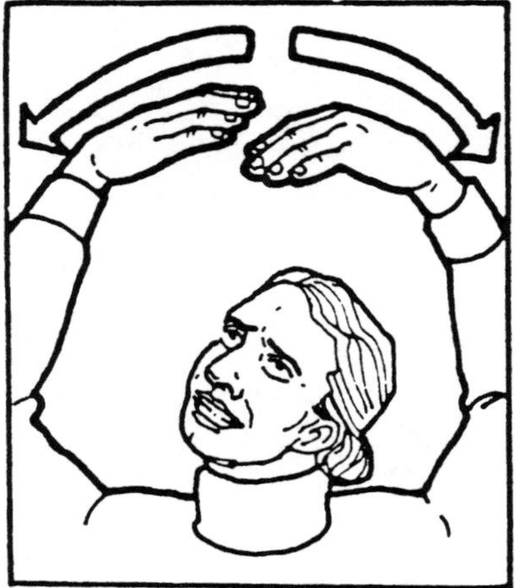

Slightly bent hands held over head sweep apart.

HEAVY

Two cupped hands move down, to indicate weight.

HEDGE

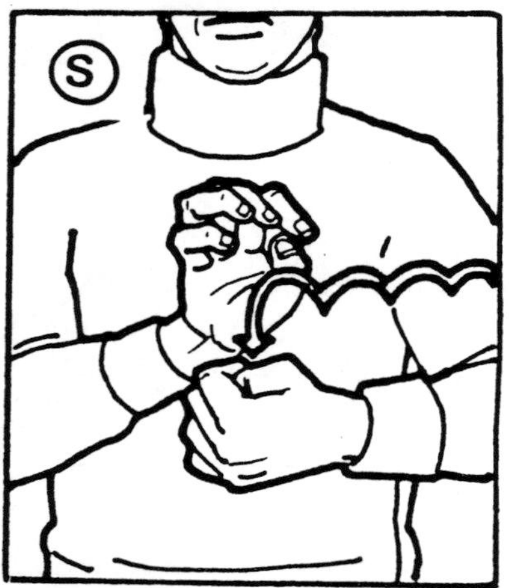

Rt. clawed hand makes hopping movement along left forearm, from elbow to wrist.

HEIGHT

Rt. bent hand moves up from shoulder.

HELICOPTER

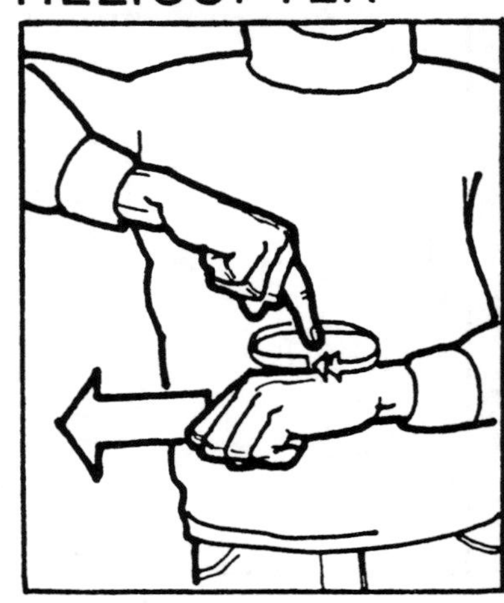

Rt. index circles above L. closed hand, as formation moves from left to right.

HELLO

Rt. flat hand sweeps right.

HELP

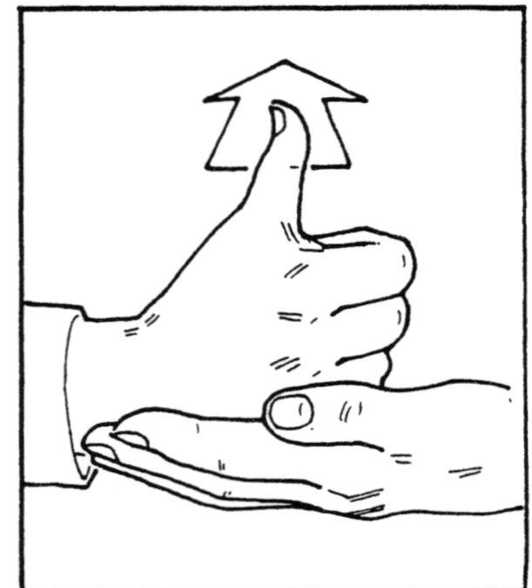

Blade of Rt. fist rests in palm of L. flat hand, formation moves up/forward. For "help me", formation moves back to self.

HEN

Rt. index and thumb open and close in front of mouth like a beak whilst elbow moves in and out.

HER (indic.)

Side of index strokes down cheek, then points to person concerned.

HER (possess.)

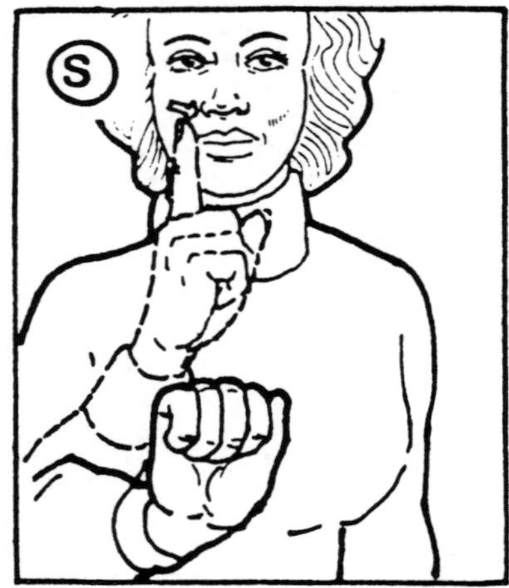

Side of index strokes down cheek, then palm forward closed hand moves forward or to person concerned.

HERD

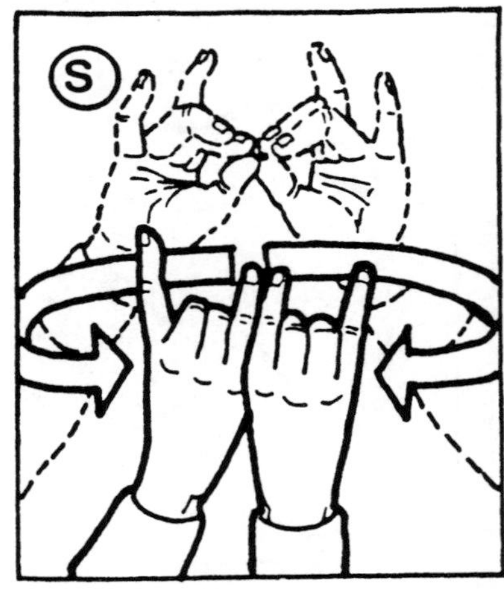

Two hands form sign for "animal", tips touching move apart in forward circle, finish blades touching.

HERE

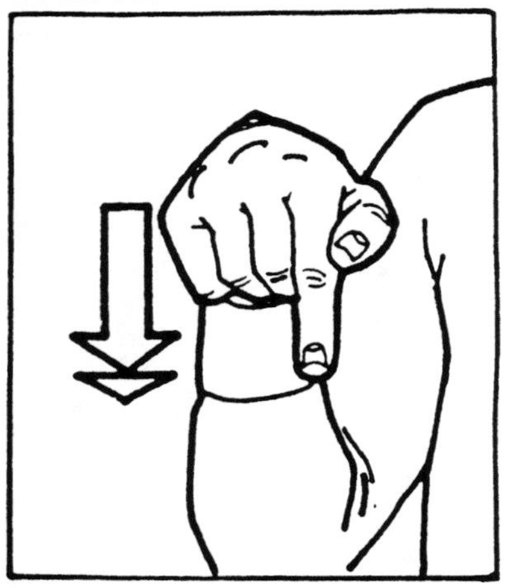

Indicate spot with extended index finger pointing down twice.

HEREDITARY

Form fingerspelt "F" and move forward/down in steps from left shoulder.

HIDE

Flat hands pointing up held in front of face, L. behind Rt. make small alternate sideways movements.

HIGH

Slightly bent hand held above head height.

HIGHCHAIR

Indicate "High" with Rt. hand then sign "chair".

HIKE

Closed hands thumbs extended held on upper chest, shoulders move to indicate walking.

HILL

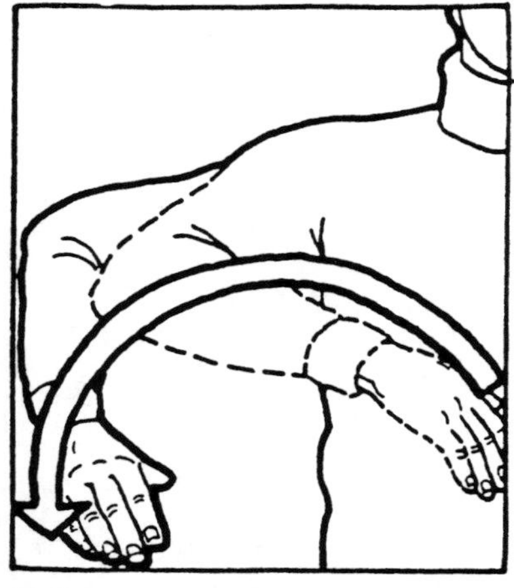

Indicate shape of hill with flat hand.

HIM

Index and thumb stroke chin, then index points to person concerned.

HIPPOPOTAMUS

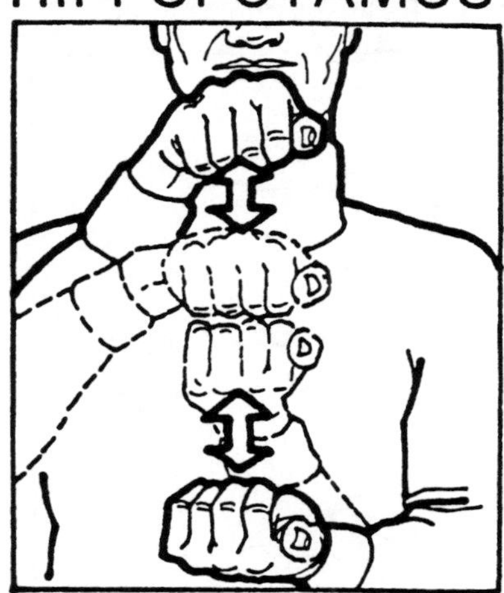

Closed hands, Rt. on L., palms facing, move apart and together to indicate jaws.

HIRE

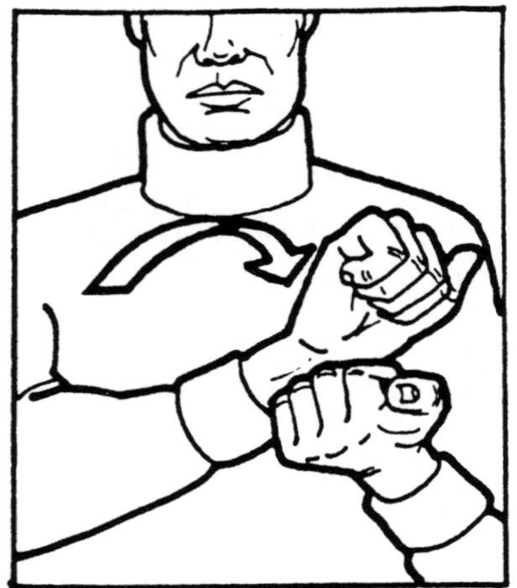

Closed hands facing each other, crossed at wrists move back/left to body in small arc.

HIS

Index and thumb stroke down chin, then palm forward closed hand moves forward, or to person concerned.

HOLD

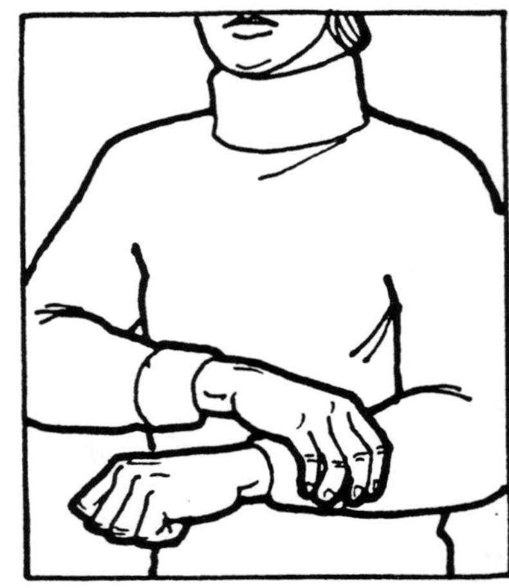

Rt. hand holds left arm.

HOLE

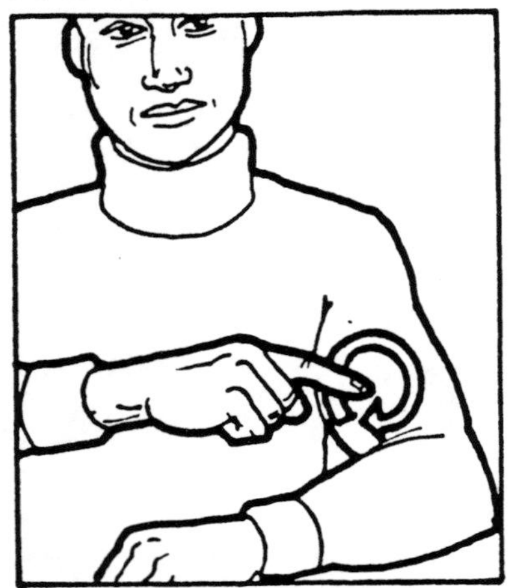

Indicate hole with Rt. index on left arm, or in appropriate place.

HOLIDAY

Rt. index pointing up makes horizontal circle at head height.

HOLLAND

Both hands on head, fingers open, move out changing to bunched hands to indicate Dutch hat.

HOLY

Rt. closed hand thumb out makes large anti clockwise circle above L. palm then drops down onto L. palm.

HOME

Rt. bent hand moves forward.

HONOUR

Flat hands touch forehead, then drop down to palm up, head slightly bent.

HOP

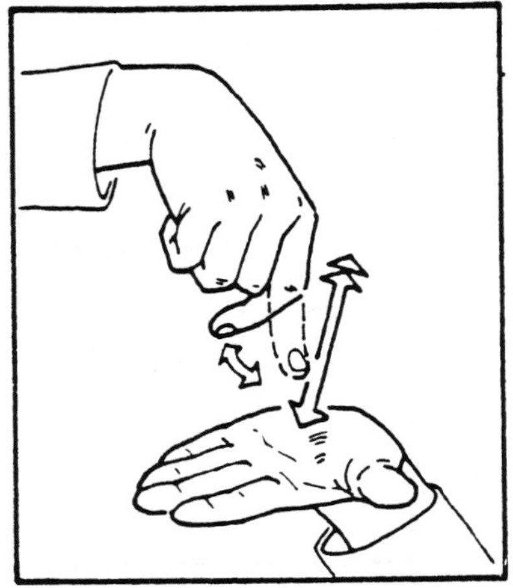

Rt. index hops on L. palm.

HOPE

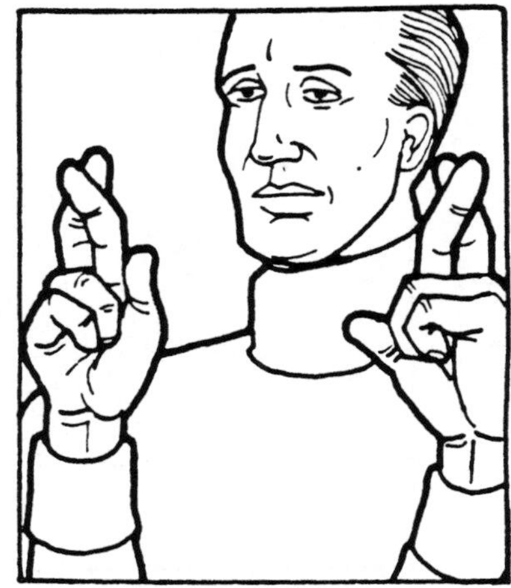

Index and middle fingers crossed, pointing up.

HORSE

Two fists held together, move up and down.

HOSPITAL

Rt. thumb makes cross on L. arm.

HOT

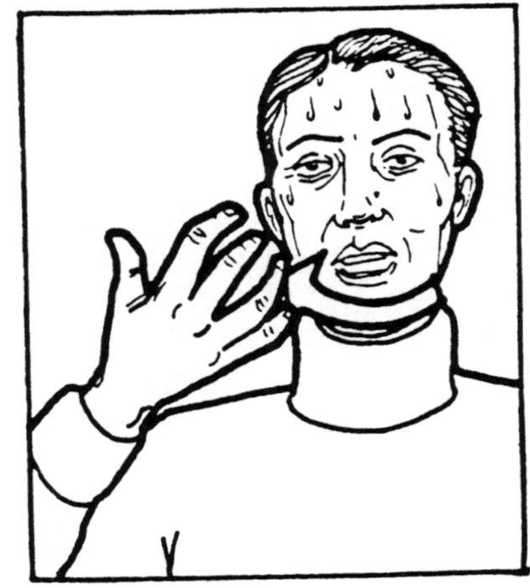

Rt. clawed hand draws across mouth from left to right.

HOTDOG

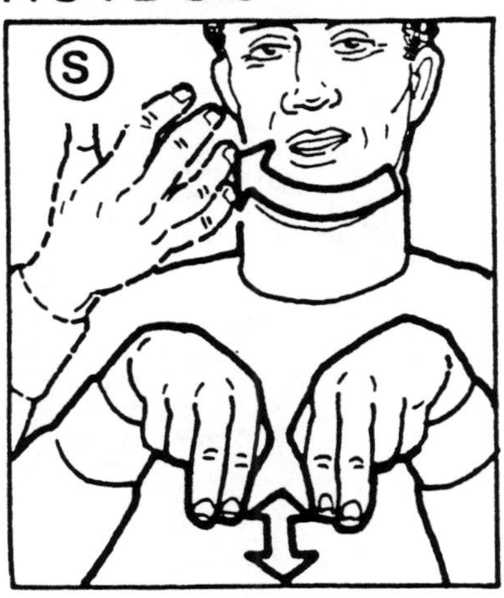

Sign "Hot", then "Dog".

HOTEL

Flat hands at sides of head, move forward/down, turning to palm down.

HOUR

Rt. index twists round in full circle over L. wrist.

HOUSE

Indicate shape of house, with two "N" hands.

HOVERCRAFT

Rt. flat hand "hovers" over L. flat hand whilst formation moves left to right.

HOW

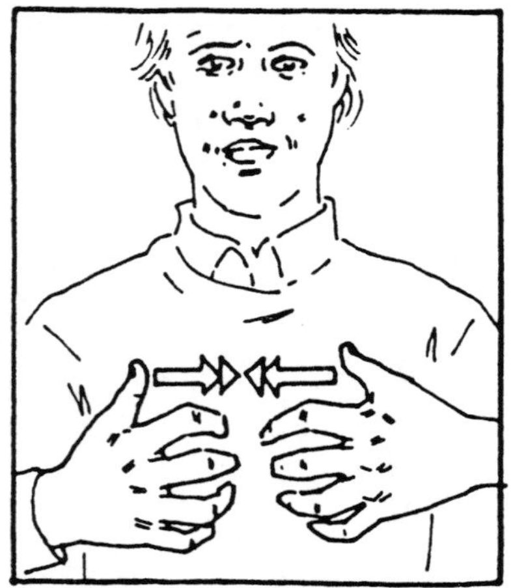

Knock 2nd knuckles of two clawed hands together twice.

HOW OLD

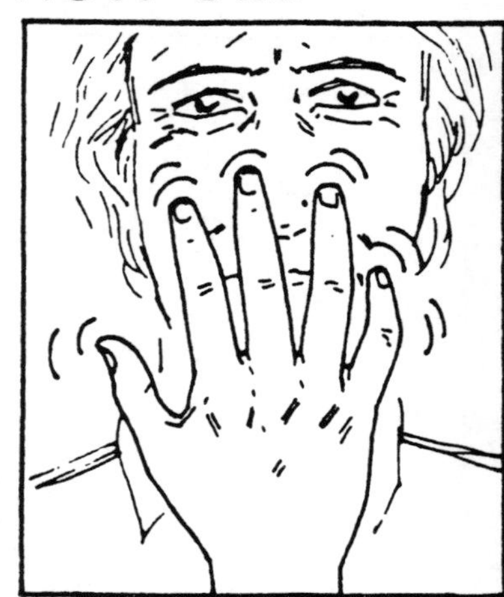

Fingers of open hand flutter in front of nose with questioning facial expression.

HUNDRED

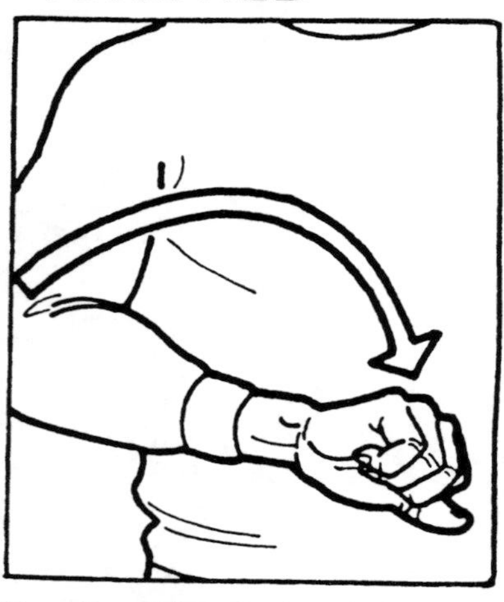

Rt. closed hand, thumb up sweeps left and twists to point down.

HUNGRY

Move hand round in circle on stomach.

HURRY

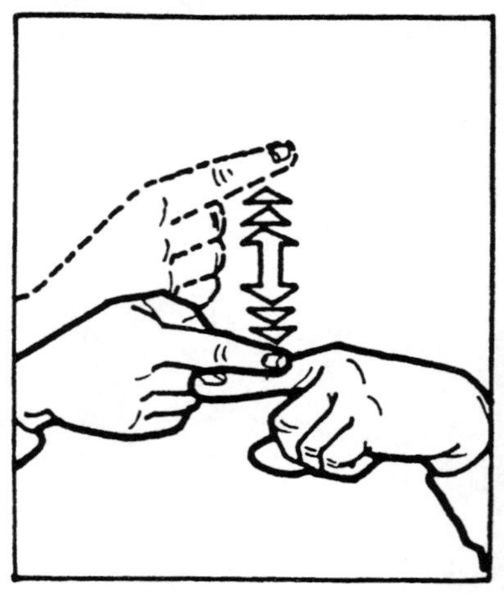

Rt. index taps on L. several times very quickly.

HURT

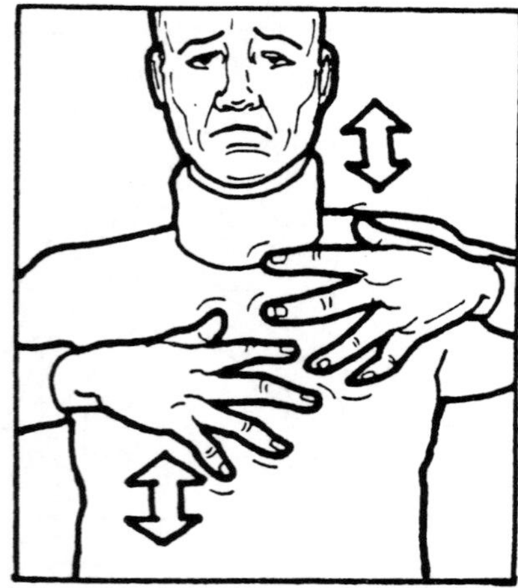

Two open hands shake up and down alternately.

HUSBAND

Sign "man" then index and thumb touch imaginary ring on finger.

I

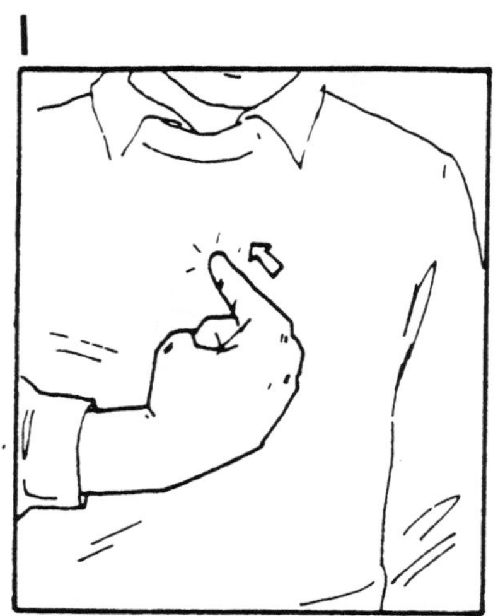

Point to self.

ICE

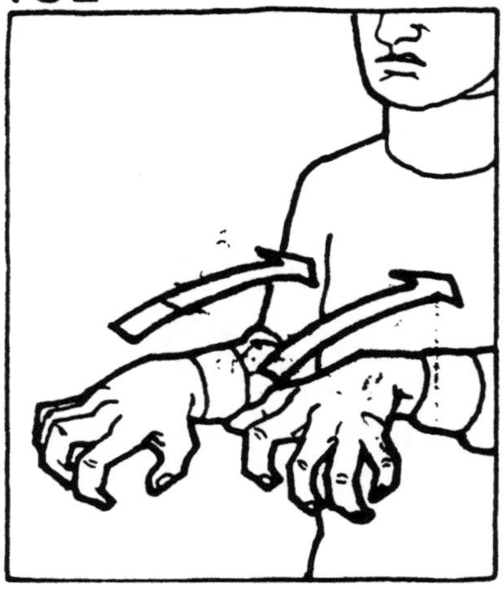

Clawed hands palms down held forward, pull back to body.

ICECREAM

Mime holding and licking an ice-cream.

IDEA

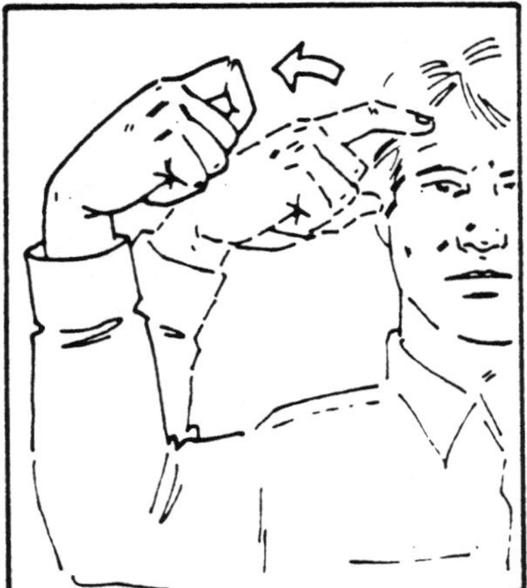

Index points to temple, then pulls out and bends.

IF

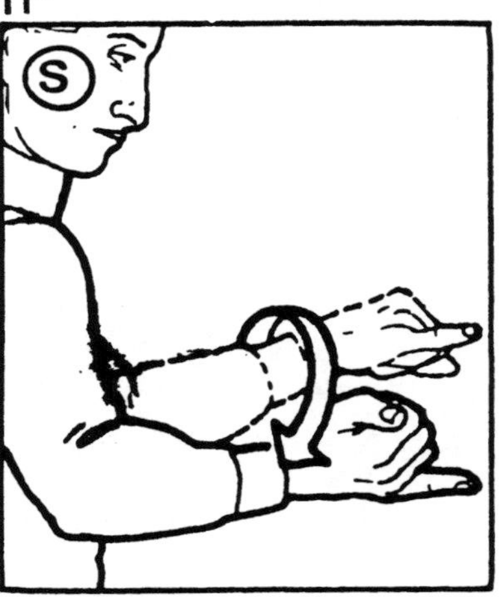

Extended little finger of Rt. hand, palm down, twist to palm left.

IGNORE

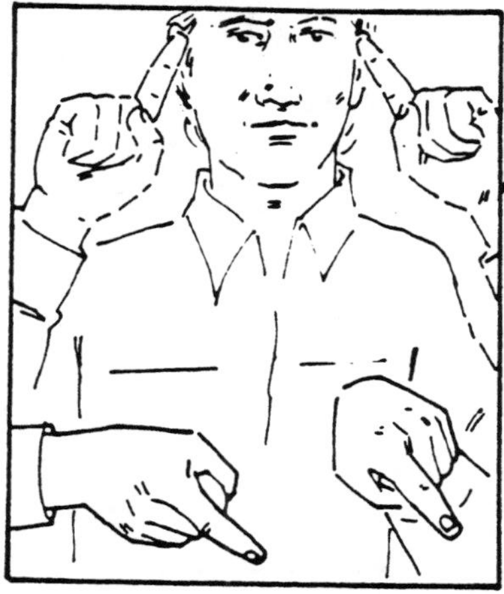

Indexes point to ears then flick sharply down and to one side, simultaneously.

ILL

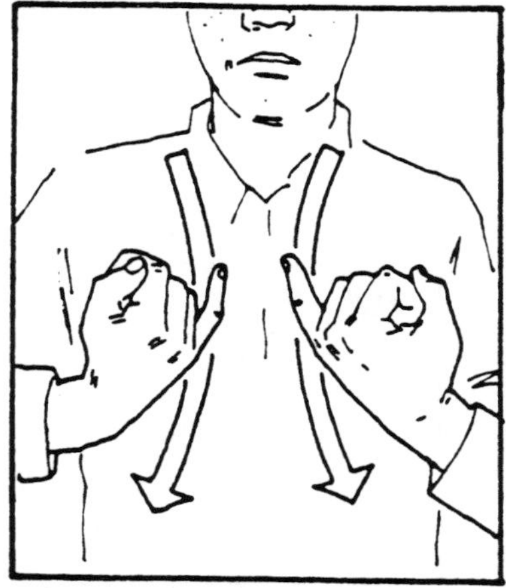

Move both hands simultaneously down chest with little fingers against body.

IMAGINE

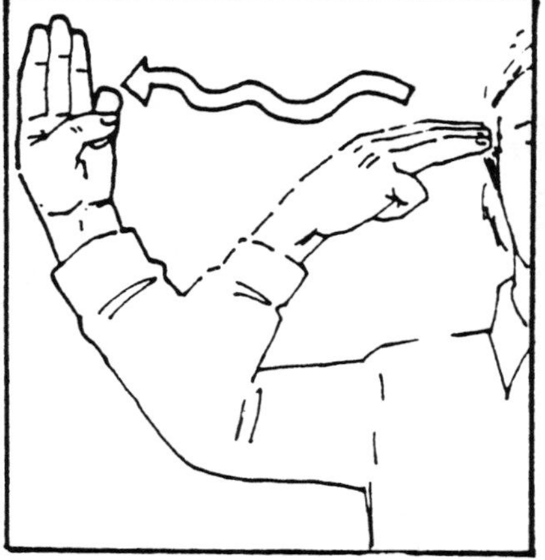

"M" hand touches temple, then moves out with slight waggling movement.

IMPORTANT

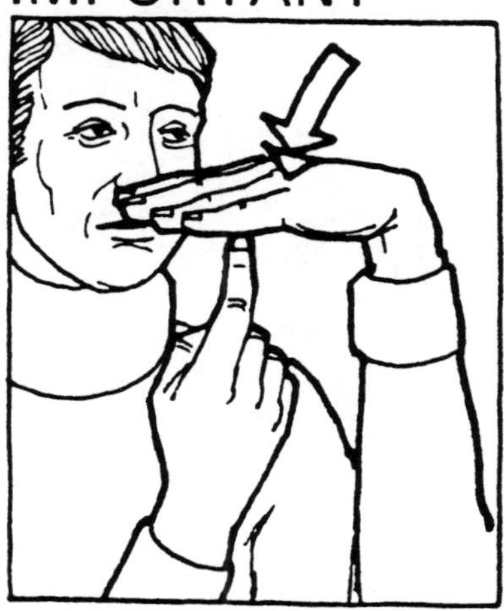

L. flat hand taps top of Rt. index twice, at head height.

IMPOSSIBLE

Indexes extended pointing up, palms forward simultaneously move down, twist over in loop, finish palms up.

IMPRESSED

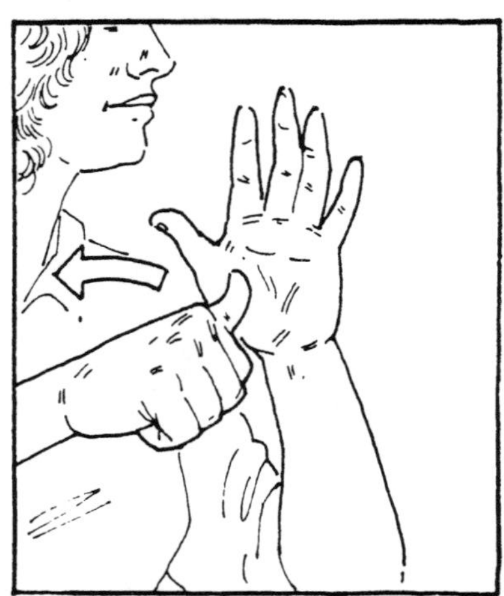

Tip of Rt. thumb contacts L. palm, and formation moves back towards body.

IMPROVE

Rt. "O" hand strokes up length of L. index and continues up a few inches.

IN

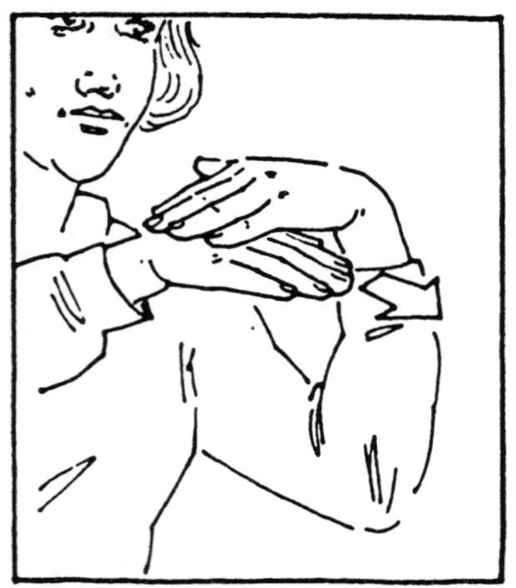

Rt. flat hand makes short movement forward/under L.

INCLUDE

Rt. flat hand pointing down, slightly bent, swings left to slot into L. hand.

INCREASE

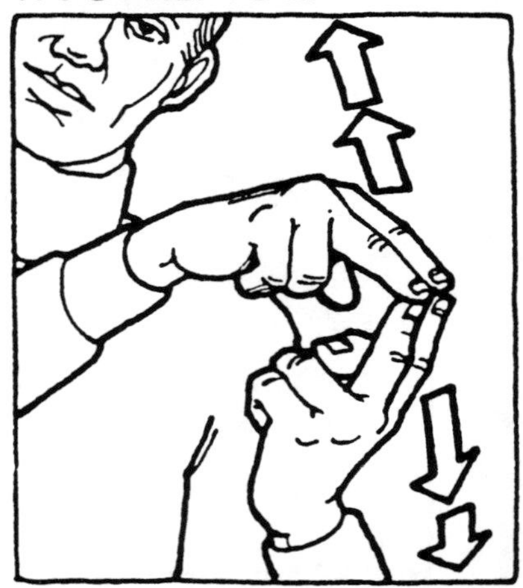

Two "N" hands, palms facing touching at tips, move apart in two movements.

INDIA

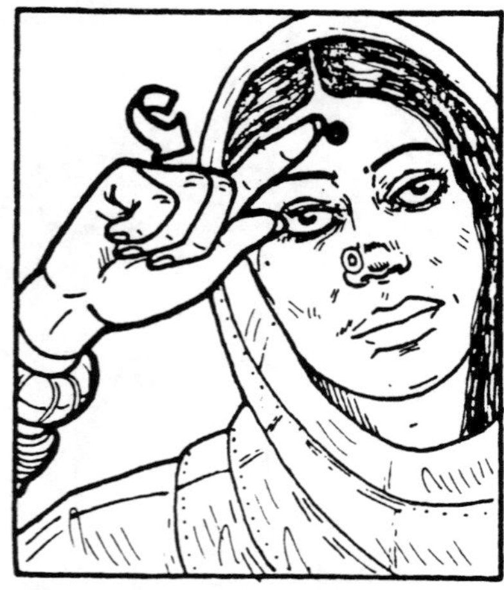

Rt. index points to middle of head and twists.

INDIAN

"V" hand held at back of head.

INDICATOR

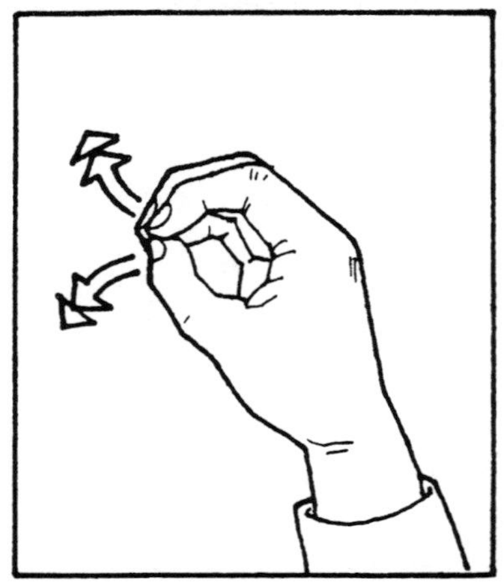

Fingers make small repeated opening movements from full "O" hand, to the right or left.

INFLUENCE

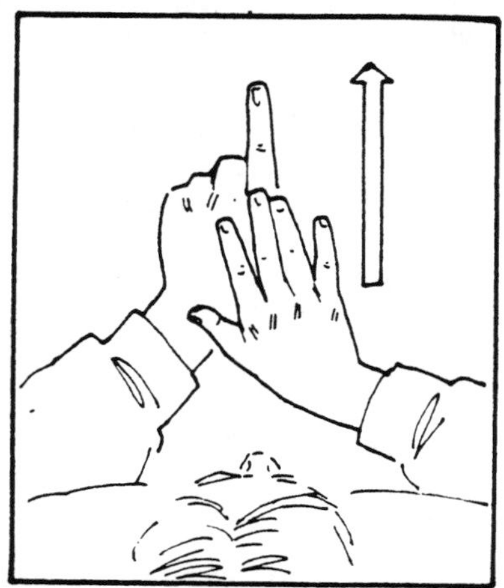

Rt. open hand moves slowly down the back of extended L. index.

INFORMATION

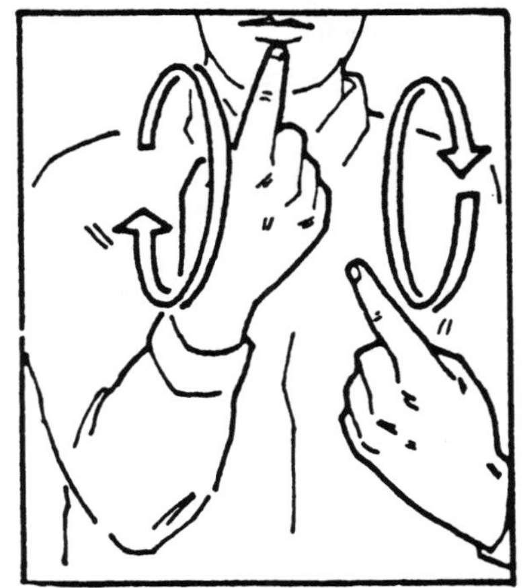

Indexes move in alternating circles from the mouth, forward or backward depending on context.

INJECT

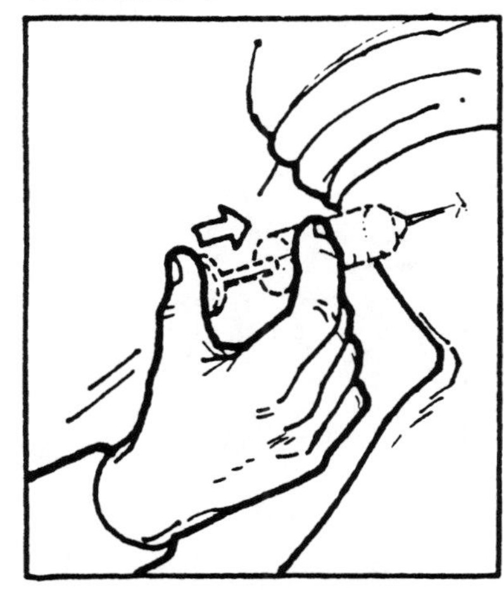

Mime injecting oneself with a syringe.

INSECT

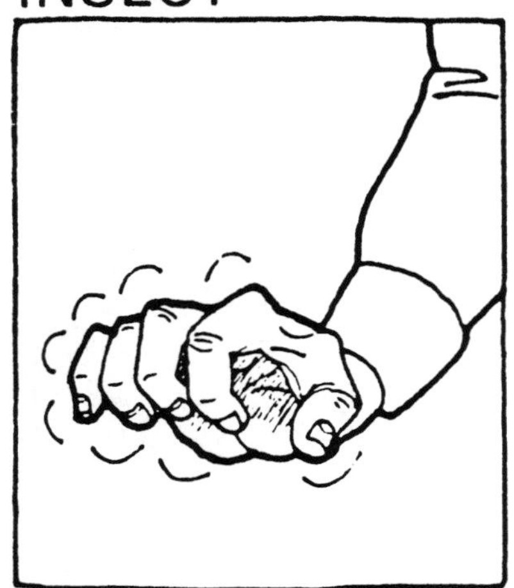

Clawed hand palm down, wriggle fingers to indicate insects legs.

INSIDE

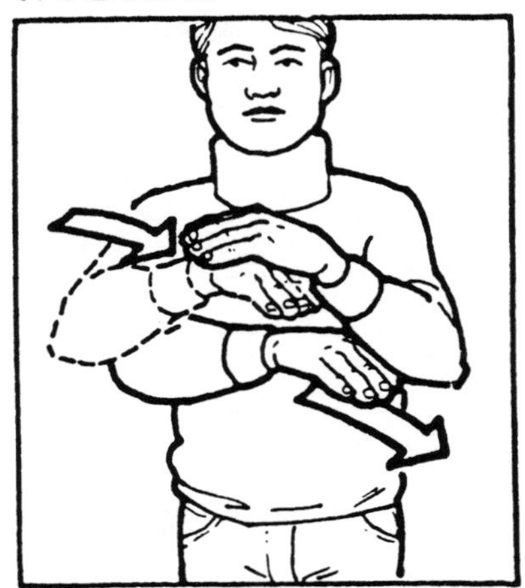

Rt. flat hand moves under L., then forward/down (two movements).

INSTEAD

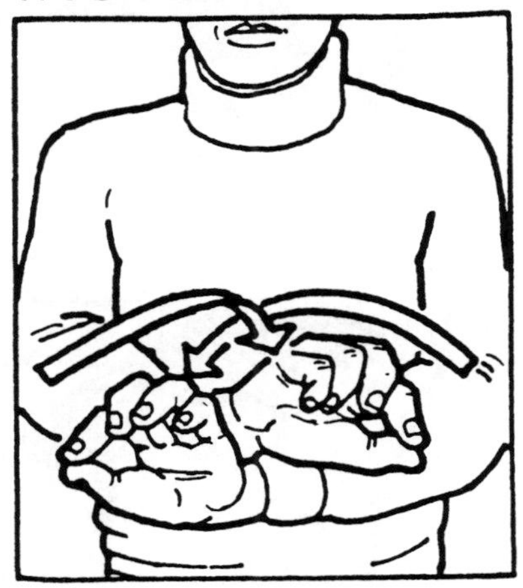

Two "O" hands, palms down move together in small arcs to cross over at wrists.

INSURE

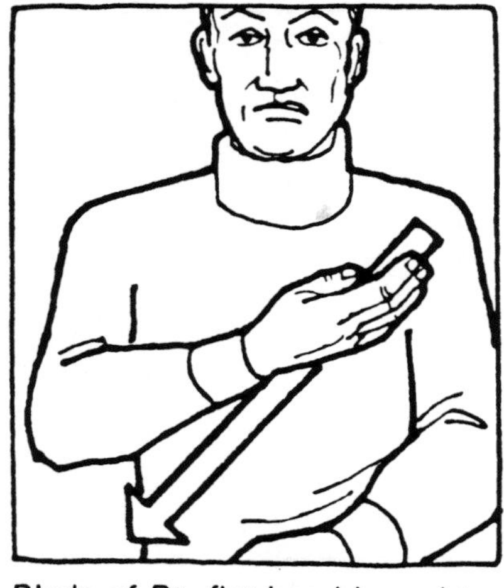

Blade of Rt. flat hand brought diagonally down body.

INTEGRATE

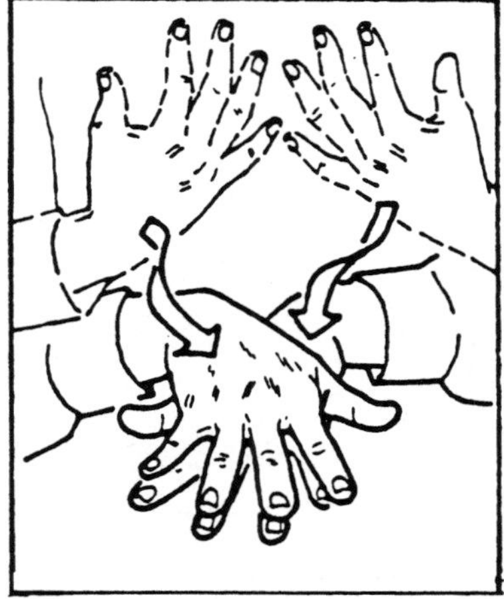

Open hands, palms back move forward whilst twisting to palm down Rt. on top of L. in one smooth movement.

INTERESTED

Hands slightly clawed rub up and down alternately on chest several times, quickly.

INTERPRET

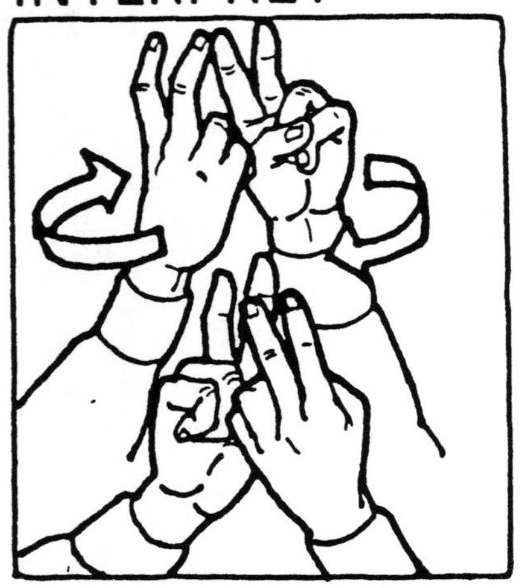

"V" hands, palms facing, Rt. in front of L., rotate to L. in front of Rt. and back again.

INTERRUPT

Fingers of Rt. hand prod sharply through L. hand fingers, forward or backward depending on context.

INTERVIEW

Indexes extended move alternately backwards and forwards to mouth.

INTO

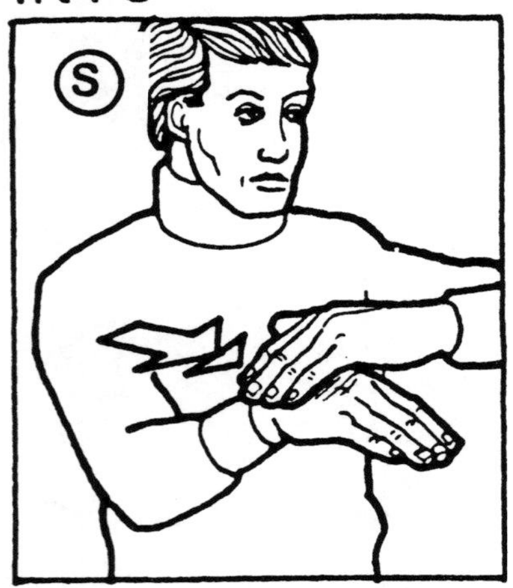

Rt. flat hand makes two short forward movements under L. hand.

INTRODUCE

Two flat hands palms up held together to right of body move left in small arc.

IRELAND

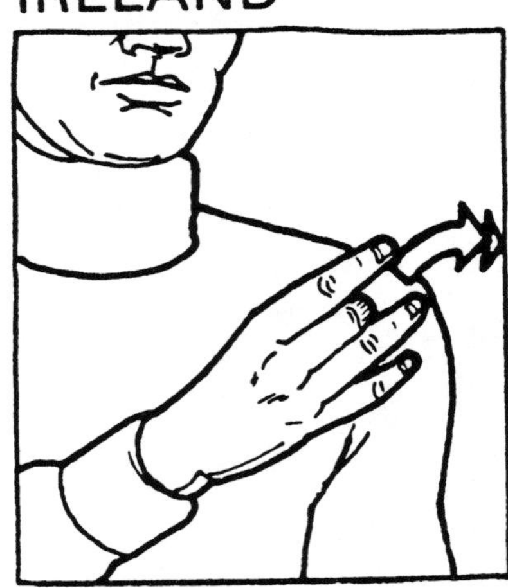

Middle finger flicks left shoulder twice.

IRON

Mime holding an iron and. ironing.

ISLAND

L. closed hand palm down indicates land, Rt. flat hand circles all round it with wavy motion indicating water.

ITALY

Rt. thumb tucked into bent index, hand moves in circular movement.

JAM

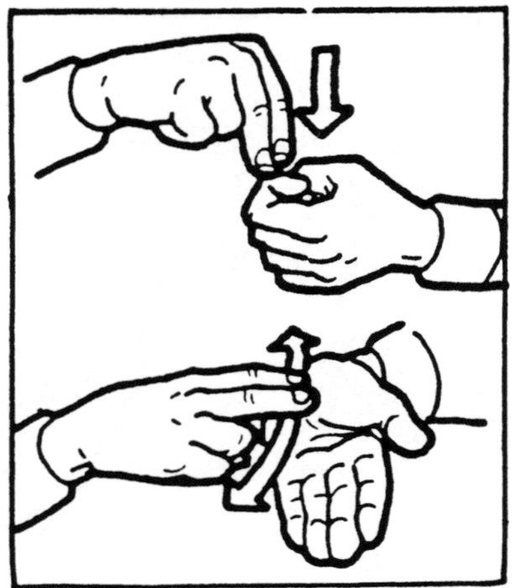

Rt. "N" hand dips into L. full "O" hand, then mimes spreading on L. palm.

JAPAN

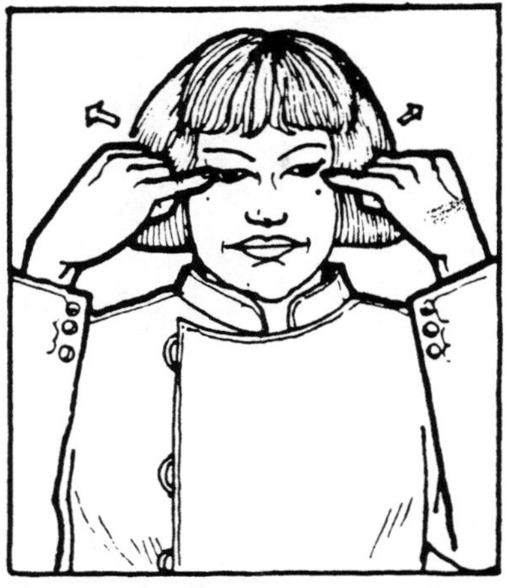

Little fingers move back slightly from corners of eyes.

JAR

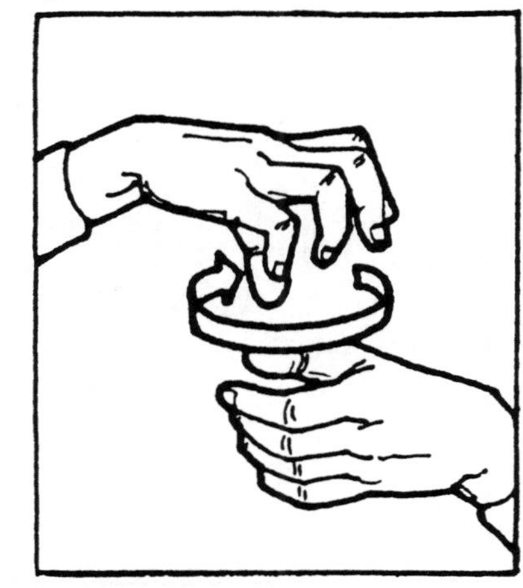

Mime unscrewing jar.

JEALOUS

Rt. clawed hand moves up across chest diagonally left to right, with emphasis.

JEANS

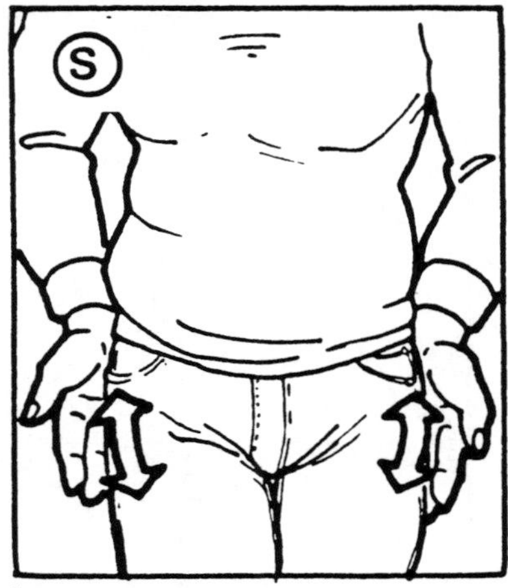

Hands rub up and down over back pockets.

JELLY

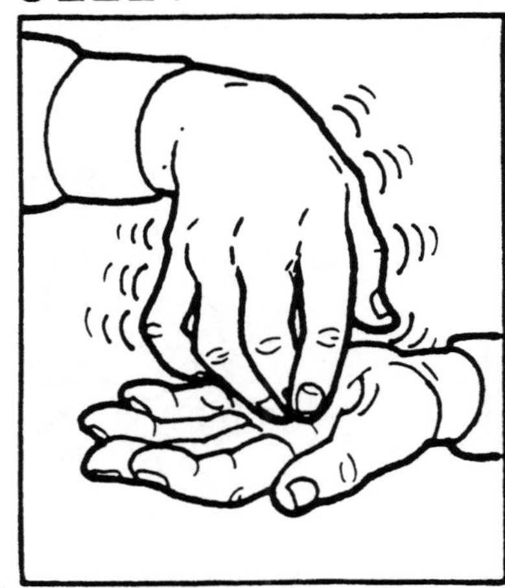

Shake Rt. loosely clawed hand on L. palm.

JESUS

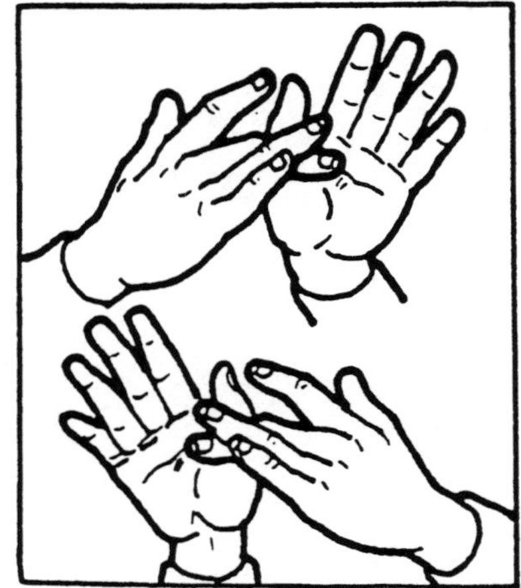

Rt. middle finger prods L. palm, then L. middle finger prods Rt.

JIGSAW

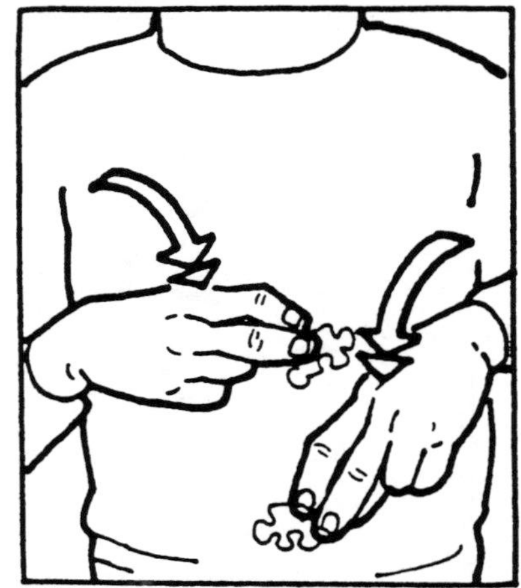

Index and middle fingers of both hands touch thumbs and mime fitting pieces down.

JOIN

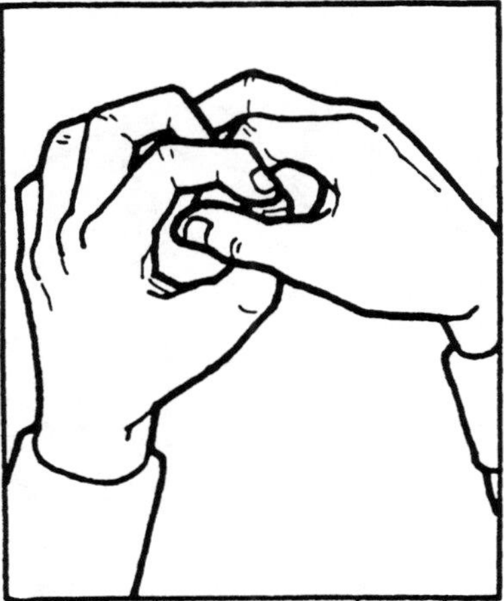

Two "O" hands interlink.

JOKE

Index, middle and thumb extended, move in small circles, thumbtip brushing nose.

JOURNEY

Two "V" hands, fingers bent, held together; Rt. hand moves forward.

JUDGE

Two full "C" hands move down sides of head to indicate wig.

JUG

Closed hand, thumb extended twists over as if pouring.

JUGGLE

Mime juggling.

JUMP

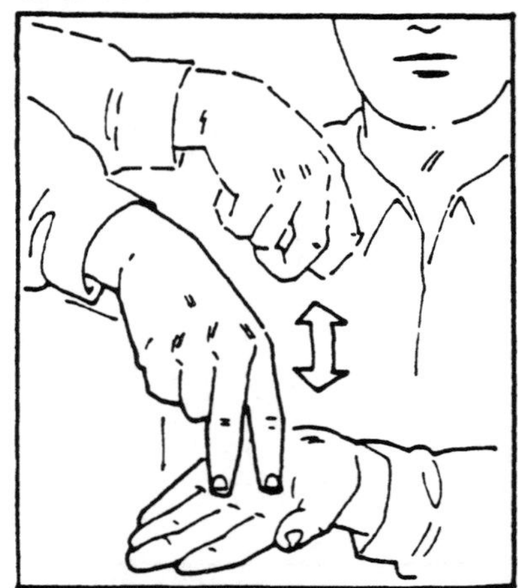

Rt. index and middle on palm of L. "jump" up, bend and land back on palm.

JUMPER

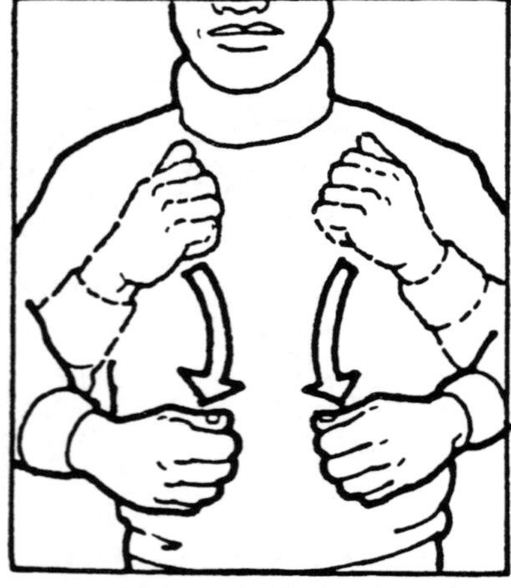

Closed hands contact upper chest, then lower chest.

JUST

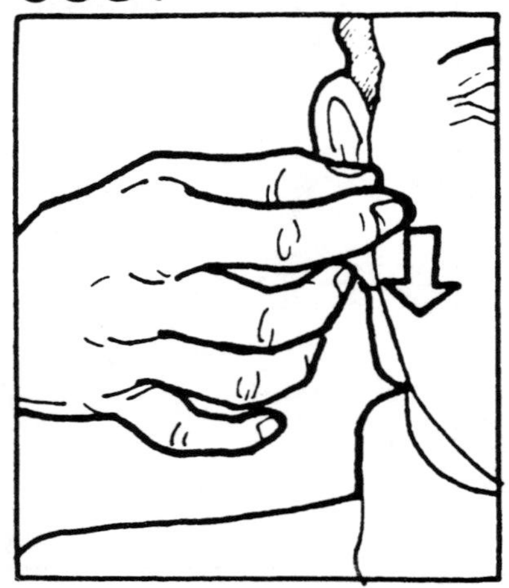

Rt. "O" hand, palm left makes short movement down cheek.

KEEN

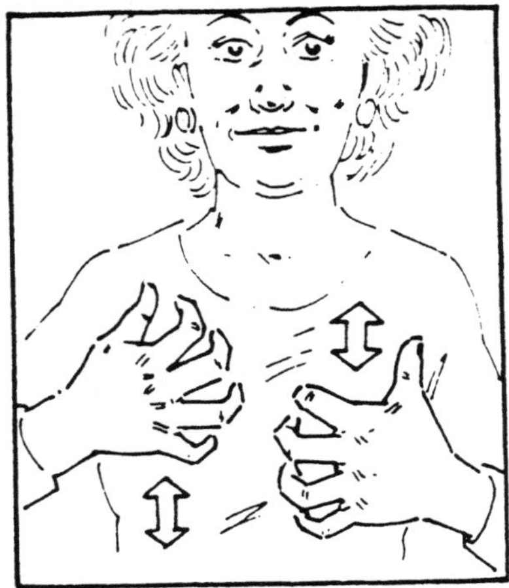

Fingers bent at second knuckles; hands rub up and down alternately, on chest, in short quick movements.

KEEP

Tap Rt. cupped hand on L. cupped hand twice.

KETCHUP

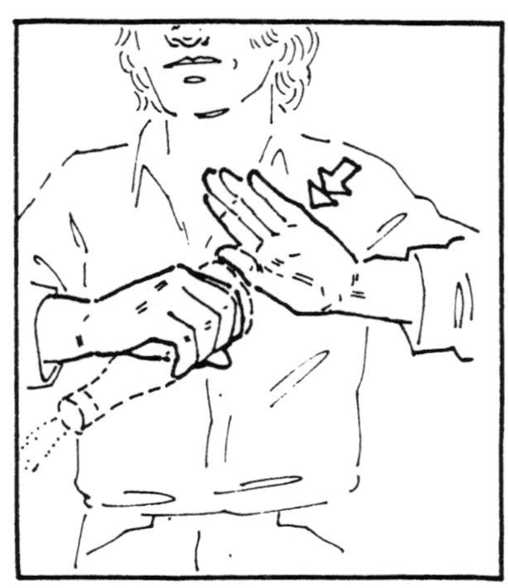

Rt. flat hand hits L. full "C" hand in action of using a ketchup bottle.

KETTLE

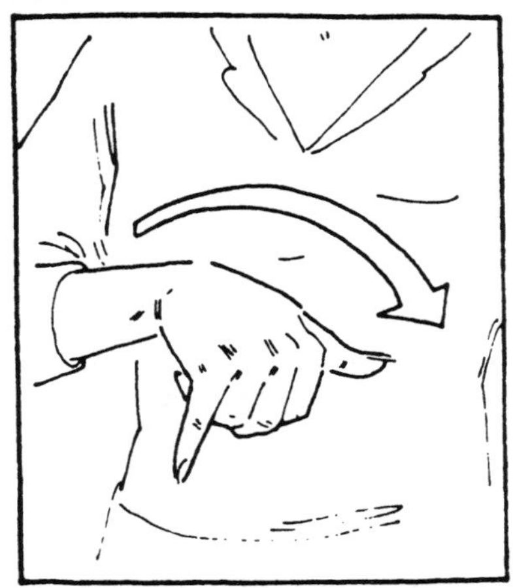

Closed hand with little finger and thumb extended moves from right to left in small arc.

KEY

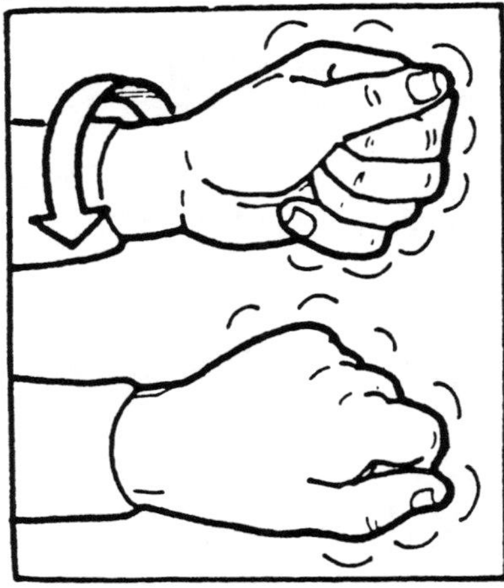

Mime turning key and waggle slightly.

KICK

Indexes pointing down, Rt. pulls slightly back as L. kicks forward.

KILL

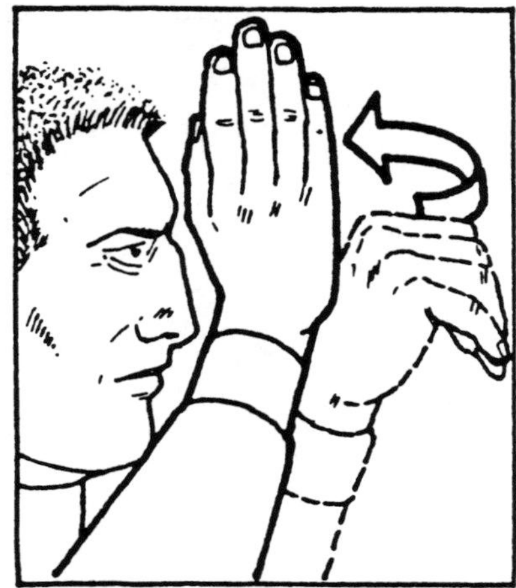

Rt. cupped hand pointing forward twists and straightens sharply to point up in front of forehead.

KIND (good)

Closed hand, thumb up over heart moves forward with slight twist.

KING

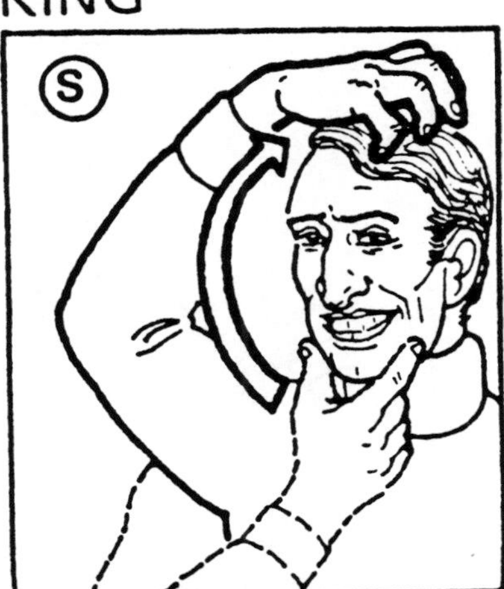

. Index and thumb stroke down chin, then clawed hand on head.

KISS

Rt. "N" hand touches lips, then tips of L. "N" hand and reverse L. on to Rt.

KITCHEN

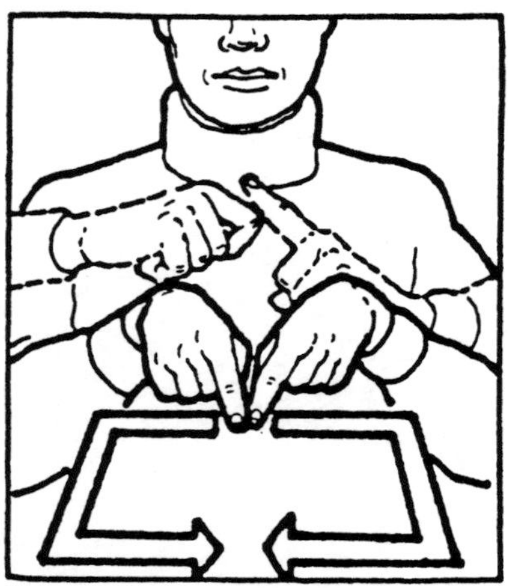

Fingerspell "K" then, indexes pointing down, outline shape of room.

KITE

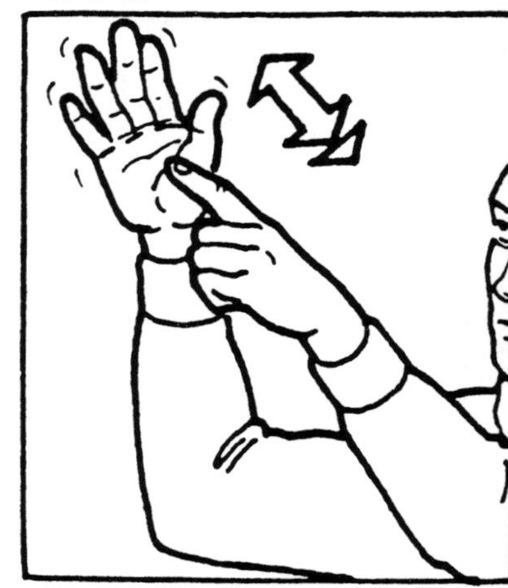

Tip of L. index in palm of Rt. hand at head height; formation makes small up/down movements.

KNEEL

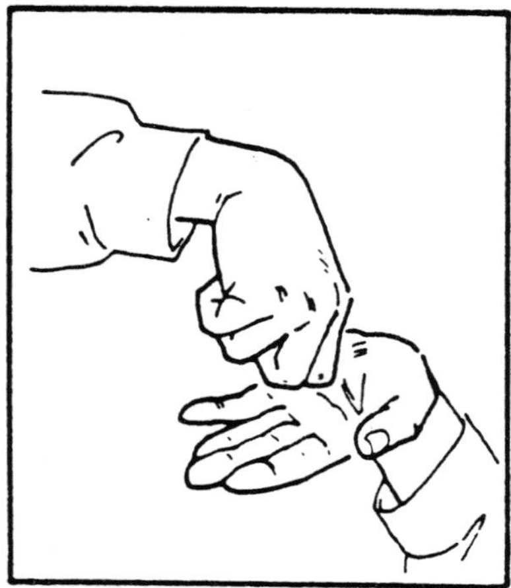

Rt. index and middle finger, bent at 2nd knuckles placed on L. palm.

KNIFE

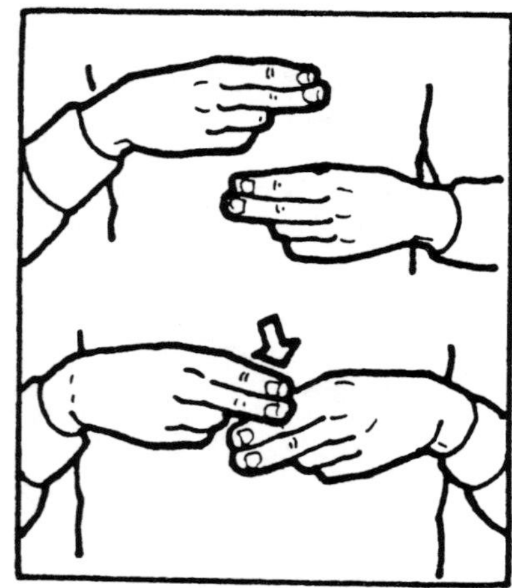

Two "N" hands; Rt. moves down to touch L. at right angle.

KNIGHT

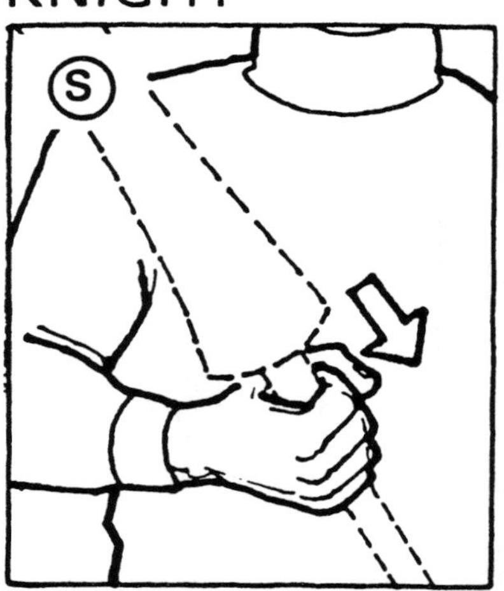

Mime holding a lance and move towards side of body.

KNIT

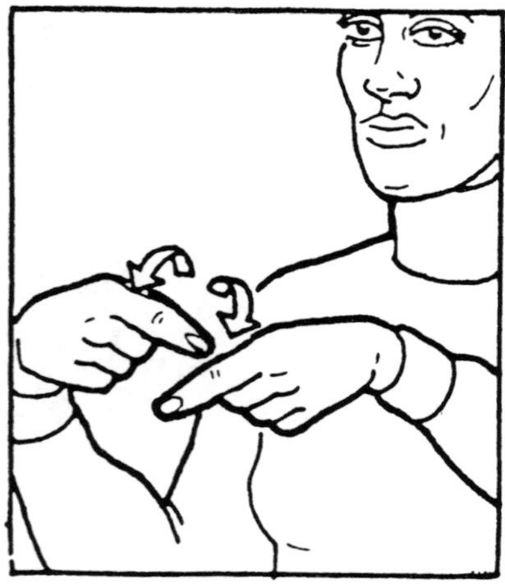

Mime knitting with index fingers.

KNOCK

Mime knocking on door.

KNOT

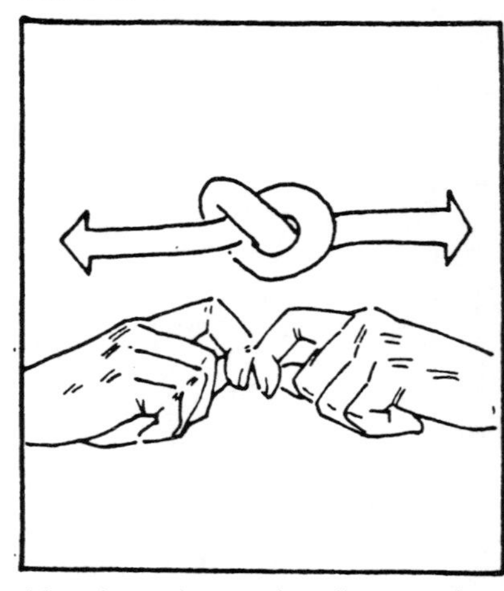

Hands twist and pull apart in action of tying a knot.

KNOW

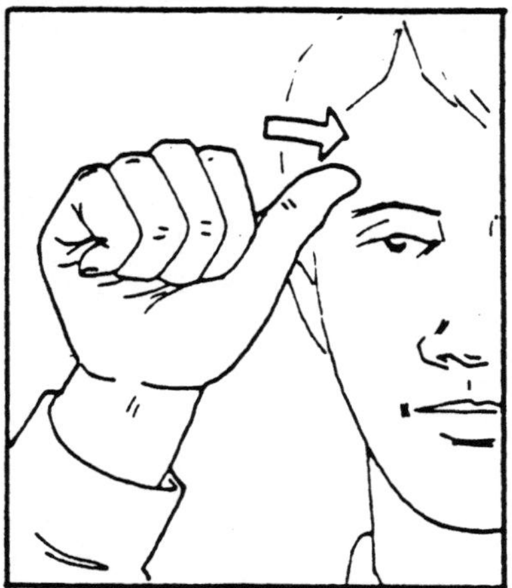

Tip of extended thumb touches side of forehead.

DON'T KNOW

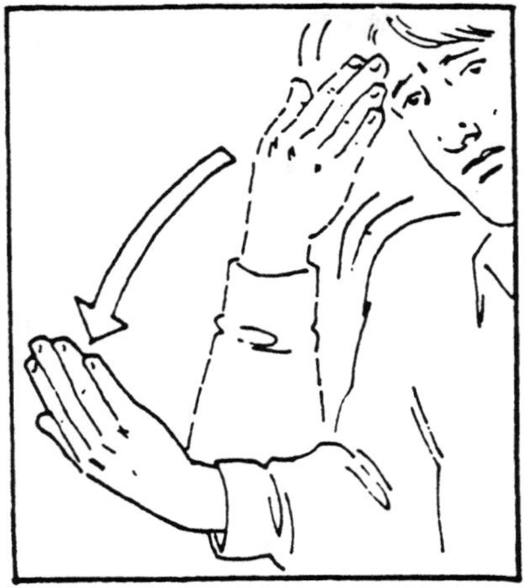

Tips of flat hand touch forehead, then move forward/down, with slight shrug of shoulders and shake of head.

LADDER

Mime climbing a ladder.

LAKE

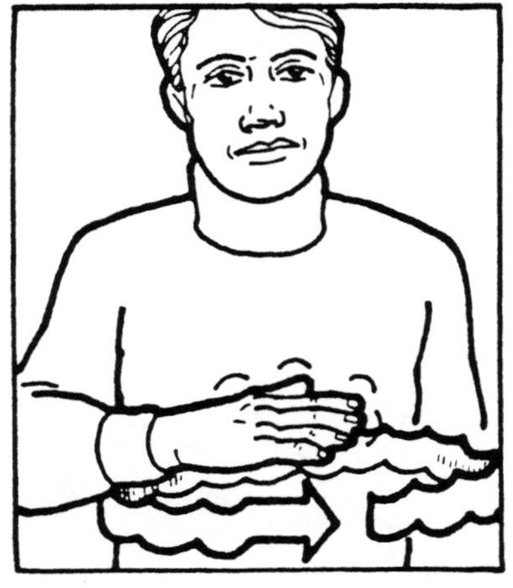

Palm down flat hand makes large circular rippling movement in front of body.

LAMP

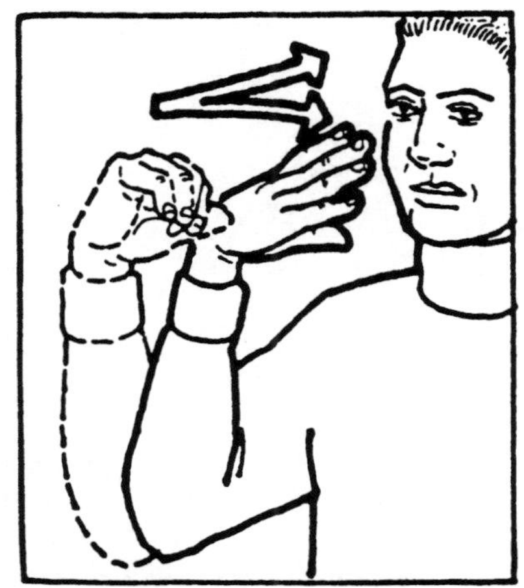

Full "O" hand moves in as it springs open near side of face.

LAND

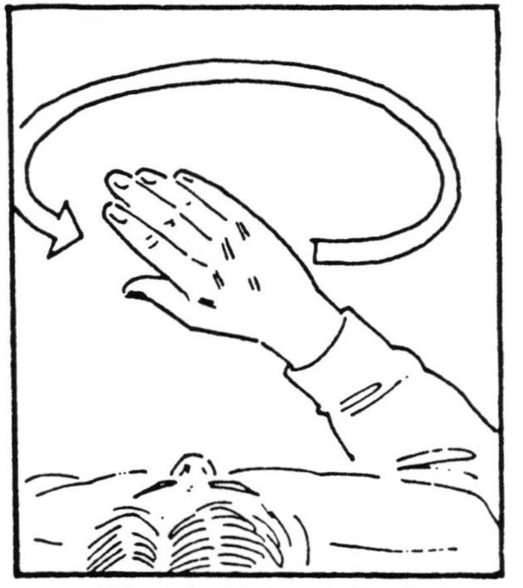

Palm down flat hand moves in horizontal circular movement.

LANGUAGE

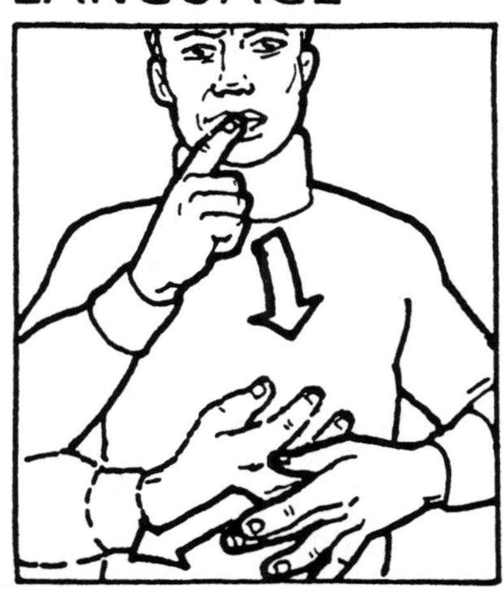

Rt. index points to mouth, moves down to open hand and brushes backs of fingers along palm of L. open hand.

LAST

Tip of Rt. little finger strikes tip of L. little finger in sharp upwards movement.

LATE

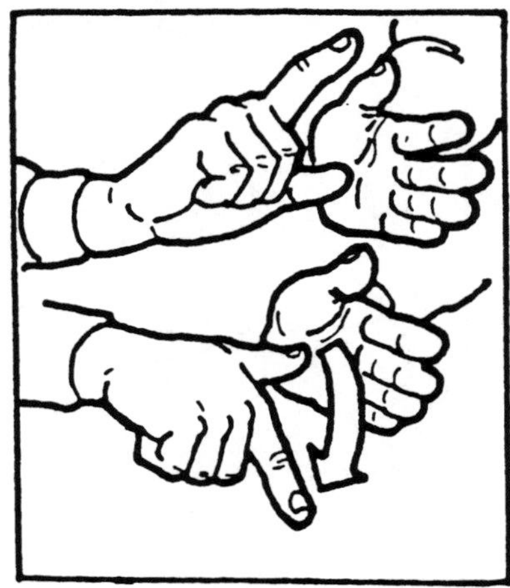

Rt. thumb and index extended. Thumb maintains contact with L. palm as index twists sharply down.

LATER

Rt. thumb and index extended, thumb in L. palm. Index twists forward then moves forward/ down away from L.

LAUGH

Index and thumb extended, and curved make small vertical circles below chin.

LAW

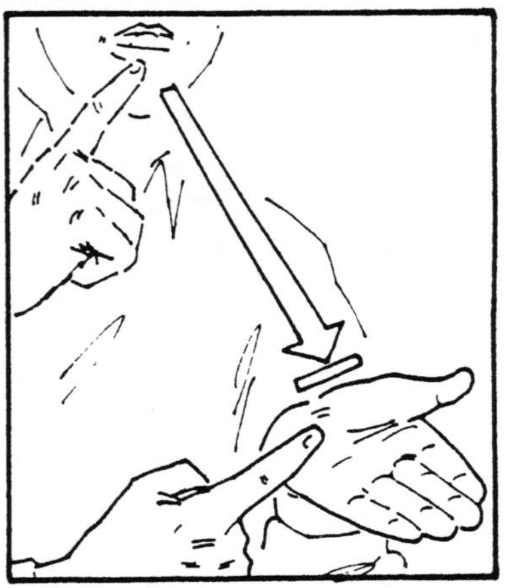

Index moves from mouth to contact L. palm with emphasis.

LAZY

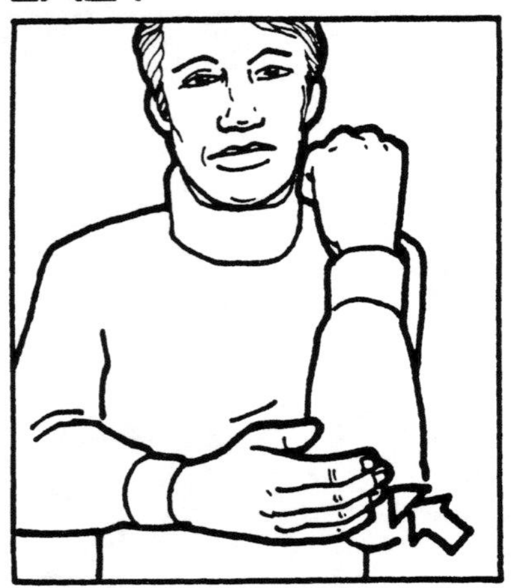

Slightly cupped Rt. hand taps left elbow twice.

LEAD

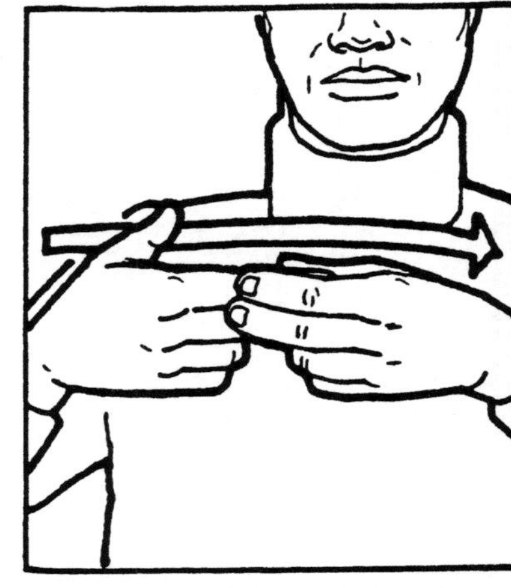

L. index, middle and thumb grasp fingers of Rt. "N" hand and pull it right to left.

LEAF

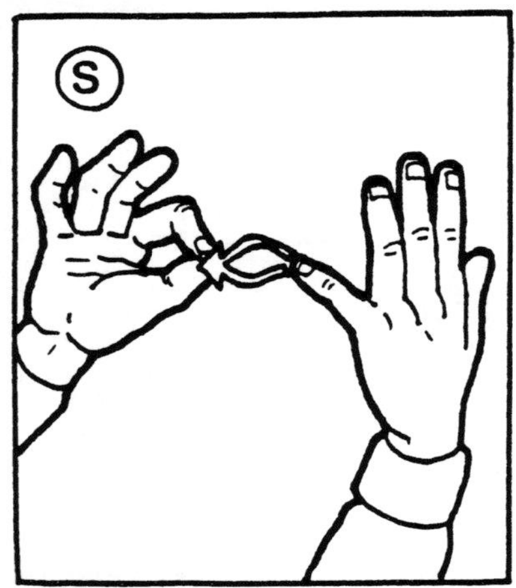

Rt. index and thumb touch L. little fingertip then move away opening then closing in shape of leaf.

LEARN

Bunched hands move up alternately to temples as if feeding the brain.

LEATHER

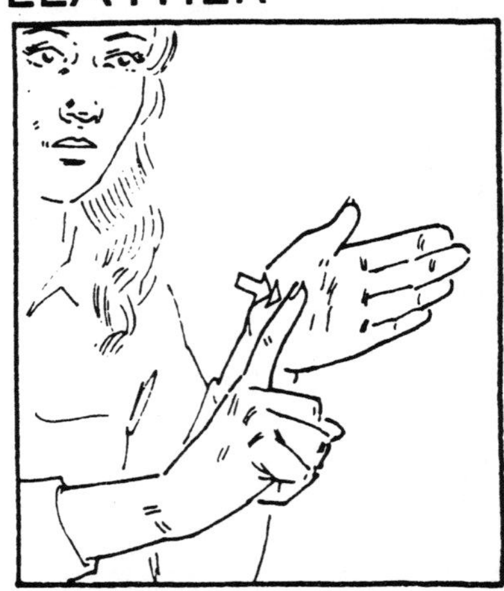

Form "L" and rub index on L. palm.

LEAVE

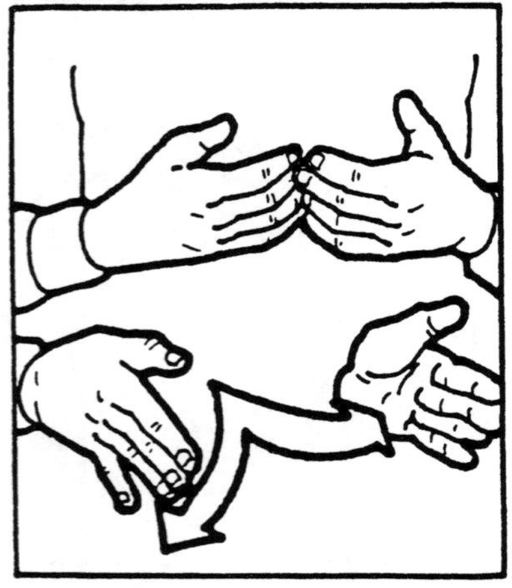

Tips of palm back hands touch, then hands spring to point forward.

LECTURE

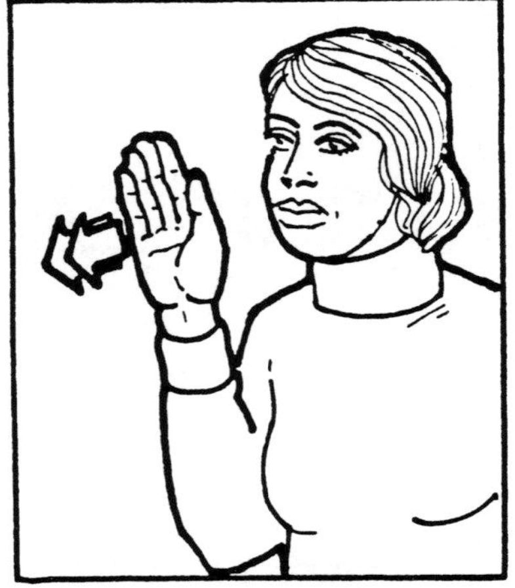

Rt. flat hand pointing up at side of head moves forward twice.

LEFT (over)

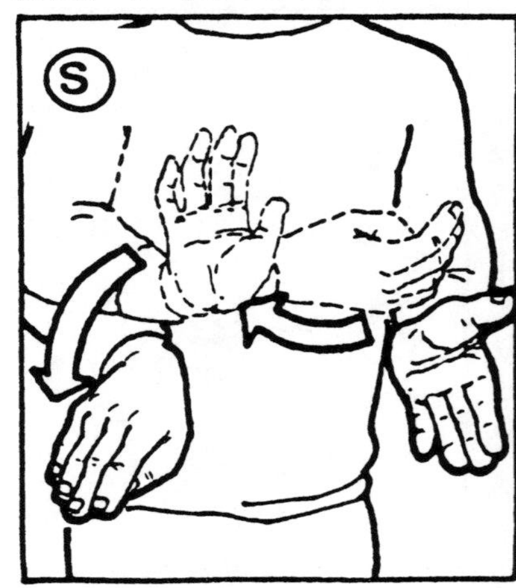

Back of Rt. hand fingertips brush along L. palm finishing palm forward, then arc over and down.

LEISURE

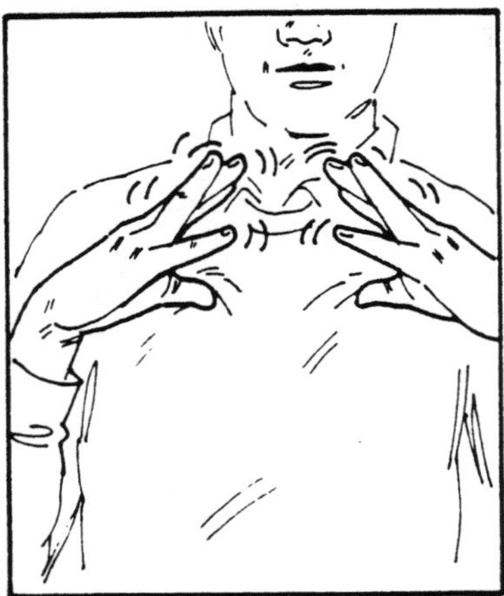

Thumb tips contact chest, as fingers waggle.

LEMON

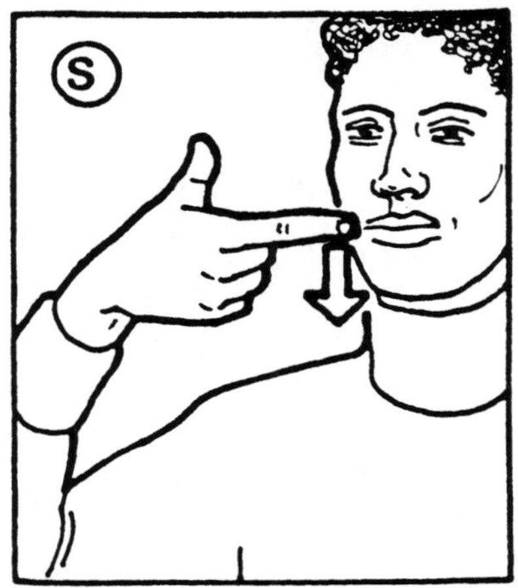

Index and thumb extended, index contacting corner of mouth; move down a few inches.

LEMONADE

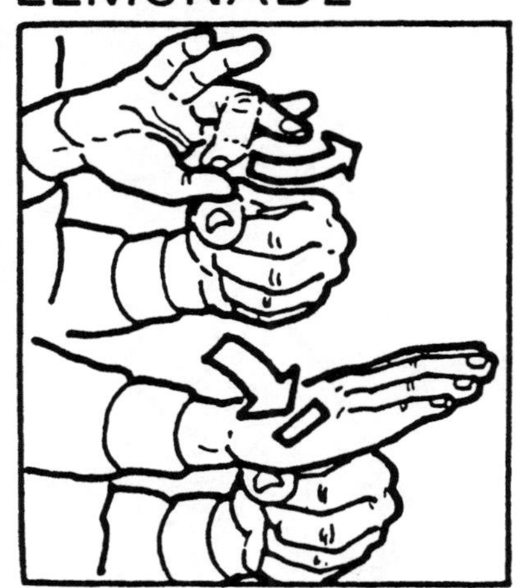

Flick top of L. full "O" hand with Rt. middle finger, then bang Rt. hand on top of L.

LEND

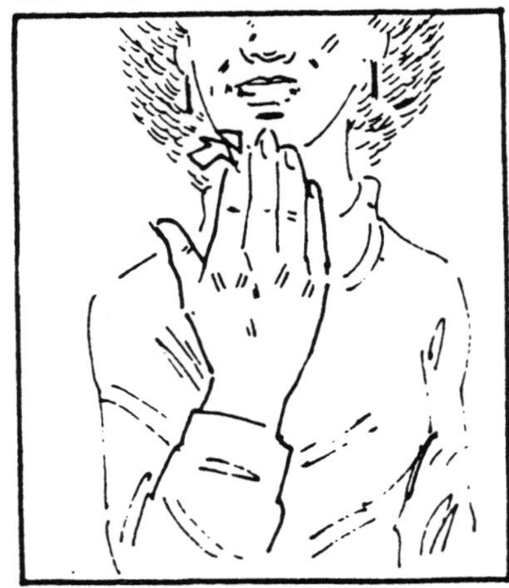

Flat hand taps chin twice.

LEOPARD

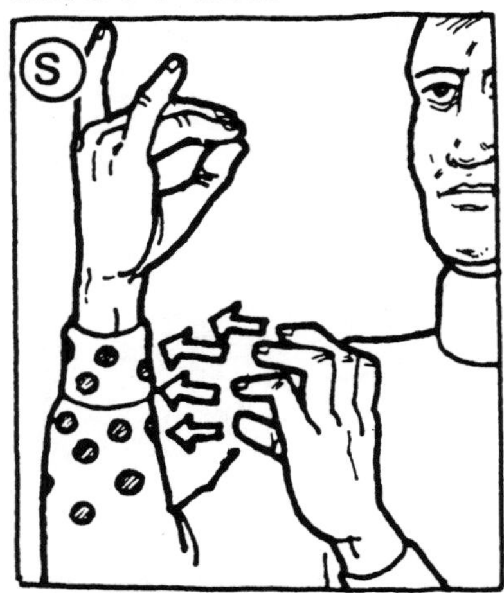

Rt. hand forms the sign for "animal" then tips of L. clawed hand tap right arm to indicate spots.

LESS

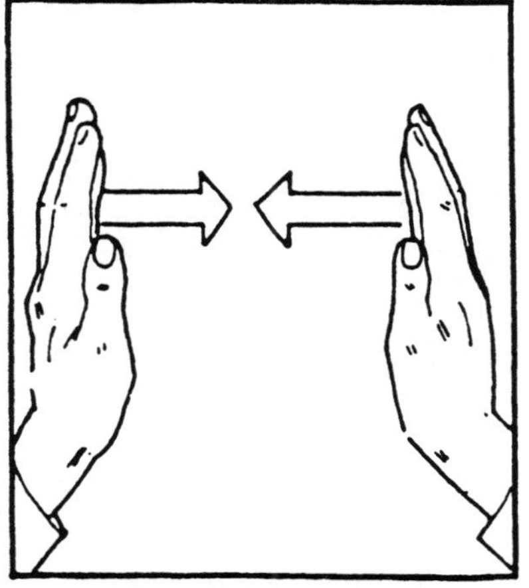

Flat hands held apart move in towards each other.

LESSON

Rt. index and thumb extended, palm forward moves down in waggling movement in front of face.

LET (allow)

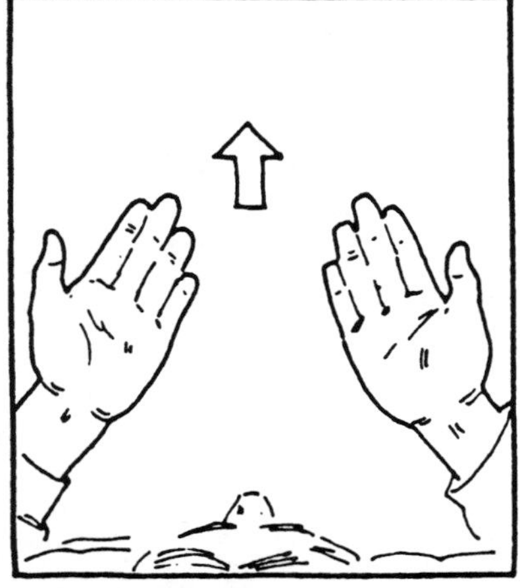

Palm up flat hands move towards person concerned. For "let me", hands move back to self.

LETTER (abc)

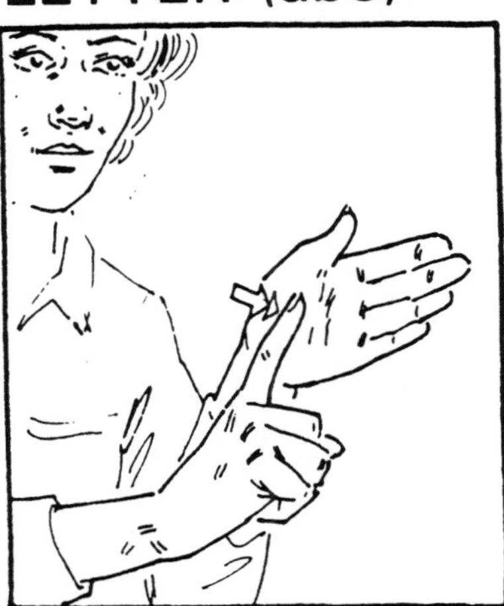

Form fingerspelt "L" and tap twice.

LETTER (post)

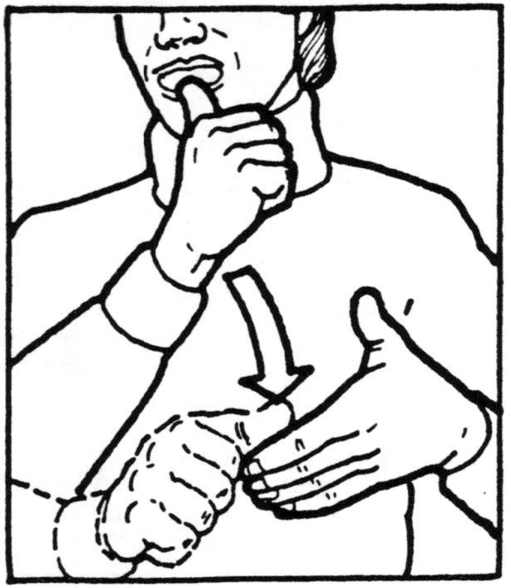

Rt. thumb touches mouth, then touches index tip of L. flat hand like sticking on a stamp.

LETTUCE

Heels of slightly cupped hands tap together twice.

LIBRARY

Palm left Rt. flat hand moves from left to right in waggling movement to indicate row of books.

LID

Mime putting lid on saucepan.

LIE (down)

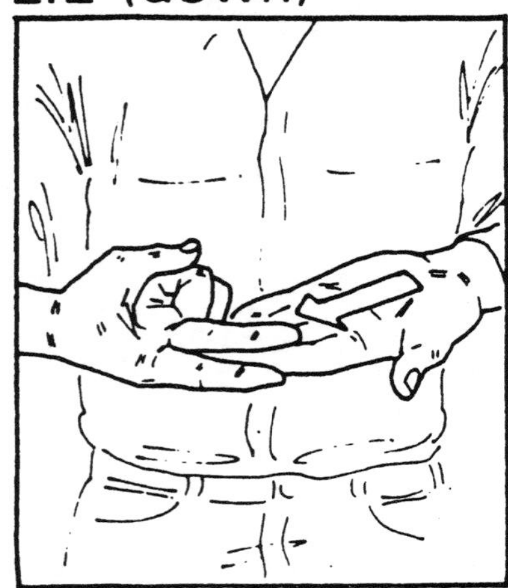

Palm up Rt. "V" hand makes small movement along L. palm.

LIE (untrue)

Rt. index pointing left pulls sharply across chin from left to right.

LIFEBOAT

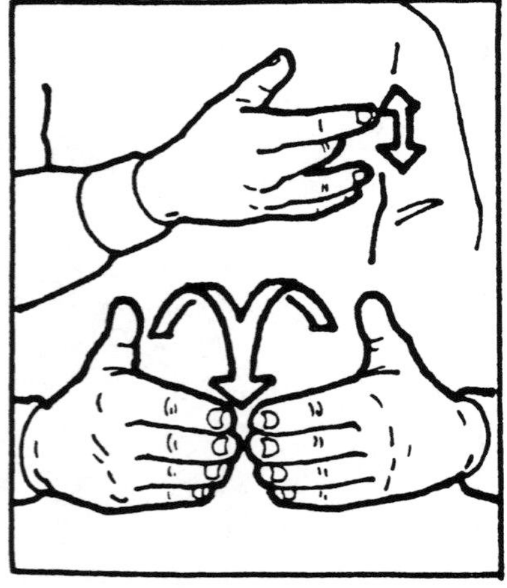

Tip of Rt. middle finger rubs up and down over heart, then both hands sign "boat".

LIFT

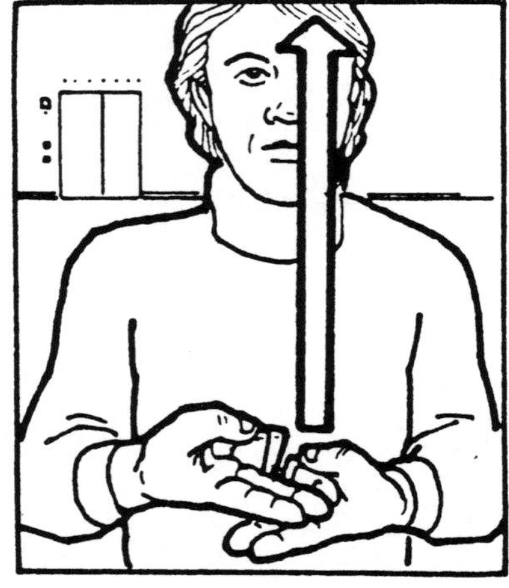

Two "N" hands, Rt. on L.; formation moves up.

LIFT (ride)

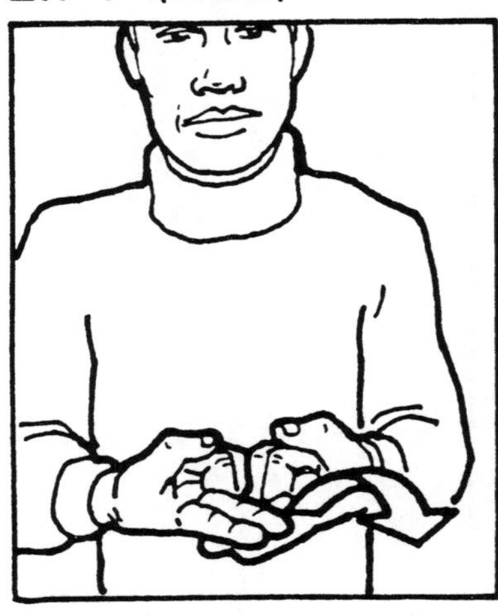

Two "N" hands, Rt. on top of L.; formation moves in small arc forward.

LIFT (raise)

Two palm up flat hands move up with slight stress.

LIGHT (lamp)

Full "O" hand moves in slightly as it springs open at head height.

LIGHT (dark)

Palm back flat hands, start crossed, then swing apart to point up.

LIGHT (weight)

Palm up flat hands make repeated, light upward movement.

LIGHTNING

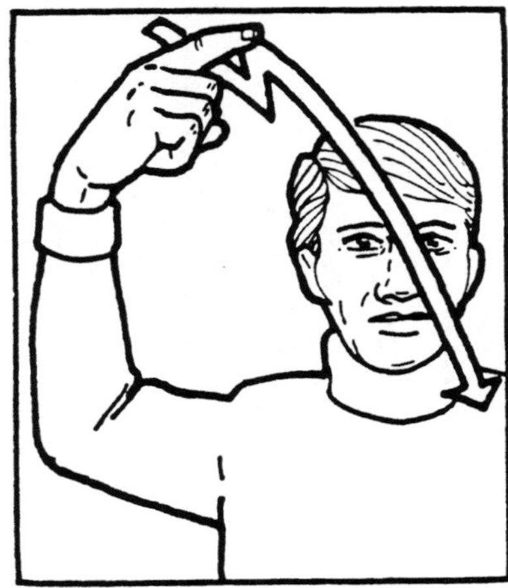

Index finger moves down sharply in zig-zag.

LIKE (similar)

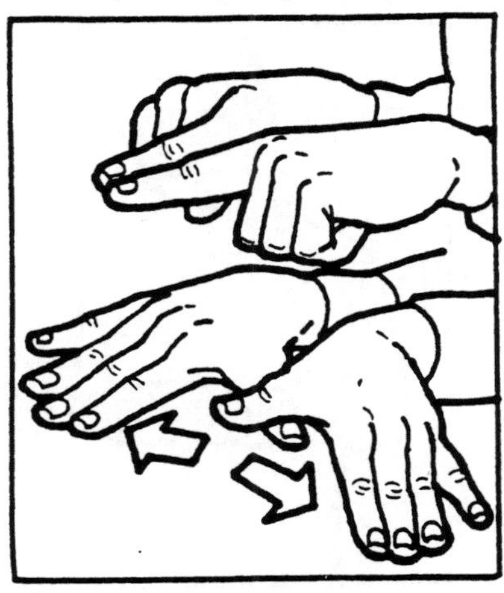

Indexes touch, pointing forward, then hands spring open and slightly apart.

LIKE (prefer)

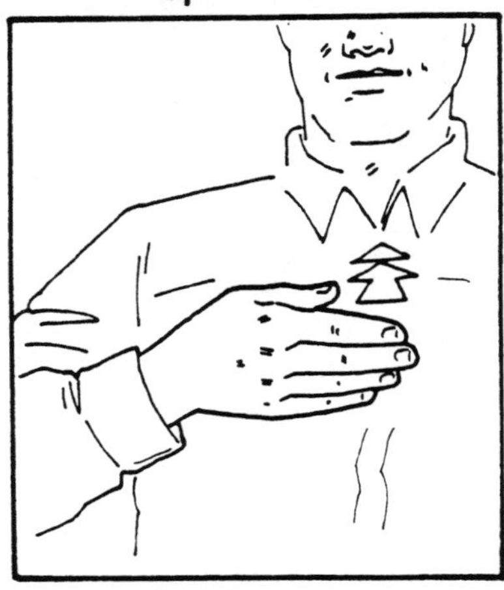

Flat hand taps chest twice.

DON'T LIKE

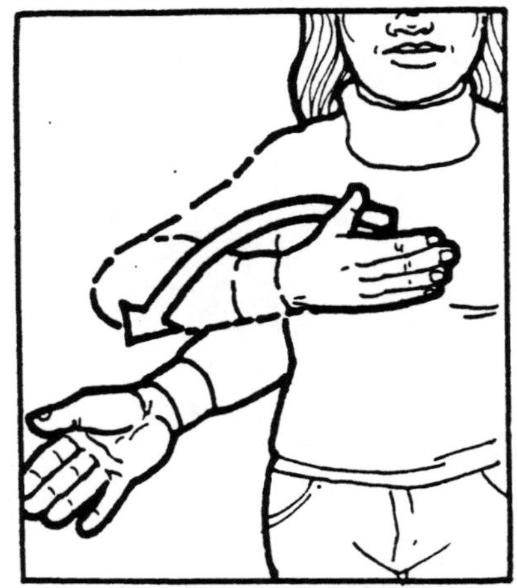

Flat hand on chest brushes up slightly and twists over moving sharply away from body.

LINE (people)

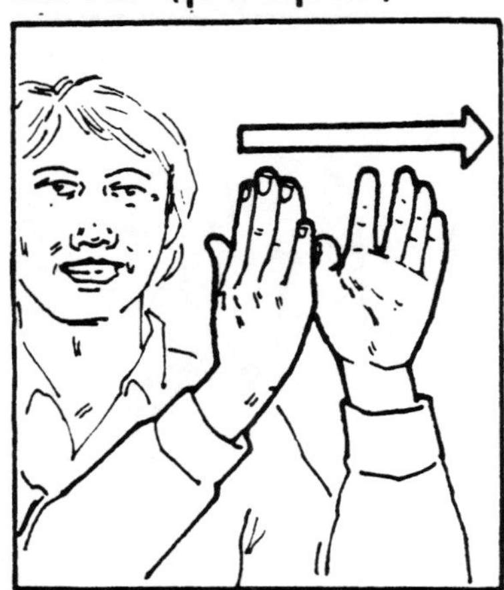

Hands move forward, one in front of the other.

LION

Clawed hands on head move out slightly and down to indicate mane, then make small alternate clawing movements.

LIST

Rt. thumb extended, pointing left moves down in waggling movement off L. flat hand.

LISTEN

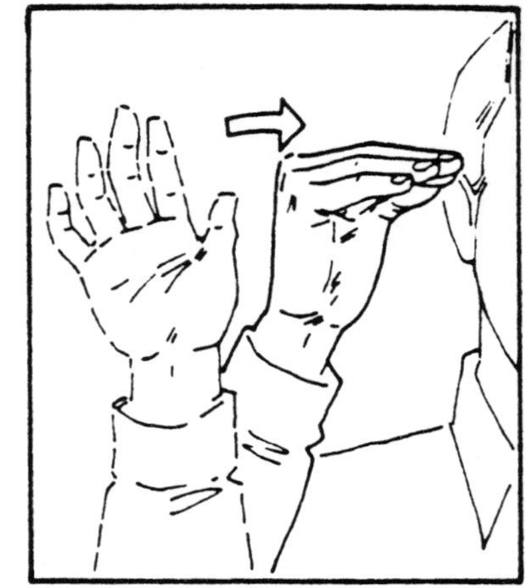

Hand closes sharply to bunched hand, at ear.

LITTLE

Flat hand palm down makes small downward movement twice.

LITTLE (bit)

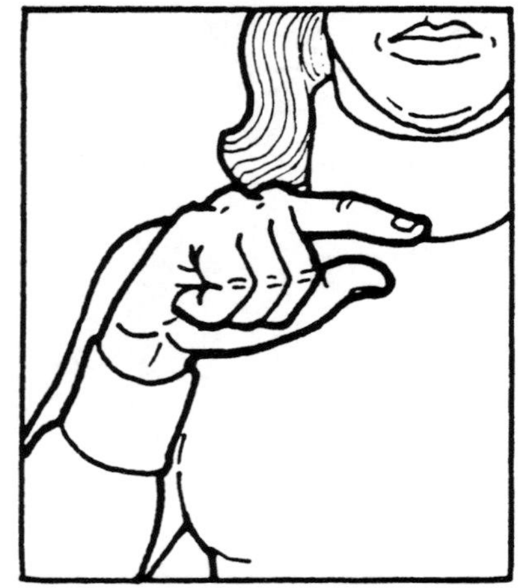

Indicate something little with index and thumb.

LIVE

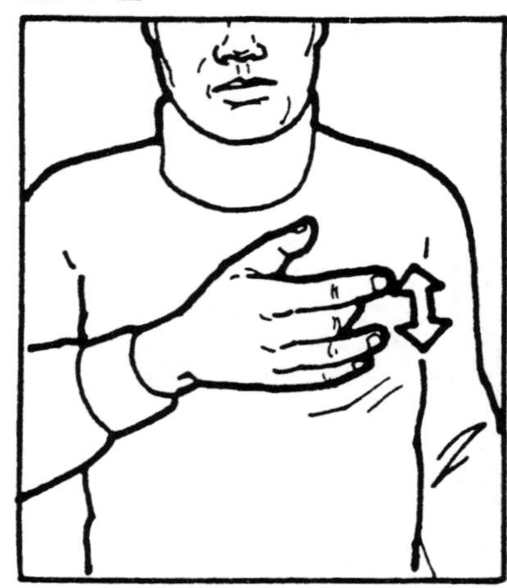

Tip of middle finger rubs up and down over heart with small quick movement.

LOCK

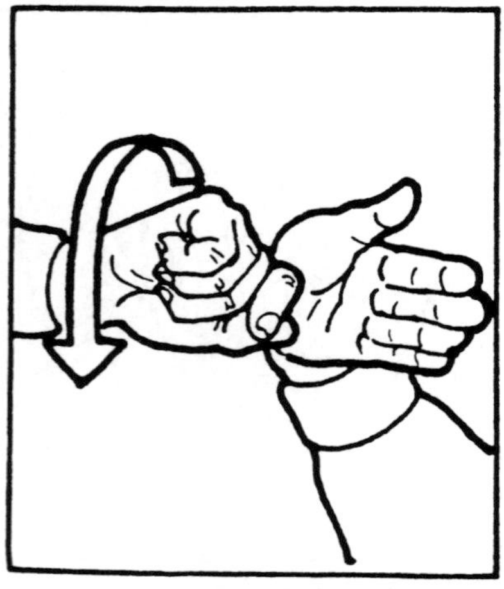

Rt. hand holds imaginary key and twists into L. palm.

LOLLY

Extended index brushes down in front of mouth.

LONDON

Index points to ear, then moves out in spiralling circles.

LONELY

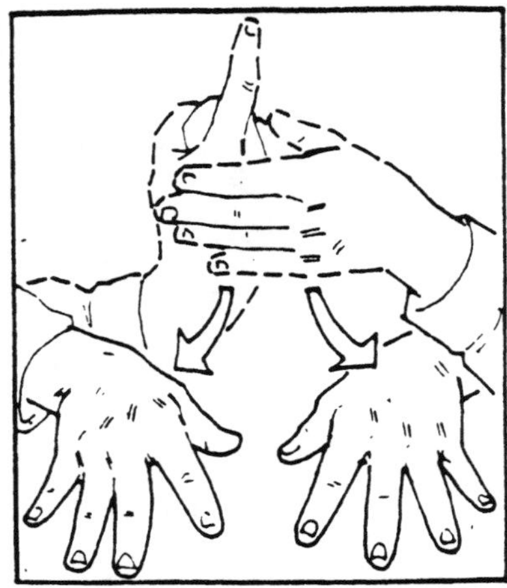

Rt. index pointing up moves down behind L. hand then both hands open and swing to point down.

LONG (time)

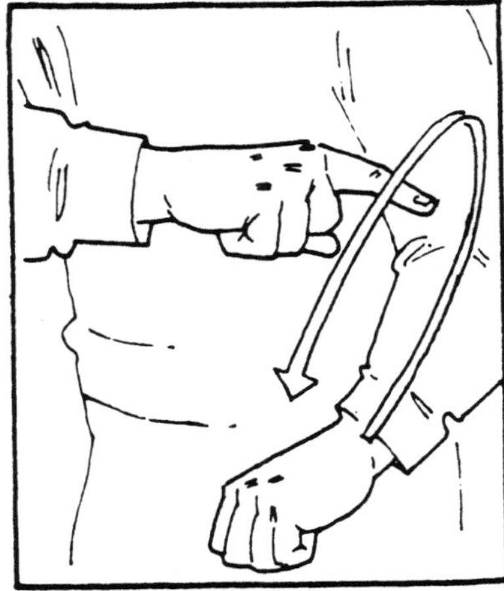

Sweep Rt. index up extended left arm, returning to wrist.

LONG (length)

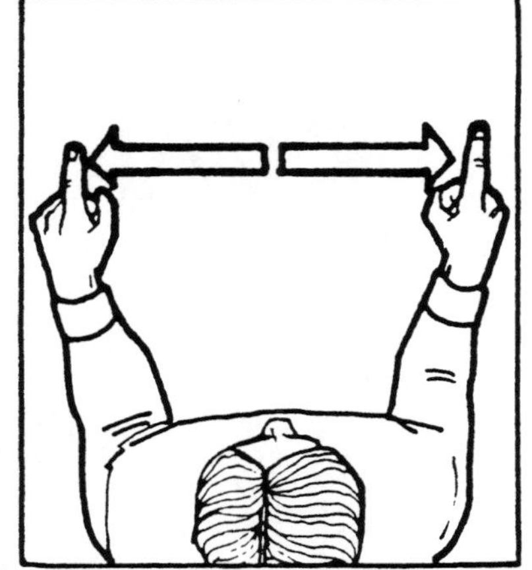

Indexes extended, palms facing, pull apart.

LONG TIME AGO

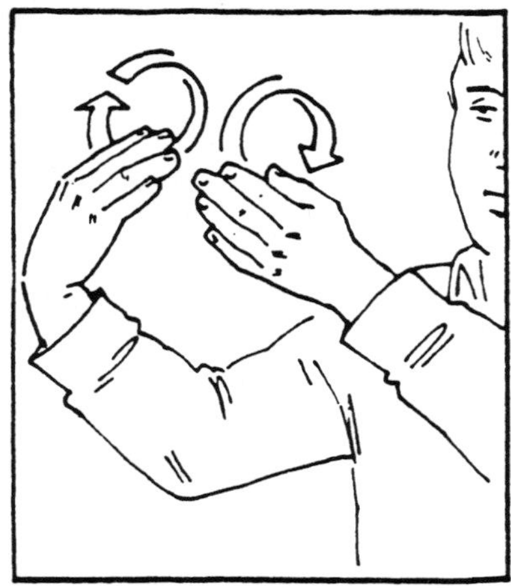

Flat hands circle round each other, backwards over right shoulder.

LOOK

"V" hand moves from eye, forward, or towards the person or thing concerned.

LOOK AFTER

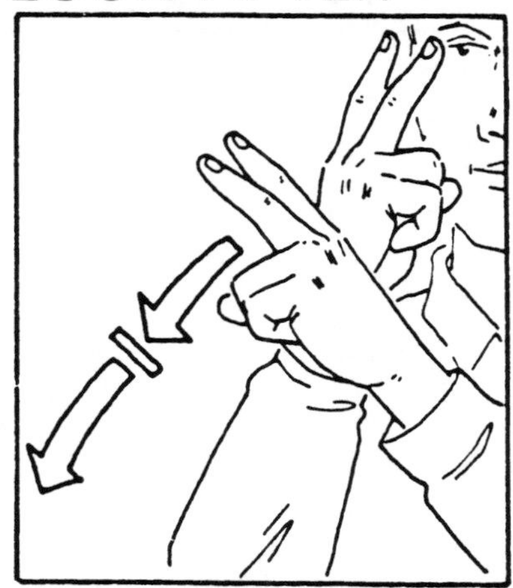

Two "V" hands, blade of Rt. on top of L.; formation moves down from eye in two movements.

LORD

Indexes held at head height make short forward movement with stress.

LORRY

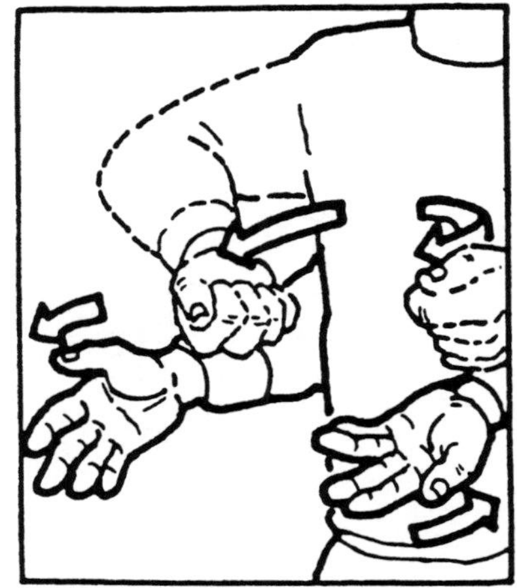

Hands hold imaginary horizontal wheel then both hands spring open, Rt. moving forward and L. back.

LOSE

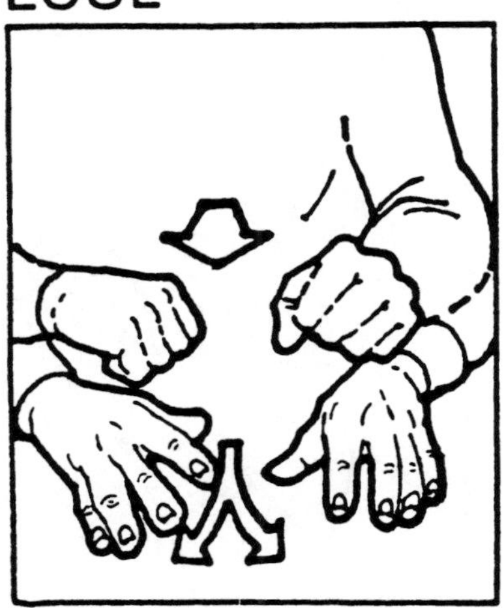

Two fists palms down move down and spring open.

LOSS OF FACE

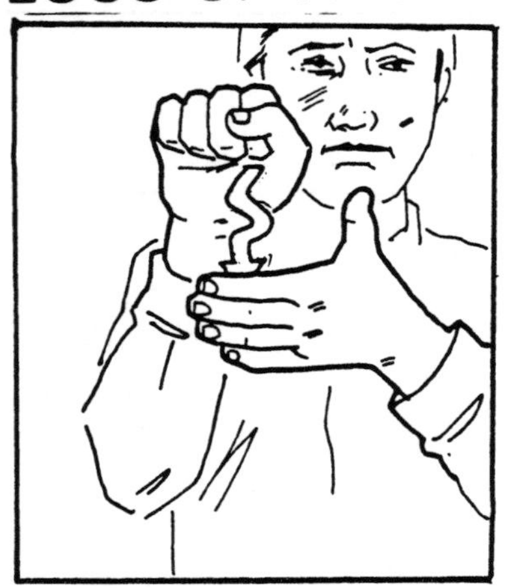

Rt. fist moves down behind L. flat hand in side to side wavering movement.

LOT (A)

Indexes and thumbs extended, index tips touching, bounce up and down whilst moving apart.

LOUD

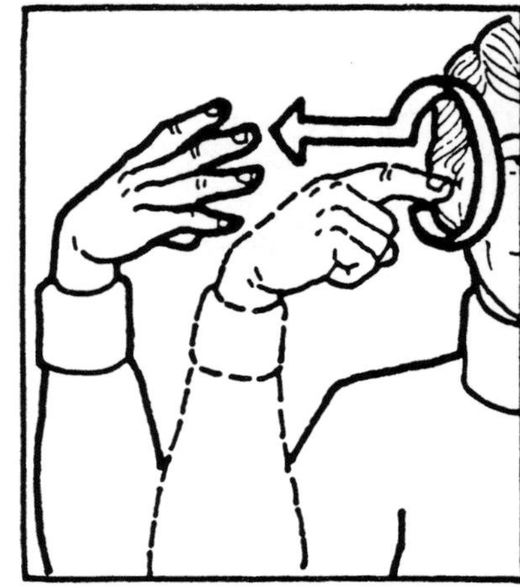

Index pointing to ear makes a circle then springs out and open.

LOVE

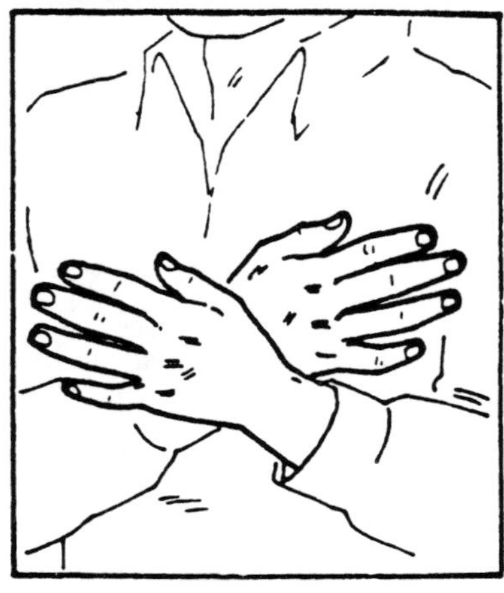

Hands crossed at wrists, held on chest.

LOVELY

Rt. index and thumb extended; draw index slowly under bottom lip left to right and close index, leaving thumb up.

LOW

Palm down hand moves down at side of body.

LUCKY

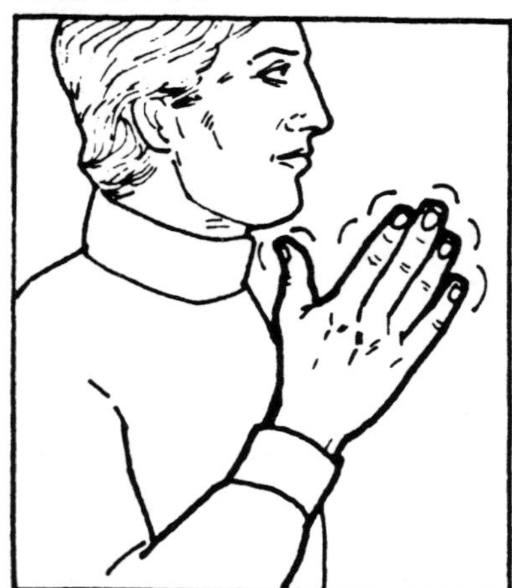

Rt. hand, palm left, makes small shaking movement near chin.

MACHINE

Closed hands, palms facing, thumbs extended make small alternate forward circles.

MAGAZINE

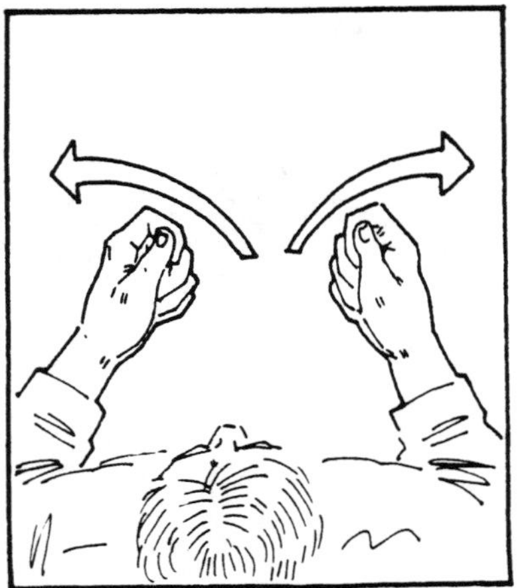

Hands move in action of holding and opening a magazine.

MAGIC

Two full "O" hands move forward and spring open.

MAKE

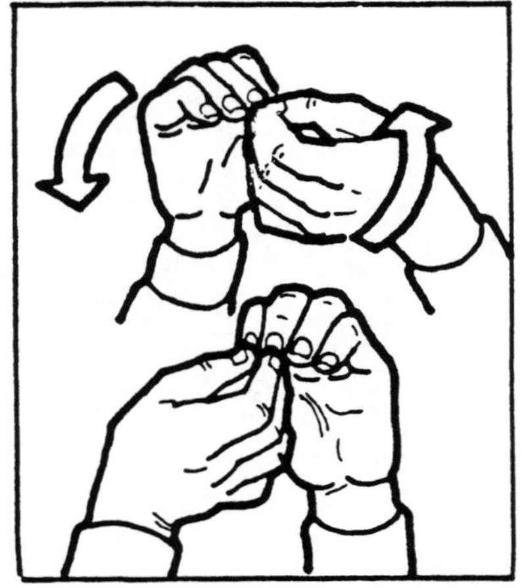

Bunched hands touch at tips and twist alternately against each other.

MAN

Full hand strokes down chin and closes to indicate beard.

MANAGE

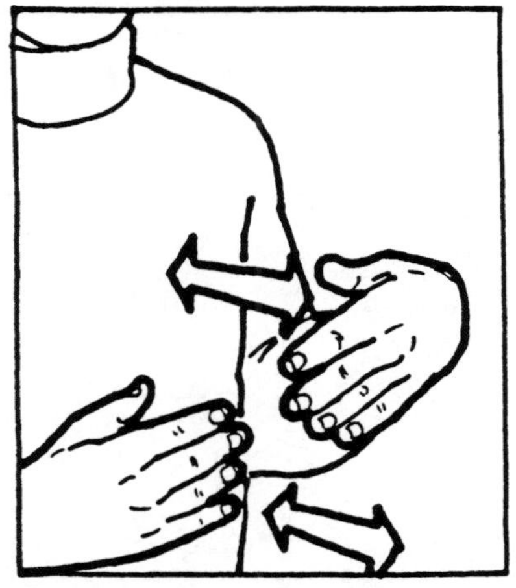

Palms back, hands pointing towards each other, fingers slightly open, move alternately backwards and forwards.

MANAGER

Closed hands, thumbs extended; thumbs jab into upper chest twice.

MANNERS

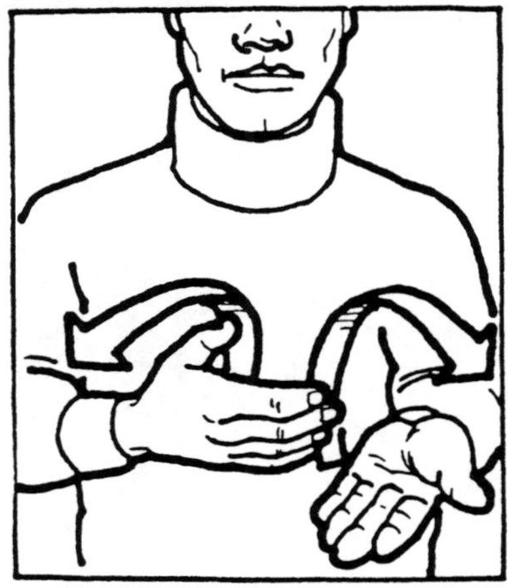

Flat hands move in alternate arcs forward and out.

MANY

Open hands move apart fingers fluttering.

MARK

Make tick on L. palm with Rt. index.

MARKET

Tips of "M" hands touch, pull apart/down, move to the side and repeat.

MARRY

Mime putting on ring, then pat back of L. hand with Rt.

MASH

Mime mashing potatoes.

MATCH

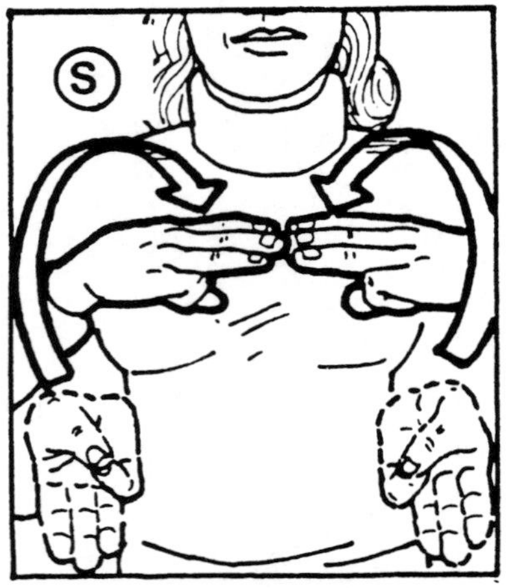

"M" hands move up and twist over to touch at tips.

MATERIAL

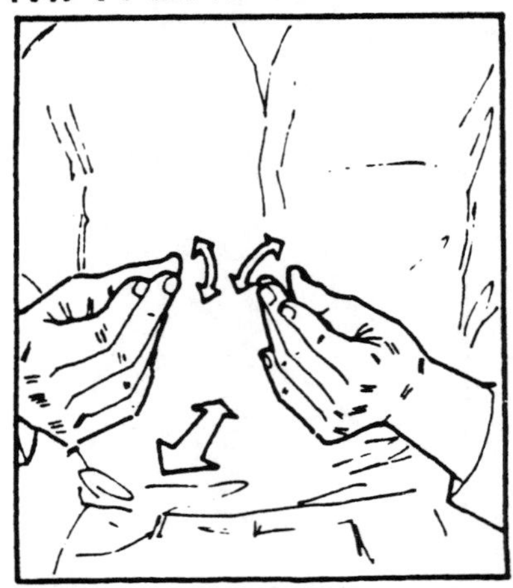

Thumbs rub along tips of fingers, and hands move slightly forwards and back.

MATHS

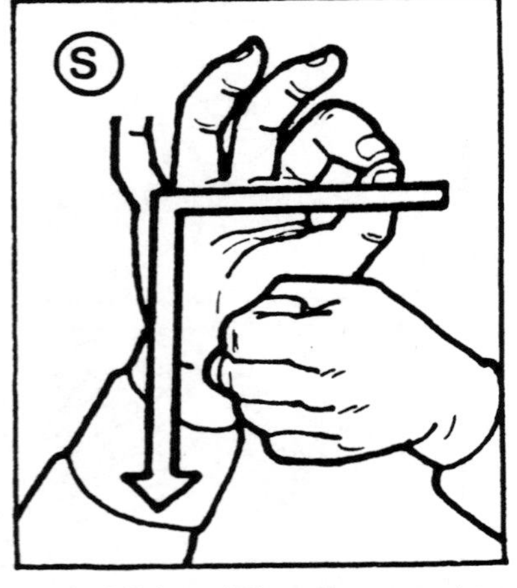

Rt. "O" hand draws across top and down side of L. fist.

MATTER (the)

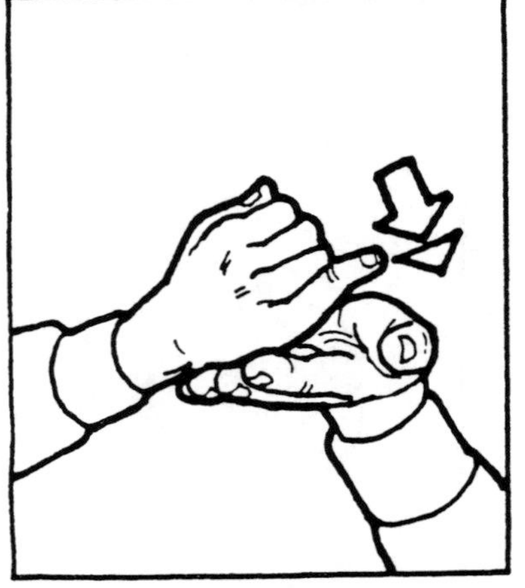

Blade of Rt. hand, little finger extended, taps L. palm twice.

MAXIMUM

Rt. closed hand moves up and contacts L. palm with stress.

MAYBE

Rt. thumb and little finger extended, palm left, waggles.

MEAL

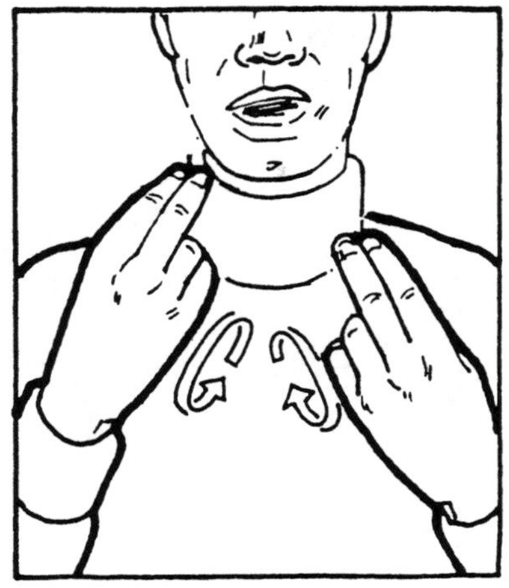

"N" hands make small alternate circular movements near the mouth.

MEAN (imply)

Flat hands, Rt. over L. move in horizontal circles alternately.

MEAN (stingy)

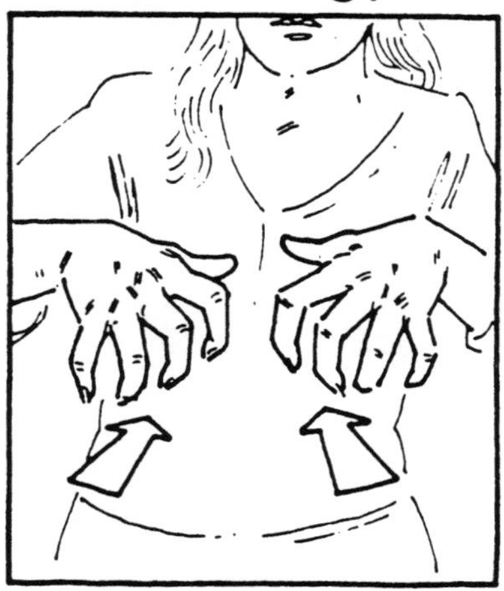

Palm down clawed hands pull back towards body.

MEASURE

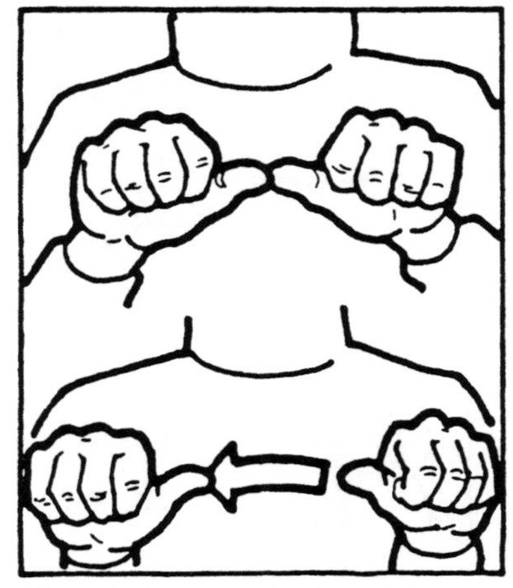

Thumbtips touch, then Rt. moves away to the right.

MEAT

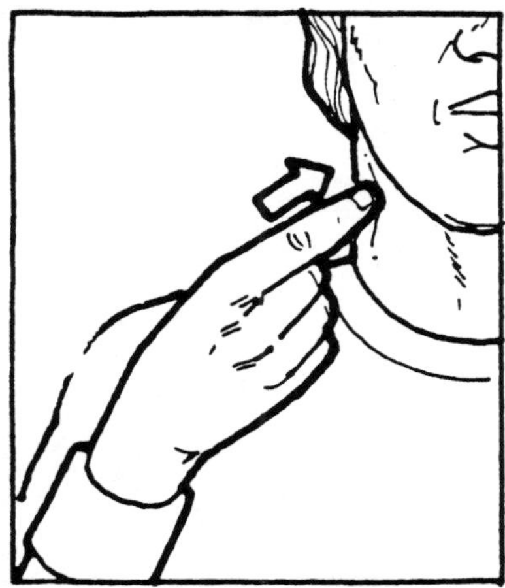

Prod side of neck with Rt. index.

MEDAL

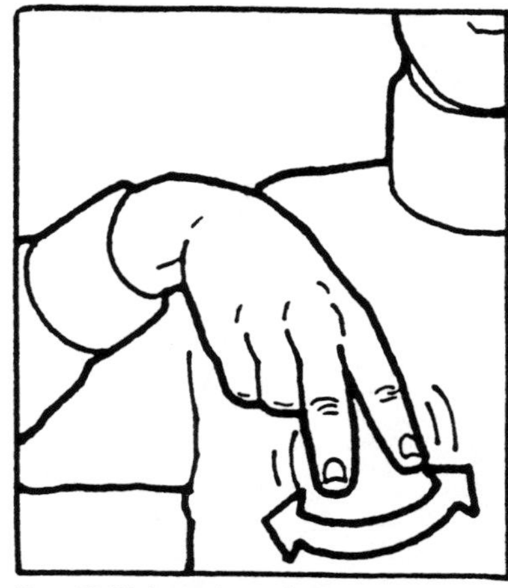

Rt. "V" hand, pointing down shakes from side to side on right upper chest.

MEDICINE

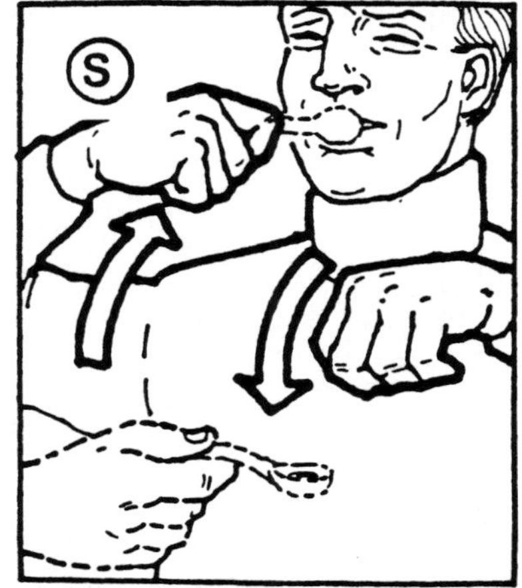

Mime pouring medicine into spoon and drinking it.

MEET

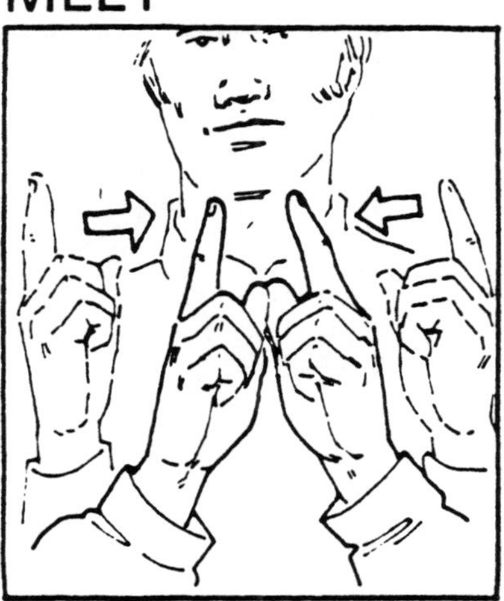

Indexes held apart move in to meet each other.

MEETING

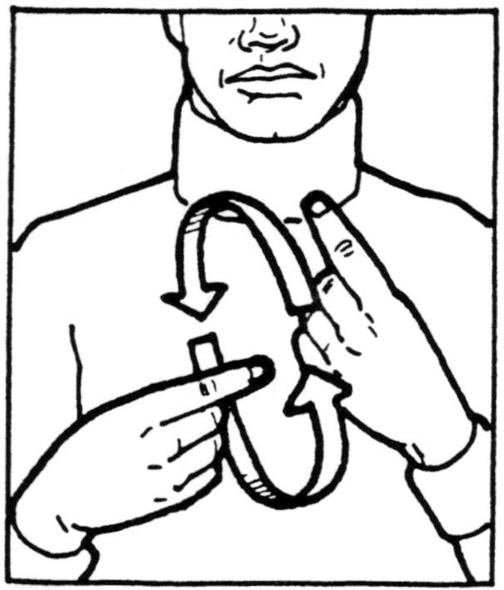

Indexes pointing up/in make alternate circles.

MELT

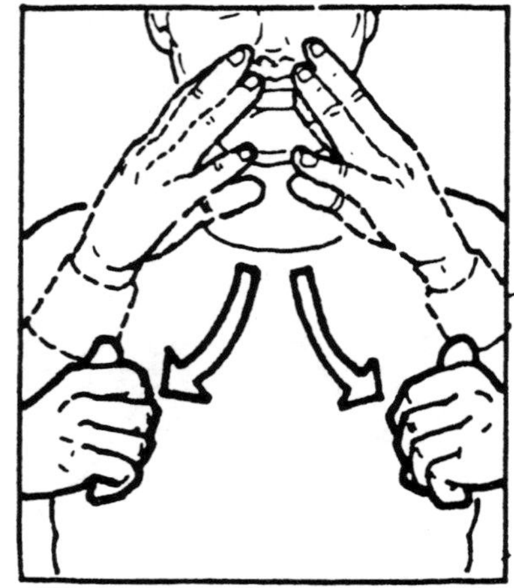

Hands move down/out as thumbs rub along fingertips from little fingers to indexes in slow movement.

MEND

Rt. closed hand twists from palm forward to palm back as it strikes top of L. closed hand, twice.

MENU

Rt. "M" hand taps L. palm and moves down tapping imaginary items on menu.

MERCY

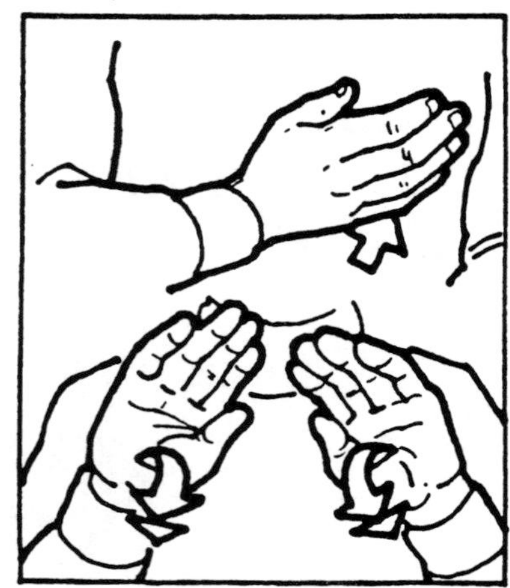

Rt. flat hand makes small movement up, over heart, then two flat hands make forward stroking movements.

MESS

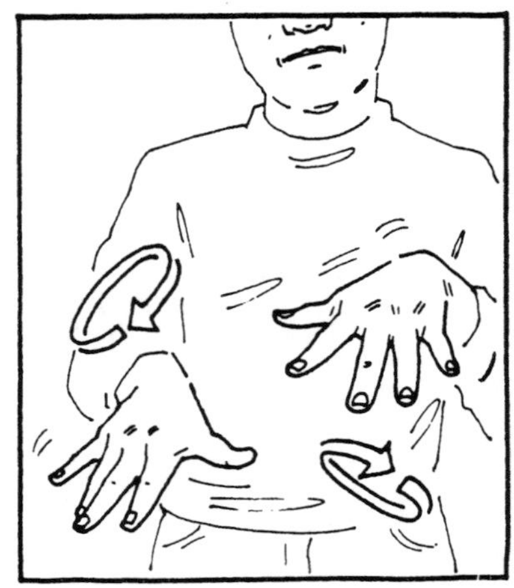

Open hands move in alternating circles.

METAL

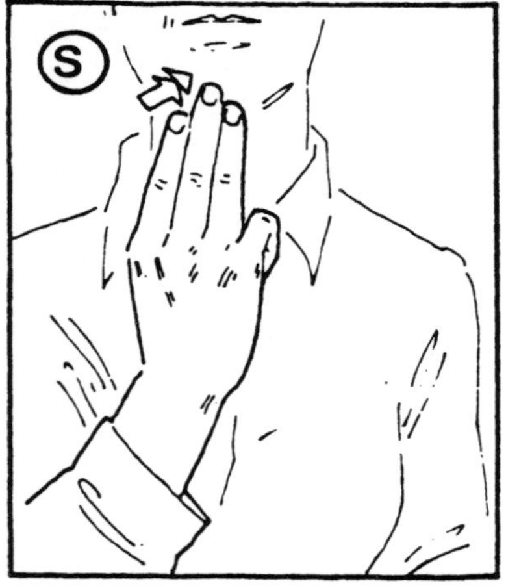

Tips of "M" hand tap chin twice.

METHOD

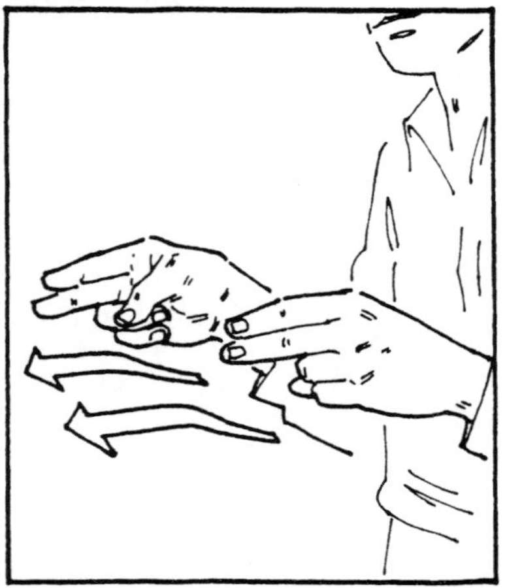

"N" hands, held parallel, move forward.

MIDDLE

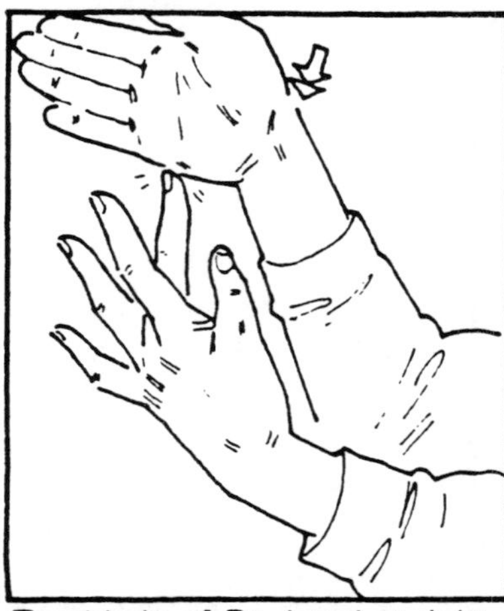

Tap blade of Rt. hand at right angle on top of L. middle finger twice.

MIGHT

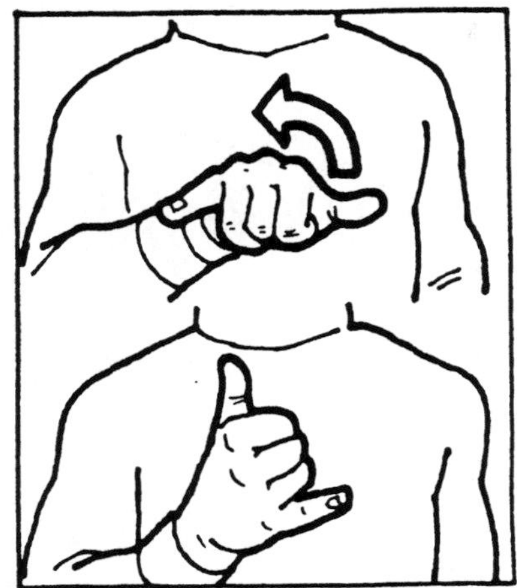

Rt. little finger and thumb extended, palm down, twists sharply to palm left.

MILE

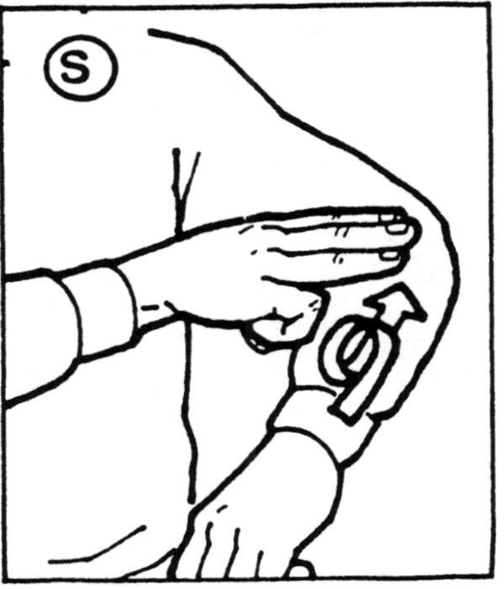

Rt. "M" hand strokes in small loop up left forearm.

MILK

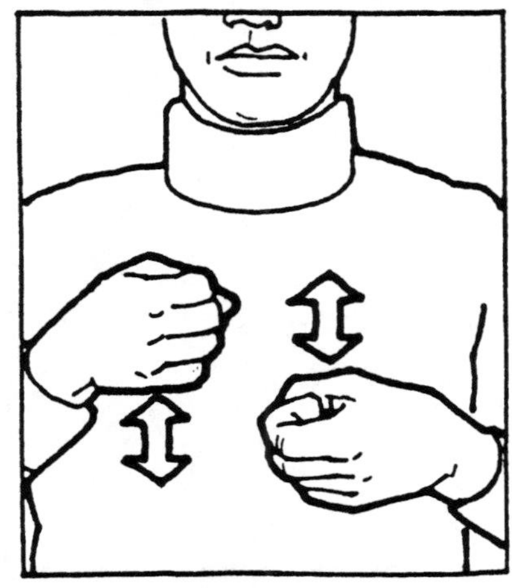

Hands move up and down alternately with squeezing movement.

MILLION

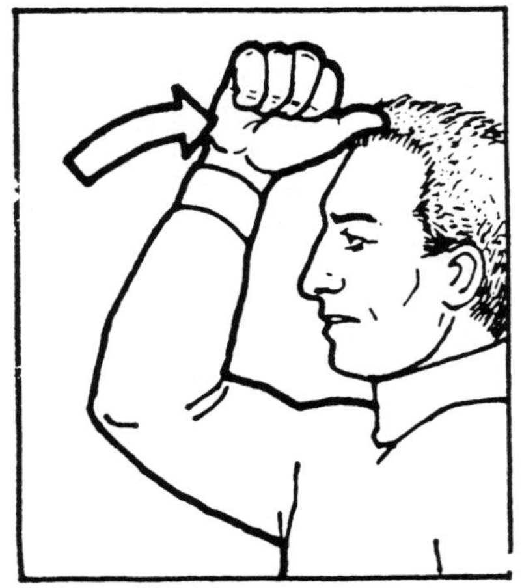

Thumb extended moves up in front of face and over head.

MINE

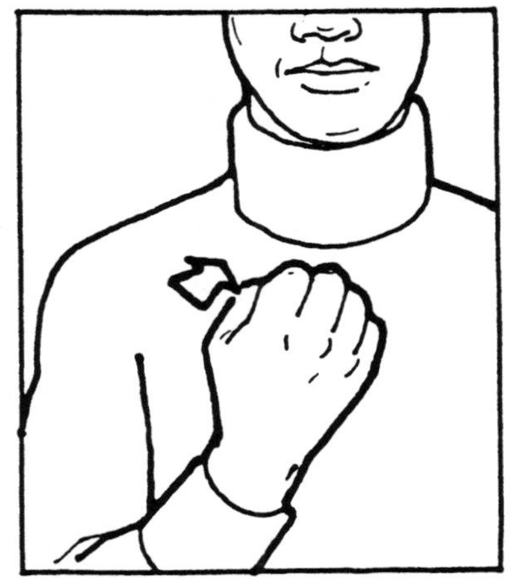

Closed hand moves to touch chest.

MINI-BUS

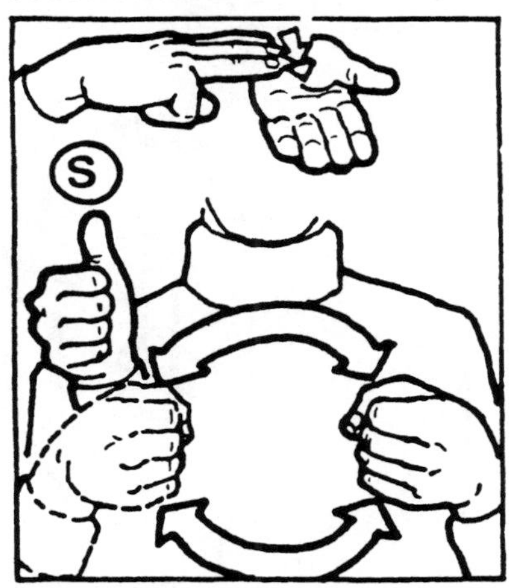

Tap "M" twice on L. palm, then sign "bus".

MINUS

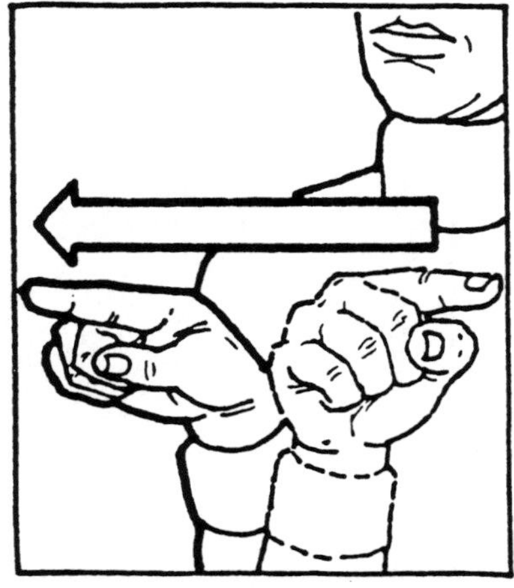

Draw minus sign in air with index.

MINUTE

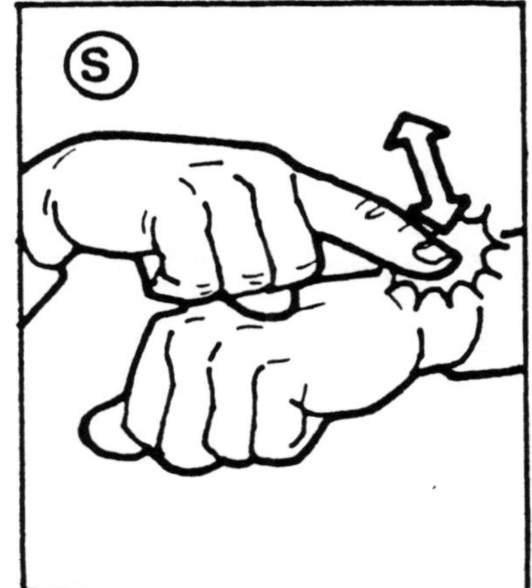

Rt. index strikes L. wrist and bounces up sharply.

MIRROR

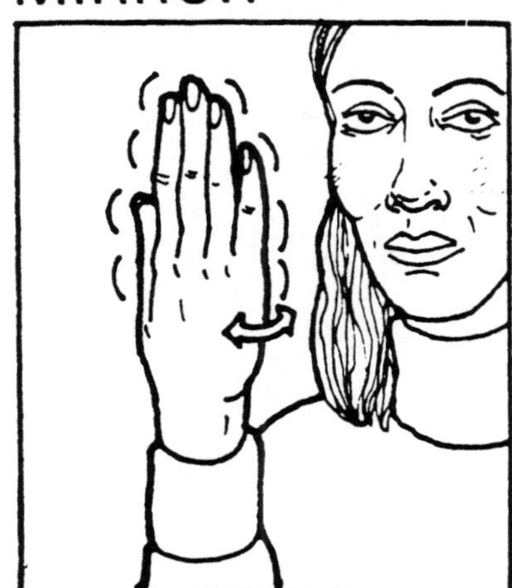

Flat hand in front of face makes very slight quick twisting movement.

MISERABLE

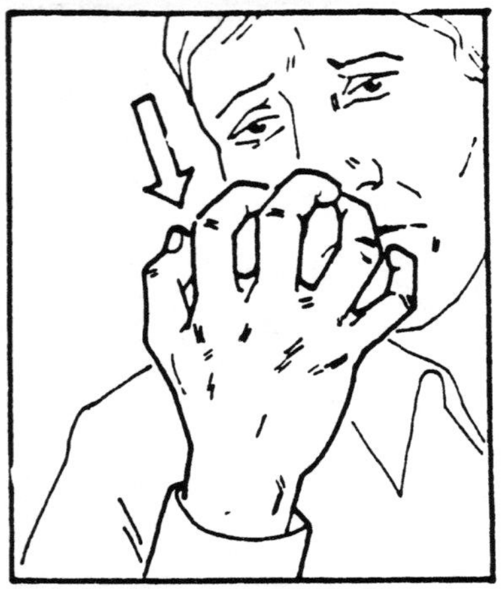

Clawed hand pulls down in front of face.

MISS

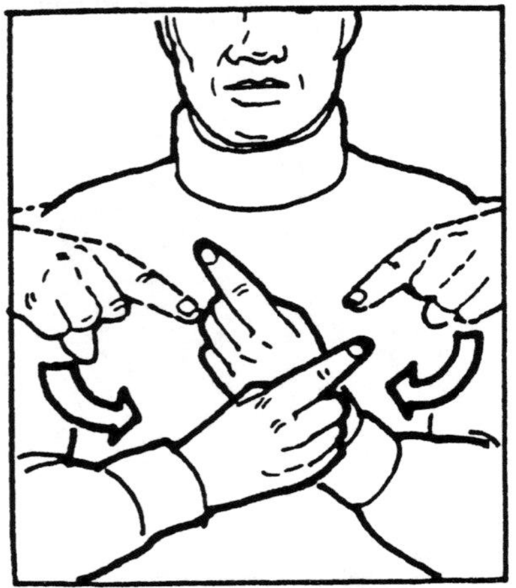

Indexes apart, pointing in, move in sharply past each other with slight twist.

MISTAKE

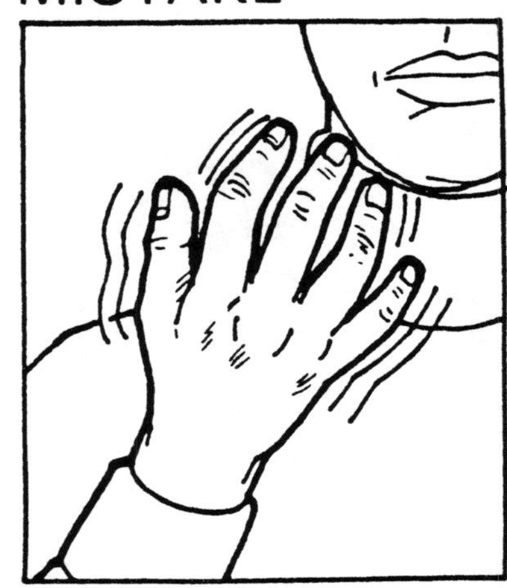

Open hand, fingers slightly bent shakes from side to side at side of chin.

MITTEN(S)

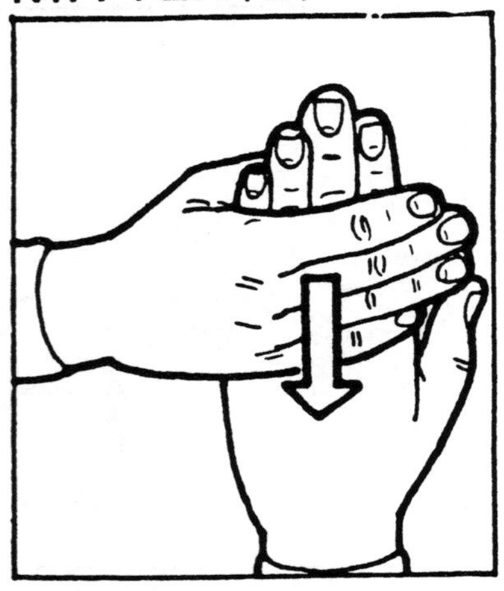

Rt. hand slides down L. like pulling on mitten. Reverse to L. down Rt. for "mittens".

MIX

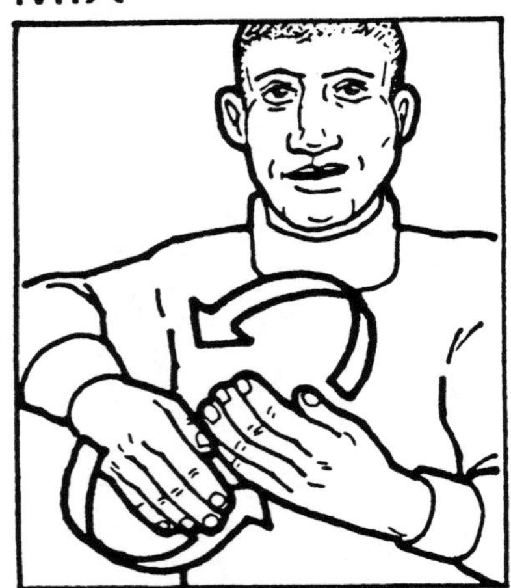

Flat hands revolve round each other at slight angle.

MONEY

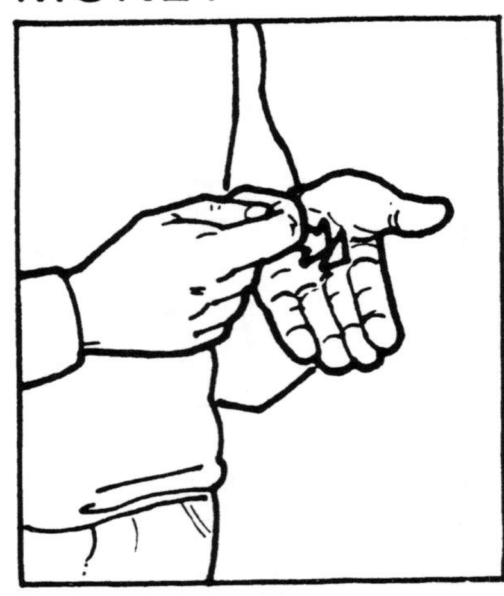

Thumb tucked into bent Rt. index; tap L. palm twice.

MONKEY

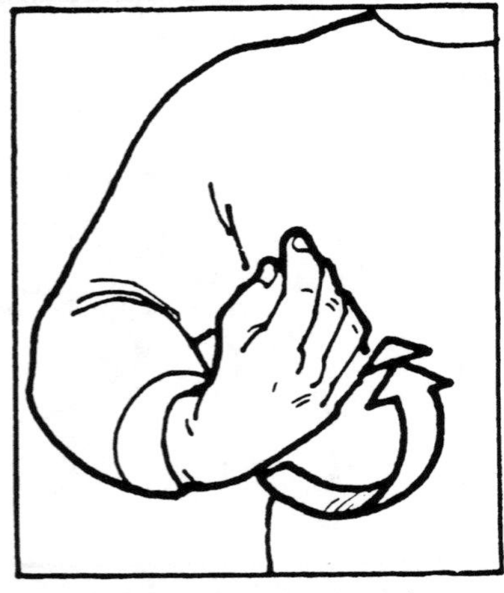

Rt. hand makes scratching movement under right arm.

MONTH

Rt. "M" moves from tips to heel of L. flat hand.

MOODY

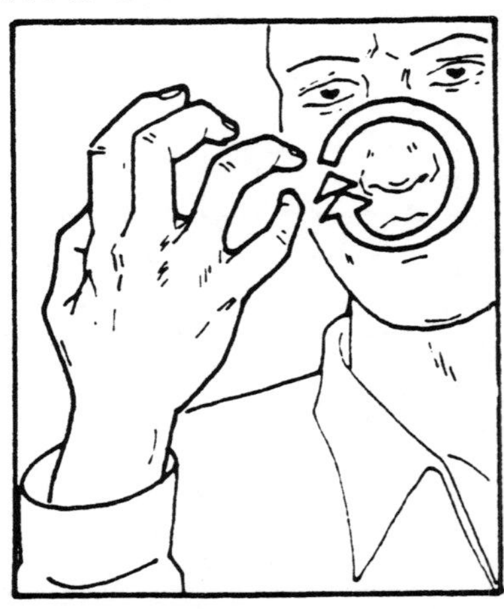

Clawed hand makes circular movement in front of face.

MOON

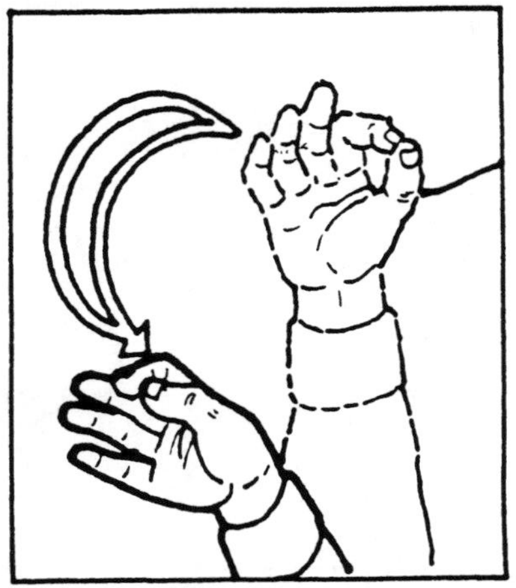

"O" hand moves in crescent shape, as fingers open then close.

MORE

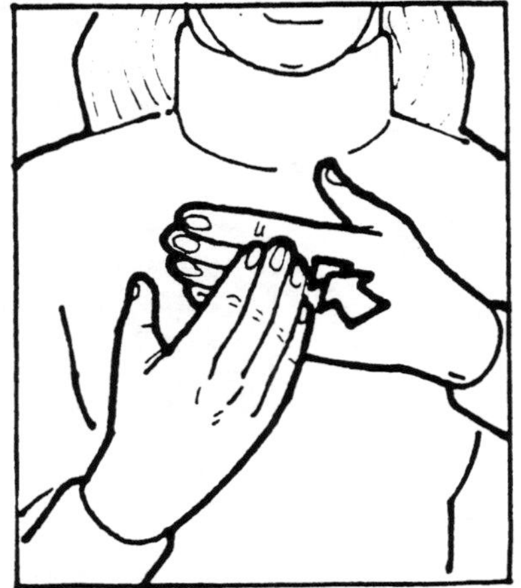

Tap palm back L. flat hand with Rt. flat hand twice.

MORNING

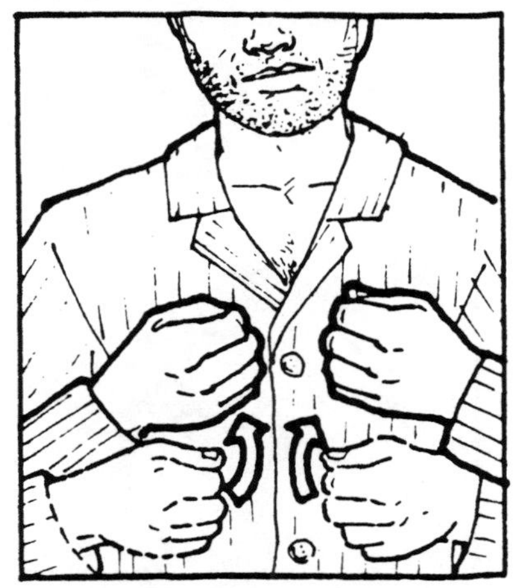

Closed hands move up body with slight twist.

MOST

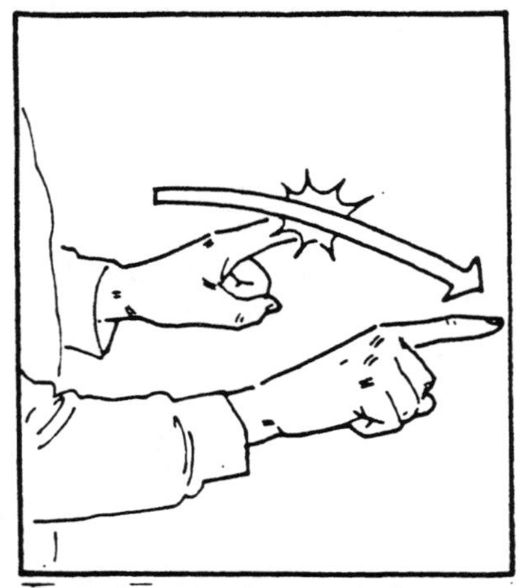

Indexes point forward, Rt. behind L., Rt. moves sharply forward hitting L. in passing.

MOTHER

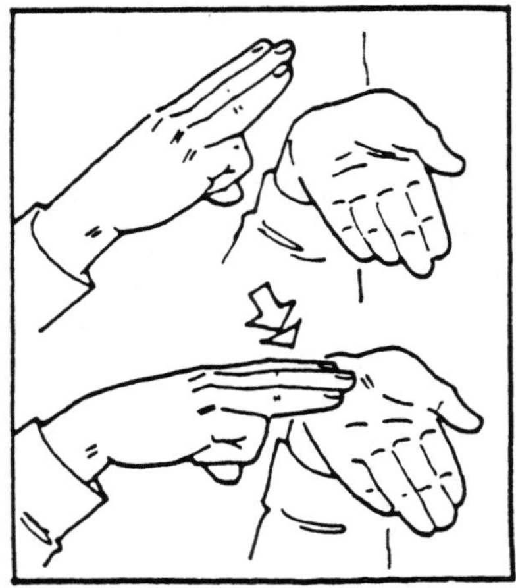

Tap "M" on L. palm twice.

MOTORBIKE

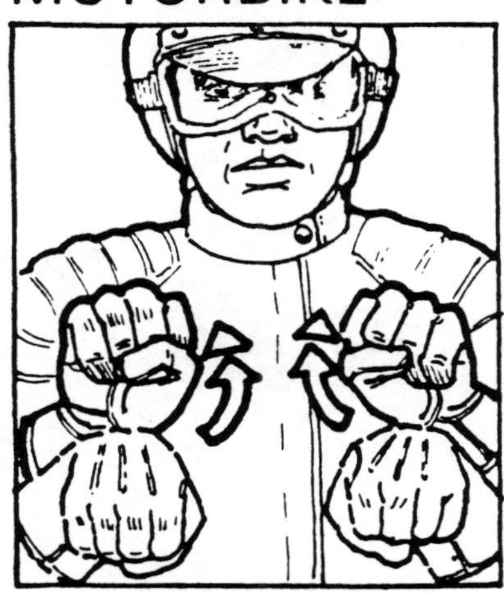

Fists twist from palm down to palm forward sharply twice.

MOUNTAIN

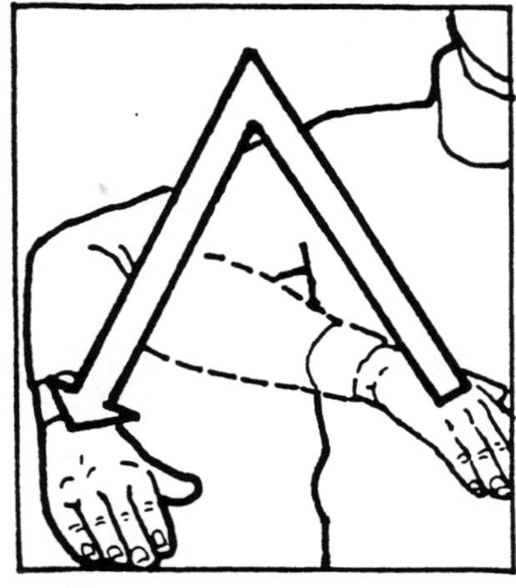

Flat hand moves up and down in outline of mountain.

MOUSE

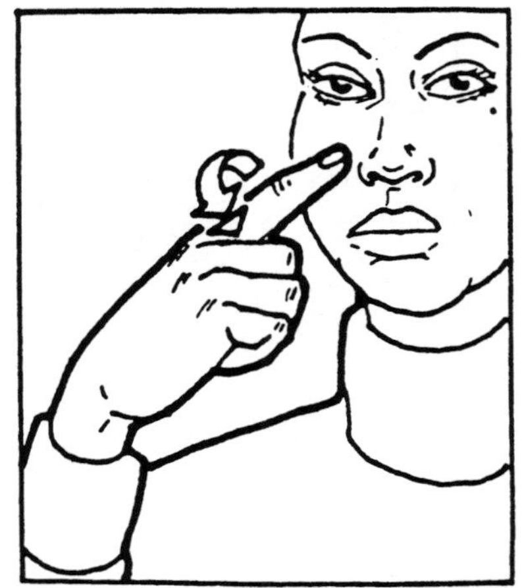

Index twists repeatedly at side of nose.

MOVE

Flat hands parallel move sharply left to right with stress.

MR.

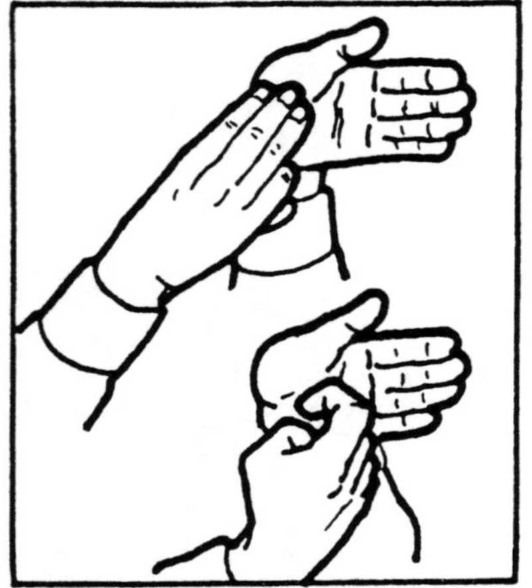

Fingerspell "M" "R".

MRS.

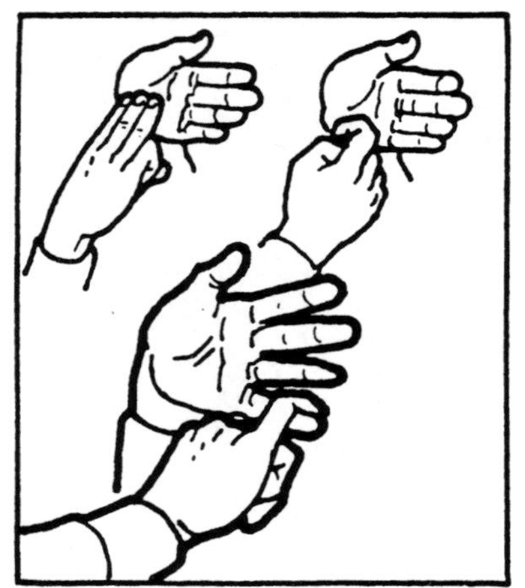

Fingerspell "M" "R" "S".

MUCH

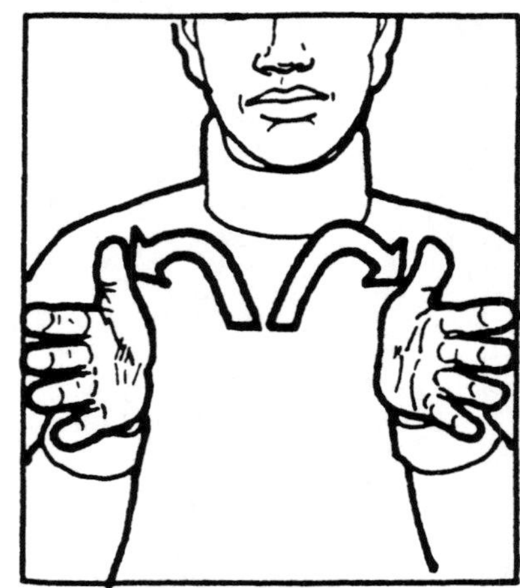

Open hands move apart in upward arc.

MUD

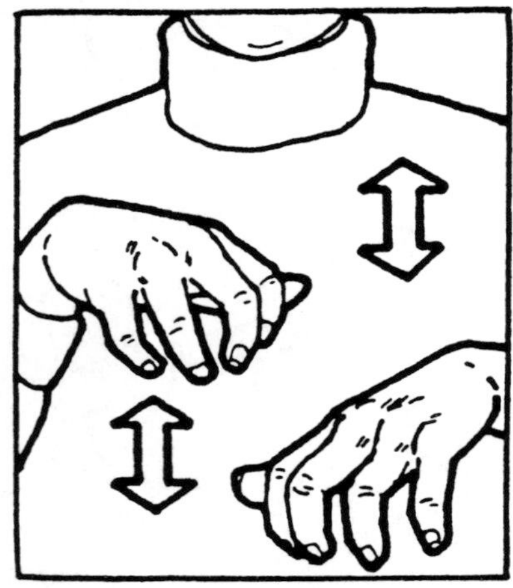

Clawed hands, palms down move alternately up and down as though stuck in mud.

MULTIPLY

Tap fingers of fingerspelt "X" together twice.

MUSHROOM

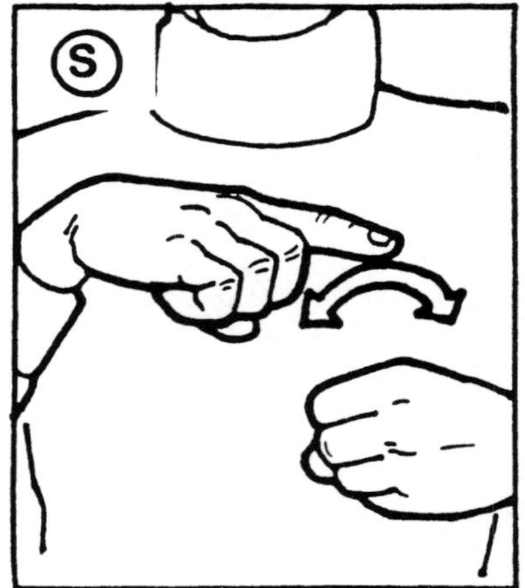

Indicate shape of top of mushroom with Rt. index over top of L. fist.

MUSIC

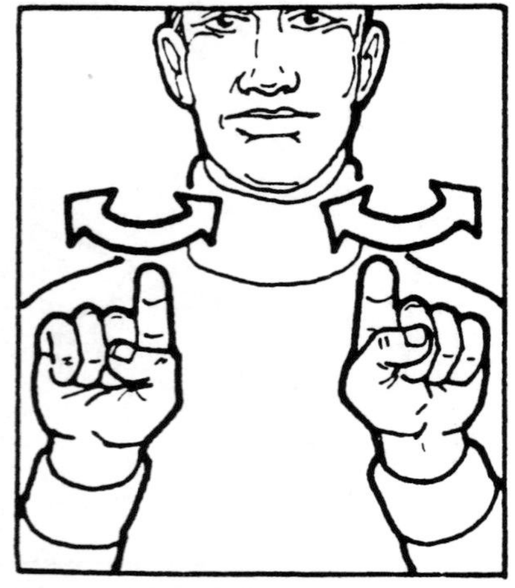

Indexes pointing forward, swing from side to side as if conducting.

MUST

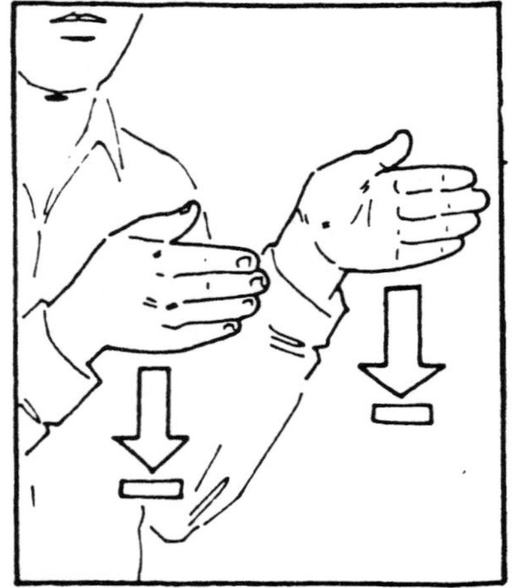

Flat hands held parallel move sharply down with stress.

MY

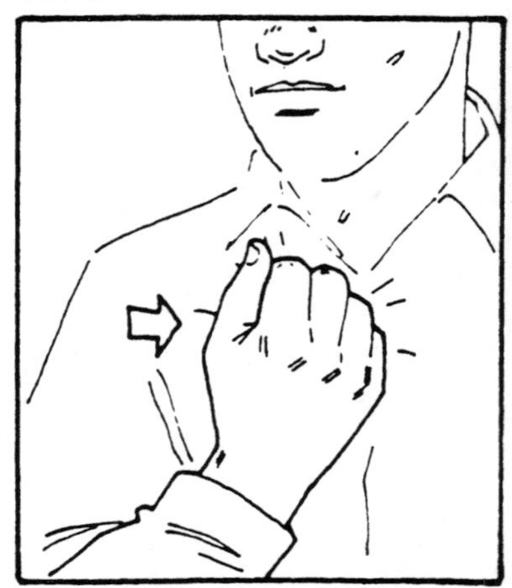

Closed hand moves to contact chest.

MY OWN

Closed hand moves back onto chest, then sharply up.

MYSELF

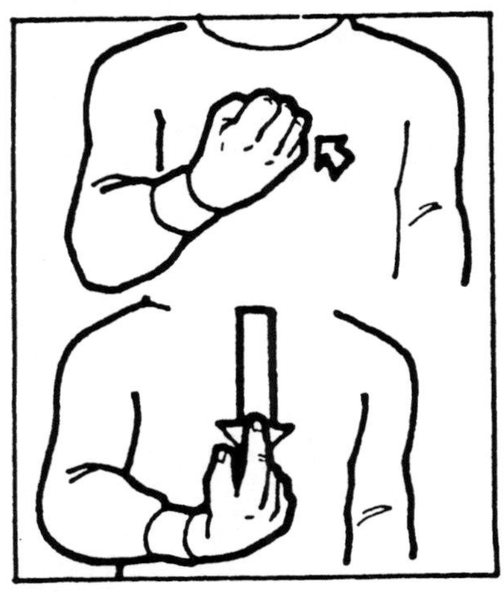

Closed hand moves to contact chest, changes to index extended brushed down chest.

NAME

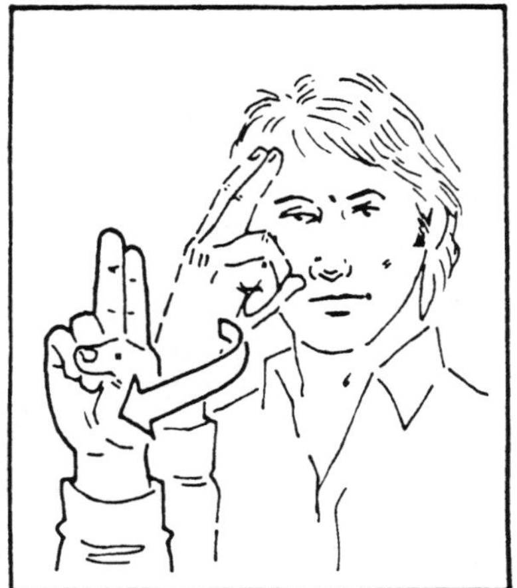

"N" hand touches side of forehead, then moves and twists forward.

NARROW

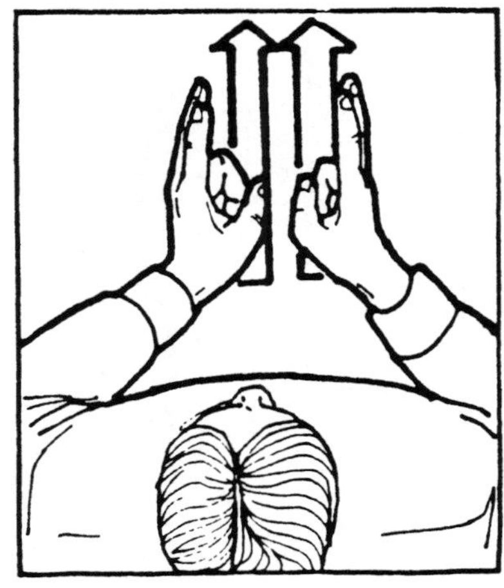

Two "N" hands palms facing, pointing forward, move forward.

NAUGHTY

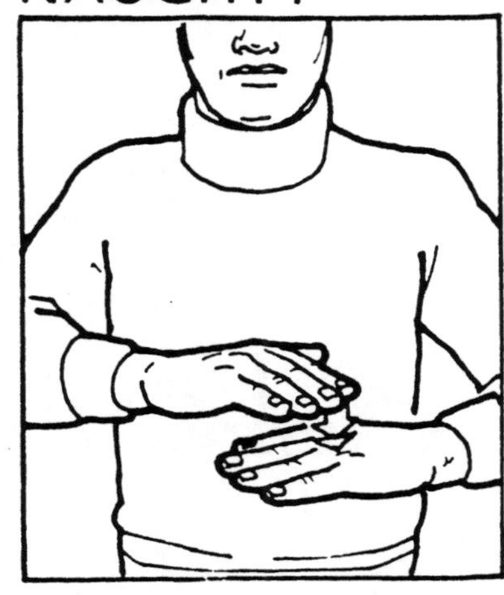

Fingertips of Rt. flat hand tap back of L. hand twice.

NAVY

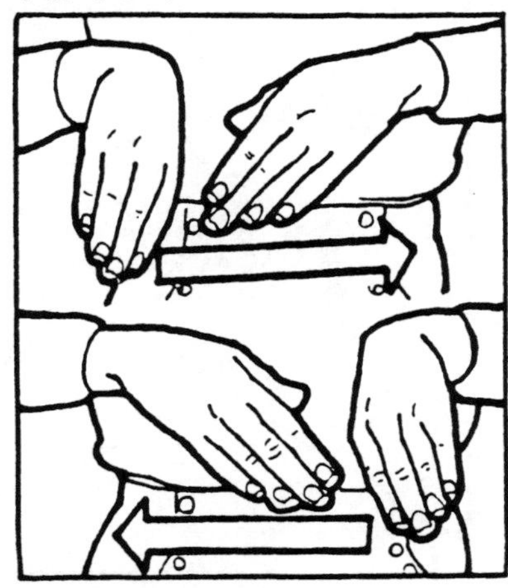

Flat hands pointing down held at right side of waist, swing to left side, then back again.

NEAR

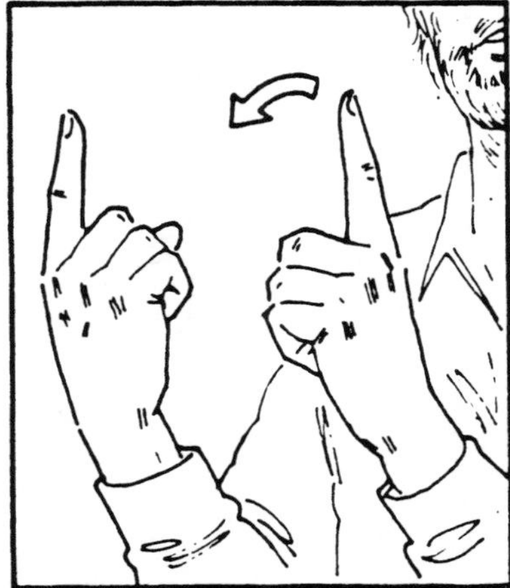

Indexes held close together, Rt. hand moves out with small twisting movement away from L.

NEARLY

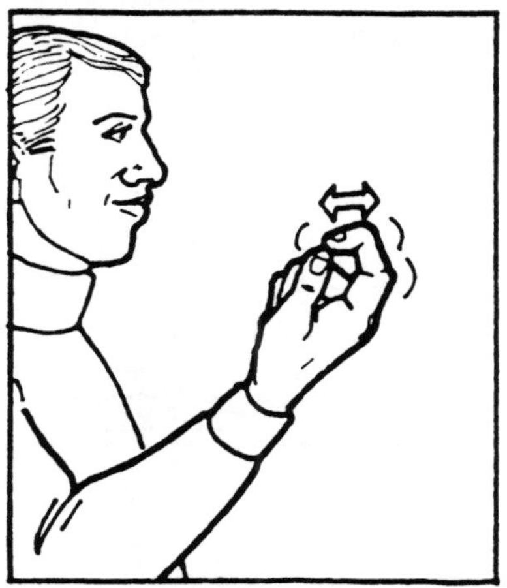

Tips of index and thumb of Rt. closed hand touch, hand makes small movement backwards and forwards.

NEED

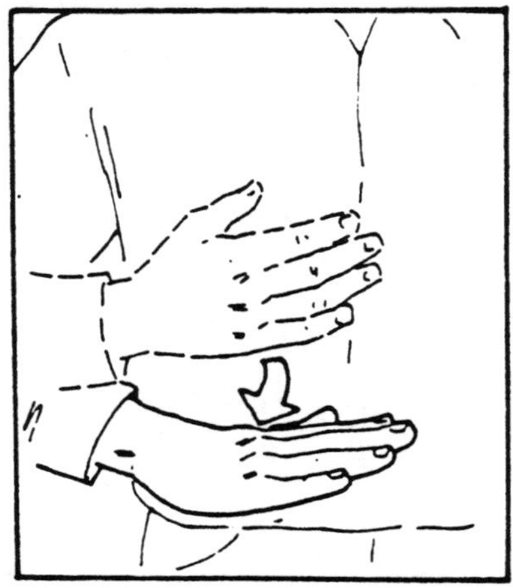

Rt. flat hand held on right side above waist brushes down, twisting to palm down.

NEEDLE

Hold imaginary needle, and make very small twisting movement.

NEGOTIATE

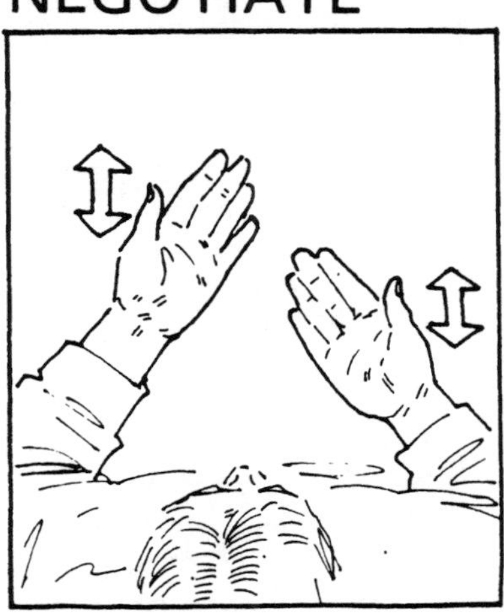

Palm up flat hands move alternately backward and forward.

NEIGHBOUR

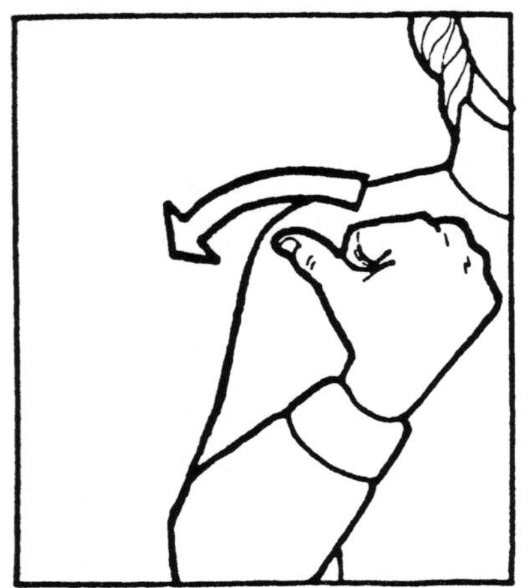

Rt. thumb extended, contacts shoulder, palm left, twists out to palm back.

NEPHEW

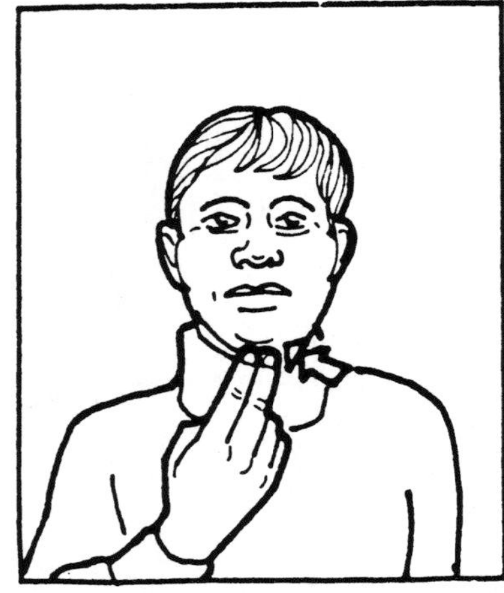

Tips of "N" hand tap chin twice.

NERVOUS

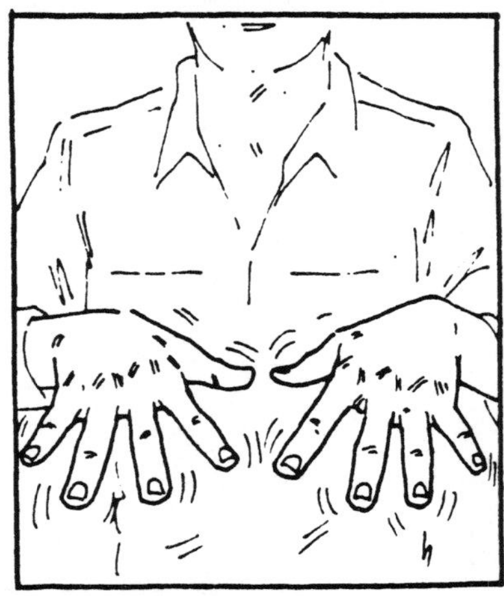

Fingers of both hands point down and shake.

NET

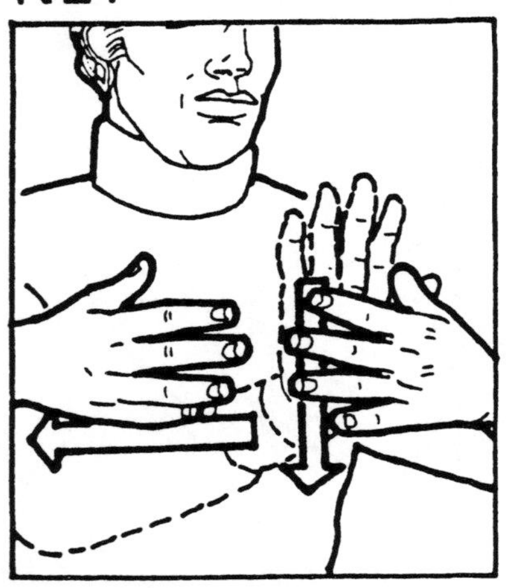

Rt. open hand palm forward brushes down behind L., twists to palm back pointing left and brushes along L. from heel to tips.

NEVER

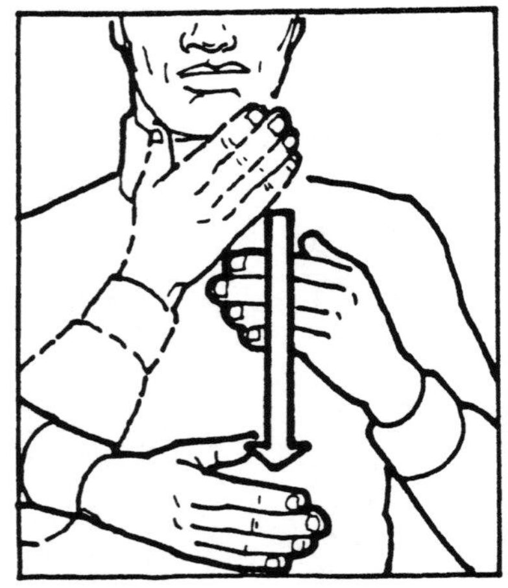

L. hand palm back; Rt. flat hand chops sharply down back of L.

NEW

Rt. flat hand brushes up back of L.

NEWS

Rt. index points to mouth, moves down to flat hand pointing forward, tips brush forward twice along fingers of L. hand.

NEWSPAPER

Hold imaginary paper and open.

NEXT

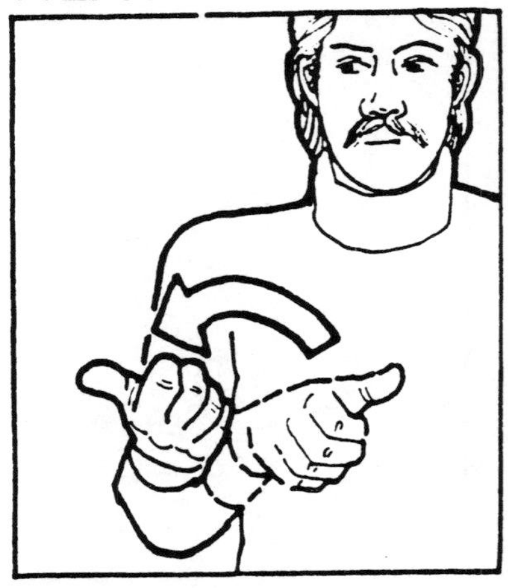

Rt. thumb extended, twists over from palm left, to palm up.

NICE

Rt. thumb moves across chin from left to right.

NIECE

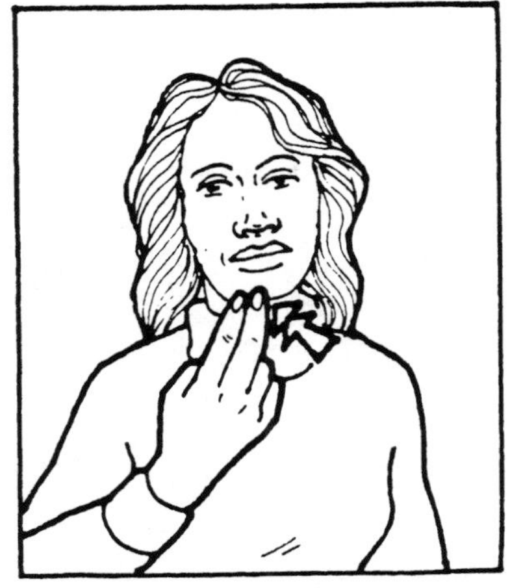

Tips of "N" hand tap chin twice.

NIGHT

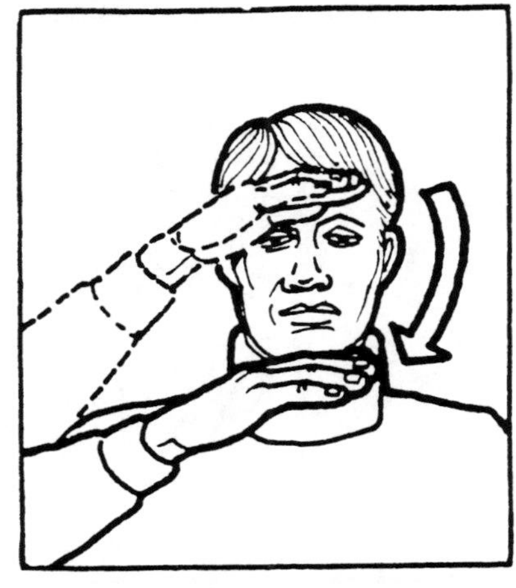

Flat hand moves down from forehead to chin in small forward arc.

LAST NIGHT

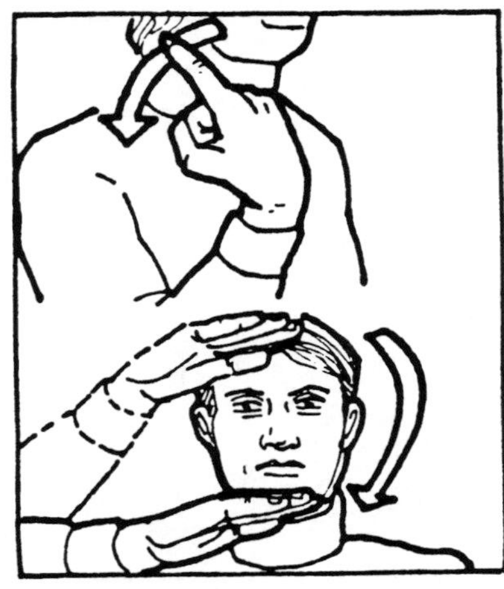

Rt. index palm back, touches cheek then drops down/back, plus sign for "night".

NIGHT-GOWN

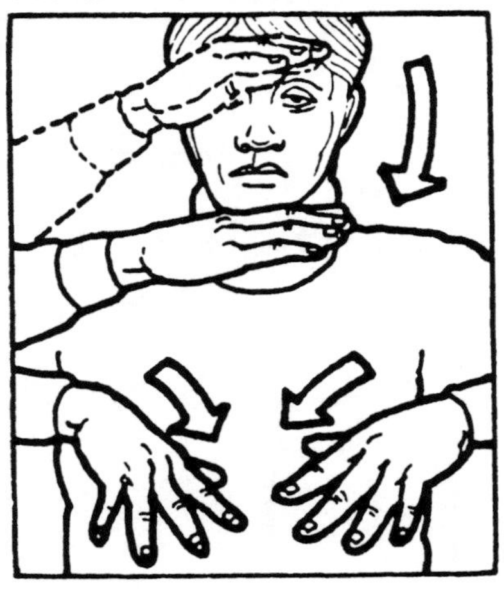

Sign "night" then brush open hands down body to indicate dress.

NO (not any)

Rt. "O" hand, palm forward.

NO (~yes)

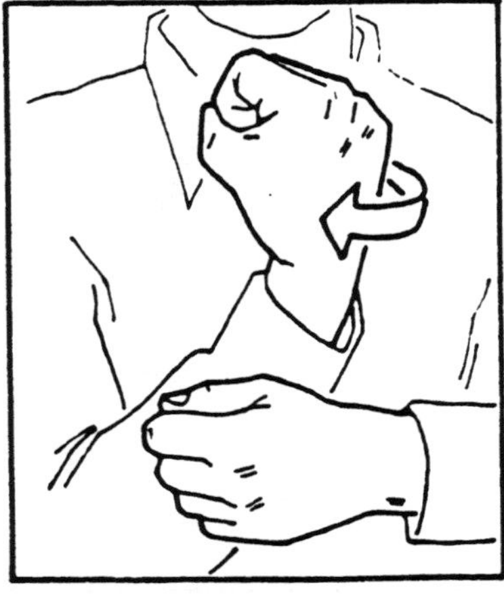

Right forearm rests on L. closed hand; Rt. fist twists sharply from palm back to palm forward.

NOISE

Index makes circular movements, around ear.

NONE

Full "O" hand.

NORWAY

"N" hand makes large "N" in the air.

NOT

Flat hands start crossed, then swing sharply apart with emphasis.

NOT YET

Closed hands, palms forward/down shake from side to side in short quick movement.

NOTE (music)

Index makes the shape of a musical note in the air.

NOTHING

"O" hand, palm forward, shakes from side to side.

NOW

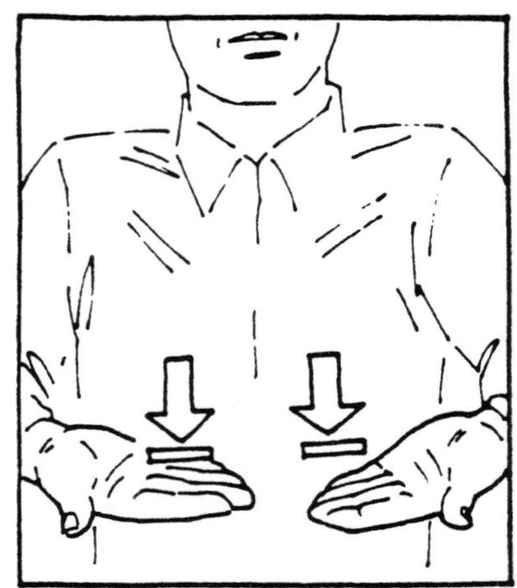

Flat hands, palms up, move down with stress.

NUMBER

Closed hand taps twice on chin.

NUN

Indexes start together in front of forehead, then move out and down to indicate veil.

NURSE

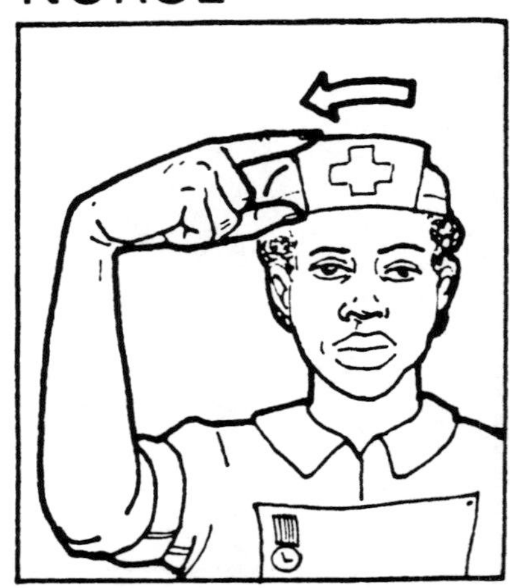

Index and thumb indicate shape of nurse's cap across forehead.

NURSERY

Tip of extended middle finger taps chin twice.

NUT

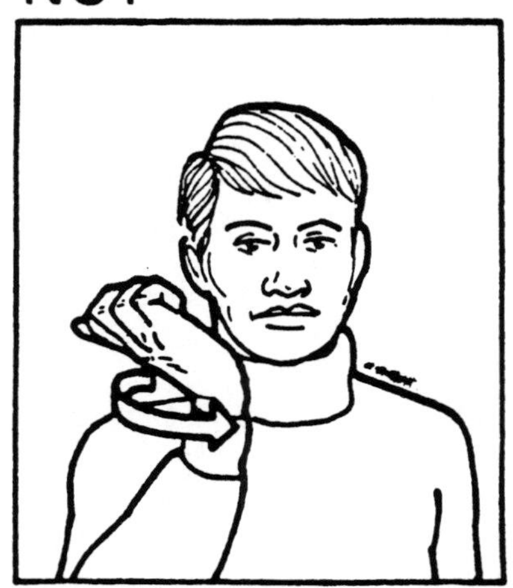

Fingers bent at second knuckles, heel of hand on side of chin, hand twists forward.

O'CLOCK

Full "O" hand opens to full "C".

OATH

Flat hand palm forward held near shoulder.

OBJECT (TO)

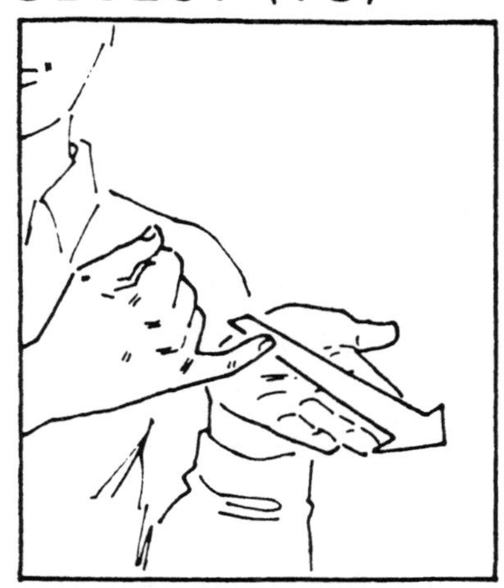

Edge of extended little finger brushes sharply forward/up along L. hand from heel to tips.

OCCUR

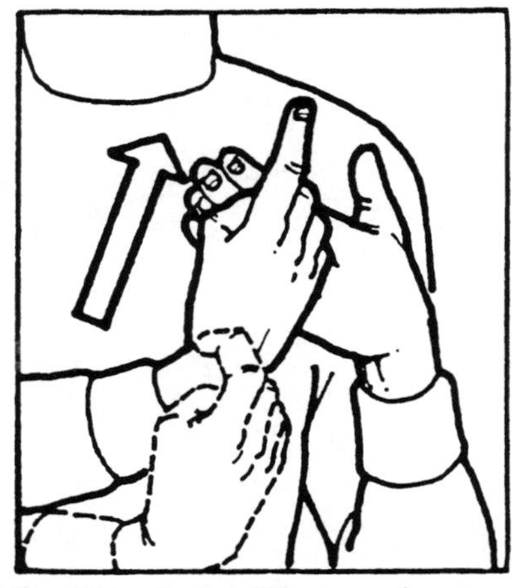

Bent Rt. index flicks up moving sharply up back of L. flat hand palm back.

OFF (absent)

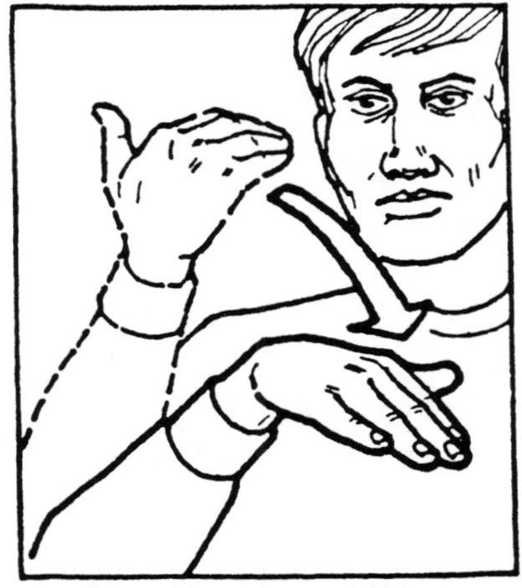

Rt. flat hand pointing back at side of neck, twists and moves sharply forward.

OFF (cancel)

Arms start crossed, then swing open.

OFF (get off)

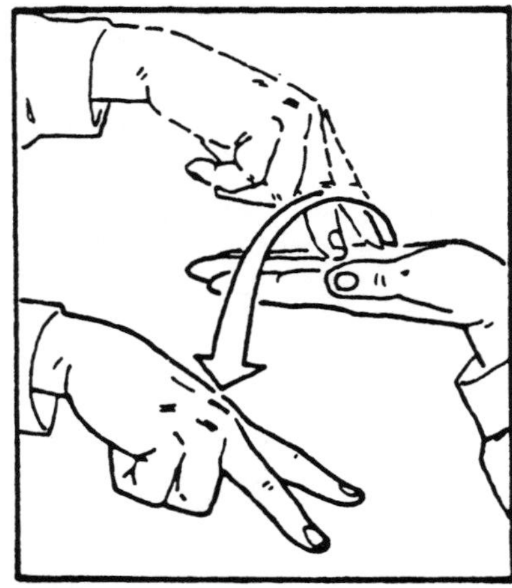

Tips of "V" hand stand on L. palm, then move off in small arc.

OFFICE

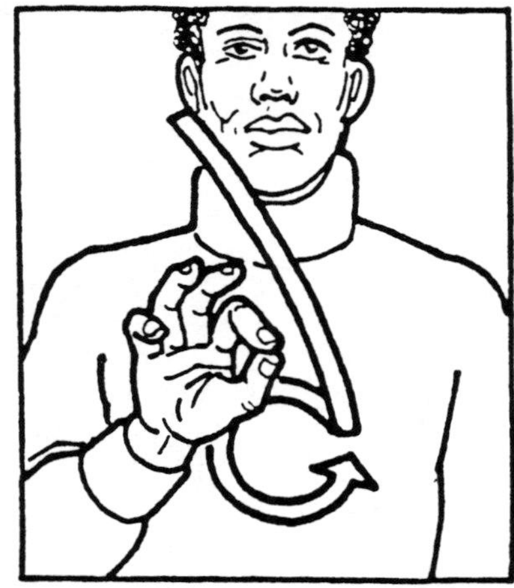

"O" hand moves down from ear and makes an "O" in the air.

OFTEN

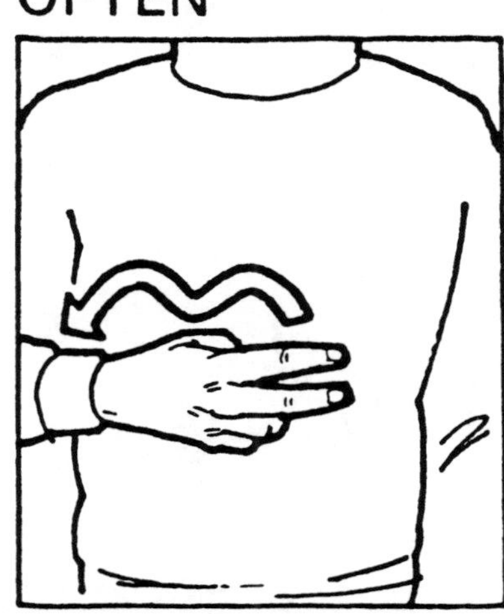

Rt. "V" hand, pointing left shakes down, hops right and shakes down again.

OLD

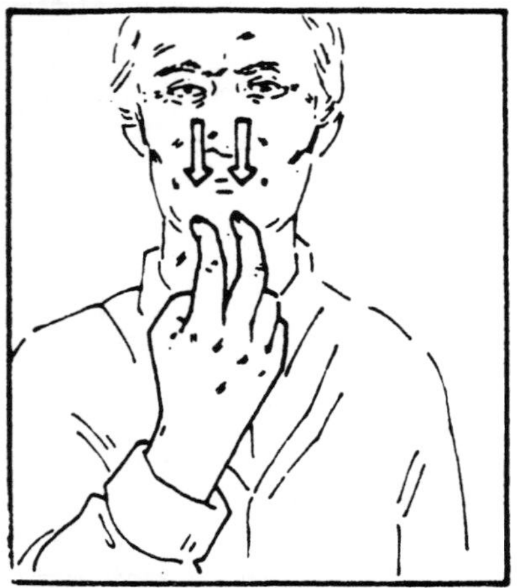

Fingers of "V" hand pull down and bend in front of nose.

ON

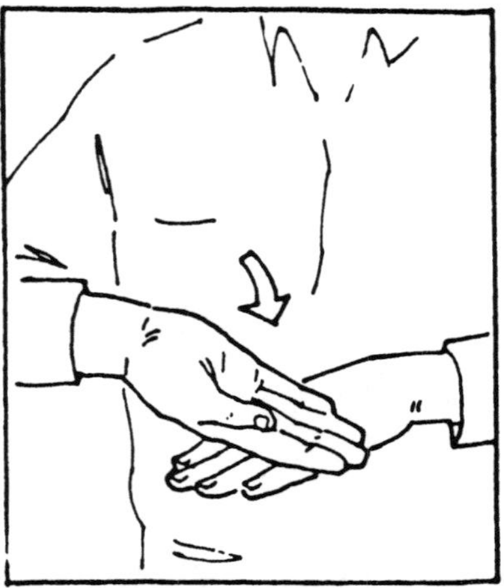

Rt. palm up flat hand placed down onto back of L. hand.

ONCE

Index, pointing up twists sharply from palm forward to palm back.

ONION

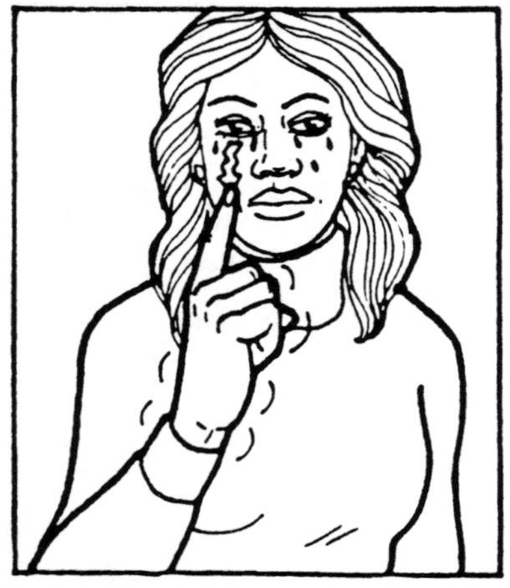

Index moves down cheek with slight twisting movement to indicate tears.

ONLY

Rt. index pointing up, palm back held above and behind L. moves down behind L. hand.

OPEN

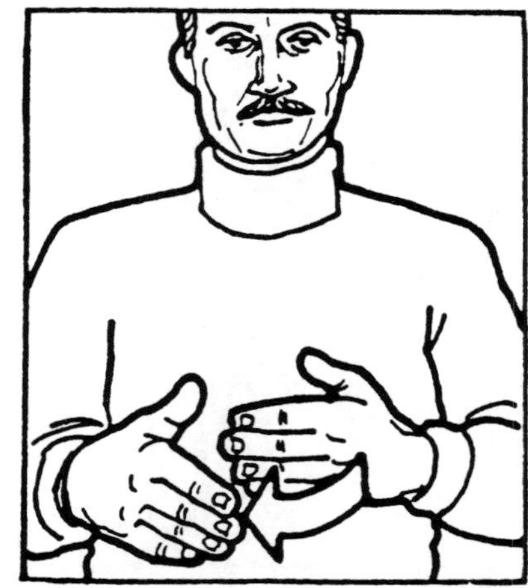

Flat hands palms back, Rt. in front of L., Rt. hand swings open.

OPERATION

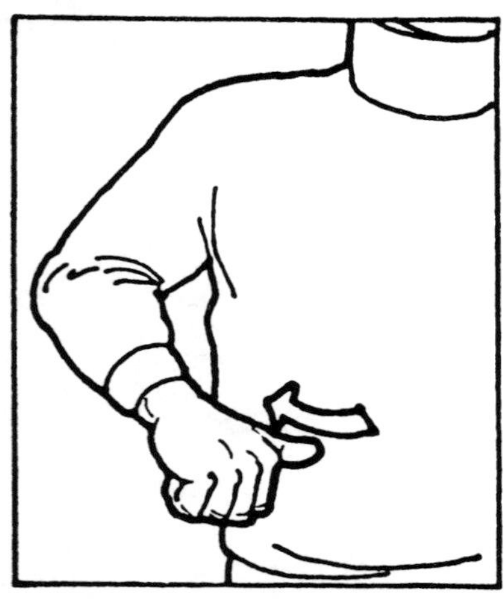

Draw tip of thumb across appropriate part of body.

OPPORTUNITY

Bent Rt. index flicks up whilst moving sharply up back of L., repeat quickly.

OPPOSE

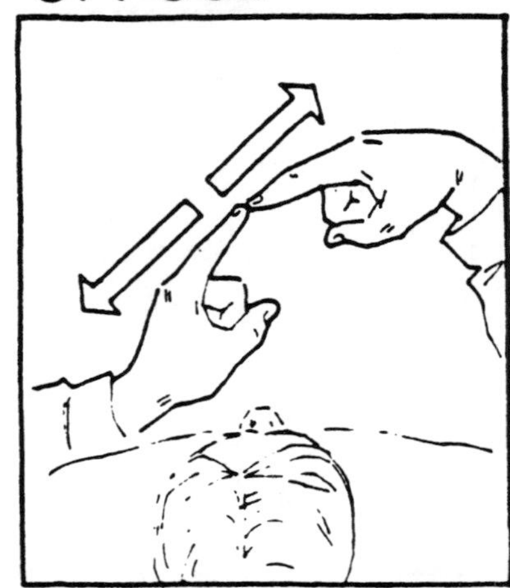

Indexes point towards each other, held diagonally in front of body, then pull apart.

OPPOSITE (idea)

Indexes point towards each other, then pull apart in small arc.

OPPOSITE (place)

Indexes point up, palms facing, Rt. in front of L., move down with slight stress.

ORAL

Bent "V" hand makes small circular movement near mouth.

ORANGE

Make repeated squeezing movement, palm forward at side of mouth.

ORANGE JUICE

Sign "Orange" then mime drinking.

ORDER (command)

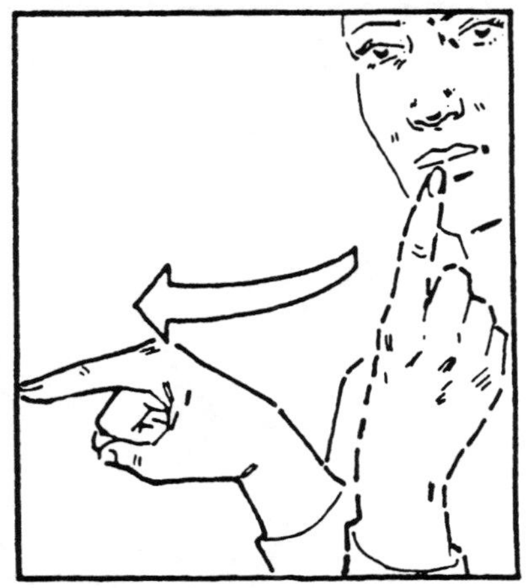

Index points to mouth then moves sharply to point forward.

ORDER (arrange)

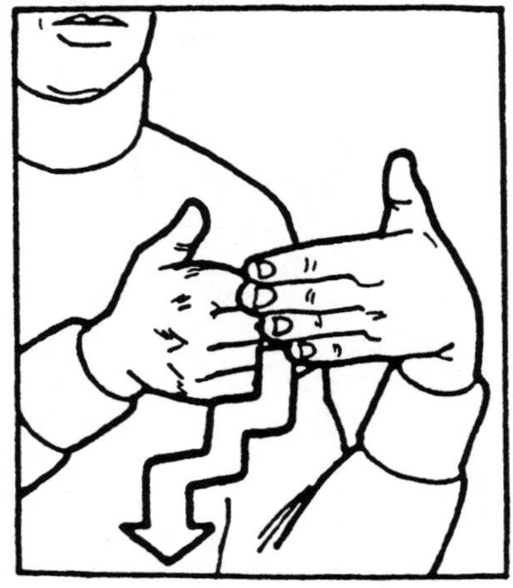

L. flat hand palm back; Rt. bent hand moves down/back towards body in steps from behind L. palm.

ORGANISE

Thumbs tucked into bent indexes; hands move backwards and forwards alternately.

OTHER

L. open hand palm back; flick back of L. ring finger with Rt. index twice.

OTHERS

L. open hand palm back; run Rt. index across backs of L. fingers, from index to little finger.

OUR

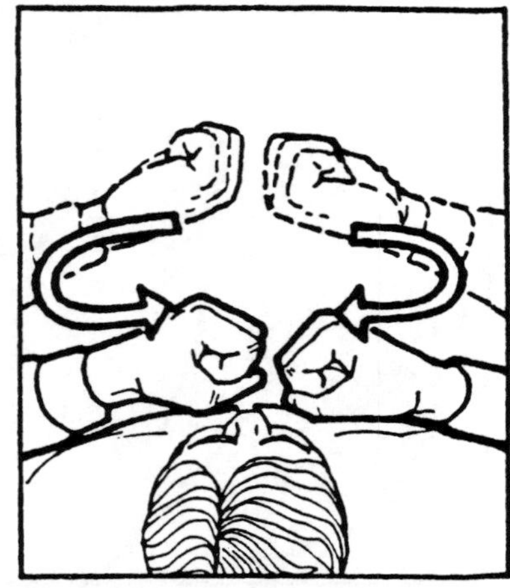

Closed hands, palms forward held out in front of body, circle back twisting to finish palms back on chest.

OUT

Rt. thumb pointing up jerks back/right.

OUTSIDE

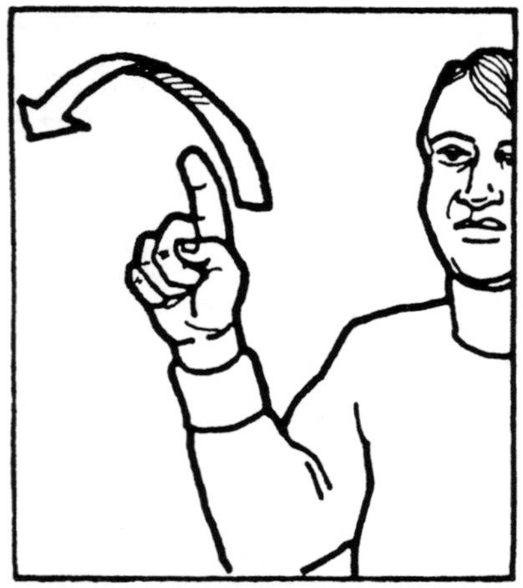

Index pointing up moves forward in upward arc to point forward.

OVER

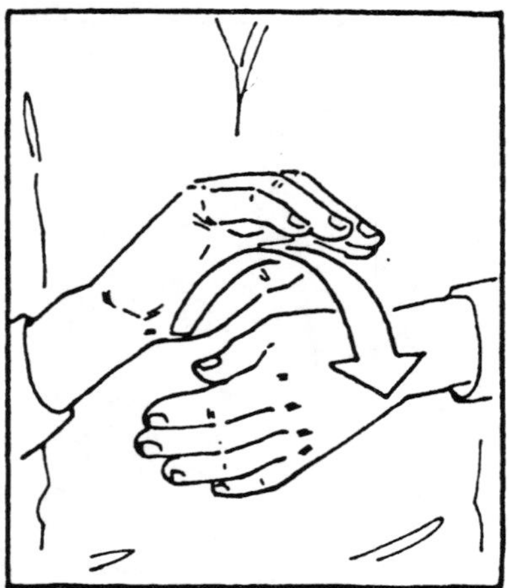

Rt. hand, slightly bent arcs over L. hand.

OVERCOME

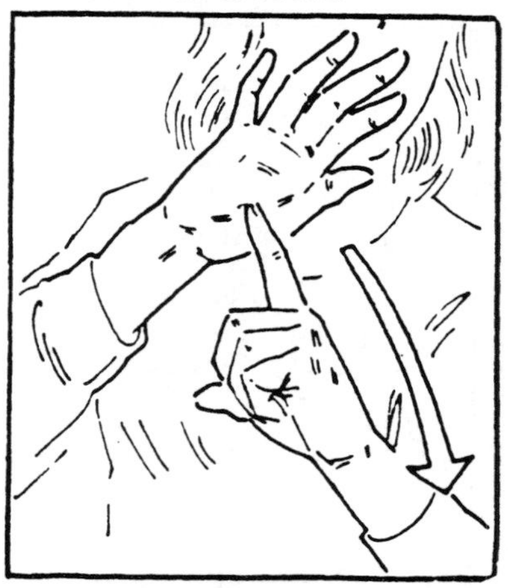

Rt. hand pushes L. index down/left.

OVERTAKE

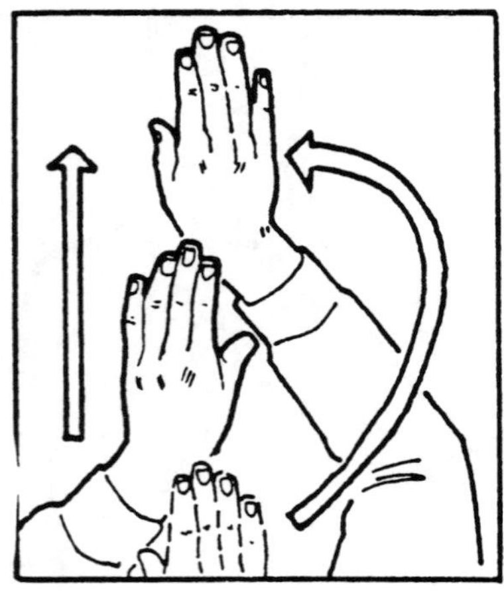

Flat hands move forward, Rt. behind L., then Rt. hand sweeps round to "overtake" the L.

OWE

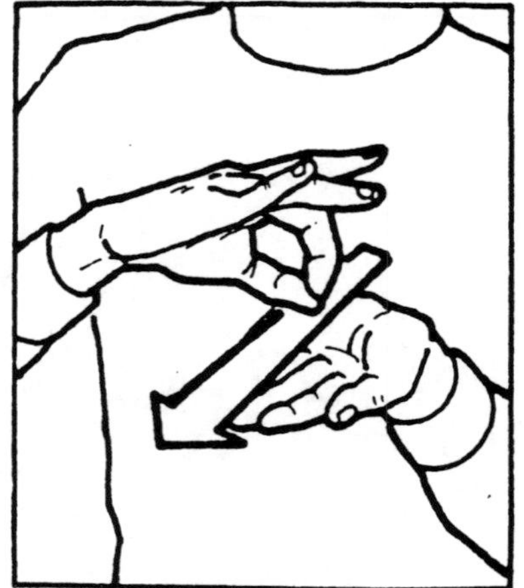

Rt. "O" hand moves forward, brushing across L. palm, towards person concerned. For "Owe me", "O" hand brushes back to self.

OWL

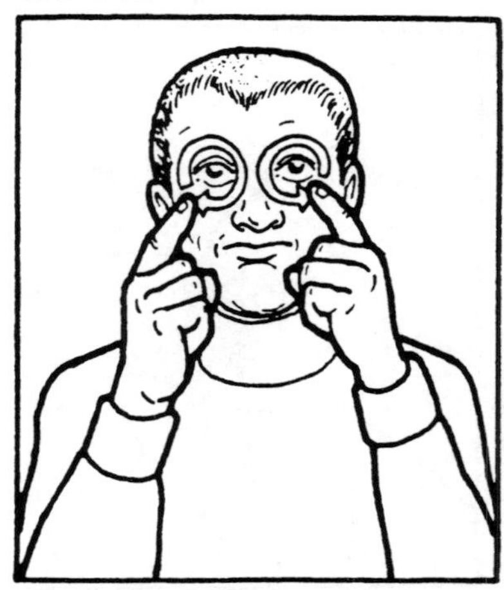

Make circles round eyes with indexes.

PACK

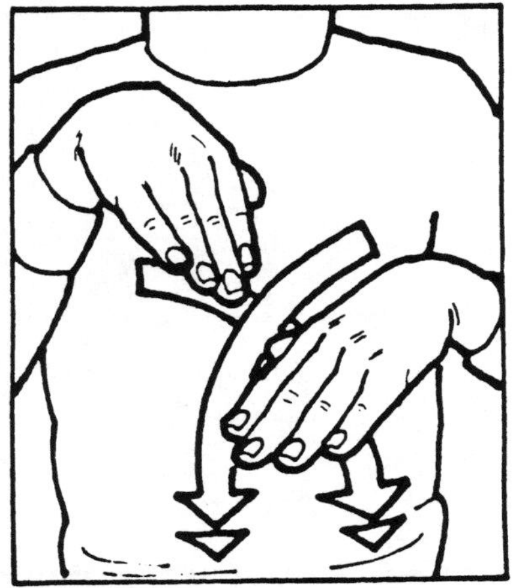

Flat hands move down/in alternately several times to indicate packing.

PAGE

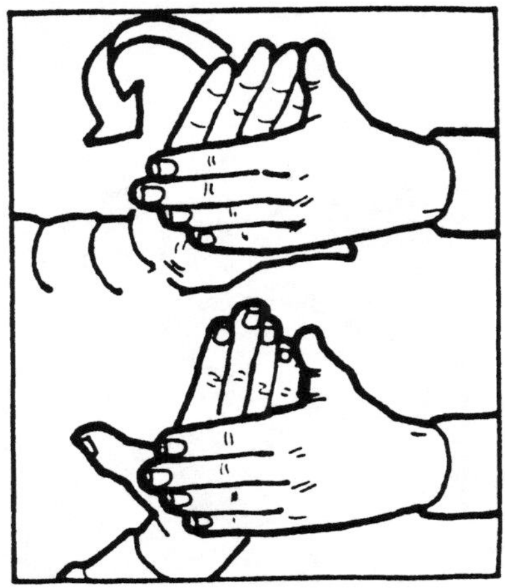

Rt. flat hand, palm down on top of L., turns over to palm up.

PAIN

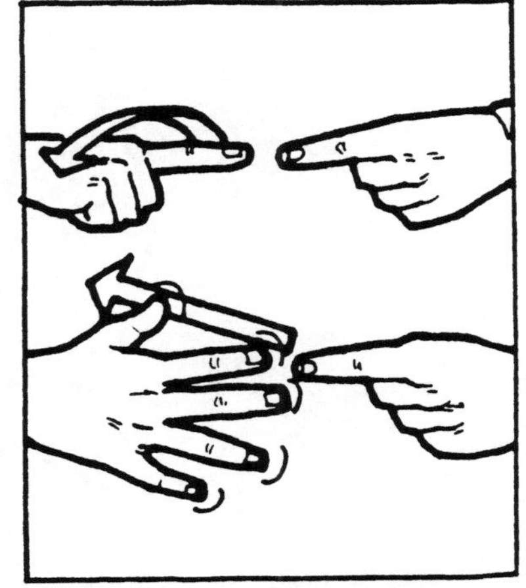

Indexes point towards each other, Rt. twists from palm down to palm back, then fingers spring open as hand pulls sharply away.

PAINT

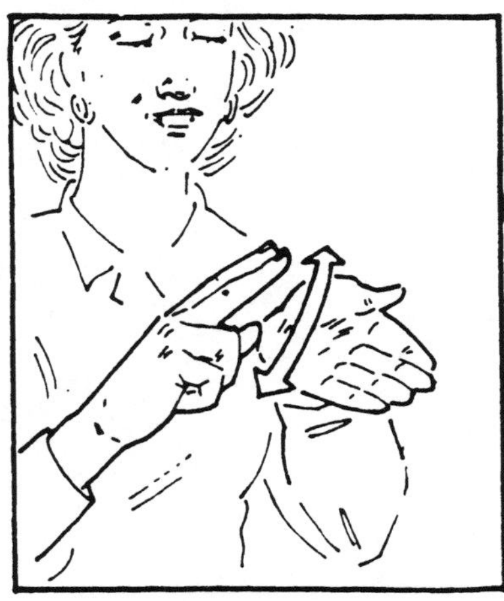

Rt. "N" hand brushes up and down L. palm.

PAIR

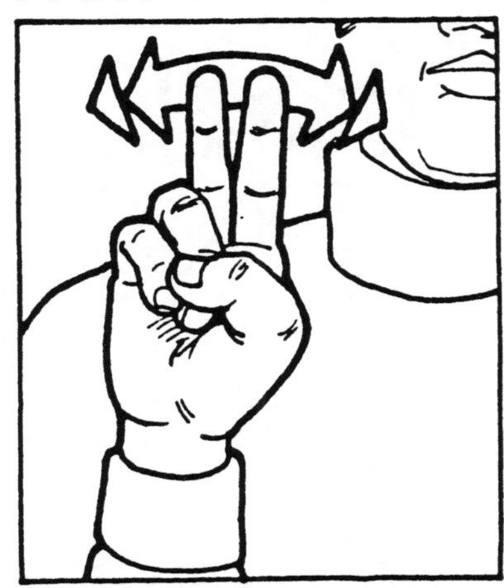

Rt. "V" hand, palm forward, shakes from side to side several times.

PANIC

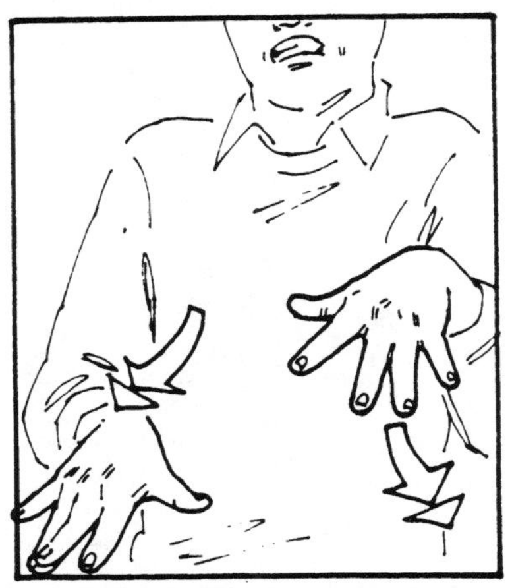

Open hands move alternately, as head moves from side to side, in an air of panic.

PAPER

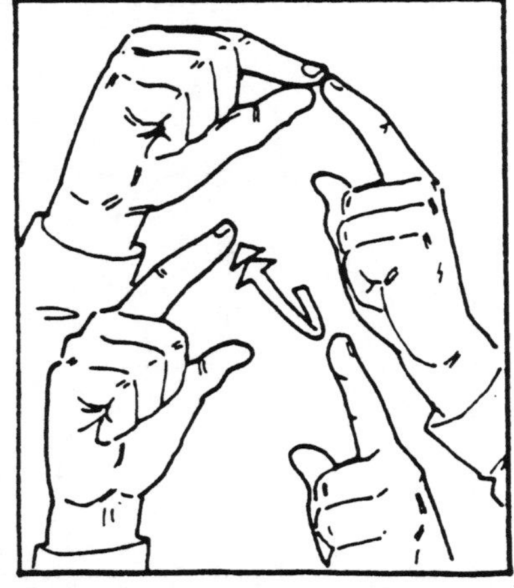

Form fingerspelt "P" then flick Rt. index and thumb open twice off end of L. index.

PARAGRAPH

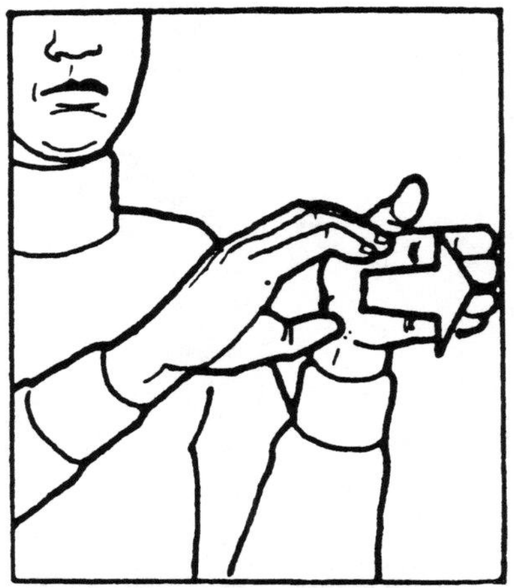

Rt. full "C" hand, indicates block of writing with short movement along L. palm.

PARALLEL

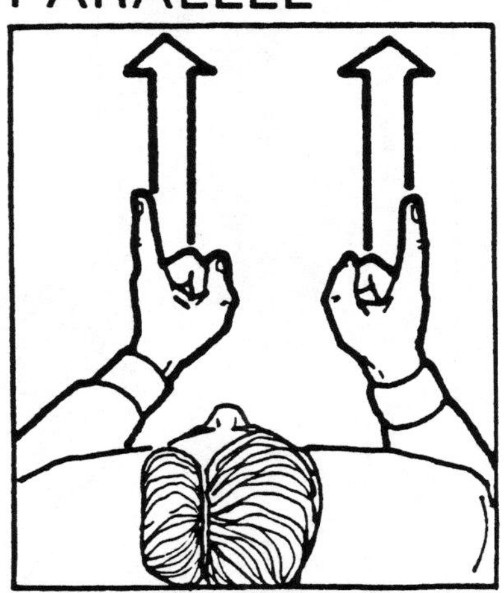

Indexes point and move forward, remaining parallel.

PARENT

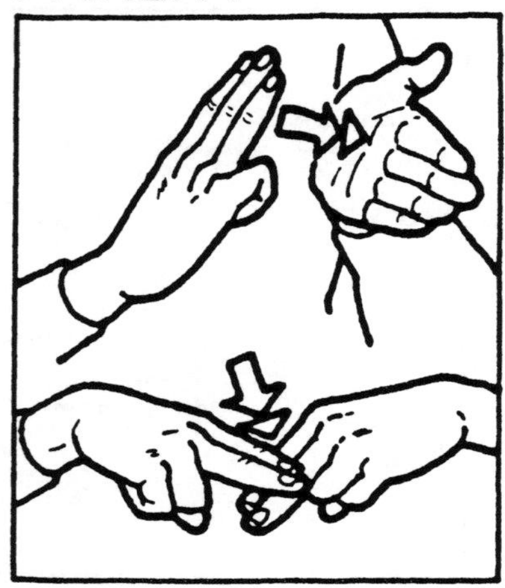

Tap "M" on L. palm twice, then tap fingers of fingerspelt "F" twice.

PARK

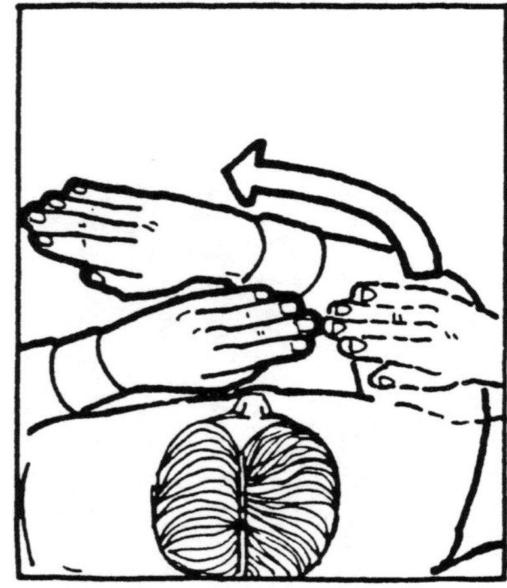

Flat hands touch at tips, palms down, then Rt. hand swings forward/left to finish in front of L. wrist.

PARK (car)

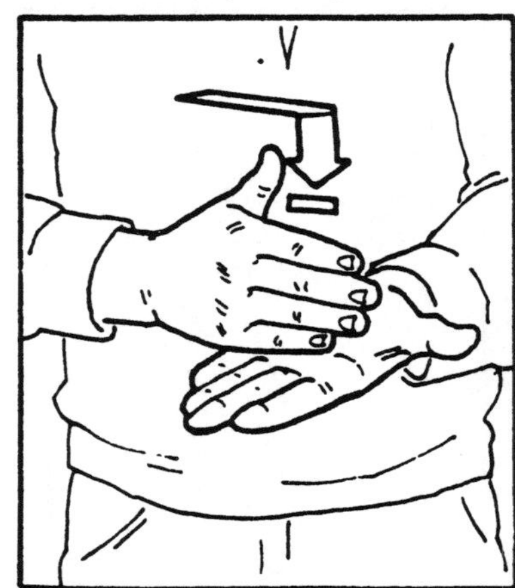

Flat hand moves forward, then down onto L. palm to represent parking a vehicle.

PART

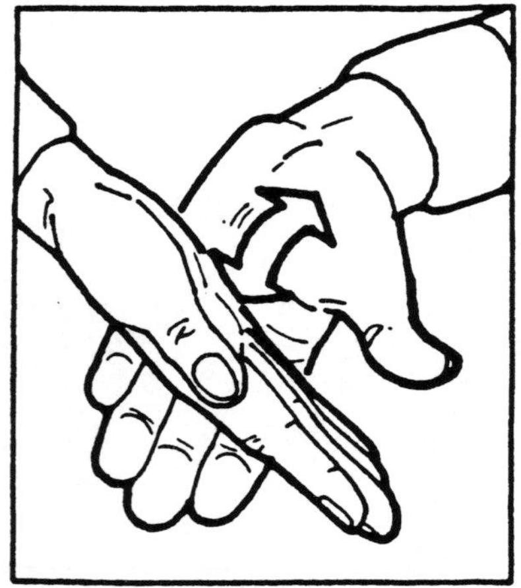

Blade of Rt. flat hand chops down onto fingers of L. flat hand, then diagonally across L. palm.

PARTICULAR

Rt. "O" moves forward to strike tip of L. index, and springs open sharply.

PARTNER

Closed hands, thumbs up, held out in front of body, move back together to left side of chest.

PARTY

Two "O" hands move up and down alternately to mouth.

PASS

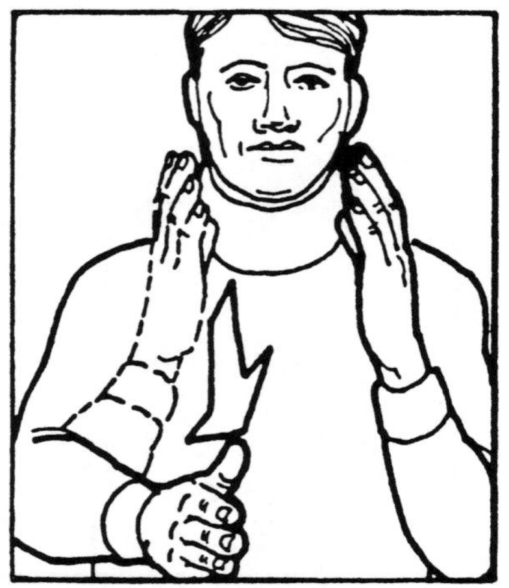

Rt. flat hand, pointing up, swings forward/down past L. flat hand.

PAST (the)

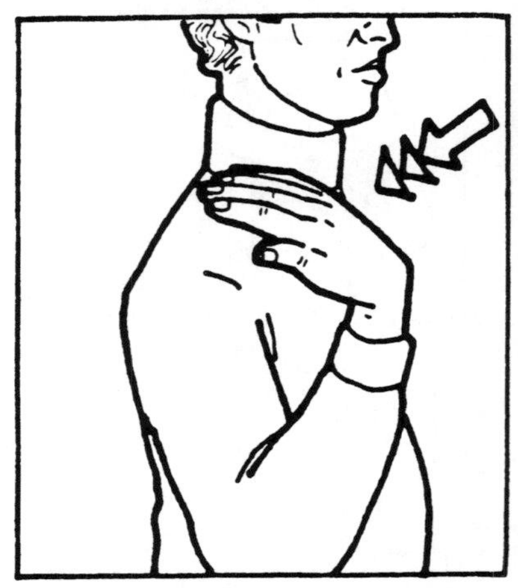

Rt. hand makes backward movement over shoulder.

PASTIE

Indexes and thumbs touch, hands pull apart as indexes close onto thumbs to indicate shape of pastie.

PATIENT (calm)

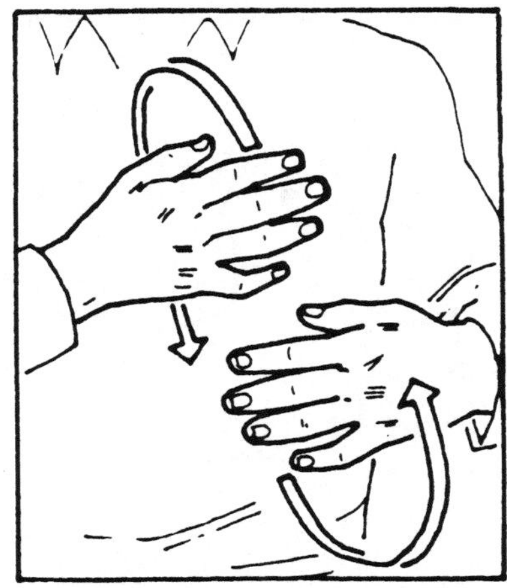

Flat hands brush alternately down body in backward circular movement.

PATTERN

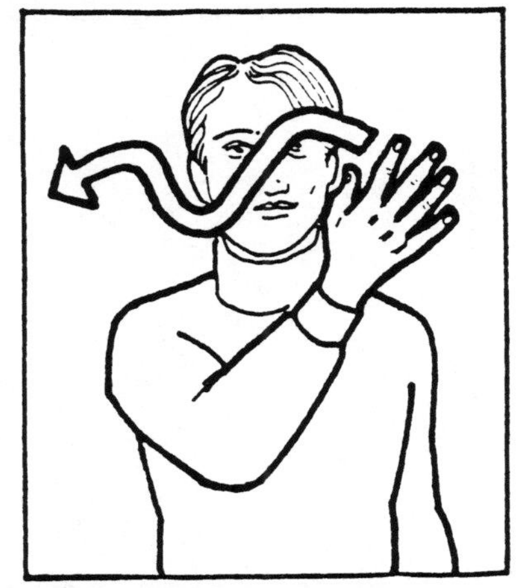

Open hand, palm back makes wavy up and down movement.

PAVEMENT

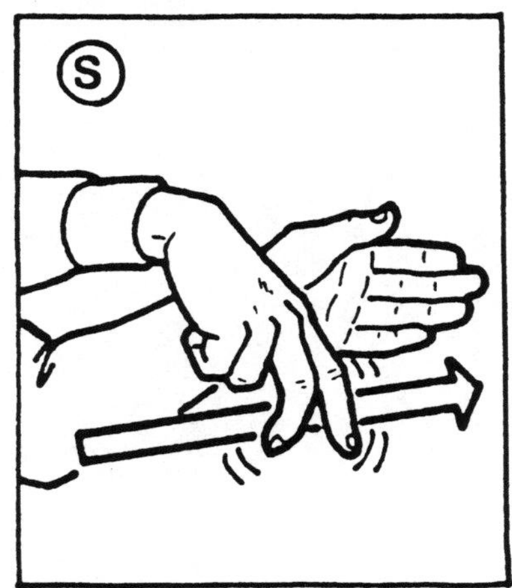

Left arm and hand point forward, Rt. index and middle fingers "walk" along side of left arm.

PAY

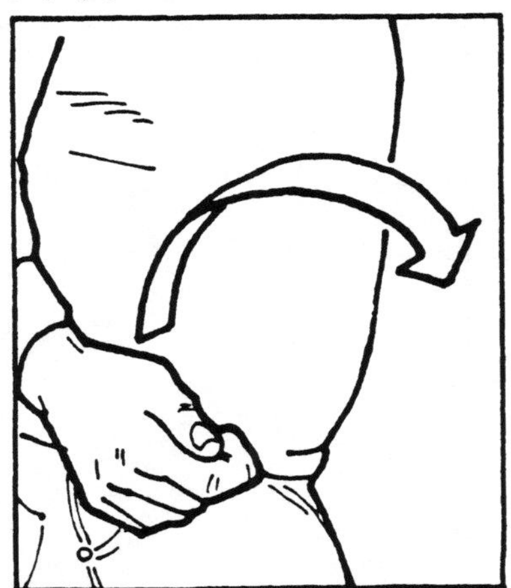

Rt. thumb tucked into bent index, hand moves forward in upward arc, from right hip.

PEACH

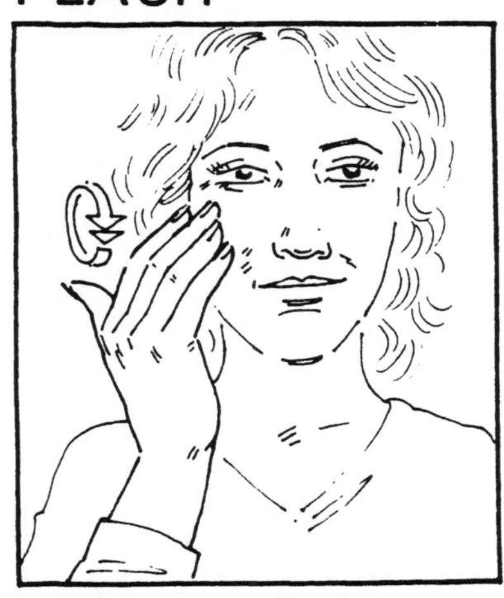

Fingers of Rt. hand make circular rubbing movement on cheek.

PEAR

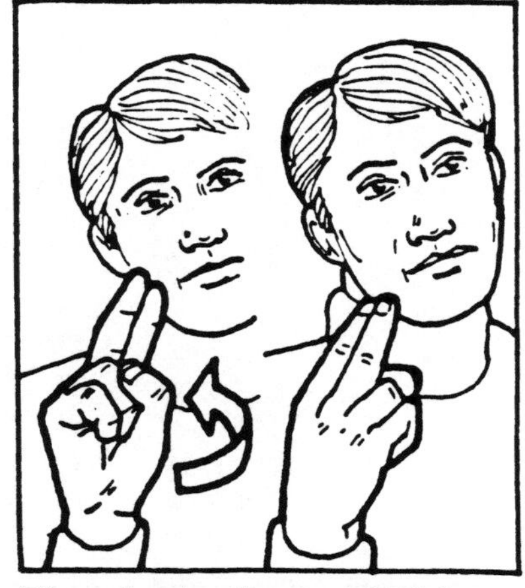

Tips of palm forward "N" hand touch side of mouth and twist to palm back.

PEAS

Rt. thumb scrapes forward several times along L. extended index, as if shelling peas.

PEDAL-CAR

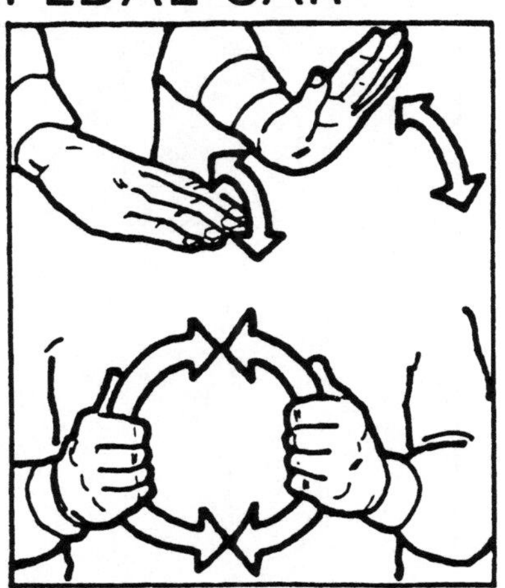

Flat hands mime pedalling movement, then sign "Car".

PEEL

L. thumb moves against Rt. hand in action of peeling.

PEN

Flex thumb of closed hand, then mime writing.

PENCIL

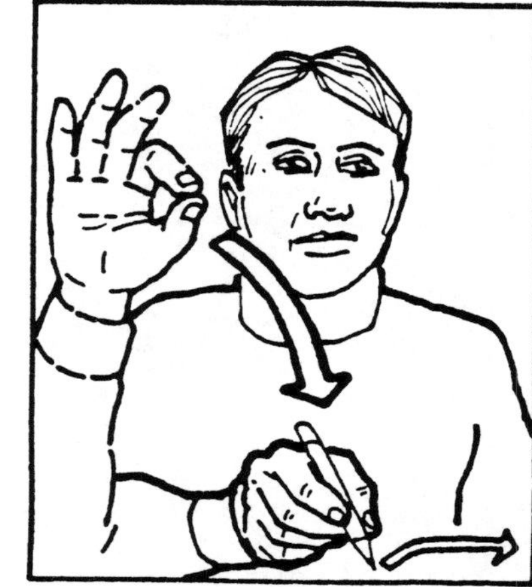

Pluck imaginary pencil from behind ear, then mime writing.

PENGUIN

Flat hands point out at sides of body, body rocks slightly from side to side.

PENNY/PENCE

Tips of Rt. full "O" hand touch tip of L. index, to form "P".

PEOPLE

Index and thumb stroke down chin, then edge of index brushes forward on cheek.

PERCENT

"O" hand makes short forward movement, moves diagonally down a few inches and makes short forward movement again.

PERFECT

"O" hand makes two short forward movements from near mouth.

PERHAPS

Rt. thumb and little finger extended, palm left. Hand waggles with quick twisting movement of wrist.

PERSON

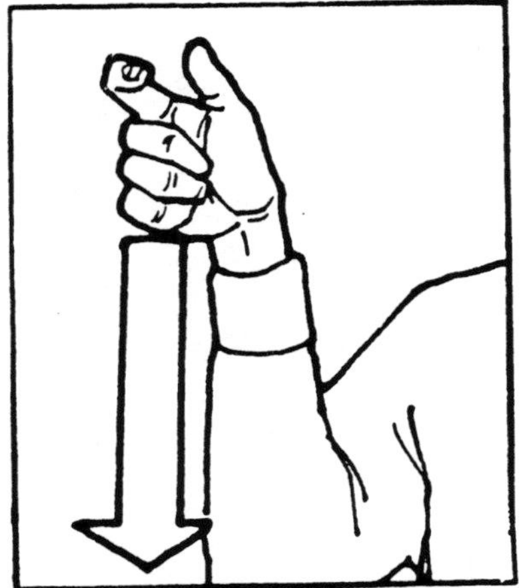

Rt. "C" hand, palm forward pointing right, moves down about 6 inches.

PERSUADE

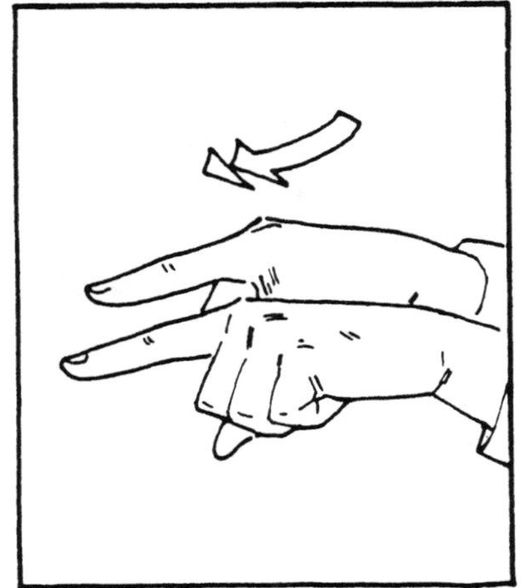

Index fingers move forward twice, simultaneously.

PET

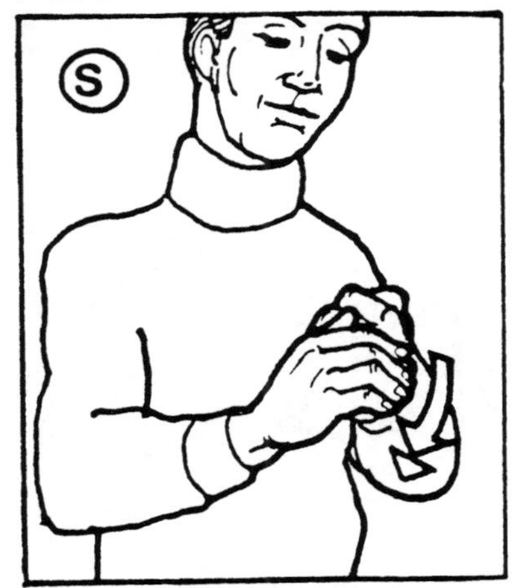

Rt. hand strokes down back of L. closed hand twice.

PETROL

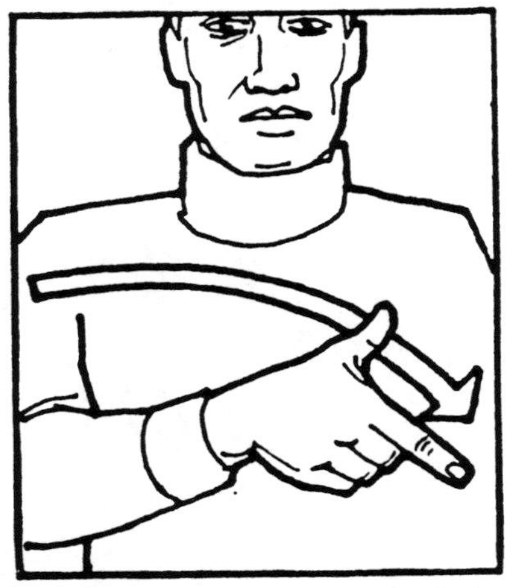

Rt. index and thumb extended, hand moves in arc, forward/ left.

PHOTO

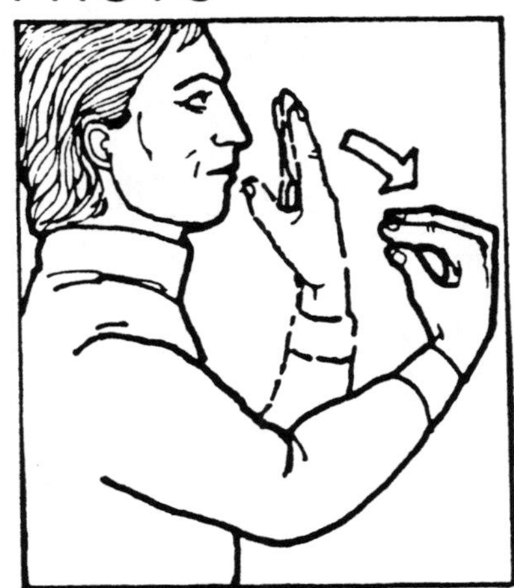

Flat hand held in front of face, thumb pointing back. Hand pulls forward sharply, closing fingers onto thumb.

PIANO

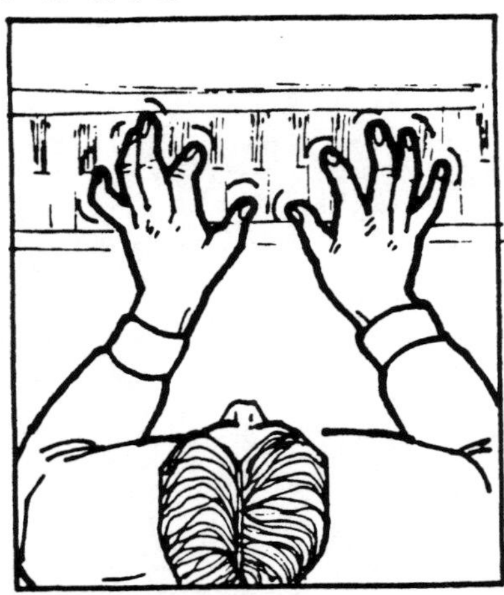

Mime playing piano.

PICK

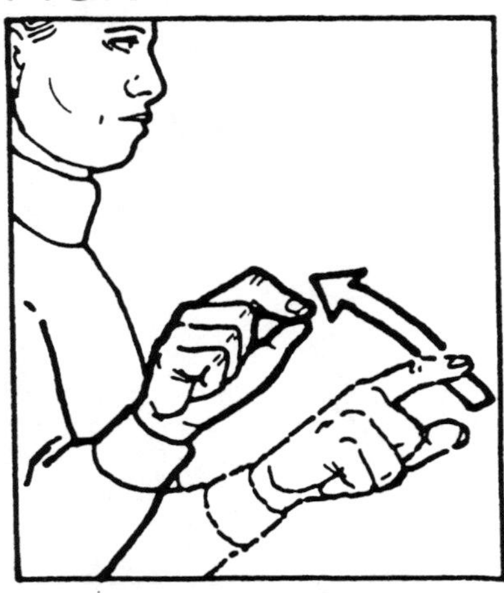

Index and thumb point forward, hand moves up/back sharply closing index and thumb tips together.

PICNIC

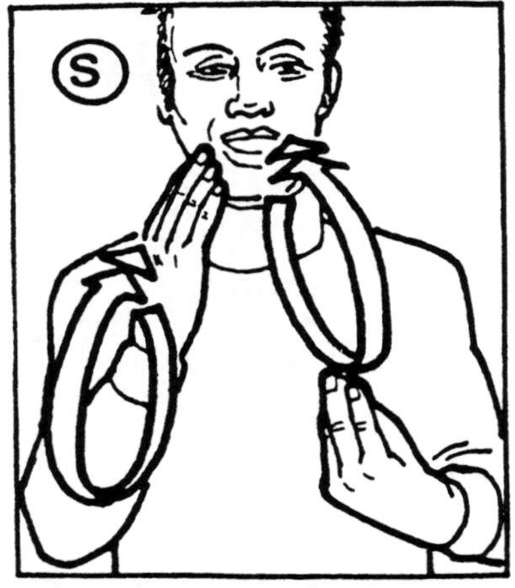

Bunched hands make alternate circular movements up to mouth.

PICTURE

Indexes make outline of picture.

PIE

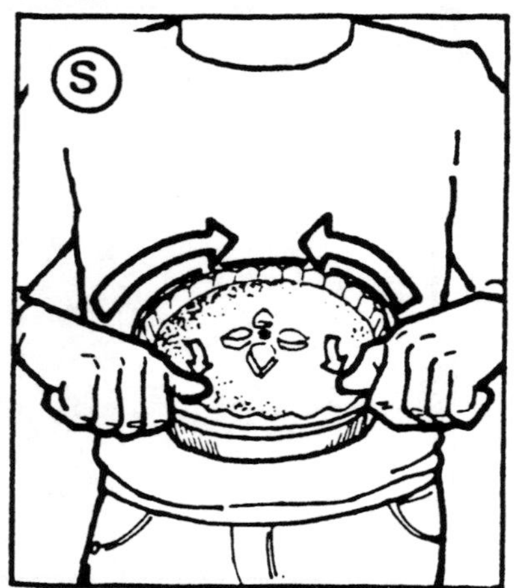

Thumbs press down in circular movement like pressing on a pie crust.

PIER

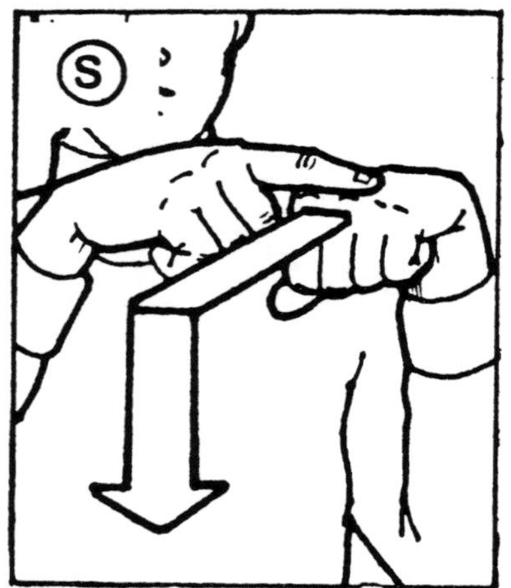

Rt. index moves forward from back of L. closed hand, then down.

PIG

Rt. fist makes small circular movement in front of nose.

PILLOW

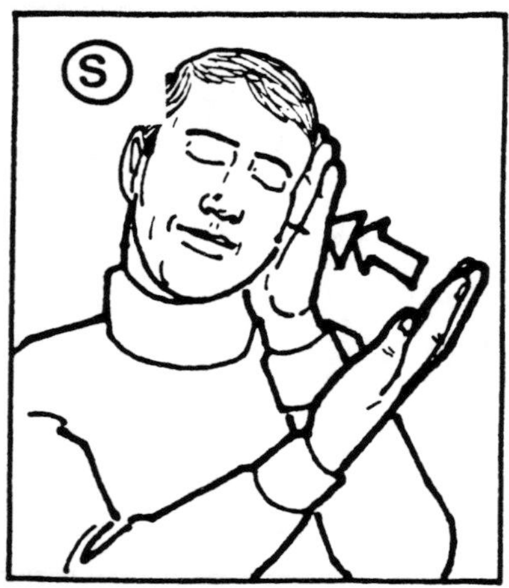

Head rests on L. flat hand, Rt. hand pats back of L. twice.

PILL(S)

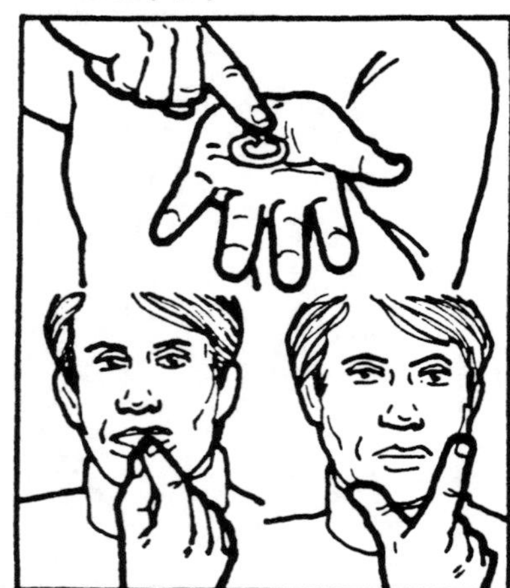

Rt. index makes small circle on L. palm, then Rt. index and thumb flick open in front of mouth.

PINEAPPLE

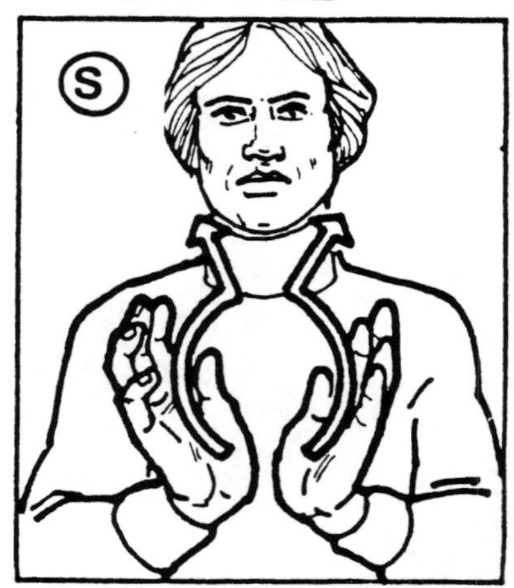

Open hands, fingers slightly bent, touch at heels, move up/out, touch again, then move slightly up/out.

PINK

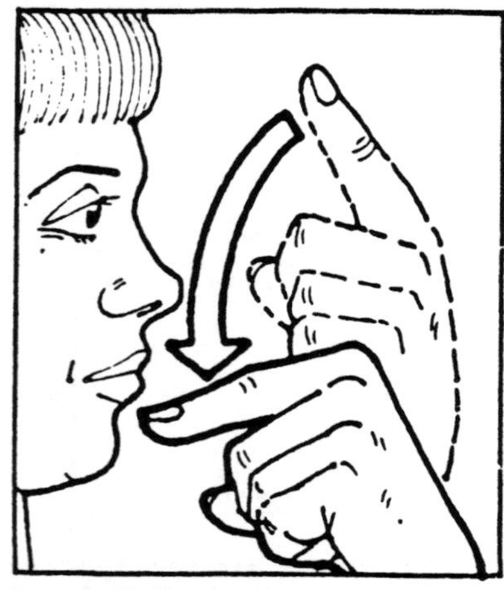

Index flicks down in front of face.

PIPE

Thumb and little finger extended, thumb taps mouth twice.

PIZZA

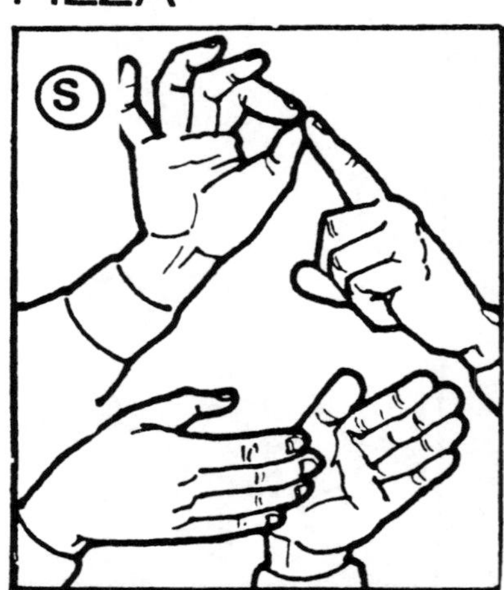

Fingerspell "P" then "Z".

PLACE

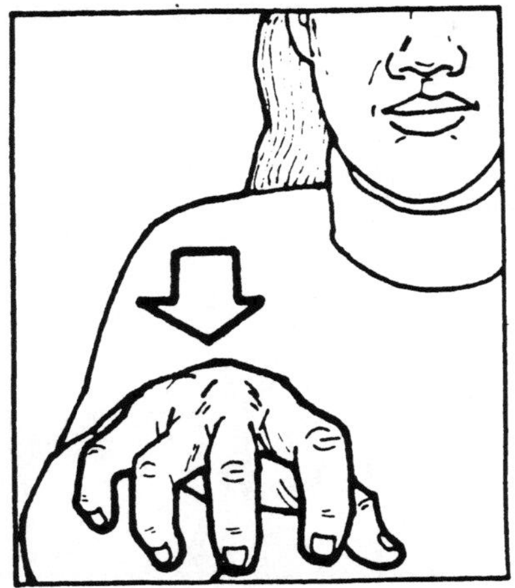

Palm down clawed hand makes short movement down.

PLAN

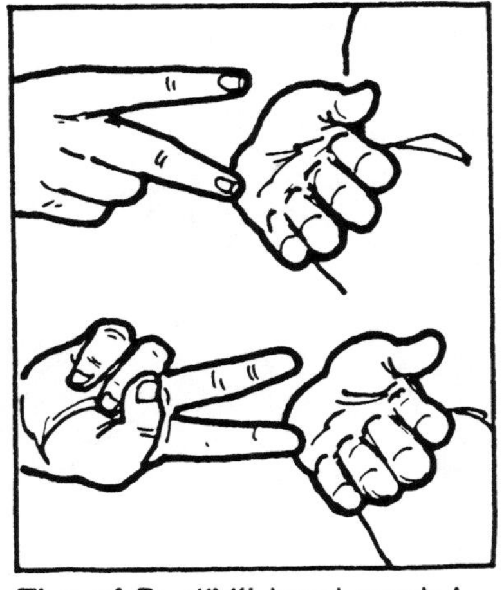

Tips of Rt. "V" hand touch L. palm alternately as Rt. hand twists from palm back to palm forward and back.

PLANT

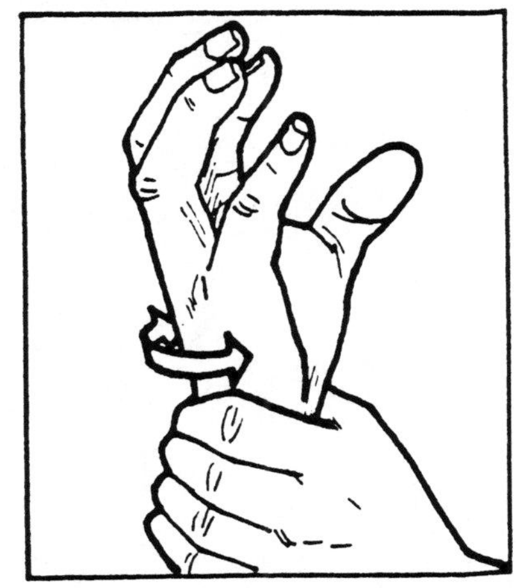

Rt. slightly clawed hand twists from wrist, supported by L. hand.

PLASTIC

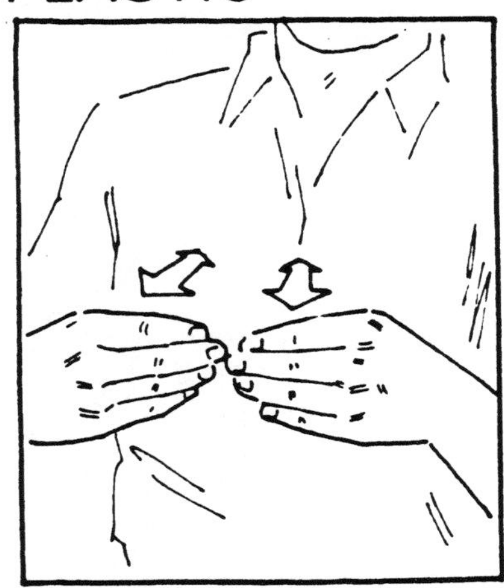

Bunched hands flex backwards and forwards simultaneously from the wrists.

PLATE

Rt. index makes a circle over L. palm.

PLAY

Flat hands move out in horizontal circles.

PLEASE

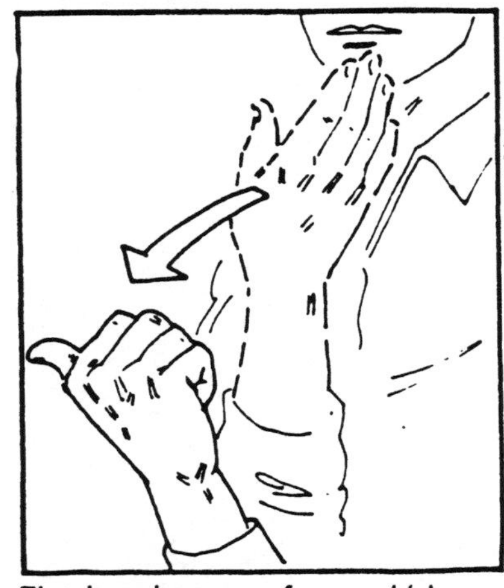

Flat hand moves forward/down from mouth.

PLEASED

Flat hand rubs in circular movement on chest.

PLENTY

Slightly bent hand strokes up/forward under chin twice.

PLUM

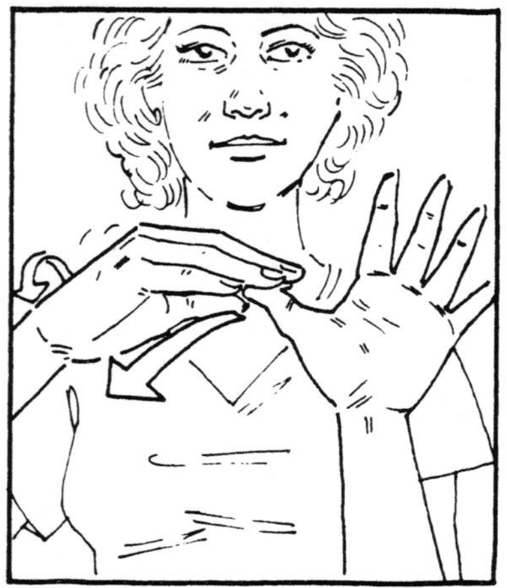

Rt. bunched hand holds and "twists off" L. thumb.

PLUS

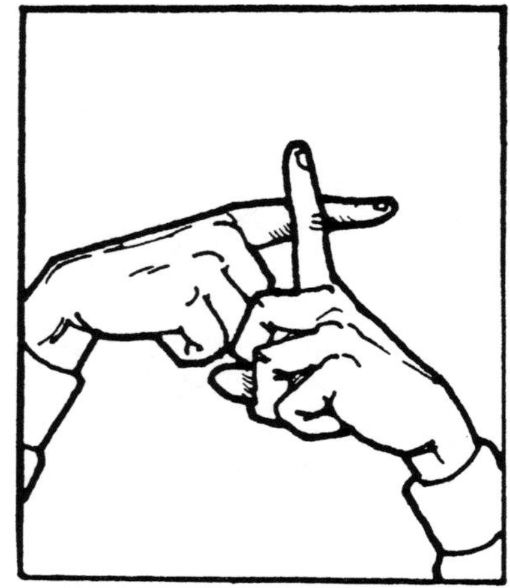

Indexes form a "plus" symbol.

POCKET

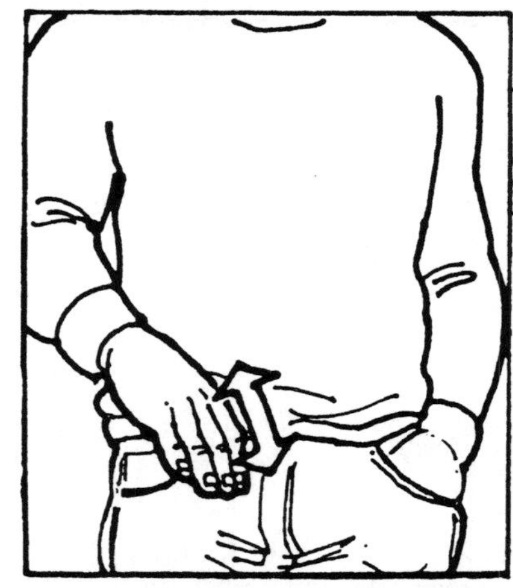

Flat hand rubs up and down over pocket.

POEM

Index points to mouth, moves forward, then moves down in slightly outward arcs.

POINT (finger)

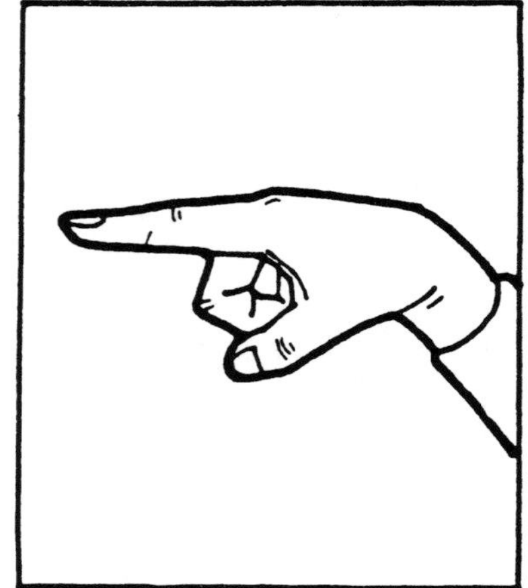

Point with index.

POINT (make a)

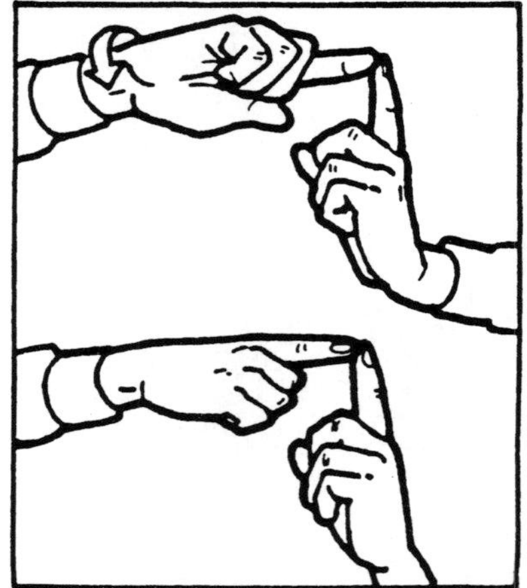

Tip of Rt. index contacts tip of L. index and twists.

POINTED

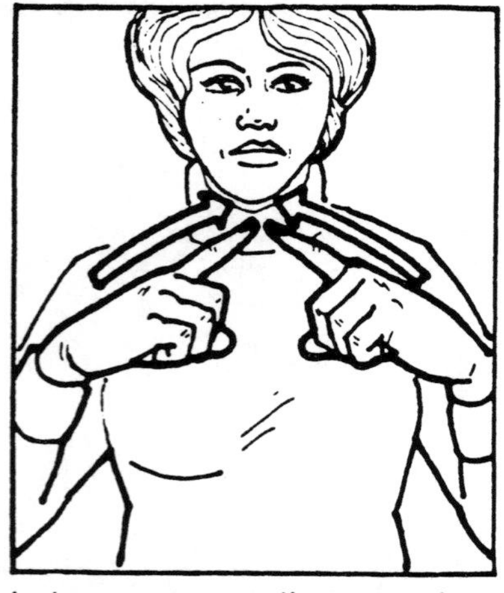

Indexes move up/in to touch at tips.

POISON

Tip of Rt. little finger makes circular movement in L. full "O" hand.

POLICE

Fingers of Rt. "V" hand pull across L. wrist and flex.

POLICE CAR

Sign "police" then "car".

POLITE

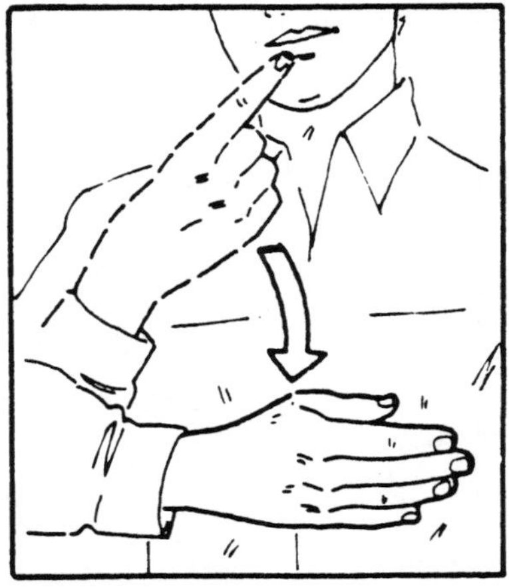

Index touches mouth, changes to flat hand and brushes down body once.

POND

Fingerspell "P", then make circular wavy movement with flat hand.

POOR

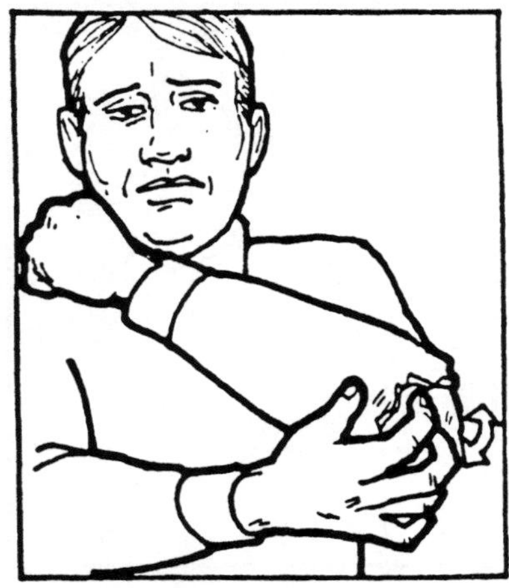

Tips of Rt. clawed hand scratch left elbow, indicating sleeve worn through.

POORLY

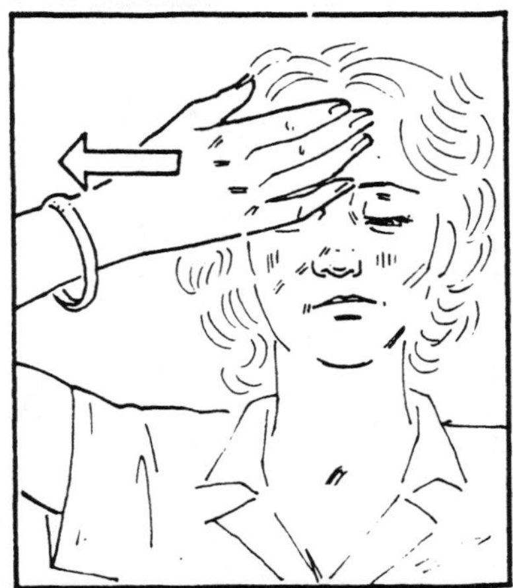

Flat hand brushes across forehead.

POPULAR

Both thumbs extended, hands move quickly in small alternate forward circles.

POSH

Index tip brushes up against tip of nose, twice.

POSSIBLE

Rt. hand palm back. Straight index closes onto thumb twice, quickly, in front of nose.

POST

Rt. bunched hand moves forward under L. and springs open.

POST OFFICE

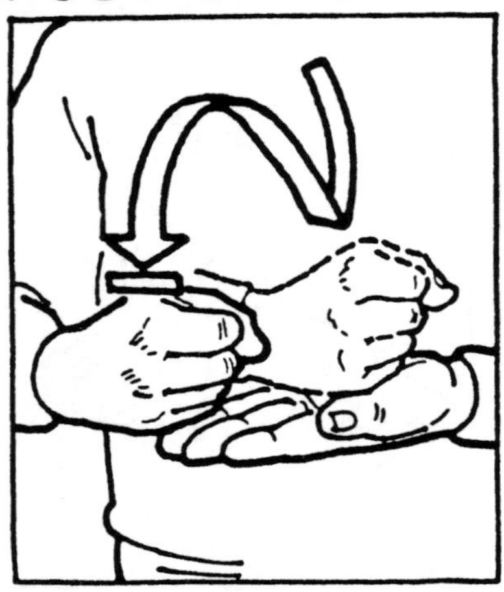

Blade of Rt. fist stamps on heel, then fingers of L. hand.

POTATO

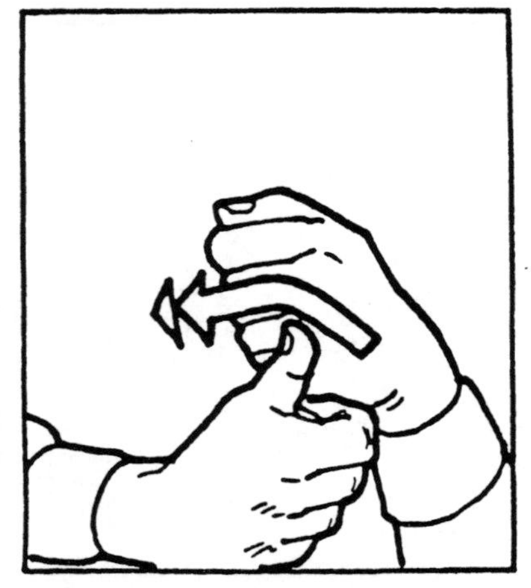

Rt. thumb scrapes up and over back of L. closed hand, twice.

POUND

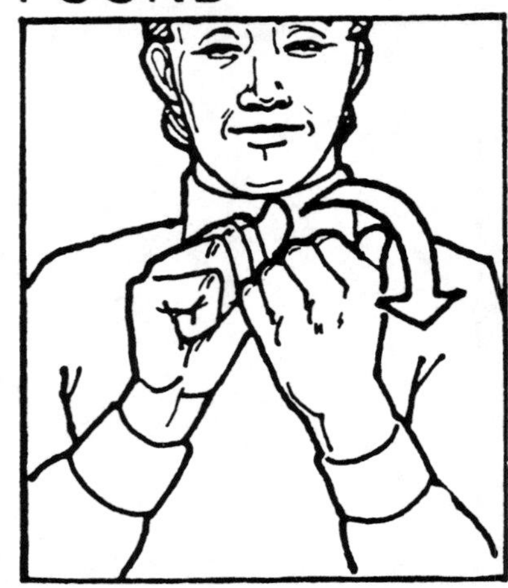

Rt. closed hand twists forward/ down over L. closed hand as if peeling note off wad.

POWER

Open hands held out sweep in and up closing to fists.

PRACTICE

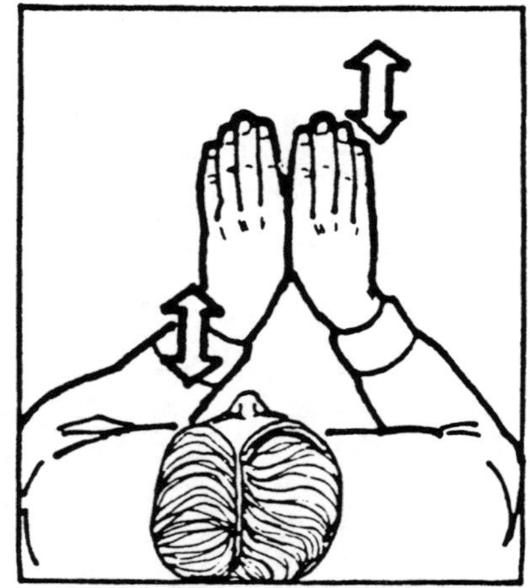

Flat hands, thumbs tucked in, rub backwards and forwards against each other.

PRAISE

Both thumbs up, hands make alternate forward circles at head height.

PRAM

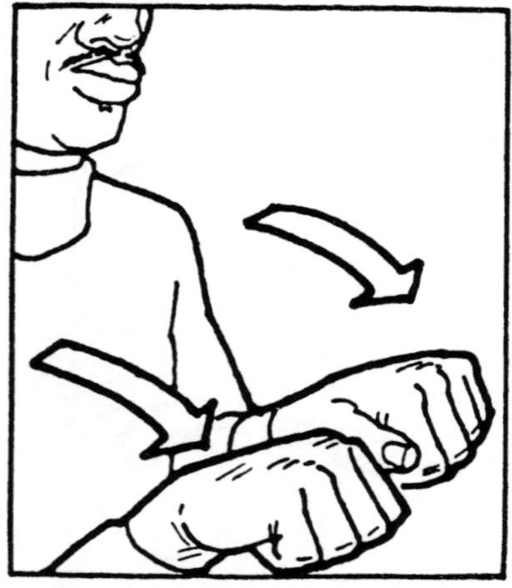

Mime pushing a pram.

PRAY

Flat hands held together, as in praying.

PREFER

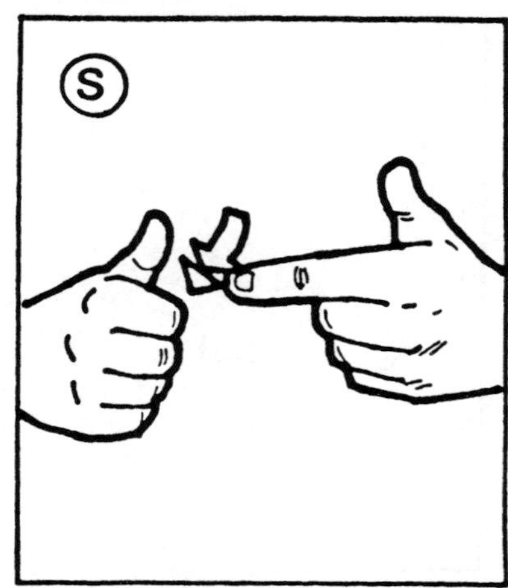

L. thumb and index extended, Rt. thumbtip brushes forward twice off tip of L. index.

PREGNANT

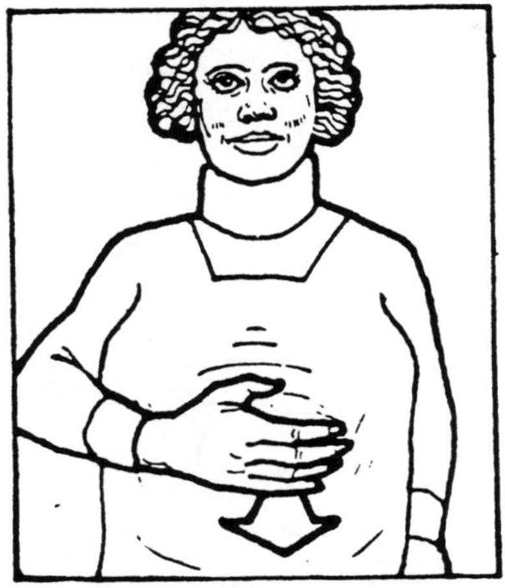

Flat hand held on stomach moves forward to indicate pregnancy.

PREPARE

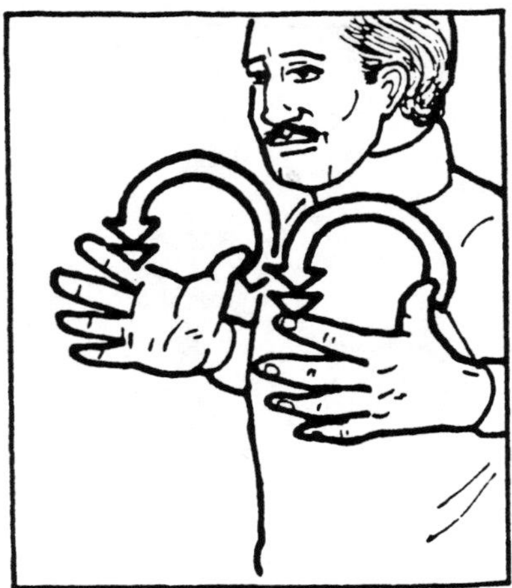

Thumbs of open hands, palms facing, brush up sides of upper chest in forward circular movement, twice.

PRESENT

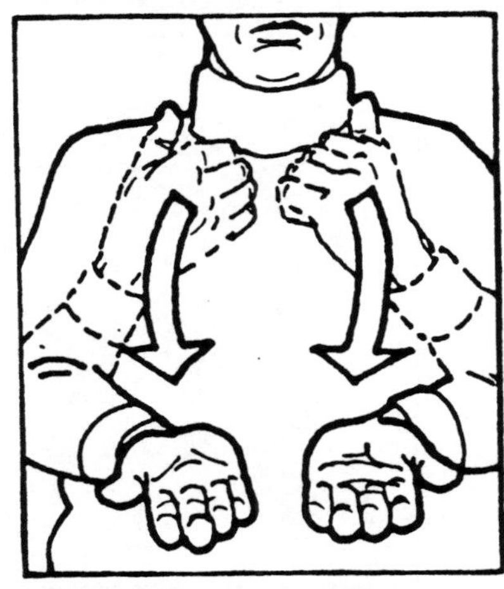

Bent hands, palms back, swing forward/down opening to flat hands.

PRETEND

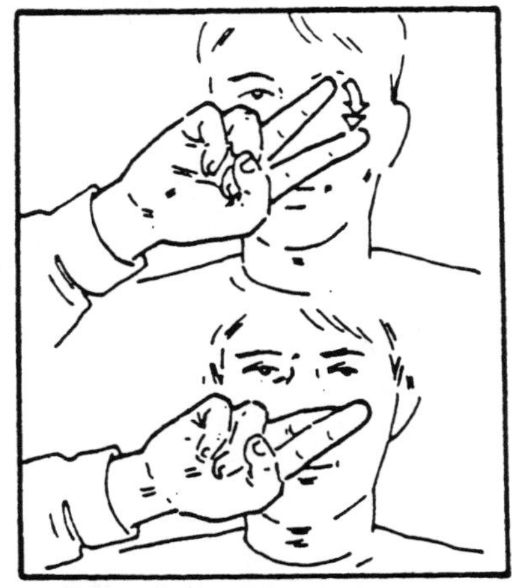

Middle finger of "V" hand brushes down nose closing behind index twice quickly.

PRETTY

Index circles face, then hand moves out slightly thumb up.

PREVENT

Rt. closed hand pushes forward to contact L. index with stress.

PRICE

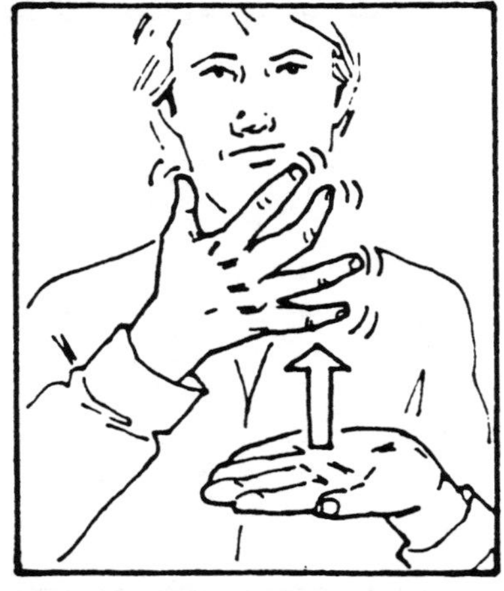

Fingers of Rt. hand move up from L. palm and flutter near chin.

PRIEST

Index and thumb tips touch then pull apart round neck to indicate clerical collar.

PRINCE

Index extended, palm forward moves across forehead in small forward arcs.

PRINCESS

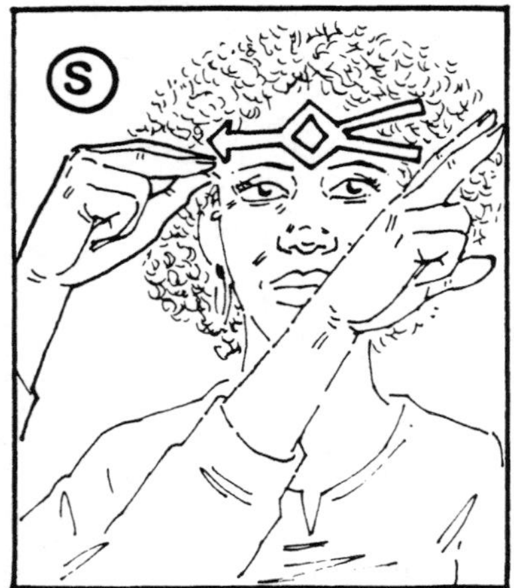

Index and middle finger, open and close onto thumb as formation moves across forehead.

PRINT

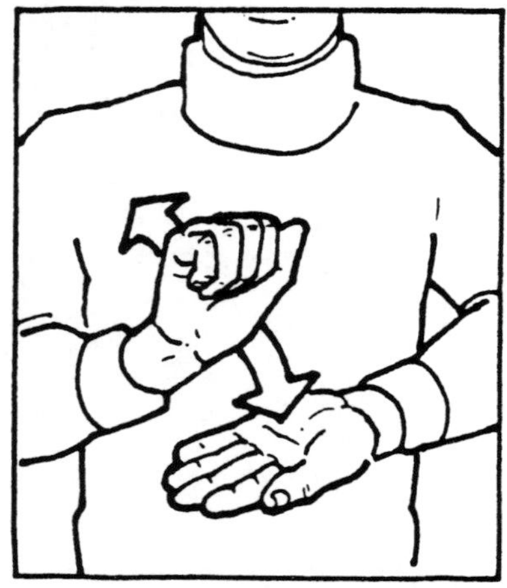

Rt. closed hand hits L. palm and bounces up.

PRISON

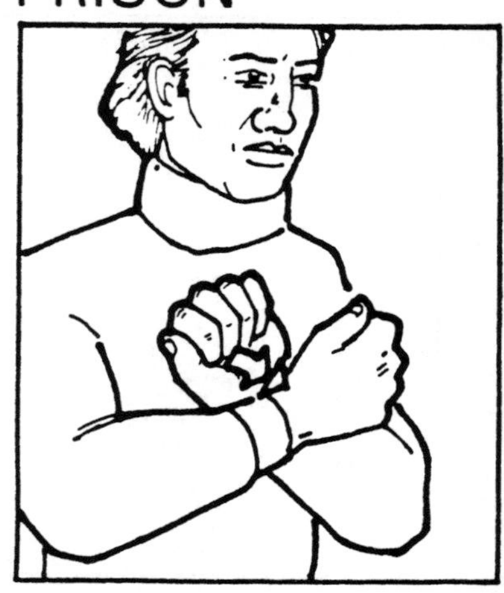

Closed hands crossed at wrists tap together twice.

PRIVATE

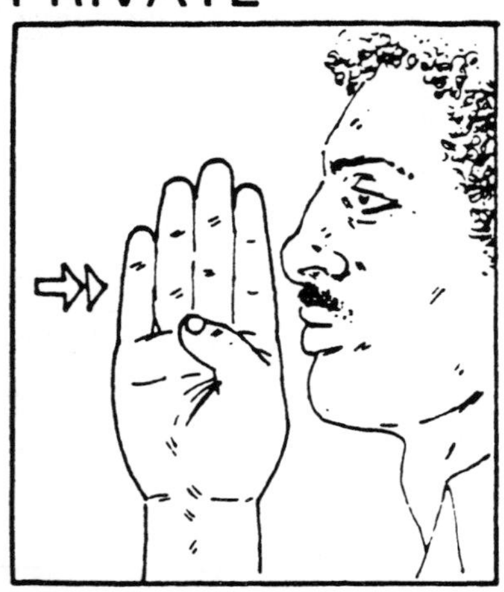

Index edge of flat hand, thumb tucked in, taps nose twice.

PRIZE (trophy)

Little fingers and thumbs extended, palms back, move up/forward as if presenting a cup.

PROFESSION

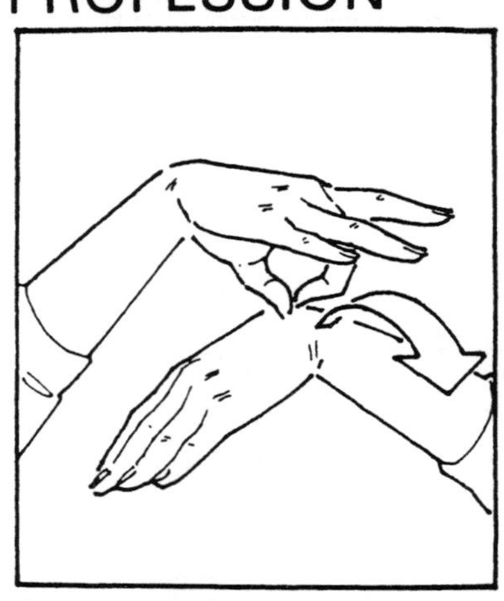

Rt. middle finger and thumb touching, contact L. wrist, then Rt. hand moves forward and opens.

PROFIT

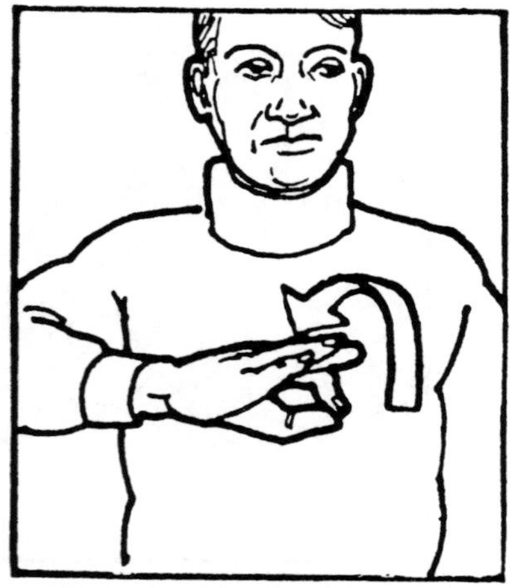

"O" hand moves back to body in small arc, twisting over from palm up, to palm down.

PROGRAMME

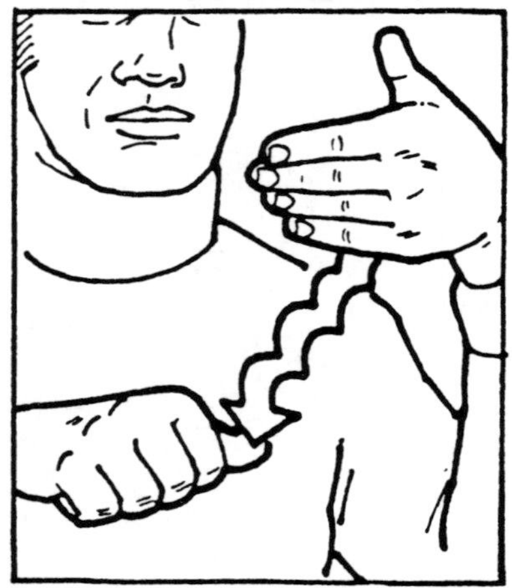

Rt. closed hand, palm down, thumb extended, moves down from L. palm in small hops.

PROGRAMME (TV)

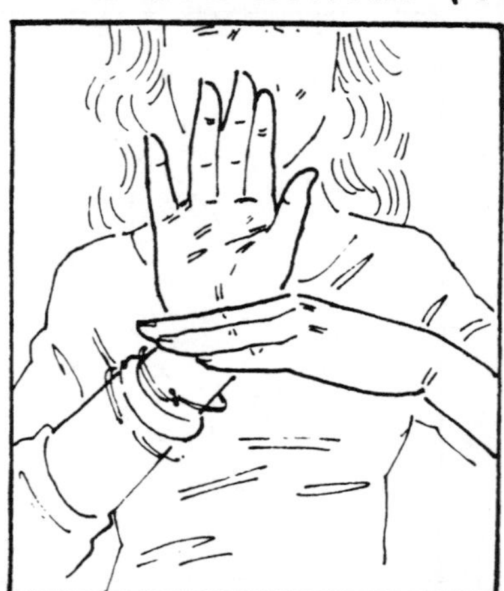

Heel of Rt. open hand contacts L. index and makes small side to side shaking movement.

PROMISE

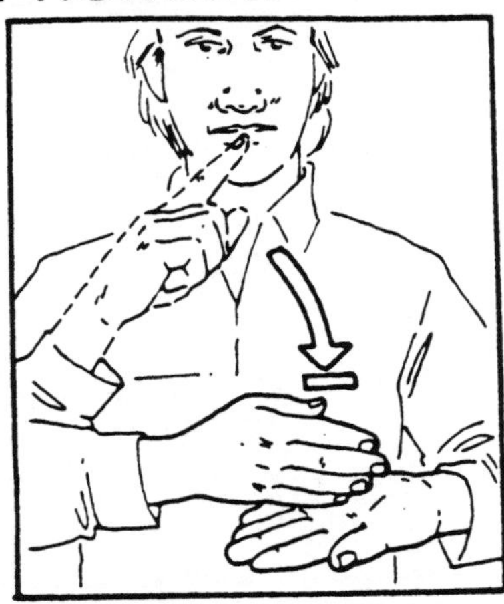

Rt. index points to mouth, then blade of Rt. flat hand hits L. palm with emphasis.

PROOF

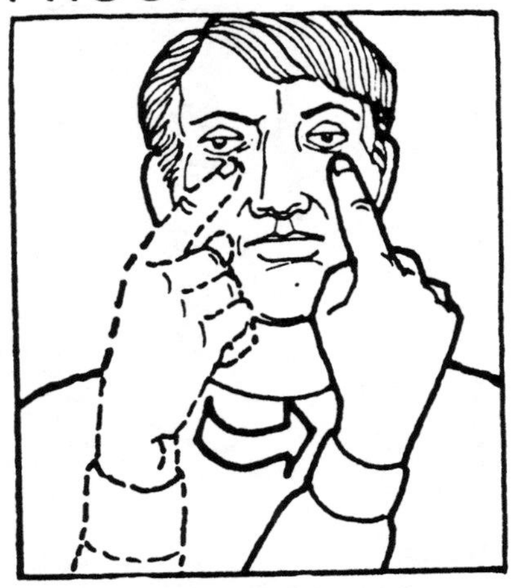

Tip of index held under right eye, then left eye.

PROTECT

Fists held back to back, Rt. palm forward in front of L.; Rt. pushes forward/out with stress.

PROTESTANT

Blade of Rt. flat hand brushes diagonally down chest from left shoulder.

PROUD

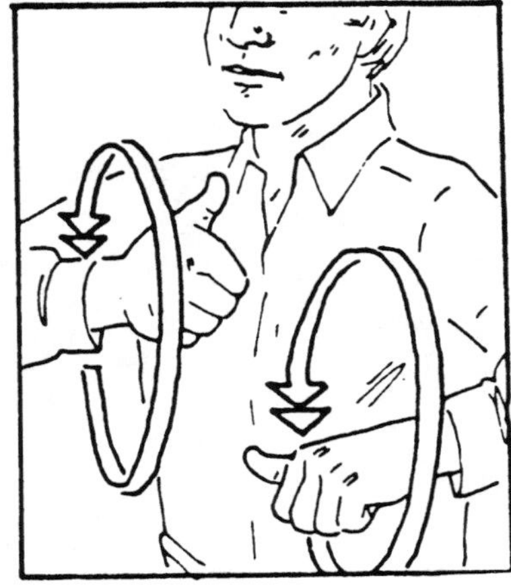

Thumbs brush down chest in alternate backward circles.

PROVOKE

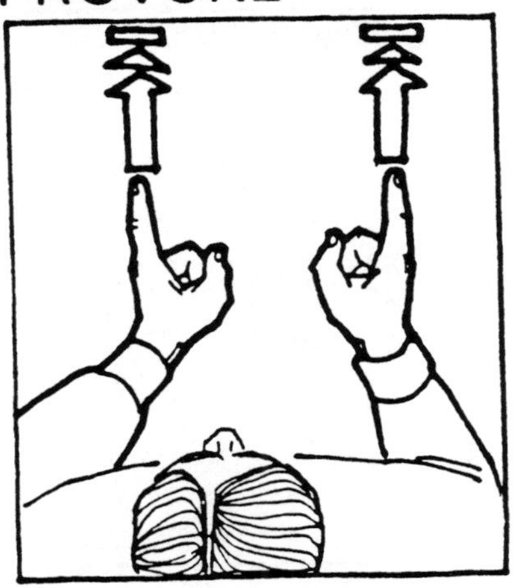

Indexes pointing forward, palms facing, jerk forward twice.

PSYCHOLOGY

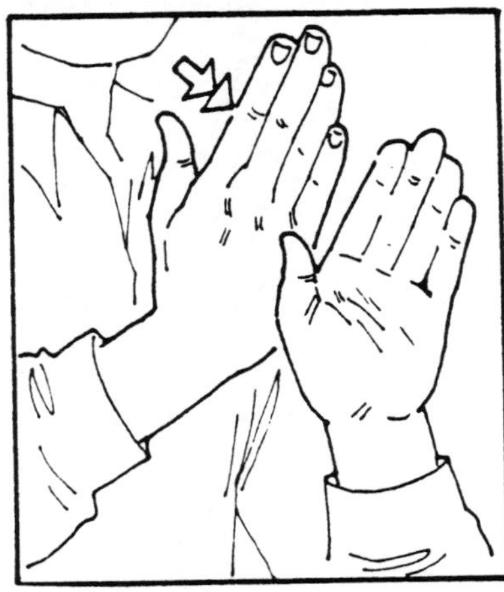

Blade of Rt. hand taps twice in between the base of L. thumb and index.

PUBLICITY

Two closed hands, held in front of mouth; Rt. hand moves forward.

PUBLISH

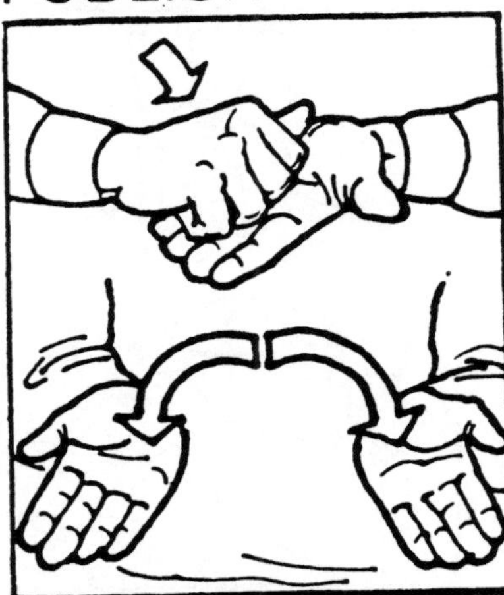

Rt. closed hand bangs on L. palm, then two flat hands move forward/apart.

PUDDING

Rt. hand mimes spooning from L. flat hand to mouth.

PULL

Mime appropriate pulling action.

PUNISH

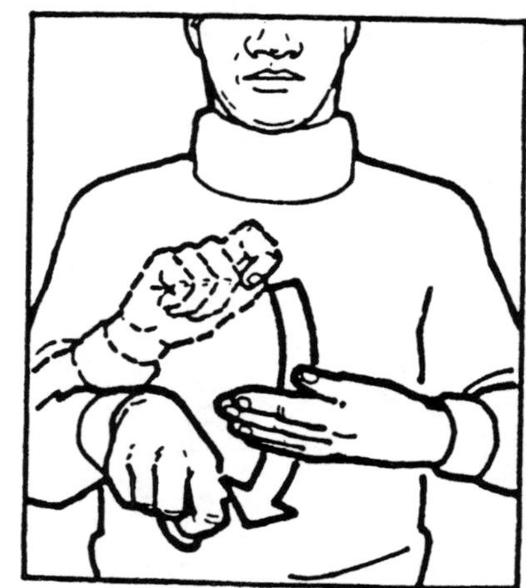

Mime holding cane and striking L. hand.

PUPPET (string)

Palm down "O" hands move alternately up and down as if pulling strings.

PURPLE

Tips of Rt. "O" hand brush forward twice off tip of L. index.

PUSH

Flat hands push forward.

PUT

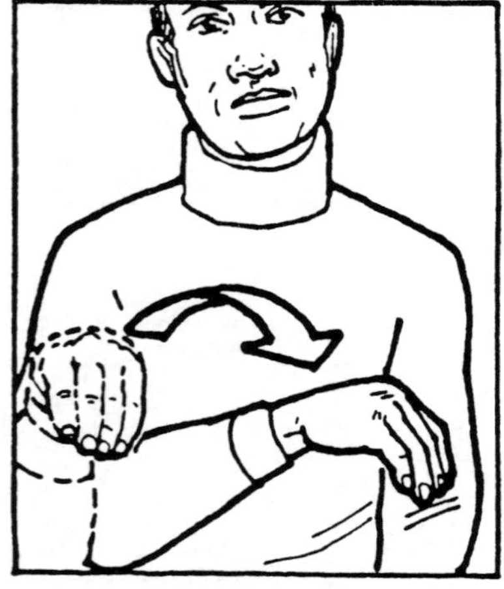

Palm down bunched hand moves in arc to put down imaginary object.

PUT OFF

Palm down "O" hands move in forward arc.

PYJAMAS

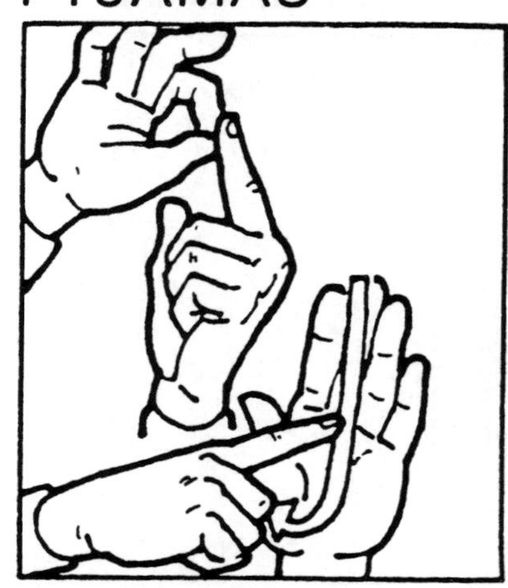

Fingerspell "P" then "J".

QUALIFICATIONS

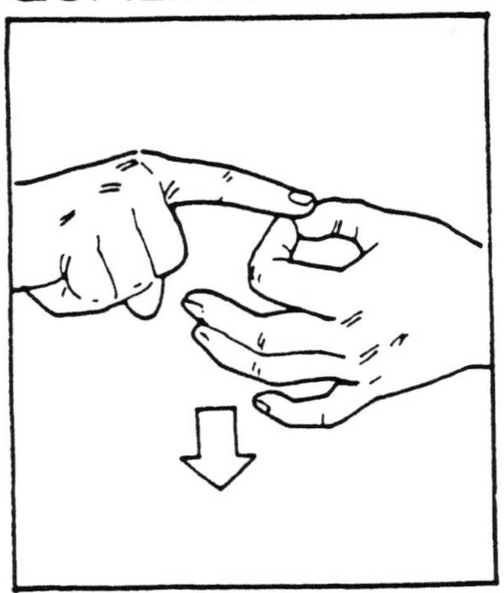

Form fingerspelt "Q" and make a small movement down.

QUARREL

"V" hands, palms facing, fingers bent, move up and down alternately, several times.

QUARTER

"O" hand moves in small, clockwise circle.

QUEEN

Index brushes forward on cheek, then clawed hand placed on head.

QUESTION

"O" hand moves in shape of question mark at head height.

QUEUE

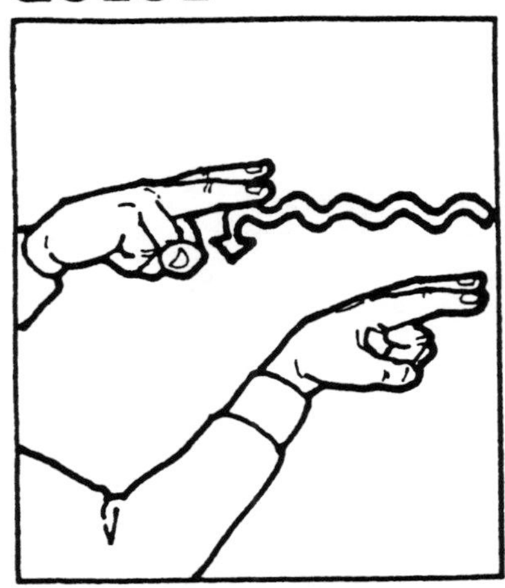

"V" hands, pointing forward, L. in front of Rt. Rt. hand moves back, bouncing up and down slightly to indicate line of people.

QUICK

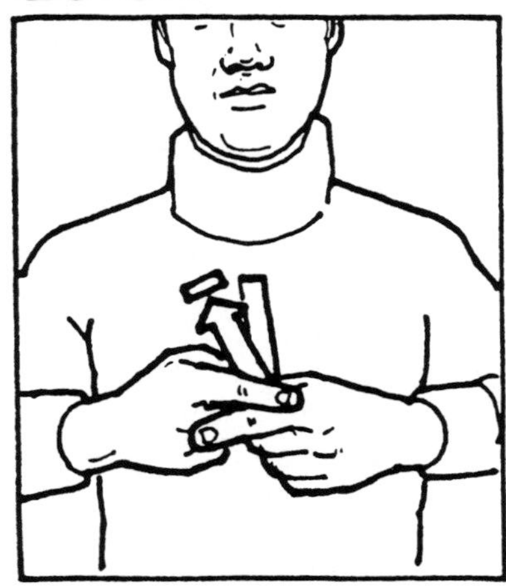

Rt. index hits L. index and bounces sharply up.

QUIET

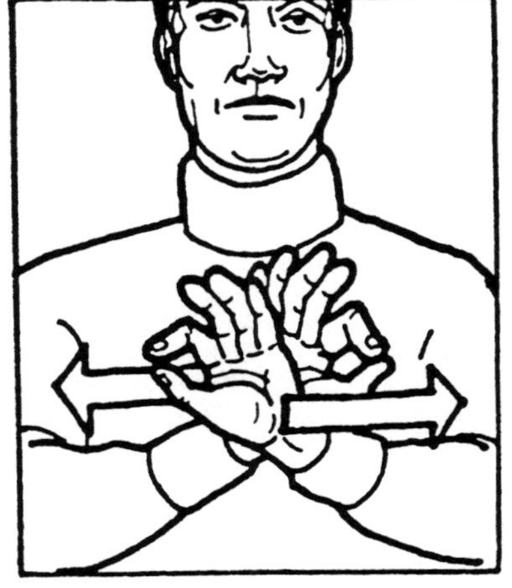

Palm forward hands start crossed, indexes close onto thumbs as hands pull slowly apart.

QUITE

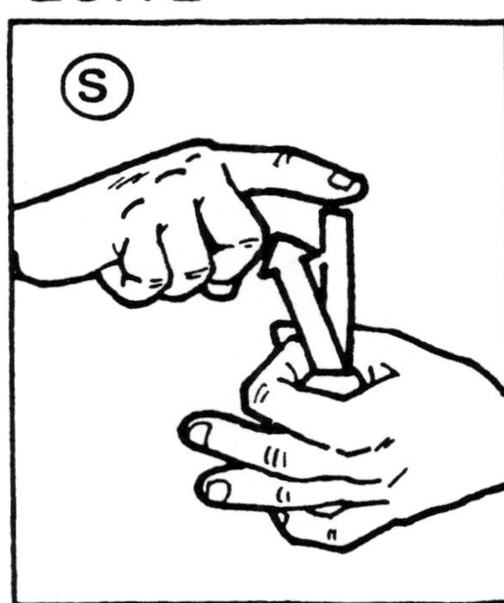

Rt. index makes quick tap on L. "O" hand.

QUOTE

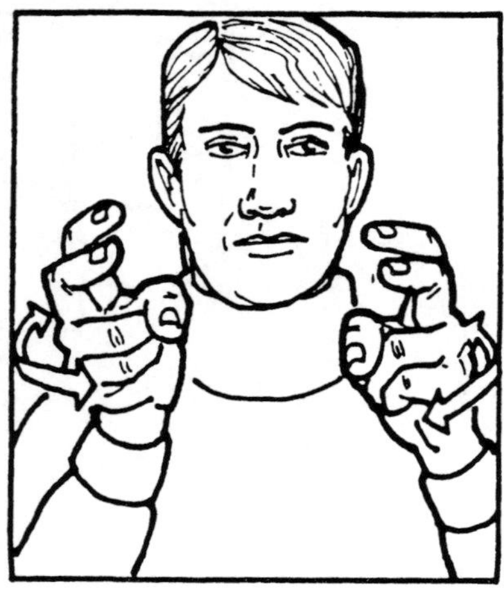

"V" hands, fingers bent, palms facing, twist at wrists to indicate quotation marks.

RABBIT

Palm forward "N" hands, held at either side of head, bend several times to indicate ears.

RADIO

Clawed hands held on ears, make small quick twisting movements.

RAFFLE

Hands make repeated alternate plucking movements.

RAILWAY

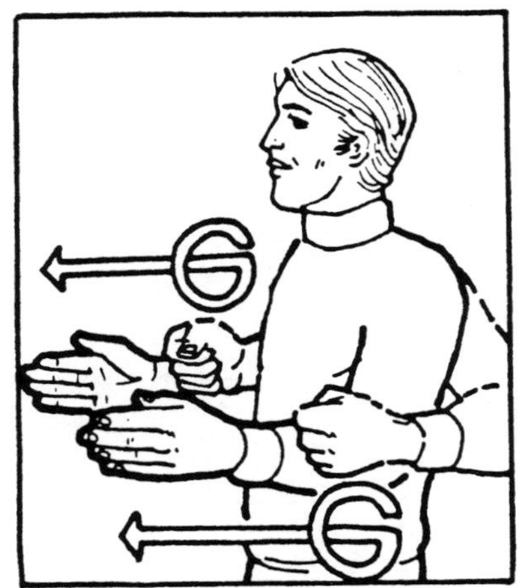

Closed hands move in forward circles, then flat hands move forward.

RAIN

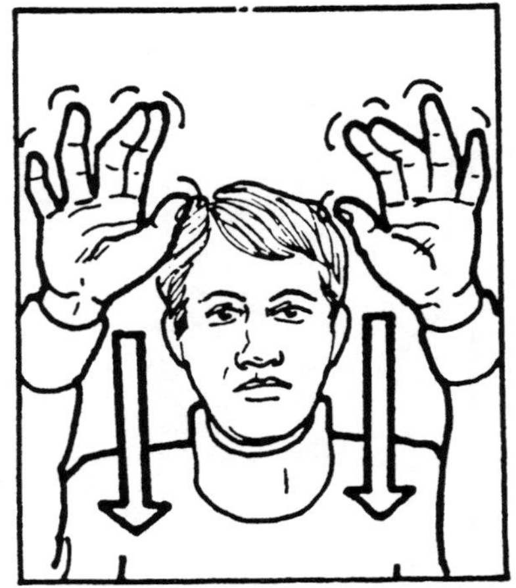

Hands move down from head height, fingers fluttering to indicate rain.

RAINBOW

Palm back open Rt. hand moves left to right in large arc over head.

RAINCOAT

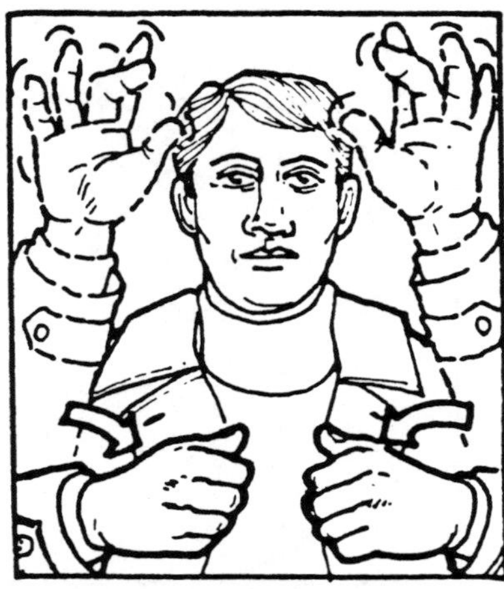

Fingers flutter down to indicate rain, then mime pulling coat over shoulders.

RAISE

Palm up flat hands move upwards.

RARELY

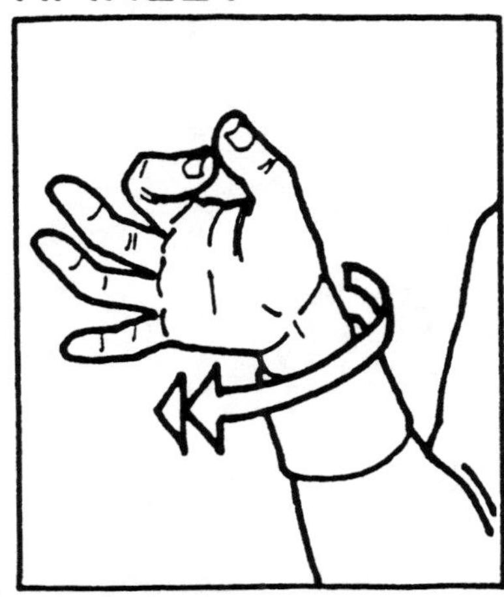

Palm left Rt. "O" hand twists to palm forward twice.

RATHER

Rt. closed hand, thumb extended, contacts L. palm twice.

RAW

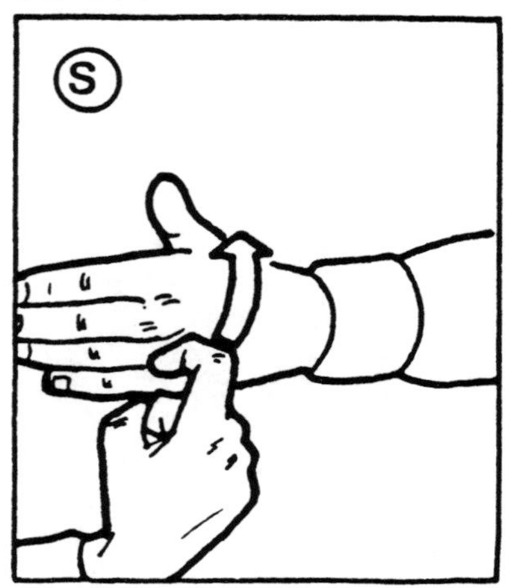

Rt. "R" hand brushes up back of L. flat hand.

READ

Rt. "V" hand moves from eye to sweep twice along L. palm.

READY

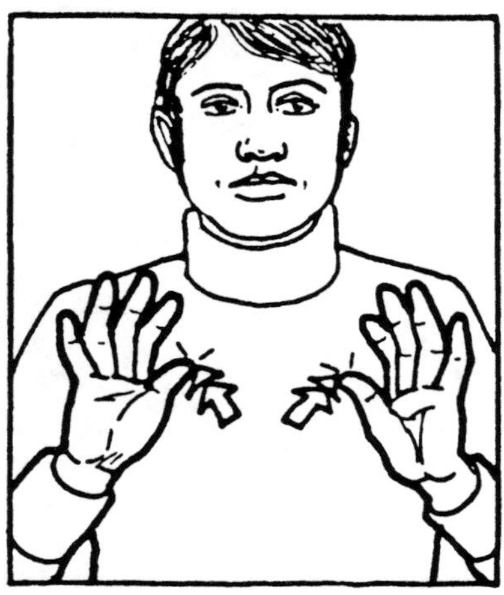

Thumbs of open hands, palms facing, contact upper chest twice, quickly.

REAL/REALLY

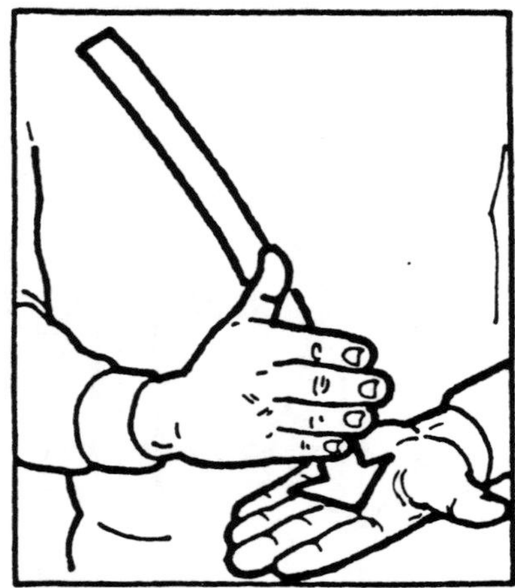

Strike L. palm with blade of Rt. flat hand, once for real, twice for really.

REASON

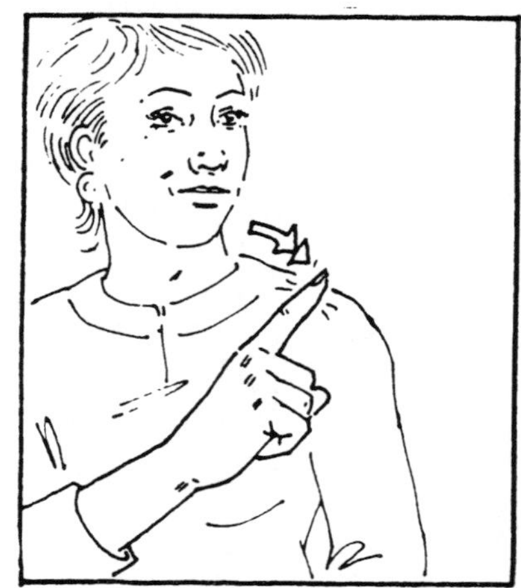

Edge of Rt. index taps left shoulder, twice.

RECEIVE

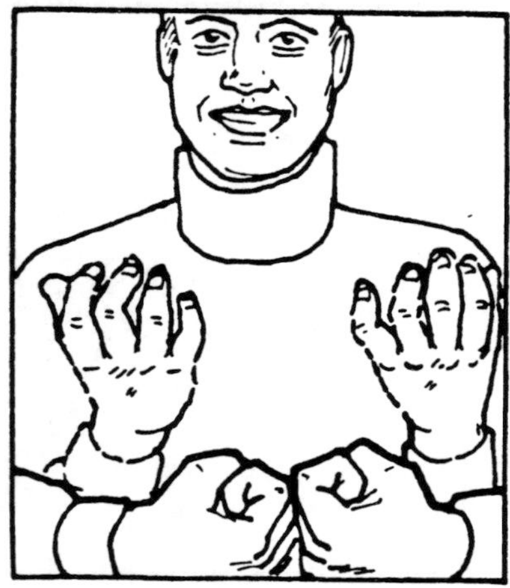

Clawed hands, held forward, move back to body, closing to fists.

RECENTLY

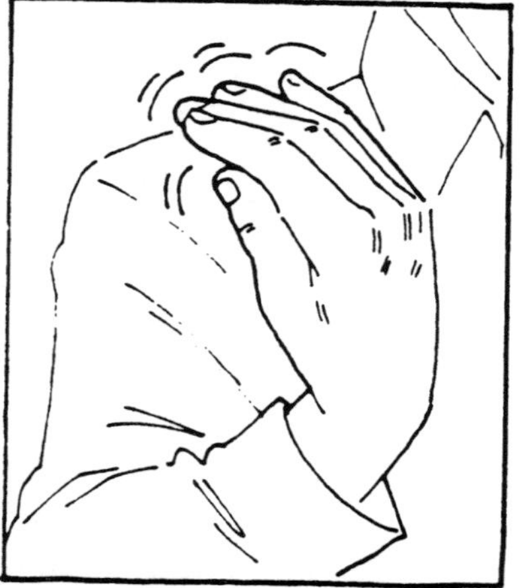

Slightly bent hand makes small backward movement over shoulder. Shoulder moves forward slightly.

RECIPE

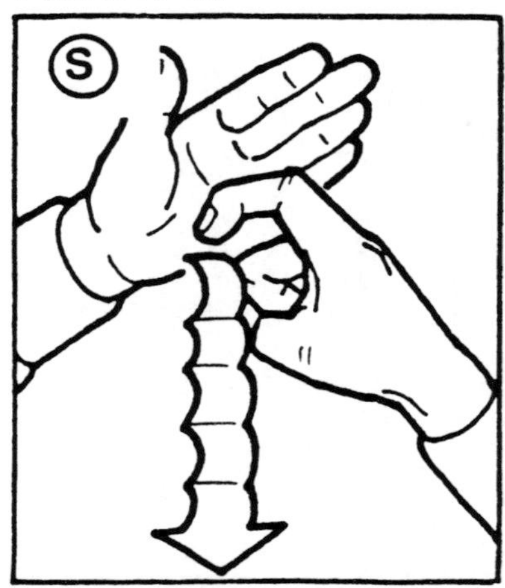

Form fingerspelt "R", and move Rt. formation down in small arcs to indicate list of items.

RECOGNISE

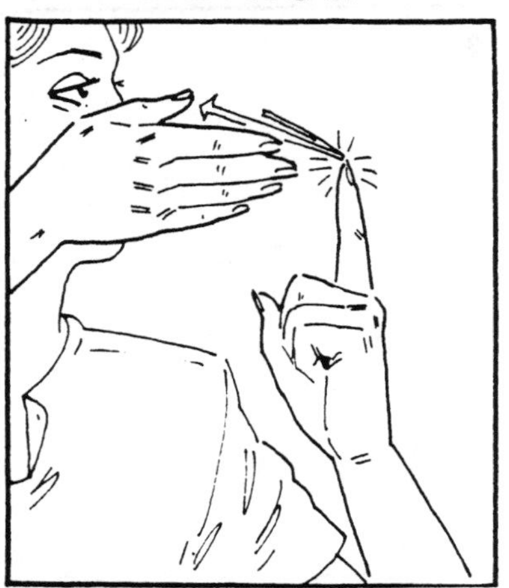

Rt. flat hand contacts L. index and springs back.

RED

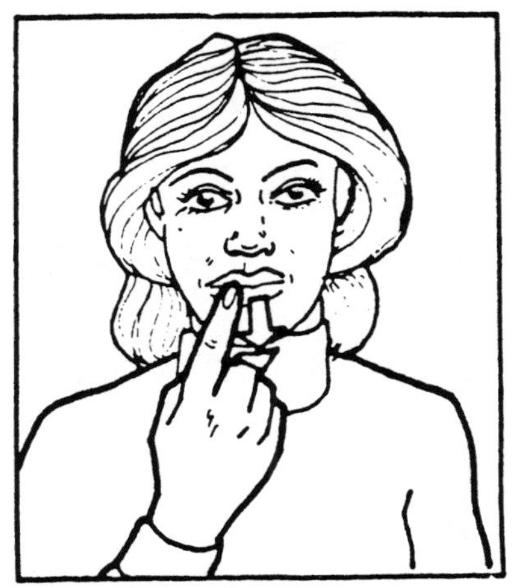

Index brushes down bottom lip twice, bending slightly.

REDUNDANT

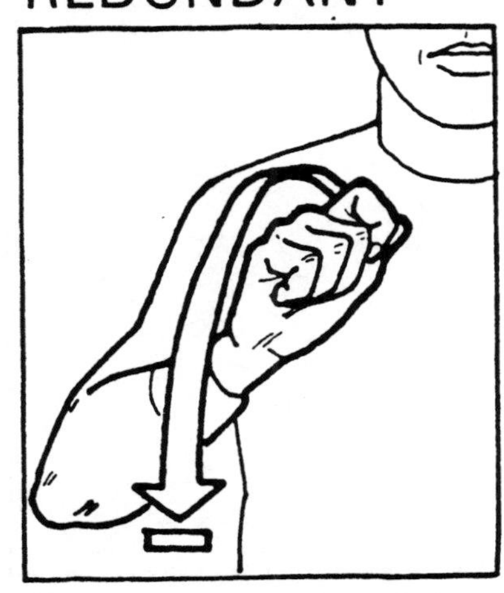

Thumb tucked into bent index, hand moves sharply forward/ down.

REFLECTION

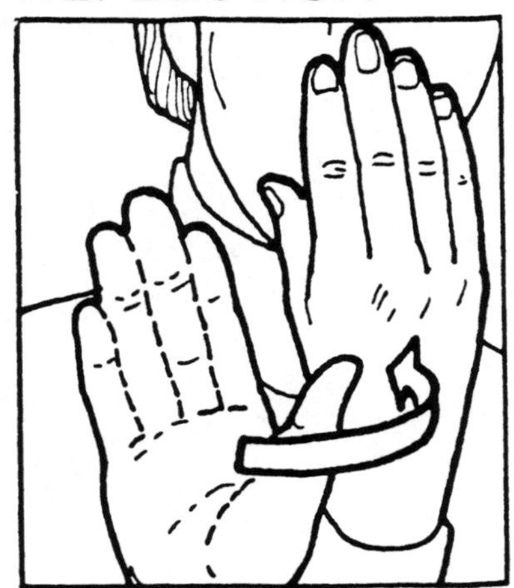

Palm forward flat hand held slightly forward to the side of face, swings to palm back in front of face.

REFUSE

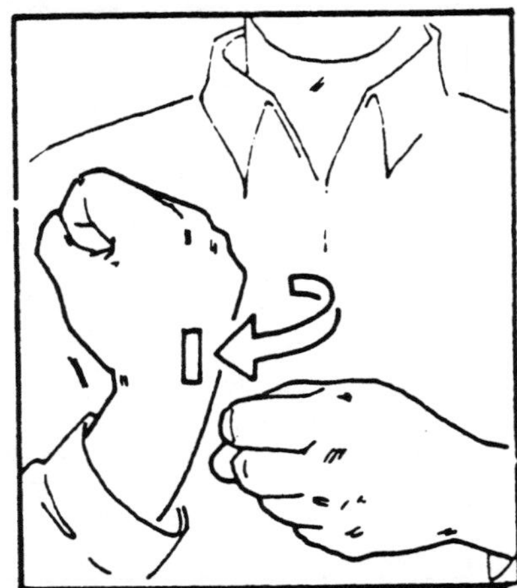

Palm back Rt. fist, resting on L. fist, twists sharply to palm forward.

REGISTER

"V" hand, fingers bent, contacts side of forehead, then L. palm, and moves down in small hops, indicating list of names.

REGULAR

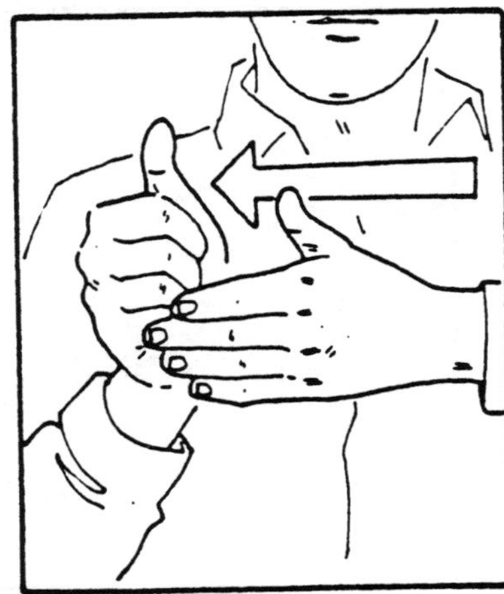

Rt. closed hand, thumb up, brushes along palm back L. hand.

RELATE

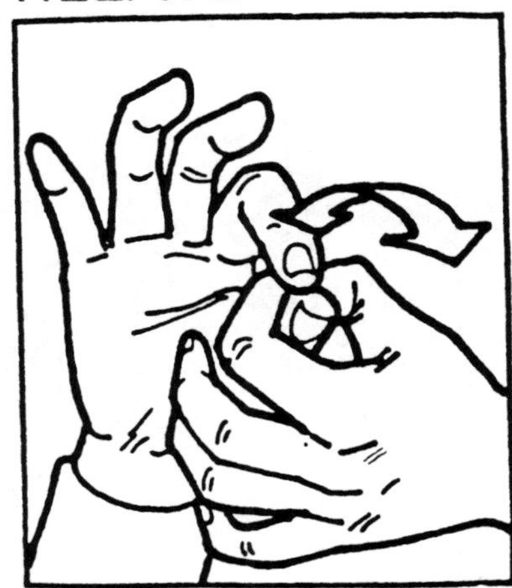

Interlink "O" hands and move forward and back.

RELEASE

"O" hands, interlinked, spring open and apart.

REMEMBER

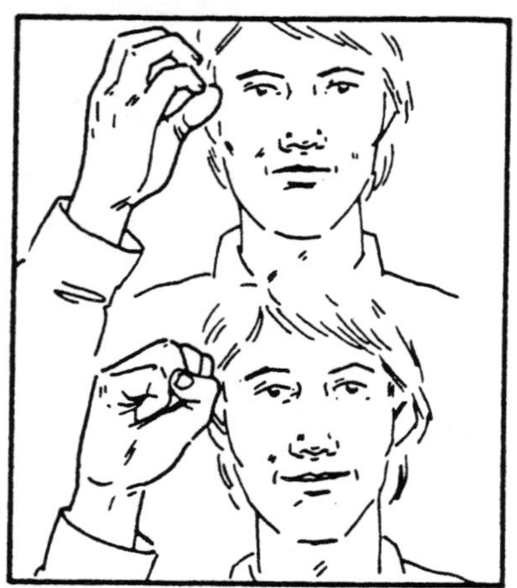

Clawed hand closes sharply to fist at temple.

REMIND

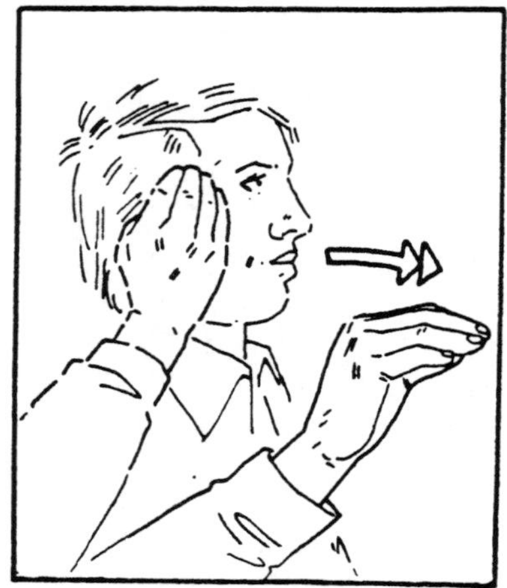

Bunched hand contacts temple, then moves towards person concerned as if tapping them. For "remind me" move from temple to tap on shoulder.

RENT

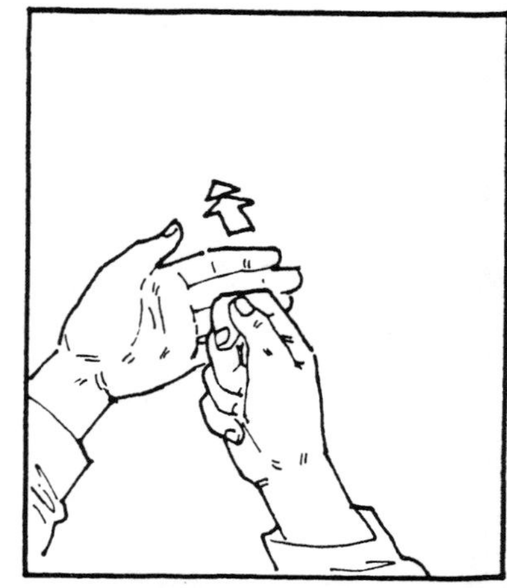

Rt. thumb tucked into bent index, hand moves forward repeatedly from L. palm.

REPEAT

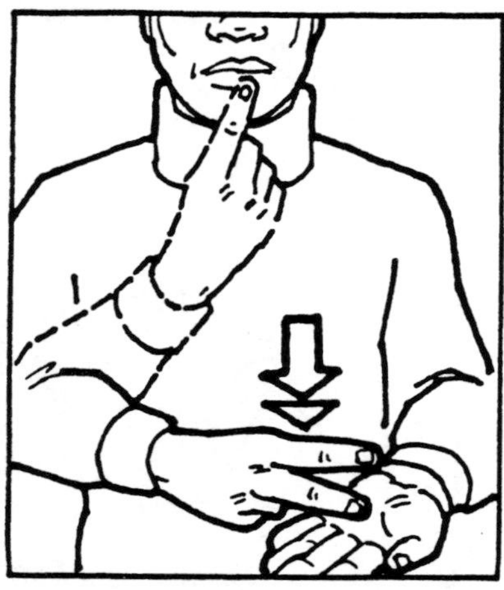

Rt. index points to mouth, then moves down, changing to "V" hand and taps L. palm twice with edge of middle finger.

REPLY

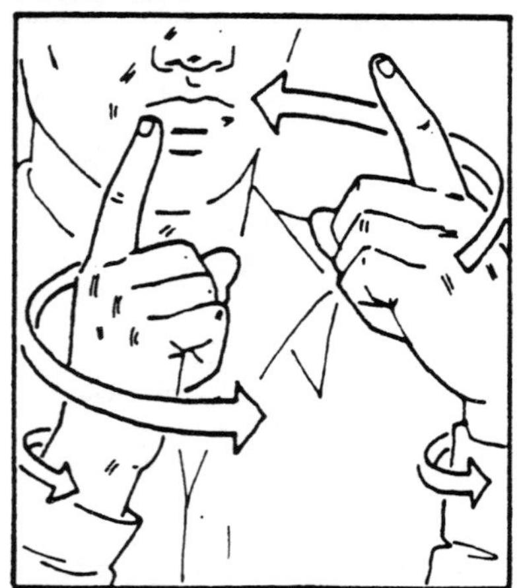

Indexes extended, Rt. on lips, L. held slightly forward. Hands twist sharply to reverse positions.

REPORT

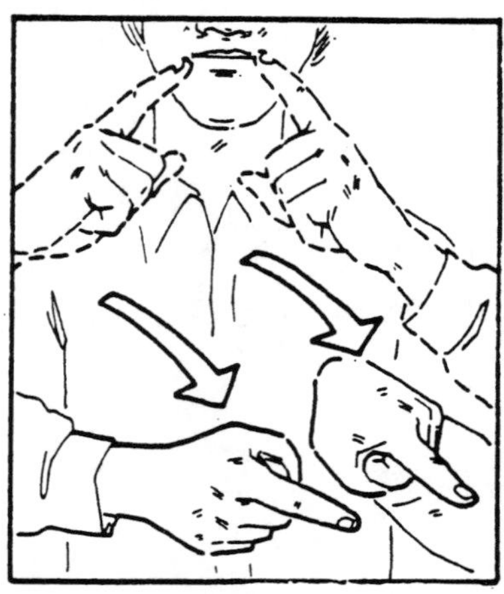

Indexes touch sides of mouth, then move forward/left.

REPRESENT

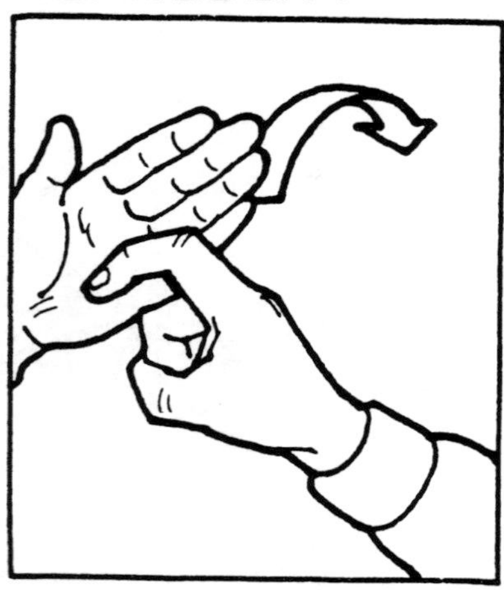

Form fingerspelt "R" and move formation forward in small arc.

RESEARCH

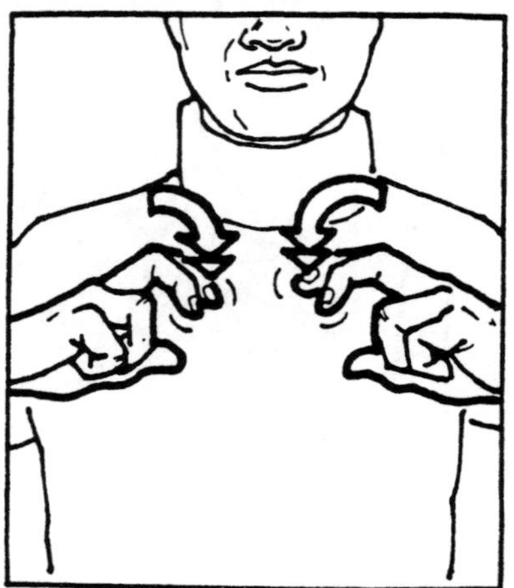

"V" hands pointing towards each other, pull apart, flexing fingers several times.

RESIGN

Closed hands, palms facing, thumbs on chest, move in forward arc, twisting to thumbs forward.

RESPONSIBILITY

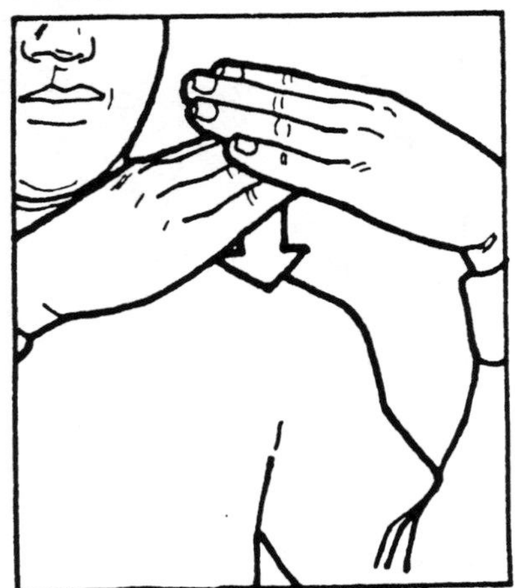

Flat hands, L. on top of Rt. held slightly above left shoulder, move down to contact top of shoulder.

REST

Flat hands pointing up/in, thumbs extended and touching upper chest. Hands swivel to point in/down.

RETIRE

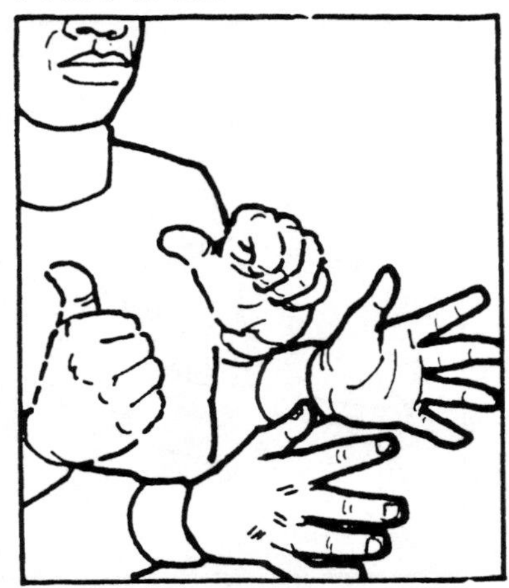

Closed hands, palms facing, thumbs on chest, move forward sharply and spring open.

REVENGE

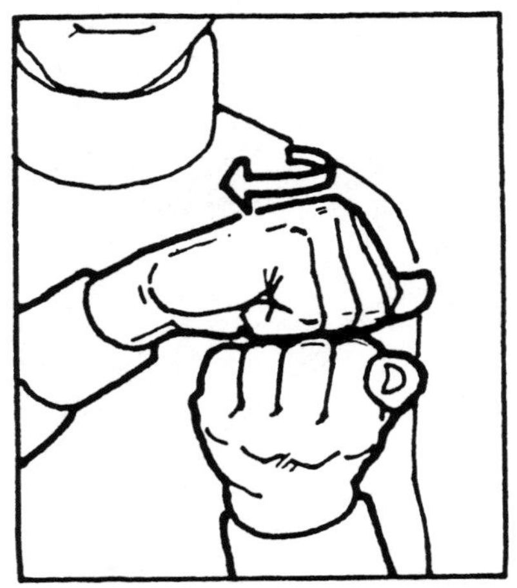

Closed hands, Rt. on top of L., at right angles. Rt. hand twists to point forward, with emphasis.

REVERSE

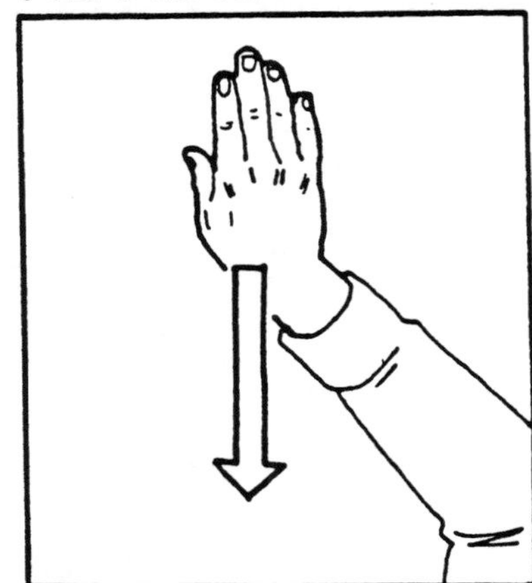

Flat hand moves backwards to represent a vehicle reversing.

RHINOCEROS

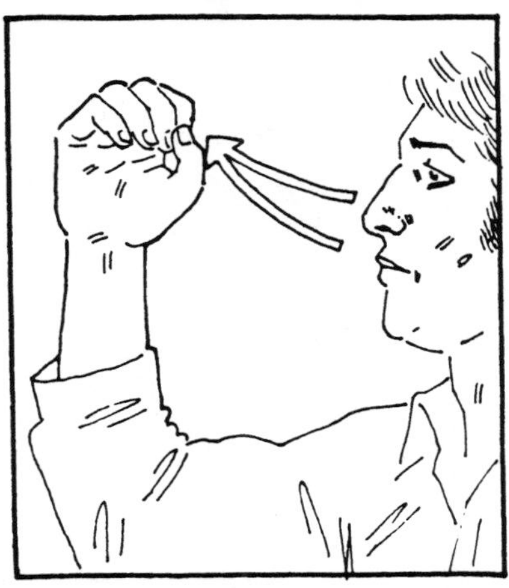

Full "C" hand moves forward/ up from nose closing to full "O" hand to indicate horn.

RICE

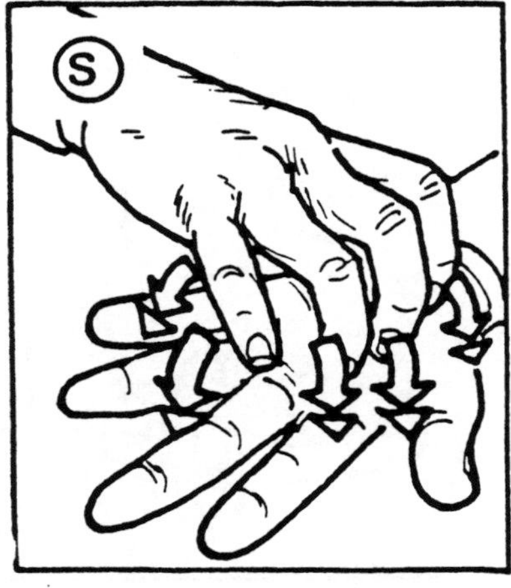

Rt. clawed hand taps down in circular movement on palm of L. open hand.

RICH

Blades of flat hands brush down body, to indicate rich clothing.

RIDE

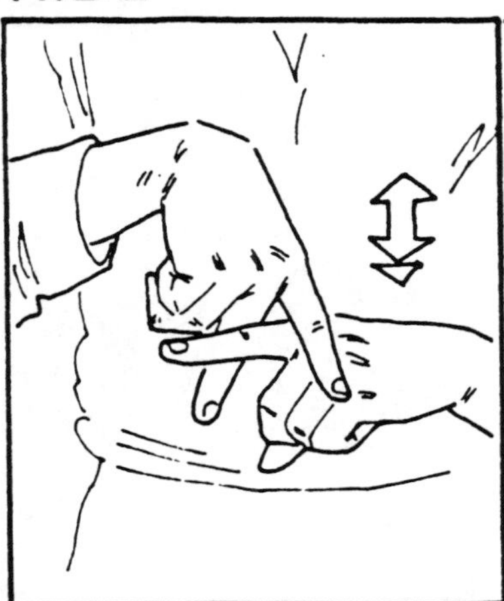

Rt. "V" hand on L. index finger. Formation moves up and down to indicate riding.

RIGHT

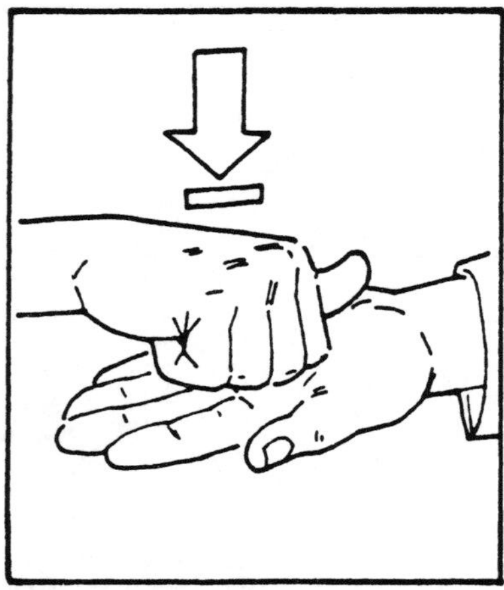

Rt. closed hand, thumb extended bangs L. palm with emphasis.

RING

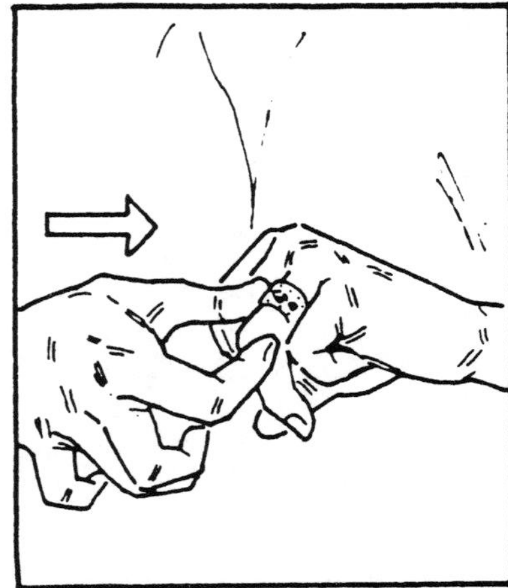

Indicate pushing a ring onto finger.

RIPE

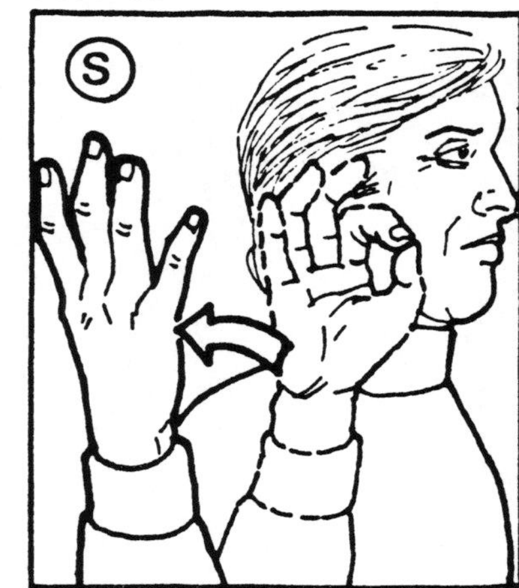

Rt. "O" hand brushes back slightly at corner of mouth, then moves out changing to open hand.

RISK

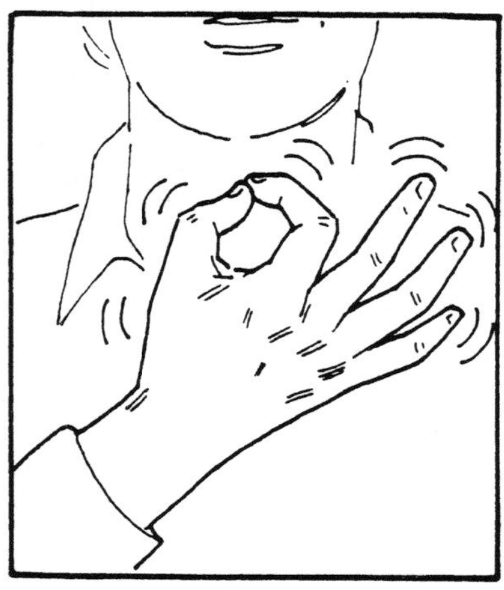

Tips of "O" hand contact front of neck with slight movement.

RIVER

Flat hands, held parallel, move forward in curving movement, to indicate a river.

ROAD

Flat hands, held parallel, move forward.

ROAST

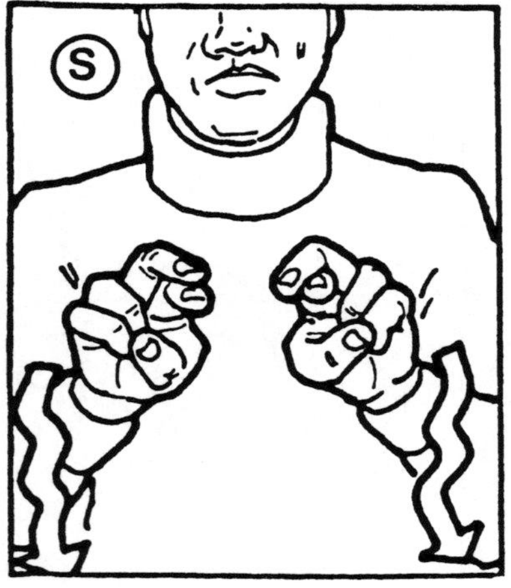

Index and middle fingers crossed. Hands move down with twisting movement.

ROCK

L. closed hand indicates ground, Rt. closed hand moves down onto L., to indicate a rock.

ROLL

Indexes, pointing in, make alternate forward circles round each other.

ROOF

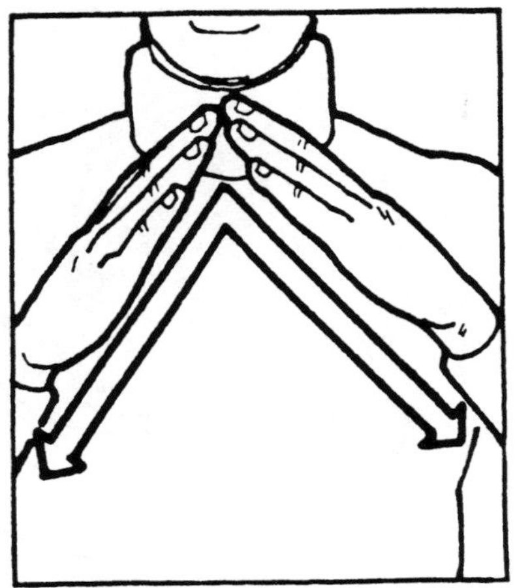

Flat hands move down/out in shape of roof.

ROOM

Indexes pointing down move out, back, then in, to indicate outline of room.

ROOT

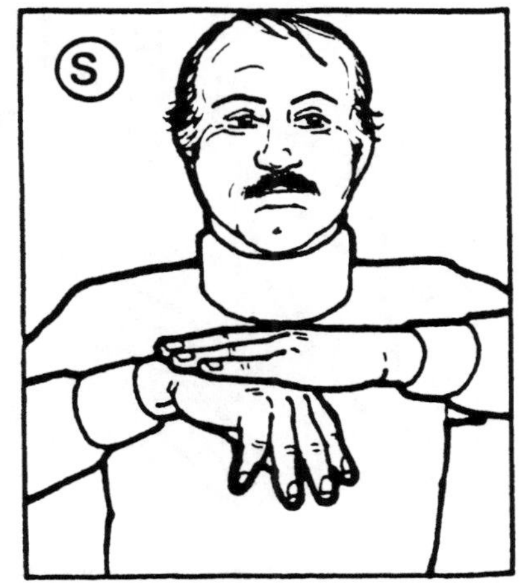

Fingers of Rt. hand open and pointing down, held under L. hand.

ROPE

Hands hold imaginary rope and pull apart twisting.

ROTTEN

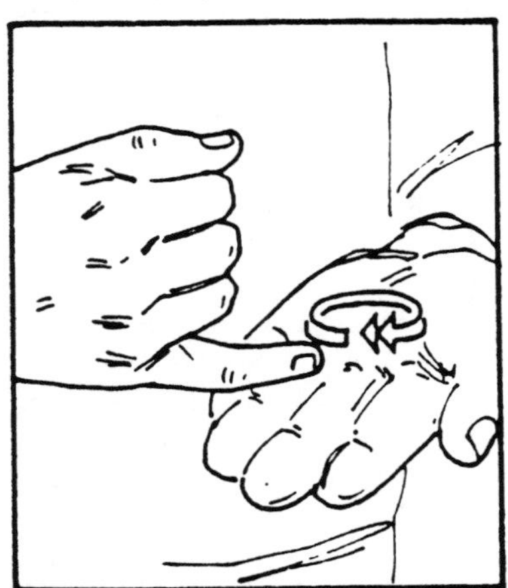

Edge of Rt. little finger makes circular movement on L. palm.

ROUGH

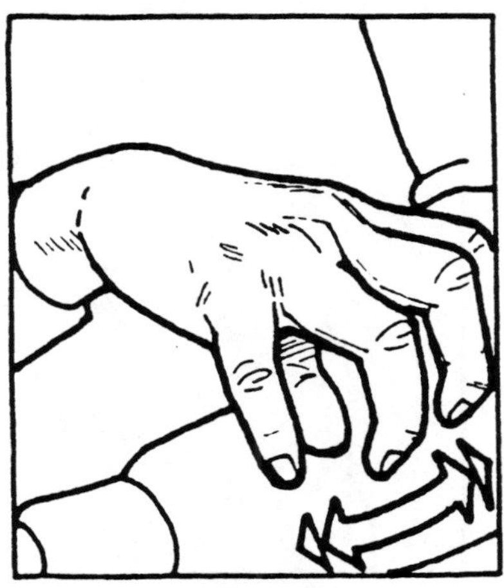

Tips of clawed hand rub up and down left forearm several times.

ROUND

Index makes circular movement.

RUBBER

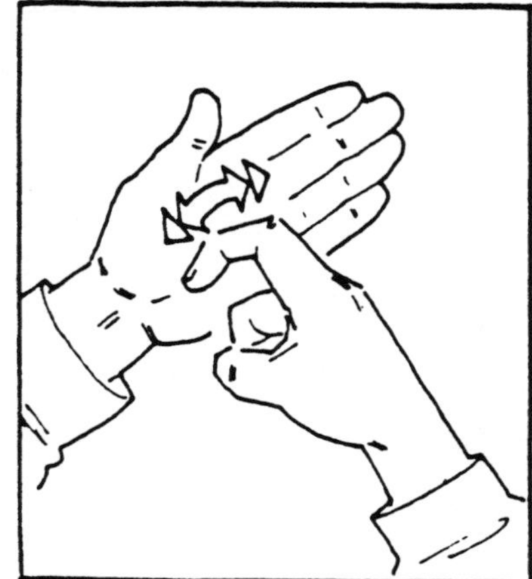

Rub Rt. "R" on L. palm.

RUBBISH (talk)

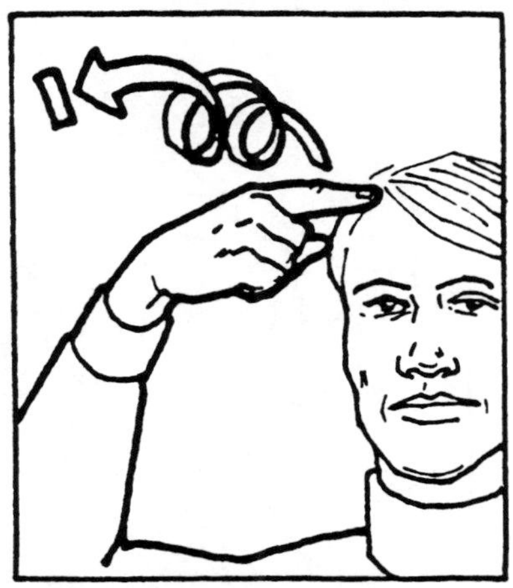

Index points to middle of forehead then moves sharply up/forward in several loops.

RUBBISH (waste)

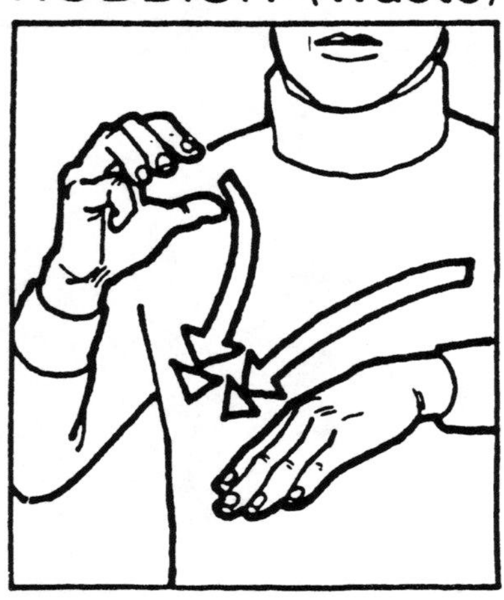

Hands move alternately in and open as if throwing rubbish in a bin.

RUDE (manners)

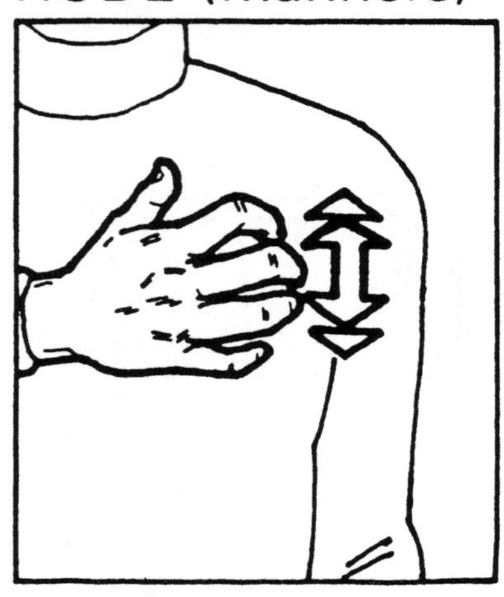

Tips of Rt. clawed hand rub up and down left upper chest.

RUDE (indecent)

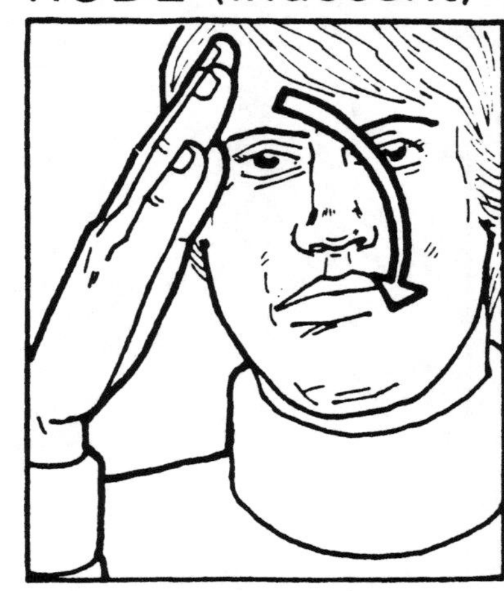

Rt. flat hand, palm left flips to palm down in front of nose.

RUGBY

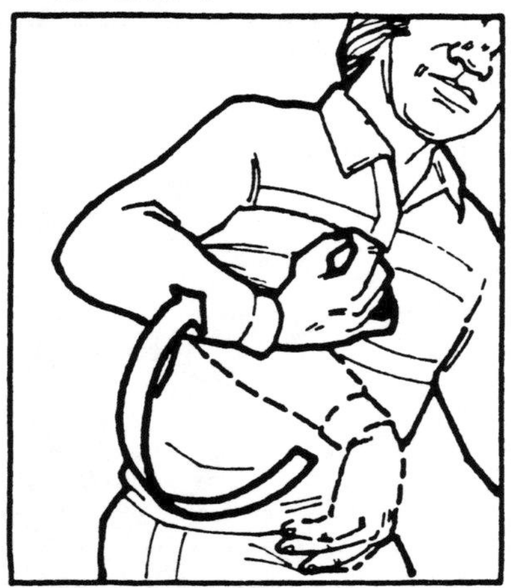

Cupped hand sweeps back and up as if scooping a rugby ball under the arm.

RULER

Indexes and thumbs pull apart indicating shape of a ruler.

RULES

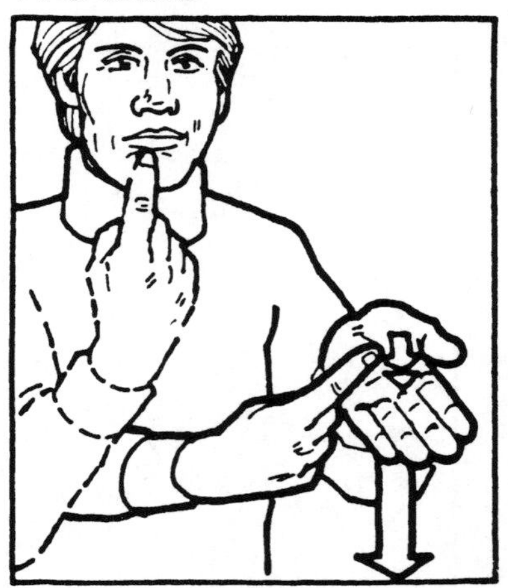

Rt. index points to mouth, then hits L. palm several times as formation moves down.

RUN

Arms move up and down to indicate running.

RUSH

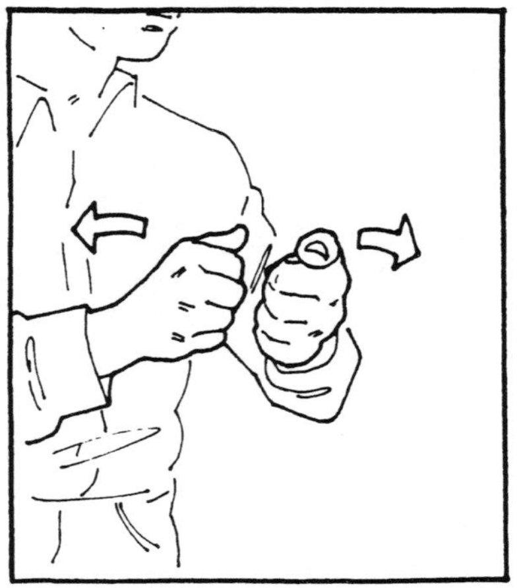

Closed hands, held together, pull sharply apart, diagonally.

RUSSIA

Fist held up at head height makes slight movement forward with stress.

SACK (TO)

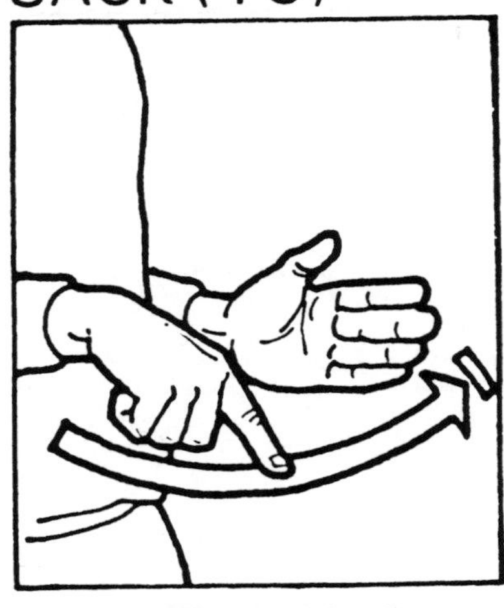

L. flat hand palm right. Rt. index pointing down moves and flicks sharply to point forward past L. palm.

SAD

Indexes make small downward movement from corners of mouth.

SAFE

Blade of Rt. cupped hand sweeps backwards onto L. palm then formation moves back to contact body, and up.

SAIL

Slightly curved Rt. hand sweeps round in small arc.

SAILOR

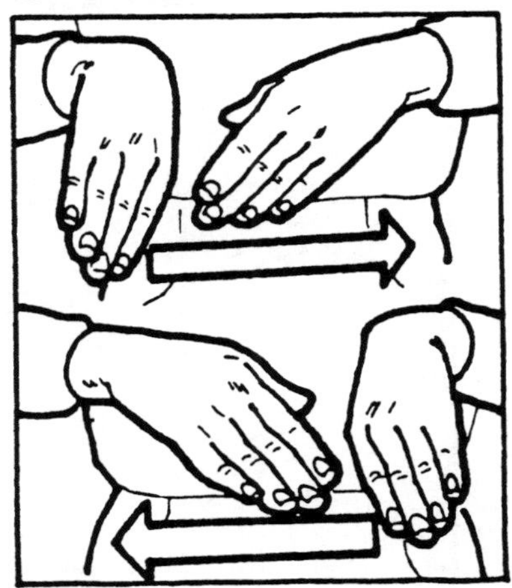

Flat hands, pointing down, held at right side of waist. Swing to left side, then back again.

SALAD

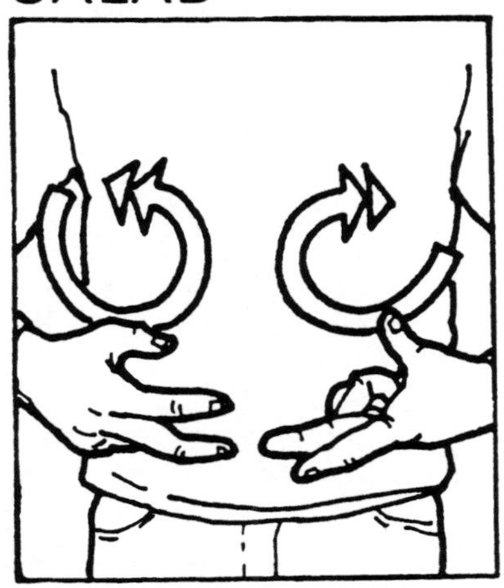

Index, middle fingers and thumbs extended, move in, in vertical circles as if tossing a salad.

SALT

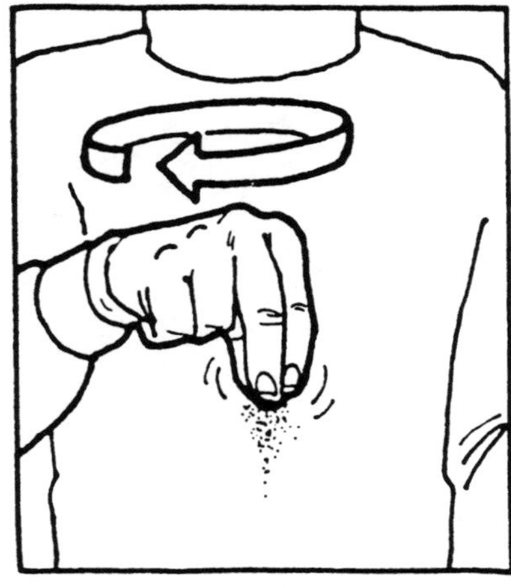

Index, middle finger and thumb tips rub together as hand moves in horizontal circle, as if sprinkling salt.

SAME

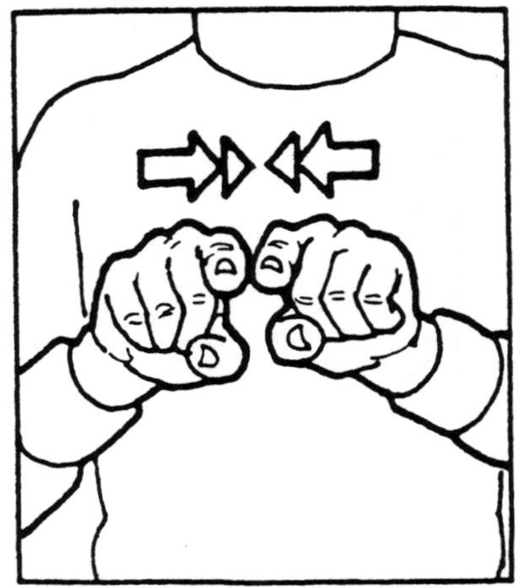

Indexes pointing forward tap together twice.

SAND

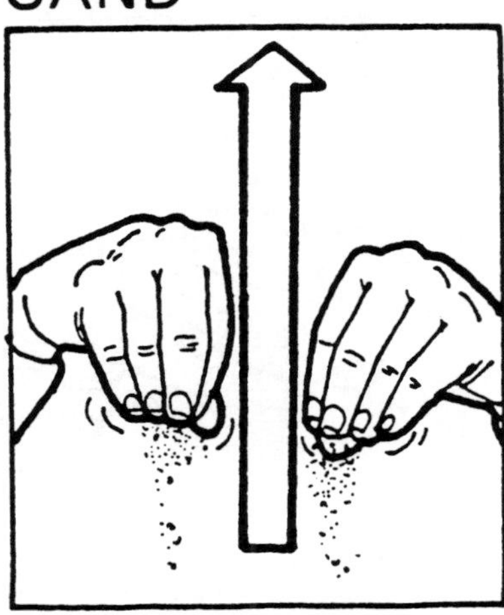

Thumbs rub along fingertips as hands move up.

SANDAL

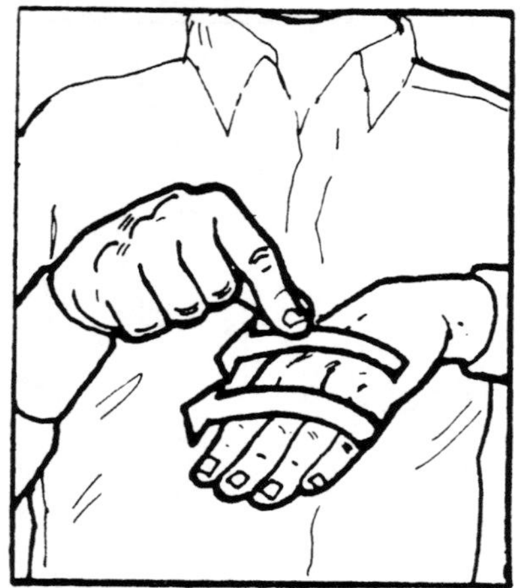

Draw tips of Rt. thumb and index across back of L. hand twice, to indicate straps.

SANDWICH

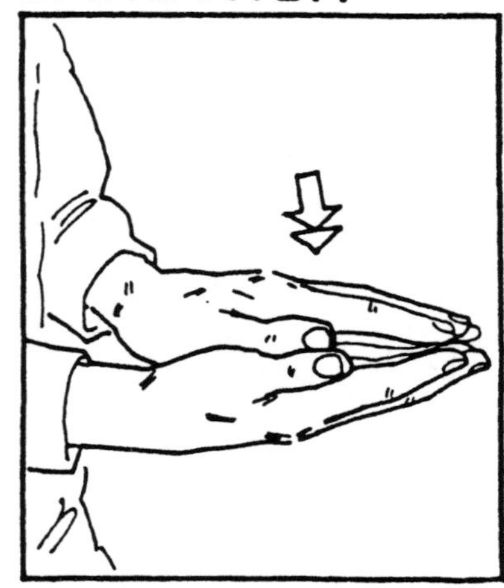

Palm together flat hands tap together twice.

SATISFIED

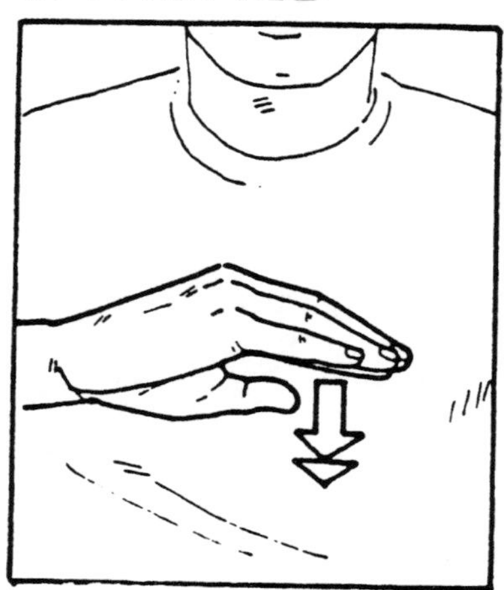

Index edge of slightly cupped hand brushes down chest, twice.

SAUCE

Mime shaking sauce from a bottle.

SAUCER

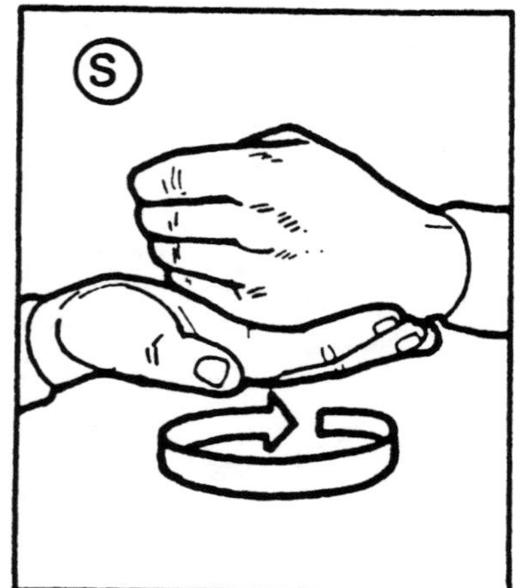

Rub Rt. flat hand in circular movement under L. full "C" hand.

SAUSAGES

Index and middle fingers close onto thumbs as hands move apart, indicating sausage links.

SAVE

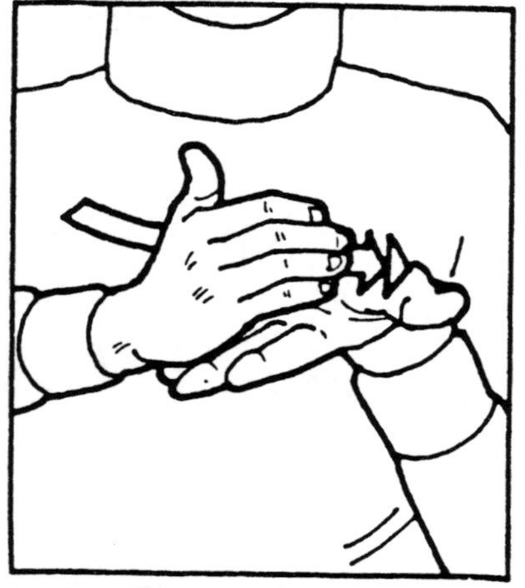

Blade of Rt. cupped hand, thumb up, brushes along L. palm, twice.

SAW (cut)

Flat hand moves in sawing action.

SAY

Index moves forward from mouth.

SCARE

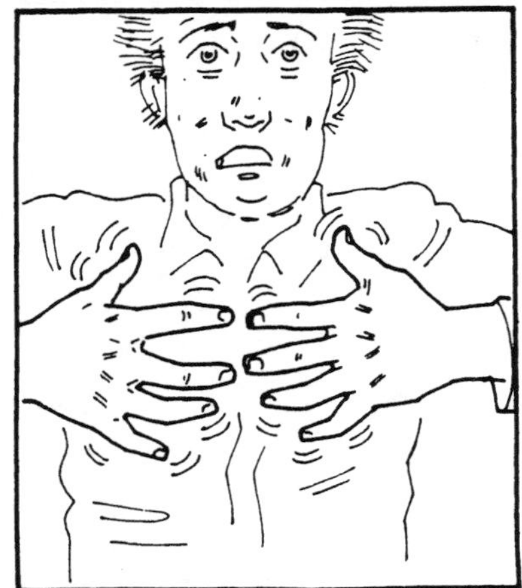

Open hands make small quick shaking movements in front of body.

SCARF

Hands move forward from sides of neck, cross and move back, as if wrapping a scarf round neck.

SCHOOL

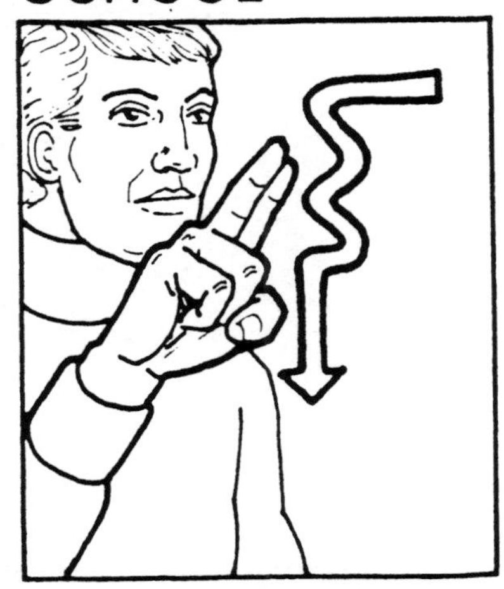

Palm forward "N" hand makes sharp side to side movement, whilst moving down in front of face.

SCIENCE

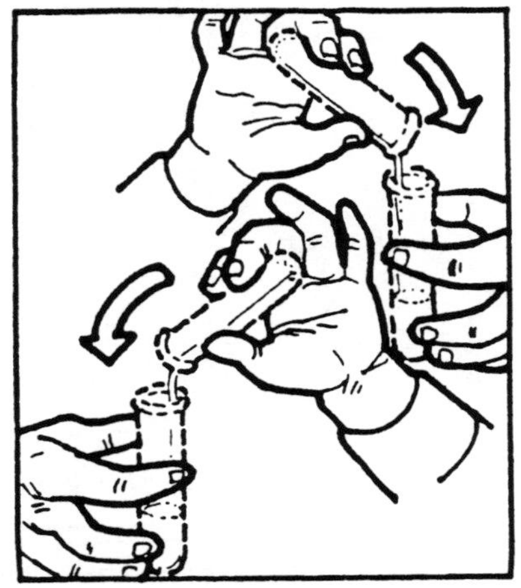

Hands mime tipping contents of one test-tube into another, then reverse.

SCISSORS

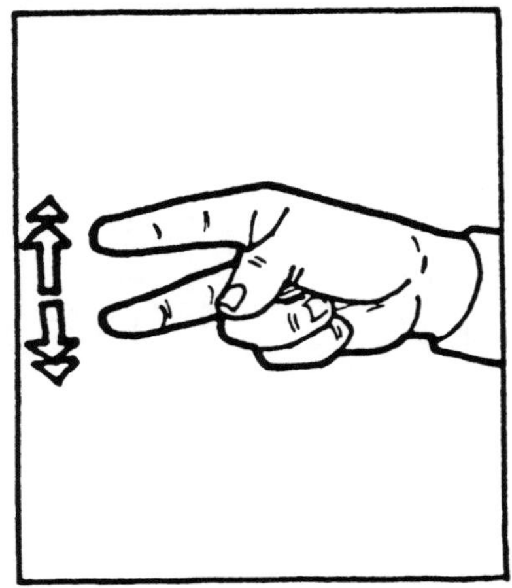

Fingers of "V" hand, open and close several times.

SCOOTER (toy)

L. fist holds imaginary handle, Rt. flat hand mimes action of foot.

SCORE

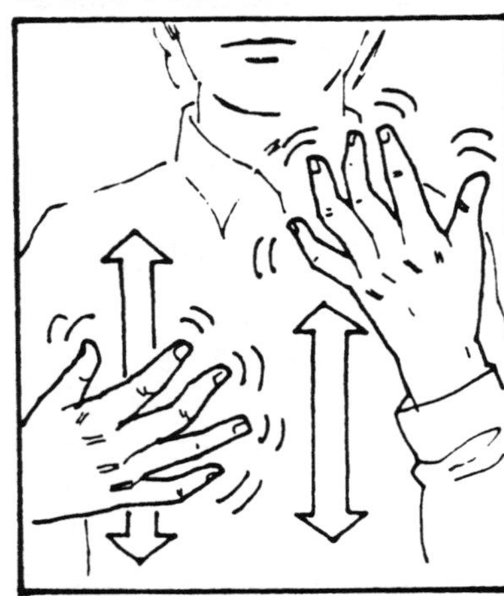

Open hands move up and down alternately with fingers fluttering.

SCOTLAND

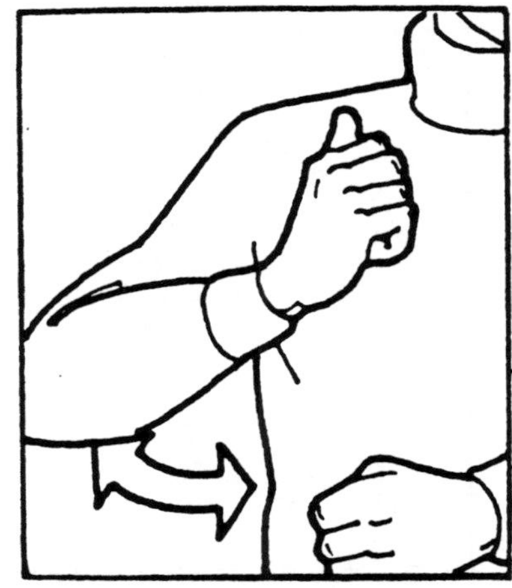

Elbow moves out and in to body to indicate bagpipes.

SCOUT

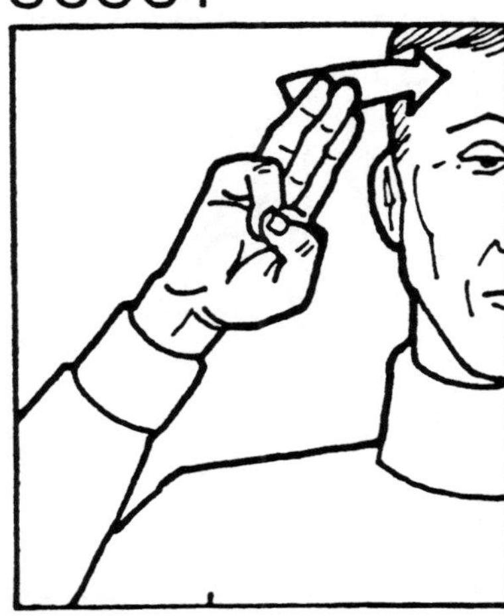

Make the scout salute.

SCREAM

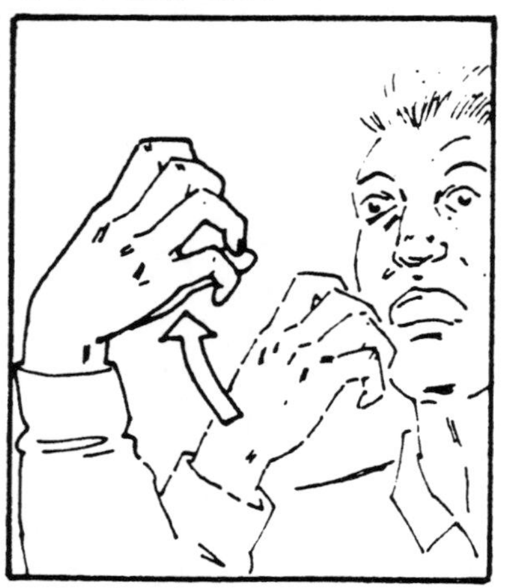

Clawed hand, palm back, moves forward/up from mouth.

SCREW

Rt. hand mimes screwing action against L. fist.

SCULPTURE

Rt. thumb extended, moves down past L. fingertips with twisting movements.

SEA

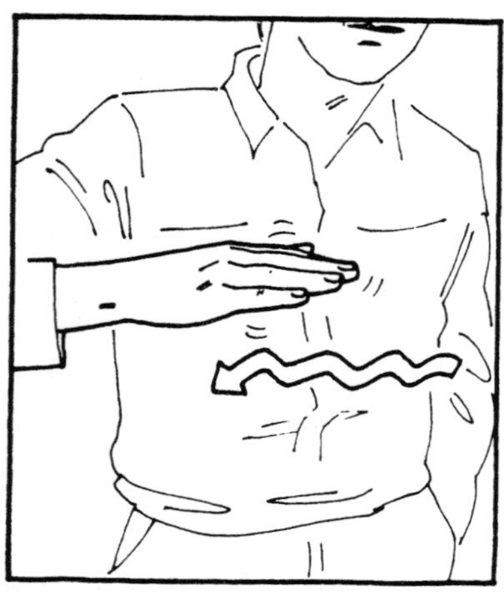

Flat hand moves horizontally in up and down wavy movement.

SEAL

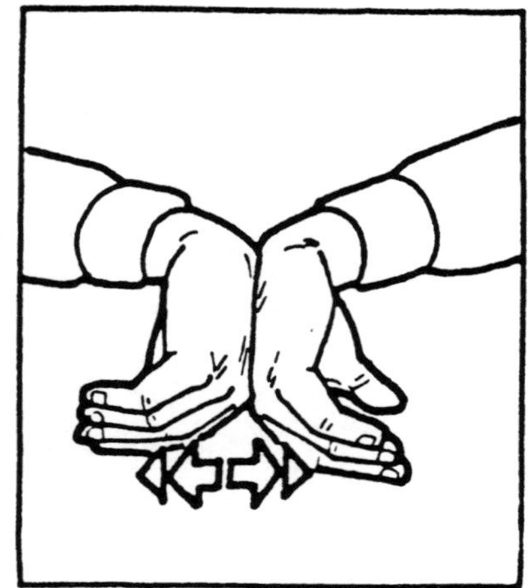

Hands held back to back, fingers flap together several times to indicate flippers.

SEARCH

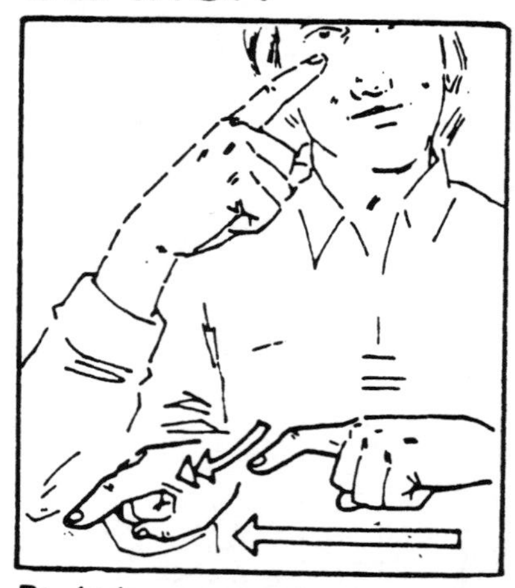

Rt. index moves from eye, to contact L. in repeated forward brushing movement, as formation moves sideways, fingers slightly bent.

SEASON

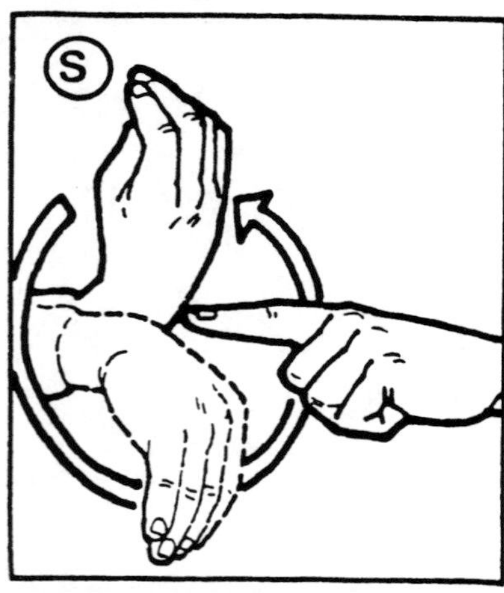

Rt. bunched hand, pointing up, held against L. index, swivels forward and round in full circle, indicating a bud's yearly cycle.

SECOND (clock)

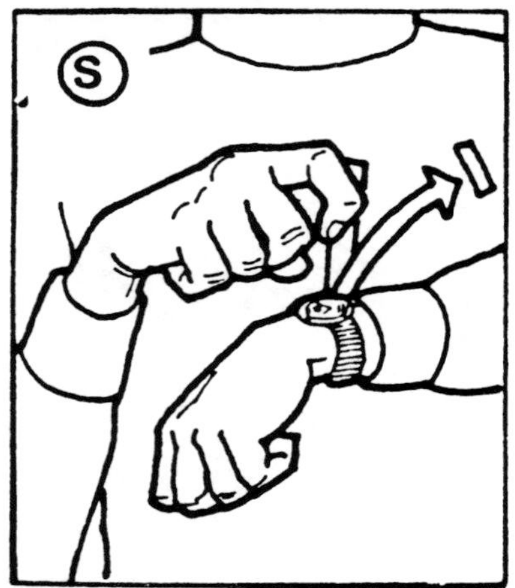

Tip of Rt. "R" hand, palm down, taps L. wrist in short, sharp movement.

SECOND (2nd)

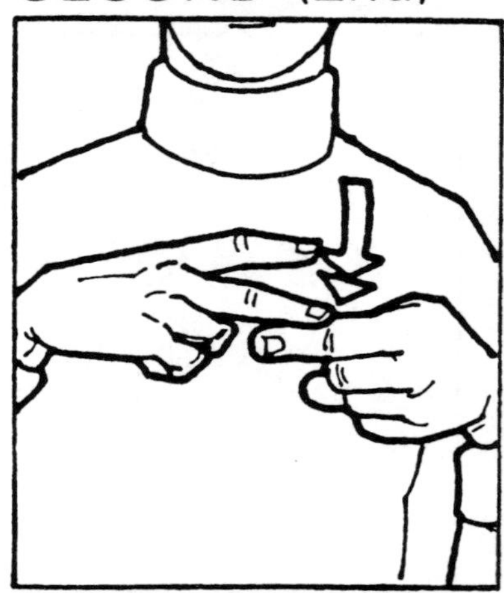

Middle finger edge of Rt. "V" hand, taps L. index, twice.

SECRET

Flat hands, edge to edge against each other, in front of mouth, move in very small alternate side to side movements.

SEE

Index moves forward from eye.

SEEDS

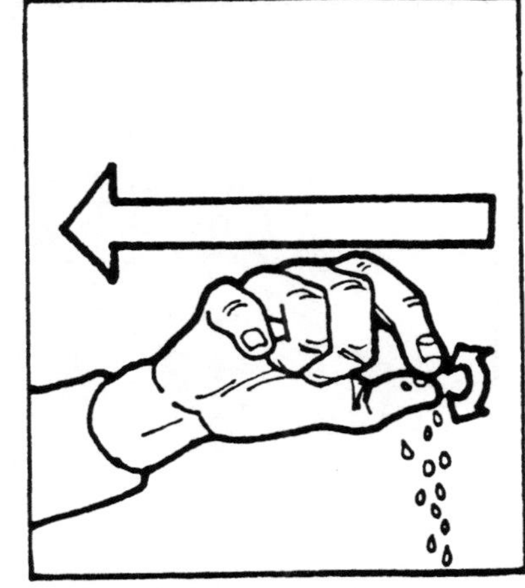

Rt. hand moves to the right as index and thumb rub together, like sprinkling seeds.

SEEM

Flat hand, palm back in front of face, drops foward/down to palm up.

SELF

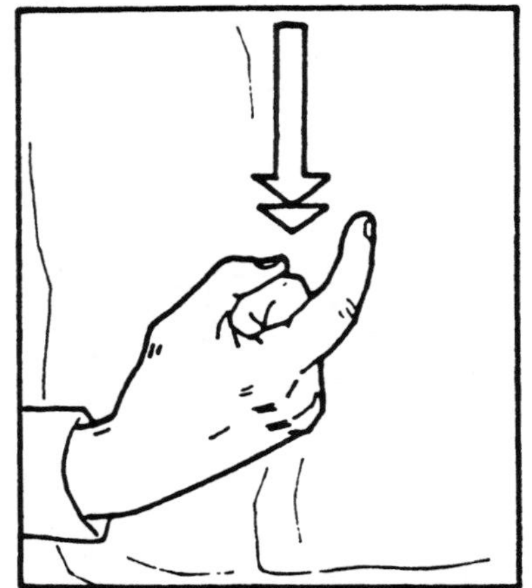

Brush extended index down body, twice, or towards person concerned.

SELFISH

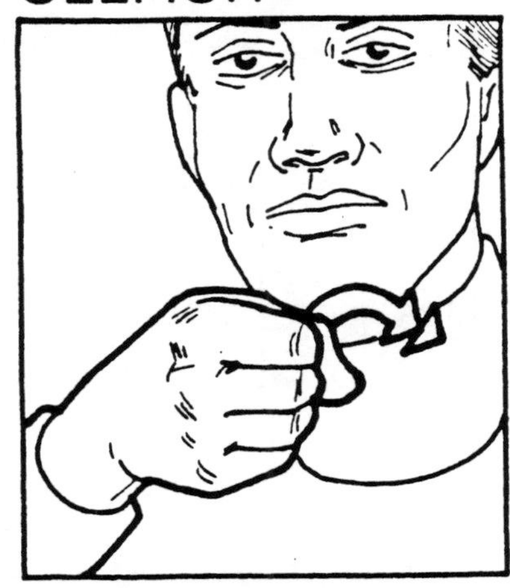

Index edge of Rt. fist makes small circular movement on chin.

SELL

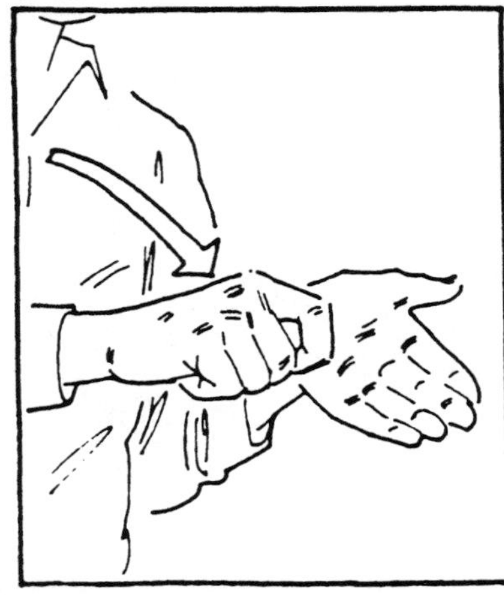

Palm down Rt. "R" hand, thumb extended, hits L. palm and bounces off

SEND

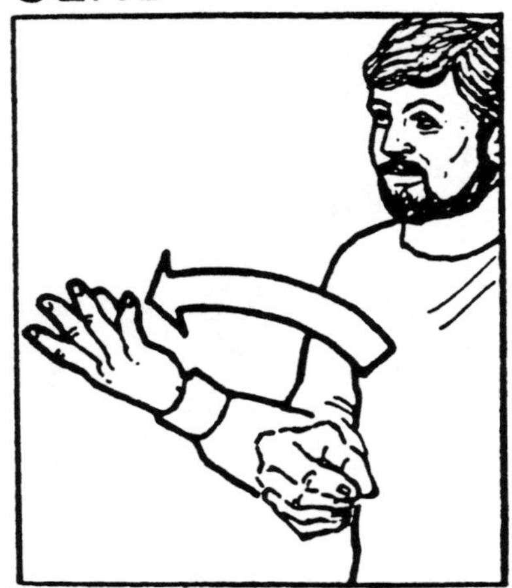

Full "O" hand moves forward sharply from near body, and springs open.

SENSIBLE

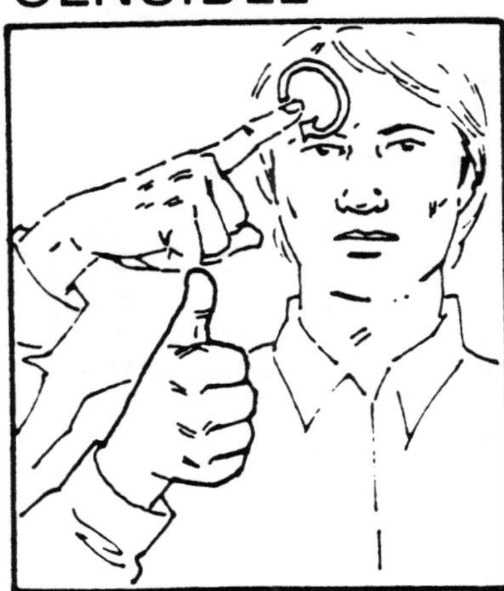

Index makes small circle on side of forehead, then moves out slightly changing to sign for "good".

SENTENCE

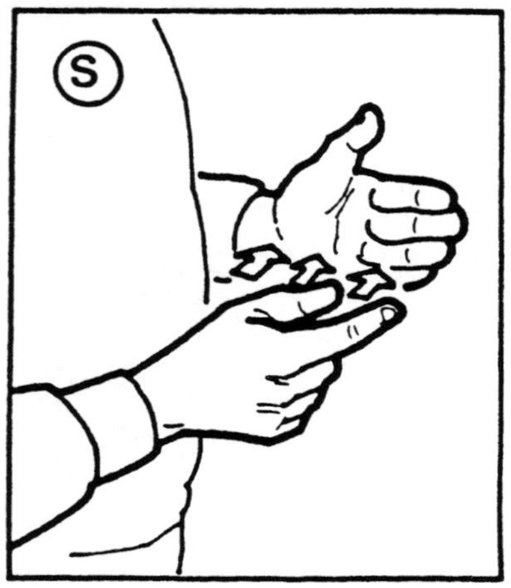

Rt. index and thumb about 1″ apart, move forward, contacting edge of L. palm several times to indicate a line of words.

SEPARATE

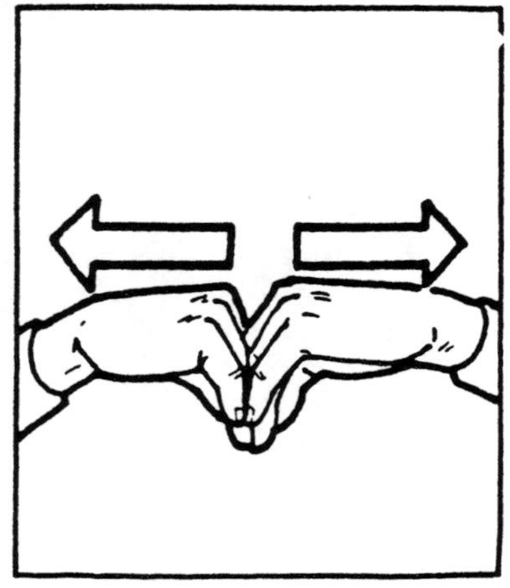

Bent hands, back to back, pull apart.

SERIES

Rt. thumb twists over repeatedly in a left to right movement.

SERIOUS

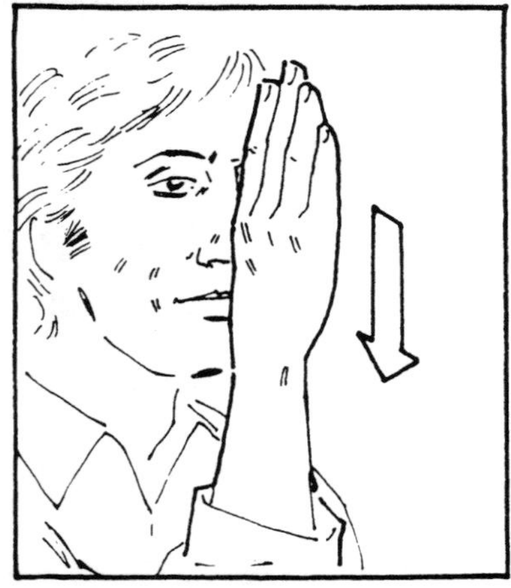

Rt. flat hand, palm left, moves down in front of nose.

SERVANT

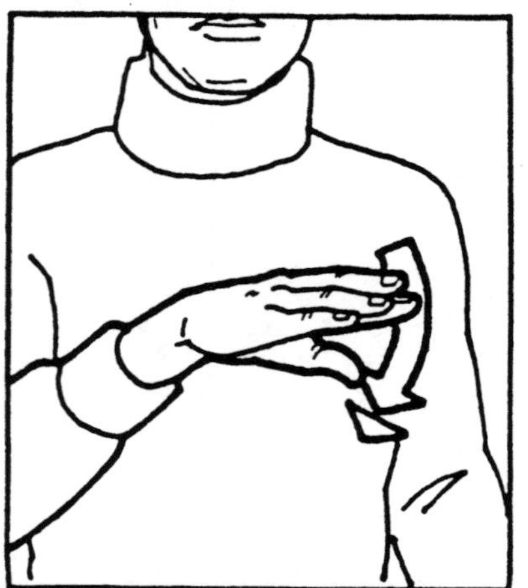

Thumb of palm down Rt. flat hand brushes down twice on left side of chest.

SET

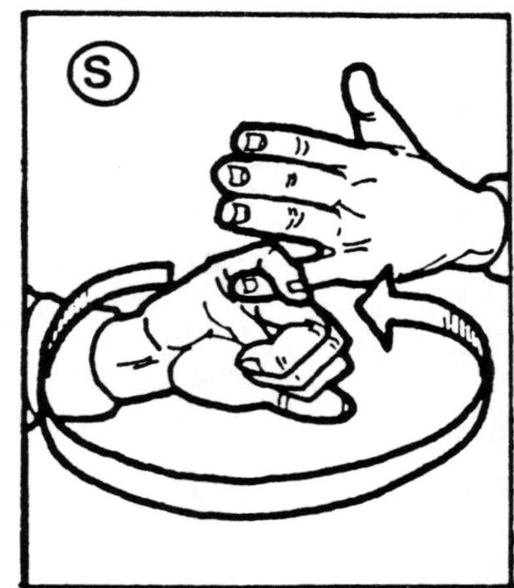

Form fingerspelt "S" and move formation round in horizontal circle.

SEVERAL

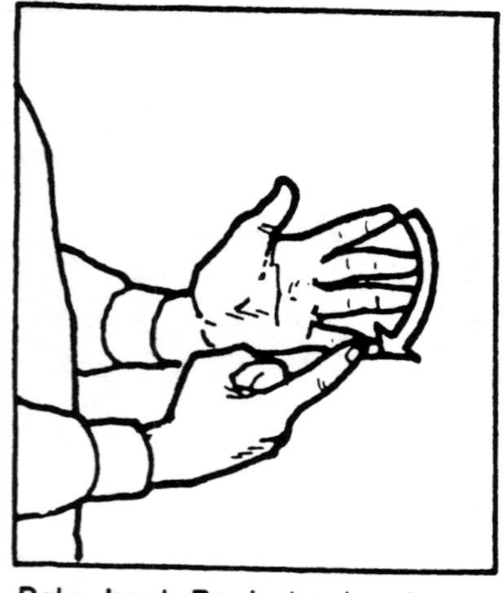

Palm back Rt. index brushes down along fingertips of L. open hand.

SEW

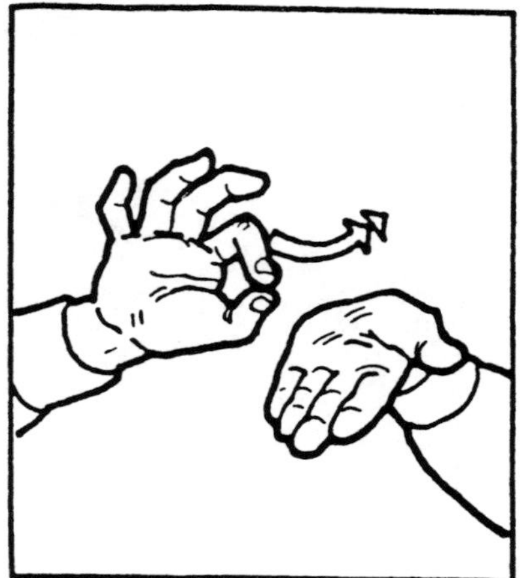

Rt. "O" hand mimes sewing action on L. palm.

SHADE

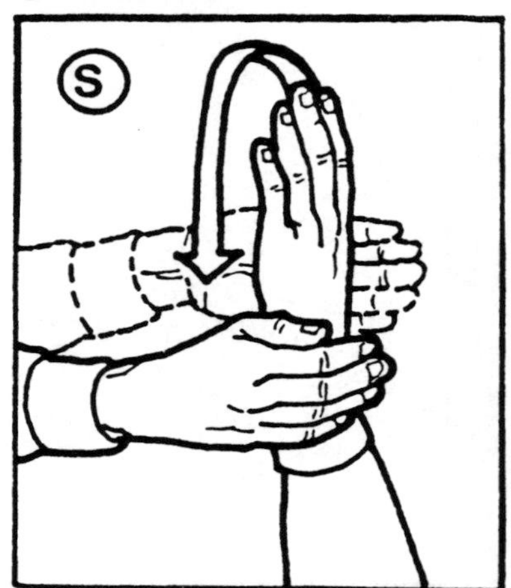

L. flat hand, palm right. Rt. cupped hand, palm forward, behind L. curves over top of L. hand to finish palm back.

SHADOW

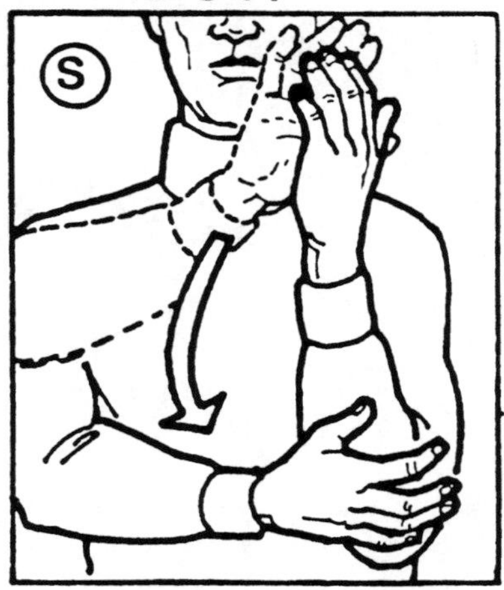

L. hand, palm back/right. Rt. open hand palm forward sweeps from behind L., forward/down, to finish palm back near left elbow.

SHALLOW

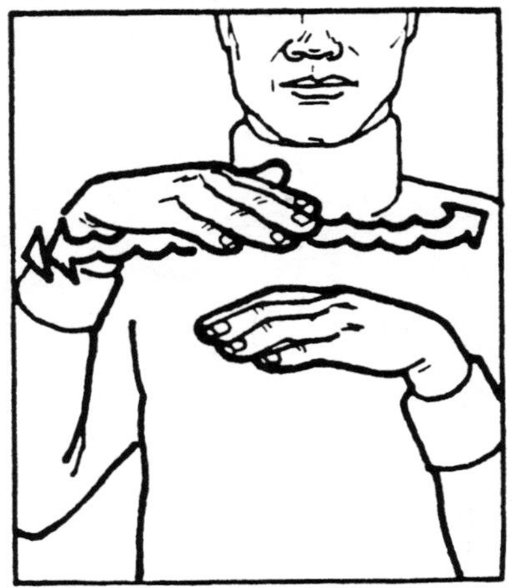

Rt. flat hand moves in wavy movement a few inches above L.

SHAME (guilt)

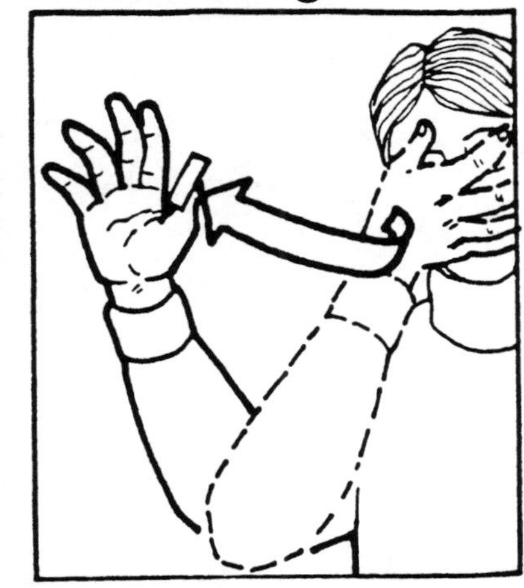

Open hand, fingers slightly bent, held palm back in front of face, moves forward, twisting to palm forward with emphasis.

SHAME (pity)

Slightly cupped hand moves back twice, as if stroking a child's head.

SHAPE

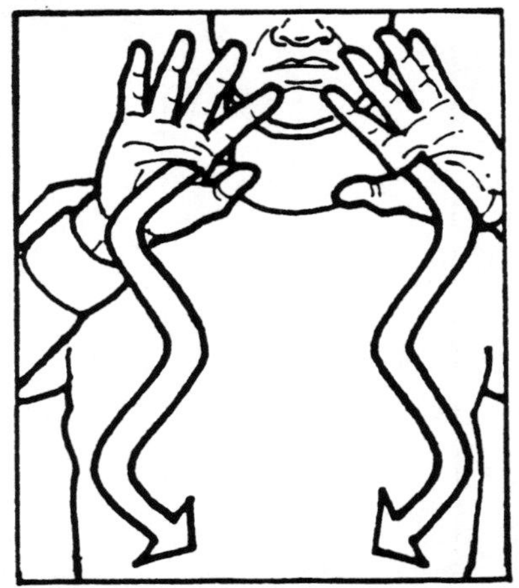

Open hands move out and in whilst moving down, to indicate shape.

SHARE

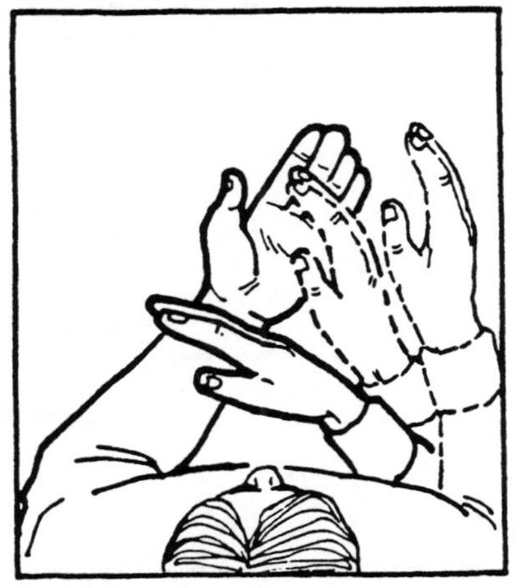

Blade of Rt. flat hand chops down three times along L. palm.

SHARP

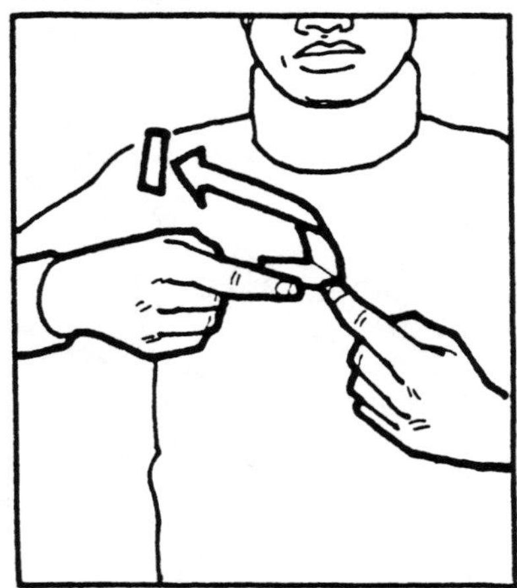

Tip of Rt. index moves to contact tip of L., then twists and sharply pulls away.

SHAVE

Edge of thumb brushes down cheek, twice.

SHE

Index brushes forward on cheek, then points forward, or to the person concerned.

SHEEP

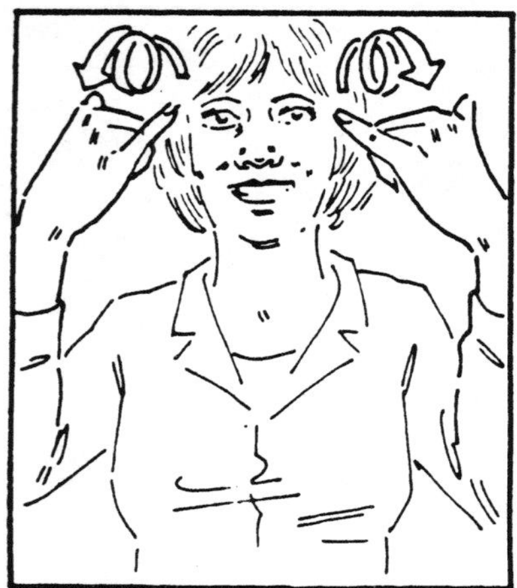

Little fingers move forward/ down in circular movement from sides of face to indicate ram's horns.

SHEET

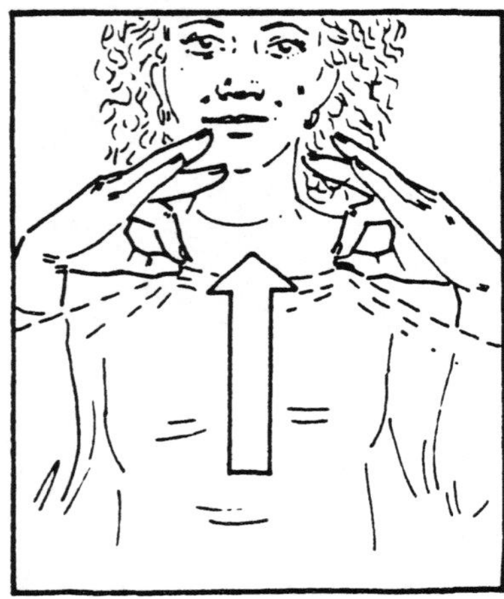

Mime pulling sheet up body.

SHELF

Bent hands pull apart, to indicate a shelf.

SHEPHERD

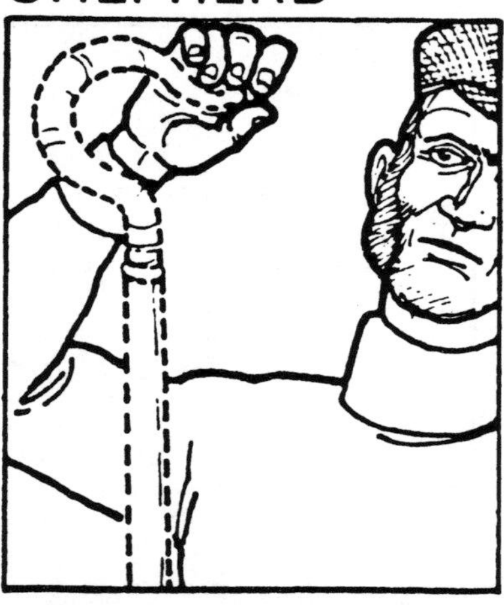

Hand moves down in shape of shepherd's crook.

SHIFT (work)

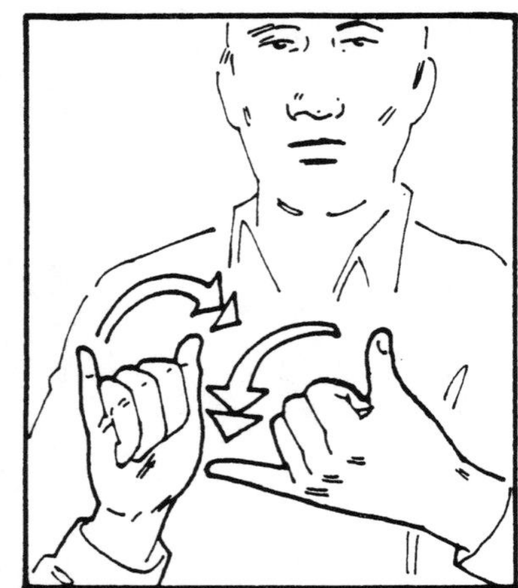

Little fingers and thumbs extended from closed hands. Hands move from side to side in alternate twisting movement.

SHINE

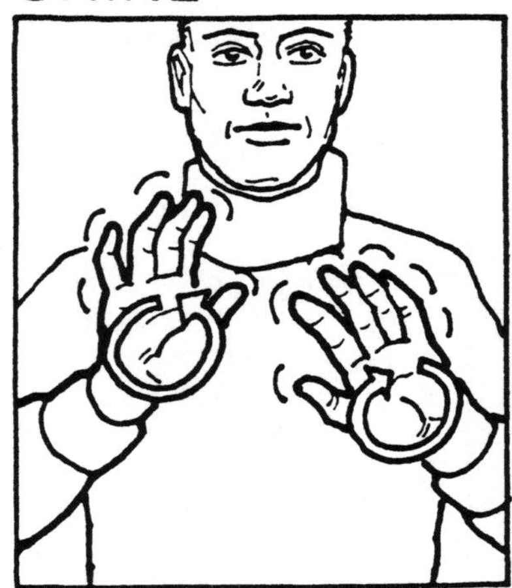

Palm forward hands move apart and round in small circles with fingers fluttering.

SHIP

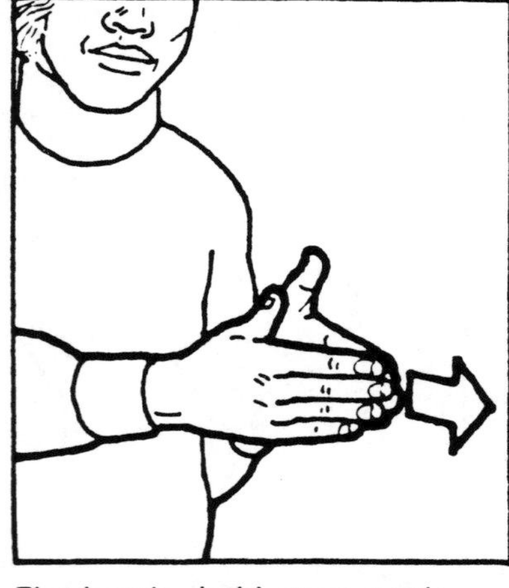

Flat hands, held at an angle, touch at tips indicating shape of ship. Formation moves forward.

SHIRT

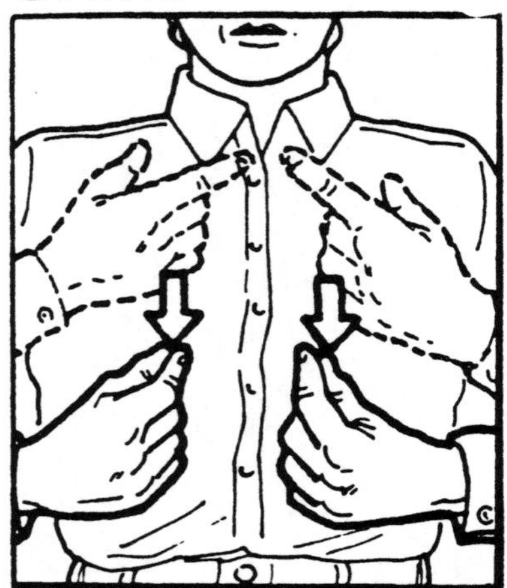

Indexes and thumbs, held open, move slightly down, closing together to indicate a shirt's collar.

SHOCK

Palm down open hands move sharply back to body with stress.

SHOE

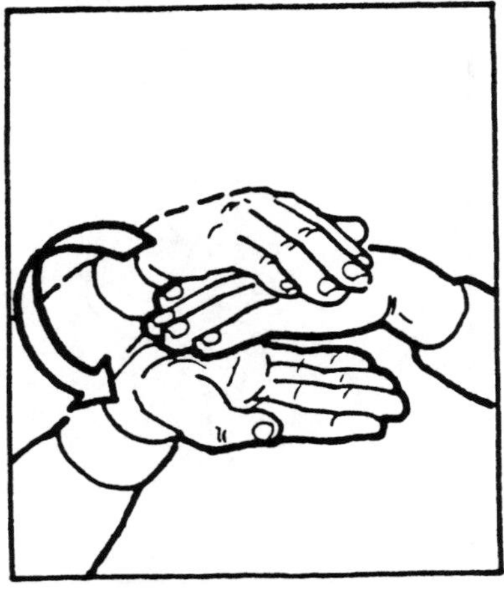

Rt. flat hand brushes along back of L. to tips, then twists to palm up under L.

SHOP

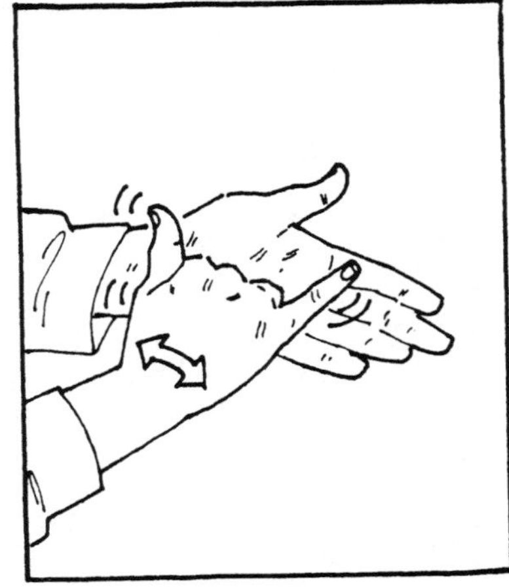

Rt. hand little finger and thumb extended, makes small, quick side to side movement on L. palm.

SHOPPING

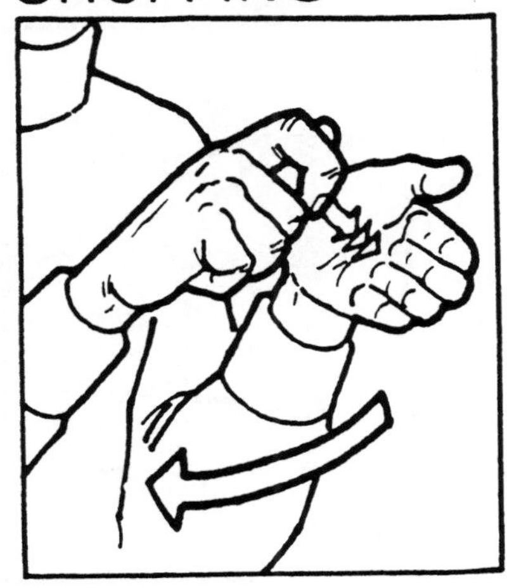

Rt. "R" hand, thumb extended, hits L. palm several times as formation moves to the right.

SHORT

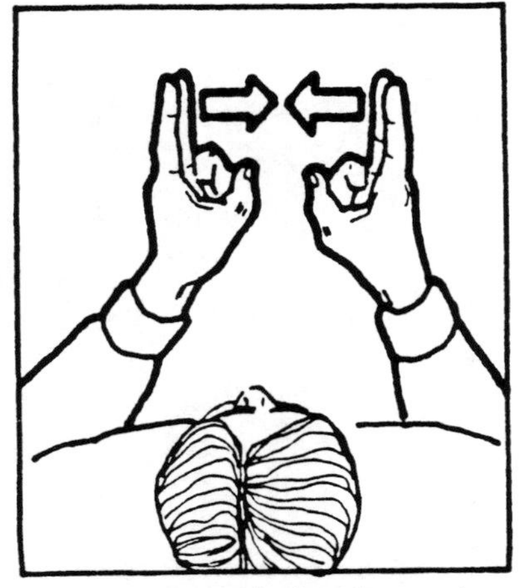

"N" hands, pointing forward, palms facing, make short movement towards each other.

SHORTS

Blades of flat hands tap against thighs.

SHOULD

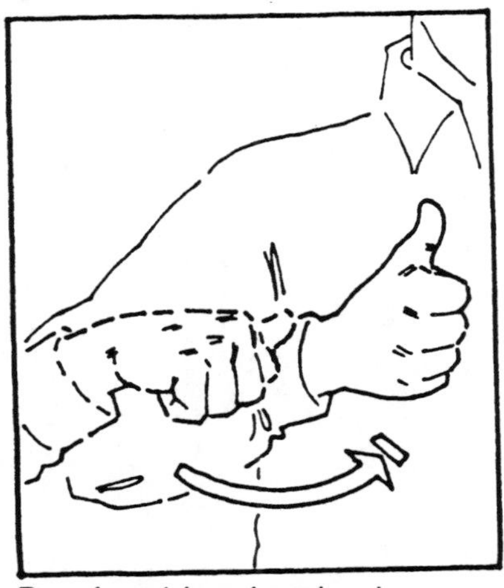

Rt. closed hand, palm down, thumb extended and pointing left, moves sharply in, twisting to palm back, thumb up, with emphasis.

SHOUT

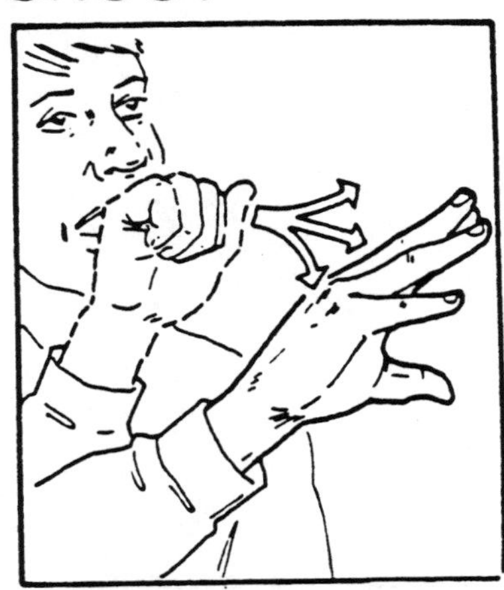

Closed hand, palm forward, in front of mouth, moves forward springing sharply open.

SHOW

Flat hands palm back, held under eyes, sweep forward/ down and apart.

SHOW-OFF

Thumbs pointing back on chest. Shoulders waggle backwards and forwards alternately in swaggering manner.

SHOWER

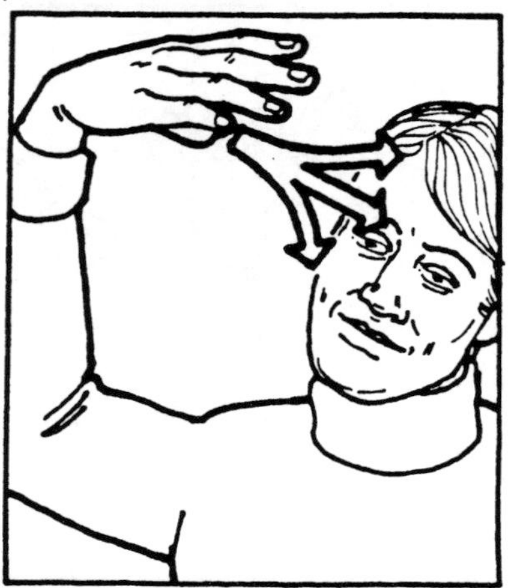

Full "O" hand springs open towards head, several times.

SHUT

Rt. flat hand closes onto back of L.

SHY

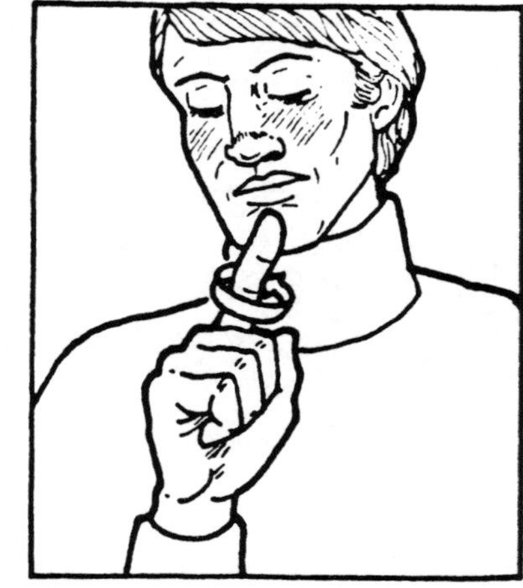

Rt. index, palm left twists to palm back on chin.

SICK

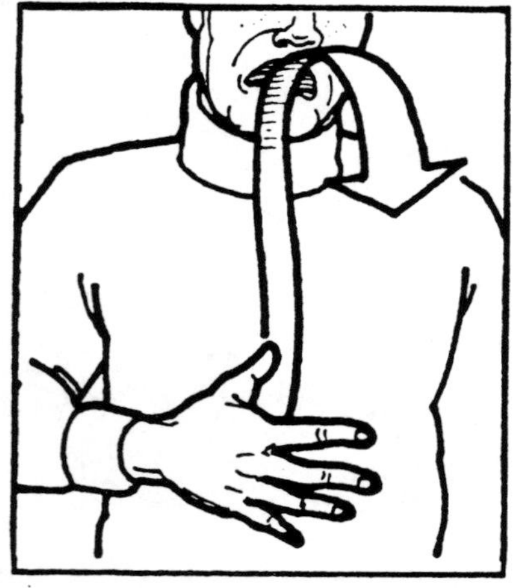

Rt. open hand brushes up body and forward from mouth.

SIDE

Hand moves down at side of body.

SIDEBOARD

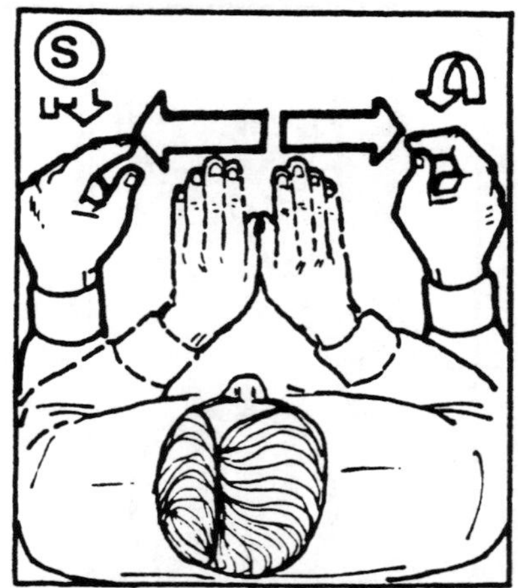

Flat hands move apart, then mime opening doors.

SIGN

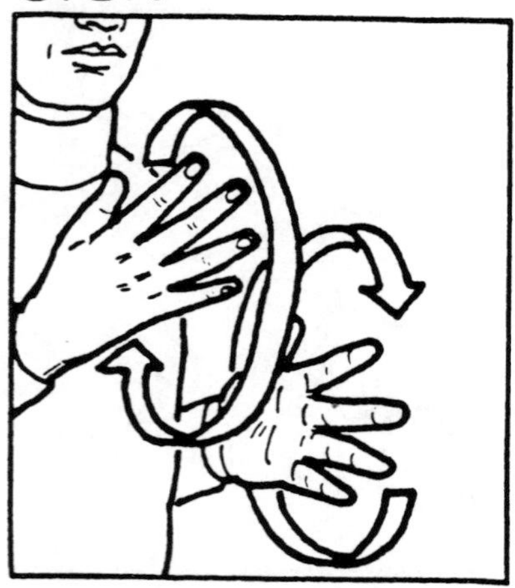

Open hands make alternate forward circles.

SILENT

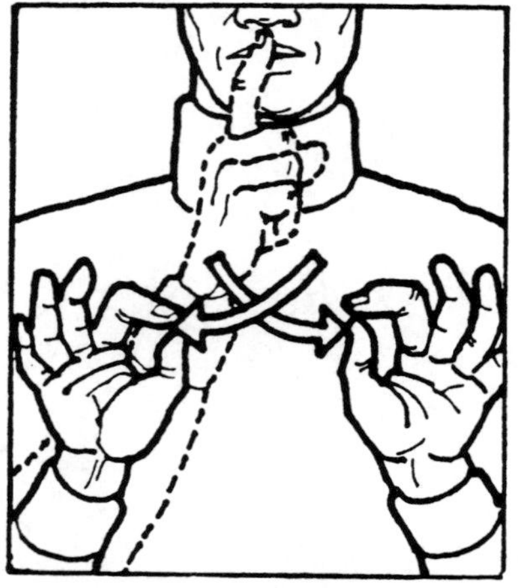

Index held on lips, then crossed "O" hands pull apart.

SILLY

Tap forehead twice, with middle finger.

SILVER

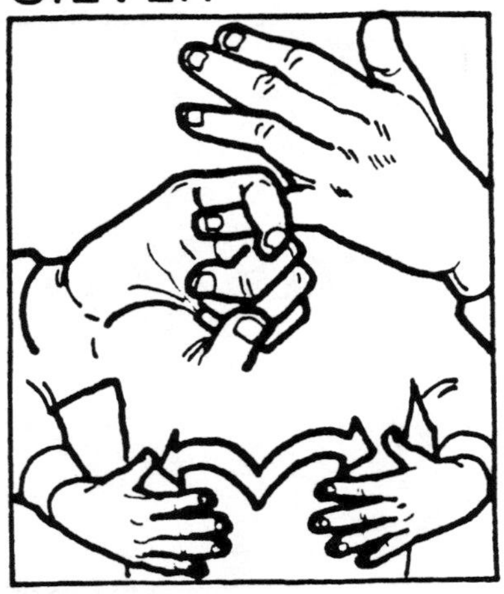

Form fingerspelt "S" then hands spring sharply open and apart.

SIMILAR

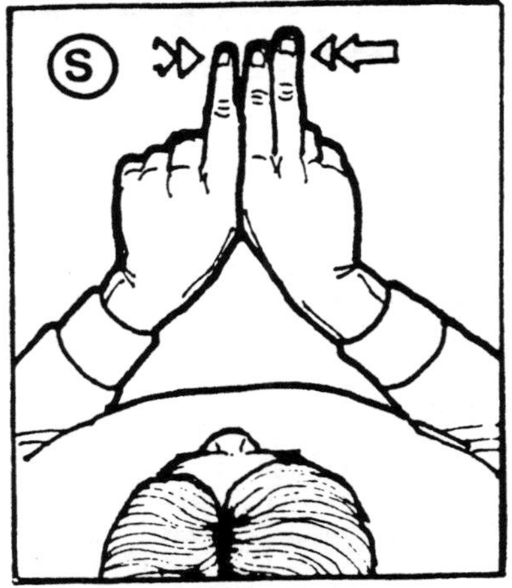

Rt. "N" hand, pointing forward, taps against L. index, twice.

SINCE

Cupped hand moves forward from shoulder.

SING

"N" hands circle alternately upwards from mouth.

SINGLE (one)

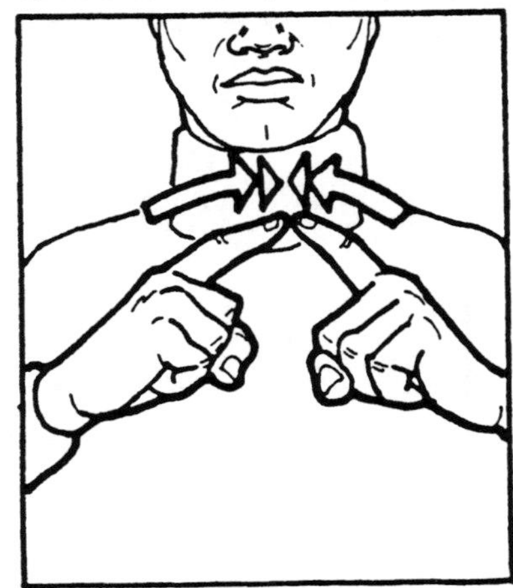

Indexes pointing up/in tap together, twice.

SINGLE (status)

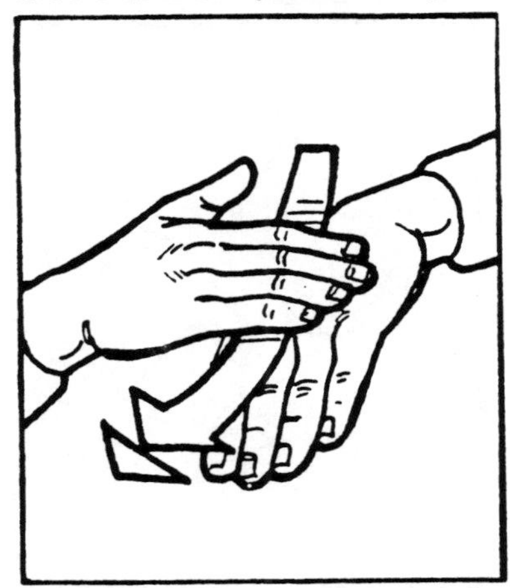

Rt. flat hand brushes forward along back of L. hand, twice.

SINK (TO)

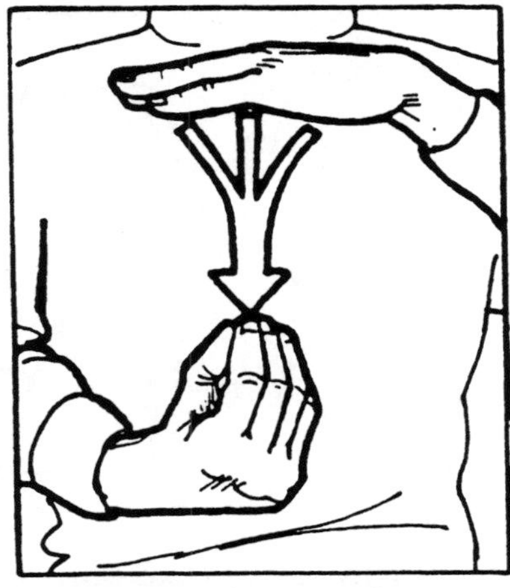

Rt. open hand moves down, closing to bunched hand, under L. flat hand.

SINK (kitchen)

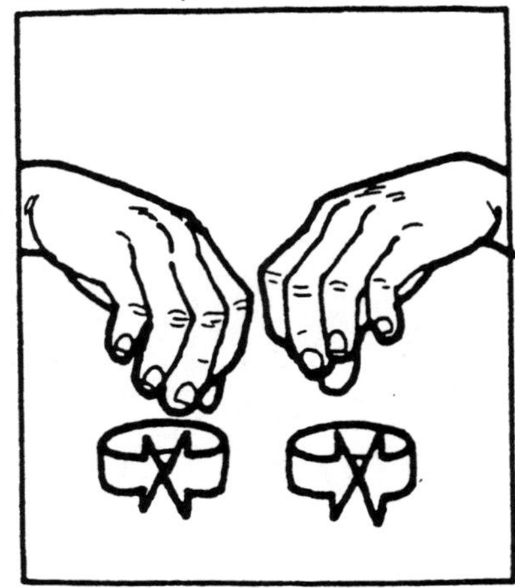

Mime turning taps.

SISTER

Tap nose twice with bent index finger.

SIT

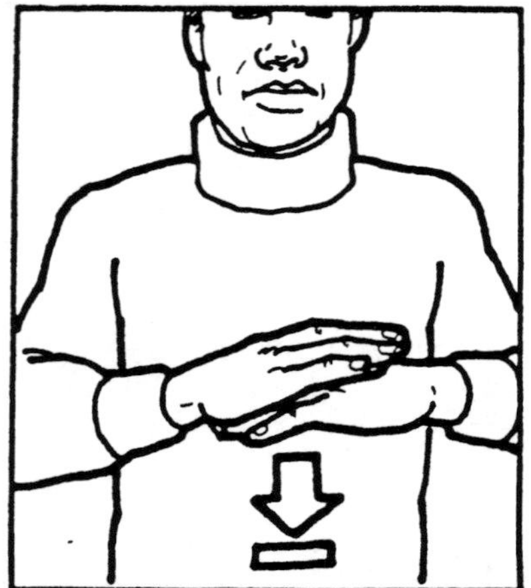

Rt. flat hand on top of L. Move down with slight stress.

SITUATION

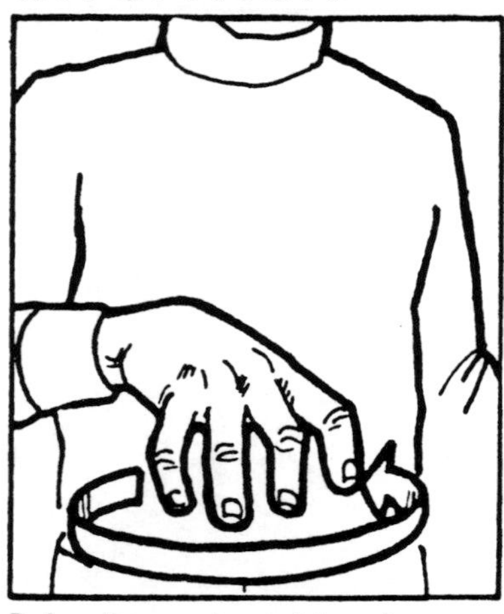

Palm down clawed hand moves round in small horizontal circle.

SIZE

Tips of Rt. hand in fingerspelt "Z" formation, tap L, palm twice.

SKATE

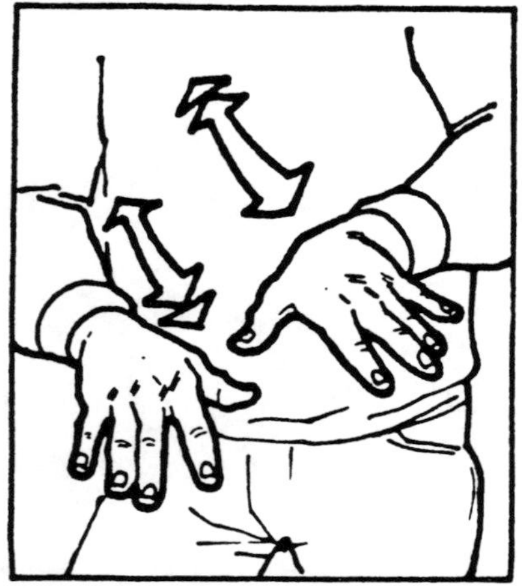

Palm down hands, move forward and back alternately in skating action.

SKILL

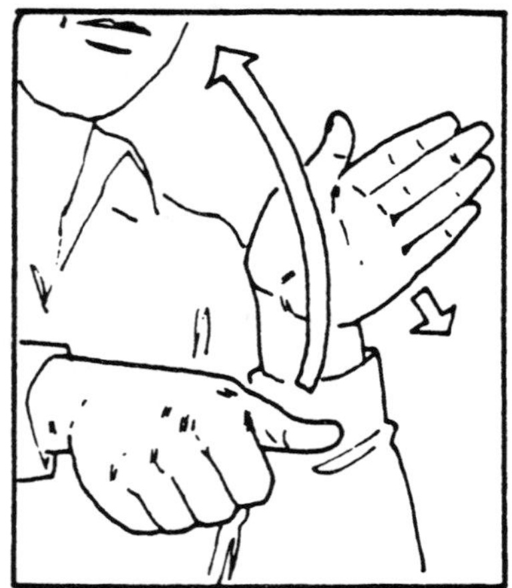

L. flat hand, palm right, makes slight downward movement, as Rt. thumb sweeps sharply up L. palm.

SKIP

Mime skipping with rope.

SKIPPING ROPE

Mime skipping, then hands pull apart as indexes and thumbs rub together to indicate rope.

SKIRT

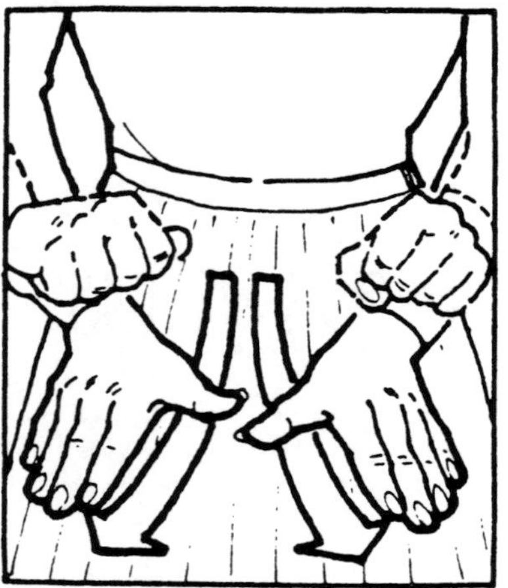

Closed hands move down from waist opening to flat hands.

SKY

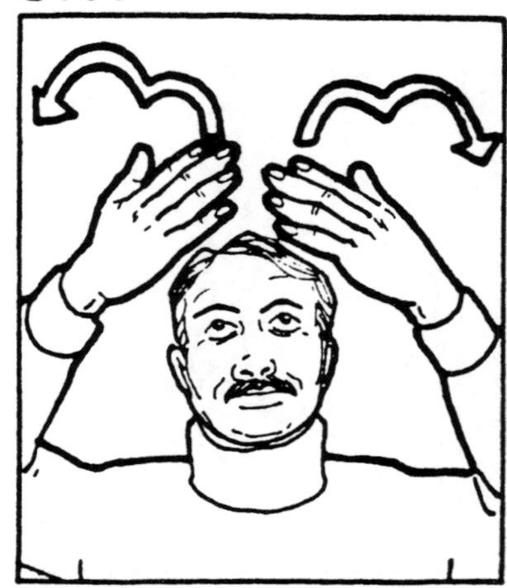

Flat hands move out in small arcs over head.

SLEEP

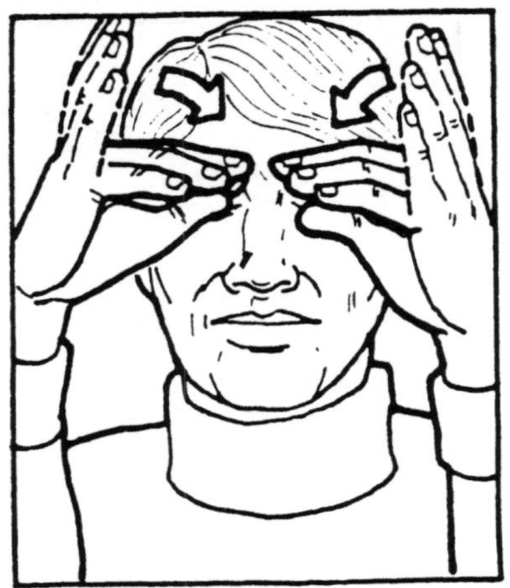

Fingers of flat hands, pointing up, close on to thumbs near eyes.

SLIDE

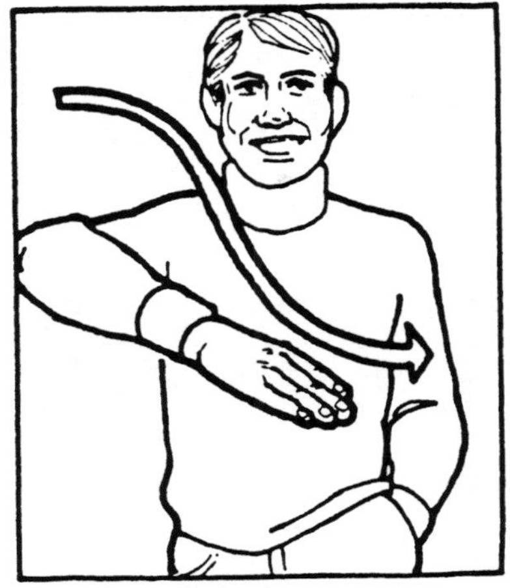

Flat hand curves down in shape of slide.

SLIP

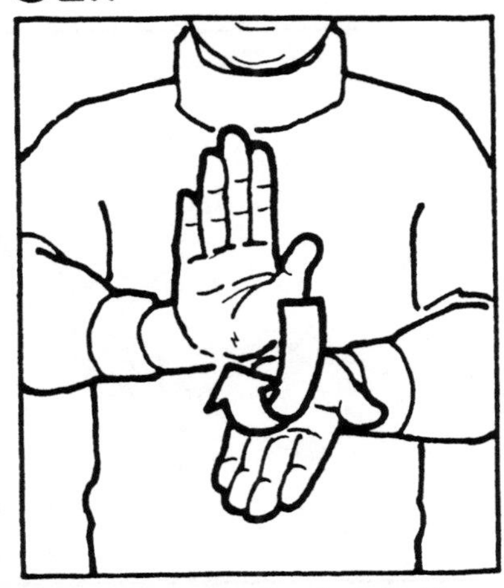

Palm down Rt. flat hand slips forward off L. twisting to palm forward.

SLIPPER

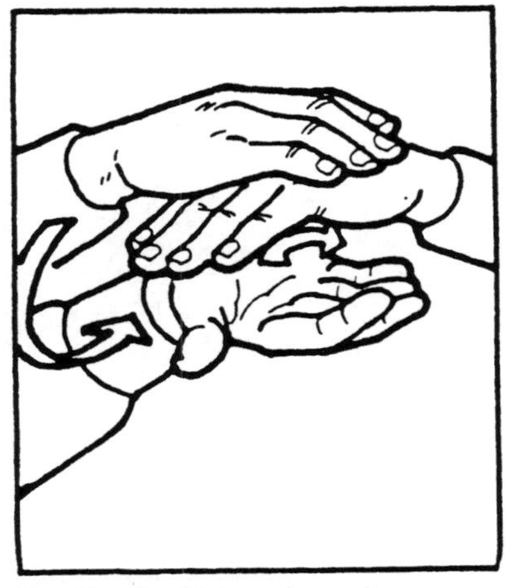

Rt. flat hand brushes along back of L. to tips, twists to palm up and rubs along underside of L. hand.

SLOW

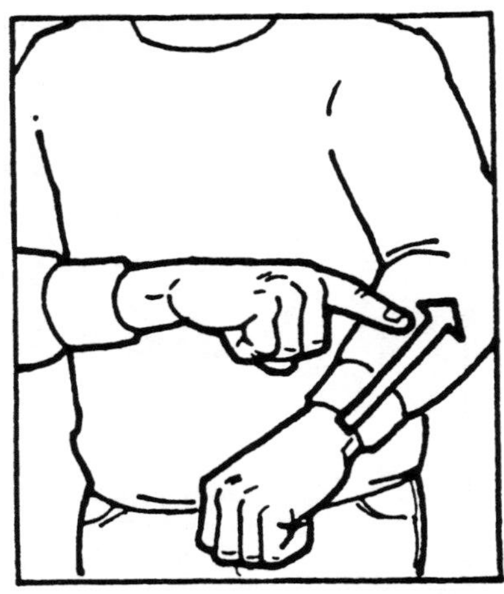

Rt. index moves slowly up left forearm.

SLY

Tip of extended thumb brushes down cheek.

SMACK

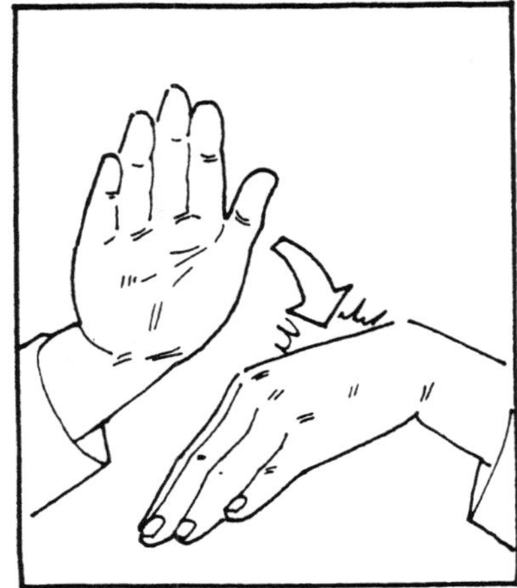

Smack back of L. hand with fingers of Rt.

SMALL

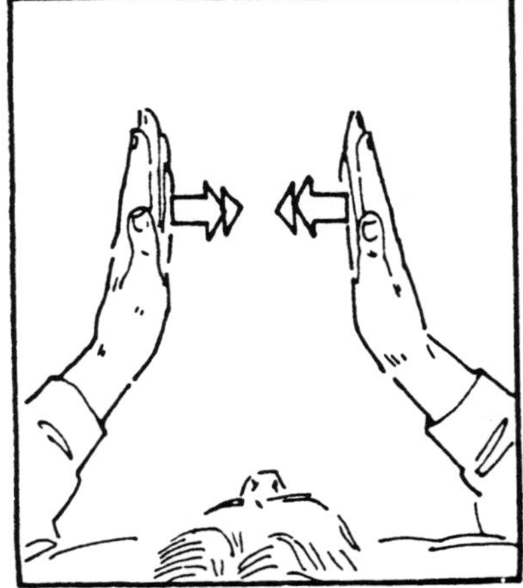

Flat hands make small repeated movement in.

SMART

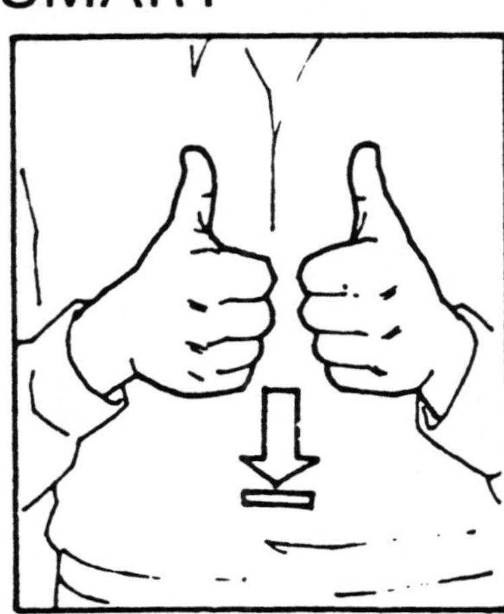

Hands held on chest, thumbs up, make short movement down, with stress.

SMOOTH

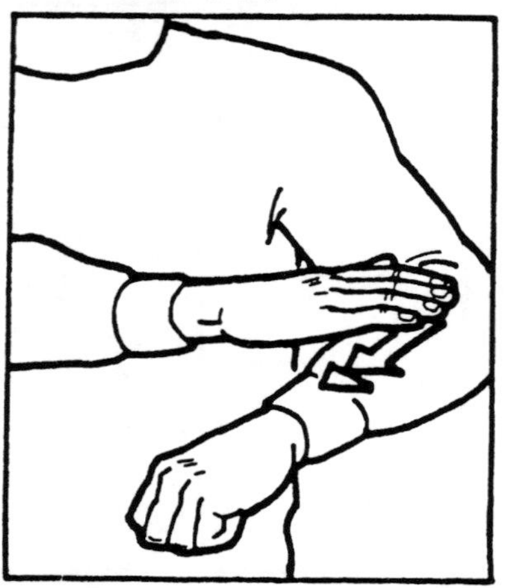

Rt. flat hand strokes down left forearm, twice.

SNAIL

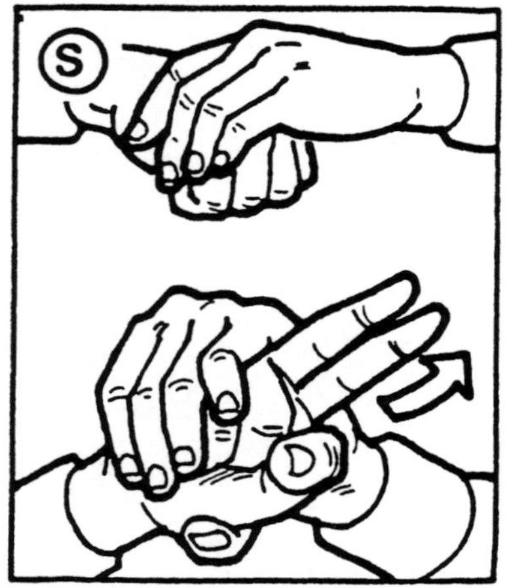

Rt. fist held under L. cupped hand makes small movement forward as index and middle fingers flick out like a snail's antennae.

SNAKE

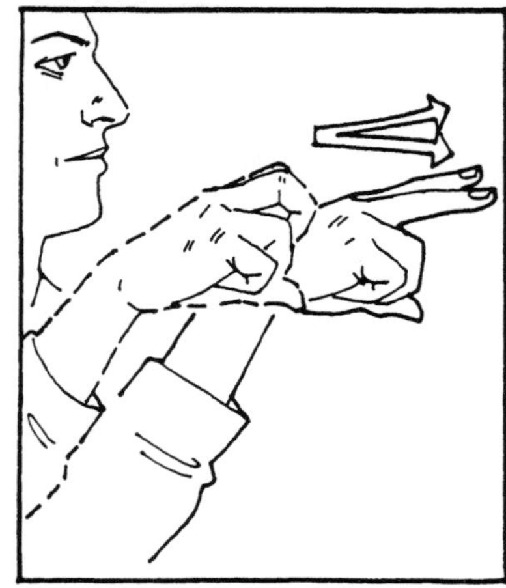

Bent "V" hand moves forward from near mouth as fingers straighten.

SNOOKER

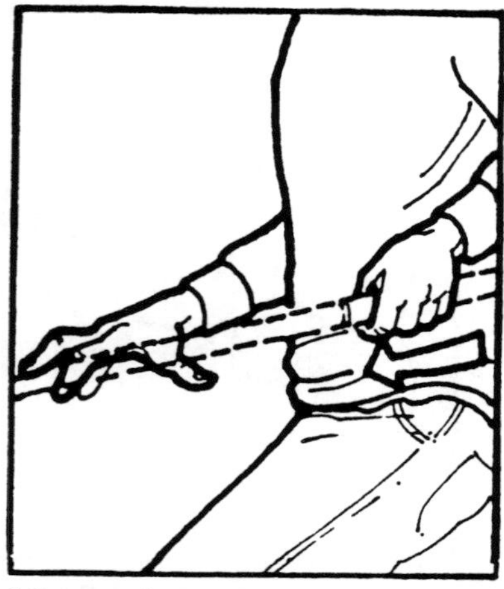

Mime using a snooker cue.

SNOW

Fingers flutter from side to side, as hands move down, like snow falling.

SOAP

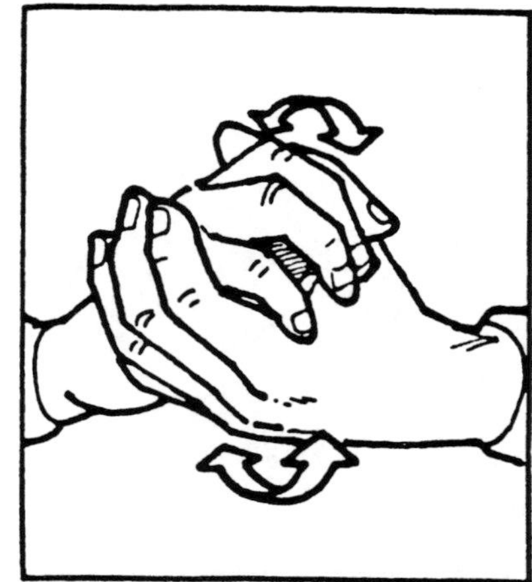

Cupped hands rub together.

SOCIAL WORKER

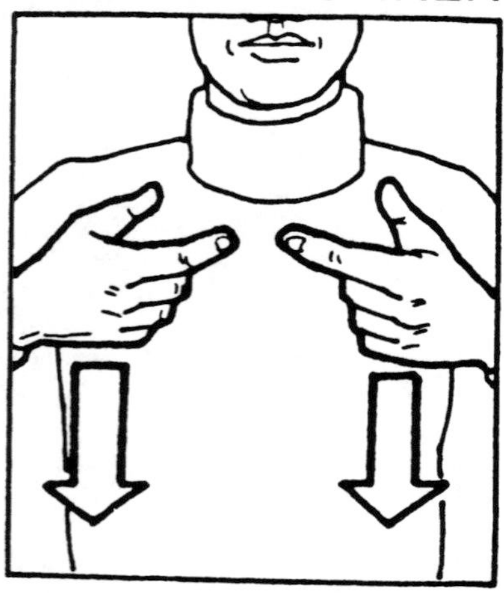

Tips of "C" hands move down upper chest.

SOCIETY (a)

Fingers of "O" hands interlocked; formation moves in horizontal circle.

SOCK

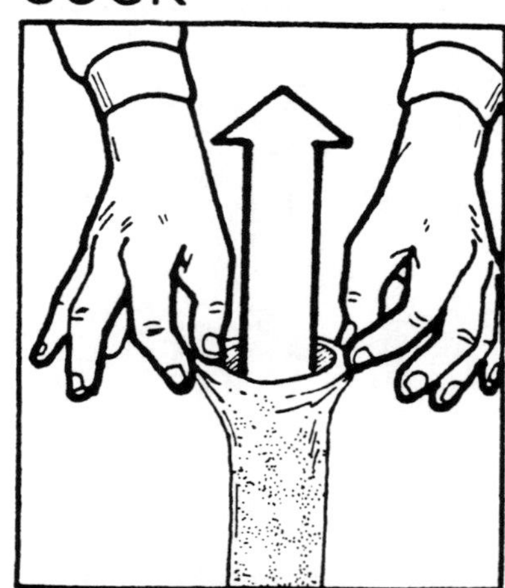

Mime pulling on sock.

SOFA

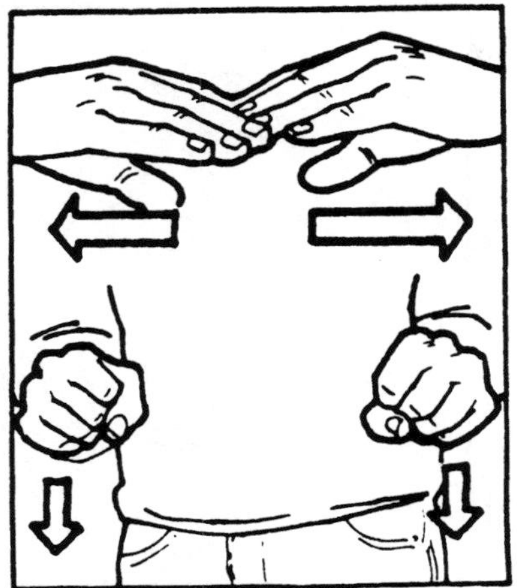

Hands pull apart, then fists make small movement down, held slightly out at sides of body.

SOFT

Index prods into cheek, once.

SOIL

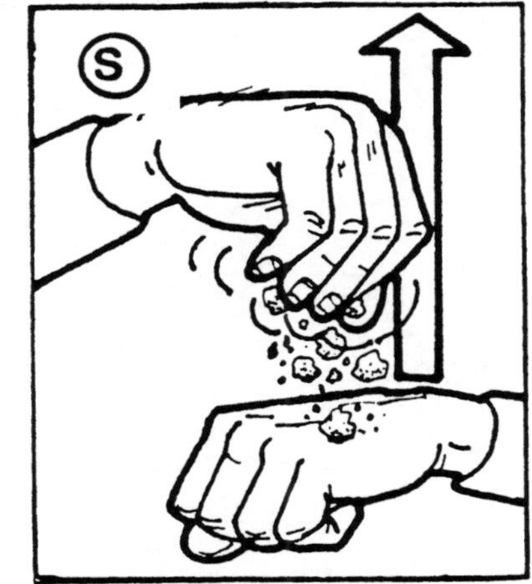

Rt. thumb rubs along fingertips several times as hand moves up from back of L. closed hand.

SOLDIER

Rt. flat hand, pointing up, contacts right side of chest, then left.

SOME

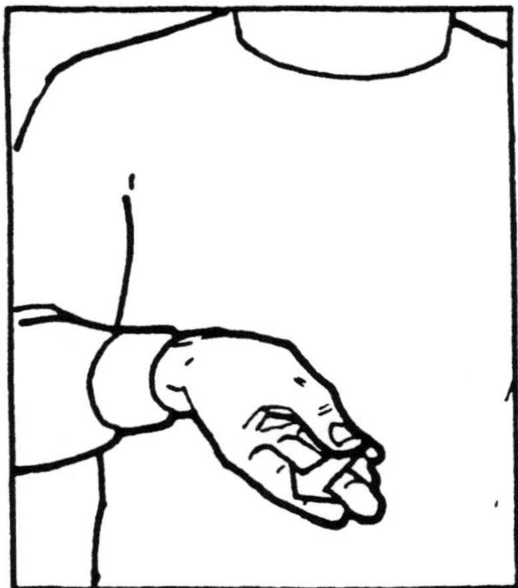

Thumb rubs along fingertips from little finger.

SOMEONE

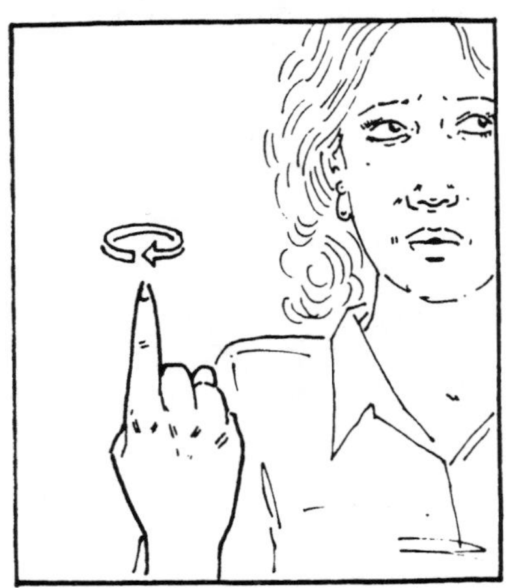

Extended index, pointing up, palm back, moves in small horizontal circles.

SOMETHING

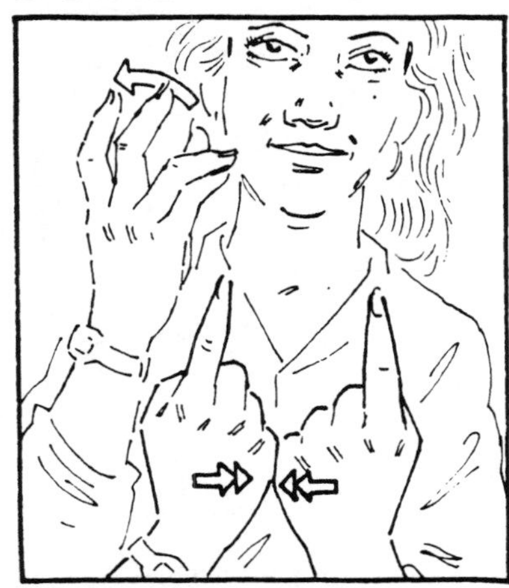

Thumb rubs along fingertips, then blades of closed hands, indexes extended, tap together twice.

SOMETIMES

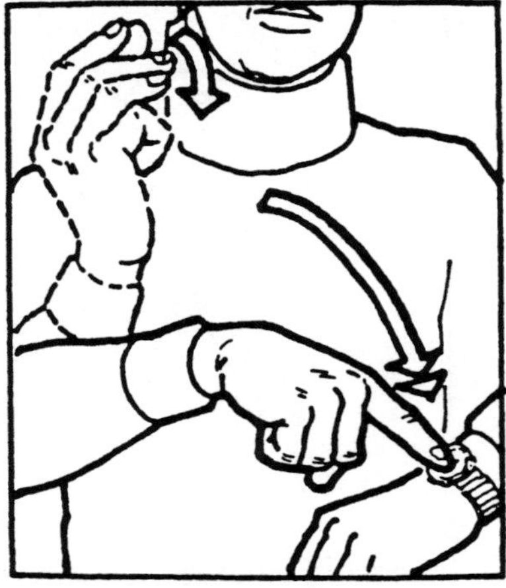

Thumb rubs along fingertips, then index taps back of L. wrist, twice.

SON

Fingerspell "S" "O" "N".

SONG

"N" hands circle alternately upwards from mouth, and stop abruptly.

SOON

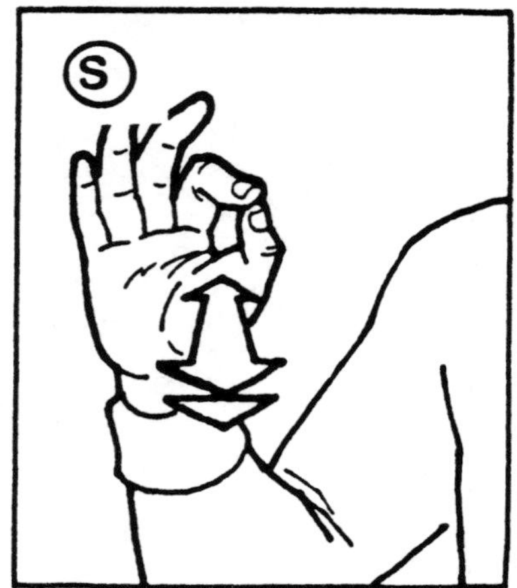

Palm forward "O" hand makes small backward and forward movement.

SORRY

Closed hand rubs in circular movement on chest.

SORT (out)

Cupped hands move in/down alternately several times, as if separating things.

SOUL

Open hand sweeps round and upwards from mouth, closing to bunched hand.

SOUND

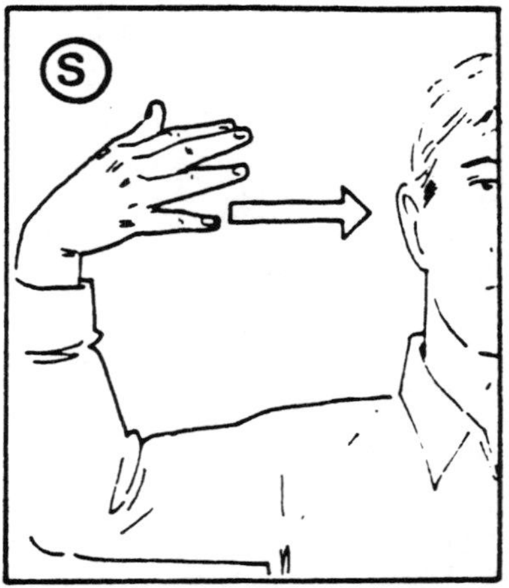

Open hand, pointing towards side of head moves sharply towards ear.

SOUP

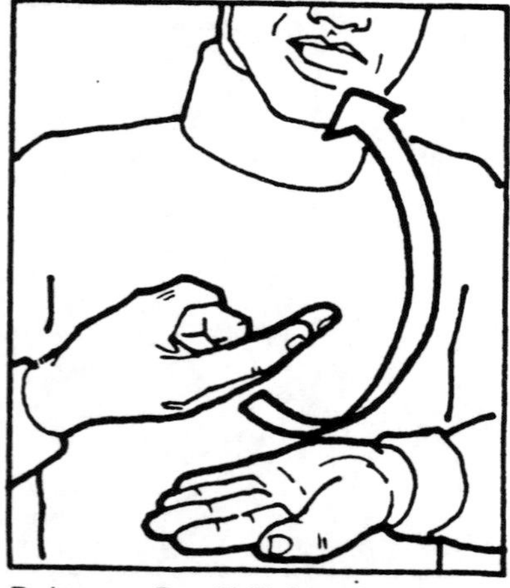

Palm up Rt. "N" hand mimes spooning soup to mouth off L. palm.

SOUR

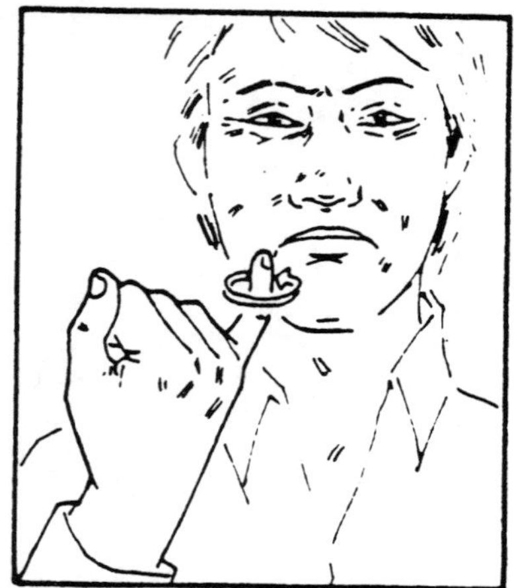

Little finger of Rt. hand, palm left, twists to palm back at corner of mouth.

SPACE

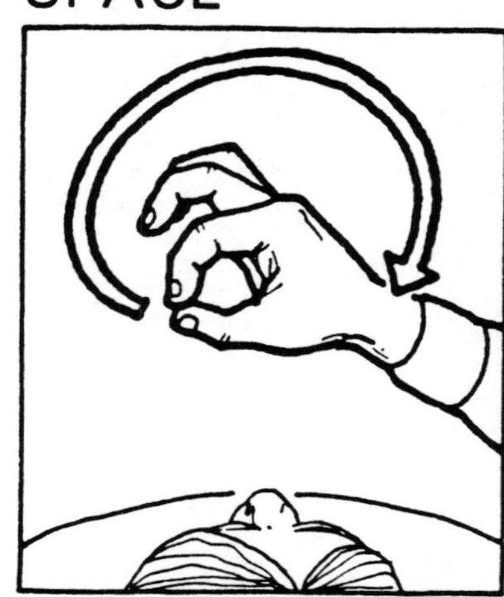

Rt. "O" hand, palm left, moves in horizontal circle.

SPADE

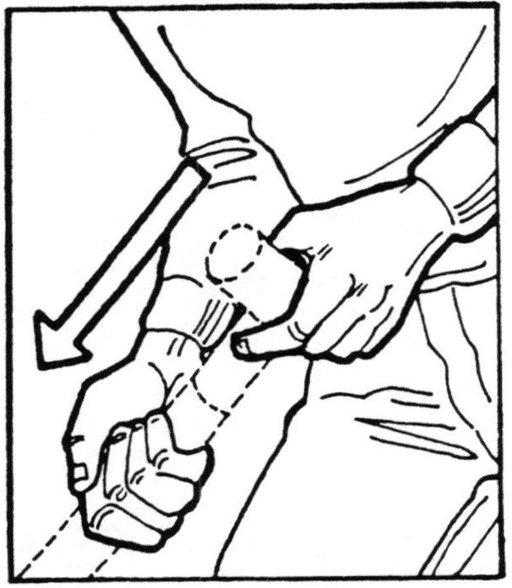

Mime holding spade and make short movement down.

SPAGHETTI

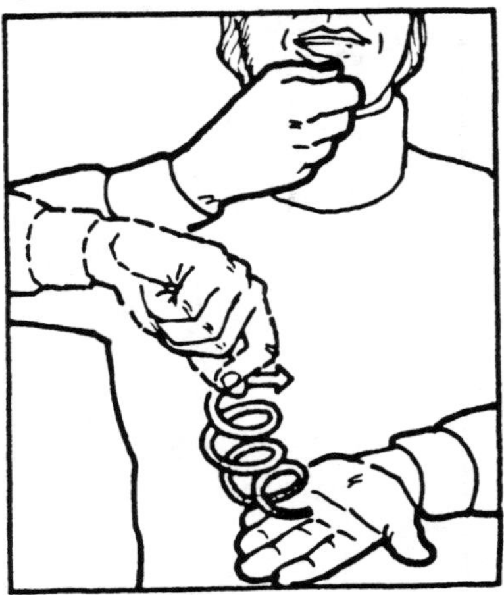

Rt. hand mimes twisting spaghetti onto fork above L. palm, then moves to mouth.

SPAIN

Mime playing castanets.

SPEAK

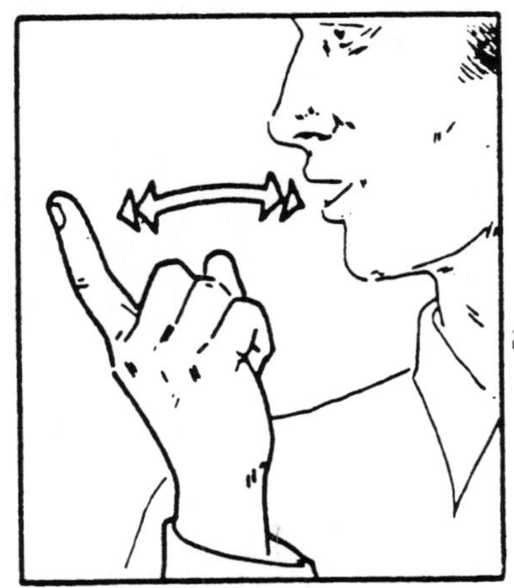

Index makes short repeated movements backwards and forward from mouth.

SPECIAL

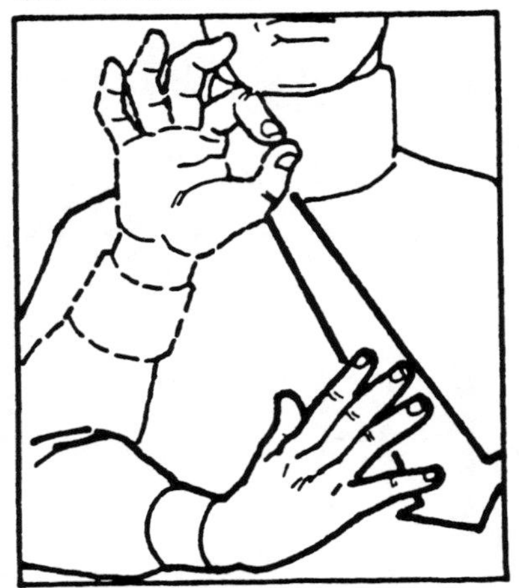

"O" hand moves forward/down, springing sharply open.

SPEND

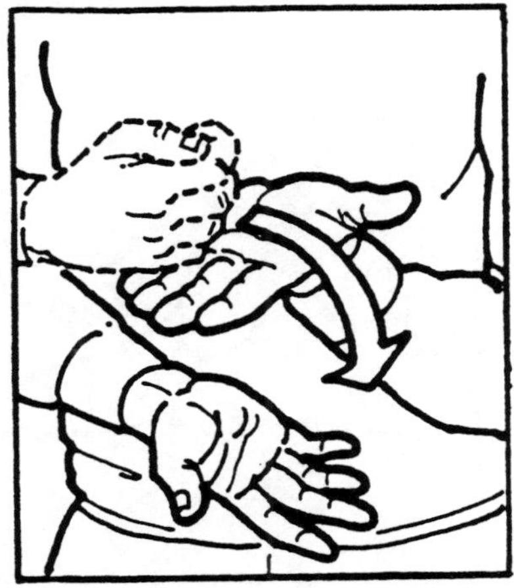

Rt. thumb tucked into bent index. Hand springs open whilst moving forward off L. palm.

SPIDER

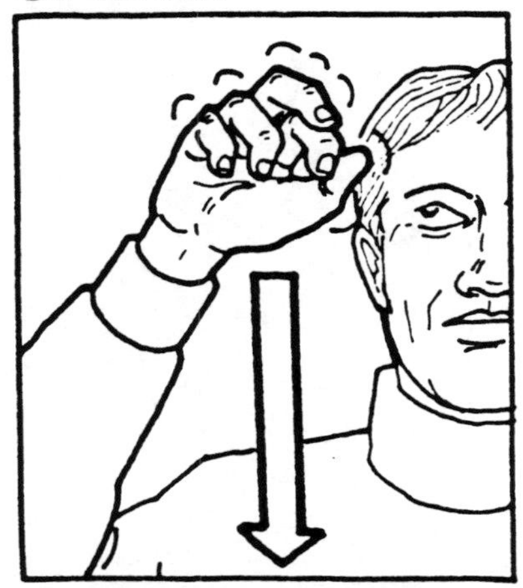

Clawed hand moves down, with fingers wriggling to indicate spider's legs.

SPILL

Rt. fist moves forward sharply and springs open.

SPIT

Index flicks out in forward movement from mouth.

SPLIT

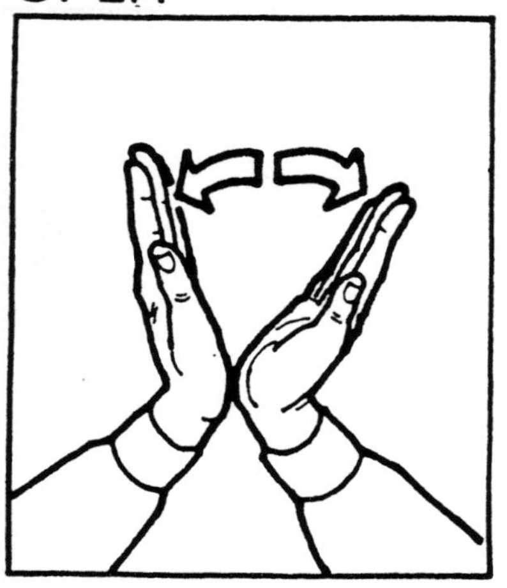

Flat hands held palms together, open, maintaining contact at heels.

SPOIL

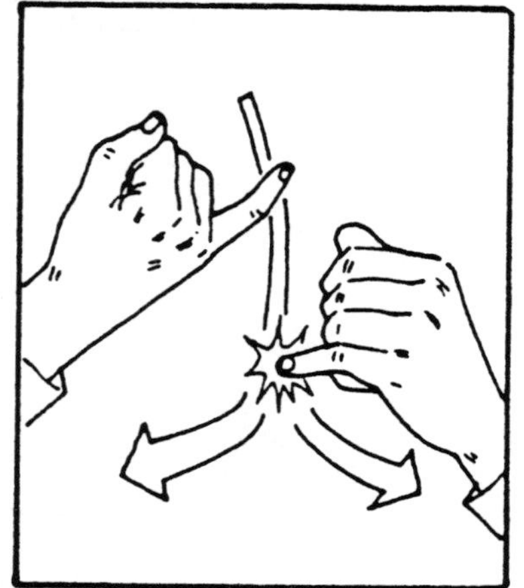

Rt. little finger moves down sharply to strike L., as both twist to point down.

SPOON

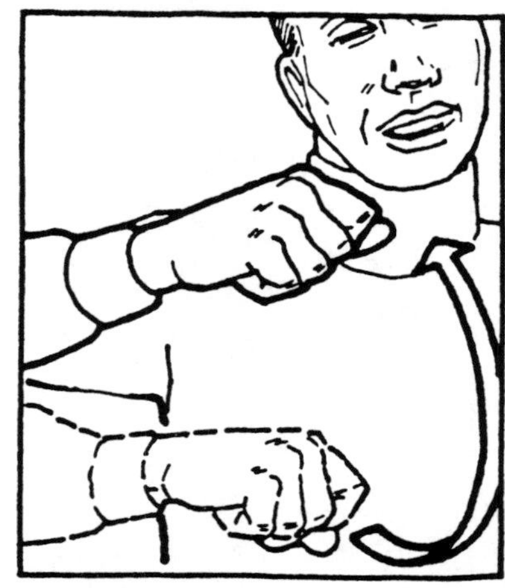

Mime holding a spoon, and move to mouth.

SPORT

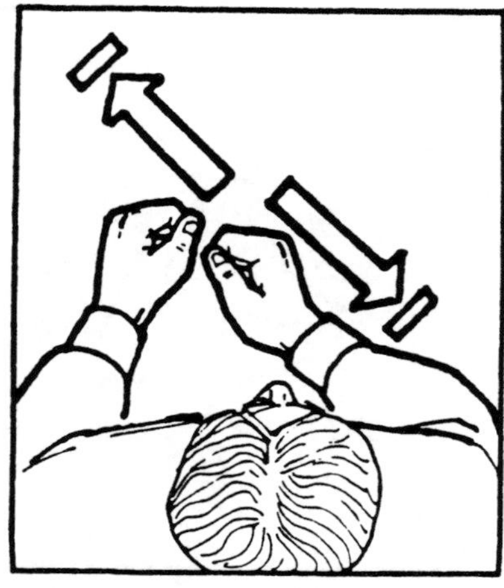

Closed hands, held together, pull sharply apart, diagonally.

SPOTS

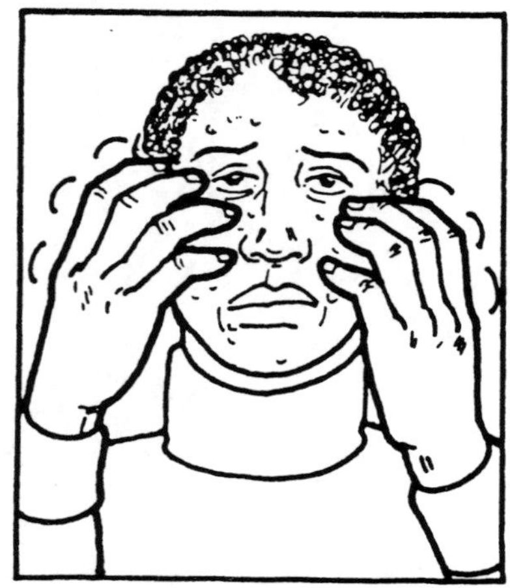

Tips of slightly clawed hands tap on face.

SPREAD

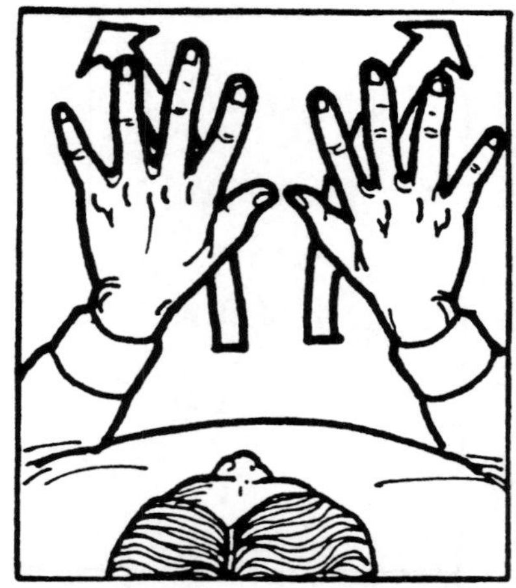

Palm down open hands move forward/out.

SPRING (season)

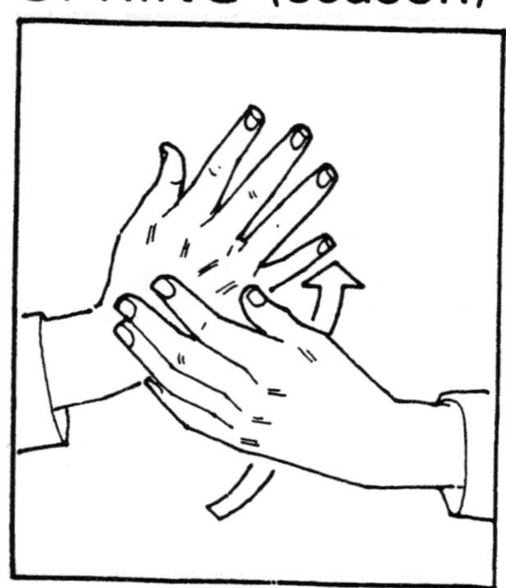

Rt. open hand swivels to point upwards, from behind L.

SQUARE

Indexes indicate outline of square.

SQUASH

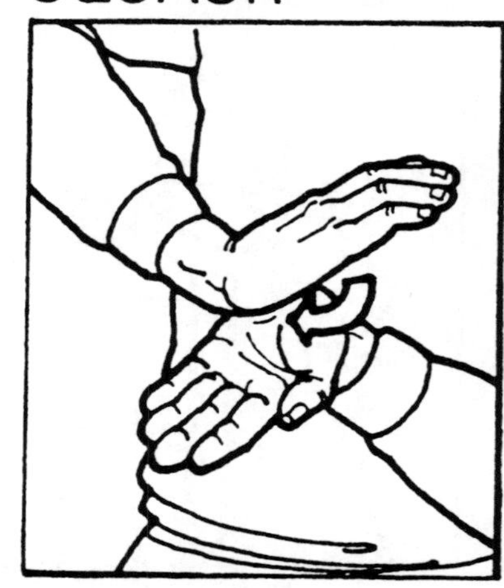

Heel of Rt. hand twist on L.

SQUIRREL

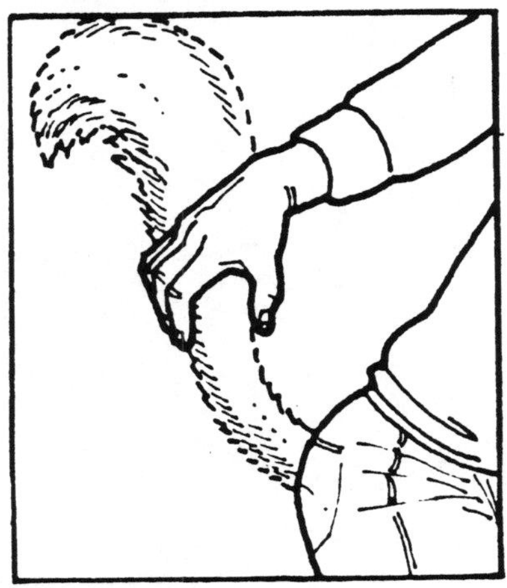

Hand moves up and out from back of body to indicate bushy tail.

STAIRS

Fingers mime walking on stairs - upwards for "upstairs", downwards for "downstairs".

STAMP (post)

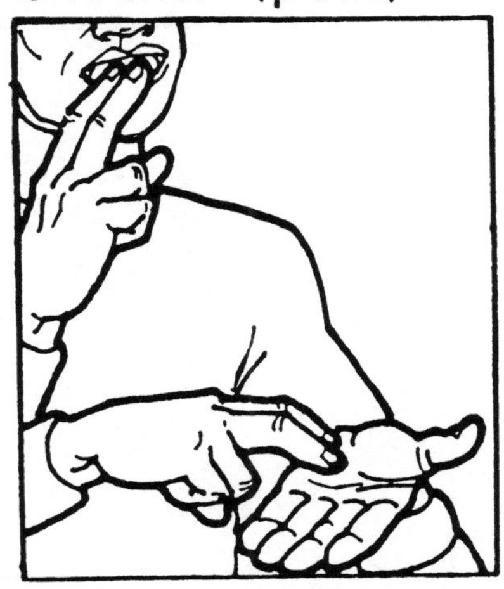

Rt. "N" hand touches mouth, then L. palm, to indicate sticking on a stamp.

STAND

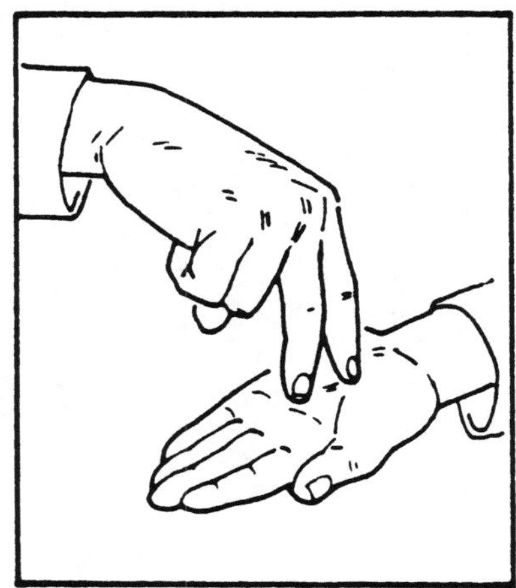

Rt. "V" hand stands on L. palm.

STARS

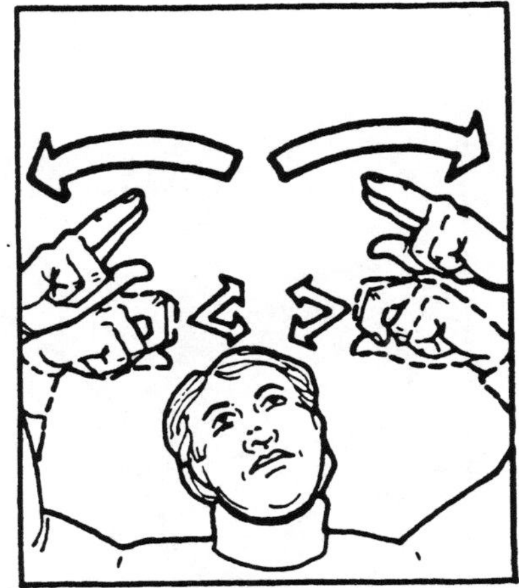

Indexes and middle fingers flexed on thumbs, flick out several times, as hands move apart, over head.

START

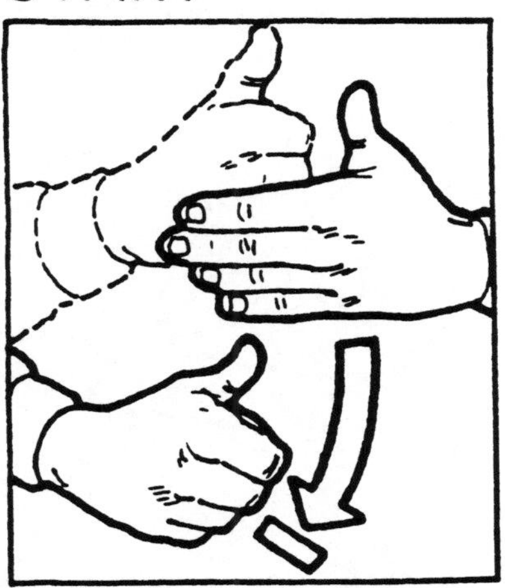

Rt. thumb up, brushes down sharply behind L. flat hand.

STATION

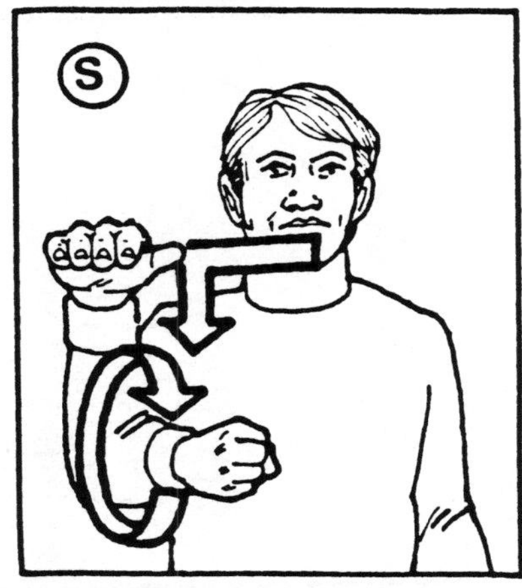

Move flat hand out then down to indicate building, then sign "train".

STAY

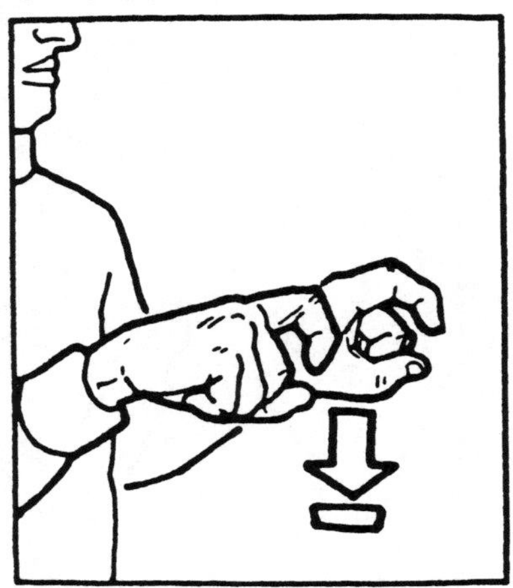

Palm down "C" hands make short movement down, with stress.

STEAL

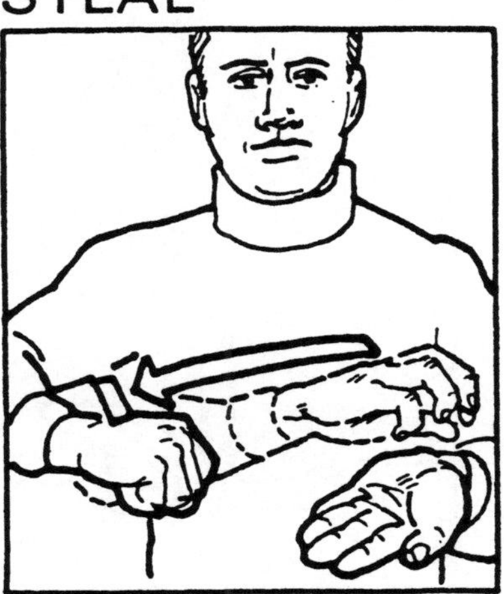

Rt. clawed hand above L. flat hand, snatches sharply back/right, closing to fist.

STEEL

Index finger tip taps against teeth.

STICKS

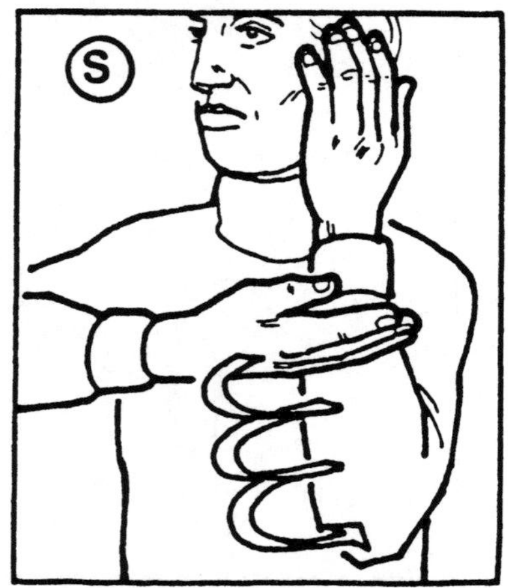

Blade of Rt. flat hand chops down left forearm several times.

STILL

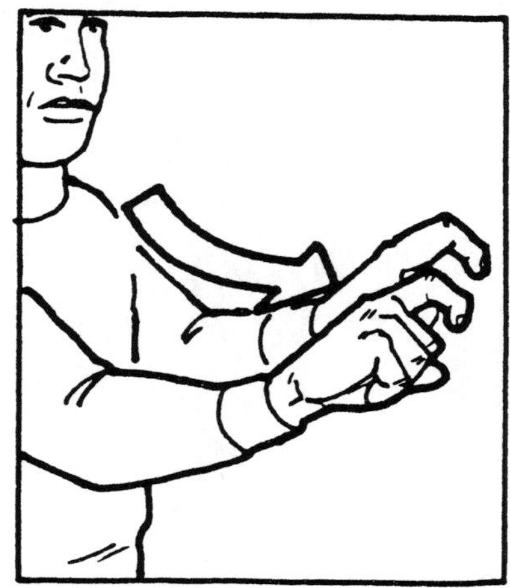

Palm down "C" hands twist to palm forward, whilst moving forward.

STING

Tips of Rt. thumb and index twist into L. palm and pull sharply away.

STOCKING

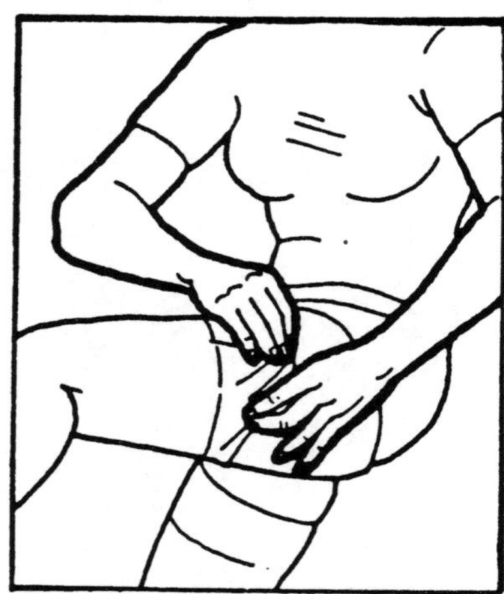

Mime pulling on stocking.

STONE

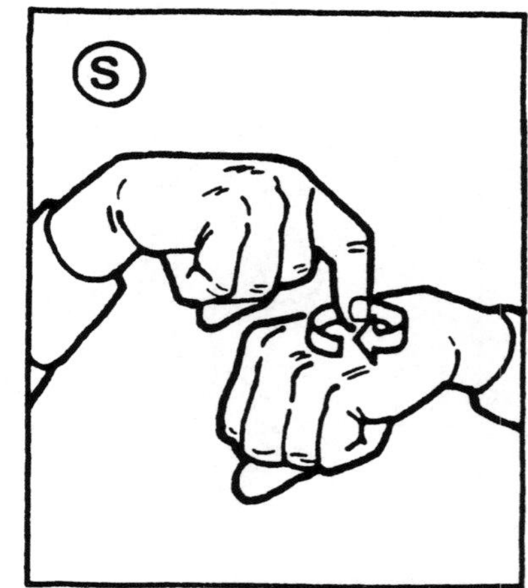

L. closed hand indicates ground, Rt. index makes small circular movement on back of L. to indicate a stone.

STOP

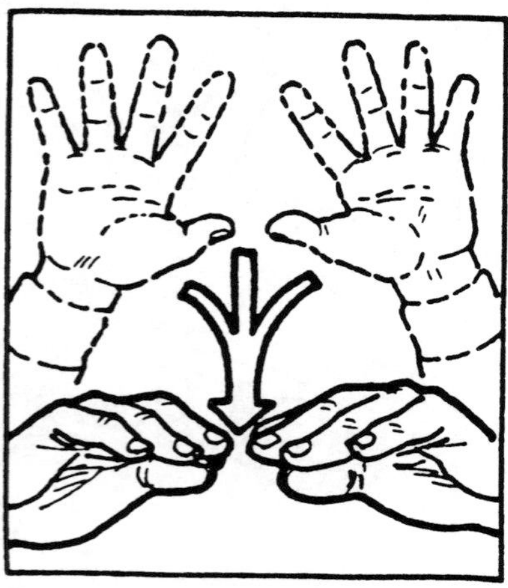

Fingers of palm forward open hands snap closed onto thumbs.

STOP (~go)

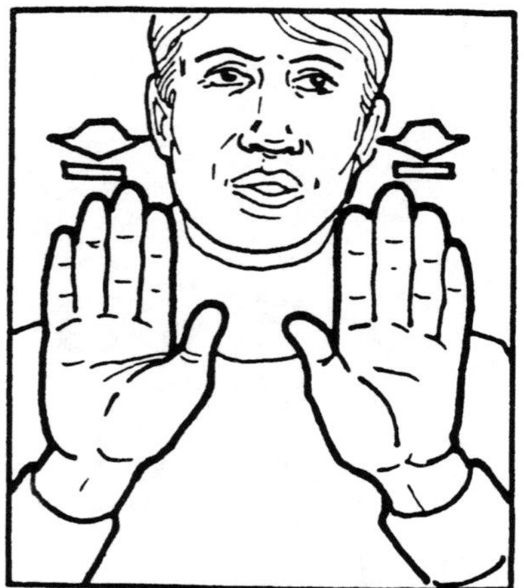

Palm forward flat hands move forward slightly with stress.

STORY

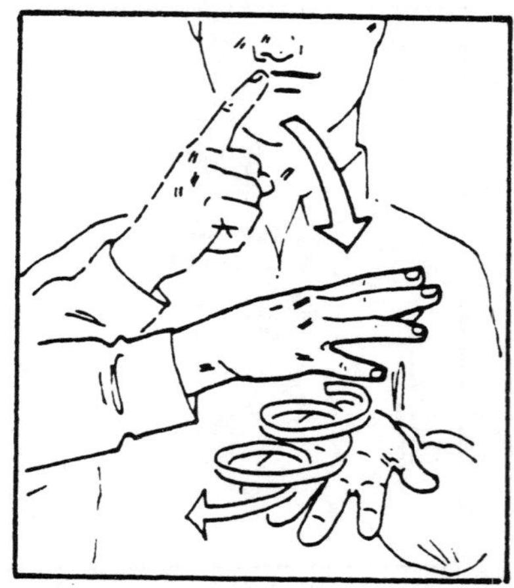

Rt. index points to mouth, moves down changing to open hand and makes two forward circular movements along L. open hand.

STRAIGHT

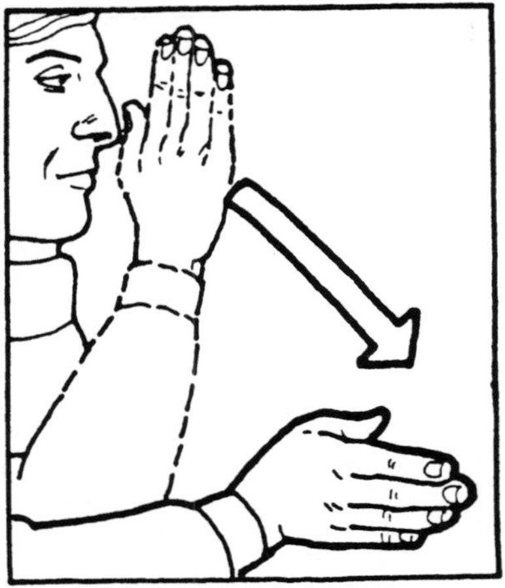

Rt. flat hand moves sharply forward/down from face.

STRANGE

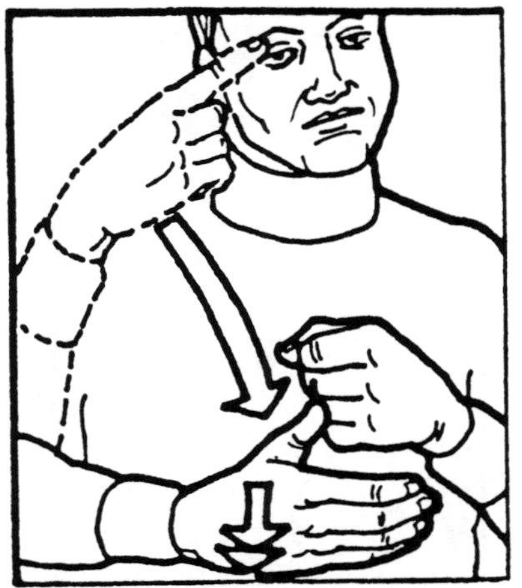

Rt. index points to eye, moves down, changing to flat hand, and brushes down knuckles of L. closed hand twice.

STRAWBERRY

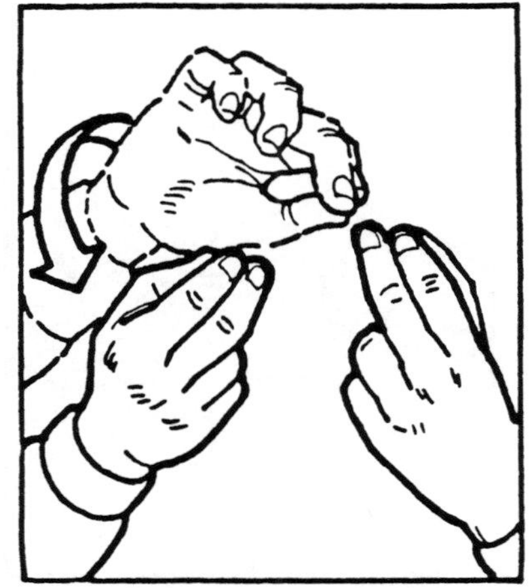

Tips of index, middle fingers and thumbs of both hands touching, Rt. hand twists off the tips of L.

STRICT

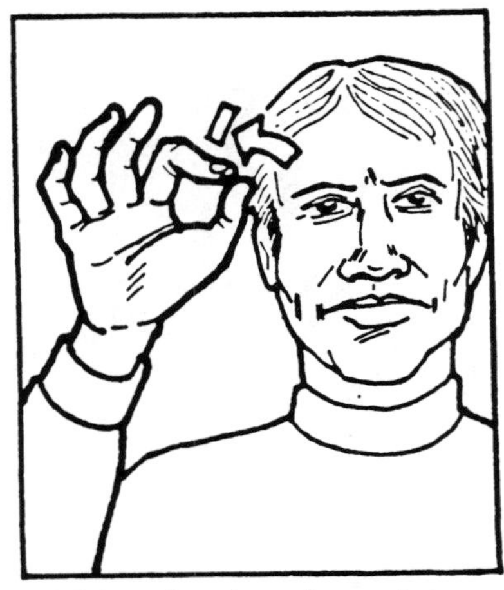

"O" hand makes short sharp movement, forward/up from temple.

STRIKE (on)

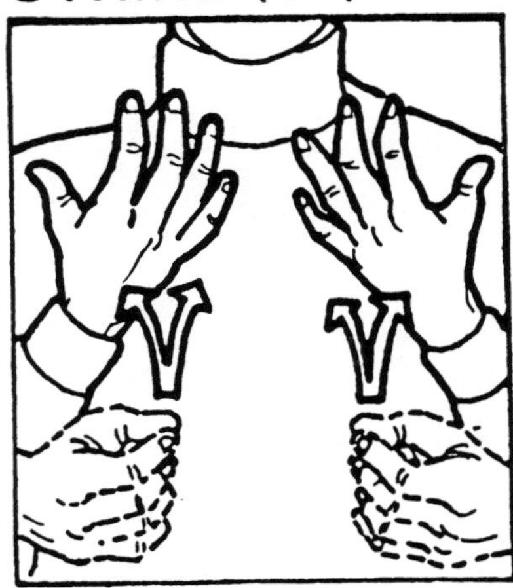

Palm back full "O" hands move up and spring open sharply.

STRING

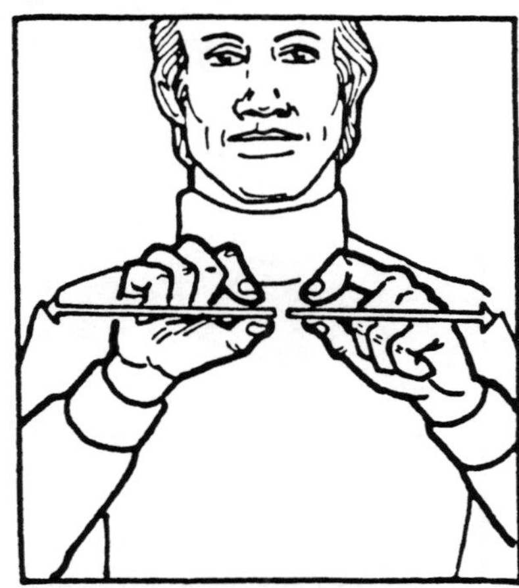

Indexes and thumbs almost touching, pull apart to indicate string.

STRONG

Fists pull upwards, as if flexing muscles.

STUCK

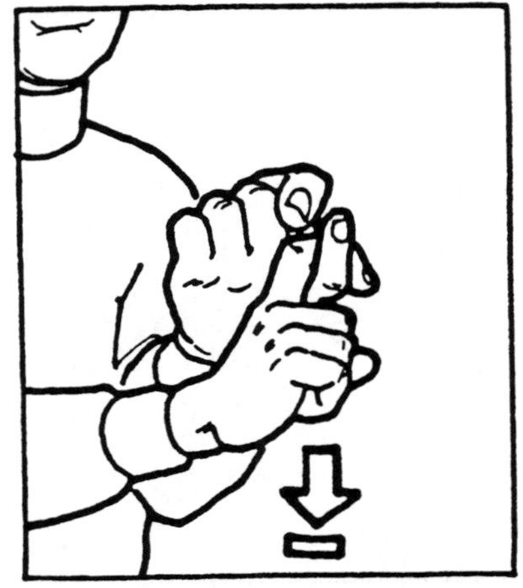

Indexes hooked together, make small movement down, with stress.

STUPID

Knuckles of closed hand tap forehead, twice.

SUBTRACT

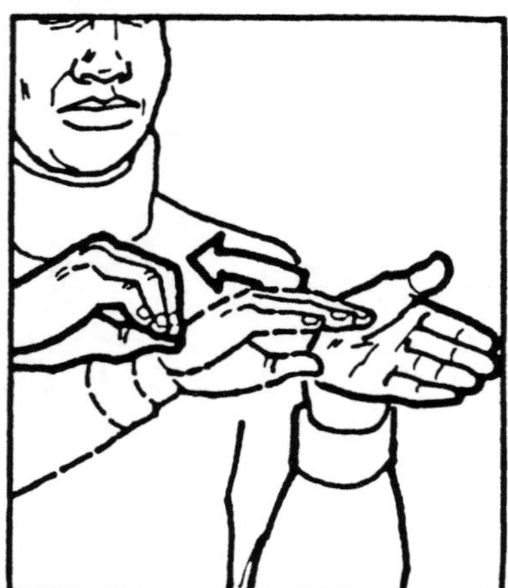

Rt. "C" hand, fingers and thumbs held straight, pull away closing to full "O" hand, off L. palm.

SUCCESS

Clawed hand, held out at head height, moves in circular movement, closing to fist.

SUCCEED

Two closed hands, thumbs extended, twist from palms facing to palms down and pull slightly apart, in quick movement.

SUGAR

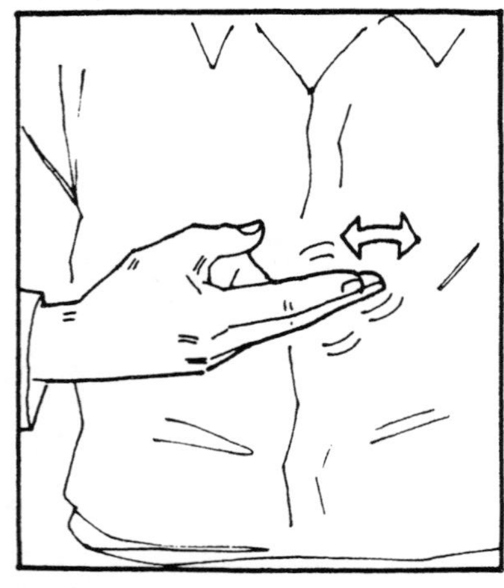

Palm up "N" hand shakes from side to side as if shaking sugar from a spoon.

SUIT

Closed hands, thumbs extended, move in to contact each other.

SUMMER

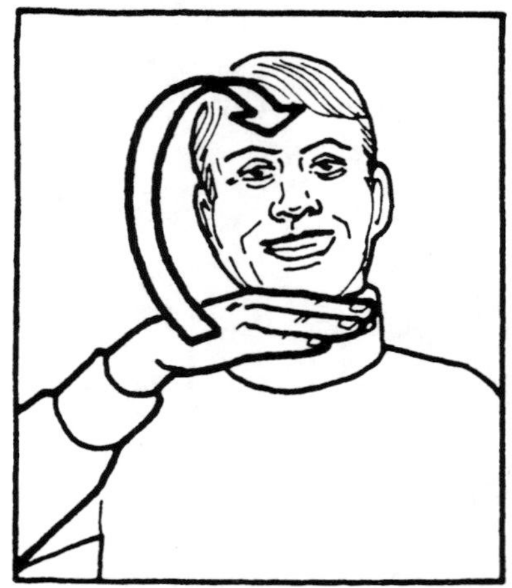

Flat hand moves up from chin to forehead, in small forward arc.

SUN

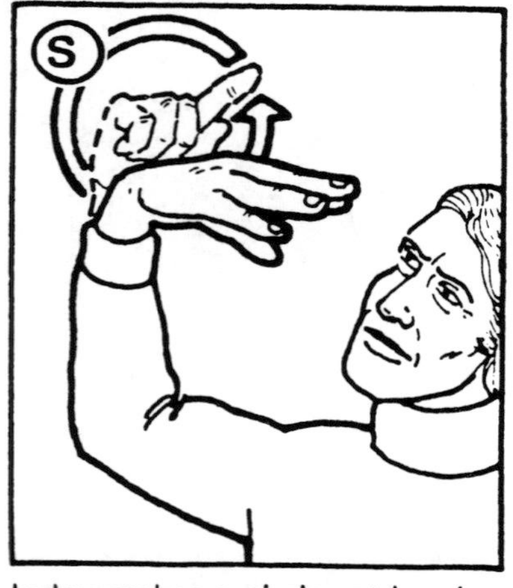

Index makes a circle, at head height, then changes to open hand pointing towards head.

SUNDAY

Flat hands tap together twice.

SUNRISE

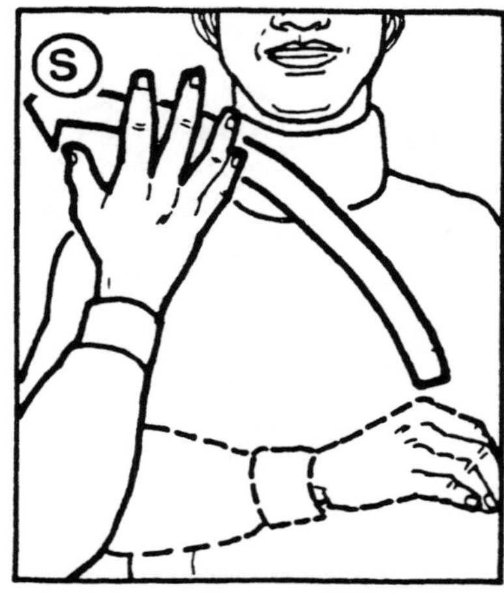

Rt. bunched hand, held across body, arcs slowly up/right as fingers open.

SUNSET

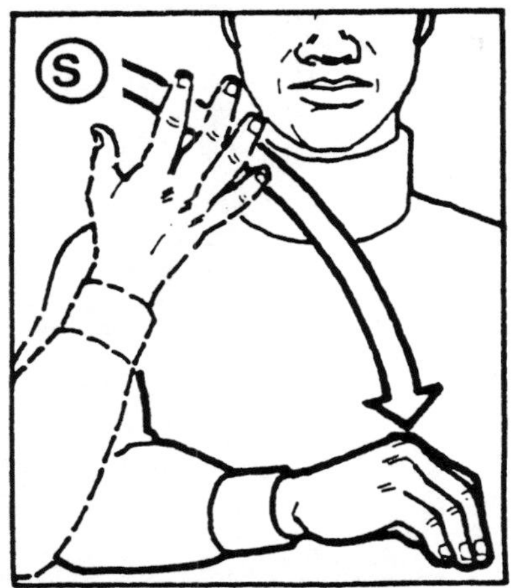

Rt. open hand arcs slowly down/left as fingers close onto thumb.

SUPERVISOR

Tips of thumb and bent index make short movement across chest to indicate name - badge.

SUPPORT

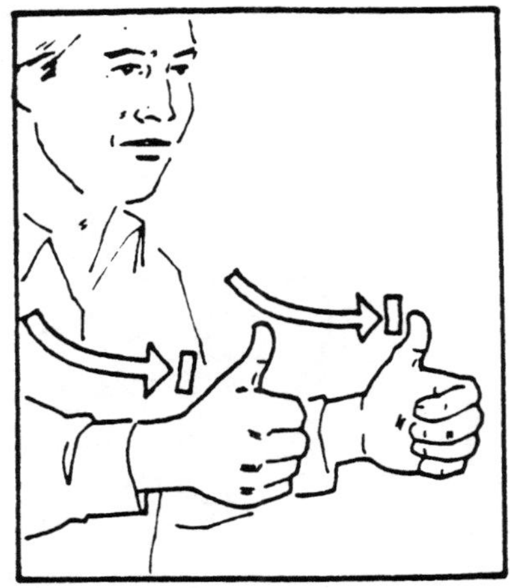

Closed hands, thumbs up, move forward in small arc, with stress.

SUPPOSE

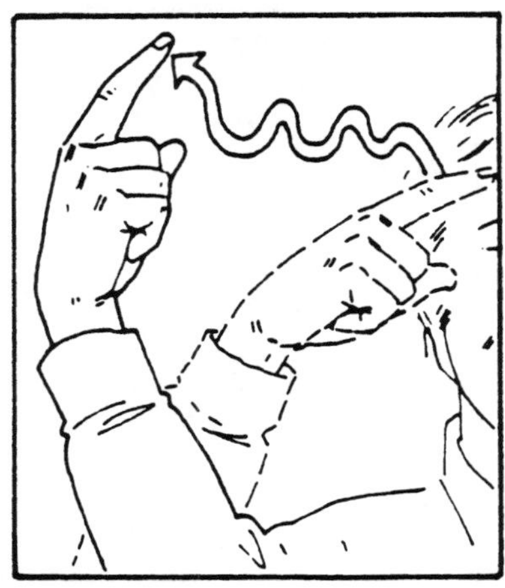

Index moves out from forehead with slight waggling movement.

SURE

Blade of Rt. flat hand strikes L. palm, sharply.

NOT SURE

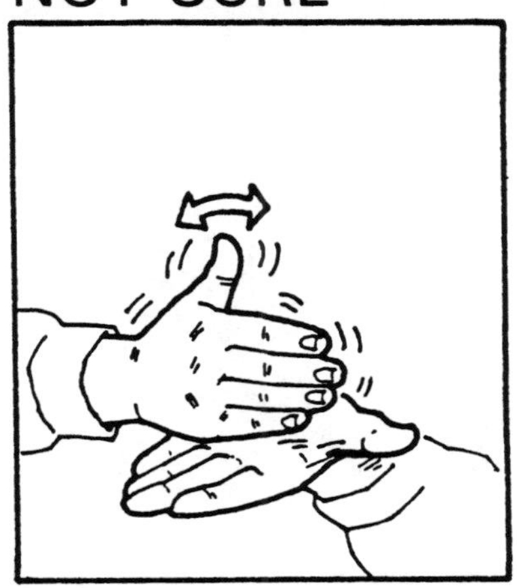

Rt. hand makes small side to side wavering movements whilst resting on L. palm.

SURPRISE

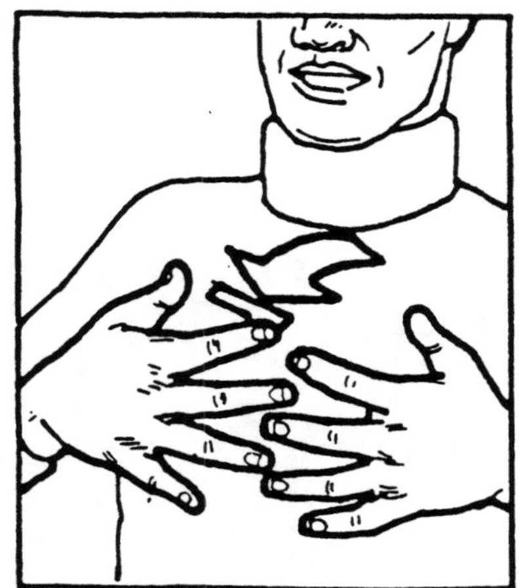

Open hands move forward from chest with emphasis.

SUSPICIOUS

Little finger makes small circular movements, on forehead.

SWAN

Right forearm held up, hand bunched, moves slowly to the left.

SWAP

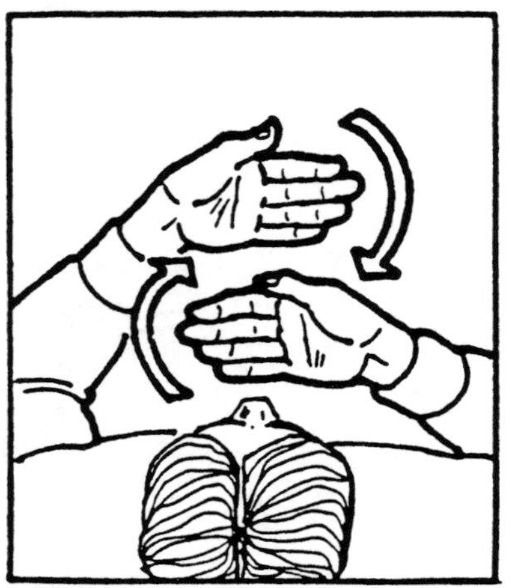

Flat hands swap positions.

SWEAR

Little finger moves forward from mouth with emphasis.

SWEDEN

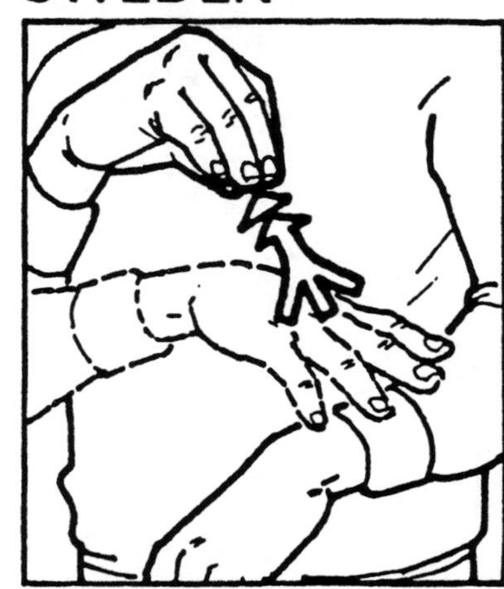

Rt. fingers and thumb tips hold L. wrist and pull away closing fingers onto thumb, twice.

SWEET(S)

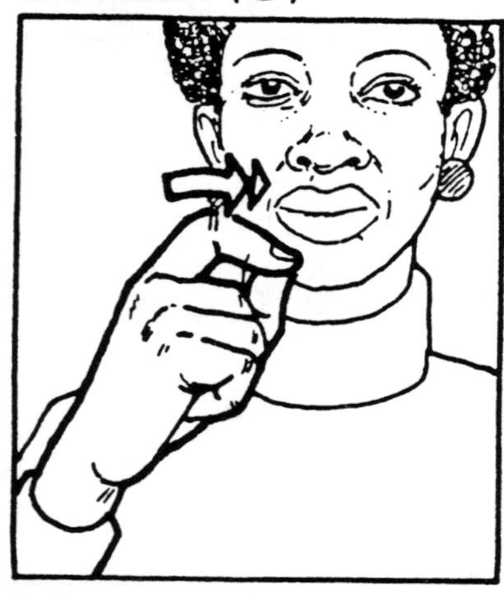

Index and thumb tips touching, tap corner of mouth, twice.

SWEET (taste)

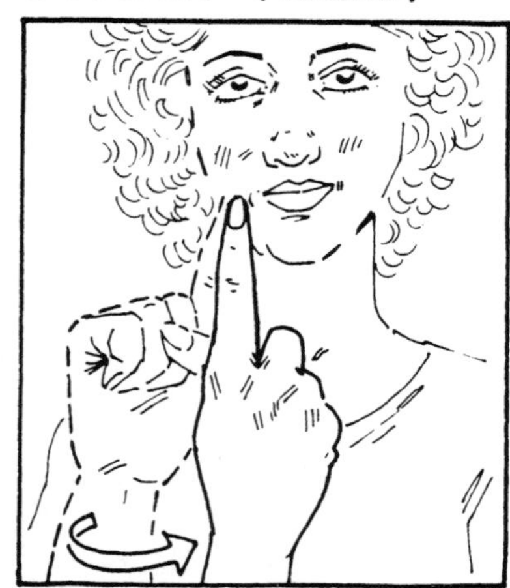

Rt. index twists from palm left, to palm back, at corner of mouth.

SWIM

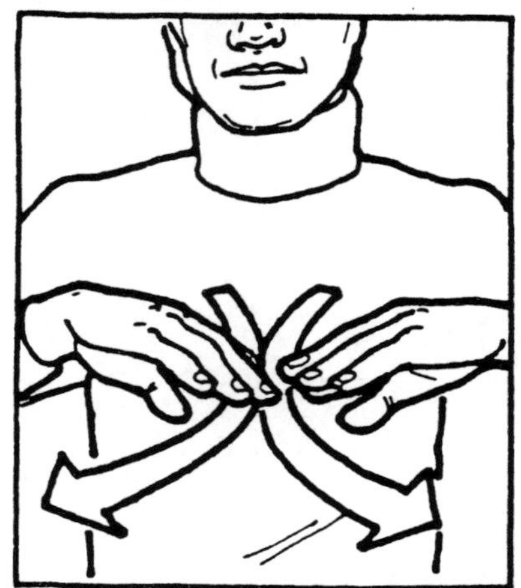

Hands mime action of swimming.

SWIMSUIT

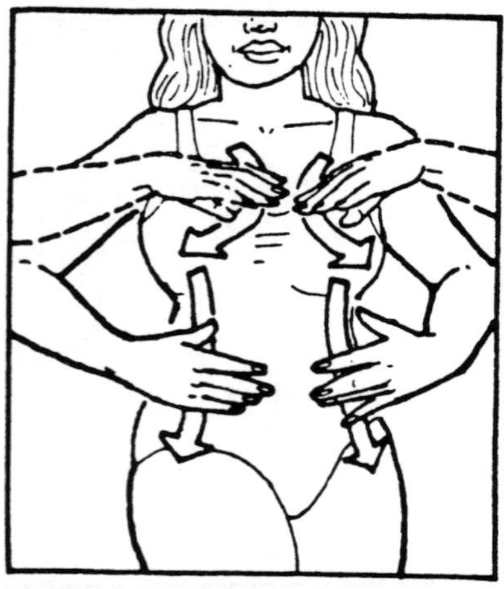

Hands mime swimming, then brush down body, to indicate costume.

SWING

Closed hands swing backwards and forwards, at sides of body.

SWITZERLAND

Tips of "C" hand move down, then across chest to indicate the cross on the Swiss flag.

T-SHIRT

Blades of flat hands tap upper arms twice.

TABLE

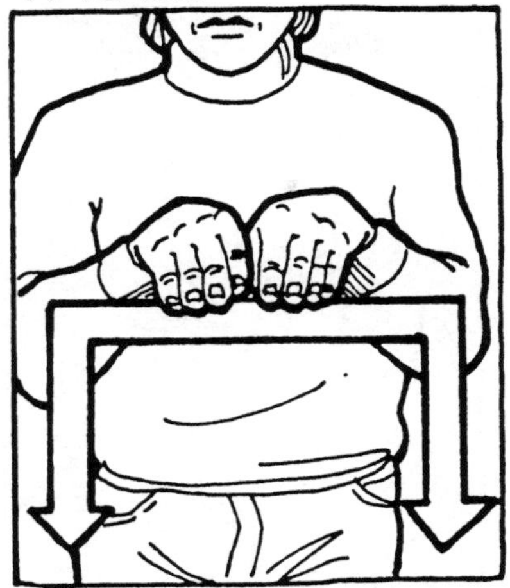

Palm down flat hands move apart, twist to palms facing and move down to indicate shape of table.

TABLET

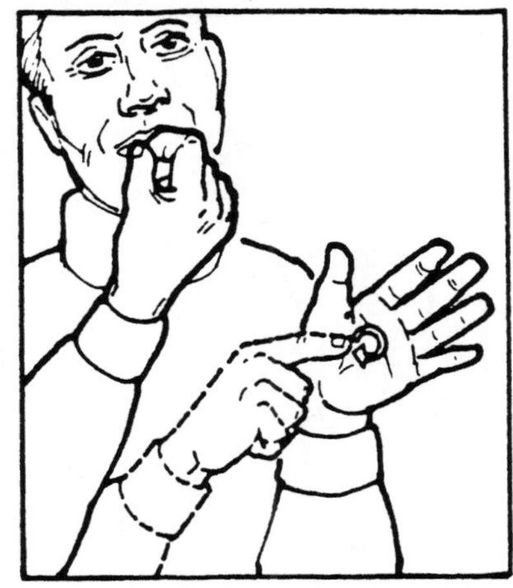

Make small circle on L. palm with Rt. index, then mime putting tablet in mouth.

TAIL

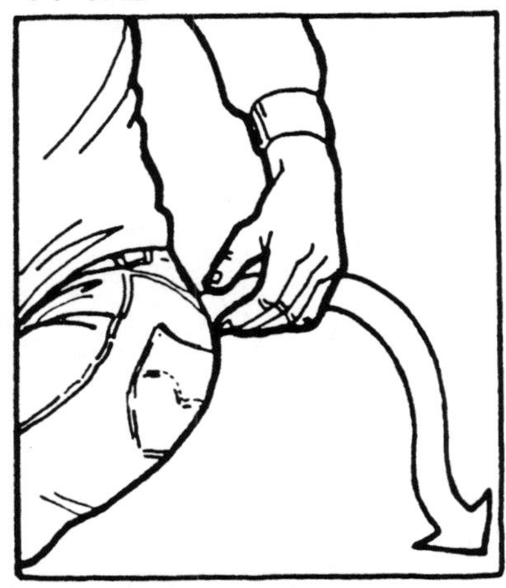

Move hand out at back of body to indicate tail.

TAKE

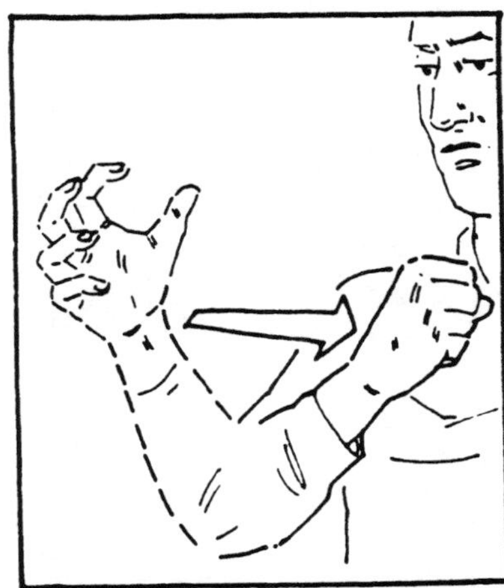

Rt. clawed hand moves to the left, closing sharply to a fist.

TAKE IN (absorb)

Flat hand with fingers and thumb pointing forward, moves back to temple as fingers close onto thumb.

TALE

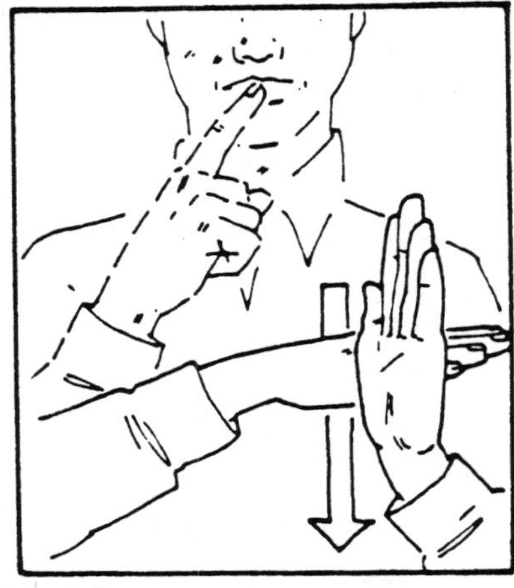

Rt. index moves down, from mouth, changing to flat hand, and brushes down index edge of L. flat hand.

TALK

Closed hands, indexes extended. Rt. hand points to mouth, then bangs top of L. hand twice, at right angles.

TALL

Rt. flat hand moves up to above head height.

TAXI

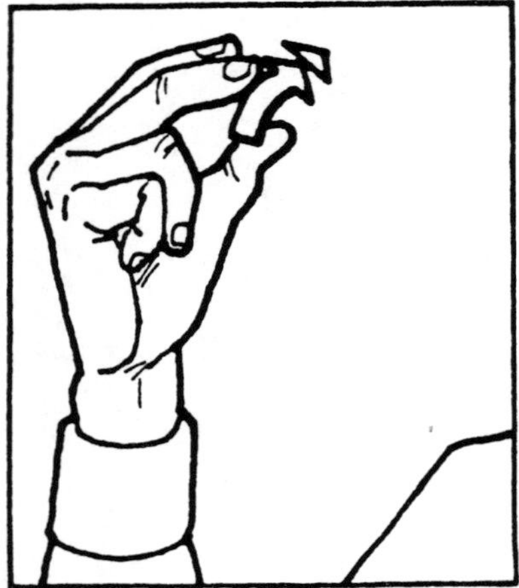

Click middle finger and thumb several times at head height as if hailing a taxi.

TEA

Rt. "O" hand moves to mouth from L. palm as if lifting a tea-cup.

TEA-SET

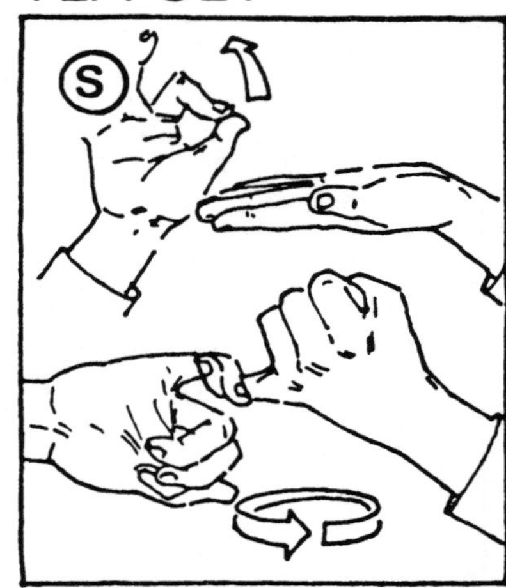

Sign "tea", then form letter "S" and move formation in horizontal circle.

TEACH

Bunched hands point to temples, then twist forward and make two short forward movements.

TEACHER

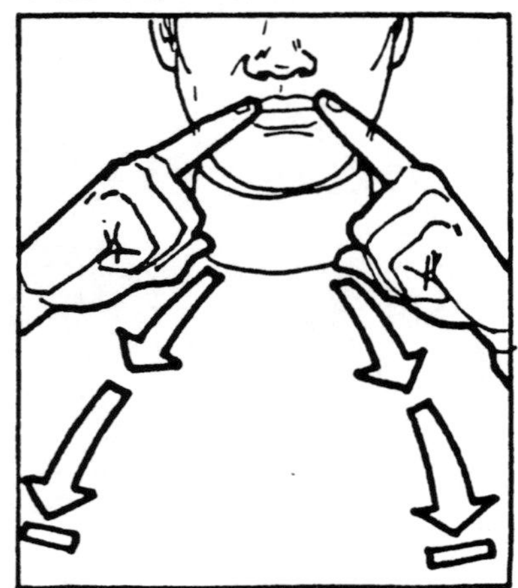

Indexes point to sides of mouth, then move forward/out in two movements.

TEAPOT

Little finger and thumb extended, hand tips in pouring action.

TEAR (rip)

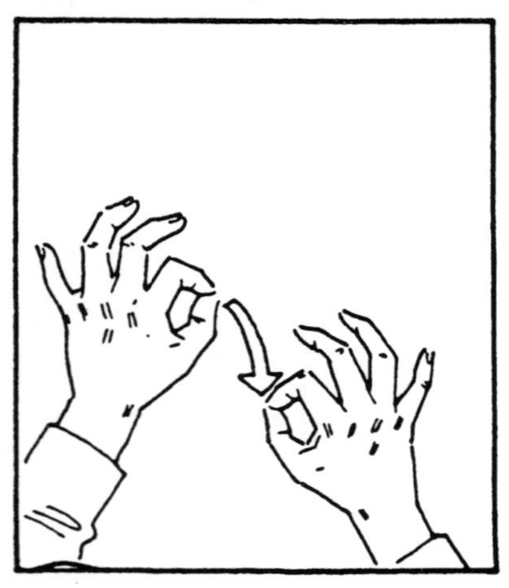

"O" hands pull apart in tearing action.

TEASE

Rt. open hand brushes forward twice along L. index towards person concerned. Hands point back and Rt. hand brushes back to self in "teasing me".

TEASPOON

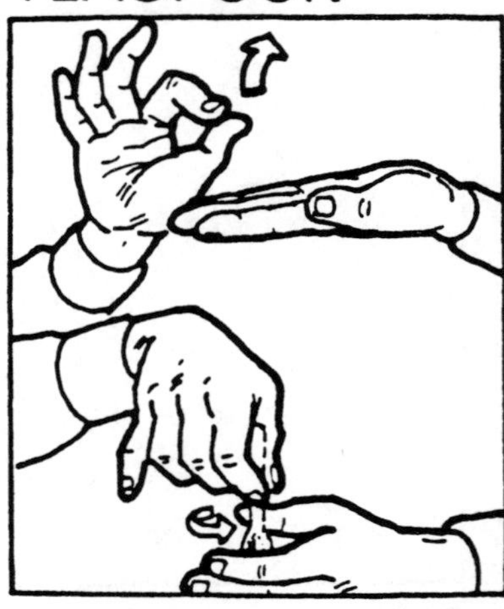

Sign "tea", then mime stirring above L. full "C" hand.

TELEPHONE

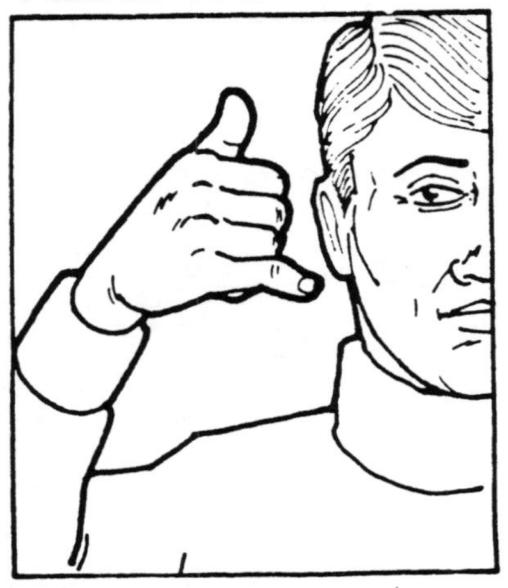

Thumb and little finger extended indicate 'phone at side of head.

TELEVISION

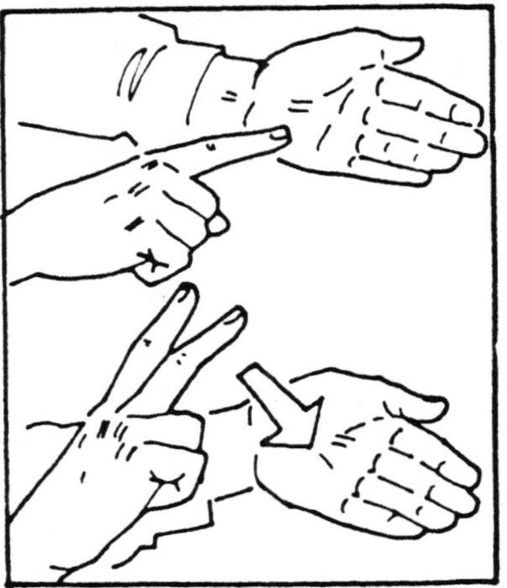

Fingerspell "T" "V".

TELL

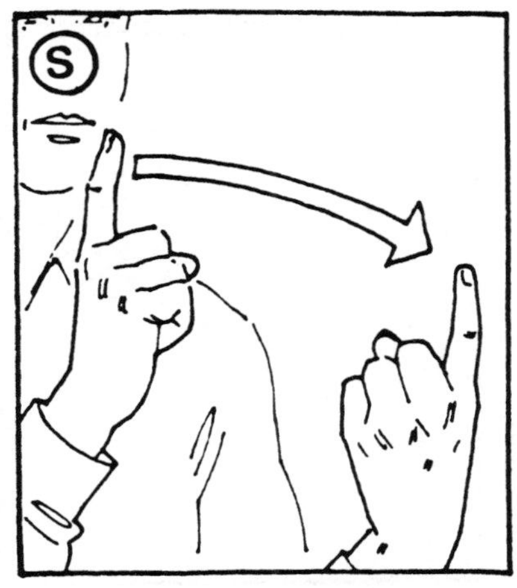

L. index held away from body; Rt. index moves forward from mouth to point to L. index.

TEMPORARY

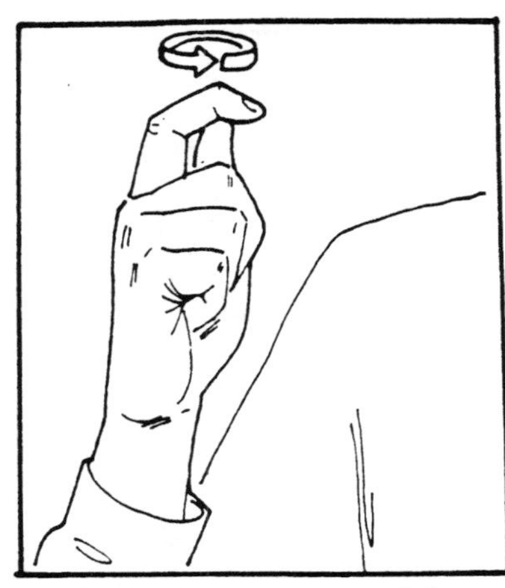

Thumb tucked into bent index. Hand moves in small horizontal circles.

TEMPT

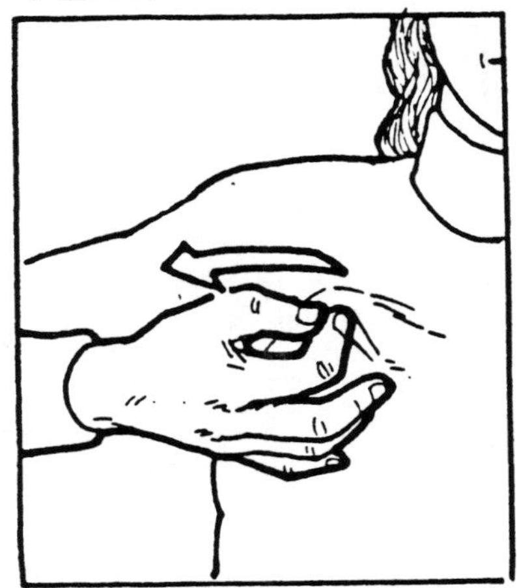

"O" hand plucks clothing and pulls forward/out. Body makes small movement in same direction.

TENT

Tips of two "V" hands touch, then move out/down in shape of tent.

TEST

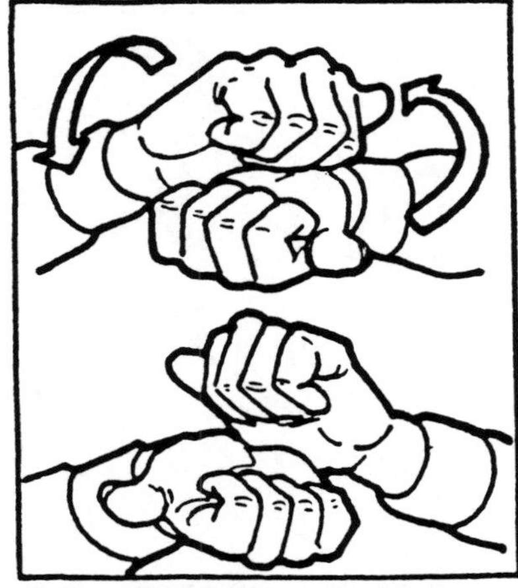

Closed hands, crossed at wrists, Rt. above L. Reverse to L. above Rt.

THAN

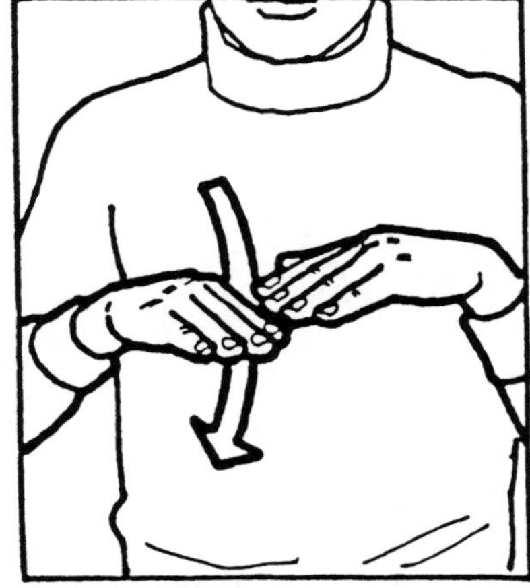

Fingers of Rt. flat hand, pointing forward, brush down past tips of L. flat hand, pointing right.

THANK YOU

Tips of flat hand touch mouth, then move forward/ down to finish palm up.

THAT

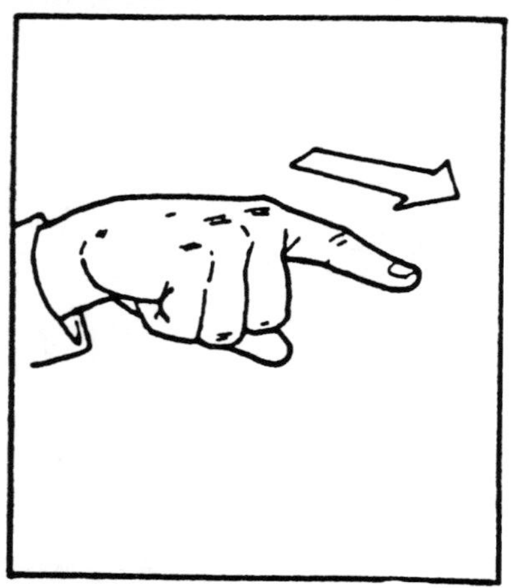

Index points forward, or to object, or person concerned.

THAT'S ALL

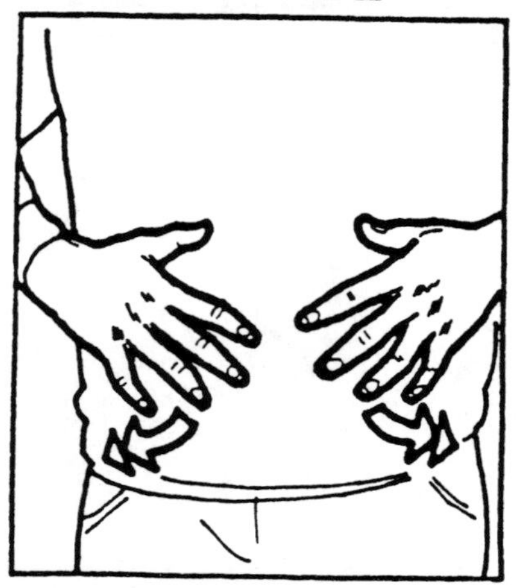

Open hands pointing in/down shake outwards twice with emphasis.

THEATRE

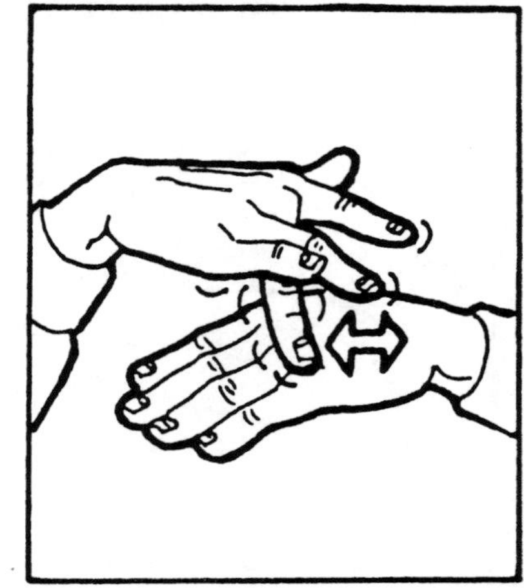

Rt. middle finger stands on back of L. hand. Tip maintains contact as Rt. hand rocks from side to side.

THEIR(S)

Closed hand sweeps sideways, palm facing persons concerned.

THEN

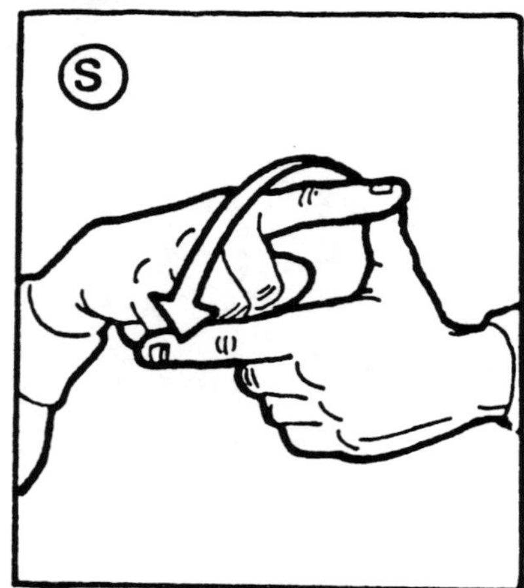

L. thumb and index extended. Rt. index makes small arc from L. thumb to index.

THEORY

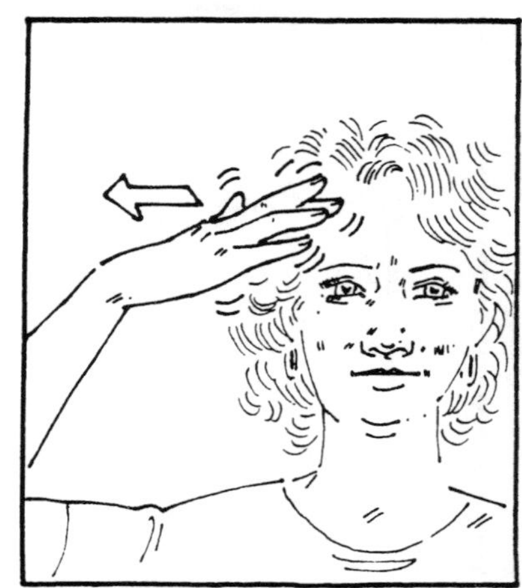

Palm down open hand moves forward from side of forehead with fingers fluttering.

THERE

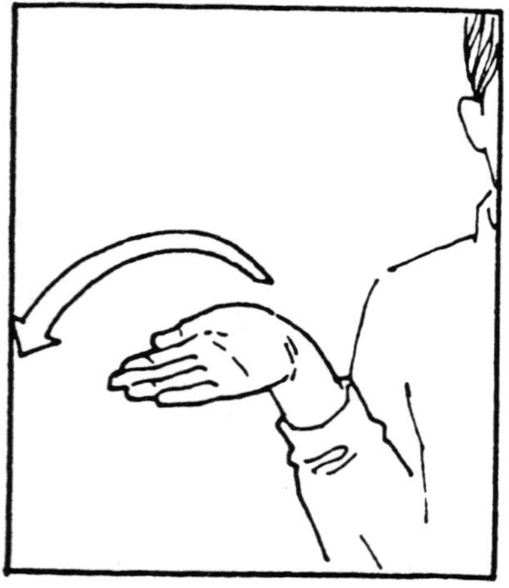

Flat hand, palm up moves in small arc forward or towards place concerned.

THEREFORE

Index makes three short movements forward to indicate "therefore" symbol.

THERMOMETER

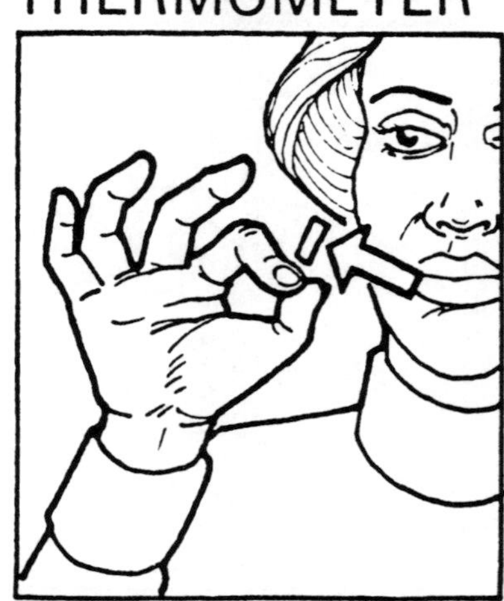

"O" hand makes short movement up/out from mouth to indicate thermometer.

THESE

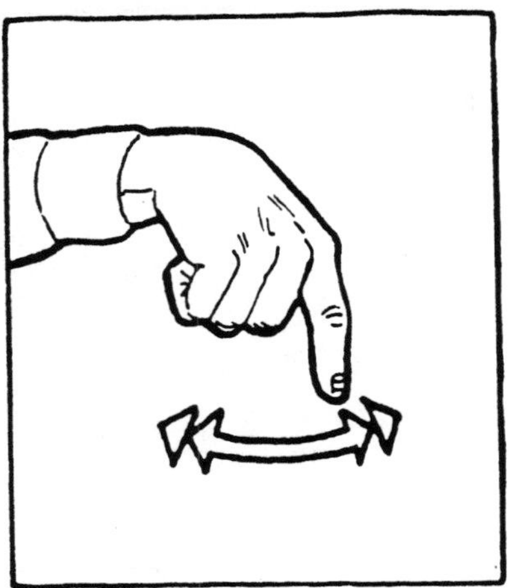

Index swings from side to side, pointing down indicating objects concerned.

THEY

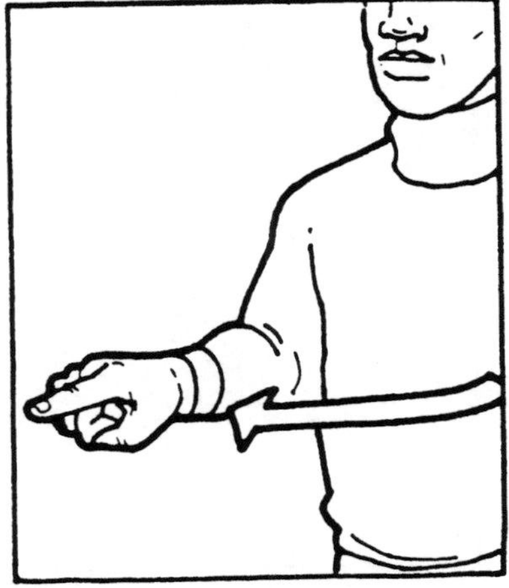

Index sweeps sideways, pointing towards persons, or objects concerned.

THICK

Full "C" hand, palm forward, makes small movement forward/down.

THIEVE

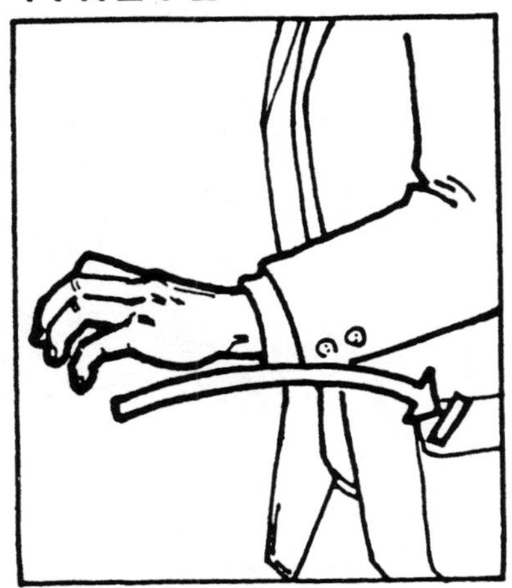

Clawed hand, held slightly out, snatches in to hip, closing to fist.

THIN

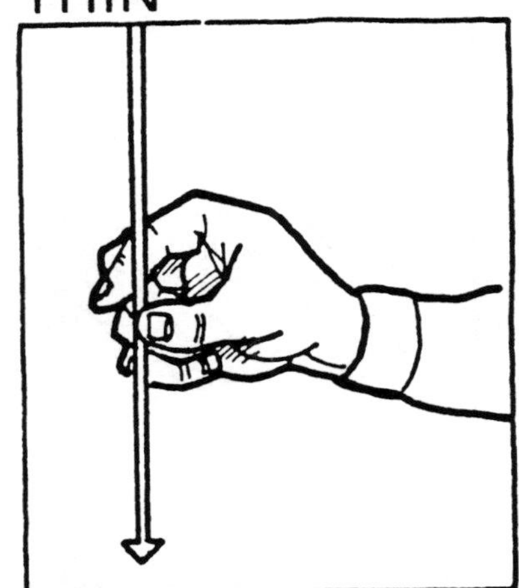

Index and thumb, almost touching, move down in straight line.

THING

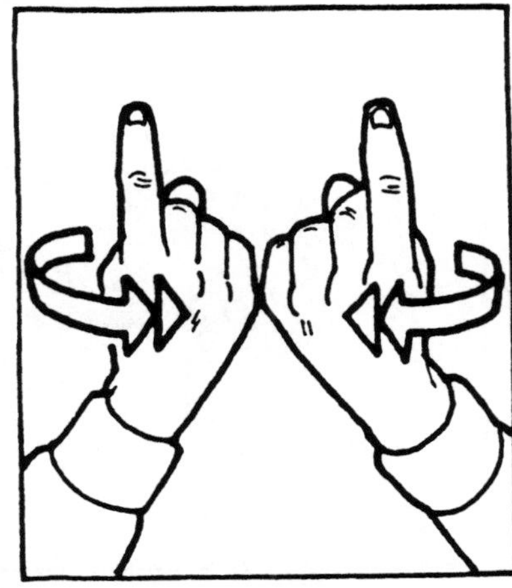

Indexes extended, palms facing, twist to palms back and knock blades together twice.

THINK

Index contacts forehead.

THIRD

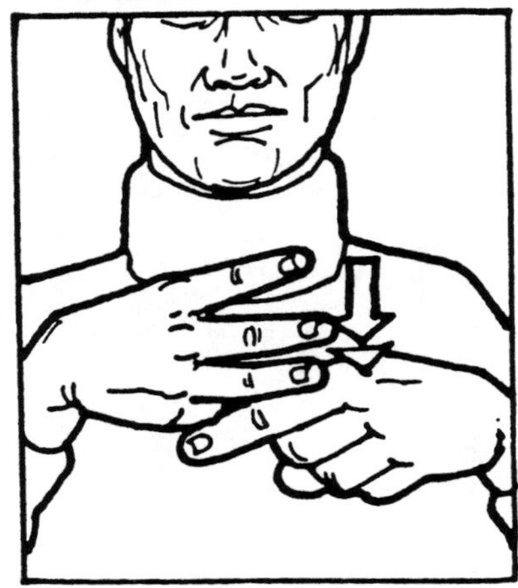

Rt. index, middle and ring fingers extended and open, tap edge of ring finger twice on L. index.

THIRSTY

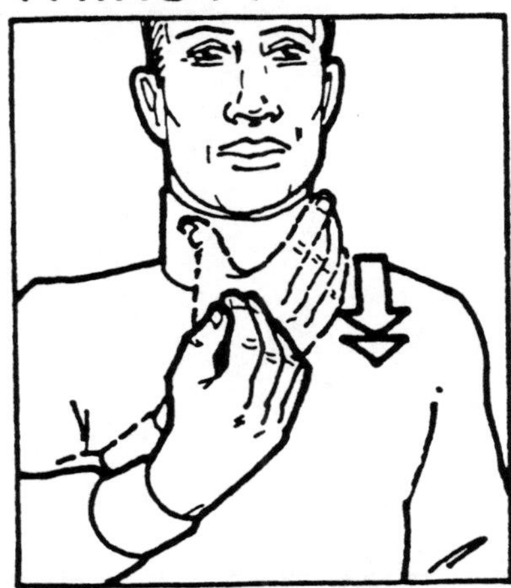

Tips of fingers and thumb on throat, pull forward and close fingers onto thumb, twice.

THIS

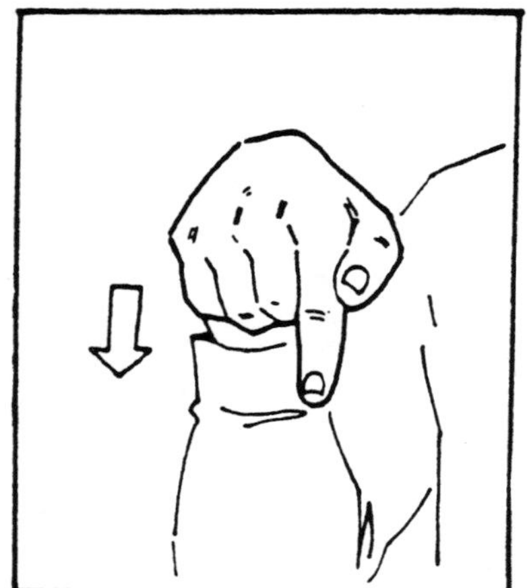

Indicate object with one downward movement of index.

THOROUGH

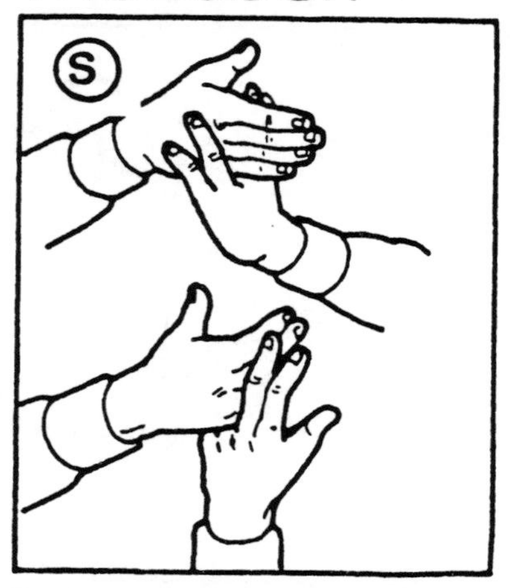

Rt. flat hand passes forward through fingers of L. hand, twists, and moves back through.

THOSE

Index swings from side to side, pointing to objects or persons concerned.

THOUGHTFUL

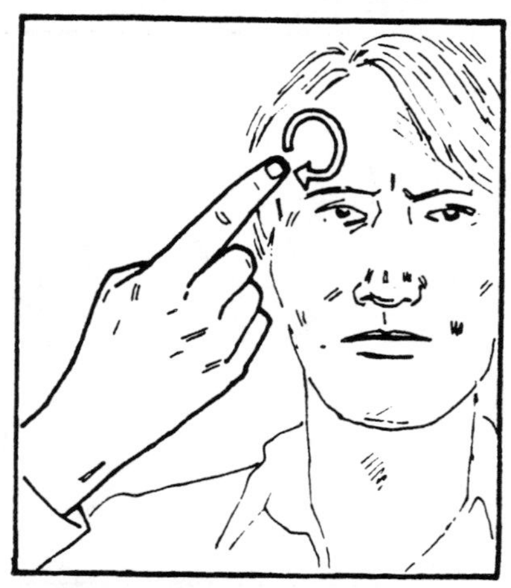

Index makes circular movement on forehead.

THOUSAND

Rt. thumb extended jabs into left upper chest.

THREAD

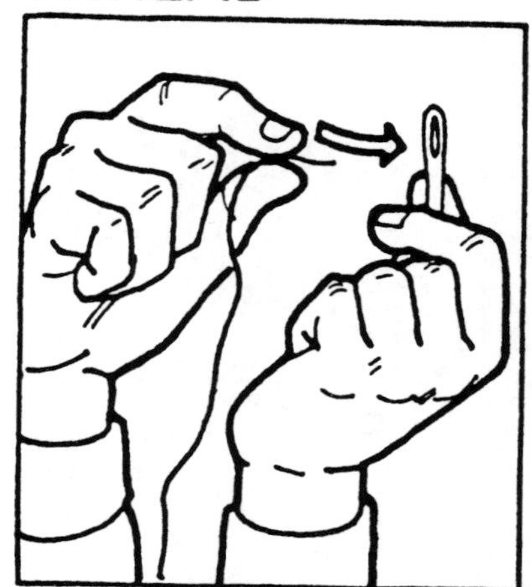

Mime threading a needle.

THREE-QUARTER

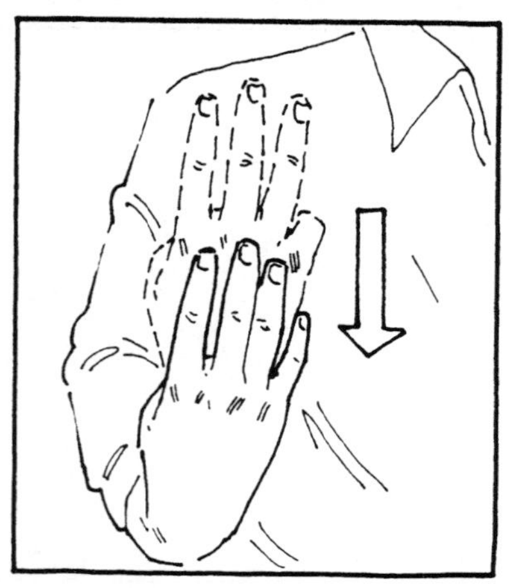

Sign "three", then drop hand slightly and sign "four".

THROUGH

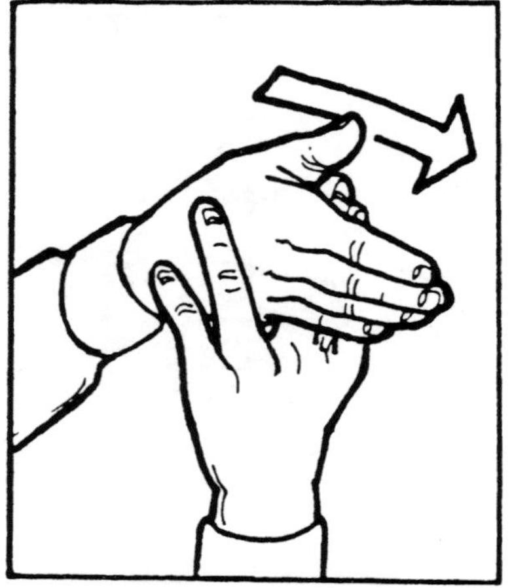

Rt. flat hand passes forward between L. ring and middle fingers.

THROW

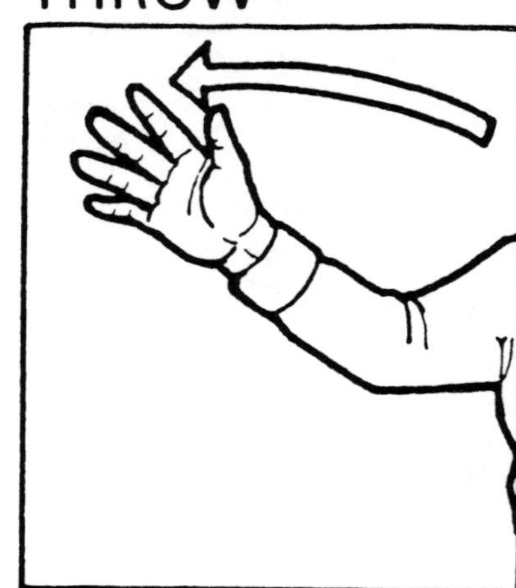

Mime throwing action.

THUNDER

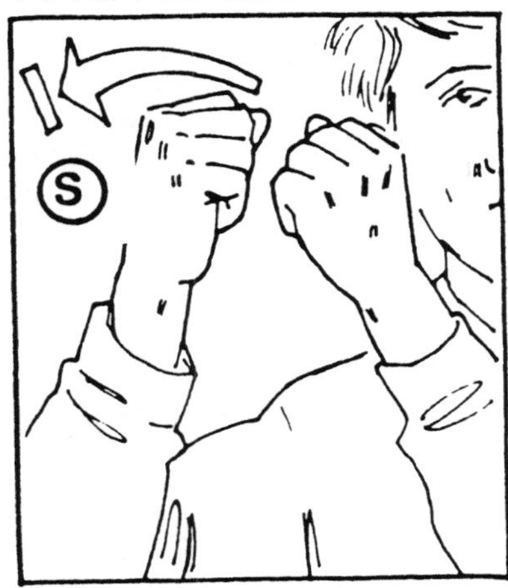

Two fists, palms facing, held at right ear. Rt. fist pulls out sharply with stress.

TICKET

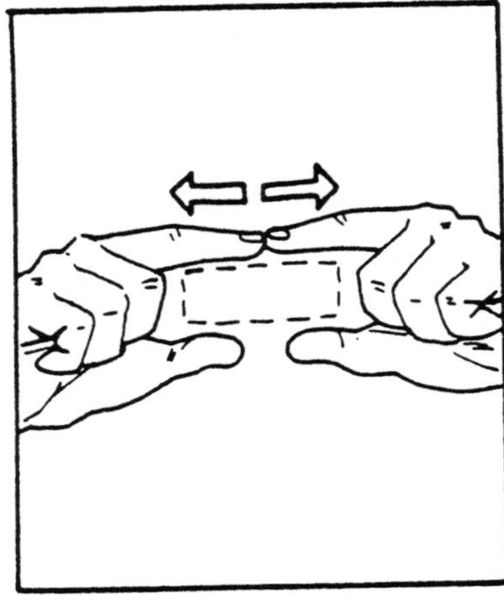

Indexes and thumbs pull slightly apart, to indicate shape of ticket.

TIDY

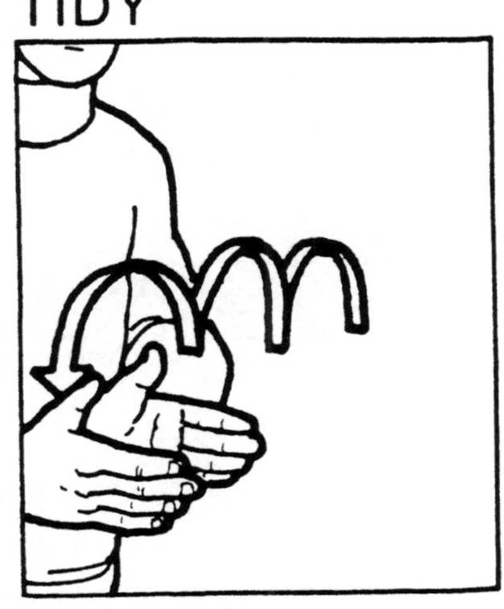

Flat hands held a few inches apart, palms facing, move sideways in several small hops.

TIE (neck)

"C" hands, L. above Rt. Rt. hand moves down to indicate tie.

TIE (string)

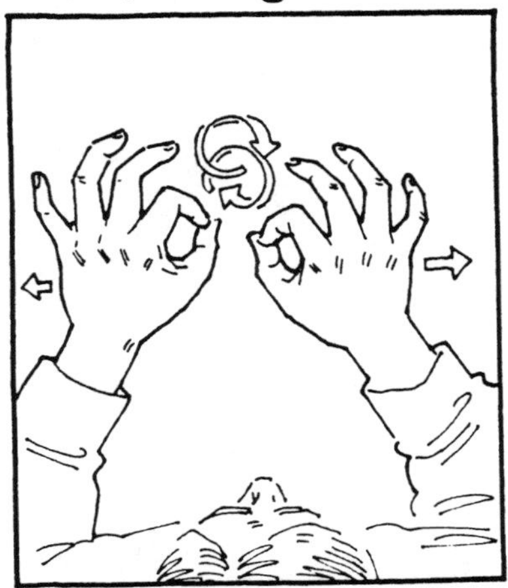

Hands twist then pull apart in tying action.

TIGER

Open hand moves across chest, to indicate stripes, then clawed hands make small alternate movements.

TIME

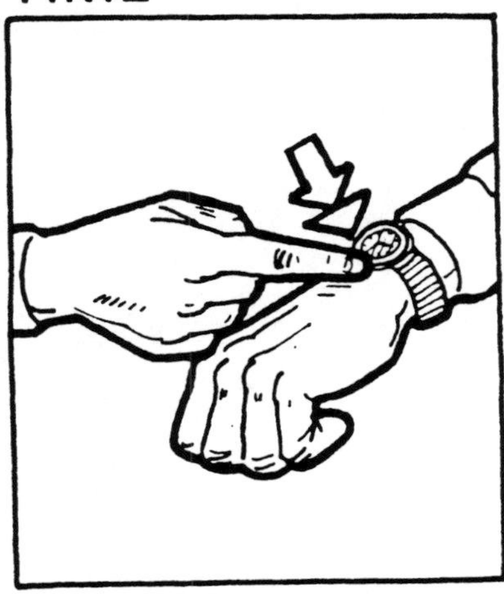

Rt. index taps back of L. wrist, twice.

TIPPER-LORRY

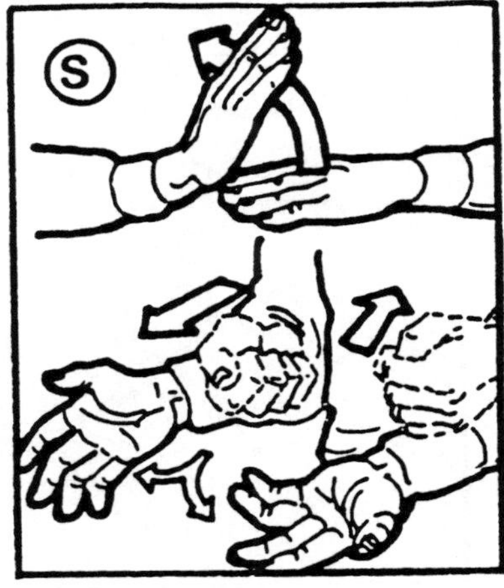

Rt. flat hand tips up on top of L., then sign "lorry".

TIRED

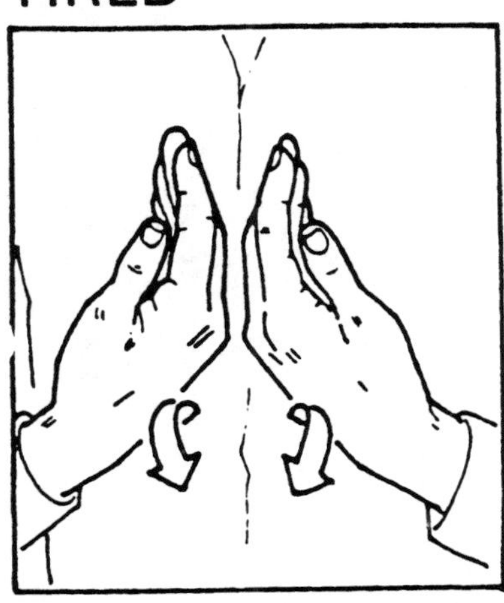

Tips of palm back bent hands on upper chest. Hands twist down so that blades contact chest.

TITLE

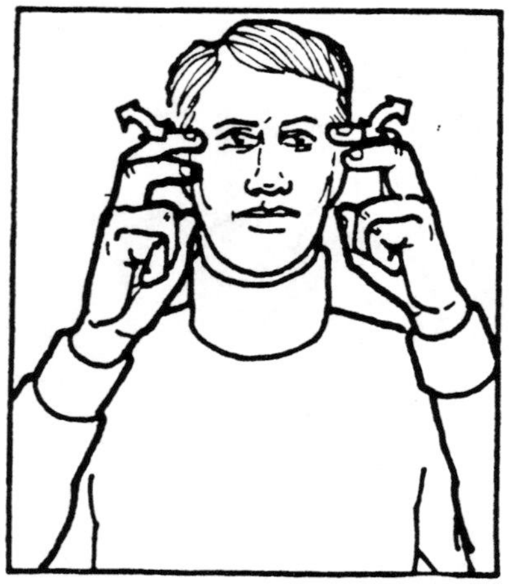

"V" hands, palms facing, held at head height. Fingers flex several times.

TOAST

Flat hands, palms down make small forward movement, then flip over to palms up and move forward again.

TODAY

Flat hands, palms up, make small downward movement twice, near waist.

TOE

Rt. index indicates shape of toe round L. index.

TOGETHER

Fingers of Rt. "V" hand close together as they move in to be held by L. index, middle finger and thumb.

TOIL

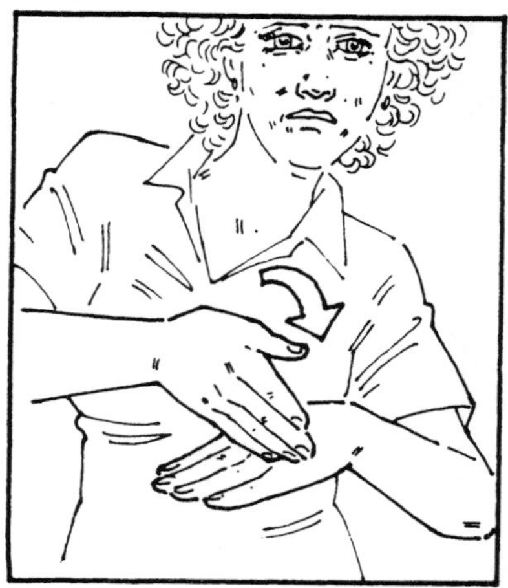

Blade of Rt. hand swivels over and down back of L. with emphasis.

TOILET

Fingerspell "T" and tap twice.

TOMATO

Tips of Rt. bunched hand twist off tips of L. bunched hand, as if removing stalk.

TOMORROW

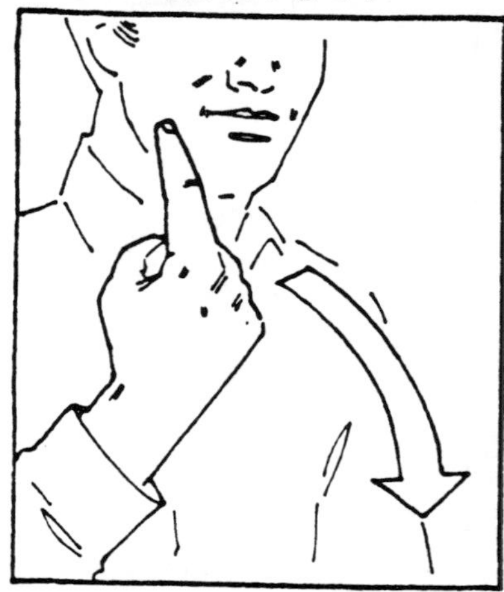

Rt. index touches side of chin, then swings forward/down, finishing palm up.

TOP

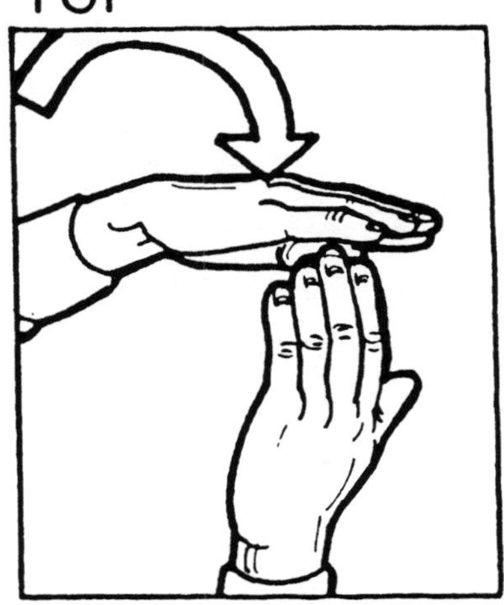

Rt. flat hand moves up in arc to land on top of L. fingertips.

TORMENT

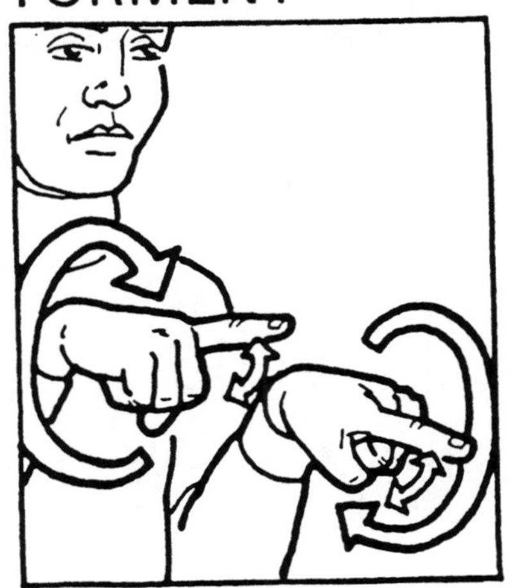

Indexes make flexing movement as hands move alternately in forward circles.

TORTOISE

Fingers of L. clawed hand flex, indicating legs and head of tortoise. Rt. hand on top indicates shell.

TOSS AND TURN

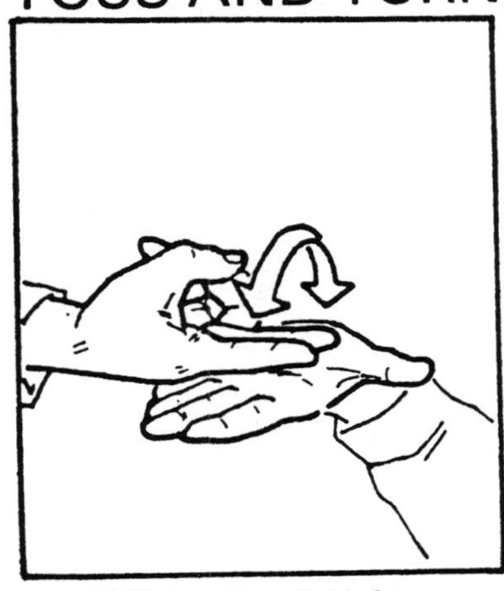

Rt. "V" hand twists from palm up to palm down in repeated contact with L. palm.

TOTAL

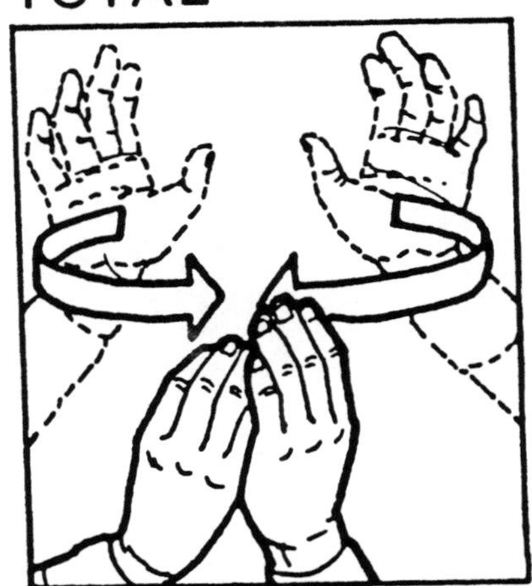

Palm forward open hands twist round/down in forward circle closing to bunched hands together.

TOUR

Fingers of "V" hand, slightly bent, move round in horizontal circle with slight flexing.

TOWARDS

L. index held slightly forward, Rt. index moves towards L.

TOWEL

Mime action of using towel.

TOWN

Rt. clawed hand moves round L. closed hand from behind in three small hops.

TRACTOR

Indexes point towards each other and make one large circle forward, then one small one, to indicate tractor's wheels.

TRAFFIC

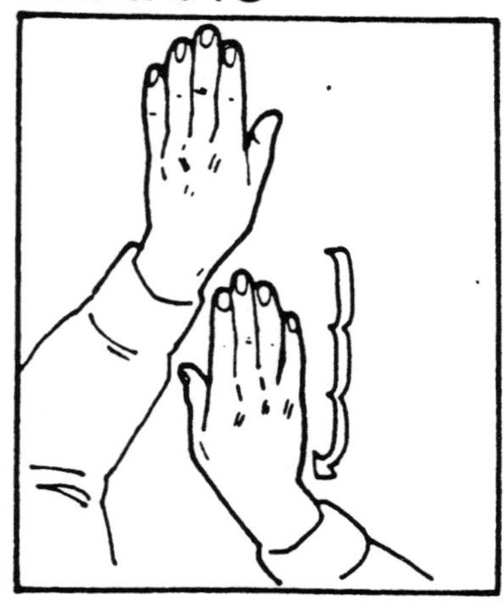

Flat hands held forward, Rt. behind L. Rt. hand moves back to body in small hops to indicate line of cars.

TRAFFIC LIGHTS

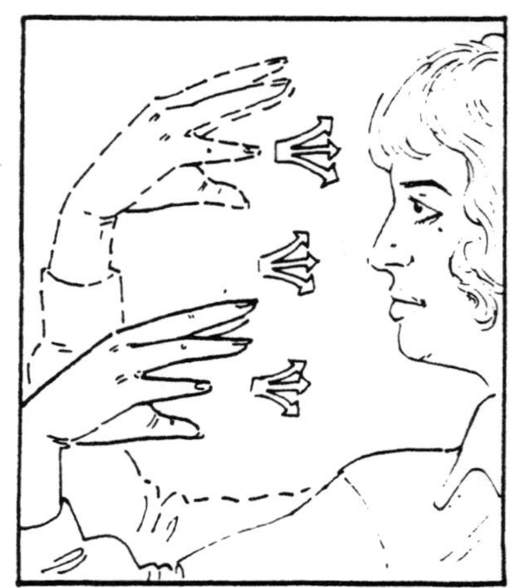

Hand held away from body, palm back, fingers spring open from full "O" hand; repeat twice, moving hand down slightly each time. Both hands may be used.

TRAIN

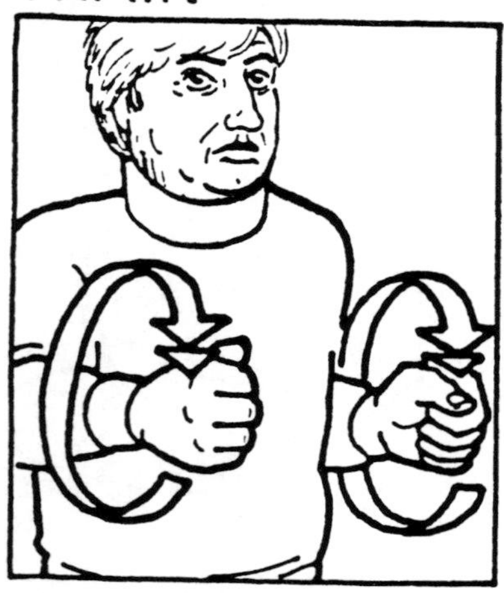

Closed hands move in forward circles, like wheels of a train.

TRANSLATE

Palm down Rt. flat hand contacts L. palm, then flips over to palm up.

TRANSPORT

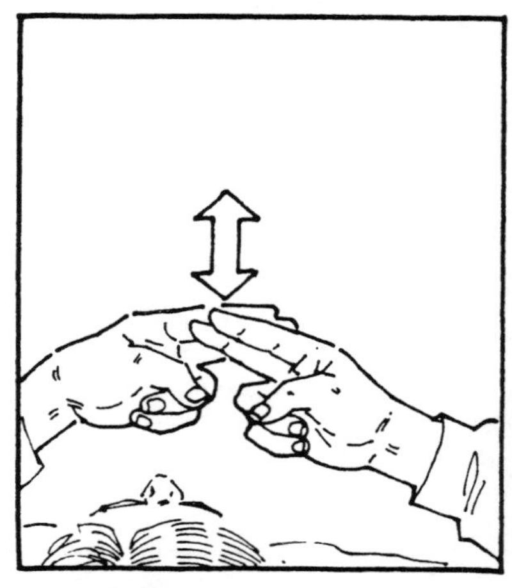

Two "N" hands, Rt. on top of L.; formation moves forward and back.

TRAVEL

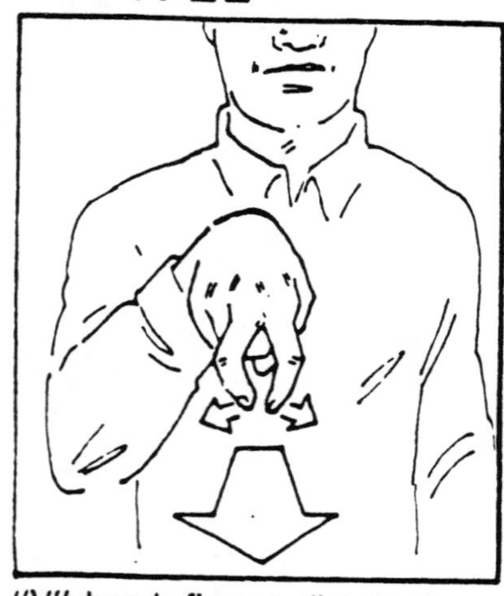

"V" hand, fingers slightly bent, moves forward twisting from side to side.

TRAY

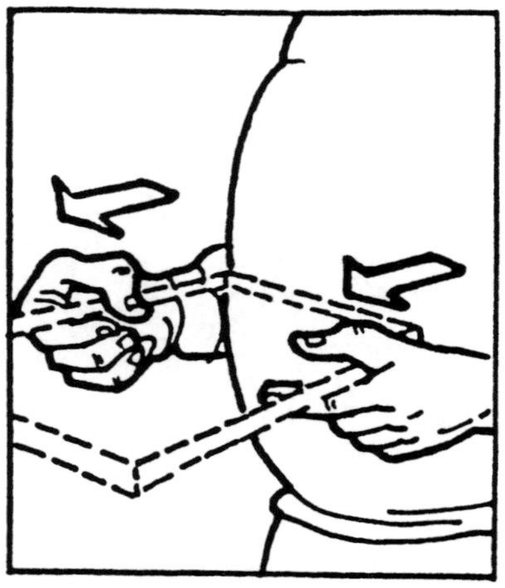

Mime holding a tray with slight forward movement.

TREBLE (3X)

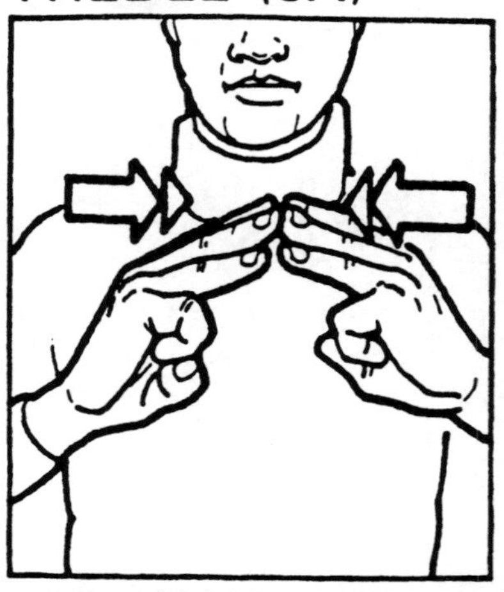

Index, middle and ring fingers extended and open, tap together twice.

TREE

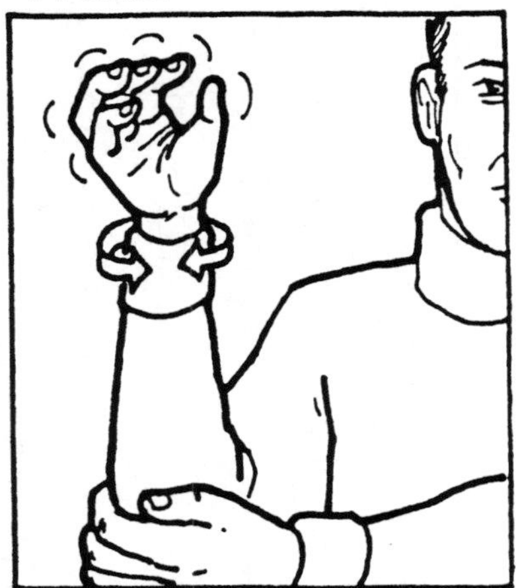

Right elbow cradled in L. hand. Rt. clawed hand, palm up/ left twists from side to side.

TRIANGLE

Indexes outline shape of triangle.

TRIP

Two "V" hands, held together, fingers bent. Rt. hand moves forward, then back.

TROUBLE

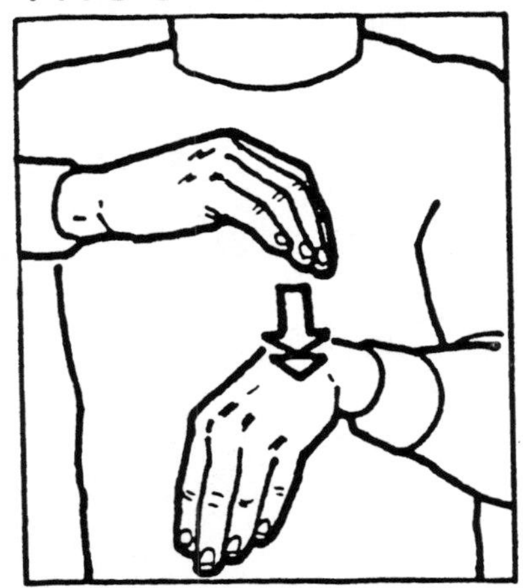

Tips of Rt. cupped hand tap twice on back of L. hand.

TROUSERS

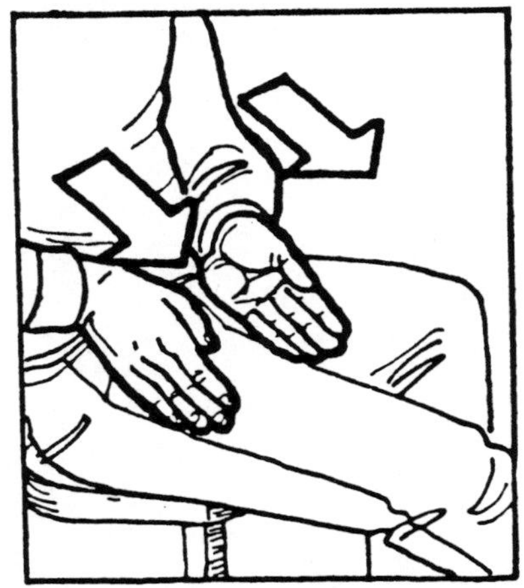

Flat hands, held parallel make short movement down one leg, then the other.

TRUE

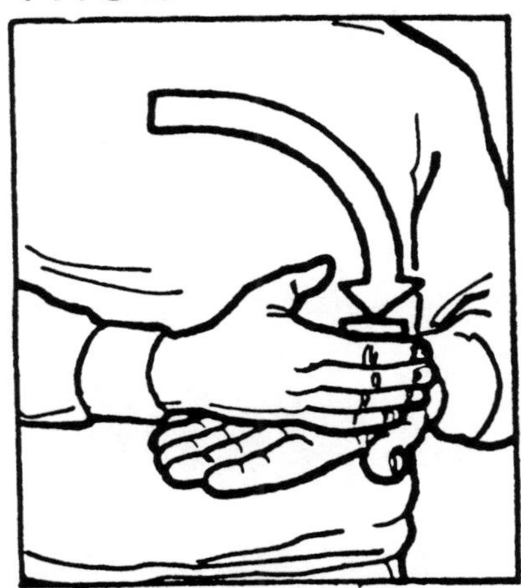

Blade of Rt. flat hand strikes L. palm with emphasis.

TRUST

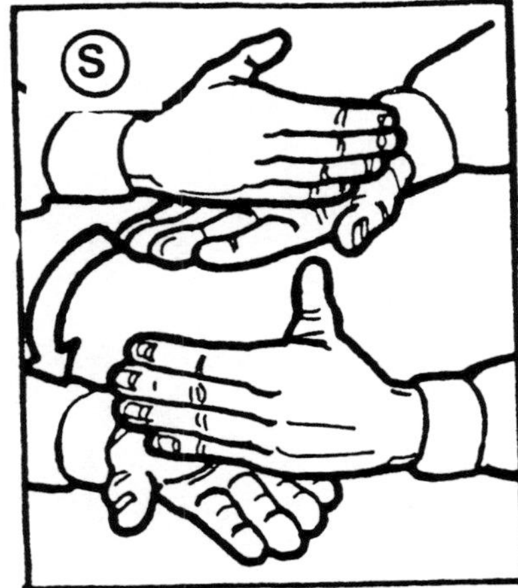

Strike L. palm with blade of Rt. flat hand, then Rt. palm with blade of L.

TRUTH

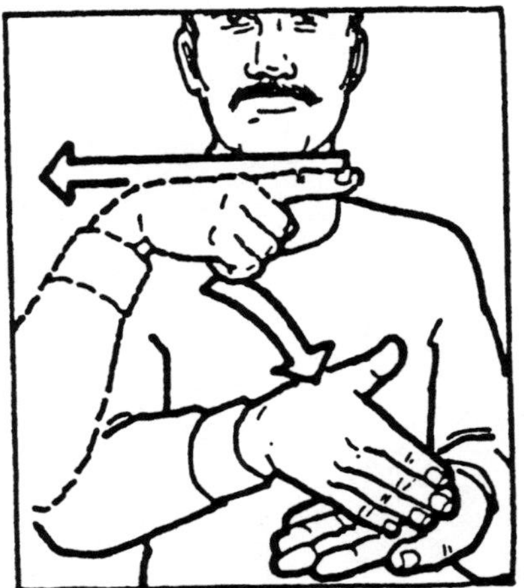

Rt. index moves left to right across the throat, then blade of Rt. flat hand strikes L. palm.

TRY

Indexes, pointing forward, rub together several times.

TURKEY

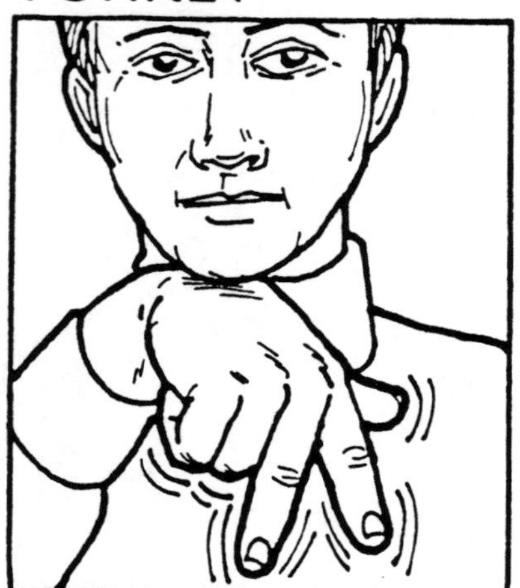

Index, middle finger and thumb, held under chin, pointing down, make shaking movement.

TURN

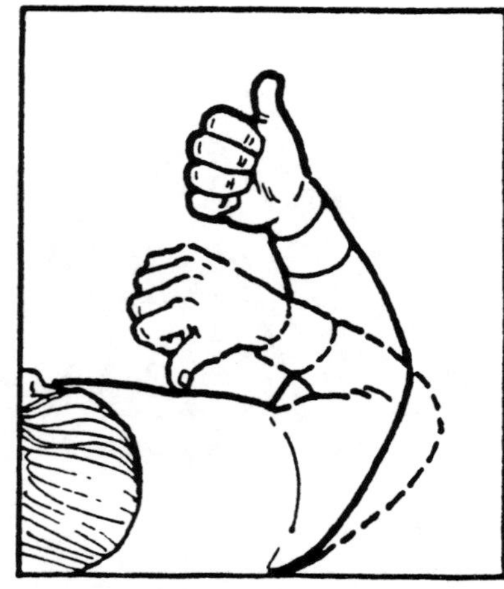

Rt. thumb, pointing back, contacts right upper chest, then moves forward, twisting to point forward.

TWICE

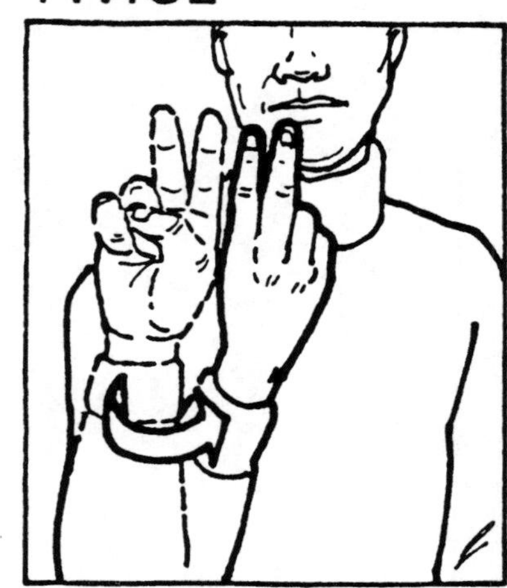

"V" hand, palm forward, twists sharply to palm back.

UGLY

Little finger circles round face.

UNCLE

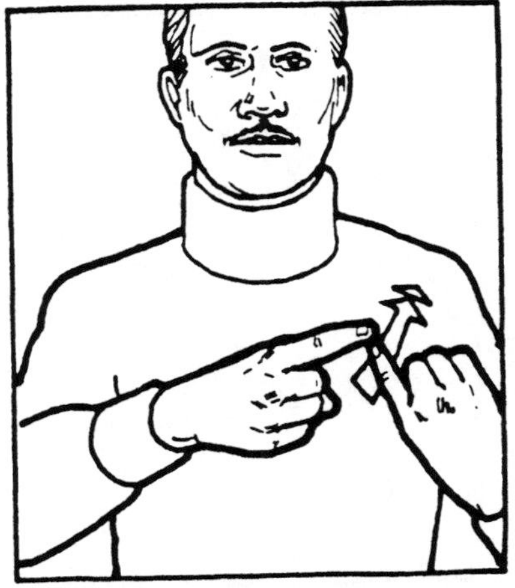

Rt. index brushes up/back off tip of extended L. little finger, twice.

UNDER

Rt. flat hand moves under L. in small arc.

UNDERGROUND TRAIN

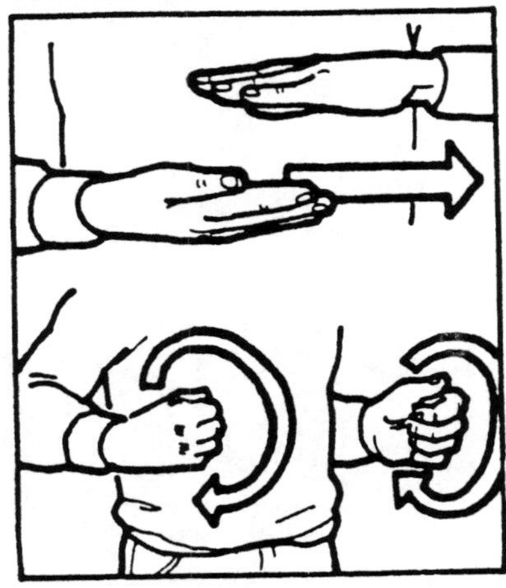

Rt. flat hand moves under L., then closed hands move in forward circles, like a train.

UNDERNEATH

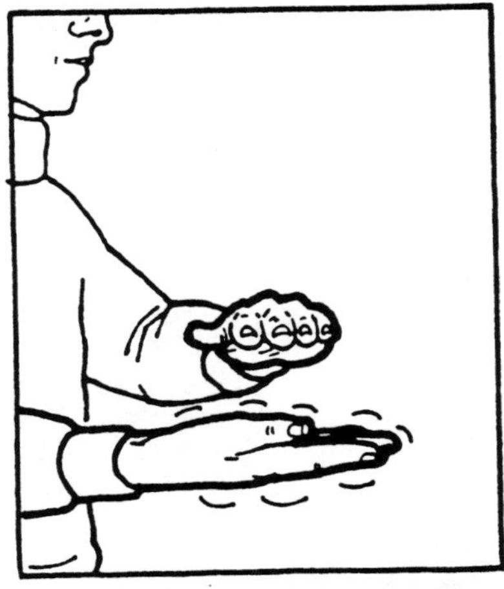

Rt. flat hand makes small side to side movements under L.

UNDERSTAND

Index flicks up at side of forehead.

UNEMPLOYED

Middle finger extended moves in small horizontal circle.

UNFORTUNATE

Little fingers extended, palms forward, move down whilst twisting over in small loop, to finish palms up.

UNIFORM

Palm down flat hands move in to touch, then brush down body.

UNIVERSITY

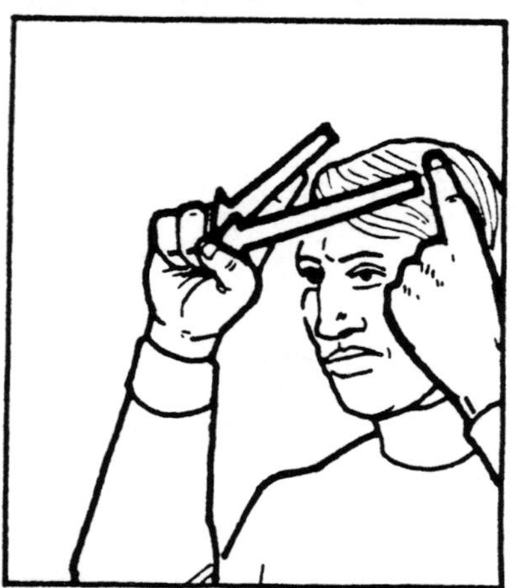

Indexes move forward/in, from sides of head, to indicate mortarboard.

UNLESS

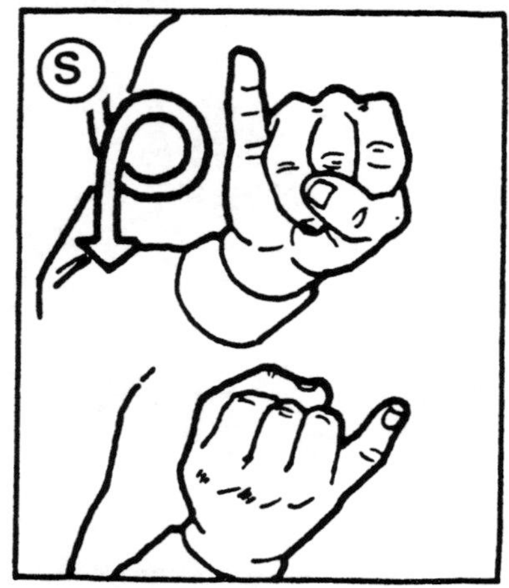

Little finger twists over in small loop, from palm down, to palm up.

UNTIL

L. closed hand, little finger extended. Rt. index sweeps right, over top of L., then down onto L. little finger.

UP

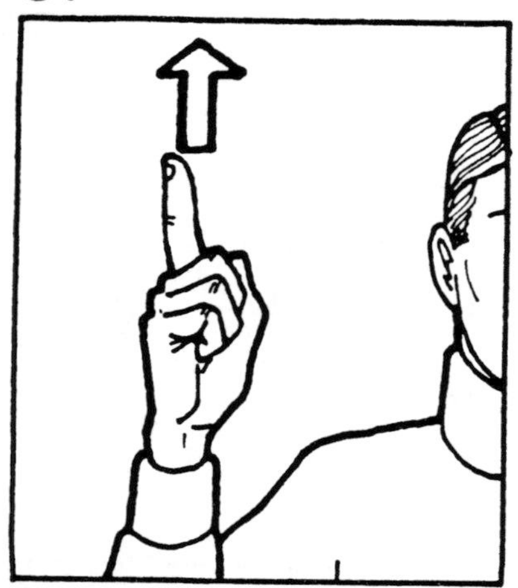

Index moves up.

UPSET

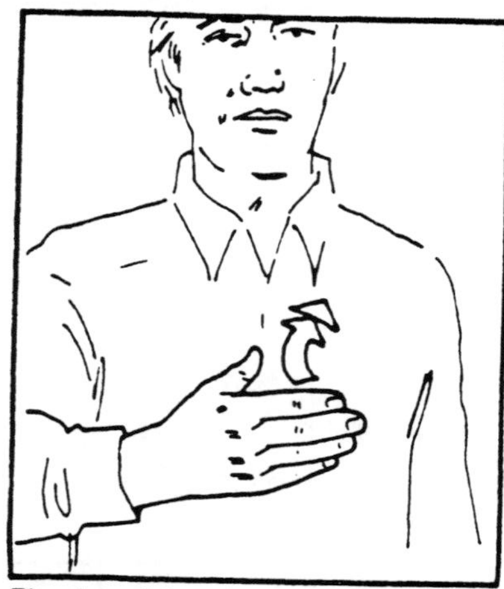

Flat hand brushes up/forward, twice, on chest, in small movement.

US

Hands held forward, indexes touch at tips, then, pointing down, move apart in circle back to touch on chest.

USE

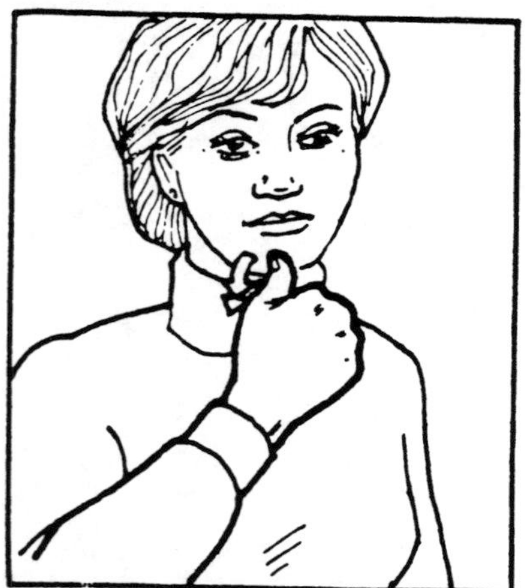

Thumb tip brushes down chin, twice.

VALLEY

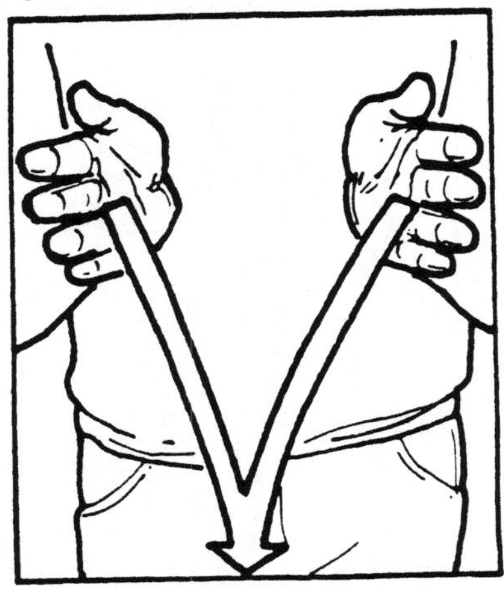

Flat hands move down/in to indicate shape of valley.

VALUE

Closed hands, held together, thumbs up, move up and down, twice.

VARIOUS

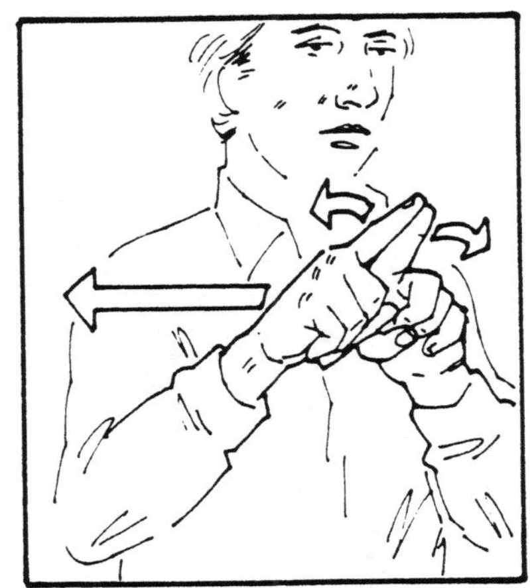

Indexes contact and repeatedly twist apart, as formation moves from left to right.

VEGETABLES

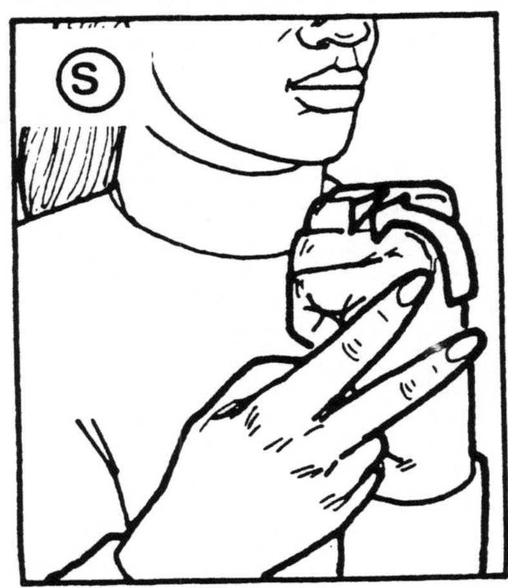

Rt. "V" hand brushes up and over back of L. fist, twice, as if peeling a vegetable.

VERY

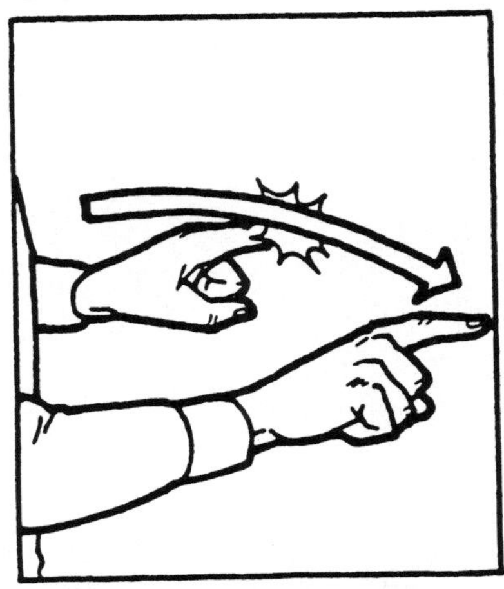

Indexes point forward, Rt. behind L., Rt. moves sharply forward hitting L. in passing.

VEST

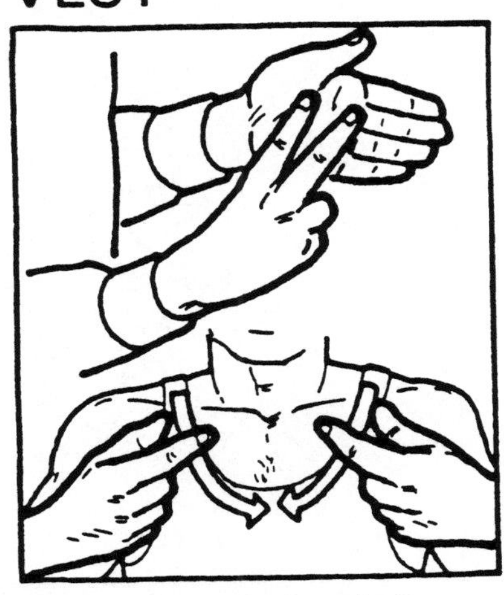

Fingerspell "V", then indicate shoulders of vest with thumbs and indexes.

VIDEO

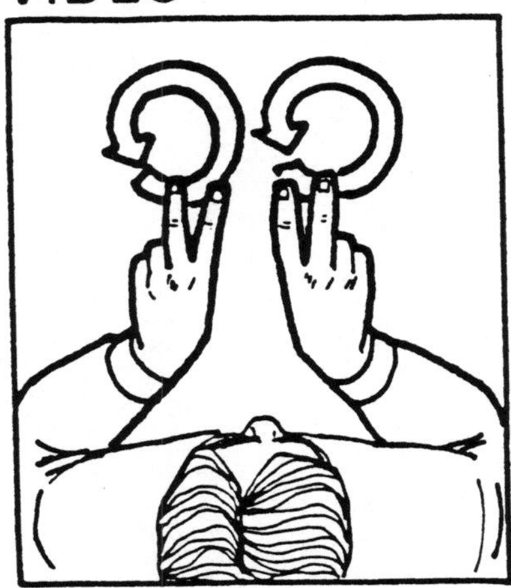

Palm down "V" hands make small horizontal circles, simultaneously.

VILLAGE

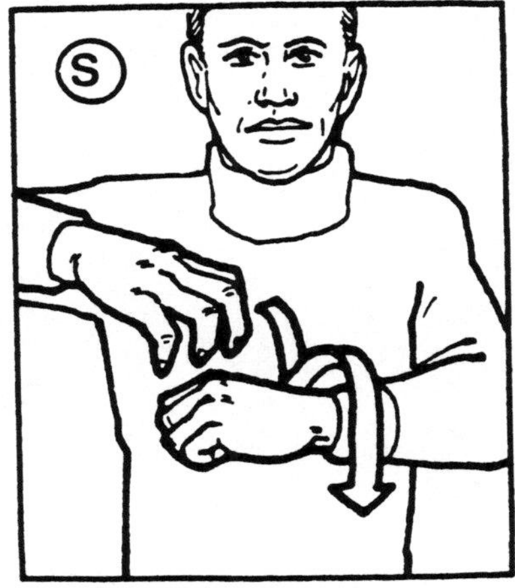

Palm down Rt. clawed hand makes small movement down behind L. closed hand, then hops over to finish in front of L.

VISIT

Rt. bent hand moves forward under L. bent hand, or towards person concerned. For "visit me", Rt. hand faces and moves back to self under L.

VOCABULARY

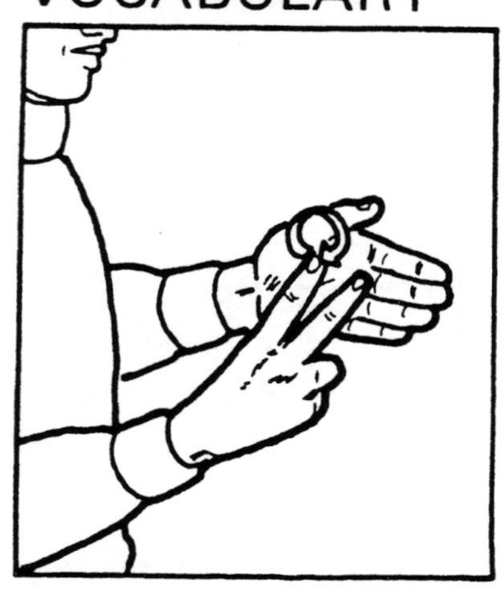

Rt. "V" hand brushes in small forward circles on L. palm, as if leafing through a book.

VOICE

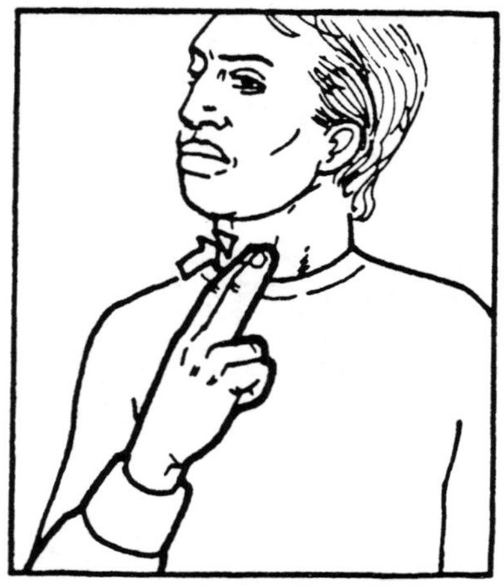

Tips of "N" hand tap voice-box, twice.

VOLUNTEER

Rt. flat hand swings up, as if volunteering.

VOTE

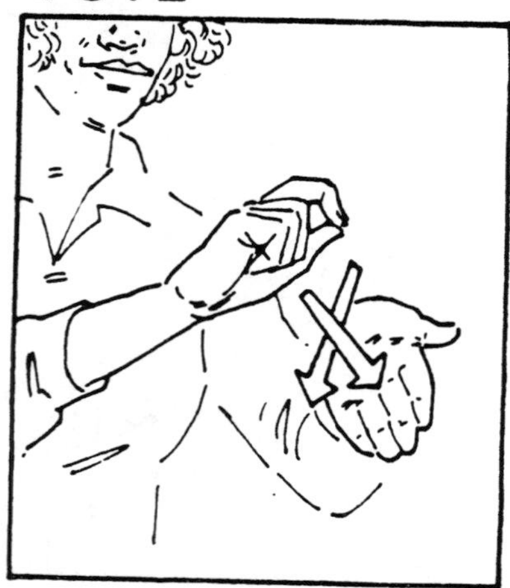

L. flat hand, palm up; make a cross on L. palm with Rt. index and thumb.

WAGES

Rt. slightly clawed hand moves down, closing sharply, onto L. palm, as both hands move slightly back to body.

WAIT

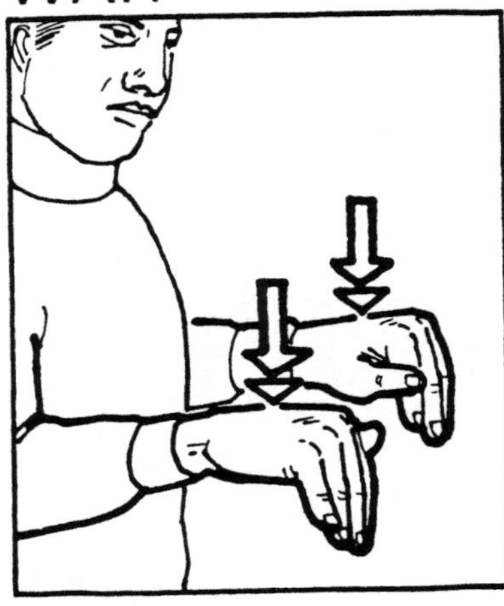

Palm down bent hands make two small movements down.

WAKE UP

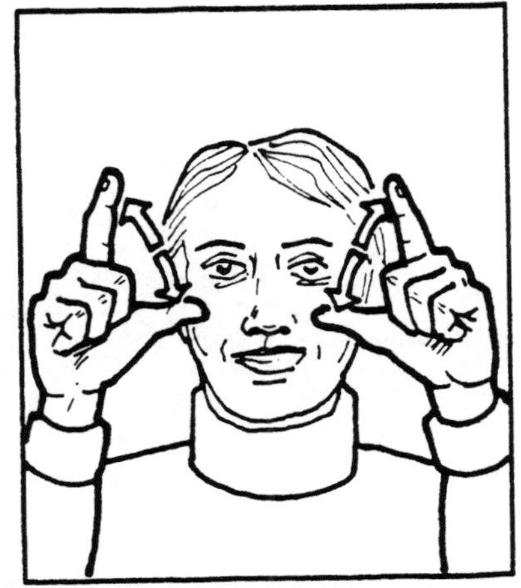

Thumbs and indexes flick open at sides of eyes.

WALES

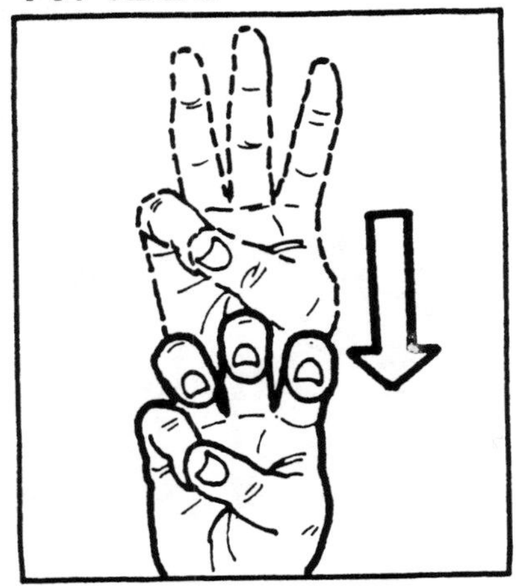

Index, middle and ring fingers, palm forward and open, make small movement down as fingers bend, indicating the Prince of Wales feathers.

WALK

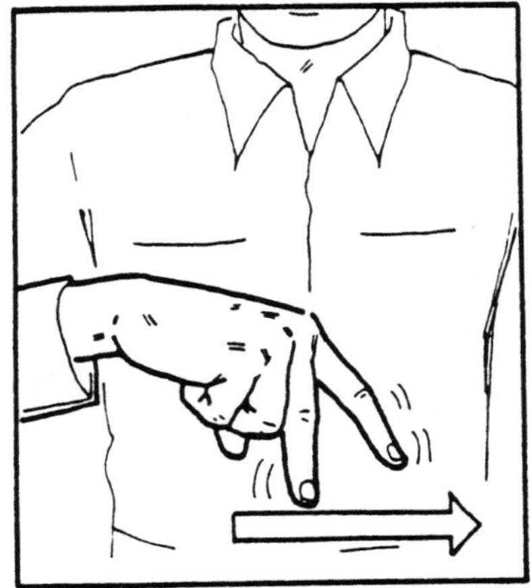

Index and middle fingers move like legs walking.

WALL

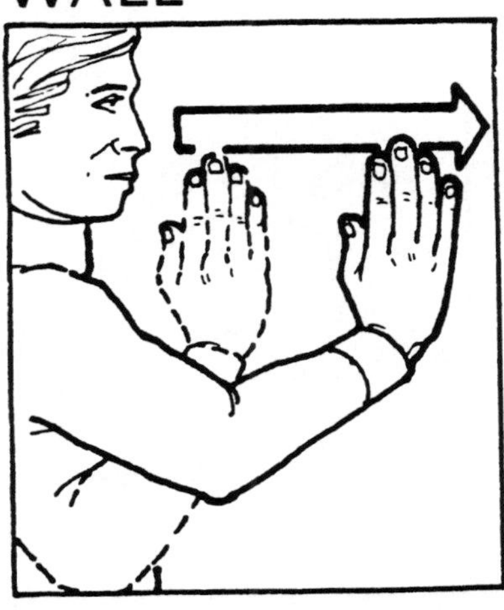

Flat hand moves forward to indicate wall.

WANT

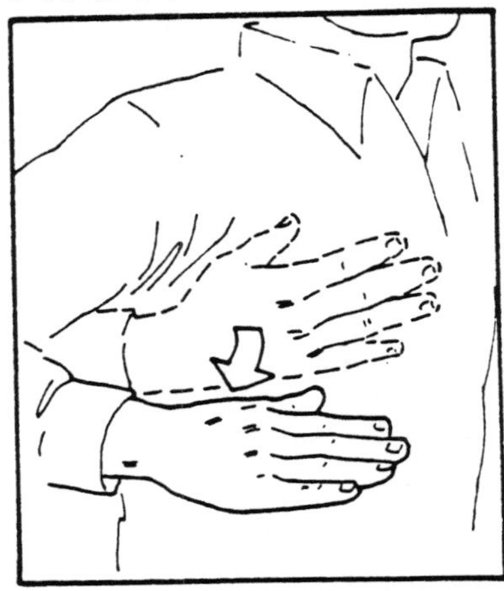

Flat hand on side of upper chest brushes down, twisting to palm down in small movement.

DON'T WANT

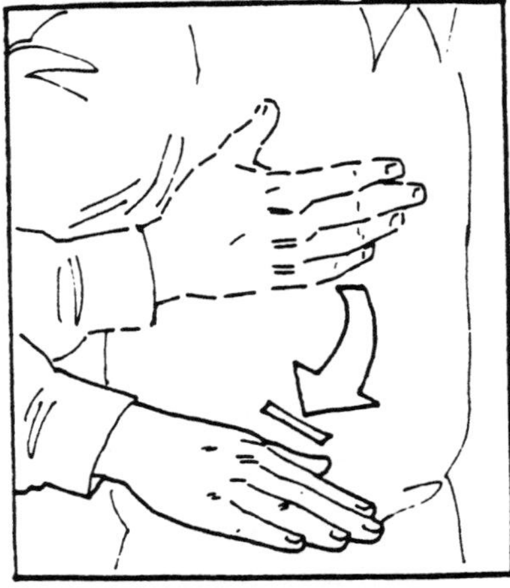

Flat hand on side of upper chest, brushes sharply down and away from body, with emphasis.

WAR

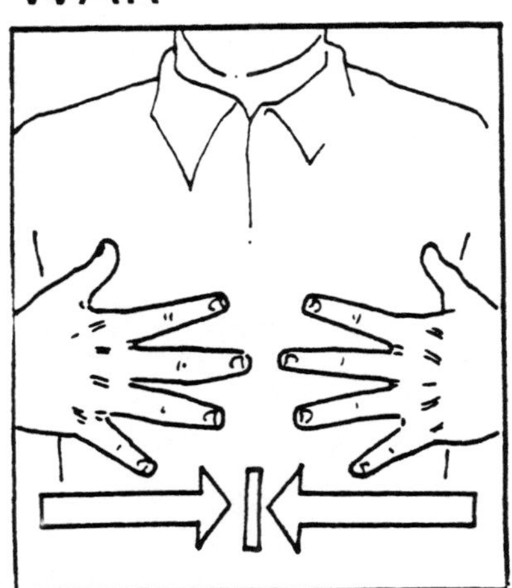

Open hands move sharply towards each other, and stop abruptly.

WARDROBE

Indexes hooked together, Rt. moves down onto L. several times, as formation moves to the right, indicating a line of coat hangers.

WARM

Clawed hand makes small circular movement in front of mouth.

WARN

Extended index finger wags forward.

WASH

Mime appropriate washing action, e.g. "wash hair" on head "wash face" on face etc. "wash hands" as illustrated.

WASHING MACHINE

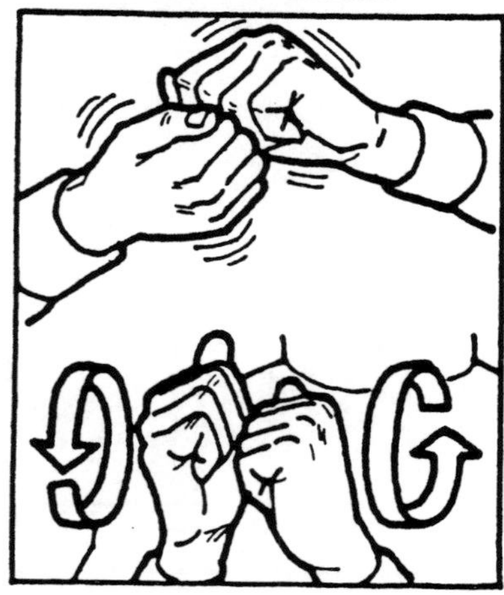

Knuckles of closed hands rub together in washing action, then move in small alternate forward circles for "machine".

WASTE

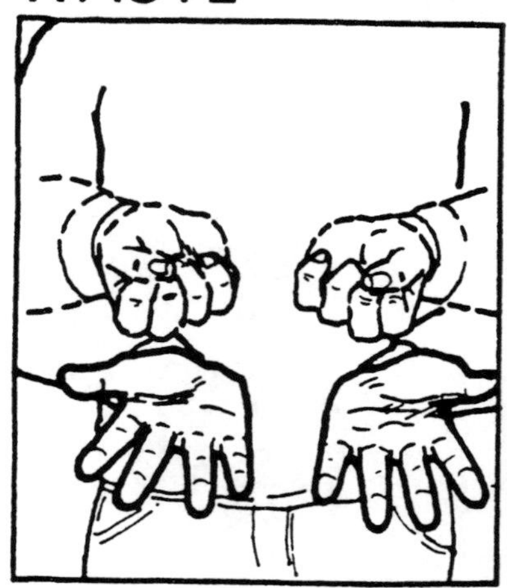

Fingers flexed behind thumbs, palms up. Hands move sharply forward/down and spring open.

WATCH (TO)

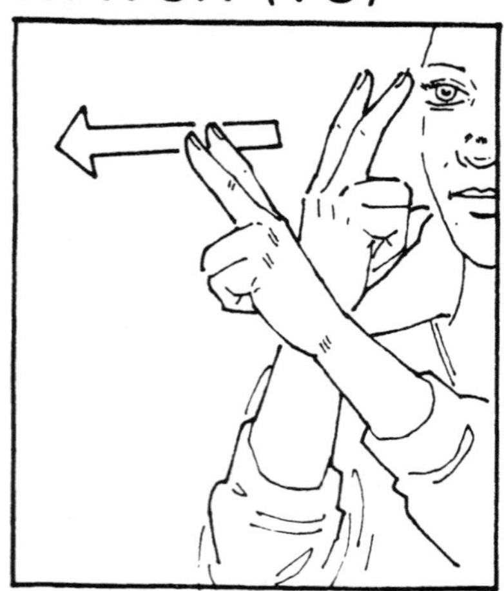

"V" hands, L. in front of Rt., move forward from eye.

WATCH (A)

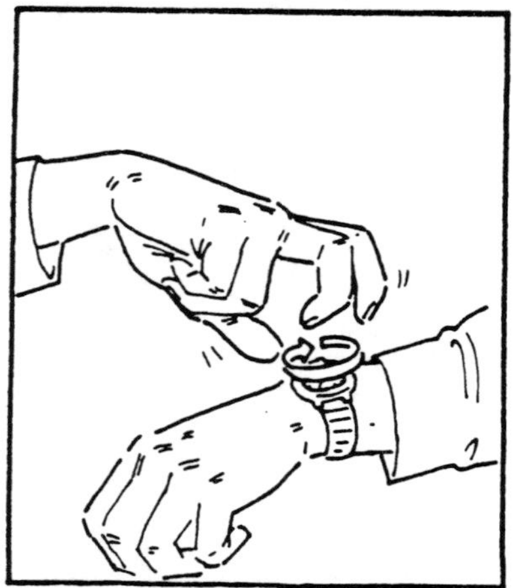

Index, middle finger and thumb extended and bent, make twisting movement over wrist.

WATER

Palm down flat hand makes wavy movement, at side of body.

WAVE

Wave hand from side to side.

WE

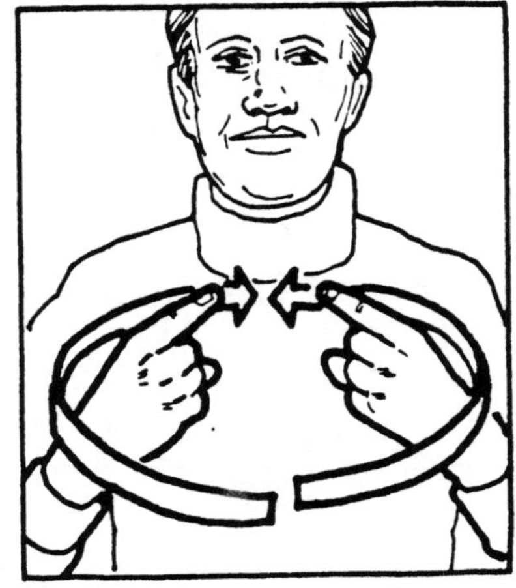

Hands held forward, indexes touch at tips, then, pointing up, move apart in circle back to touch on chest.

WEAK

Rt. little finger moves down left upper arm.

WEAR

Open hands move alternately up and down on body.

WEATHER

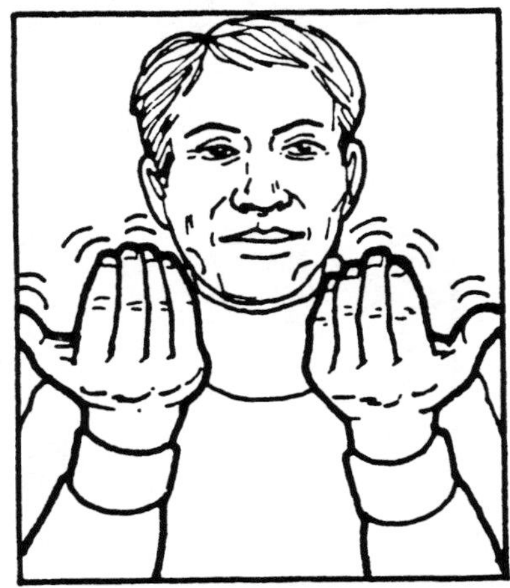

Fingers of cupped hands make very small quick backward movements near face.

WEEK

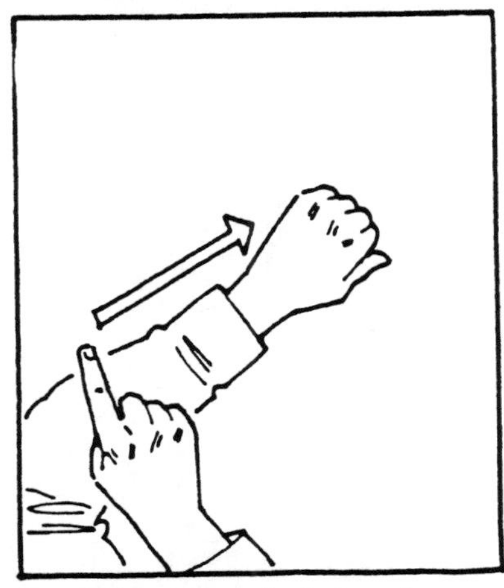

Rt. index extended, hand moves down left forearm. "In 2 weeks, 3 weeks" etc., same movement with appropriate fingers extended.

LAST WEEK

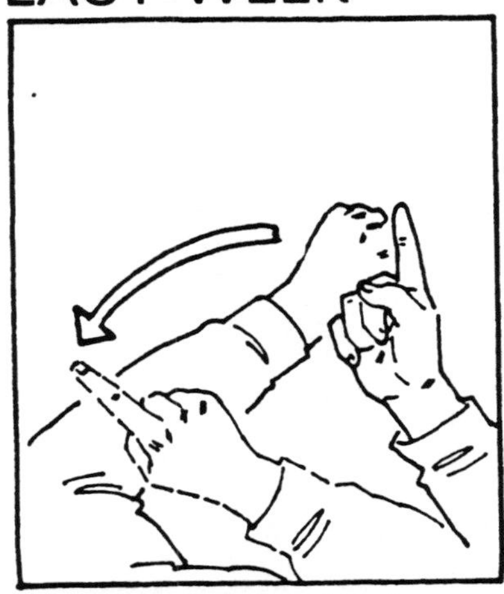

Rt. index extended, hand moves in arc up left forearm. "2 weeks ago, 3 weeks ago" etc., same movement with appropriate fingers extended.

NEXT WEEK

Rt. thumb extended, hand moves in arc down left forearm, twisting from palm down, to palm up.

THIS WEEK

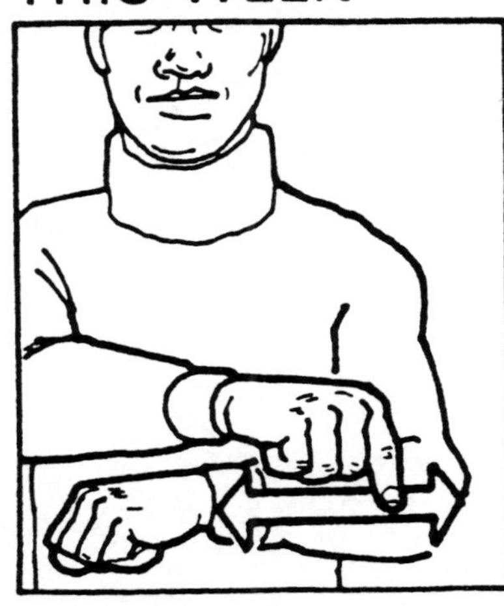

Rt. index, pointing down, in front of left elbow, moves along forearm to wrist, and back again.

WEEKEND

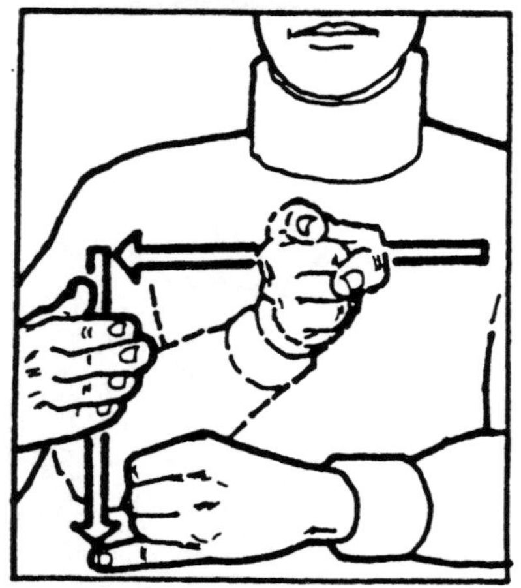

L. little finger extended. Rt. extended index moves along, above left forearm, changes to flat hand, and brings blade down onto L. little finger.

WEIGH

Palm up cupped hands move up and down alternately, like scales.

WELCOME

Bent hands held slightly forward. Fingers straighten and bend at 3rd knuckles, as if beckoning.

WELD

Index and thumb extended, hand moves side to side in downward movement.

WELDER

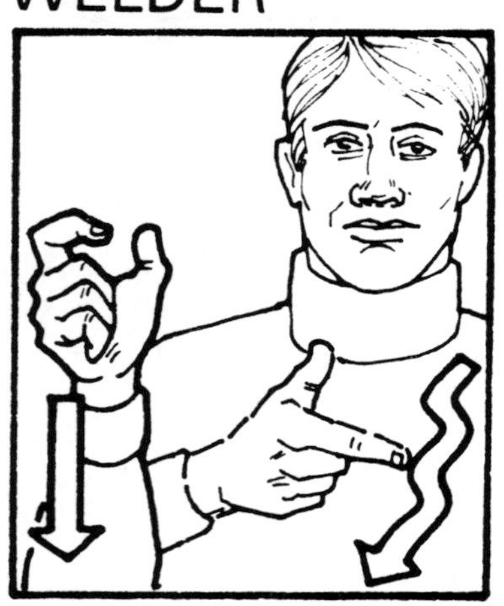

Index and thumb extended, hand moves side to side, then "C" hand moves down to indicate person.

WELL

Thumbs move down upper chest, then twist forward.

WEST

L. flat hand moves to left.

WET

Rt. fngertips touch lips, then thumbs rub across tips of fingers, several times, quickly.

WHAT

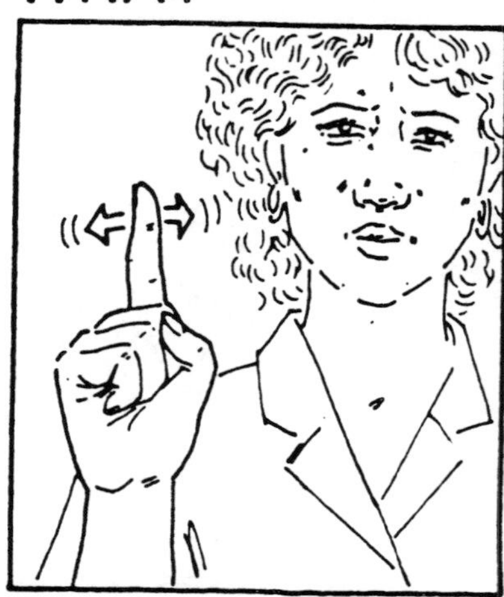

Index pointing up, palm forward, shakes from side to side, in small, quick movement.

WHEELCHAIR

Closed hands move forward, and open, at sides of body, as if turning wheels.

WHEN

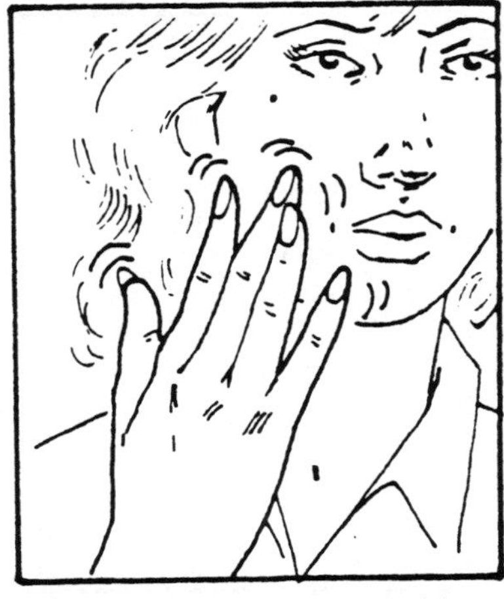

Fingers flutter at side of chin.

WHERE

Palm up flat hand moves in small vertical circles.

WHICH

Thumb and little finger extended, hand moves from side to side, or between the items referred to.

WHILE

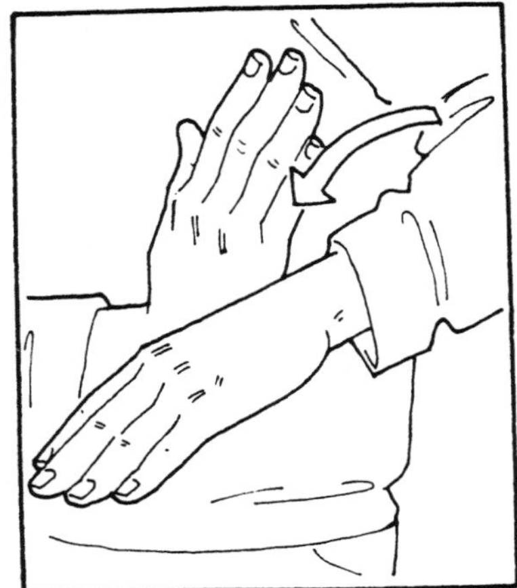

Flat hand makes a small arc on left forearm, near wrist.

WHISPER

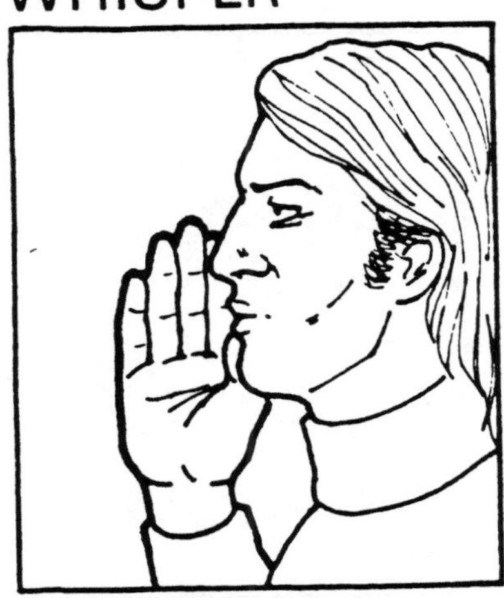

Flat hand held at side of mouth.

WHISTLE

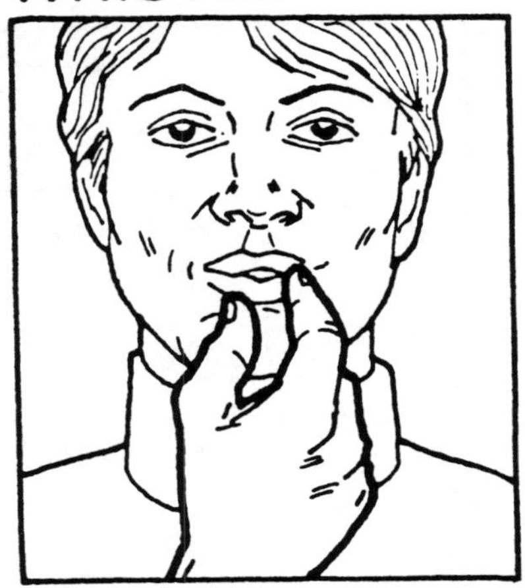

Bent thumb and index hold imaginary whistle to mouth.

WHITE

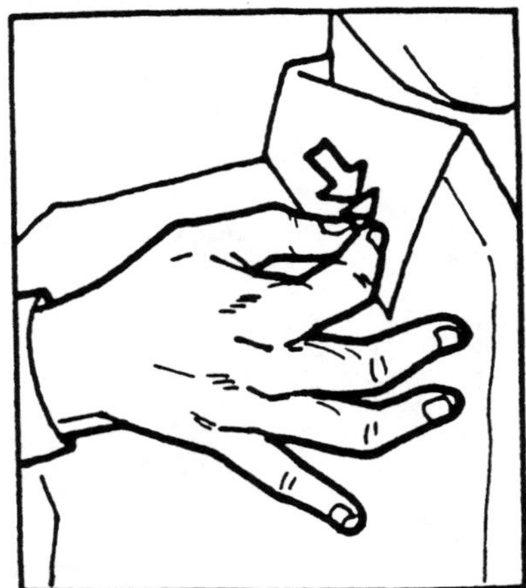

Tips of "O" hand brush down near neck, indicating white collar.

WHO

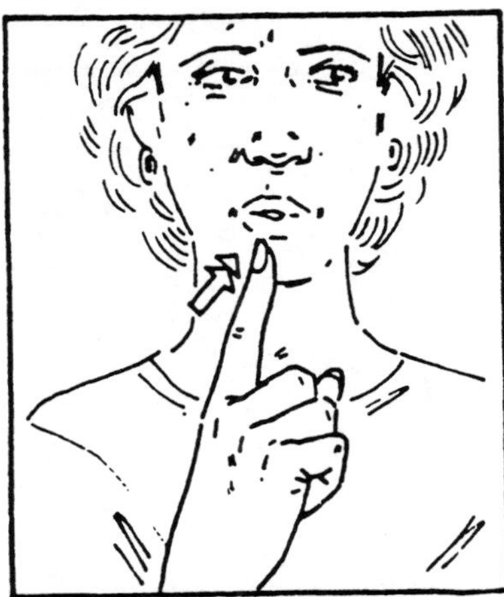

Rt. index extended, palm left, taps chin, twice.

WHOSE

Palm left Rt. index touches chin, then moves forward, changing to closed hand, palm forward.

WHY

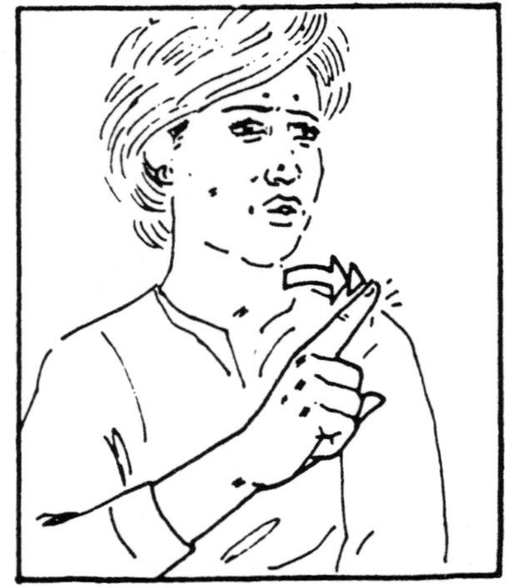

Edge of Rt. index taps left shoulder, with questioning facial expression.

WIDE

Open hands move apart.

WIFE

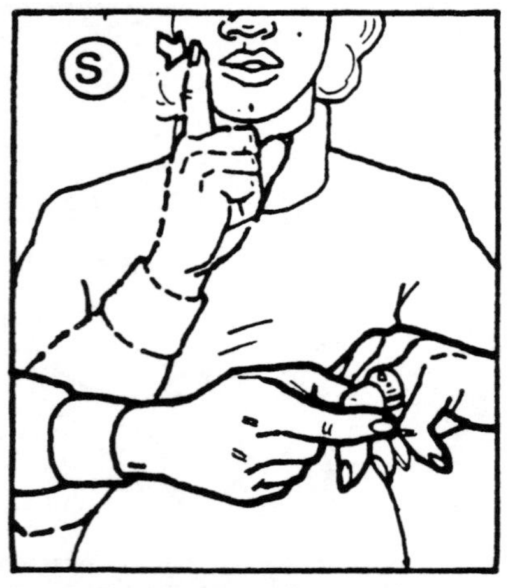

Rt. index brushes forward on cheek, then Rt. thumb and index move onto L. ring finger.

WILL

Palm forward closed hand twists forward at side of chin.

WIN

Rt. thumb brushes sharply down right side of chest, twisting to palm down.

WIND

Open hands sway from side to side, at head height.

WINDOW

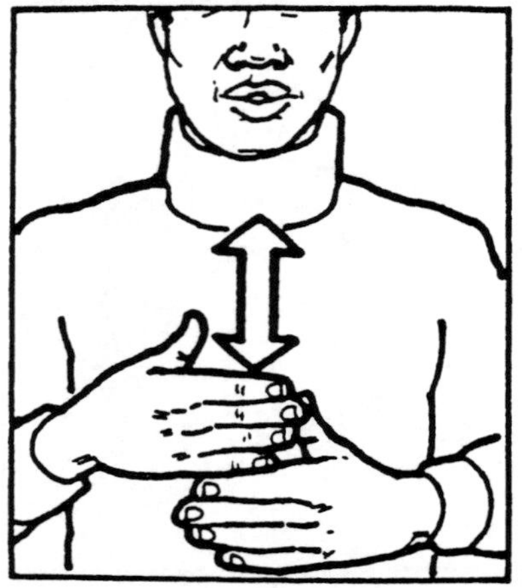

Palm back flat hands, edge to edge, Rt. on top of L. Rt. hand moves up, and back down onto L.

WINE

Thumb and little finger extended, hand tilts into mouth, as if pouring from wine container.

WINTER

Closed hands held close together on chest; elbows pull into body in shivering action.

WISE

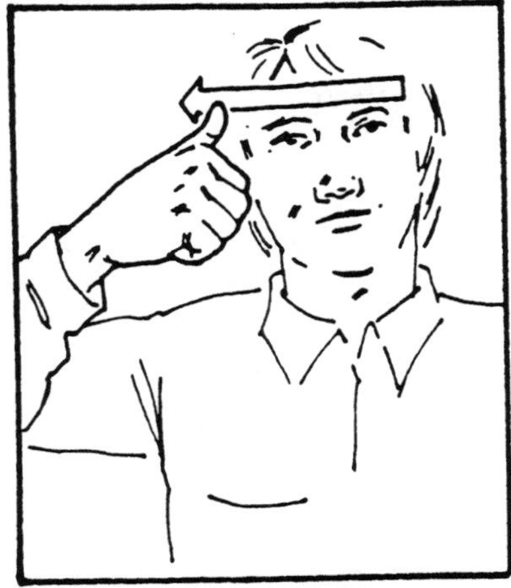

Rt. thumb moves across forehead, left to right.

WISH

Tips of fingers and thumbs hold throat, then pull forward, closing fingers onto thumb.

WITH

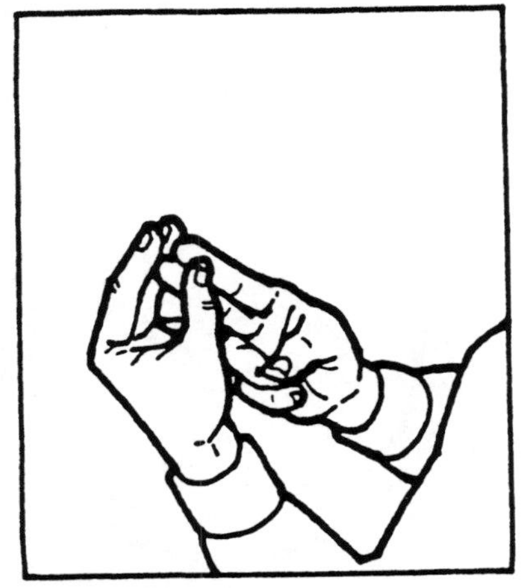

Hold fingers of Rt. "N" hand with L. index, middle finger and thumb.

WITHDRAW

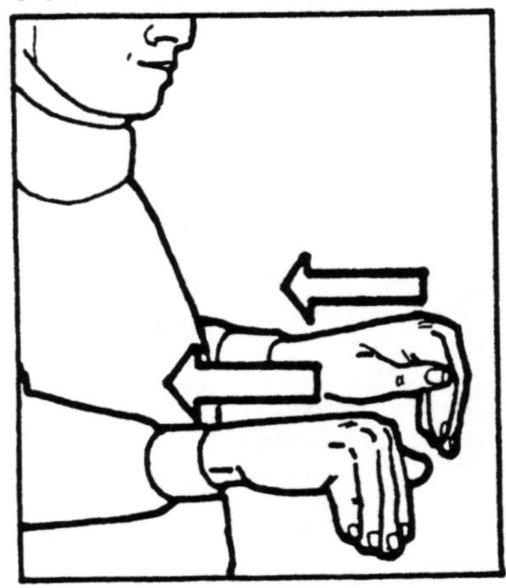

Palm down bent hands pull back towards body.

WITHOUT

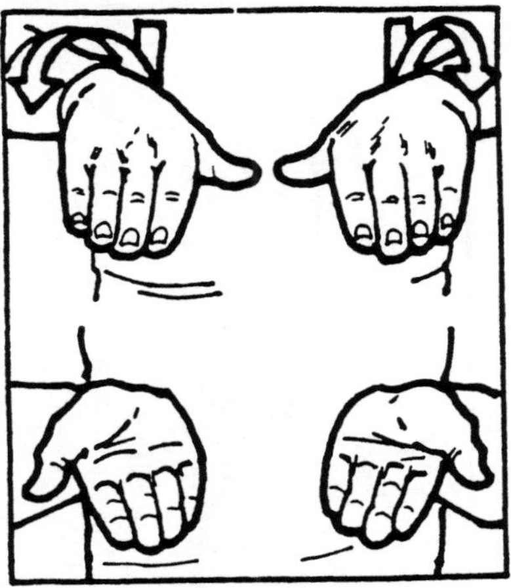

Palm down flat hands make small movement down, then up twisting over to palm up.

WOLF

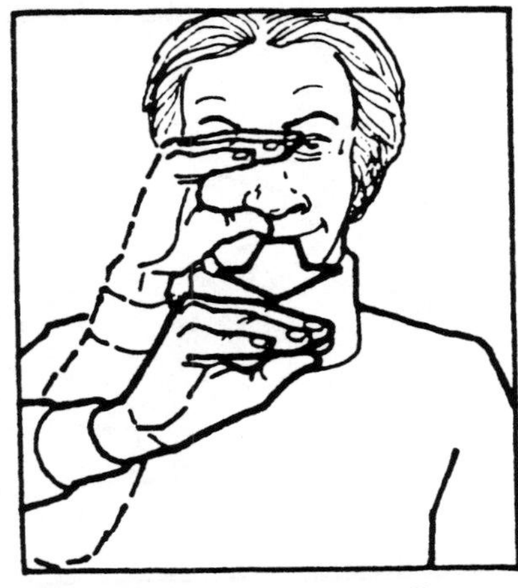

Palm left Rt. "C" hand, fingers held straight, moves forward from face, snapping fingers onto thumb.

WOMAN

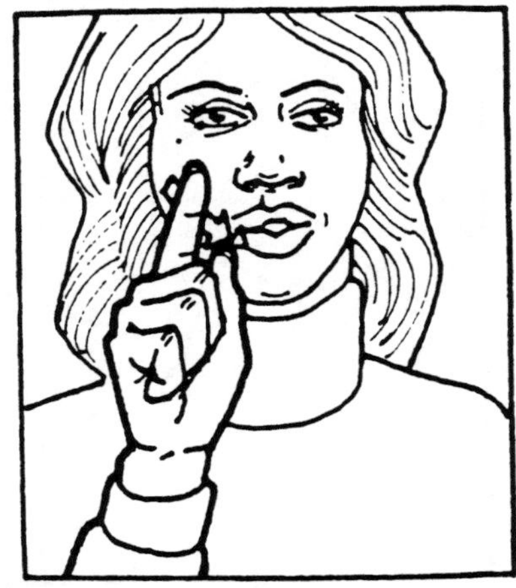

Edge of index brushes forward, twice, on cheek.

WON'T

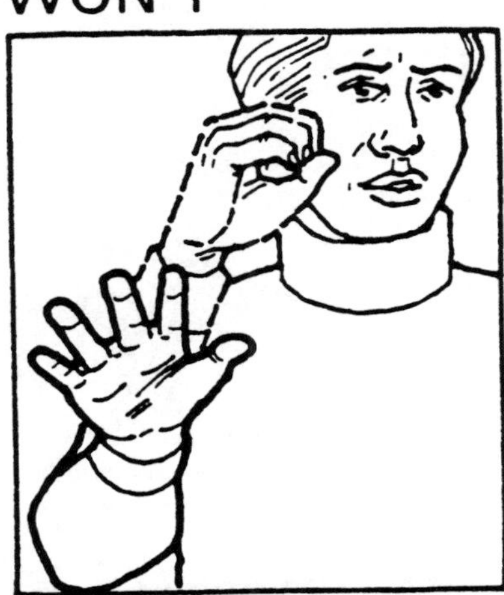

Fingers flexed behind thumb, hand moves sharply forward/down, from side of chin, and springs open.

WONDERFUL

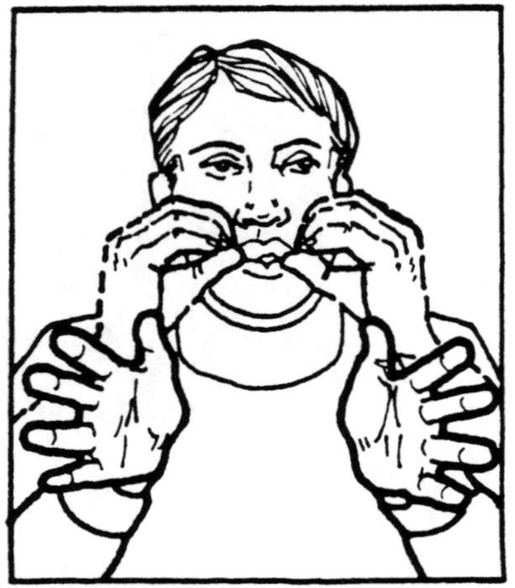

Full "O" hands held at sides of mouth, move forward and spring open sharply.

WOOD

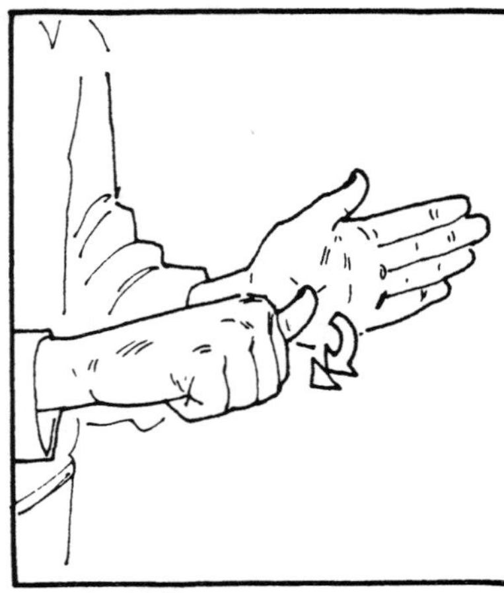

Tip of Rt. thumb twists into L. palm, like carving wood.

WOOL

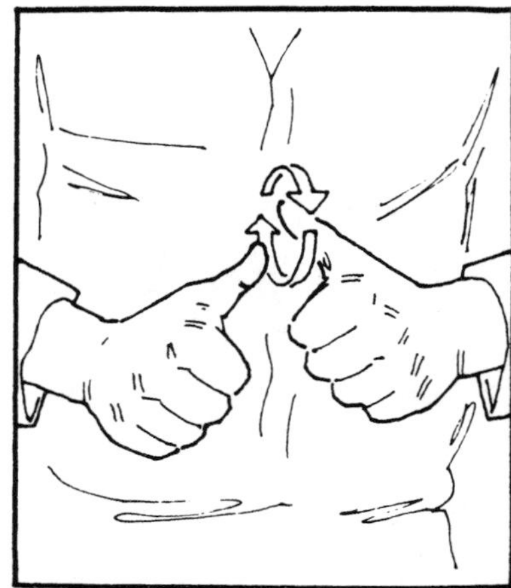

Thumbs move in small circular movements round each other, like winding wool.

WORD

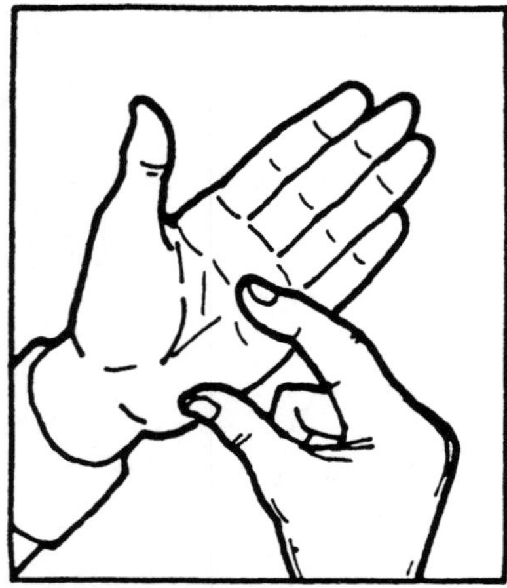

Rt. index and thumb contact L. palm.

WORK

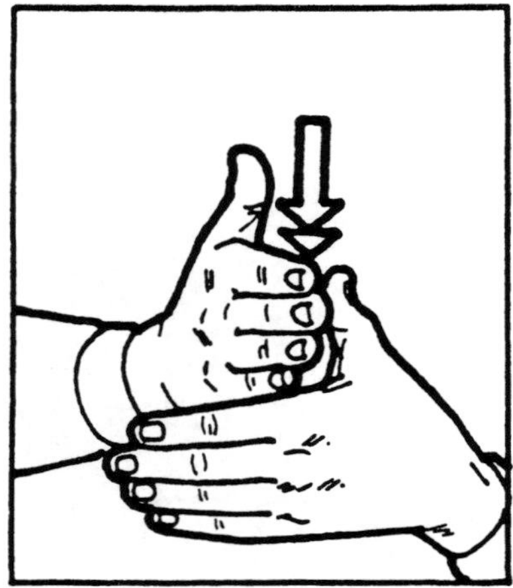

Blade of Rt. flat hand chops down twice on index edge of L. flat hand, at right angles.

WORLD

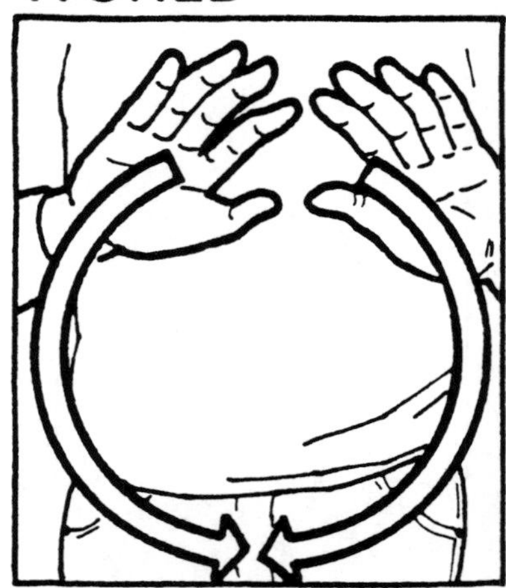

Hands sweep round in large circle, to indicate globe.

WORM

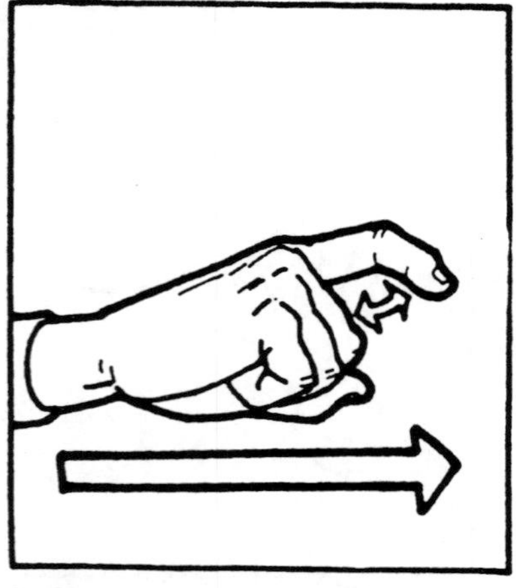

Index straightens and bends, as hand moves slowly forward, like a worm.

WORRY

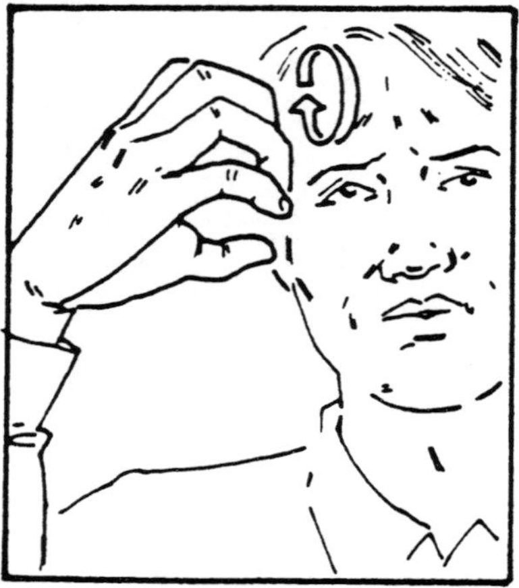

Clawed hand makes circular movement near temple.

WORSE

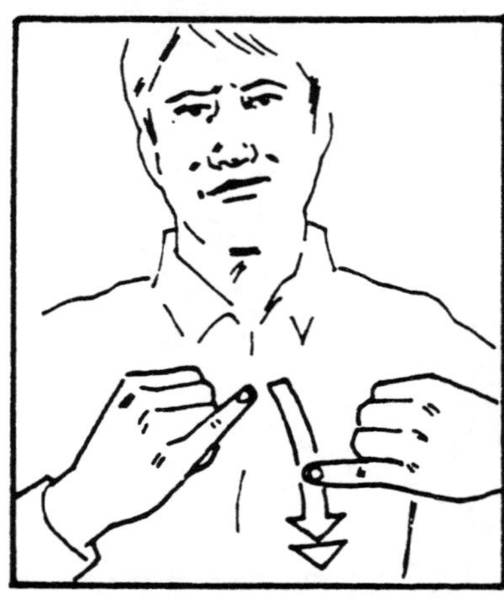

Rt. little finger tip brushes forward/down against L. little finger tip, twice.

WORST

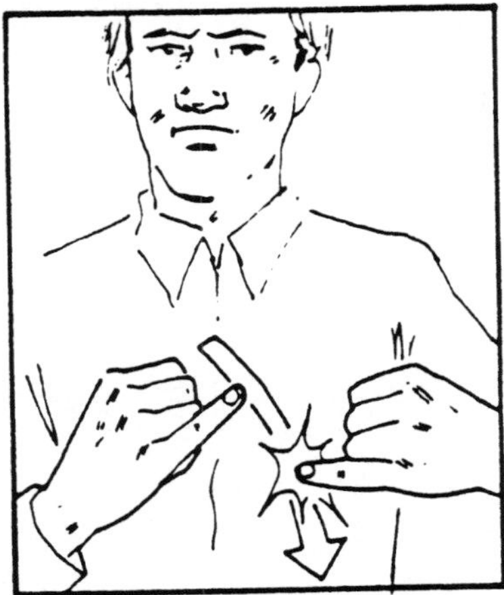

Rt. little finger tip brushes sharply forward/down against L. little finger tip.

WORTH

Closed hands, held together, thumbs up, move down with slight stress.

WRITE

Mime writing.

WRONG

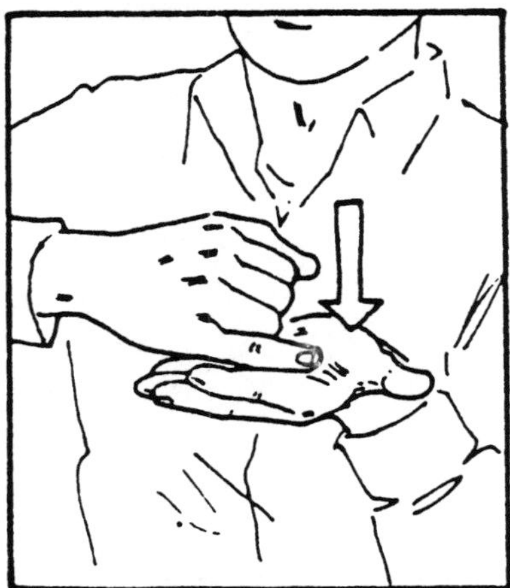

Bring edge of Rt. little finger sharply down on L. palm.

X-RAY

Fingerspell "X" "R" "A" "Y".

XYLOPHONE

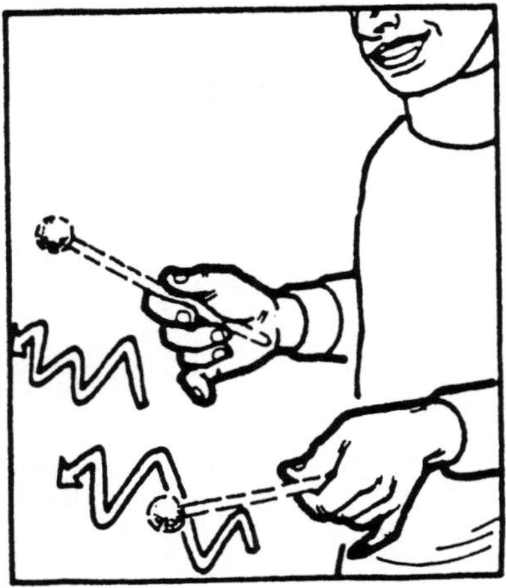

Mime playing a xylophone.

YEAR

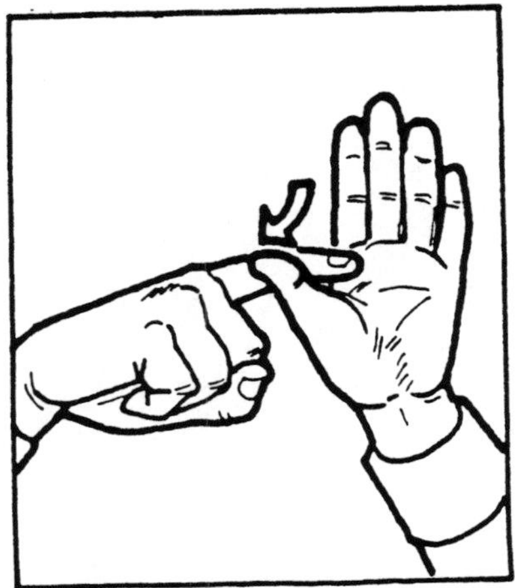

Form fingerspelt "Y" and brush Rt. index down slightly.

LAST YEAR

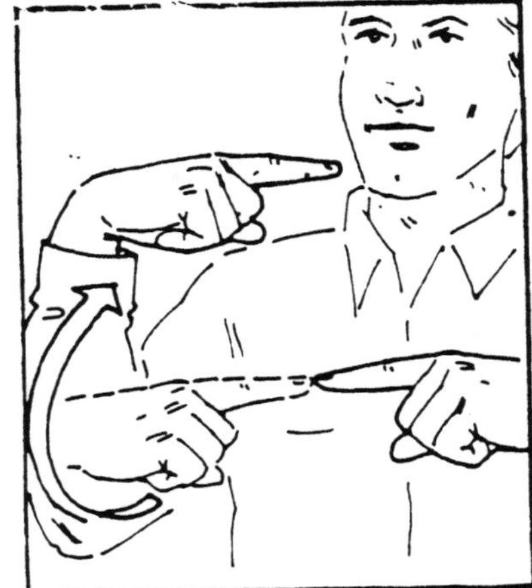

Index tips touch, then Rt. moves in backward circle, finishing over right shoulder. "2, 3 years ago" etc., same movement with appropriate fingers extended.

NEXT YEAR

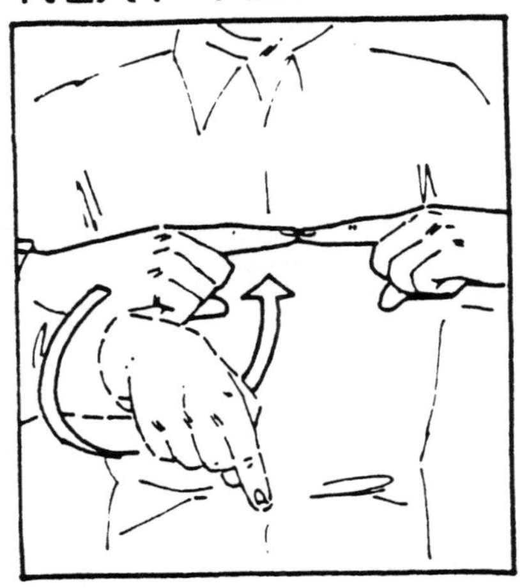

Index tips touch, then Rt. moves in full forward circle. "In 2, 3 years" etc., same movement with appropriate fingers extended.

YELLOW

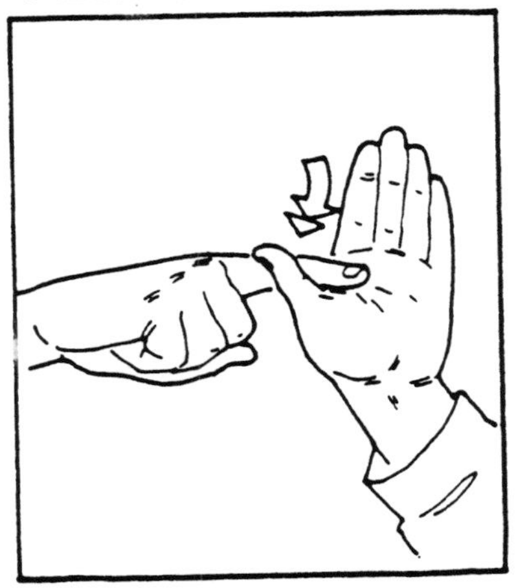

Form fingerspelt "Y" and brush Rt. index down slightly, twice.

YES

Rt. closed hand supported by L. index, twists from palm forward, to palm down, like a head nodding.

YESTERDAY

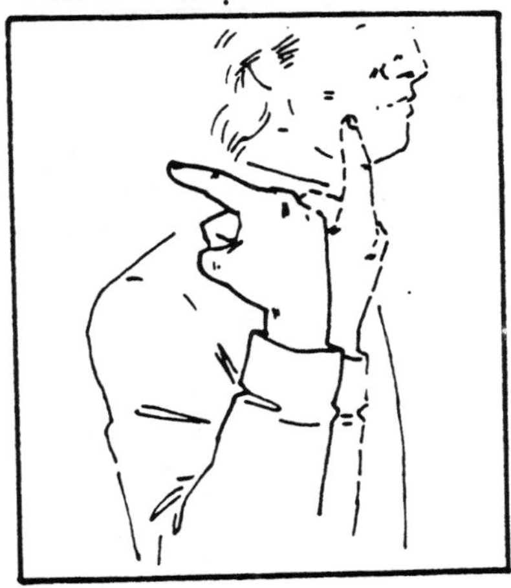

Rt. index held on side of chin, drops down/back.

YOGHURT

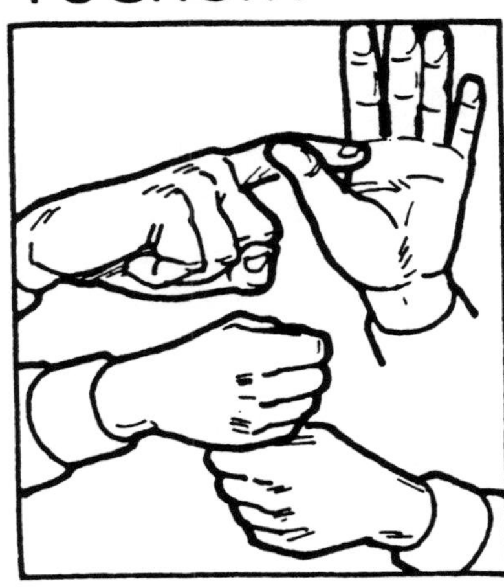

Fingerspell "Y" "G".

YOU

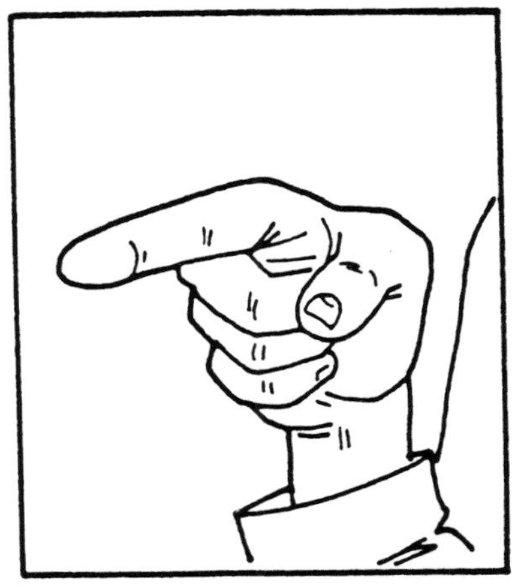

Point to person, or persons concerned.

YOUNG

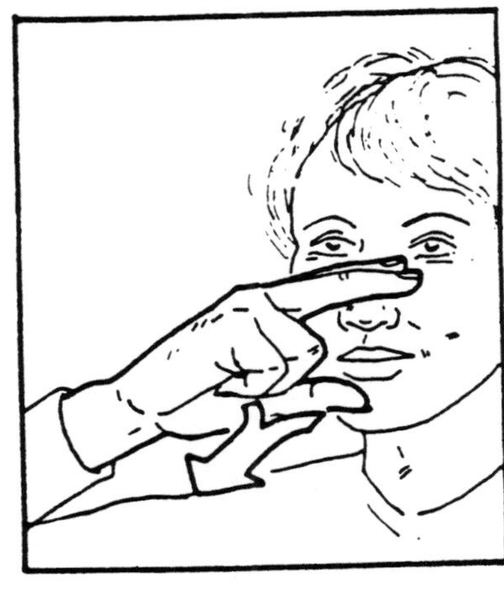

Rt. index, middle finger and thumb extended, move slightly forward, closing fingers onto thumb, in front of nose.

YOUR

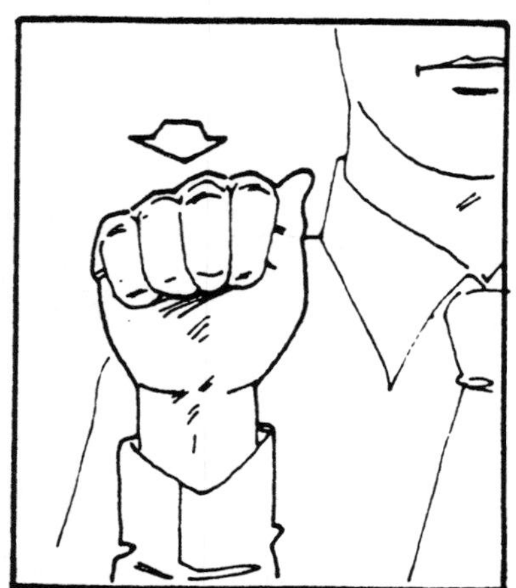

Palm forward closed hand moves towards person, or persons concerned.

YOUR OWN

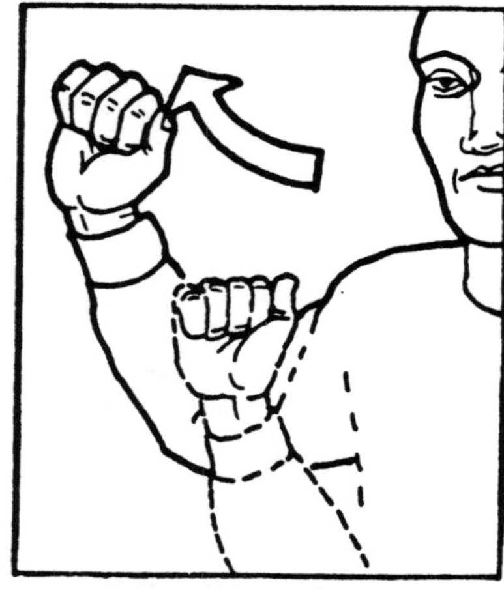

Palm forward closed hand moves towards person(s) concerned, then moves slightly upwards.

YOURSELF

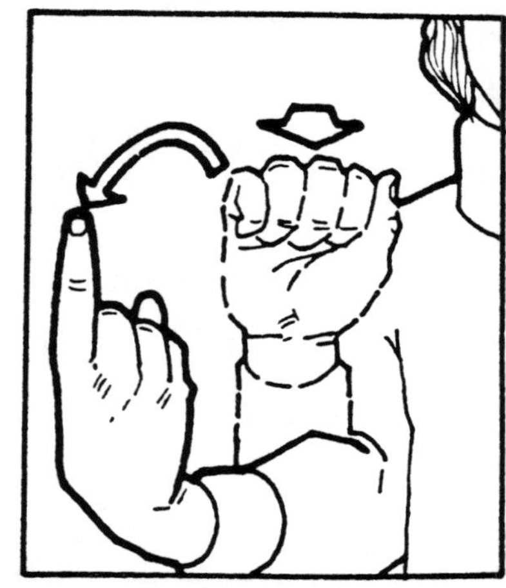

Palm forward closed hand moves towards person concerned, twists to palm back, index extended and moves down.

YOURSELVES

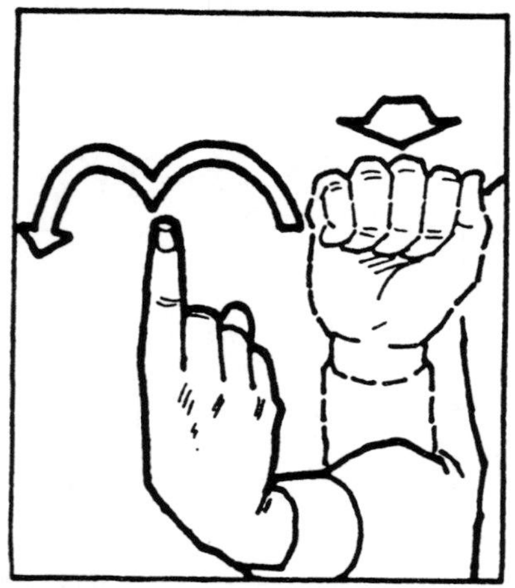

Palm forward closed hand moves towards persons concerned, twists to palm back, index extended, and moves down several times, whilst moving to the right.

ZEBRA

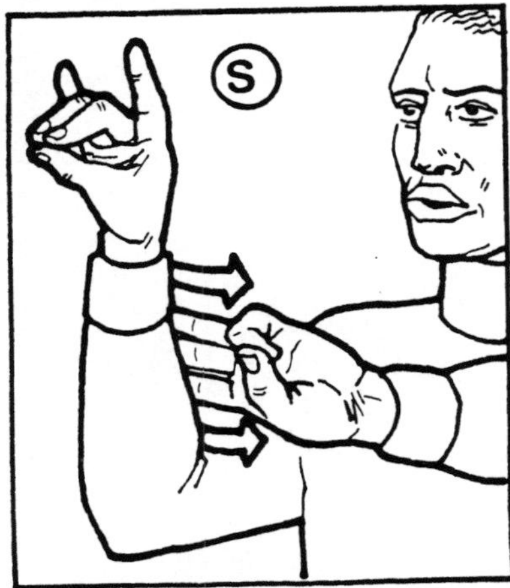

Rt. hand forms the sign for "animal", as L. index, middle and ring fingers stroke across back of right forearm, to indicate stripes.

ZOO

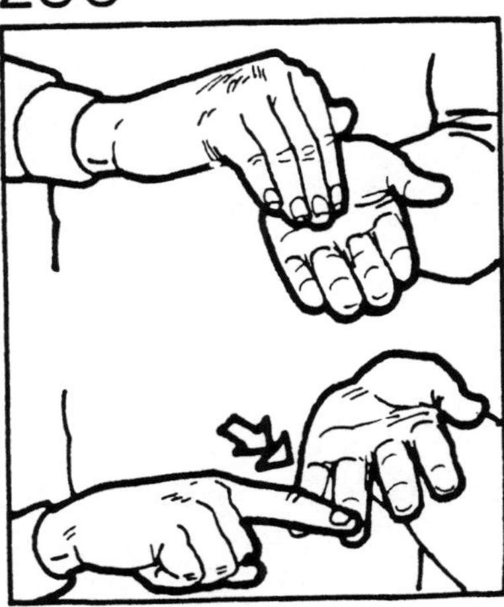

Fingerspell "Z" "O" "O".

FURTHER INFORMATION
USEFUL ADDRESS

Alliance of Deaf Service Users and Providers
Centre for Deaf People, Centenary House, North Street, Leeds LS2 8AY. (Tel: 0532 438328 Voice/Minicom)

Association for the Catholic Deaf of Great Britain and Ireland
Henesy House, 104 Denmark Road, Manchester M15 6JS. (Tel: 061-226 7139 Voice)

Association of British Sign Language Tutors (ABSLT)
c/o 119, Kingsmead Avenue, Worcester Park, Surrey KT4 8UT.

Association of Sign Language Interpreters (ASLI)
c/o 97, Wesley Close, Harrow, Middlesex HA2 0QE. (Tel: 081-423 4924 Voice/Minicom)

Association of Teachers of Lip-reading to Adults (ATLA)
c/o 3, Halons Road, Eltham, London SE9 5BS. (Tel: 081-850 4006)

Breakthrough Trust Deaf Hearing Integration
Selly Oak Colleges, Birmingham B29 6LE. (Tel: 021-472 6447/471 1001 Voice/ Minicom/Vistel)

The British Association of the Hard of Hearing (Hearing Concern)
7-11 Armstrong Road, London W3 7JL. (Tel: 081-743 1110 Voice/Minicom)

British Association of Teachers of the Deaf
Icknield High School Hearing Impaired Unit, Riddy Lane, Luton, Bedfordshire LU3 2AH. (Tel: 0582 596599 Voice)

British Deaf Association
38 Victoria Place, Carlisle, Cumbria CA1 1HU. (Tel: 0228 48844 Voice, 0228 28719 Minicom)

British Society of Hearing Therapists
The Leicester Royal Infirmary, Leicester, Leicestershire LE1 5WW. (Tel: 0533 541414 ext 5578 Voice)

Centre for Deaf Studies, School of Education
University of Bristol, 22 Berkeley Square, Bristol, Avon BS8 1HP. (Tel: 0272 303030 Ext. 17377 Voice/Minicom)

Christian Council of Workers with People who are Deaf
Halwyn House, 55 Bustleholme Lane, West Bromwich, West Midlands B71 3BD. (Tel: 021-588 6417/3722 Voice/Minicom)

Church of England General Synod Council for the Deaf
Church House, Great Smith Street, London SW1P 3NZ. (Tel: 071-222 9011 ext 329/223 1153 Voice/Qwerty)

Council for the Advancement of Communication with Deaf People
Pelaw House, School of Education, University of Durham, Durham DH1 1 TA. (Tel: 091-374 3607 Voice/Minicom)

Deaf Accord, A Consortium of Deaf Consumer Organisations
Charity Base, The Chandlery, 50 Westminster Bridge Road, London SE1 7QY. (Tel: 071-721 7689)

Deaf Broadcasting Council
c/o Ruth Myers, 70 Blacketts Wood Drive, Chorleywood, Rickmansworth, Hertfordshire WD3 5QQ.

Deaf Studies Research Unit
University of Durham, Department of Sociology and Social Policy, Elvet Riverside 2, New Elvet, Durham, DH1 3JT. (Tel: 091-374 2304/2314/2306 Minicom/Voice)

'Earshot'
Channel 4 Television, c/o 22 Carlton Green, Redhill, Surrey RH1 2DA.

Friends for the Young Deaf
FYD Communication Centre, East Court Mansion Council Offices, College Lane, East Grinstead, West Sussex RH19 3LT. (Tel: 0342 323444/312639 Voice/Minicom)

Hard of Hearing Christian Fellowship
43 Stoneham Close, Tilehurst, Reading, Berkshire RG3 4HB. (Tel: 0734 428988 Voice)

Hearing Dogs for the Deaf
Training Centre, London Road (A40), Lewknor, Oxfordshire OX9 5RY. (Tel: 0844 53898 Voice/Minicom)

Irish Deaf Society
Carmichael House Place, North Brunswick Street, Dublin 7, Eire. (Tel: 010 353 1 2735702/2725748 Voice/Minicom)

LASER: The Language of Sign as an Educational Resource
c/o 8 Church Lane, Kimpton, Hitchen, Hertfordshire SG4 8RP. (Tel: 0438 832676 Voice/Minicom)

National Association of Deafened People
103 Heath Road, Widnes, Cheshire WA8 7NU.

National Deaf-Blind League
18 Rainbow Court, Paston Ridings, Peterborough, Crambridgeshire PE4 6UP. (Tel: 0733 73511 Voice)

The National Deaf Children's Society
National Office, 45 Hereford Road, London W2 5AH. (Tel: 071-229 9272 Voice and Text)

NDCS Family Services Centre
Carlton House, 24 Wakefield Road, Rothwell Haigh, Leeds, LS26 0SF. (Tel: 0532 823458 Voice and Text)

NDCS Technology Information Centre
4 Church Road, Edgbaston, Birmingham B15 3TD. (Tel: 021-454 5151 Voice and Text. Parents freephone 1-5pm weekdays: 0800 424 545)

National Deaf Children's Sports Association
Braidwood School for the Deaf, Perry Common Road, Erdington, Birmingham, West Midlands. (Tel: 021 373 5558 Voice)

'Read Hear'
BBC News and Current Affairs, PO Box 701, Glasgow G42 9XG. (Tel: 041-632 0024 Voice/TDD)

The Royal National Institute for Deaf People
105 Gower Street, London WC1E 6AH. (Tel: 071-387 8033. Text 071-388 6038 (Qwerty 300 Baud) 071-383 3154 Minicom)

Scottish Association of Sign Language Interpreters (SASLI)
c/o 31 York Place, Edinburgh EH1 3HP. (Tel: 031-557 6370)

SENSE: The National Deaf-Blind and Rubella Association
311 Gray's Inn Road, London WC1X 8PT. (Tel: 071-278 1005)

Sign Language Information Centre (SLIC)
31 High Street, Carluke ML8 4AL. (Tel: 0555 70297)

Sound Advantage plc
1 Metro Centre, Welbeck Way, Peterborough PE2 0UH. (Tel: 0733 361199. Text 0733 238020)

TYPE TALK: National Telephone Relay Service
Pauline Ashley House, Ravenside Retail Park, Speke, Liverpool L24 8QB. (Tel: 051-494 1000. Text 051-494 1794)

Wales Council for the Deaf
Maritime Offices, Woodland Terrace, Maesycoed, Pontypridd, Mid Glamorgan, Wales CF37 1DZ. (Tel: 0443 485687/485686 Voice/Minicom)

RECOMMENDED READING

FLETCHER, L. (1987) *Language for Ben: A deaf child's right to sign.* London: Souvenir Press.

GREGORY, S. AND HARTLEY, G. (1991). *Constructing Deafness.* Pinter Publishers in association with the Open University.

JACKSON, P. (1990). *Britain's Deaf Heritage.* Edinburgh: The Pentland Press Limited.

KLIMA, E. AND BELLUGI, U. (1979). *The signs of Language.* Harvard University Press.

KYLE, J.G. AND WOLL, B. (1985). *Sign Language: The study of deaf people and their language.* Cambridge University Press.

LANE, H. (1987). *When the Mind Hears: A history of the deaf.* London: Souvenir Press.

MILES, D. (1988). *British Sign Language: A beginner's guide.* London: BBC Books.

OPEN UNIVERSITY D251 (1991). *Issues in Deafness. Course Units.* Milton Keynes: The Open University.

Unit 1: *Perspectives on Deafness: An introduction* . Prepared for the course team by George Taylor and Susan Gregory.

Unit 2: *The Deaf Community.* Prepared for the course team by Jim Kyle.

Unit 3: *British Sign Language, Communication and Deafness.* Prepared for the course team by Susan Gregory and Dorothy Miles.

ROBINSON, K. (1991). *Children of Silence.* London: Penguin Books.

SACKS, O. (1990). *Seeing Voices: A journey into the world of the deaf.* London: Pan Books Ltd.

SMITH, C. (1990). *Signs Make Sense: A Guide to British Sign Language.* London: Souvenir Press.

SMITH, C. (1992). Sign In Sight: A Step into the Deaf World. London: Souvenir Press.

TAYLOR, G. AND GREGORY, S. (1991). B*eing Deaf: the experience of deafness.* Pinter Publishers in association with the Open University.

WOLL, B. KYLE, J. and DEUCHAR, M. (1981). *Perspectives on British Sign Language and Deafness.* London: Croom Helm.

VIDEOS

British Sign Language: A beginner's guide. BBC Video, PO Box 100, Nailsea, Bristol BS19 1AM.
Sign 1-10: An Introduction to British Sign Language (BSL), Moray House College of Further Education, Holyrood Road, Edinburgh EH8 8AQ.

Video materials are also available to students of BSL through the Council for the Advancement of Communication with Deaf People (CACDP), Pelaw House, School of Education, University of Durham, Durham City DH1 1TA.

PERIODICALS

The British Deaf News. Published monthly. Journal of the British Deaf Association, 38 Victoria Place, Carlisle, Cumbria CA1 1HU.
Hark. Published quarterly. Journal of the British Association for the Hard of Hearing, 7-11 Armstrong Road, London W3 7JL.
See Hear. Published quarterly. Journal of the Royal Institute for Deaf People, 105 Gower Street, London WC1E 6AH.
TALK. Published quarterly. Journal of the National Deaf Children's Society, 45 Hereford Road, London W2 5AH.
Talking Sense. Published quarterly. Journal of the National Deaf-Blind and Rubella Association, 311 Gray's Inn Road, London WC1 8PT.

INFORMATION BOOKLETS

LISTENING EYE. Tyne Tees Television production for Channel 4. (1990). *Signs of Our Times.*
LISTENING EYE. Tyne Tees Television production for Channel 4. (1991). *Looking to the Future.*
ROCHESTER INSTITUTE OF TECHNOLOGY. *Tips for Communication with Deaf People.* Rochester: New York.

INFORMATION PACKS/LEAFLETS

British Telecom's Guide to Equipment and Services for Disabled Customers 1991. The British Deaf Association Information Pack.
The Council for the Advancement of Communication with Deaf People Information Pack.
Deaf Accord: A Consortium of Deaf Consumer Organisations Information Leaflet.
LASER: Language of Sign as an Educations Resource Information Leaflet.
The National Deaf Children's Society Information Pack.
The Royal National Institute for the Deaf Information Pack.
SENSE: The National Deaf-Blind and Rubella Association Information Pack.

TELEVISION PROGRAMMES AND TELETEXT INFORMATION SERVICES

BBC Television 'See Hear!'.
Tyne Tees Television for Channel 4 'Sign On'.
BBC Television 'Read Hear'.
Channel 4 'Earshot'.

VOCABULARY INDEX

85
HERE
HEREDITARY
HIDE
HIGH
HIGHCHAIR
HIKE
HILL
HIM
HIPPOPOTAMUS

86
HIRE
HIS
HOLD
HOLE
HOLIDAY
HOLLAND
HOLY
HOME
HONOUR

87
HOP
HOPE
HORSE
HOSPITAL
HOT
HOTDOG
HOTEL
HOUR
HOUSE

88
HOVERCRAFT
HOW
HOW OLD
HUNDRED
HUNGRY
HURRY
HURT
HUSBAND

89
I
ICE
ICECREAM
IDEA
IF
IGNORE
ILL
IMAGINE
IMPORTANT

90
IMPOSSIBLE
IMPRESSED
IMPROVE
IN
INCLUDE
INCREASE
INDIA
INDIAN
INDICATOR

91
INFLUENCE
INFORMATION
INJECT
INSECT
INSIDE
INSTEAD
INSURE
INTEGRATE
INTERESTED

92
INTERPRET
INTERRUPT
INTERVIEW
INTO
INTRODUCE
IRELAND
IRON
ISLAND
ITALY

93
JAM
JAPAN
JAR
JEALOUS
JEANS
JELLY
JESUS
JIGSAW
JOIN

94
JOKE
JOURNEY
JUDGE
JUG
JUGGLE
JUMP
JUMPER
JUST

95
KEEN
KEEP
KETCHUP
KETTLE
KEY
KICK
KILL
KIND (good)
KING

96
KISS
KITCHEN
KITE
KNEEL
KNIFE
KNIGHT
KNIT
KNOCK
KNOT

97
KNOW
DON'T KNOW

99
LADDER
LAKE
LAMP
LAND
LANGUAGE
LAST
LATE
LATER
LAUGH

100
LAW
LAZY
LEAD
LEAF
LEARN
LEATHER
LEAVE
LECTURE
LEFT (over)

101
LEISURE
LEMON
LEMONADE
LEND
LEOPARD
LESS
LESSON
LET (allow)
LETTER (abc)

102
LETTER (post)
LETTUCE
LIBRARY
LID
LIE (down)
LIE (untrue)
LIFEBOAT
LIFT
LIFT (ride)

103
LIFT (raise)
LIGHT (lamp)
LIGHT (dark)
LIGHT (weight)
LIGHTNING
LIKE (prefer)
LIKE (similar)
DON'T LIKE
LINE (people)

104
LION
LIST
LISTEN
LITTLE
LITTLE (bit)
LIVE
LOCK
LOLLY
LONDON

105
LONELY
LONG (time)
LONG (length)
LONG TIME AGO
LOOK
LOOK AFTER
LORD
LORRY
LOSE

106
LOSS OF FACE
LOT (a)
LOUD
LOVE
LOVELY
LOW
LUCKY

107
MACHINE
MAGAZINE
MAGIC
MAKE
MAN
MANAGE
MANAGER
MANNERS
MANY

108
MARK
MARKET
MARRY
MASH
MATCH
MATERIAL
MATHS
MATTER (the)
MAXIMUM

109
MAYBE
MEAL
MEAN (imply)
MEAN (singly)
MEASURE
MEAT
MEDAL
MEDICINE
MEET

110
MEETING
MELT
MEND
MENU
MERCY
MESS
METAL
METHOD
MIDDLE

111
MIGHT
MILE
MILK
MILLION
MINE
MINI-BUS
MINUS
MINUTE
MIRROR

112
MISERABLE
MISS
MISTAKE
MITTEN(S)
MIX
MONEY
MONKEY
MONTH
MOODY

113
MOON
MORE
MORNING
MOST
MOTHER
MOTORBIKE
MOUNTAIN
MOUSE
MOVE

114
MR.
MRS.
MUCH
MUD
MULTIPLY
MUSHROOM
MUSIC
MUST
MY

115
MY OWN
MYSELF

117
NAME
NARROW
NAUGHTY
NAVY
NEAR
NEARLY
NEED
NEEDLE
NEGOTIATE

118
NEIGHBOUR
NEPHEW
NERVOUS
NET
NEVER
NEW
NEWS
NEWSPAPER
NEXT

119
NICE
NIECE
NIGHT
LAST NIGHT
NIGHT-GOWN
NO (not any)
NO (- yes)
NOISE
NONE

120
NORWAY
NOT
NOT YET
NOTE (music)
NOTHING
NOW
NUMBER
NUN
NURSE

121
NURSERY
NUT

123
O'CLOCK
OATH
OBJECT (to)
OCCUR
OFF (absent)
OFF (cancel)
OFF (get off)
OFFICE
OFTEN

124
OLD
ON
ONCE
ONION
ONLY
OPEN
OPERATION
OPPORTUNITY
OPPOSE

125
OPPOSITE (idea)
OPPOSITE (place)
ORAL
ORANGE
ORANGE JUICE
ORDER (command)
ORDER (arrange)
ORGANISE
OTHER

126
OTHERS
OUR
OUT
OUTSIDE
OVER
OVERCOME
OVERTAKE
OWE
OWL

127
PACK
PAGE
PAIN
PAINT
PAIR
PANIC
PAPER
PARAGRAPH
PARALLEL

128
PARENT
PARK
PARK (car)
PART
PARTICULAR
PARTNER
PARTY
PASS
PAST (the)

129
PASTIE
PATIENT (calm)
PATTERN
PAVEMENT
PAY
PEACH
PEAR
PEAS
PEDAL-CAR

130
PEEL
PEN
PENCIL
PENGUIN
PENNY/PENCE
PEOPLE
PERCENT
PERFECT
PERHAPS

131
PERSON
PERSUADE
PET
PETROL
PHOTO
PIANO
PICK
PICNIC
PICTURE

132 PIE
PIER
PIG
PILLOW
PILLS
PINEAPPLE
PINK
PIPE
PIZZA

133 PLACE
PLAN
PLANT
PLASTIC
PLATE
PLAY
PLEASE
PLEASED
PLENTY

134 PLUM
PLUS
POCKET
POEM
POINT (finger)
POINT (make a)
POINTED
POISON
POLICE

135 POLICE CAR
POLITE
POOL
POOR
POORLY
POPULAR
POSH
POSSIBLE
POST

136 POST OFFICE
POTATO
POUND
POWER
PRACTICE
PRAISE
PRAM
PRAY
PREFER

137 PREGNANT
PREPARE
PRESENT
PRETEND
PRETTY
PREVENT
PRICE
PRIEST
PRINCE

138 PRINCESS
PRINT
PRISON
PRIVATE
PRIZE (trophy)
PROFESSION
PROFIT
PROGRAMME
PROGRAMME (TV)

139 PROMISE
PROOF
PROTECT
PROTESTANT
PROUD
PROVOKE
PSYCHOLOGY
PUBLICITY
PUBLISH

140 PUDDING
PULL
PUNISH
PUPPET (string)
PURPLE
PUSH
PUT
PUT OFF
PYJAMAS

141 QUALIFICATIONS
QUARREL
QUARTER
QUEEN
QUESTION
QUEUE
QUICK
QUIET
QUITE

142 QUOTE

143 RABBIT
RADIO
RAFFLE
RAILWAY
RAIN
RAINBOW
RAINCOAT
RAISE
RARELY

144 RATHER
RAW
READ
READY
REAL/REALLY
REASON
RECEIVE
RECENTLY
RECIPE

145 RECOGNISE
RED
REDUNDANT
REFLECTION
REFUSE
REGISTER
REGULAR
RELATE
RELEASE

146 REMEMBER
REMIND
RENT
REPEAT
REPLY
REPORT
REPRESENT
RESEARCH
RESIGN

147 RESPONSIBILITY
REST
RETIRE
REVENGE
REVERSE (car)
RHINOCEROS
RICE
RICH
RIDE

148 RIGHT
RING
RIPE
RISK
RIVER
ROAD
ROAST
ROCK
ROLL

149 ROOF
ROOM
ROOT
ROPE
ROTTEN
ROUGH
ROUND
RUBBER
RUBBISH (talk)

150 RUBBISH (waste)
RUDE (manners)
RUDE (indecent)
RUGBY
RULER
RULES
RUN
RUSH
RUSSIA

151 SACK (to)
SAD
SAFE
SAIL
SAILOR
SALAD
SALT
SAME
SAND

152 SANDAL
SANDWICH
SATISFIED
SAUCE
SAUCER
SAUSAGES
SAVE
SAW (cut)
SAY

153 SCARE
SCARF
SCHOOL
SCIENCE
SCISSORS
SCOOTER
SCORE
SCOTLAND
SCOUT

154 SCREAM
SCREW
SCULPTURE
SEA
SEAL
SEARCH
SEASON
SECOND (clock)
SECOND (2nd)

155 SECRET
SEE
SEEDS
SEEM
SELF
SELFISH
SELL
SEND
SENSIBLE

156 SENTENCE
SEPARATE
SERIES
SERIOUS
SERVANT
SET
SEVERAL
SEW
SHADE

157 SHADOW
SHALLOW
SHAME (guilt)
SHAME (pity)
SHAPE
SHARE
SHARP
SHAVE
SHE

158 SHEEP
SHEET
SHELF
SHEPHERD
SHIFT (work)
SHINE
SHIP
SHIRT
SHOCK

159 SHOE
SHOP
SHOPPING
SHORT
SHORTS
SHOULD
SHOUT
SHOW
SHOW OFF

160 SHOWER
SHUT
SHY
SICK
SIDE
SIDEBOARD
SIGN
SILENT
SILLY

161 SILVER
SIMILAR
SINCE
SING
SINGLE (one)
SINGLE (status)
SINK (TO)
SINK (kitchen)
SISTER

162 SIT
SITUATION
SIZE
SKATE
SKILL
SKIP
SKIPPING ROPE
SKIRT
SKY

163 SLEEP
SLIDE
SLIP
SLIPPER
SLOW
SLY
SMACK
SMALL
SMART

164 SMOOTH
SNAIL
SNAKE
SNOOKER
SNOW
SOAP
SOCIAL WORKER
SOCIETY (a)
SOCK

165 SOFA
SOFT
SOIL
SOLDIER
SOME
SOMEONE
SOMETHING
SOMETIMES
SON

166 SONG
SOON
SORRY
SORT (out)
SOUL
SOUND
SOUP
SOUR
SPACE

167 SPADE
SPAGHETTI
SPAIN
SPEAK
SPECIAL
SPEND
SPIDER
SPILL
SPIT

168 SPLIT
SPOIL
SPOON
SPORT
SPOTS
SPREAD
SPRING (season)
SQUARE
SQUASH

169 SQUIRREL
STAIRS
STAMP (post)
STAND
STARS
START
STATION
STAY
STEAL

170 STEEL
STICKS
STILL
STING
STOCKING
STONE
STOP
STOP (- go)
STORY

171 STRAIGHT
STRANGE
STRAWBERRY
STRICT
STRIKE (on)
STRING
STRONG
STUCK
STUPID

172 SUBTRACT
SUCCESS
SUCCEED
SUGAR
SUIT
SUMMER
SUN
SUNDAY
SUNRISE